THE WESTERN HERITAGE

THE WESTERN HERITAGE
Seventh Edition

VOLUME A
TO 1527

DONALD KAGAN
YALE UNIVERSITY

STEVEN OZMENT
HARVARD UNIVERSITY

FRANK M. TURNER
YALE UNIVERSITY

Prentice
Hall

UPPER SADDLE RIVER, NEW JERSEY 07458

Library of Congress Cataloging–in–Publication Data

Kagan, Donald
    The Western heritage / Donald Kagan, Steven Ozment, Frank M. Turner.—
    Combined Volume, 7th ed.
        p.   cm.
    Includes bibliographical references and index.
    ISBN 0-13-027718-5
    1. Civilization, Western. I. Ozment, Steven E. II. Turner, Frank M. (Frank Miller), 1944-III. Title.
    CB245.K28 2001
    909′.09812—dc21
                                    00-026148

Editorial Director: Charlyce Jones Owen
Editor-in-Chief, Development: Susanna Lesan
Development Editor: Roberta Meyer
Director of Production
   and Manufacturing: Barbara Kittle
Production Editor: Joseph Scordato
Prepress and Manufacturing Manager:
   Nick Sklitsis
Prepress and Manufacturing Buyer: Lynn Pearlman

Creative Design Director: Leslie Osher
Interior and Cover Designer: Nancy Wells
Electronic Page Layout: Scott Garrison, Joh Lisa,
   Thomas Benfatti
Photo Director: Beth Boyd
Photo Research: Barbara Salz
Cartographer: Carto-Graphics
Copy Editor: Write With, Inc.
Art Manager: Guy Ruggiero

Cover Art: *Mese de Dicembre, Castello de Buonconsiglio.* Trento/Scala/Art Resource, NY

This book was set in 10/12 Trump Mediaeval by the HSS in-house formatting
and production services group and was printed and bound by RR Donnelley & Sons.
The cover was printed by Phoenix Color Corp.

Printed in the United States of America
10 9 8 7 6 5 4 3 2

ISBN 0-13-027282-5

Prentice-Hall International (UK) Limited, *London*
Prentice-Hall of Australia Pty. Limited, *Sydney*
Prentice-Hall Canada Inc., *Toronto*
Prentice-Hall Hispanoamericana, S.A., *Mexico*
Prentice-Hall of India Private Limited, *New Delhi*
Prentice-Hall of Japan, Inc. *Tokyo*
Pearson Education Asia Pte. Ltd., *Singapore*
Editora Prentice-Hall do Brasil, Ltda., *Rio de Janeiro*

TIME LINE PHOTO CREDITS:

Time Line 1: page 0, (left) Gary Cralle/The Image Bank;
(right) Winfield I. Parks Jr./National Geographic Image Collection; page 1, The Granger Collection; page 2, *Battle of
Alexander the Great at Issus.* Roman mosaic. Museo Archeologico Nazionale, Naples, Italy. Scala/Art Resource; p. 3,
Robert Frerck/Woodfin Camp & Associates.

Time Line 2: page 192, Marvin Trachtenberg; page 193,
Bayeus, Musée de l'Eveche. "With special authorization
of the City of Bayeaux." Giraudon/Art Resource.

Time Line 3: page 288, *Elizabeth I, Armada Portrait,* c. 1588
(oil on panel) by George Gower (1540–96) (attr. to). Woburn
Abbey, Bedfordshire, UK/Bridgeman Art Library, Lon-
don/New York; p. 289, The Granger Collection.

Time Line 4: page 586, Philosopher, dramatist, poet, historian, and populizer of scientific ideas, Voltaire
(1694–1778). Bildarchiv Preussischer Kulterbesitz; page
587, By Permission of Musée de la Legion d'Honneur.

Time Line 5: page 778, Corbis; page 779, The Bridgeman
Art Library International.

Time Line 6: page 992, (left) Hulton Getty/Archive Pho-
tos; (right) Franklin D. Roosevelt Library; page 993, (left)
Corbis Sygma Photo News; (right, top) John Launois/
Black Star; (right, bottom) Reuters/Natalie Behring/
Archive Photos.

Brief Contents

Detailed Contents

PART 6   GLOBAL CONFLICT, COLD WAR, AND NEW DIRECTIONS   992

Documents

Maps

Art & the West

The West & the World

Preface

As we enter the twenty-first century, the heritage of Western civilization is a major point of departure for understanding our own epoch. The unprecedented globalization of daily life has occurred in large measure through the spread of Western technological, economic, and political influences. From the sixteenth through the end of the twentieth century the West exerted vast influences throughout the globe for both good and ill, and the global citizens of this new century live in the wake of that impact. It is the goal of this book to introduce its readers to the Western heritage so that they may be better informed and more culturally sensitive citizens of the emerging global age.

Since *The Western Heritage* first appeared, we have sought to provide our readers with a work that does justice to the richness and variety of Western civilization. We hope that such an understanding of the West will foster lively debate on its character, values, institutions, and global influence. Indeed, we believe such a critical outlook on their own culture has characterized the peoples of the West since its earliest history. Through such debates we define ourselves and the values of our culture. Consequently, we welcome the debate and hope that *The Western Heritage*, seventh edition, can help to foster a genuinely informed discussion through its overview of Western civilization, its strengths, weaknesses, and the controveries surrounding it.

Human beings make, experience, and record their history. In this edition as in past editions, our goal has been to present Western civilization fairly, accurately, and in a way that does justice to that great variety of human enterprise. History has many facets, no one of which alone can account for the others. Any attempt to tell the story of the West from a single overarching perspective, no matter how timely, is bound to neglect or suppress some important part of that story. Like all authors, we have had to make selections for an introductory text, but we have attempted to provide the broadest possible coverage suitable to that task of introduction. To that end we hope that the vast array of documents included in this book will allow the widest possible spectrum of people over the course of the centuries to give personal voice to their experience and to allow our readers to enter into that experience.

We also believe that any book addressing the experience of the West must also look beyond its historical European borders. The students reading this book are drawn from a wide variety of cultures and experiences. They live in a world characterized by highly interconnected economies and instant communication between cultures. In this emerging multicultural society it seems both appropriate and necessary to recognize the ways in which Western civilization has throughout its history interacted with other cultures, influencing other societies and being influenced by them. Examples of this two-way interaction, such as that with Islam, appear throughout the text. To further highlight the theme of interaction, *The Western Heritage* includes a series of comparative essays, *The West & the World*. (For a fuller description, see below.)

Goals of the Text

Our primary goal has been to present a strong, clear narrative account of the central developments in Western history. We have also sought to call attention to certain critical themes:

- The capacity of Western civilization from the time of the Greeks to the present to generate transforming self-criticism.
- The development of political freedom, constitutional government, and concern for the rule of law and individual rights.
- The shifting relations among religion, society, and the state.
- The development of science and technology and their expanding impact on thought, social institutions, and everyday life.
- The major religious and intellectual currents that have shaped Western culture.

We believe that these themes have been fundamental in Western civilization, shaping the past and exerting a continuing influence on the present.

FLEXIBLE PRESENTATION *The Western Heritage*, seventh edition, is designed to accommodate a variety of approaches to a course in Western civilization, allowing teachers to stress what is most important to them. Some teachers will ask students to read all the chapters. Others will select among them to reinforce assigned readings and lectures. We have re-organized and rewritten the last two chapters (30 and 31) to permit instructors to end their course by emphasizing either social or political factors in the twentieth-century experience.

INTEGRATED SOCIAL, CULTURAL, AND POLITICAL HISTORY *The Western Heritage* provides one of the richest accounts of the social history of the West available today, with strong coverage of family life, the changing roles of women, and the place of the family in relation to broader economic, political, and social developments. This coverage reflects the explosive growth in social historical research in the past quarter century, which has enriched virtually all areas of historical study. In this edition we have again expanded both the breadth and depth of our coverage of social history through revisions of existing chapters, the addition of major new material, and the inclusion of new documents.

While strongly believing in the study of the social experience of the West, we also share the conviction that internal and external political events have shaped the Western experience in fundamental and powerful ways. The experiences of Europeans in the twentieth century under fascism, national socialism, and communism demonstrate that influence, as has, more recently, the collapse of communism in the former Soviet Union and eastern Europe. We have also been told repeatedly by teachers that no matter what their own historical specialization, they believe that a political narrative gives students an effective tool to begin to organize their understanding of the past. Consequently, we have made every effort to integrate the political with the social, cultural, and intellectual.

No other survey text presents so full an account of the religious and intellectual development of the West. People may be political and social beings, but they are also reasoning and spiritual beings. What they think and believe are among the most important things we can know about them. Their ideas about God, society, law, gender, human nature, and the physical world have changed over the centuries and continue to change. We cannot fully grasp our own approach to the world without understanding the intellectual currents of the past and their influence on our thoughts and conceptual categories.

CLARITY AND ACCESSIBILITY Good narrative history requires clear, vigorous prose. As in earlier editions, we have paid careful attention to the quality of our writing, subjecting every paragraph to critical scrutiny. Our goal was to make our presentation fully accessible to students without compromising vocabulary or conceptual level. We hope this effort will benefit both teachers and students.

Changes in the Seventh Edition

INTRODUCING *ART & THE WEST* A beautiful and important new feature enhances students' understanding of the artistic heritage of the West. In every chapter we highlight a work of art or architecture and discuss how the work illuminates and reflects the period in which it was created. In Chapter 5, for example, a portrait of a young woman on the wall of a house in Pompeii and the accompanying essay provide a glimpse into the life of well-to-do young women in the Roman Empire (p. 161). In Chapter 7, two views of Salisbury Cathedral illustrate an essay on Gothic architecture (p. 248). In Chapter 16, two paintings tell contrasting stories about domestic life in eighteenth-century France (p. 526), and in Part 4, works by Turner, Manet, and Seurat illustrate both the power of the new industrialism and its effects on European social life. Part 5 includes discussions of paintings by Grosz, Magritte, and Picasso. In Chapter 30, *Bread*, painted by the Soviet realist Tatjiana Yablonskaya, and Jackson Pollock's *One (Number 31, 1950)*, offer starkly contrasting views of twentieth-century culture (p. 1040). (See p. xxiv for a complete list of *Art & The West* essays.)

THE WEST & THE WORLD In this feature, we focus on six subjects, comparing Western institutions with those of other parts of the world, or discussing the ways in which developments in the West have influenced cultures in other areas of the globe. In the seventh edition, the essays are:

Part 1: Ancient Warfare (new) (p. 186)
Part 2: The Invention of Printing in China and Europe (new) (p. 284)
Part 3: The Columbian Exchange (new) (p. 582)
Part 4: The Abolition of Slavery in the Transatlantic Economy (p. 736)
Part 5: Imperialism: Ancient and Modern (p. 928)
Part 6: Energy and the Modern World (new) (p. 1116)

RECENT SCHOLARSHIP As in previous editions, changes in this edition reflect our determination to incorporate the most recent developments in historical scholarship and the concerns of professional historians. Of particular interest are expanded discussions of:

• **Women in the history of the West.** Adding to our longstanding commitment to the inclusion of the experience of women in Western civilization, this edition presents new scholarship on women in the ancient world and the Middle Ages, women and the scientific revolution, and women under the authoritarian governments of the twentieth century. (See, especially, chapters 3, 4, 5, 7, 14, 30.)

- **The Scientific Revolution.** Chapter 14, which addresses the rise of the new science, has been wholly revised and rewritten to clarify the new scientific theory arising from the Copernican revolution, the new understanding of the Galileo case, the role of women in the new science, and the social institutions of the new science.

- **The Dutch Golden Age.** A new section in Chapter 15 discusses the United Netherlands during the seventeenth and eighteenth centuries.

- **Africa and the transatlantic economy.** An extensive section in Chapter 17 explores the relationship of Africa to the transatlantic economy of the sixteenth through eighteenth centuries. We examine the role of African society and politics in the slave trade, the experience of Africans forcibly transported to the Americas, and the incorporation of elements of African culture into the New World.

- **Jewish thinkers in the Enlightenment.** A new section in Chapter 18 discusses the thought of Spinoza and Moses Mendelsohn as they relate to the role of Jewish religion and society in the wider European culture.

- **The Holocaust.** The discussion of the Holocaust has been significantly expanded in two ways. Chapter 29 provides more analysis of the causes of the Holocaust, and Chapter 30 includes an extensive new narrative of the particular case of the destruction of the Jews of Poland.

- **Twentieth-century social history.** The seventh edition of *The Western Heritage* presents the most extensive treatment of twentieth-century social history available in a survey text. We examine, in Chapter 30, the experiences of women under authoritarian governments, the collectivization of Soviet agriculture, the destruction of the Polish Jewish community, and European migration. The chapter concludes with a new section on the coming of the computer and the impact of new technology on European life.

- **The history of the Cold War and Europe at the start of the twenty-first century.** Chapter 31, on the Soviet–American rivalry and the collapse of communism, has been wholly rewritten and includes the conflict in the former Yugoslavia. Instructors may close their course with either of the twentieth-century chapters, depending on the issues they wish to emphasize.

Chapter-by-Chapter Revisions

Chapter 1 The treatment of the origins of humankind has been completely rewritten to reflect the newest scholarship.

Chapters 3, 4, 5 contain new sections on Women in Homeric Society; Aspasia, Pericles' Common-law Wife; Greek Slavery; Women in Early Rome; Women of the Upper Classes in later Roman history.

Chapter 9 contains a discussion of medieval Russia.

Chapter 12 includes a shorter, rewritten discussion of The Thirty Years' War.

Chapter 14 has a wholly rewritten discussion of the Scientific Revolution and of the impact of the Scientific Revolution on philosophy, new or extensively rewritten sections on women and early modern science, the new institutions associated with the emerging scientific knowledge, religious faith and the new science, with an expanded discussion of the Galileo case.

Chapter 15 contains an extensive new section on the Dutch Golden Age, including the impact of its overseas empire on its prosperity.

Chapter 16 has a new section on The Impact of the Agricultural and Industrial Revolutions on Working Women.

Chapter 17 includes a much expanded and revised section on African Slavery, the experiences of Africans in the Americas, and the cultural institutions they brought with them.

Chapter 18 has a new section on Jewish Thinkers in the Age of Enlightenment with emphasis on Spinoza and Moses Mendelsohn.

Chapter 22 has a refocused discussion of Karl Marx's thought.

Chapter 25 expands the treatment of racial thinking and the non-Western world.

Chapter 28 includes a rewritten discussion of the Soviet Experience in the 1930s.

Chapter 29 expands the discussion of the Holocaust.

Chapter 30 is a largely new chapter on twentieth-century social history, with major new sections on state violence, women under authoritarian governments, the collectivization of Soviet agriculture, the destruction of the Polish Jews, and the impact of the computer.

Chapter 31 has been extensively rewritten and reorganized to reflect the latest scholarship on the Cold War through the collapse of communism. It ends with a discussion of Europe at the Opening of the Global Century.

The last two chapters are written so that instructors, though teaching both chapters, may choose to close their course with either, depending upon their personal emphasis. Those instructors wishing to emphasize social history might end the course with Chapter 30 and those wishing to emphasize political development and great power relations may choose to conclude with Chapter 31.

MAPS AND ILLUSTRATIONS   To help students understand the relationship between geography and history, we have added relief features to approximately one-half of the maps. All 90 maps have been carefully edited for accuracy. The text also contains close to 500 color and black and white illustrations, many of them new to the seventh edition.

PEDAGOGICAL FEATURES   This edition retains the pedagogical features of the last edition, including part-opening comparative timelines, a list of key topics at the beginning of each chapter, chapter review questions, and questions accompanying the more than 200 source documents in the text. Each of these features is designed to make the text more accessible to students and to reinforce key concepts.

- **Illustrated timelines** open each of the six parts of the book summarizing, side-by-side, the major events in politics and government, society and economy, and religion and culture.

- **Primary source documents**, more than one third new to this edition, acquaint students with the raw material of history and provide intimate contact with the people of the past and their concerns. Questions accompanying the source documents direct students toward important, thought-provoking issues and help them relate the documents to the material in the text. They can be used to stimulate class discussion or as topics for essays and study groups.

- Each chapter includes an **outline**, a **list of key topics**, and an **introduction**. Together these features provide a succinct overview of each chapter.

- **Chronologies** follow each major section in a chapter, listing significant events and their dates.

- *In Perspective* sections summarize the major themes of each chapter and provide a bridge to the next chapter.

- **Chapter review questions** help students review the material in a chapter and relate it to broader themes. They too can be used for class discussion and essay topics.

- **Suggested readings lists** following each chapter have been updated with new titles reflecting recent scholarship.

A NOTE ON DATES AND TRANSLITERATIONS   This edition of *The Western Heritage* continues the practice of using B.C.E. (before the common era) and C.E. (common era) instead of B.C. (before Christ) and A.D. (*anno domini*, the year of the Lord) to designate dates. We also follow the most accurate currently accepted English transliterations of Arabic words. For example, today Koran is being replaced by the more accurate Qur'an; similarly Muhammad is preferable to Mohammed and Muslim to Moslem.

Ancillary Instructional Materials

The ancillary instructional materials that accompany *The Western Heritage* include print and multimedia supplements that are designed to reinforce and enliven the richness of the past and inspire students with the excitement of studying the history of Western civilization.

Print Supplements for the Instructor

INSTRUCTOR'S MANUAL WITH TEST ITEMS   The Instructor's Manual contains chapter summaries, key points and vital concepts, and information on audio-visual resources that can be used in developing and preparing lecture presentations. Also included is a test item file that offers multiple-choice, identification, and essay test questions.

PRENTICE HALL CUSTOM TEST   This commercial-quality computerized test management program, for Windows and Macintosh environments, allows users to create their own tests using items from the printed Test Item File. The program allows users to edit the items in the Test Item File and to add their own questions. Online testing is also available.

TRANSPARENCY PACKAGE   This collection of full-color transparency acetates provides the maps, charts, and graphs from the text for use in classroom presentations.

ADMINISTRATIVE HANDBOOK by Jay Boggis provides instructors with resources for using *The Western Heritage* with Annenberg/CPB telecourse, *The Western Tradition*.

Print Supplements for the Student

STUDY GUIDE, VOLUMES I AND II   The study guide includes commentaries, definitions, and a variety of exercises designed to reinforce the concepts in the chapter. These exercises include: identification, map exercises, and short-answer and essay questions.

DOCUMENTS SET, VOLUMES I AND II   This carefully selected and edited set of documents provides over 100 additional primary source readings. Each document includes a brief introduction as well as questions to encourage critical analysis of the reading and to relate it to the content of the text.

MAP WORKBOOK   This brief workbook gives students the opportunity to increase their knowledge of geography through identification and other map exercises. It is available free to students when shrink-wrapped with the text.

HISTORICAL ATLAS OF THE WORLD   This four-color historical atlas provides additional map resources to reinforce concepts in the text. It is available for a nominal fee when shrink-wrapped with the text.

UNDERSTANDING AND ANSWERING ESSAY QUESTIONS Prepared by Mary L. Kelley, San Antonio College. This brief guide suggests helpful study techniques as well as specific analytical tools for understanding different types of essay questions and provides precise guidelines for preparing well-crafted essay answers. This guide is available free to students when shrink-wrapped with the text.

READING CRITICALLY ABOUT HISTORY: A GUIDE TO ACTIVE READING   Prepared by Rose Wassman and Lee Ann Rinsky. This guide focuses on the skills needed to learn the essential information presented in college history textbooks. Material covered includes  vocabulary skills, recognizing organizational patterns, critical thinking skills, understanding visual aids, and practice sections. This guide is available free to students when shrink-wrapped with the text.

THEMES OF THE TIMES   *The New York Times* and Prentice Hall are sponsoring *Themes of the Times*, a program designed to enhance student access to current information of relevance in the classroom. Through this program, the core subject matter provided in the text is supplemented by a collection of current articles from one of the world's most distinguished newspapers, *The New York Times*.

These articles demonstrate the vital, ongoing connection between what is learned in the classroom and what is happening in the world around us. To enjoy the wealth of information of *The New York Times* daily, a reduced subscription rate is available. For information call toll-free: 1-800-631-1222.

Prentice Hall and *The New York Times* are proud to co-sponsor *Themes of the Times*. We hope it will make the reading of both textbooks and newspapers a more dynamic, involving process.

TELECOURSE STUDY GUIDE, VOLUMES I AND II, by Jay Boggis correlates *The Western Heritage* with the Annenberg/CPB telecourse, *The Western Tradition*.

Multimedia Supplements

HISTORY ON THE INTERNET   This guide focuses on developing the critical thinking skills necessary to evaluate and use online sources. The guide also provides a brief introduction to navigating the Internet, along with complete references related specifically to the History discipline and how to use the *Companion Website*™ available for *The Western Heritage*. This supplementary book is free to students when shrink-wrapped with the text.

COMPANION WEBSITE™
ADDRESS: WWW.PRENHALL.COM/KAGAN
Students can now take full advantage of the World Wide Web to enrich their study of Western Civilization through *The Western Heritage Companion Website*™. Features of the website include, for each chapter in the text, objectives, study questions, map labeling exercises, related links, and document exercises. A faculty module provides material from the Instructor's Manual and the maps and charts from the text in Powerpoint™ format.

POWERPOINT™ IMAGES CD ROM   Available for Windows and Macintosh environments, this resource includes the maps, charts, and graphs from the text for use in Powerpoint™ . Organized by chapters in the text, this collection of images is useful for classroom presentations and lectures.

IRC WESTERN CIVILIZATION CD ROM   Available for Windows 95 and 3.1, this lecture and presentation resource includes a library of over 3000 images, each with a descriptive caption, plus film clips, maps, and sound recordings. A correlation guide lists the images as they correspond to the chapters of *The Western Heritage*. Contact your local Prentice Hall representative for information about the adoption requirements for this resource.

COURSE MANAGEMENT SYSTEMS   For instructors interested in distance learning, Prentice Hall offers fully customizable, online courses with enhanced content, www links, online testing, and many other course management features using the best available course management systems available, including WebCT, Blackboard, and ecollege online course architecture. Contact your local Prentice Hall representative or visit our special Demonstration Central Website at http://www.prenhall.com/demo for more information.

Acknowledgments

We are grateful to the scholars and teachers whose thoughtful and often detailed comments helped shape this revision:

Lenard R. Berlanstein, University of
  Virginia, Charlottesville
Margaret Bostwick, John Jay College
Stephanie Christelow, Idaho State University
Samuel Willard Crompton, Holyoke
  Community College
Mary Beth Emmerichs, University of Wisconsin–
  Sheboygan
Robert L. Ervin, San Jacinto Community College
Benjamin Foster, Yale University
Joseph Gonzales, Moorpark College
Victor Davis Hanson, California State
  University, Fresno
John Hinde, Malaspina University-College
William I. Hitchcock, Wellesley College
Pardaic Kenny, University of Colorado, Boulder
Raymond F. Kierstead, Reed College

Steven Leibo, Russell Sage College
David Lindberg, University of
  Wisconsin, Madison
Eleanor McCluskey, Palm Beach Atlantic College
  and Broward Community College
Robert J. Mueller, Hastings College
John Nicols, University of Oregon, Eugene
W. Gary Nichols, The Citadel
Sandra J. Peacock, State University of New York,
  Binghamton
John Powell, Pennsylvania State University
Richard R. Rivers, Macomb Community College
Robert A. Schneider, Catholic University
Hugo Schwyzer, Pasadena City College
Sidney R. Sherter, Long Island University
Roger P. Snow, College of Great Falls

Ilicia J. Sprey, Blue Ridge Community College

Rachel Stocking, Southern Illinois University at
  Carbondale

Finally, we would like to thank the dedicated people who helped produce this revision. Our acquisitions editor, Charlyce Jones Owen; our development editor, Roberta Meyer; our production editor, Joe Scordato; Nancy Wells, who created the handsome new design of this edition; Scott Garrison, who formatted the pages; Lynn Pearlman, our manufacturing buyer; and Barbara Salz, photo researcher.

D.K.
S.O.
F.M.T.

About the Authors

DONALD KAGAN is Hillhouse Professor of History and Classics at Yale University, where he has taught since 1969. He received the A.B. degree in history from Brooklyn College, the M.A. in classics from Brown University, and the Ph.D. in history from Ohio State University. During 1958–1959 he studied at the American School of Classical Studies as a Fulbright Scholar. He has received three awards for undergraduate teaching at Cornell and Yale. He is the author of a history of Greek political thought, *The Great Dialogue* (1965); a four-volume history of the Peloponnesian war, *The Origins of the Peloponnesian War* (1969); *The Archidamian War* (1974); *The Peace of Nicias and the Sicilian Expedition* (1981); *The Fall of the Athenian Empire* (1987); and a biography of Pericles, *Pericles of Athens and the Birth of Democracy* (1991); and *On the Origins of War* (1995). He is coauthor, with Frederick W. Kagan of *While America Sleeps* (2000). With Brian Tierney and L. Pearce Williams, he is the editor of *Great Issues in Western Civilization*, a collection of readings.

STEVEN OZMENT is McLean Professor of Ancient and Modern History at Harvard University. He has taught Western Civilization at Yale, Stanford, and Harvard. He is the author of ten books. *The Age of Reform, 1250–1550* (1980) won the Schaff Prize and was nominated for the 1981 American Book Award. *Magdalena and Balthasar: An Intimate Portrait of Life in Sixteenth Century Europe* (1986), *Three Behaim Boys: Growing Up in Early Modern Germany* (1990), *Protestants: The Birth of a Revolution* (1992), and *The Burgermeister's Daughter: Scandal in a Sixteenth Century German Town* (1996) were selections of the History Book Club, as is his most recent book, *Flesh and Spirit: Private Life in Early Modern Germany* (1999).

FRANK M. TURNER is John Hay Whitney Professor of History at Yale University, where he served as University Provost from 1988 to 1992. He received his B.A. degree at the College of William and Mary and his Ph.D. from Yale. He has received the Yale College Award for Distinguished Undergraduate Teaching. He has directed a National Endowment for the Humanities Summer Institute. His scholarly research has received the support of fellowships from the National Endowment for the Humanities and the Guggenheim Foundation and the Woodrow Wilson Center. He is the author of *Between Science and Religion: The Reaction to Scientific Naturalism in Late Victorian England* (1974), *The Greek Heritage in Victorian Britain* (1981), which received the British Council Prize of the Conference on British Studies and the Yale Press Governors Award, and *Contesting Cultural Authority: Essays in Victorian Intellectual Life* (1993). He has also contributed numerous articles to journals and has served on the editorial advisory boards of *The Journal of Modern History, Isis,* and *Victorian Studies.* He edited *The Idea of a University*, by John Henry Newman (1996). Since 1996 he has served as a Trustee of Connecticut College.

Part 1

1,000,000 B.C.E.–400 C.E.

	POLITICS AND GOVERNMENT	SOCIETY AND ECONOMY	RELIGION AND CULTURE
1,000,000–3500 B.C.E.		ca. 1,000,000–10,000 B.C.E. **Paleolithic Age** ca. 8,000 B.C.E. **Earliest Neolithic settlements**	ca. 30,0000–6000 B.C.E. **Paleolithic art**
3500–2200 B.C.E.	ca. 3100–2700 B.C.E. **Egyptian Early Dynastic Period; unification of Upper and Lower Egypt** ca. 2800–2340 B.C.E. **Sumerian city-states' Early Dynastic period** 2700–2200 B.C.E. **Egyptian Old Kingdom** ca. 2370 B.C.E. **Sargon established Akkadian Empire**	ca. 3500 B.C.E. **Earliest Sumerian settlements** ca. 3000 B.C.E. **First urban settlements in Egypt and Mesopotamia; Bronze Age begins in Mesopotamia and Egypt** ca. 2900–1150 B.C.E. **Bronze Age Minoan society on Crete; Helladic society on Greek mainland**	ca. 3000 B.C.E. **Invention of writing** ca. 3000 B.C.E. **Temples to gods in Mesopotamia; development of ziggurat temple architecture** 2700–2200 B.C.E. **Building of pyramids for Egyptian god-kings, development of hieroglyphic writing in Egypt**
2200–1600 B.C.E.	2200–2052 B.C.E. **Egyptian First Intermediate Period** 2052–1786 B.C.E. **Egyptian Middle Kingdom** 1792–1760 B.C.E. **Reign of Hammurabi; height of Old Babylonian Kingdom; publication of Code of Hammurabi** 1786–1575 B.C.E. **Egyptian Second Intermediate Period** ca. 1700 B.C.E. **Hyksos' invasion of Egypt**	ca. 2000 B.C.E. **Hittites arrive in Asia Minor** ca 1900 B.C.E. **Amorites in Babylonia**	2200–1786 B.C.E. **Rise of Amon-Re as chief Egyptian god** ca. 1900 B.C.E. **Traditional date for Hebrew patriarch Abraham**  Sumerian clay tablet
1600–1100 B.C.E.	ca. 1600 B.C.E. **Fall of Old Babylonian Kingdom** 1575–1087 B.C.E. **Egyptian New Kingdom (or Empire)** ca. 1400–1200 B.C.E. **Height of Hittite Empire** ca. 1400–1200 B.C.E. **Height of Mycenaean power** 1367–1350 B.C.E. **Amenhotep IV (Akhenaten) in Egypt**  Queen Nefertiti ca. 1250 B.C.E. **Sack of Troy (?)** 1087–30 B.C.E. **Egyptian Post-Empire Period**	ca. 1200 B.C.E. **Hebrews arrive in Palestine**	1367–1360 B.C.E. **Religious revolution led by Akhenaten makes Aton chief Egyptian god** 1347–1339 B.C.E. **Tutankhamen restores worship of Amon-Re**

THE FOUNDATIONS OF WESTERN CIVILIZATION IN THE ANCIENT WORLD

1,000,000 B.C.E.–400 C.E.

	POLITICS AND GOVERNMENT	SOCIETY AND ECONOMY	RELIGION AND CULTURE
1100– 500 B.C.E.	ca. 1000– 961 B.C.E. **Reign of King David in Israel**	ca. 1100– 750 B.C.E. **Greek "Dark Ages"**	
	ca. 961–922 **Reign of King Solomon in Israel**	ca. 1000 B.C.E. **Italic peoples enter Italy**	
	ca. 1100– 615 B.C.E. **Assyrian Empire**	ca. 800 B.C.E. **Etruscans enter Italy**	
	ca. 800–400 B.C.E. **Height of Etruscan culture in Italy**	ca. 750–700 B.C.E. **Rise of *Polis* in Greece**	ca. 750 B.C.E. **Hebrew prophets teach monotheism**
	ca. 650 B.C.E. **Spartan constitution formed**	ca. 750–600 B.C.E. **Great age of Greek colonization**	ca. 750 B.C.E. **Traditional date for Homer**
	722 B.C.E. **Israel (northern kingdom) falls to Assyrians**	ca. 700 B.C.E. **Invention of hoplite phalanx**	ca. 750 B.C.E. **Greeks adapt Semitic script and invent the Greek alphabet**
	ca. 700–500 B.C.E. **Rise and decline of tyranny in Greece**		ca. 750–600 B.C.E. **Panhellenic shrines established at Olympia, Delphi, Corinth, and Nemea; athletic festivals attached to them**
	621 B.C.E. **First written law code in Athens**		
	612–539 B.C.E. **Neo-Babylonian (Chaldean) Empire**		
	594 B.C.E. **Solon's constitutional reforms, Athens**	ca. 600–550 B.C.E. **Spartans adopt new communitarian social system**	ca. 700 B.C.E. **Traditional date for Hesiod**
	586 B.C.E. **Destruction of Jerusalem; fall of Judah (southern kingdom); Babylonian Captivity**	ca. 600–500 B.C.E. **Athens develops commerce and a mixed economy**	ca. 675–500 B.C.E. **Development of Greek lyric and elegiac poetry**
	ca. 560–550 B.C.E. **Peloponnesian League begins**		ca. 570 B.C.E. **Birth of Greek philosophy in Ionia**
	559–530 B.C.E. **Reign of Cyrus the Great in Persia**		ca. 550 B.C.E. **Oracle of Apollo at Delphi grows to great influence**
	546 B.C.E. **Persia conquers Lydian Empire of Croesus, including Greek cities of Asia Minor**		ca. 550 B.C.E. **Cult of Dionysus introduced to Athens**
	539 B.C.E. **Persia conquers Babylonia; temple at Jerusalem restored; exiles return from Babylonia**		539 B.C.E. **Restoration of temple in Jerusalem; return of exiles**
	521–485 B.C.E. **Reign of Darius in Persia**		 Hercules taming Cerberus, Greek, 530 B.C.E.
	509 B.C.E. **Kings expelled from Rome; Republic founded**		
	508 B.C.E. **Clisthenes founds Athenian democracy**		
500–336 B.C.E.	490 B.C.E. **Battle of Marathon**	ca. 500–350 B.C.E. **Spartan population shrinks**	ca. 500–400 B.C.E. **Great age of Athenian tragedy**
	485–465 B.C.E. **Reign of Xerxes in Persia**	ca. 500–350 B.C.E. **Rapid growth in overseas trade**	469–399 B.C.E. **Life of Socrates**

1,000,000 B.C.E.–400 C.E.

	POLITICS AND GOVERNMENT	SOCIETY AND ECONOMY	RELIGION AND CULTURE
500–336 B.C.E. (cont.)	480–479 B.C.E. **Xerxes invades Greece**	477–431 B.C.E. **Vast growth in Athenian wealth**	ca. 450–400 B.C.E. **Great influence of Sophists in Athens**
	478–477 B.C.E. **Delian League founded**		ca. 450–385 B.C.E. **Great age of Athenian comedy**
	ca. 460–445 B.C.E. **First Peloponnesian War**		448–432 B.C.E. **Periclean building program on Athenian acropolis**
	450–449 B.C.E. **Laws of the Twelve Tables, Rome**		
	431–404 B.C.E. **Great Peloponnesian War**	431–400 B.C.E. **Peloponnesian War casualties cause decline in size of lower class in Athens, with relative increase in importance of upper and middle classes**	429–347 B.C.E. **Life of Plato**
	404–403 B.C.E. **Thirty Tyrants rule at Athens**		ca. 425 B.C.E. **Herodotus' history of the Persian Wars**
	400–387 B.C.E. **Spartan war against Persia**		ca. 400 B.C.E. **Thucydides' history of the Peloponnesian War**
	398–360 B.C.E. **Reign of Agesilaus at Sparta**		ca. 400–325 B.C.E. **Life of Diogenes the Cynic**
	395–387 B.C.E. **Corinthian War**		386 B.C.E. **Foundation of Plato's Academy**
	392 B.C.E. **Romans defeat Etruscans**		384–322 B.C.E. **Life of Aristotle**
	378 B.C.E. **Second Athenian Confederation**		
	371 B.C.E. **Thebans end Spartan hegemony**		
	362 B.C.E. **Battle of Mantinea; end of Theban hegemony**		
	338 B.C.E. **Philip of Macedon conquers Greece**		
336–31 B.C.E.	336–323 B.C.E. **Reign of Alexander III (the Great)**		336 B.C.E. **Foundation of Aristotle's Lyceum**
	334 B.C.E. **Alexander invades Asia**		342–271 B.C.E. **Life of Epicurus**
	330 B.C.E. **Fall of Persepolis; end Achaemenid rule in Persia**	 Alexander the Great & Darius III	335–263 B.C.E. **Life of Zeno the Stoic**
	323–301 B.C.E. **Ptolemaic Kingdom (Egypt), Seleucid Kingdom (Syria), and Antigonid Dynasty (Macedon) founded**	ca. 300 B.C.E.– 150 C.E. **Growth of international trade and development of large cities in Hellenistic/Roman world**	ca. 287–212 B.C.E. **Life of Archimedes of Syracuse**
	287 B.C.E. **Laws passed by Plebeian Assembly made binding on all Romans; end of Struggle of the Orders**		ca. 275 B.C.E. **Foundation of museum and library make Alexandria the center of Greek intellectual life**
	264–241 B.C.E. **First Punic War**		
	218–202 B.C.E. **Second Punic War**	ca. 218–135 B.C.E. **Decline of family farm in Italy; growth of tenant farming and cattle ranching**	ca. 250 B.C.E. **Livius Andronicus translates the *Odyssey* into Latin**
	215–168 B.C.E. **Rome establishes rule over Hellenistic world**		106–43 B.C.E. **Life of Cicero**

1,000,000 B.C.E.–400 C.E.

	POLITICS AND GOVERNMENT	SOCIETY AND ECONOMY	RELIGION AND CULTURE
336–31 B.C.E. (cont.)	154–133 B.C.E. **Roman wars in Spain**	ca. 150 B.C.E. **Growth of slavery as basis of economy in Roman Republic**	ca. 99–55 B.C.E. **Life of Lucretius**
	133 B.C.E. **Tribunate of Tiberius Gracchus**		86–35 B.C.E. **Life Sallust**
	123–122 B.C.E. **Tribunate of Gaius Gracchus**		ca. 84–54 B.C.E. **Life Catullus**
	82 B.C.E. **Sulla assumes dictatorship**		70–19 B.C.E. **Life of Vergil**
	60 B.C.E. **First Triumvirate**		65–8 B.C.E. **Life of Horace**
	46–44 B.C.E. **Caesar's dictatorship**		59 B.C.E.–17 C.E. **Life of Livy**
	43 B.C.E. **Second Triumvirate**		43 B.C.E.–18 C.E. **Life of Ovid**
31 B.C.E.– 400 C.E.	31 B.C.E. **Octavian and Agrippa defeat Anthony at Actium**		9 B.C.E. **Ara Pacis dedicated at Rome**
	27 B.C.E.–14 C.E. **Reign of Augustus**		ca. 4 B.C.E. **Birth of Jesus of Nazareth**
	14–68 C.E. **Reigns of Julio-Claudian Emperors**		ca. 30 C.E. **Crucifixion of Jesus**
	69–96 C.E. **Reigns of Flavian Emperors**		64 C.E. **Christians persecuted by Nero**
	96–180 C.E. **Reigns of "Good Emperors"**		66–135 C.E. **Romans suppress rebellions of Jews**
	180–192 C.E. **Reign of Commodus**		ca. 70–100 C.E. **Gospels written**
	284–305 C.E. **Reign of Diocletian; reform and division of Roman Empire**	ca. 150–400 C.E. **Decline of slavery and growth of tenant farming and serfdom in Roman Empire**	ca. 150 C.E. **Ptolemy of Alexandria establishes canonical geocentric model of the universe**
	306–337 C.E. **Reign of Constantine**	ca. 250–400 C.E. ***Coloni* (Roman tenant farmers) increasingly tied to the land**	ca. 250–260 C.E. **Severe persecutions by Decius and Valerian**
	330 C.E. **Constantinople new capital of Roman Empire**	301 C.E. **Edict of Maximum Prices at Rome**	303 C.E. **Persecution of Christians by Diocletian**
	361–363 C.E. **Reign of Julian the Apostate**		311 C.E. **Galerius issues Edict of Toleration**
	379–395 C.E. **Reign of Theodosius**		312 C.E. **Constantine converts to Christianity**
	376 C.E. **Visigoths enter Roman Empire**		325 C.E. **Council of Nicaea**
			348–420 C.E. **Life of St. Jerome**
			354–430 C.E. **Life of St. Augustine**
			395 C.E. **Christianity becomes official religion of Roman Empire**

The Roman Forum

This limestone statue depicts the head of Queen Nefertiti (about 1348–1345 B.C.E.), wife of the rebel pharaoh Akhenaten of the Eighteenth Egyptian Dynasty in the period of the New Kingdom. It was discovered at the modern site called Tell el-Amarna, the ancient city of Akhetaten founded by the pharaoh as his new capital and the center of the new worship of Aten, the disc of the sun. The queen appears to have had unusual importance, serving, along with the pharaoh, as one of the only mediators between the god and the people.

Gary Cralle/The Image Bank

The Birth of Civilization

KEY TOPICS

- The earliest history of humanity, including the beginnings of human culture in the Paleolithic Age, the agricultural revolution and the shift from food gathering to food production, and the emergence of civilization in the great river valleys of the Near East and Asia

- The ancient civilizations of Mesopotamia and Egypt

- The great Near Eastern empires, 1500–539 B.C.E.

- The emergence of Judaism

- The difference in outlook between ancient Near Eastern civilization and ancient Greek civilization

H*istory, in its two senses—as the events of the past that make up the human experience on earth and as the written record of those events—is a subject of both interest and importance. We naturally want to know how we came to be who we are, and how the world we live in came to be what it is. But beyond its intrinsic interest, history provides crucial insight into present human behavior. To understand who we are now, we need to know the record of the past and to try to understand the people and forces that shaped it.*

For hundreds of thousands of years after the human species emerged, people lived by hunting, fishing, and collecting wild plants. Only some 10,000 years ago did they learn to cultivate plants, herd animals, and make airtight pottery for storage. These discoveries transformed them from gatherers to producers and allowed them to grow in number and to lead a settled life.

About 5,000 years ago humans learned how to control the waters of great river valleys, making possible much richer harvests and supporting a further increase in population. The peoples of these river valley societies created the earliest civilizations. They invented writing, which, among other things, enabled them to keep inventories of food and other resources. They discovered the secret of smelting metal to make tools and weapons of bronze far superior to the stone implements of earlier times. They came together in towns and cities, where industry and commerce flourished. Complex religions took form, and social divisions increased. Kings—considered to be representatives of the gods or to be themselves divine—emerged as rulers, assisted by priests and defended by well-organized armies.

The first of these civilizations appeared among the Sumerians before 3500 B.C.E. in the Tigris–Euphrates Valley we call Mesopotamia. From the Sumerians to the Assyrians and Babylonians, a series of peoples ruled Mesopotamia, each shaping and passing along its distinctive culture, before the region fell under the control of great foreign empires. A second early civilization emerged in the Nile Valley around 3100 B.C.E. Egyptian civilization developed a remarkably continuous pattern, in part because Egypt was largely protected from invasion by the formidable deserts surrounding the valley. The essential character of Egyptian civilization changed little for nearly 3000 years. Influences from other areas, however, especially Nubia to the south, Syria–Palestine to the northeast, and the Aegean to the north, may be seen during many periods of Egyptian history.

By the fourteenth century B.C.E., several powerful empires had arisen and were vying for dominance in regions that included Egypt, Mesopotamia, and Asia Minor. Northern warrior peoples, among them the Hittites, the Kassites, and the Mitannians, conquered and ruled peoples in various areas. The Hittites dominated in Asia Minor, the Kassites in southern Mesopotamia, and the Mitannians in northern Mesopotamia and Syria. For two centuries, the Hittite and Egyptian Empires struggled with each other for control of Syria–Palestine. By about 1200 B.C.E., however, both these empires had collapsed. Beginning about 850 B.C.E., the Assyrians arose in northern Mesopotamia and ultimately established a mighty new empire, even invading Egypt in the early seventh century B.C.E. The Assyrians were dominant until the late seventh century B.C.E., when they fell to a combination of enemies. Their vast empire was overtaken by the Babylonians, but these people, too, would soon become only a small, though important, part of the enormous empire of Persia.

Among all these great empires nestled a people called the Israelites, who maintained a small independent kingdom in the region between Egypt and Syria for several centuries. This kingdom ultimately fell to the Assyrians and later remained subject to other conquerors. The Israelites possessed little worldly power or wealth, but they created a powerful religion, Judaism, the first certain and lasting worship of a single god in a world of polytheism. Judaism was the seedbed of two other religions that have played a mighty role in the history of the world: Christianity and Islam. The great empires have collapsed, their power forgotten for millennia until the tools of archaeologists uncovered their remains, but the religion of the Israelites, in itself and through its offshoots, has endured as a powerful force.

Early Humans and Their Culture

Scientists estimate that the earth may be as many as 6 billion years old and that creatures very much like humans appeared perhaps 3 to 5 million years ago, probably in Africa. Some 1 to 2 million years ago, erect and tool-using early humans spread over much of Africa, Europe, and Asia. Our own species, *Homo sapiens*, probably emerged some 200,000 years ago, and the earliest remains of fully modern humans date to about 90,000 years ago.

Humans, unlike other animals, are cultural beings. *Culture* may be defined as the ways of living built up by a group and passed on from one generation to another. It includes behavior such as courtship or child-rearing practices; material things such as tools, clothing, and shelter; and ideas, institutions, and beliefs. Language, apparently a uniquely human trait, lies behind our ability to create ideas and institutions and to transmit culture from one generation to another. Our flexible and dexterous hands enable us to hold and make tools and so to create the material artifacts of culture. Because culture is learned and not inherited, it permits rapid adaptation to changing conditions, making possible the spread of humanity to almost all the lands of the globe.

The Paleolithic Age

Anthropologists designate early human cultures by their tools. The earliest period—the Paleolithic (from Greek, "old stone")—dates from the earliest use of stone tools some one million years ago to about 10,000 B.C.E. During this immensely long period, people were hunters, fishers, and gatherers, but not producers, of food. They learned to make and use increasingly sophisticated tools of stone and

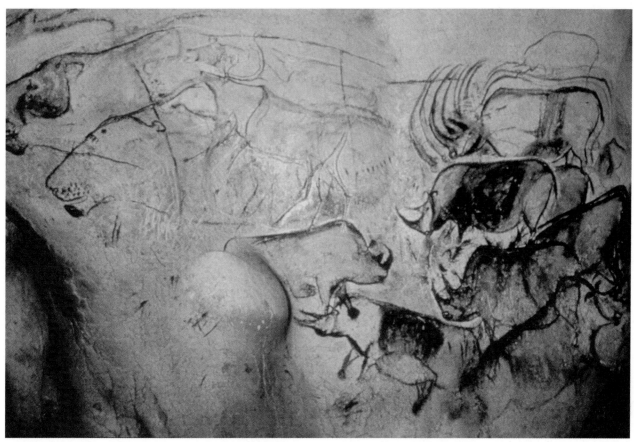

In Chauvet cave, near Avignon, France, Paleolithic artists decorated the walls with exquisite drawings of animals. Jean Clottes/Corbis Sygma Photo News

perishable materials like wood; they learned to make and control fire; and they acquired language and the ability to use it to pass on what they had learned.

These early humans, dependent on nature for food and vulnerable to wild beasts and natural disasters, may have developed responses to the world rooted in fear of the unknown—of the uncertainties of human life or the overpowering forces of nature. Religious and magical beliefs and practices may have emerged in an effort to propitiate or coerce the superhuman forces thought to animate or direct the natural world. Evidence of religious faith and practice, as well as of magic, goes as far back as archaeology can take us. Fear or awe, exultation, gratitude, and empathy with the natural world must all have figured in the cave art and in the ritual practices, such as burial, that we find evidenced at Paleolithic sites around the globe. The sense that there is more to the world than meets the eye—in other words, the religious response to the world—seems to be as old as humankind.

The style of life and the level of technology of the Paleolithic period could support only a sparsely settled society. If hunters were too numerous, game would not suffice. In Paleolothic times, people were subject to the same natural and ecological constraints that today maintain a balance between wolves and deer in Alaska.

Evidence from Paleolithic art and from modern hunter–gatherer societies suggests that human life in the Paleolitic Age was probably characterized by a division of labor by sex. Men engaged in hunting, fishing, making tools and weapons, and fighting against other families, clans, and tribes. Women, less mobile because of childbearing, gathered nuts, berries, and wild grains, wove baskets, and made clothing. Women gathering food probably discovered how to plant and care for seeds. This knowledge eventually made possible the development of agriculture and animal husbandry.

The Neolithic Age

Only a few Paleolithic societies made the initial shift from hunting and gathering to agriculture. Anthropologists and archaeologists disagree as to why, but however it happened, some 10,000 years ago parts of what we now call the Near East began to change from a nomadic hunter–gatherer culture to a more settled agricultural one. Because the shift to agriculture coincided with advances in stone tool technology—

At Ain Ghazal, a Neolithic site in Jordan, several pits contained male and female statues made of clay modeled over a reed framework. Similar figures have been found at Jericho and other sites, all from the same period, about 8500–7000 B.C.E. They were probably used in religious rituals, perhaps connected with ancestor worship, as were plastered skulls, masks, carved heads, and other artifacts. Archeological Museum, Amman, Jordan,kingdom/Art Resource. ©Photograph by Erich Lessing

the development of greater precision, for example, in chipping and grinding—this period is called the Neolithic Age (from Greek, "new stone"). Productive animals, such as sheep and goats, and food crops, such as wheat and barley, were first domesticated in the mountain foothills where they already lived or grew in the wild. Once domestication had taken place, people could move to areas where these plants and animals did not occur naturally, such as the river valleys of the Near East. The invention of pottery during the Neolithic enabled people to store surplus foods and liquids and to transport them, as well as to cook agricultural products that were difficult to eat or digest raw. Cloth was made from flax and wool. Crops required constant care from planting to harvest, so Neolithic farmers built permanent dwellings. The earliest of these tended to be circular huts, large enough to house only one or two people and clustered in groups around a central storage place. Later people built square and rectangular family-sized houses with individual

storage places and enclosures to house livestock. Houses in a Neolithic village were normally all the same size and were built on the same plan, suggesting that most Neolithic villagers had about the same level of wealth and social status. A few items, such as stones and shells, were traded long distance, but Neolithic villages tended to be self-sufficient.

Two larger Neolithic settlements do not fit this village pattern. One was found at Çatal Höyük, in a fertile agricultural region about 150 miles south of Ankara, the capital of present-day Turkey. This was a large town covering over fifteen acres, with a population probably well over 6,000 people. The houses were clustered so closely that they had no doors, but were entered by ladders from the roofs. Many were decorated inside with sculptures of animal heads and horns, as well as paintings that were apparently redone regularly. Some appear to depict ritual or festive occasions involving men and women. One is the world's oldest landscape picture, showing a nearby volcano exploding. The agriculture, arts, and crafts of this town were astonishingly diversified and at a much higher level of attainment than other, smaller settlements of the period. The site of Jericho, an oasis around a spring near the Dead Sea, was occupied as early as 12,000 B.C.E. Around 8000 B.C.E. a town of eight to ten acres grew up, surrounded by a massive stone wall with at least one tower against the inner face. Although this wall may have been for defense, its use is disputed because no other Neolithic settlement has been found with fortifications. The inhabitants of Neolithic Jericho had a mixed agricultural, herding, and hunting economy and may have traded salt. They had no pottery, but plastered the skulls of their dead to make realistic memorial portraits of them. These two sites show that the economy and the settlement patterns of the Neolithic period may be more complicated than many scholars have thought.

Throughout the Paleolithic Age, the human population had been small and relatively stable. The shift from food gathering to food production may not have been associated with an immediate change in population, but over time in the regions where agriculture and animal husbandry appeared, the number of human beings grew at an unprecedented rate. One reason for this is that farmers usually had larger families than hunters. Their children began to work and matured at a younger age than the children of hunters. When animals and plants were domesticated and brought to the river valleys, the relationship between human beings and nature was changed forever. People had learned to control nature, a vital prerequisite for the emergence of civilization. But farmers had to work harder and longer than hunters did, and they had to stay in one place. Herders, on the other hand, often moved from place to place in search of pasture and water, returning to their villages in the spring. Some scholars refer to the dramatic changes in subsistence, settlement, technology, and population of this time as the "Neolithic Revolution." The earliest Neolithic societies appeared in the Mideast about 8000 B.C.E., in China about 4000 B.C.E., and in India about 3600 B.C.E. Neolithic agriculture was based on wheat and barley in the Mideast, on millet and rice in China, and on corn in Mesoamerica, several millennia later.

The Bronze Age and the Birth of Civilization

Neolithic agricultural villages and herding cultures gradually replaced Paleolithic culture in much of the world. Then another major shift occurred, first in the plains along the Tigris and Euphrates Rivers in the region the Greeks and Romans called Mesopotamia (modern Iraq), later in the valley of the Nile River in Egypt, and somewhat later in India and the Yellow River basin in China. This shift was associated initially with the growth of towns alongside villages, creating a hierarchy of larger and smaller settlements in the same region. Some towns then grew into much larger urban centers and often drew population into them, so that nearby villages and towns declined. The urban centers, or cities, usually had monumental buildings, such as temples and fortifications. These were vastly larger than individual houses and could be built only by the sustained effort of hundreds and even thousands of people over many years. Elaborate representational artwork appeared, sometimes made of rare and imported materials. New technologies, such as smelting and the manufacture of metal tools and weapons, were characteristic of urban life. Commodities like pottery and textiles that had been made in individual houses in villages were mass produced in cities, which also were characterized by social stratification—that is, different classes of people based on factors such as control of resources, family, religious or political authority, and personal wealth. The earliest writing is also associated with the growth of cities. Writing, like representational art, was a powerful means of communicating over space and time and was probably invented to deal with urban problems of management and record keeping. These attributes—urbanism; technological, industrial, and social change; long-distance trade; and new methods of symbolic communication—are defining characteristics of the form of human culture called *civilization*. At about the time the earliest civilizations were emerging, someone discovered how to combine tin and copper to make a stronger and more useful material—bronze. Archaeologists coined the term Bronze Age to refer to the period 3100–1200 B.C.E. in the near East and eastern Mediterranean.

Early Civilizations to about 1000 B.C.E.

By 4000 years B.C.E., people had settled in large numbers in the river-watered lowlands of Mesopotamia and Egypt. By about 3000 B.C.E., when the invention of writing gave birth to history, urban life and the organization of society into centralized states were well established in the valleys of the Tigris and Euphrates Rivers in Mesopotamia and of the Nile River in Egypt.

Much of the population of cities consists of people who do not grow their own food, so urban life is possible only where farmers and stockbreeders can be made to produce a substantial surplus beyond their own needs. Also, some process has to be in place so that this surplus can be collected and redeployed to sustain city dwellers. Efficient farming of plains alongside rivers, moreover, requires intelligent management of water resources for irrigation. In Mesopotamia, irrigation was essential, because in the south (Babylonia), there was not enough rainfall to sustain crops. Furthermore, the rivers, fed by melting snows in Armenia, rose to flood the fields in the spring, about the time for harvest, when water was not needed. When water was needed for the autumn planting, less was available. This meant that people had to build dikes to keep the rivers from flooding the fields in the spring and had to devise means to store water for use in the autumn. The Mesopotamians became skilled at that activity early on. In Egypt, on the other hand, the Nile River flooded at the right moment for cultivation, so irrigation was simply a matter of directing the water to the fields. In Mesopotamia, villages, towns, and cities tended to be strung along natural watercourses and, eventually, man-made canal systems. Thus, control of water could be important in warfare, because an enemy could cut off water upstream of a city to force it to submit. Since the Mesopotamian plain was flat, branches of the rivers often changed their courses, and people would have to abandon their cities and move to new locations. Archeologists once believed that urban life and centralized government arose in response to the need to regulate irrigation. This theory supposed that only a strong central authority could construct and maintain the necessary waterworks. However, archeologists have now shown that large-scale irrigation appeared only long after urban civilization had already developed, so major waterworks were a *consequence* of urbanism, not a cause of it.

Mesopotamian Civilization

The first civilization appears to have arisen in Mesopotamia. The region is divided into two ecological zones, roughly north and south of modern

Baghdad. In the south (Babylonia), as noted, irrigation is vital; in the north (Assyria), agriculture is possible with rainfall and wells. The south has high yields from irrigated lands, while the north has lower yields, but much more land under cultivation, so it can produce more than the south. The oldest Mesopotamian cities seem to have been founded by a people called the Sumerians during the fourth millennium B.C.E. in the land of Sumer, which is the southern half of Babylonia. By 3000 B.C.E., the Sumerian city of Uruk was the largest city in the world (see Map 1–1). Colonies of people from Uruk built cities and outposts in northern Syria and southern Anatolia. One of these, at Habubah Kabirah on the Euphrates River in Syria, was built on a regular plain on virgin ground, with strong defensive walls, but was abandoned after a few generations and never inhabited again. No one knows how the Sumerians were able to establish colonies so far from their homeland or even what their purpose was. They may have been trading centers.

From about 2800 to 2370 B.C.E., in what is called the Early Dynastic period, several Sumerian city–states existed in southern Mesopotamia, arranged in north–south lines along the major watercourses. Among these cities were Uruk, Ur, Nippur, Shuruppak, and Lagash. Some of the city–states formed leagues among themselves that apparently had both political and religious significance. Quarrels over water and agricultural land led to incessant warfare, and in time, stronger towns and leagues conquered weaker ones and expanded to form kingdoms ruling several city–states.

Peoples who, unlike the Sumerians, mostly spoke Semitic languages (that is, languages in the same family as Arabic and Hebrew) occupied northern Mesopotamia and Syria. The Sumerian language is not related to any language known today. Many of these Semitic peoples absorbed aspects of Sumerian culture, especially writing. At the western end of this broad territory, at Ebla in northern Syria, scribes kept records using Sumerian writing and studied Sumerian word

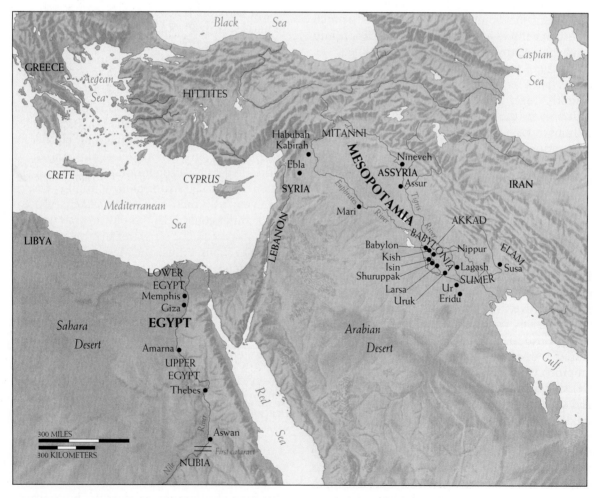

MAP 1–1   THE ANCIENT NEAR EAST   *There were two ancient river valley civilizations. While Egypt was united into a single state, Mesopotamia was long divided into a number of city-states.*

lists. In northern Babylonia, the Mesopotamians believed that the large city of Kish had the first kings in history. In the far east of this territory, not far from modern Baghdad, a people known as the Akkadians established their own kingdom at a capital city called Akkade, under their first king, Sargon, who had been a servant of the king of Kish.

The Akkadians conquered all the Sumerian city–states and invaded southwestern Iran and northern Syria. This was the first empire in history, having a heartland, provinces, and an absolute ruler. It included numerous peoples, cities, languages, and cultures, as well as different ecological zones, under one rule. Sargon's name became legendary as the first great conqueror of history. His grandson, Naram-Sin, ruled from the Persian Gulf to the Mediterranean Sea, with a standardized administration, unheard-of wealth and power, and a grand style that to later Mesopotamians was a high point of their history. Naram-Sin even declared himself a god and had temples built to himself, something no Sumerian ruler had ever done. (See "Art and the West.") External attack and internal weakness destroyed the Akkadian empire, but several smaller states flourished independently, notably Lagash in Sumer, under it's ruler Gudea.

About 2125 B.C.E. the Sumerian city of Ur rose to dominance, and the rulers of the Third Dynasty of Ur established an empire built on the foundation of the Akkadian empire, but far smaller. In this period, Sumerian culture and literature flourished. Epic poems were composed, glorifying the deeds of the ancestors of the kings of Ur. A highly centralized administration kept detailed records of agriculture, animal husbandry, commerce, and other matters. Over a hundred thousand of these documents have been found in the ruins of Sumerian cities. After little more than a century of prominence, the kingdom of Ur disintegrated in the face of famine and invasion. From the east, the Elamites attacked the city of Ur and captured the king. From the north and west, a Semitic-speaking people, the Amorites, invaded Mesopotamia in large numbers, settling around the Sumerian cities and eventually founding their own dynasties in some of them, such as at Uruk, Babylon, Isin, and Larsa.

The fall of the Third Dynasty of Ur put an end to Sumerian rule, and the Sumerians gradually disappeared as an identifiable group. The Sumerian language survived only in writing as the learned language of Babylonia taught in schools and used by priests and scholars. So great was the respect for Sumerian, that seventeen centuries after the fall of Ur, when Alexander the Great arrived in Babylon, Sumerian was still used as a scholarly and religious language there.

This statue of Gudea, city ruler of Lagash after the fall of the Akkadian empire, shows him as a pious Sumerian ruler. It was carved of very hard imported black stone. A brief historical inscription is visible on his cloak. Gudea built a major temple to a local deity at Lagash, Ningirsu, and describes the work, step by step, in one of the longest Sumerian poems known today. Scala/Art Resource, NY

For some time after the fall of Ur, there was relative peace in Babylonia under the Amorite kings of Isin, who used Sumerian at their court and considered themselves the successors of the kings of Ur. Eventually, another Amorite dynasty at the city of Larsa contested control of Babylonia, and a period of warfare began, mostly centering around attacks on strategic points on waterways. A powerful new dynasty at Babylon defeated Isin, Larsa, and other rivals and dominated Mesopotamia for nearly 300 years. Its high point was the reign of its most famous king, Hammurabi (r. ca. 1792–1750 B.C.E.), best known today for the collection of laws that bears his name. Hammurabi destroyed the great city of Mari on the Euphrates and created a kingdom embracing most of Mesopotamia.

A Monument to a King's Triumph:
The Victory Stele of Naram-Sin

The Victory Stele of the Akkadian ruler Naram-Sin commemorates the king's campaign against the Lullubi, a people living in the northern Zagros Mountains, along the eastern frontier of Mesopotamia. Kings set up monuments like this one in the courtyards of temples to record their deeds. They were also left in remote corners of the empire to warn distant peoples of the death and enslavement awaiting the king's enemies. On a slab of limestone over six feet high, the sculptor posed Naram-Sin so that the ruler's size and placement dominate the scene. The king, wearing the horned helmet denoting divine power, strides forward at the head of his army. Beneath his feet are the trampled bodies of defeated Lullubi. He seems oblivious to the hide-clad survivors to the right, who beg for mercy. Originally, a cuneiform inscription describing the king's triumph occupied much of the sky area, but it is now so abraded that it is barely visible.

The mountain summit bears a second cuneiform inscription, this one added in the twelfth century B.C. when the Elamites captured the stele and took it back to their capital of Susa, in southwestern Iran. The seizure of artifacts as war booty was common practice in the ancient world, with monuments often being destroyed or mutilated in the process. This piece was spared that fate, as was the Stele of the Laws of Hammurabi,

which the Elamites also brought to Susa. Modern archaeologists discovered both stelae, along with other Mesopotamian works of art, in the ruins of Susa.

The Stele of Naram-Sin is one of the finest sculptures to survive from the Akkadian period. The Akkadians built the first empire known to history, and new features in their art, many of which we can see in this piece, reflect that imperialism. Sumerian art confined figures to horizontal rows, or registers. Here Naram-Sin and his army move diagonally across the space, energetically ascending and conquering. For the first time, Mesopotamian art shows a sense of landscape, with the rocky terrain and gnarled trees signaling how far distant from Mesopotamia Naram-Sin has pushed the borders of his empire. The human figures, even those of the enemy, are naturalistically modeled, in sharp contrast to the Sumerian emphasis on gesture at the expense of anatomy.

The portrayal of the gods on this stele is especially striking. They appear at the top, three stars symbolizing Naram-Sin's patron deities. In a comparable Sumerian victory stele, made just a few generations earlier, the god of the successful city, shown in anthropomorphic form, occupies nearly one entire side, holding enemy prisoners in a net. In contrast, the Akkadian focus here is on Naram-Sin, warrior–king and deified ruler.

The Victory Stele of Naram–Sin, King of Akkad, over the mountain-dwelling Lullubi, Mesopotamian, Akkadian Period, c. 2230 B.C.E. (pink sandstone). Louvre, Paris, France. The Bridgeman Art Library International Ltd.

Collections of laws existed as early as the Third Dynasty of Ur, and Hammurabi's owed much to earlier models and different legal traditions. His collection of laws, now referred to as the Code of Hammurabi, reveals a society divided by class. There were nobles, commoners, and slaves, and the law did not treat all of them equally. In general, punishments were harsh, based literally on the principle of "an eye for an eye, a tooth for a tooth," whereas Sumerian law often levied fines instead of bodily mutilation or death. Disputes over property and other complaints were heard in the first instance by local city assemblies of leading citizens and heads of families. Professional judges heard cases for a fee and held court near the city gate. In Mesopotamian trials, witnesses and written evidence had to be produced and a written verdict issued. False testimony was punishable by death. Sometimes the contesting parties would submit to an oath before the gods, on the theory that no one would risk swearing a false oath. In cases where evidence or oath could not establish the truth, the contesting parties might take an ordeal, such as being thrown into the river for the god to decide who was telling the truth. Cases of capital punishment could be appealed to the king. Hammurabi was closely concerned with the details of his kingdom, and his surviving letters often deal with minor local disputes.

About 1600 B.C.E., the Babylonian kingdom fell apart under the impact of invasions from the north by the Hittites, Hurrians, and Kassites, all non-Mesopotamian peoples.

GOVERNMENT From the earliest historical records, it is clear that the Sumerians were ruled by monarchs in some form. The earliest Sumerian rulers are shown in their art leading an army, killing prisoners, and making offerings to the gods. The type of rule varied at different times and places. In later Assyria, for example, the king served as chief priest, while in Babylonia the priesthood was separate from royalty. Royal princesses were sometimes appointed as priestesses of important gods. One of the most famous of these was Enheduanna, daughter of Sargon of Akkad. She is the first author in history whose writings can be identified with a real person. Although she was an Akkadian, she wrote complicated, passionate, and intensely personal poetry in the Sumerian language, in which she tells of important historical events that she experienced. In one passage, she compares the agony of writing a poem to giving birth.

The government and the temples cultivated large areas of land to support their staffs and retinue. Laborers of low social status who were given rations of raw foods and other commodities to sustain them and their families did some of the work on this land. Citizens leased some land for a share of the crop and a cash payment. These lands were carefully surveyed, and sometimes the crop could be estimated in advance. The government and temples owned large herds of sheep, goats, cattle, and donkeys. The Sumerian city–states exported wool and textiles to buy metals, such as copper, that were not available in Mesopotamia. Families and private individuals often owned their own farmland or houses in the cities, which they bought and sold as they liked.

A Letter Home

In this letter from a son to his mother, the young man argues for a new suit of clothes.

❖ *What seems to be the most important reason he needs new clothes? Are his old ones worn out? In Mesopotamia, when you wrote a petition, you saved the strongest argument for last. What does he hope will really move his mother? If you were his mother, how would you respond to his letter?*

Tell the Lady Zinû: Iddin-Sin sends the following message:

May the gods Shamash, Marduk, and Ilabrat keep you forever in good health for my sake.

From year to year, the clothes of the [young] gentlemen here become better, but you let my clothes get worse from year to year. Indeed, you persisted(?) in making my clothes poorer and more scanty. At a time when in our house wool is used up like bread, you have made me poor clothes. The son of Adad-iddinam, whose father is only an assistant of my father, (has) two new sets of clothes...while you fuss even about a single set of clothes for me. In spite of the fact that you bore me and his mother only adopted him, his mother loves him, while you, you do not love me!

From translation by A. Leo Oppenheim in *Letters from Mesopotamia* (Chicago: The University of Chicago Press), p. 85.

The Babylonian Story of the Flood

The passage that follows is part of the Babylonian Epic of Gilgamesh. *It did not form a part of the original Epic, but was added at some point from an earlier independent Babylonian* Story of the Flood, *which suggested that the gods sent a flood as a drastic effort at population control because there were too many people on the earth. The gods realized their mistake when there were no more people to provide for them, so they made sure that everyone would die sooner or later, and they restricted childbirth through various social and medical means. A version of this story was later combined with the* Epic of Gilgamesh. *Gilgamesh was a legendary king who became terrified of death when his best friend and companion died. He resolved to locate Utanapishtim, who, with his wife, was the only survivor of the great flood, in order to ask him how he, too, could escape death. After many adventures, Gilgamesh crossed the distant ocean and the "waters of death" to ask Utanapishtim the secret of eternal life. In response, Utanapishtim narrated the story of the great flood, to show that his own immortality derived from a one-time event in the past, so that Gilgamesh could not share his destiny. Note the similarities between this and the biblical story of Noah, as well as the important differences between them.*

❖ *How is this tale similar to the story of Noah in the* Book of Genesis *in the Hebrew Bible? How is it different?*

Six days and seven nights
The wind continued, the deluge and windstorm
  levelled the land.
When the seventh day arrived,
The windstorm and deluge left off their battle,
Which had struggled, like a woman in labor.
The sea grew calm, the tempest stilled, the deluge ceased.
I looked at the weather, stillness reigned,
And the whole human race had turned into clay.
The landscape was flat as a rooftop.
I opened the hatch, sunlight fell upon my face.
Falling to my knees, I sat down weeping,
Tears running down my face.
I looked at the edges of the world, the borders
  of the sea,
At twelve times sixty double leagues the periphery emerged.

The boat had come to rest on Mount Nimush,
Mount Nimush held the boat fast, not letting
  it move.
One day, a second day Mount Nimush held the
  boat fast, not letting it move.
A third day, a fourth day Mount Nimush held
  the boat fast, not letting it move.
A fifth day, a sixth day Mount Nimush held the
  boat fast, not letting it move.
When the seventh day arrived,
I brought out a dove and set it free.
The dove went off and returned,
No landing place came to its view, so it
  turned back.
I brought out a swallow and set it free,
The swallow went off and returned,
No landing space came to its view, so it
  turned back.

WRITING AND MATHEMATICS   Government, business, and scholarship required a good system of writing. The Sumerians invented the writing system now known as *cuneiform* (from the Latin *cuneus*, "wedge") because of the wedge-shaped marks they made by writing on clay tablets with a cut reed stylus. At first the writing system was sketchy, giving only a few elements of a sentence to help a reader remember something that he probably already know. Later, people thought to write whole sentences in the order in which they were to be spoken, so writing could communicate new information to a reader. The Sumer-ian writing system used several thousand characters, some of which stood for words and some for sounds. Some characters stood for many different sounds or words, and some sounds could be written using a choice of many different characters. The result was a writing system that was difficult to learn. Sumerian students were fond of complaining about their unfair teachers, how hard their schoolwork was, and their too-short vacations. Sumerian and Babylonian schools emphasized language and literature, accounting, legal practice, and mathematics, especially geometry, along with memorization of much abstract knowledge that

I brought out a raven and set it free.
The raven went off and saw the ebbing of the
waters.
It ate, preened, left droppings, did not turn back.
I released all to the four directions,
I brought out an offering and offered it to the
four directions.
I set up an incense burner on the summit of
the mountain,
I arranged seven and seven cult vessels,
I heaped reeds, cedar, and myrtle in their bowls.
The gods smelled the savor,
The gods smelled the sweet savor,
The gods crowded round the sacrificer like flies.
As soon as the Belet-ili arrived,
She held up the great fly-ornaments that Anu
had made in his ardor:
'O ye gods, as surely as I shall not forget
these lapis pendants on my neck,
'I shall be mindful of these days and not for-
get, not ever!
'The gods should come to the incense burner,
'But Enlil should not come to the incense
burner,
'For he, irrationally, brought on the flood,
'And marked my people for destruction!'
As soon as Enlil arrived,
He saw the boat, Enlil flew into a rage,
He was filled with fury at the gods:
'Who came through alive? No man was to
survive destruction!'
Ninurta made ready to speak,
Said to the valiant Enlil:
'Who but Ea could contrive such a thing?
'For Ea alone knows every artifice.'
Ea made ready to speak,

Said to the valiant Enlil:
'You, O valiant one, are the wisest of the gods,
'How could you, irrationally, have brought
on the flood?
'Punish the wrong-doer for his wrong-doing,
'Punish the transgressor for his transgression,
'But be lenient, lest he be cut off,
'Bear with him, lest he [...].
'Instead of your bringing on a flood,
'Let the lion rise up to diminish the
human race!
'Instead of your bringing on a flood,
'Let the wolf rise up to diminish the
human race!
'Instead of your bringing on a flood,
'Let famine rise up to wreak havoc in the land!
'Instead of your bringing on a flood,
'Let pestilence rise up to wreak havoc in
the land!
'It was not I who disclosed the secret of the
great gods,
'I made Atrahasis have a dream and so he
heard the secret of the gods.
'Now then, make some plan for him.'
Then Enlil came up into the boat,
Leading me by the hand, he brought me up too.
He brought my wife up and had her kneel be-
side me.
He touched our brows, stood between us to
bless us:
'Hitherto Utanapishtim has been a human
being,
'Now Utanapishtim and his wife shall be-
come like us gods.
'Utanapishtim shall dwell far distant at the
source of the rivers.'

had no relevance to everyday life. The ability to read and write was restricted to an elite who could afford to go to school. Success in school, however, and factors such as good family connections, meant that a literate Sumerian could find employment as a clerk, surveyor, teacher, diplomat, or administrator.

The Sumerians also began the development of mathematics. The earliest Sumerian records suggest that before 3000 B.C.E. people had not yet thought of the concept of number independently of counting specific things. Therefore, the earliest writing used different numerals for counting different things, and the nu-

merals had no independent value. (The same sign could be 10 or 18, for example, depending on what was counted.) Once an independent concept of number was established, mathematics developed rapidly. The Sumerian system was based on the number 60 ("sexagesimal"), rather than the number 10 ("decimal"), the system in general use today. Sumerian counting survives in the modern 60-minute hour and the circle of 360 degrees. By the time of Hammurabi, the Mesopotamians were expert in many types of mathematics, including mathematical astronomy. The calendar the Mesopotamians used had twelve lunar months of thirty days each. To keep it in accordance with the solar year and the seasons, the Mesopotamians occasionally introduced a thirteenth month.

RELIGION   The Sumerians and their successors worshiped many gods and goddesses. They were visualized in human form, with human needs and weaknesses. Most of the gods were identified with some natural phenomenon such as the sky, fresh water, or storms. They differed from humans in their greater power, sublime position in the universe, and immortality. The Mesopotamians believed that the human race was created to serve the gods and to relieve the gods of the necessity of providing for themselves. The gods were considered universal, but also residing in specific places, usually one important god or goddess in each city. Mesopotamian temples were run like great households where the gods were fed lavish meals, entertained with music, and honored with devotion and ritual. There were gardens for their pleasure and bedrooms to retire to at night. The images of the gods were dressed and adorned with the finest

This clay tablet from the Neo-Babylonian period (612–539 B.C.E.) shows a map of the world as seen by the Babylonians. The "Salt Sea" is shown as a circle. An arc inside it is labeled "Mountains." Below it is a rectangular box marked "Babylon," and to the right of the box is a small circle marked "Assyria." Courtesy of the Trustees of the British Museum. © The British Museum

materials. Theologians organized the gods into families and generations. Human social institutions, such as kingship, or crafts, such as carpentry, were associated with specific gods, so the boundaries between human and divine society were not always clearly drawn. Since the great gods were visualized like human rulers, remote from the common people and their concerns, the Mesopotamians imagined another more personal intercessor god who was supposed to look after a person, rather like a guardian spirit. The public festivals of the gods were important holidays, with parades, ceremonies, and special foods. People wore their best clothes and celebrated their city and its gods. The Mesopotamians were religiously tolerant and readily accepted the possibility that different people might have different gods.

The Mesopotamians had a vague and gloomy picture of the afterworld. The winged spirits of the dead were recognizable as individuals. They were confined to a dusty, dark netherworld, doomed to perpetual hunger and thirst unless someone offered them food and drink. Some spirits escaped to haunt human beings. There was no preferential treatment in the afterlife for those who had led religious or virtuous lives—everyone was in equal misery. Mesopotamian families often had a ceremony to remember and honor their dead. People were usually buried together with goods such as pottery and ornaments. In the Early Dynastic period, certain kings were buried with a large retinue of attendants, including soldiers and musicians, who apparently took poison during the funeral ceremony and were buried where they fell. But this practice soon disappeared. Children were sometimes buried under the floors of houses. Some families used burial vaults, others large cemeteries. No tombstones or inscriptions identified the deceased. Mesopotamian religion focused on problems of this world and how to lead a good life before dying.

The Mesopotamian peoples who came after the Sumerians believed that the gods revealed a person's destiny to those who could understand the omens, or indications of what was going to happen. The Babylonians therefore developed an elaborate science of divination based on chance observations, such as a cat walking in the street, and on ritual procedures, such as asking a question of the gods then slaughtering a sheep to examine its liver and entrails for certain marks and features. Some omens, such as monstrous births or eclipses, were thought to apply to the government, while others, such as birds flying over a person's house, were thought to apply to the individual. Thousands of omens, including both the observation and the outcome thereof, were compiled into huge encyclopedias that scholars could consult.

Divination was often done before making major decisions and to discover the causes of illness, unhappiness, and failure. The hope was to avert unfavorable future events by discovering them in time and carrying out rituals or avoiding certain actions. Diviners were paid professionals, not priests. Witchcraft was also widely feared and blamed for illnesses and harm to people. There were many rituals against witchcraft, such as making a figurine of a witch and burning it, thereby burning up the witchcraft.

Religion played a large part in the literature and art of Mesopotamia. Epic poems told of the deeds of the gods, such as how the world was created and organized, of a great flood the gods sent to wipe out the human race, and of the hero–king Gilgamesh, who tried to escape death by going on a fantastic journey to find the sole survivor of the great flood. (See "The Babylonian Story of the Flood.") There were also many literary and artistic works that were not religious in character, so we should not imagine that religion dominated all aspects of the Mesopotamians' lives. Religious architecture took the form of great temple complexes in the major cities. The most imposing religious structure was the *ziggurat*, a tower in stages, sometimes with a small chamber on top. The terraces may have been planted with trees to resemble a mountain. Poetry about ziggurats often compares them to mountains, with their peaks in the sky and their roots in the netherworld, linking heaven to earth, but their precise purpose is not known. Eroded remains of many of these monumental structures still dot the Iraqi landscape. Through the Bible, they have entered western tradition as "the tower of Babel."

SOCIETY   Hundreds of thousands of cuneiform texts from the early third millenium B.C.E. until the third century B.C.E. give us a full and detailed picture of how peoples in ancient Mesopotamia conducted their lives and of the social conditions in which they lived. From the time of Hammurabi, for example, there are many royal letters to and from the various rulers of the age, letters from the king to his subordinates, administrative records from many different cities, and numerous letters and documents belonging to private families.

Categorizing the laws of Hammurabi according to the aspects of life with which they deal reveals much about Babylonian life in his time. The third largest category of laws deals with commerce, relating to such issues as contracts, debts, rates of interest, security, and default. Business documents of Hammurabi's time show how people invested their money in land, moneylending, government contracts, and international trade. Some of these laws regulate professionals, such as builders, judges, and surgeons. The second largest category of laws deals with land tenure, especially land given by the king to soldiers and

This stele preserves the laws of Hammurabi. In the relief carving at the top, Hammurabi, standing prayerfully to the left, receives a rod and ring, perhaps symbols of justice, from the sun god, who is seated and wears the special crown of the gods. The text of the laws is inscribed below "to administer the law of the land, to prescribe the ordinances of the land, to give justice to the oppressed." Reunion des Musèes Nationaux

marines in return for their service. The letters of Hammurabi that deal with land tenure show that he was concerned to uphold individual rights of landholders against powerful officials who tried to take their land from them. The largest category of laws relates to the family and its maintenance and protection, including marriage, inheritance, and adoption.

Parents usually arranged marriages, and betrothal was followed by the signing of a marriage contract. The bride usually left her own family to join her husband's. The husband-to-be could make a bridal payment, and the father of the bride-to-be provided a dowry for his daughter in money, land, or objects. A

Key Events and People in Mesopotamian History	
ca. 3500 B.C.E.	Development of Sumerian cities, especially Uruk
ca. 2800–2370 B.C.E.	Early Dynastic period of Sumerian city–states
ca. 2370 B.C.E.	Sargon establishes Akkadian dynasty and empire
ca. 2125–2027 B.C.E.	Third Dynasty of Ur
ca. 2000–1800 B.C.E.	Establishment of Amorites in Mesopotamia
ca. 1792–1750 B.C.E.	Reign of Hammurabi
ca. 1550 B.C.E.	Establishment of Kassite Dynasty at Babylon

An Assyrian Woman Writes to Her Husband, ca. 1800 B.C.E.

The wives of early Assyrian businessmen were often active in their husbands' business affairs. They made extra money for themselves by having slave girls weave textiles that the husbands then sold on business trips. Their letters are one of the largest groups of women's records from the ancient world. The woman writing this letter, Taram-Kubi, complains of her husband's selfishness and points out all the matters she has worked on during his absence on business.

❖ *What functions did this woman perform on behalf of the family? How do you judge her real power in regard to her husband? On what evidence do you base that judgment? What does this document reveal about the place of women in Assyrian society?*

You wrote to me saying, "You'll need to safeguard the bracelets and rings which are there so they'll be available [to buy] food." In fact, you sent [the man] Ilum-bani a half pound of gold! Which are the bracelets you left me? When you left, you didn't leave me an ounce of silver, you picked the house clean and took away everything! After you left, there was a severe famine in the city. Not so much as a quart of grain did you leave me, I always had to buy grain for our food. Besides that, I paid the assessment for the divine icon(?); in fact, I paid for my part in full. Besides that, I paid over to the Town Hall the grain owed [the man] Atata. What is the extravagance you keep writing to me about? There is nothing for us to eat—we're the ones being extravagant? I picked up whatever I had to hand and sent it to you—today I'm living in an empty house. It's high time you sent me the money realized on my weavings, in silver, from what you have to hand, so I can buy ten quarts of grain!

Translation, Benjamin R. Foster, 1999.

marriage started out monogamous, but a husband whose wife was childless or sickly could take a second wife. Sometimes husbands also sired children from domestic slave women. Women could own their own property and do business on their own. Women divorced by their husbands without good cause could get their dowry back. A woman seeking divorce could also recover her dowry if her husband could not convict her of wrongdoing. A married woman's place was thought to be in the home, but hundreds of letters between wives and husbands show them as equal partners in the ventures of life. (See "An Assyrian Woman Writes to Her Husband, ca. 1800 B.C.E.") Single women who were not part of families could set up in business on their own, often as tavern owners or moneylenders, or could be associated with temples, sometimes working as midwives and wetnurses, or taking care of orphaned children.

SLAVERY: CHATTEL SLAVES AND DEBT SLAVES   There were two main types of slavery in Mesopotamia: chattel and debt slavery. Chattel slaves were bought like any other piece of property and had no legal rights. They had to wear their hair in a certain way and were sometimes branded or tatooed on their hands. They were often non-Mesopotamians bought from slave merchants. Prisoners of war could also be enslaved. Chattel slaves were expensive luxuries during most of Mesopotamian history. They were used in domestic service rather than in production, such as fieldwork. A wealthy household might have five or six slaves, male and female.

Debt slavery was more common than chattel slavery. Rates of interest were high, as much as $33\frac{1}{3}$, so people often defaulted on loans. One reason the interest rates were so high was that the government periodically canceled certain types of debts, debt slavery, and obligations, so lenders ran the risk of losing their money. If debtors had pledged themselves or members of their families as surety for a loan, they became the slave of the creditor; their labor went to pay the interest on the loan. Debt slaves could not be sold, but could redeem their freedom by paying off the loan. True chattel slavery did not become common until the Neo-Babylonian period (612–539 B.C.E.).

Although laws against fugitive slaves or slaves who denied their masters were harsh—the Code of Hammurabi permits the death penalty for anyone who sheltered or helped a runaway slave to escape—Mesopotamian slavery appears enlightened compared with other slave systems in history. Slaves were generally of the same people as their masters. They had been enslaved because of misfortune from which their masters were not immune, and they generally labored alongside them. Slaves could engage in business and, with certain restrictions, hold property. They could marry free men or women, and the resulting children would normally be free. A slave who acquired the means could buy his or her freedom. Children of a slave by a master might be allowed to share his property after his death. Nevertheless, slaves were property, subject to an owner's will and had little legal protection.

Egyptian Civilization

As Mesopotamian civilization arose in the valley of the Tigris and Euphrates, another great civilization emerged in Egypt, centered on the Nile River. From its sources in Lake Victoria and the Ethiopian highlands, the Nile flows north some 4,000 miles to the Mediterranean. Ancient Egypt included the 750-mile stretch of smooth, navigable river from Aswan to the sea. South of Aswan the river's course is interrupted by several cataracts—rocky areas of rapids and whirlpools.

The Egyptians recognized two sets of geographical divisions in their country. Upper (southern) Egypt consisted of the narrow valley of the Nile. Lower (northern) Egypt referred to the broad triangular area, named by the Greeks after their letter "delta," formed by the Nile as it branches out to empty into the Mediterranean. (See Map 1–2.) They also made a distinction between what they termed the "black land," the dark fertile fields along the Nile, and the "red land," the desert cliffs and plateaus bordering the valley.

The Nile alone made agriculture possible in Egypt's desert environment. Each year the rains of central Africa caused the river to rise over its floodplain, cresting in September and October. In places the plain extends several miles on either side, while elsewhere the cliffs slope down to the water's edge. When the floodwaters receded, they left a rich layer of organically fertile silt. The construction and maintenance of canals, dams, and irrigation ditches to control the river's water, together with careful planning and organization of planting and harvesting, produced agricultural prosperity unmatched in the ancient world.

The Nile served as the major highway connecting Upper and Lower Egypt. There was also a network of desert roads running north and south, as well as routes across the eastern desert to the Sinai and the Red Sea. Other tracks led to oases in the western desert. Thanks to geography and climate, Egypt was more isolated and enjoyed far more security than Mesopotamia. This security, along with the predictable flood calendar, gave Egyptian civilization a more optimistic outlook than

One of the hallmarks of the early river civilizations was the development of techniques to increase harvests. This statue from the Old Kingdom in Egypt (ca. 2700–2200 B.C.E.) shows a woman grinding wheat for bread. Kenneth Garrettings/National Geographic Society

the civilizations of the Tigris and Euphrates, which were more prone to storms, flash floods, and invasions.

The 3,000-year span of ancient Egyptian history is traditionally divided into thirty-one royal dynasties, from the first, said to have been founded by Menes, the king who originally united Upper and Lower Egypt, to the last, conquered by Alexander the Great in 332 B.C.E. (as we shall see in Chapter 3). Ptolemy, one of Alexander's generals, founded the Ptolemaic Dynasty, whose last ruler was Cleopatra. In 30 B.C.E. the Romans defeated Egypt, effectively ending the independent existence of a civilization that had lasted three millennia.

The unification of Upper and Lower Egypt was vital, for it meant that the entire river valley could benefit from an unimpeded distribution of resources. Three times in its history, Egypt experienced a century or more of political and social disintegration, known as Intermediate Periods. During these eras, rival dynasties often set up separate power bases in Upper and Lower Egypt until a strong leader reunified the land.

The three largest pyramids of Egypt, located at Giza, near Cairo, are the colossal tombs of pharaohs of the Fourth Dynasty (ca. 2640–2510 B.C.E.): Khufu (right), Chafre (center), and Menkaure (left). The small pyramids and tombs at their bases were those of the pharaohs' queens and officials. Pictor

THE OLD KINGDOM (2700–2200 B.C.E.)   The Old Kingdom represents the culmination of the cultural and historical developments of the Early Dynastic period. For over 400 years, Egypt enjoyed internal stability and great prosperity. During this period, the pharaoh (the term comes from the Egyptian for "great house," much as we use "White House" to refer to the President) was a king who was also a god. From his capital at Memphis, the god–king administered Egypt according to set principles, prime among them being *maat*, an ideal of order, justice, and truth. In return for the king's building and maintaining temples, the gods preserved the equilibrium of the state and ensured the king's continuing power, which was absolute. Since the king was obligated to act infallibly in a benign and beneficent manner, the welfare of the people of Egypt was automatically guaranteed and safeguarded.

Nothing better illustrates the nature of Old Kingdom royal power than the pyramids built as pharaonic tombs. Beginning in the Early Dynastic period, kings constructed increasingly elaborate burial complexes in Upper Egypt. Djoser, a Third Dynasty king, was the first to erect a monumental six-step pyramid of hard stone. Subsequent pharaohs built other stepped pyramids until Snefru, the founder of the Fourth Dynasty, converted a stepped to a true pyramid over the course of putting up three monuments.

His son Khufu (Cheops in the Greek version of his name) chose the desert plateau of Giza, south of Memphis, as the site for the largest pyramid ever constructed. Its dimensions are prodigious: 481 feet high, 756 feet long on each side, and its base covering 13.1 acres. The pyramid is made of 2,300,000 stone blocks averaging 2.5 tons each. It is also a geometrical wonder, deviating from absolutely level and square only by the most minute measurements using the latest modern devices. Khufu's successors, Khafre (Chephren) and Menkaure (Mycerinus), built equally perfect pyramids at Giza, and together, the three constitute one of the most extraordinary achievements in human history. Khafre also built the huge composite creature, part lion and part human, which the Greeks named the Sphinx. Recent research has shown that the Sphinx played a crucial role in the solar cult aspects of the pyramid complex.

The pyramids are remarkable not only for the great technical skill they demonstrate, but also for the concentration of resources they represent. They are evidence that the pharaohs controlled vast wealth and had the power to focus and organize enormous human effort over the years it took to build each pyramid. They also provide a visible indication of the nature of the Egyptian state: The pyramids, like the pharaohs, tower above the land, while the low tombs at their base, like the officials buried there, seem to huddle in relative unimportance.

Originally, the pyramids and their associated cult buildings contained statuary, offerings, and all that the pharaoh needed for the afterlife. Despite great precautions and ingenious concealment methods, tomb robbers took nearly everything, leaving little for modern archeologists to recover. Several full-size wooden boats have been found, however, still in their own graves at the base of the pyramids, ready for the pharaoh's journeys in the next world. Recent excavations have uncovered remains of the large town built to house the thousands of pyramid builders, including the farmers who worked at Giza during the annual flooding of their fields.

Numerous officials, both members of the royal family and nonroyal men of ability, aided the god–kings. The highest office was the *vizier* (a modern term from Arabic). Central offices dealing with granaries, surveys, assessments, taxes, and salaries administered the land. Water management was local rather than on a national level. Upper and Lower Egypt were divided into *nomes*, or districts, each governed by a *nomarch*, or governor, and his local officials. The kings could also appoint royal officials to oversee groups of nomes or to supervise pharaonic land holdings throughout Egypt.

THE FIRST INTERMEDIATE PERIOD AND MIDDLE KINGDOM (2200–1630 B.C.E.)

Towards the end of the Old Kingdom, for a combination of political and economic reasons, absolute pharaonic power waned as the nomarchs and other officials became more independent and influential. About 2200 B.C.E. the Old Kingdom collapsed and gave way to the decentralization and disorder of the First Intermediate Period, which lasted until about 2025 B.C.E. Eventually, the kings of Dynasty 11, based in Thebes in Upper Egypt, defeated the rival Dynasty 10, based in a city south of Giza.

Amunemhet I, the founder of Dynasty 12 and the Middle Kingdom, probably began his career as a successful vizier under an Eleventh Dynasty king. After reuniting Upper and Lower Egypt, he turned his attention to making three important and long-lasting administrative changes. First, he moved his royal residence from Thebes to a brand new town, just south of the old capital at Memphis, signaling a fresh start rooted in past glories. Second, he reorganized the nome structure by more clearly defining the nomarchs' duties to the state, granting them some local autonomy within the royal structure. Third, he established a coregency system to smooth transitions from one reign to another.

Amunemhet I and the other Middle Kingdom pharaohs sought to evoke the past by building pyramid complexes like those of the later Old Kingdom rulers. Yet the events of the First Intermediate Period had irrevocably changed the nature of Egyptian kingship. Gone was the absolute, distant god–king; the king was now more directly concerned with his people. In art, instead of the supremely confident faces of the Old Kingdom pharaohs, the Middle Kingdom rulers seem thoughtful, careworn, and brooding.

Egypt's relations with its neighbors became more aggressive during the Middle Kingdom. To the south, royal fortresses were built to control Nubia and the growing trade in African resources. To the north and east, Syria and Palestine increasingly came under Egyptian influence, even as fortifications sought to prevent settlers from the Levant from moving into the Delta.

THE SECOND INTERMEDIATE PERIOD AND THE NEW KINGDOM (1630–1075 B.C.E.)

For some unknown reason, during Dynasty 13, the kingship changed hands rapidly and the western Delta established itself as an independent Dynasty 14, ushering in the Second Intermediate Period. The eastern Delta, with its expanding Asiatic populations, came under the control of the Hyksos (Dynasty 15) and minor Asiatic kings (Dynasty 16). Meanwhile, the Dynasty 13 kings left their northern capital and regrouped in Thebes (Dynasty 17).

Though much later sources describe the Hyksos ("chief of foreign lands" in Egyptian) as ruthless invaders from parts unknown, they were almost certainly Amorites from the Levant, part of the gradual infiltration of the Delta during the Middle Kingdom. Ongoing excavations at the Hyksos capital of Avaris in the eastern Delta have revealed architecture, pottery, and other goods consistent with that cultural

Seated Egyptian scribe, height 21" (53 cm.) painted limestone, fifth dynasty, c. 2510–2460 B.C.E. One of the hallmarks of the early river valley civilizations was the development of writing. Ancient Egyptian scribes had to undergo rigorous training, but were rewarded with a position of respect and privilege.
Musée de Louvre, Paris. © Giraudon/Art Resource, N.Y.

Love Poems From the New Kingdom

Numerous love poems from ancient Egypt reveal the Egyptians' love of life through their frank sensuality.

❖ *How does the girl in the first poem propose to escape the supervision of her parents? What ails the young man in the second poem?*

SHE: Love, how I'd love to slip down to the
    pond, bathe with you close by on the bank.
Just for you I'd wear my new Memphis swim-
    suit, made of sheer linen, fit for a queen—
Come see how it looks in the water!
Couldn't I coax you to wade in with me? Let
    the cool creep slowly around us?
Then I'd dive deep down and come up for you
    dripping,
Let you fill your eyes with the little red fish
    that I'd catch.
And I'd say, standing there tall in the shallows:
Look at my fish, love, how it lies in my hand,

How my fingers caress it, slip down its sides...
But then I'd say softer, eyes bright with your
    seeing:
A gift, love. No words.
Come closer and look, it's all me.

HE: I think I'll go home and lie very still, feign-
    ing terminal illness.
Then the neighbors will all troop over to stare,
    my love, perhaps, among them.
How she'll smile while the specialists snarl in
    their teeth!—
she perfectly well knows what ails me.

From *Love Songs of the New Kingdom*, translated from the Ancient Egyptian by John L. Foster, copyright © 1969, 1970, 1971, 1972, 1973, and 1974 by John L. Foster, p. 20 and p. 72. Reprinted by permission of the University of Texas Press.

background. After nearly a century of rule, the Hyksos were expelled, a process begun by Kamose, the last king of Dynasty 17, and completed by his brother Ahmose, the first king of the Eighteenth Dynasty and the founder of the New Kingdom.

During the Eighteenth Dynasty, Egypt pursued foreign expansion with renewed vigor. Military expeditions reached as far north as the Euphrates in Syria, with frequent campaigns in the Levant. To the south, major Egyptian temples were built in the Sudan, almost 1,300 miles from Memphis. Egypt's economic and political power was at its height.

Egypt's position was reflected in the unprecedented luxury and cosmopolitanism of the royal court and in the ambitious palace and temple projects undertaken throughout the country. Perhaps to foil tomb robbers, the Eighteenth Dynasty pharaohs were the first to cut their tombs deep into the rock cliffs of a desolate valley in Thebes, known today as the Valley of the Kings. To date, only one intact royal tomb has been discovered there, that of the young Eighteenth Dynasty king Tutankhamun, and even it had been disturbed shortly after his death. The thousands of goods buried with him, many of them marvels of craftsmanship, give an idea of Egypt's material wealth during this period.

Following the premature death of Tutankhamun in 1323 B.C.E., a military commander named Horemheb assumed the kingship, which passed in turn to his own army commander, Ramses I. The Ramessides of Dynasty 19 undertook numerous monumental projects, among them Ramses II's rock-cut temples at Abu Simbel, south of the First Cataract, which had to be moved to a higher location when the Aswan High Dam was built in the 1960s. There and elsewhere, Ramses II left textual and pictorial accounts of his battle in 1285 B.C.E. against the Hittites at Kadesh on the Orontes in Syria. Sixteen years later, the Egyptians and Hittites signed a formal peace treaty, forging an alliance against an increasingly volatile political situation in the Mideast and Eastern Mediterranean during the thirteenth century B.C.E.

Merneptah, one of the hundred offspring of Ramses II, held off a hostile Libyan attack, as well as incursions by the Sea Peoples, a loose coalition of Mediterranean raiders who seem to have provoked and taken advantage of unsettled conditions. One of Merneptah's inscriptions commemorating his military triumphs contains the first known mention of Israel.

Despite his efforts, by the end of the Twentieth Dynasty, Egypt's period of imperial glory had passed. The next thousand years witnessed a Third Intermediate Period, a Saite Renaissance, Persian domination, conquest by Alexander the Great, the Ptolemaic period, and finally, defeat at the hands of Octavian in 30 B.C.E.

LANGUAGE AND LITERATURE. Writing first appears in Egypt about 3000 B.C.E. While the impetus for the first Egyptian writing probably came from Mesopotamia, the Egyptians may have invented it on their own. The writing system, dubbed *hieroglyphs* ("sacred carvings") by the Greeks, was highly sophisticated, involving hundreds of picture signs that remained relatively constant in the way they were rendered for over 3,000 years. Many of them formed a syllabary of one, two, or three consonantal sounds, while some conveyed a word's meaning or category, either independently or added to the end of the word. Texts were usually written horizontally from right to left, but could be written from left to right, as well as vertically from top to bottom in both horizontal directions. A cursive version of hieroglyphs was used for business documents and literary texts, which were penned rapidly in black and red ink. The Egyptian language, part of the Afro–Asiatic (or Hamito–Semitic) family, evolved through several stages—Old, Middle, and Late Egyptian, Demotic, and Coptic—thus giving it a history of continuous recorded use well into the medieval period.

Egyptian literature includes narratives, myths, books of instruction in wisdom, letters, religious texts, and poetry, written on papyri, limestone flakes, and postherds. (See "Love Poems from the New Kingdom.") Unfortunately only a small fraction of this enormous literature has survived, and many texts are incomplete. Though they surely existed, we have no epics or dramas from ancient Egypt. Such nonliterary documents as lists of kings, autobiographies in tombs, wine jar labels, judicial records, astronomical observations, and medical and other scientific texts are invaluable for our understanding of Egyptian history and civilization.

RELIGION: GODS AND TEMPLES Egyptian religion encompasses a multitude of concepts that often seem mutually contradictory to us. Three separate explanations for the origin of the universe were formulated, each based in the philosophical traditions of a venerable Egyptian city. The cosmogony of Heliopolis, north of Memphis, held that the creator sun god Atum (also identified as Re) emerged from the darkness of a vast sea to stand upon a primeval mound, containing within himself the life force of the gods he was to create. At Memphis, it was the god Ptah who created the other gods by uttering their names. Further south, at Hermopolis, eight male and female entities

The Egyptians believed in the possibility of life after death through the god Osiris. Aspects of each person's life had to be tested by 42 assessor-gods before the person could be presented to Osiris. In this scene from a papyrus manuscript of the Book of the Dead *the deceased and his wife (on the left) watch the scales of justice weighing his heart (on the left side of the scales) against the feather of truth. The jackal-headed god Anubis also watches the scales, while the ibis-headed god Thoth keeps the record.* British Museum, London/The Bridgeman Art Library International Ltd.

within a primordial slime suddenly exploded, and the energy that resulted created the sun and Atum, from which the rest came.

The Egyptian gods, or pantheon, similarly defy neat categorization, in part because of the common tendency to combine the character and function of one or more gods. Amun, one of the eight entities in the Hermopolitan cosmogony, provides a good example. Thebes, Amun's cult center, rose to prominence in the Middle Kingdom. In the New Kingdom, Amun was elevated above his seven cohorts and took on aspects of the sun god Re to become Amun-Re.

Not surprisingly in a nearly rainless land, solar cults and mythologies were highly developed. Much thought was devoted to conceptualizing what happened as the sun god made his perilous way through the underworld in the night hours between sunset and sunrise. Three long texts trace Re's journey as he vanquishes immense snakes and other foes.

The Eighteenth Dynasty was one of several periods during which solar cults were in ascendancy. Early in his reign, Amunhotep IV promoted a single, previously minor aspect of the sun, the Aten ("disk") above Re himself and the rest of the gods. He declared that the Aten was the creator god who brought life to mankind and all living beings, with himself and his queen Nefertiti the sole mediators between the Aten and the people. For religious and political reasons still imperfectly understood, he went further, changing his name to Akhenaten ("the effective spirit of the Aten"), building a new capital called Akhetaten ("the horizon of the Aten") near Amarma north of Thebes, and chiseling out the name of Amun from inscriptions everywhere. Shortly after his death, Amarna was abandoned and partially razed. A large diplomatic archive of tablets written in Akkadian was left at the site, which give us a vivid, if one-sided, picture of the political correspondence of the day. During the reigns of Akhenaten's successors, Tutankhamun (born Tutankhaten) and Horemheb, Amun was restored to his former position, and Akhenaten's monuments were defaced and even demolished.

In representations, Egyptian gods have human bodies, possess human or animal heads, and wear crowns, celestial disks, or thorns. The lone exception is the Aten, made nearly abstract by Akhenaten, who altered its image to a plain disk with solar rays ending in small hands holding the hieroglyphic sign for life to the nostrils of Akhenaten and Nefertiti. The gods were thought to reside in their cult centers, where, from the New Kingdom on, increasingly ostentatious temples were built, staffed by full-time priests. At Thebes, for instance, successive kings enlarged the great Karnak temple complex dedicated to Amun for over 2,000 years. Though the ordinary person could not enter a temple precinct, great festivals took place for all to see. During Amun's major festival of Opet, the statue of the god traveled in a divine boat along the Nile, whose banks were thronged with spectators.

WORSHIP AND THE AFTERLIFE   For most Egyptians, worship took place at small local shrines. They left offerings to the chosen gods, as well as votive inscriptions with simple prayers. Private houses often had niches containing busts for ancestor worship and statues of household deities. The Egyptians strongly believed in the power of magic, dreams, and oracles, and they possessed a wide variety of amulets to ward off evil.

The Egyptians thought that the afterlife was full of dangers, which could be overcome by magical means, among them the spells in the *Book of the Dead*. The goals were to join and be identified with the gods, especially Osiris, or to sail in the "boat of millions." Originally only the king could hope to enjoy immortality with the gods, but gradually this became available to all. Since the Egyptians believed that the preservation of the body was essential for continued existence in the afterlife, early on they developed mummification, a process that took seventy days by the New Kingdom. How lavishly tombs were prepared and decorated varied over the course of Egyptian history and in accordance with the wealth of a family. A high-ranking Dynasty 18 official, for example, typically had a Theban rock-cut tomb of several rooms embellished with scenes from daily life and funerary texts, as well as provisions and equipment for the afterlife, statuettes of workers, and a place for descendants to leave offerings.

WOMEN IN EGYPTIAN SOCIETY   It is difficult to assess the position of women in Egyptian society, because our pictorial and textual evidence comes almost entirely from male sources. Women's prime roles were connected with the management of the household. They could not hold office, go to scribal schools, or become artisans. Nevertheless, women could own and control property, sue for divorce, and, at least in theory, enjoy equal legal protection.

Major Periods in Ancient Egyptian History (Dynasties in Roman Numerals)	
3100–2700 B.C.E.	Early Dynastic Period (I–II)
2700–2200 B.C.E.	Old Kingdom (III–VI)
2200–2025 B.C.E.	First Intermediate Period (VII–XI)
2025–1630 B.C.E.	Middle Kingdom (XII–XIII)
1630–1550 B.C.E.	Second Intermediate Period (XIV–XVII)
1550–1075 B.C.E.	New Kingdom (XVIII–XX)

This painting from the Theban tomb of a high-ranking Eighteenth Dynasty official shows him, accompanied by his wife and daughter, on a hunting trip through the papyrus marshes, an activity the family enjoyed during their lives on earth and would continue in the afterlife. Courtesy of the Trustees of the British Museum. Copyright The British Museum

Royal women often wielded considerable influence, particularly in the Eighteenth Dynasty. The most remarkable was Hatshepsut, daughter of Thutmosis I and widow of Thutmosis II, who ruled as pharaoh for nearly 20 years. Many Egyptian queens held the title "god's wife of Amun," a power base of great importance.

In art, royal and nonroyal women are conventionally shown smaller than their husbands or sons (see illustration above). Yet it is probably of greater significance that they are so frequently depicted in such a wide variety of contexts. Much care was lavished on details of their gestures, clothing, and hairstyles. With their husbands, they attend banquets, boat in the papyrus marshes, make and receive offerings, and supervise the myriad affairs of daily life.

SLAVES   Slaves did not become numerous in Egypt until the growth of Egyptian imperial power in the Middle Kingdom (2052–1786 B.C.E.). During that period, black Africans from Nubia to the south and Asians from the east were captured in war and brought back to Egypt as slaves. The great period of Egyptian imperial expansion, the New Kingdom (1550–1075 B.C.E.), vastly increased the number of slaves and captives in Egypt. Sometimes an entire people was enslaved, as the Bible says the Hebrews were.

Slaves in Egypt performed many tasks. They labored in the fields with the peasants, in the shops of artisans, and as domestic servants. Others worked as policemen and soldiers. Many slaves labored to erect the great temples, obelisks, and other huge monuments of Egypt's imperial age. As in Mesopotamia, slaves were branded for identification and to help prevent their escape. Slaves could be freed in Egypt, but manumission seems to have been rare. Nonetheless, former slaves were not set apart and could expect to be assimilated into the mass of the population.

This Egyptian wallpainting, in the tomb of Menna, shows men carrying grain while, in the background, two slaves fight over the leftovers. Menna was scribe of the fields and estate inspector under Pharaoh Thutmosis IV 15th century B.C.E. (18th Dynasty). Archaeological Site, Luxor–Thebes, Egypt. © Photograph by Erich Lessing. Art Resource

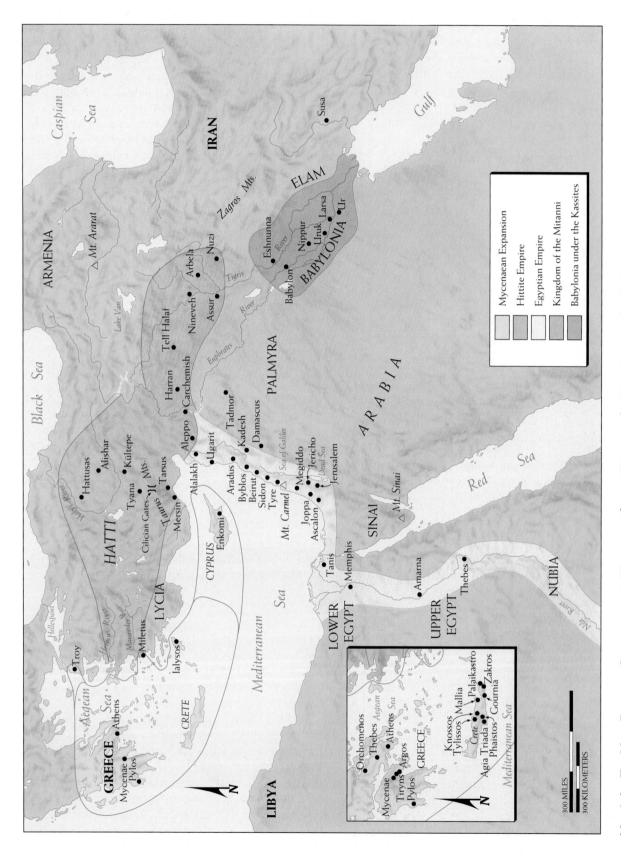

MAP 1–2   THE NEAR EAST AND GREECE ABOUT 1400 B.C.E.   About 1400 B.C.E., the Near East was divided among four empires. Egypt went south to Nubia and north through Palestine and Phoenicia. Kassites ruled in Mesopotamia, Hittites in Asia Minor, and the Mitannians in Assyrian lands. In the Aegean, the Mycenaean kingdoms were at their height.

Ancient Near Eastern Empires

In the time of the Eighteenth Dynasty in Egypt, new groups of peoples had established themselves in the Near East: the Kassites in Babylonia, the Hittites in Asia Minor, and the Mitannians in northern Syria and Mesopotamia. (See Map 1–2.) The Kassites and Mitannians were warrior peoples who ruled as a minority over more civilized folk and absorbed their culture. The Hittites established a kingdom of their own and forged an empire that lasted some 200 years.

The Hittites

The Hittites were an Indo-European people, speaking a language related to Greek and Sanskrit. By about 1500 B.C.E., they established a strong, centralized government with a capital at Hattusas (near Ankara, the capital of modern Turkey). Between 1400 and 1200 B.C.E., they emerged as a leading military power in the Mideast and contested and contested Egypt's ambitions to control Palestine and Syria. This struggle culminated in a great battle between the Egyptian and Hittite armies at Kadesh in northern Syria (1285 B.C.E.) and ended as a standoff. The Hittites also broke the power of the Mitannian state in northern Syria. The Hittites adopted Mesopotamian writing and many aspects of Mesopotamian culture, especially through the Hurrian peoples of northern Syria and southern Anatolia. Their extensive historical records are the first to mention the Greeks, whom the Hittites called Ahhiyawa (the Achaeans of Homer). The Hittite kingdom disappeared by 1200 B.C.E., swept away in the general invasions and collapse of the Mideastern nation–states at that time. Successors to the empire, called the Neo-Hittite states, flourished in southern Asia Minor and northern Syria until the Assyrians destroyed them in the first millennium B.C.E.

The government of the Hittites was different from that of Mesopotamia in that Hittite kings did not claim to be divine or even to be the chosen representatives of the gods. In the early period, a council of nobles limited the king's power, and the assembled army had to ratify his succession to the throne.

THE DISCOVERY OF IRON An important technological change took place in northern Anatolia, somewhat earlier than the creation of the Hittite Kingdom, but perhaps within its region. This was the discovery of how to smelt iron and the decision to use it to manufacture weapons and tools in preference to copper or bronze. Archaeologists refer to the period after 1100 B.C.E. as the Iron Age.

The Kassites

The Kassites were a people of unknown origin, speaking their own Kassite language, who established a dynasty at Babylon that ruled for nearly 500 years. The Kassites were organized into large tribal families and carved out great domains for themselves in Babylonia. They promoted Babylonian culture, and many of the most important works of Babylonian literature were written during their rule. Under the Kassites, Babylonia became one of the great nation–states of the late Bronze Age, along with Mitanni on the Upper Euphrates, Assyria, Egypt, and the empire of the Hittites in Anatolia. The kings of these states wrote frequently to each other and exchanged lavish gifts. They supported a military aristocracy based on horses and chariots, the prestige weaponry of the age. Though equally matched in power, the kings of this time conspired against each other, with Egypt and the Hittites hoping to control Syria and Palestine, and Babylonia and Assyria testing each other's borders, but wars were often inconclusive.

The Mitannians

The Mitannians belonged to a large group of people called the Hurrians, some of whom had been living in Mesopotamia and Syria in the time of the kings of Akkad and Ur. Their language is imperfectly understood, and the location of their capital city, Washukanni, is uncertain. The Hurrians were important mediators of Mesopotamian culture to Syria and Anatolia. They developed the art of chariot warfare and horse training to a high degree and created a large state that reached from the Euphrates to the foothills of Iran. The Hittites destroyed their kingdom, and the Assyrian empire eventually incorporated what was left of it.

The Assyrians

The Assyrians were originally a people living in Assur, a city in northern Mesopotamia on the Tigris River. They spoke a Semitic language closely related to Babylonian. They had a proud, independent culture heavily influenced by Babylonia. Assur had been an early center for trade, but emerged as a political power during the fourteenth century B.C.E., after the decline of Mitanni. The first Assyrian empire spread north and west against the Neo-Hittite states, but was brought to an end in the general collapse of Near Eastern states at the end of the second millennium. A people called the Arameans, a Semitic nomadic and agricultural people originally from northern Syria who spoke a language called Aramaic, invaded As-

This eighth-century B.C.E. relief of a hero gripping a lion formed part of the decoration of an Assyrian palace. The immense size of the figure and his powerful limbs and muscles may well have suggested the might of the Assyrian king. Giraudon/Art Resource, N.Y.

syria. Aramaic is still used in parts of the Near East and is one of the languages of medieval Jewish and Mideastern Christian culture.

The Second Assyrian Empire

After 1000 B.C.E., the Assyrians began a second period of expansion, and by 665 B.C.E. they controlled all of Mesopotamia, much of southern Asia Minor, Syria, Palestine, and Egypt to its southern frontier. They succeeded thanks to a large, well-disciplined army and a society that valued military skills. Some Assyrian kings boasted of their atrocities, so that

their names inspired terror throughout the Near East. They constructed magnificent palaces at Nineveh and Nimrud (near modern Mosul, Iraq), surrounded by parks and gardens. The walls of the reception rooms and hallways were decorated with stone reliefs and inscriptions proclaiming the power and conquests of the king.

The Assyrians organized their empire into provinces with governors, military garrisons, and administration for taxation, communications, and intelligence. Important officers were assigned large areas of land throughout the empire, and agricultural colonies were set up in key regions to store up supplies for military actions beyond the frontiers. Vassal kings had to send tribute and delegations to the Assyrian capital every year. Tens of thousands of people were forcibly displaced from their homes and resettled in other areas of the empire, partly to populate sparsely inhabited regions, partly to diminish resistance to Assyrian rule. People of the kingdom of Israel, which the Assyrians invaded and destroyed, were among them.

The empire became too large to govern efficiently. The last years of Assyria are obscure, but civil war apparently divided the country. The Medes, a powerful people from western and central Iran, had been expanding across the Iranian plateau. They were feared for their cavalry and archers, against which traditional Mideastern armies were ineffective. The Medes attacked Assyria and were joined by the Babylonians, who had always been restive under Assyrian rule, under the leadership of a general named Nebuchadnezzar. They eventually destroyed the Assyrian cities, including Nineveh in 612 B.C.E., so thoroughly that Assyria never recovered. The ruins of the great Assyrian palaces lay untouched until archaeologists began to explore them in the nineteenth century.

The Neo-Babylonians

The Medes did not follow up on their conquests, so Nebuchadnezzar took over much of the Assyrian empire. Under him and his successors, Babylon grew into one of the greatest cities of the world. The Greek traveler Herodotus described its wonders, including its great temples, fortification walls, boulevards, parks, and palaces, to a Greek readership that had never seen the like. Babylon prospered as a center of world trade, linking Egypt, India, Iran, and Syria–Palestine by land and sea routes. For centuries, an astronomical center at Babylon kept detailed records of observations that were the longest-running chronicle of the ancient world. Nebuchadnezzar's dynasty did not last long, and the government passed to various men in rapid succession. The last independent king of Babylon set up a second capital in the Arabian desert and tried to force the Babylonians to honor the Moon-god above all

Key Events in the History of Ancient Near Eastern Empires

ca. 1400–1200 B.C.E.	Hittite Empire
ca. 1100 B.C.E.	Rise of Assyrian power
732–722 B.C.E.	Assyrian conquest of Syria–Palestine
671 B.C.E.	Assyrian conquest of Egypt
612 B.C.E.	Destruction of Assyrian capital at Nineveh
612–539 B.C.E.	Neo-Babylonian (Chaldean) Empire

other gods. He allowed dishonest or incompetent speculators to lease huge areas of temple land for their personal profit. These policies proved unpopular—some said that the king was insane—and many Babylonians may have welcomed the Persian conquest that came in 539 B.C.E. After that, Babylonia began another, even more prosperous phase of its history as one of the most important provinces of another great Eastern empire, that of the Persians. We shall return to the Persians in Chapter 2.

Palestine

None of the powerful kingdoms of the ancient Near East had as much influence on the future of Western civilization as the small stretch of land between Syria and Egypt, the land called Palestine for much of its history. The three great religions of the modern world outside the Far East—Judaism, Christianity, and Islam—trace their origins, at least in part, to the people who arrived there a little before 1200 B.C.E. The book that recounts their experiences is the Hebrew Bible.

The Canaanites and the Phoenicians

Before the Israelites arrived in their promised land, it was inhabited by groups of people speaking a Semitic language called Canaanite. The Canaanites lived in walled cities and were farmers and seafarers. They had their own writing system, an alphabet that may have originated among people who were impressed by Egyptian writing, but wanted something much simpler to use. Instead of the hundreds of characters required to read Egyptian or cuneiform, their alphabet used between twenty and thirty. The Canaanites, like the other peoples of Syria–Palestine, worshiped many gods, especially gods of weather and fertility, whom they thought resided in the clouds atop the high mountains of northern Syria. The invading Israelites destroyed various Canaanite cities and holy places and may have forced some of the population to move north and west, though Canaanite and Israelite culture also intermingled.

The Phoenicians were the descendants of the Canaanites and other peoples of Syria–Palestine, especially those who lived along the coast. They played an important role in Mediterranean trade, sailing to ports in Cyprus, Asia Minor, Greece, Italy, France, Spain, Egypt, and North Africa, as far as Gibraltar and possibly beyond. They founded colonies throughout the Mediterranean as far west as Spain. The most famous of these colonies was Carthage, near modern Tunis in North Africa. Sitting astride the trade routes, the Phoenician cities were important sites for the transmission of culture from east to west. The Greeks, who had long forgotten their older writing system of the Bronze Age, adopted a Phoenician version of the Canaanite alphabet that is the origin of our present alphabet.

The Israelites

The history of the Israelites must be pieced together from various sources. They are mentioned only rarely in the records of their neighbors, so we must rely chiefly on their own account, the Hebrew Bible. This is not a history in our sense, but a complicated collection of historical narrative, pieces of wisdom, poetry, law, and religious witness. Scholars of an earlier time tended to discard it as a historical source, but the most recent trend is to take it seriously while using it with caution.

According to tradition, the patriarch Abraham came from Ur and wandered west to tend his flocks in the land of the Canaanites. Some of his people settled there, and others wandered into Egypt. By the thirteenth century B.C.E., led by Moses, they had left Egypt and wandered in the desert until they reached and conquered Canaan. They established a united kingdom that reached its peak under David and

The Israelites

ca. 1000–961 B.C.E.	Reign of King David
ca. 961–922 B.C.E.	Reign of King Solomon
722 B.C.E.	Assyrian conquest of Israel (northern kingdom)
586 B.C.E.	Destruction of Jerusalem; fall of Judah (southern kingdom); Babylonian Captivity
539 B.C.E.	Restoration of temple; return of exiles

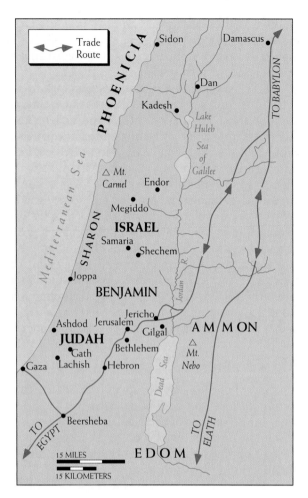

MAP 1–3   ANCIENT PALESTINE   *The Hebrews estab-lished a unified kingdom in Palestine under Kings David and Solomon in the tenth century B.C.E.. After the death of Solomon, however, the kingdom was di-vided into two parts—Israel in the north and Judah, with its capital, Jerusalem, in the south. Along the coast, especially to the north, were the great commer-cial cities of the Phoenicians, such as Sidon and Tyre.*

Solomon in the tenth century B.C.E. The sons of Solomon could not maintain the unity of the king-dom, and it split into two parts: Israel in the north and Judah, with its capital at Jerusalem, in the south. (See Map 1–3.) The rise of the great empires brought disaster to the Israelites. The northern kingdom fell to the Assyrians in 722 B.C.E., and its people—the "ten lost tribes"—were scattered and lost forever. Only the kingdom of Judah remained. It is from this time that we may call the Israelites Jews.

In 586 B.C.E., Judah was defeated by the Neo-Baby-lonian king Nebuchadnezzar II. He destroyed the great temple built by Solomon and took thousands of hostages off to Babylon. When the Persians de-feated Babylonia, they ended this Babylonian cap-tivity of the Jews and allowed them to return to their homeland. After that, the area of the old kingdom of

the Jews in Palestine was dominated by foreign peo-ples for some 2,500 years, until the establishment of the State of Israel in 1948 C.E.

The Jewish Religion

The fate of the small nation of Israel would be of little interest were it not for its unique religious achieve-ment. The great contribution of the Jews is the devel-opment of monotheism—the belief in one universal God, the creator and ruler of the universe. This idea may be as old as Moses, as the Jewish tradition asserts, and it certainly dates as far back as the prophets of the eighth century B.C.E. The Jewish God is neither a nat-ural force nor like human beings or any other crea-tures; He is so elevated, that those who believe in Him may not picture Him in any form. The faith of the Jews is given special strength by their belief that God made a covenant with Abraham that his progeny would be a chosen people who would be rewarded for following God's commandments and the law He re-vealed to Moses. (See "The Second Isaiah Defines He-brew Monotheism.")

A novelty of Jewish religious thought is the pow-erful ethical element it introduced. God is a severe, but just, judge. Ritual and sacrifice are not enough to achieve His approval. People must be righteous, and God Himself appears to be bound to act righteously. The Jewish prophetic tradition was a powerful ethi-cal force. The prophets constantly criticized any falling away from the law and the path of righteous-ness. They placed God in history, blaming the mis-fortunes of the Jews on God's righteous and necessary intervention to punish the people for their misdeeds. The prophets also promised the redemption of the Jews if they repented, however. The prophetic tradi-tion expected the redemption to come in the form of a Messiah who would restore the house of David. Christianity, emerging from this tradition, holds that Jesus of Nazareth was that Messiah.

Jewish religious ideas influenced the future de-velopment of the West, both directly and indirect-ly. The Jews' belief in an all-powerful creator (who is righteous Himself and demands righteousness and obedience from humankind) and a universal God (who is the father and ruler of all peoples) is a criti-cal part of the Western heritage.

General Outlook of Mideastern Cultures

Our brief account of the history of the ancient Mideast so far reveals that its various peoples and cultures were different in many ways. Yet the distance between all of them and the emerging culture of the Greeks

The Second Isaiah Defines Hebrew Monotheism

The strongest statement of Hebrew monotheism is found in these words of the anonymous prophet whom we call the Second Isaiah. He wrote during the Hebrew exile in Babylonia, 597–539 B.C.E.

❖ *How is the deity in this passage different from the deities of the Mesopotamian and Egyptian societies? Are there any similarities? Many peoples have claimed that a single god was the greatest and the ruler over all others. What is there in this selection that claims a different status for the Hebrew deity?*

42

[5]Thus says God, the Lord
who created the heavens and stretched them out,
who spread forth the earth and what comes
 from it,
who gives breath to the people upon it and spirit
to those who walk in it:
[6]"I am the Lord, I have called you in righteousness,
I have taken you by the hand and kept you;
I have given you as a covenant to the people, a
 light to the nations,
[7]to open the eyes that are blind,
to bring out the prisoners from the dungeon,
from the prison those who sit in darkness.
[8]I am the Lord, that is my name;
my glory I give to no other,
nor my praise to graven images.
[9]Behold, the former things have come to pass,
 and new things I now declare;
before they spring forth I tell you of them."

44

[6]Thus says the Lord, the King of Israel and his
 Redeemer, the Lord of hosts:
"I am the first and I am the last; besides me
 there is no god.
[7]Who is like me? Let him proclaim it,
let him declare and set it forth before me.
Who has announced of old the things to come?
Let them tell us what is yet to be.
[8]Fear not, nor be afraid;
have I not told you from of old and declared it?

And you are my witnesses!
Is there a God besides me?
There is no Rock; I know not any."

49

[22]Thus says the Lord God:
"Behold, I will lift up my hand to the nations,
and raise my signal to the peoples;
and they shall bring your sons in their bosom,
and your daughters shall be carried on their
 shoulders
[23]Kings shall be your foster fathers,
and their queens your nursing mothers.
With their faces to the ground they shall bow
 down to you,
and lick the dust of your feet.
Then you will know that I am the Lord;
those who wait for me shall not be put to
 shame."
[24]Can the prey be taken from the mighty, or the
 captives of a tyrant be rescued?
[25]Surely, thus says the Lord:
"Even the captives of the mighty shall be taken,
and the prey of the tyrant be rescued,
for I will contend with those who contend
 with you
and I will save your children.
[26]I will make your oppressors eat their own flesh,
and they shall be drunk with their own blood as
 with wine.
Then all flesh shall know
that I am the Lord your Savior,
and your Redeemer, the Mighty One of Jacob."

Bible, Revised Standard Version (New York: Division of Christian Education, National Council of Churches, 1952).

(Chapter 2) is striking. We can see this distance best by comparing the approach of the other cultures with that of the Greeks on several fundamental human problems: What is the relationship of humans to nature? To the gods? To other humans? These questions involve attitudes toward religion, philosophy, science, law, justice, politics, and government in general.

Humans and Nature

For the peoples of the Mideast, there was no simple separation between humans and nature or even between animate creatures and inanimate objects. Humanity was part of a natural continuum, and all things partook of life and spirit. These peoples imagined the universe to be dominated by gods more or less in the shape of humans, and the world they ruled was irregular and unpredictable, subject to divine whims. The gods were capricious because nature seemed capricious.

A Babylonian story of creation makes it clear that humanity's function is merely to serve the gods. The creator Marduk says:

I shall compact blood, I shall cause bones to be,
I shall make stand a human being, let "Man" be
    its name.
I shall create humankind,
They shall bear the gods' burden that those
    may rest.[1]

In a world ruled by powerful deities of this kind, human existence was precarious. Disasters that we would think human in origin the Mesopotamians saw as the product of divine will. Thus, a Babylonian text depicts the destruction of the city of Ur by invading Elamites as the work of the gods, carried out by the storm god Enlil:

Enlil called the storm.
The people mourn.
Exhilarating winds he took from the land.
The people mourn.
Good winds he took away from Sumer.
The people mourn.
He summoned evil winds.
The people mourn.
Entrusted them to Kingaluda, tender of storms.
He called the storm that will annihilate the land.
The people mourn.
He called disastrous winds.
The people mourn.
Enlil—choosing Gibil as his helper—
Called the (great) hurricane of heaven.
The people mourn.[2]

The vulnerable position of humankind in the face of divine powers is clearly shown in both the Egyptian and the Babylonian versions of the destruction of mankind. In one Egyptian tale, Re, the god who had created humans, decided to destroy them because they were plotting evil against him. He sent the goddess Sekhmet to accomplish the deed, and she was resting in the midst of her task, having enjoyed the work and waded in a sea of blood, when Re changed his mind. He ordered 7,000 barrels of blood-colored beer poured in Sekhmet's path. She quickly became too drunk to continue

the slaughter and thus preserved humanity. In the Babylonian story of the flood, the motive for the destruction of humanity is given as follows:

The land had grown numerous, the peoples
    had increased,
The land was bellowing like a bull.
The god was disturbed by their uproar,
The god Enlil heard their clamor.
He said to the great gods,
"The clamor of mankind has become burdensome
    to me,
"I am losing sleep to their uproar!"[3]

Utanapishtim and his wife survived because he was friendly with Enki, the god of wisdom, who helped him to pull through by a trick.

In such a universe, humans could not hope to understand nature, much less control it. At best, they could try by magic to use uncanny forces against others. An example of this device is provided by a Mesopotamian incantation to cure sickness. The sufferer tries to use magical powers by acting out the destruction of the powers he thinks caused his illness:

As this garlic is peeled off and thrown into
    the fire,
[And the Fire God] burns it up with fire,
Which will not be cultivated in a garden patch,
Whose roots will not take hold in the ground,
Whose sprout will not come forth nor see the sun,
Which will not be used for the repast of god or king,
[So] may the curse, something evil, revenge,
    interrogation,
The sickness of my suffering, wrong-doing,
    crime, misdeed, sin
The sickness which is in my body, flesh, and sinews
Be peeled off like this garlic,
May [the Fire God] burn it with fire this day,
May the wicked thing go forth, that I may see light.[4]

Humans and the Gods, Law, and Justice

Human relationships to the gods were equally humble. There was no doubt that the gods could destroy human beings and might do so at any time for no good reason. Humans could—and, indeed, had to—try to win the gods over by prayers and sacrifices, but there was no guarantee of success. The gods were bound by no laws and no morality. The best behavior and the greatest devotion to the cult of the gods were no defense against the divine and cosmic caprice.

[1]Benjamin R. Foster, *From Distant Days, Myths, Tales, and Poetry of Ancient Mesopotamia* (Bethesda, MD: CDL Press, p. 38).

[2]Thorkild Jacobsen in Henri Frankfort et al., *Before Philosophy* (Baltimore: Penguin, 1949), pp. 154.

[3]Foster, pp. 170–171.

[4]Foster, p. 412.

In the earliest civilizations, human relations were guided by laws, often set down in written codes. The basic question about law concerned its legitimacy: Why, apart from the lawgiver's power to coerce obedience, should anyone obey the law? For Old Kingdom Egyptians, the answer was simple: The king was bound to act in accordance with *maat*, and so his laws were righteous. For the Mesopotamians, the answer was almost the same: The king was a representative of the gods, so that the laws he set forth were authoritative. The prologue to the most famous legal document in antiquity, the Code of Hammurabi, makes this plan:

I am the king who is preeminent among kings;
my words are choice; my ability has no equal.
By the order of Sharnash, the great judge of heaven
   and earth,
may my justice prevail in the land;
by the word of Marduk, my lord,
may my statutes have no one to rescind them.[5]

The Hebrews introduced some important new ideas. Their unique God was capable of great anger and destruction, but He was open to persuasion and subject to morality. He was therefore more predictable and comforting, for all the terror of His wrath. The biblical version of the flood story, for instance, reveals the great difference between the Hebrew God and the Babylonian deities. The Hebrew God was powerful and wrathful, but He was not arbitrary. He chose to destroy His creatures for their moral failures, for the reason that

the wickedness of man was great in the earth, and that every imagination of the thought of His heart was evil continually...the earth was corrupt in God's sight and the earth was filled with violence.[6]

When He repented and wanted to save someone, He chose Noah because "Noah was a righteous man, blameless in his generation."[7]

That God was bound by His own definition of righteousness is neatly shown in the biblical story of Sodom and Gomorrah. He had chosen to destroy these wicked cities, but felt obliged by His covenant to inform Abraham first.[8] In this passage, Abraham calls on God to abide by His own moral principles, and God sees Abraham's point.

In such a world, there is the possibility of order in the universe and on this earth. There is also the possibility of justice among human beings, for the Hebrew God had provided His people with law. Through

his prophet Moses, He had provided humans with regulations that would enable them to live in peace and justice. If they would abide by the law and live upright lives, they and their descendants could expect happy and prosperous lives. This idea was quite different from the uncertainty of the Babylonian view, but like it and its Egyptian partner, it left no doubt of the certainty of the divine. Cosmic order, human survival, and justice were all dependent on God.

Toward the Greeks and Western Thought

Greek thought offered different approaches and answers to many of the concerns we have been discussing. Calling attention to some of those differences will help convey the distinctive outlook of the Greeks and the later cultures within Western civilization that have drawn heavily on Greek influence.

It is important to recognize that Greek ideas had much in common with the ideas of earlier peoples. The Greek gods had most of the characteristics of the Mesopotamian deities, magic and incantations played a part in the lives of most Greeks, and Greek law, like that of earlier peoples, was usually connected with divinity. Many, if not most, Greeks in the ancient world must have lived their lives with notions similar to those held by other peoples. The surprising thing is that some Greeks developed ideas that were strikingly different and, in so doing, set a part of humankind on an entirely new path.

As early as the sixth century B.C.E., some Greeks living in the Ionian cities of Asia Minor raised questions and suggested answers about the nature of the world that produced an intellectual revolution. In their speculations, they made guesses that were completely naturalistic and made no reference to supernatural powers. One historian of Greek thought, discussing the views of Thales, the first Greek philosopher, put the case particularly well:

In one of the Babylonian legends it says: "All the lands were sea...Marduk bound a rush mat upon the face of the waters, he made dirt and piled it beside the rush mat." What Thales did was to leave Marduk out. He, too, said that everything was once water. But he thought that earth and everything else had been formed out of water by a natural process, like the silting up of the Delta of the Nile....It is an admirable beginning, the whole point of which is that it gathers into a coherent picture a number of observed facts without letting Marduk in.[9]

By putting the question of the world's origin in a naturalistic form, Thales, in the sixth century B.C.E.,

[5]James B. Pritchard, *Ancient Near Eastern Texts Related to the Old Testament*, 3d ed. (Princeton: Princeton University Press, 1969), pp. 164.

[6]Genesis 6:5–11.

[7]Genesis 6:9.

[8]Genesis 18:20–33.

[9]Benjamin Farrington, *Greek Science* (London: Penguin Books, 1953), p. 37.

may have begun the unreservedly rational investigation of the universe and, in so doing, initiated both philosophy and science.

The same relentlessly rational approach was used even in regard to the gods themselves. In the same century as Thales, Xenophanes of Colophon expressed the opinion that humans think of the gods as resembling themselves, that, like themselves, they were born, that they wear clothes like theirs, and that they have voices and bodies like theirs. If oxen, horses, and lions had hands and could paint like humans, Xenophanes argued, they would paint gods in their own image; the oxen would draw gods like oxen and the horses like horses. Thus, Africans believed in flat-nosed, black-faced gods, and the Thracians in gods with blue eyes and red hair.[10] In the fifth century B.C.E., Protagoras of Abdera went so far in the direction of agnosticism as to say, "About the gods I can have no knowledge either that they are or that they are not or what is their nature."[11]

This rationalistic, skeptical way of thinking carried over into practical matters as well. The school of medicine led by Hippocrates of Cos (about 400 B.C.E.) attempted to understand, diagnose, and cure disease without any attention to supernatural forces or beings. One of the Hippocratics wrote, of the mysterious disease epilepsy,

It seems to me that the disease is no more divine than any other. It has a natural cause, just as other diseases have. Men think it divine merely because they do not understand it. But if they called everything divine which they do not understand, why, there would be no end of divine things.[12]

By the fifth century B.C.E., it was also possible for the historian Thucydides to analyze and explain the behavior of humans in society completely in terms of human nature and chance, leaving no place for the gods or supernatural forces.

The same absence of divine or supernatural forces characterized Greek views of law and justice. Most Greeks, of course, liked to think that, in a vague way, law came ultimately from the gods. In practice, however, and especially in the democratic states, they knew very well that laws were made by humans and should be obeyed because they represented the expressed consent of the citizens. Law, according to the fourth-century-B.C.E. statesman Demosthenes, is "a general covenant of the whole State, in accordance with which all men in that State ought to regulate their lives."[13]

In Perspective

The statement of the following ideas, so different from any that came before the Greeks, opens the discussion of most of the issues that appear in the long history of Western civilization and that remain major concerns in the modern world. What is the nature of the universe, and how can it be controlled? Are there divine powers, and if so, what is humanity's relationship to them? Are law and justice human, divine, or both? What is the place in human society of freedom, obedience, and reverence? These and many other matters were either first considered or first elaborated on by the Greeks.

The Greeks' sharp departure from the thinking of earlier cultures marked the beginning of the unusual experience that we call Western civilization. Nonetheless, they built on a foundation of lore that people in the Near East had painstakingly accumulated over millennia. From ancient Mesopotamia and Egypt, they borrowed important knowledge and skills in mathematics, astronomy, art, and literature. From Phoenicia, they learned the art of writing. The discontinuities, however, are more striking than the continuities.

The great civilizations of the river valleys were ruled by hereditary monarchies often elevated by the aura of divinity. Powerful priesthoods presented yet another bastion of privilege that stood between the ordinary person and the knowledge and opportunity needed for freedom and autonomy. Religion was an integral part of the world of the ancient Near East, in the kingdoms and city–states of Palestine, Phoenicia, and Syria just as in the great empires of Egypt and Mesopotamia. The secular, reasoned questioning that sought understanding of the world in which people lived—that tried to find explanations in the natural order of things rather than in the supernatural acts of the gods—was not characteristic of the older cultures. Nor would it appear in similar societies at other times in other parts of the world. The new way of looking at things was uniquely the product of the Greeks. We now need to see whether there was something special in their experience that made them raise fundamental questions in the way that they did.

REVIEW QUESTIONS

1. How would you define "history"? What different academic disciplines do historians rely on, and why is the study of history important?

2. How was life during the Paleolithic Age different from that in the Neolithic Age? What advancements in agriculture and human development had

[10]Henri Frankfort et al. *Before Philosophy* (Baltimore: Penguin, 1949), pp. 14–16.

[11]Hermann Diels, *Fragmente der Vorsokratiker*, 5th ed., ed. by Walter Krantz (Berlin: Weidmann, 1934–38), Frg. 4.

[12]Diels, Frgs. 14–16.

[13]Demosthenes, *Against Aristogeiton*, 16.

taken place by the end of the Neolithic era? Is it valid to speak of a "Neolithic Revolution"?

3. Describe, generally, the differences in the political and intellectual outlooks of the civilizations of Egypt and Mesopotamia. Compare especially their religious views. In what ways did geography influence the religious outlooks of these two civilizations?

4. To what extent did the Hebrew faith bind the Jews politically? Why was the concept of monotheism so radical for Near Eastern civilizations?

5. Why were the Assyrians so successful in establishing their Near Eastern empire? How did their empire differ from that of the Hittites or Egyptians? In what ways did this empire benefit the civilized Middle East? Why did the Assyrian Empire ultimately fail to survive?

6. In what ways did Greek thought develop along different lines from that of Near Eastern civilizations? What new questions about human society were asked as a result of Greek influence?

SUGGESTED READINGS

J. BAINES AND J. MÁLEK, *Atlas of Ancient Egypt* (1980). An authoritative, well-illustrated guide to archaeological sites and cultural matters, with special treatment of thematic issues.

W. V. DAVIES, *Egyptian Hieroglyphs* (1987). A good introduction to the ancient Eygptian language, scripts, and grammar of ancient Egyptian.

R. DE VAUX, *Ancient Israel: Its Life and Institutions* (1961). A fine account of social institutions.

M. EHRENBERG, *Women in Prehistory* (1989). An account of the role of women in early times.

H. FRANKFORT ET AL., *Before Philosophy* (1949). A brilliant examination of the mind of the ancients from the Stone Age to the Greeks.

O. R. GURNEY, *The Hittites* (1954). A good survey.

W. W. HALLO AND W. K. SIMPSON, *The Ancient Near East: A History* (1998). A fine survey of Egyptian and Mesopotamian history.

W. W. HALLO AND L. YOUNGER, ED., *The Context of Scripture, Canonical Compositions from the Biblical World* (1997). A good collection of literary works translated from Egyptian, Hittite, Sumerian, Babylonian, and other ancient Near Eastern languages, with introductions and explanatory notes.

G. HART, *Egyptian Myths* (1990). A clear presentation of major myths and religious literature.

D. C. JOHNSON AND M. R. EDEY, *Lucy: The Beginnings of Mankind* (1981). A study of the first human creatures based on remains found in Africa.

B. J. KEMP, *Ancient Egypt: Anatomy of a Civilization* (1989). A thought-provoking assessment of Egypt's social and intellectual history.

S. N. KRAMER, *The Sumerians: Their History, Culture and Character* (1963). A readable general account of Sumerian history.

A. KUHRT, *The Ancient Near East, c. 3000–330 B.C.* (1995). The best compact and reliable history of the ancient Near East, including Egypt and Israel, with extensive bibliographies.

S. LLOYD, *The Archaeology of Mesopotamia*, rev. ed. (1984). An account of the material remains of Mesopotamia and their meaning from the Old Stone Age to the Persian Conquest.

K. R. NEMET-NEJAT, *Daily Life in Ancient Mesopotamia* (1998). Excellent introduction for the general reader.

D. OATES AND J. OATES, *The Rise of Civilization* (1976). A study of the emergence of urban life in southern Mesopotamia, placed in a broad context and well illustrated with photographs.

J. OATES, *Babylon*, rev. ed. (1986). An introduction to the history and archaeology of Babylonia, revised to make use of newly discovered evidence.

J. N. POSTGATE, *The First Empires* (1977). A fine account of Mesopotamian history from the dawn of history to the Persian conquest.

J. N. POSTGATE, *Early Mesopotamia* (1992). An excellent study of Mesopotamian economy and society from the earliest times to about 1500 B.C.E., helpfully illustrated with drawings, pictures, and translated documents.

D. B. REDFORD, *Akhenaten* (1987). A new study of the controversial pharaoh.

C. L. REDMAN, *The Rise of Civilization* (1978). An attempt to use the evidence provided by anthropology, archaeology, and the physical sciences to illuminate the development of early urban society.

G. ROBINS, *Women in Ancient Egypt* (1993). A comprehensive study of the role of women in Egyptian society.

N. K. SANDARS, *The Sea Peoples* (1985). A lively account of the collection of peoples who disrupted established Mediterranean civilization in the thirteenth century B.C.E.

D. C. SNELL, *Life in the Ancient Near East, 3100–332 B.C.E.* (1997). Imaginative study focusing on social and economic history.

A. J. SPENCER, *Early Egypt: The Rise of Civilisation in the Nile Valley* (1993). An up-to-date account of the latest research on the Predynastic and Early Dynastic periods.

B. G. TRIGGER ET AL., *Ancient Egypt: A Social History* (1982).

M. Van De Mieroop, *The Ancient Mesopotamian City* (1997). Written for the general historian, a concise survey of Mesopotamian urban life, including political and social structures, economy, government, and the arts.

Chapter 2

The ruins of the sanctuary of Apollo at Delphi, dating from the sixth century B.C.E. Greeks and foreigners traveled great distances to worship Apollo and to consult the famous Delphic oracle for clues to the future. Josè Fuste Raga/The Stock Market

The Rise of Greek Civilization

KEY TOPICS

- The Bronze Age civilizations that ruled the Aegean area before the development of Hellenic civilization

- The rise, development, and expansion of the *polis*, the characteristic political unit of Hellenic Greece

- The early history of Sparta and Athens

- The wars between the Greeks and the Persians

About 2000 B.C.E., Greek-speaking peoples settled the lands surrounding the Aegean Sea and established a style of life and formed a set of ideas, values, and institutions that spread far beyond the Aegean corner of the Mediterranean Sea. Preserved and adapted by the Romans, Greek culture powerfully influenced the society of western Europe in the Middle Ages and dominated the Byzantine Empire in the same period. It would ultimately spread across Europe and cross the Atlantic to the Western Hemisphere.

At some time in their history, the Greeks of the ancient world founded cities on every shore of the Mediterranean Sea. Pushing on through the Dardanelles, they placed many settlements on the coasts of the Black Sea in southern Russia and as far east as the approaches to the Caucasus Mountains. The center of Greek life, however, has always been the Aegean Sea and the islands in and around it. This location at the eastern end of the Mediterranean very early put the Greeks in touch with the more advanced and earlier civilizations of Mesopotamia, Egypt, Asia Minor, and Syria–Palestine.

The Greeks acknowledged the influence of these predecessors. A character in one of Plato's dialogues says, "Whatever the Greeks have acquired from foreigners they have, in the end, turned into something finer."[1] This is a proud statement, but it also shows that the Greeks were aware of how much they had learned from other civilizations.

The Bronze Age Minoan culture of Crete contributed to Greek civilization, and the mainland Mycenaean culture, which conquered Minoan Crete, contributed even more. Both these cultures, however, had more in common with the cultures of the Near East than with the new Hellenic culture established by the Greeks in the centuries after the end of the Bronze Age in the twelfth century B.C.E.

The rugged geography of the Greek peninsula and its nearby islands isolated the Greeks of the early Iron Age from their richer and more culturally advanced neighbors, shaping, in part, their way of life and permitting them to develop that way of life on their own. The aristocratic world of the "Greek Dark Ages" (1150–750 B.C.E.) produced impressive artistic achievements, especially in the development of painted pottery and most magnificently, in the epic poems of Homer. In the eighth century B.C.E., social, economic, and military changes profoundly influenced the organization of Greek political life; the Greek city–state, the polis, *came into being and thereafter dominated the cultural development of the Greek people.*

This change came in the midst of turmoil, for the pressure of a growing population led many Greeks to leave home and establish colonies far away. Those who remained often fell into political conflict, from which tyrannies sometimes emerged. These tyrannies, however, were in all cases transitory, and the Greek cities emerged from them as self-governing polities, usually ruled by an oligarchy, broad or narrow. The two most important states, Athens and Sparta, developed in different directions. Sparta formed a mixed constitution in which a very small part of the population dominated the vast majority, and Athens developed the world's first democracy.

The Bronze Age on Crete and on the Mainland to about 1150 B.C.E.

The Bronze Age civilizations in the region that the Greeks would rule arose on the island of Crete, on the islands of the Aegean, and on the mainland of Greece. Crete was the site of the earliest Bronze Age settlements, and modern scholars have called the

civilization that arose there Minoan, after the legendary king of Crete. A later Bronze Age civilization was centered at the mainland site of Mycenae and is called Mycenaean.

The Minoans

With Greece to the north, Egypt to the south, and Asia to the east, Crete was a cultural bridge between the older civilizations and the new one of the Greeks. The Bronze Age came to Crete not long after 3000 B.C.E., and the Minoan civilization, which powerfully influenced the islands of the Aegean and the mainland of Greece, arose in the third and second millennia B.C.E.

Scholars have established links between stratigraphic layers at archaeological sites on Crete and specific styles of pottery and other artifacts found in the layers. On this basis they have divided the Bronze Age on Crete into three major periods—Early, Middle, and Late Minoan—with some subdivisions. Dates for Bronze Age settlements on the Greek mainland, for which the term *Helladic* is used, are derived from the same chronological scheme.

(a)

(b)

(a) The Minoan-period Palace at Cnossus on the island of Crete. (b) A fresco painting from the east wing of the palace. The fresco shows acrobats leaping over a charging bull. It is not known whether such acrobatic displays were only for entertainment or part of some religious ritual.
(a) D. A. Harissiadis Photography, Benaki Museum, Photographic Department; (b) Leaping bull. Minoan fresco. Archeological Museum, Heraklion, Crete, Greece. Scala/Art Resource, N.Y.

[1]Plato, *Epinomis*, 987 d.

During the Middle and Late Minoan periods in the cities of eastern and central Crete, a civilization developed that was new and unique in its character and beauty. Its most striking creations are the palaces uncovered at such sites as Phaestus, Haghia Triada, and, most important, Cnossus. Each of these palaces was built around a central court surrounded by a labyrinth of rooms. Some sections of the palace at Cnossus were as tall as four stories high. The basement contained many storage rooms for oil and grain, apparently paid as taxes to the king. The main and upper floors contained living quarters, as well as workshops for making pottery and jewelry. There were sitting rooms and even bathrooms, to which water was piped through excellent plumbing. Lovely columns, which tapered downward, supported the ceilings, and many of the walls carried murals showing landscapes and seascapes, festivals, and sports. The palace design and the paintings show the influence of Syria, Asia Minor, and Egypt, but the style and quality are unique to Crete.

In contrast to the Mycenaean cities on the mainland of Greece, Minoan palaces and settlements lacked strong defensive walls. This evidence that the Minoans built without defense in mind has raised questions and encouraged speculation. Some scholars, pointing also to evidence that Minoan religion was more matriarchal than the patriarchal religion of the Mycenaeans and their Greek descendants, have argued that the civilizations of Crete, perhaps reflecting the importance of women, were inherently more tranquil and pacific than others. An earlier and very different explanation for the absence of fortifications was that the protection provided by the sea made them unnecessary. The evidence is not strong enough to support either explanation, and the mystery remains.

Along with palaces, paintings, pottery, jewelry, and other valuable objects, excavations have revealed clay writing tablets like those found in Mesopotamia. The tablets, preserved accidentally when a great fire that destroyed the royal palace at Cnossus hardened them, have three distinct kinds of writing on them: a kind of picture writing called *hieroglyphic*, and two different linear scripts called Linear A and Linear B. The languages of the two other scripts remain unknown, but Linear B proved to be an early form of Greek. The contents of the tablets, primarily inventories, reveal an organization centered on the palace and ruled by a king who was supported by an extensive bureaucracy that kept remarkably detailed records.

This sort of organization is typical of early civilizations in the Near East, but as we shall see, is nothing like that of the Greeks after the Bronze Age.

A Linear B tablet from Cnossus, dated about 1200 B.C.E. First discovered late in the nineteenth century, Linear B was not deciphered until 1952, when a brilliant young Briton, Michael Ventris, demonstrated that it was an early Greek dialect. This tablet is part of a palace inventory. It survived because it was hardened in a fire when the palace at Cnossus was destroyed by invaders.
Hirmer Fotoarchiv

Yet the inventories were written in a form of Greek. If they controlled Crete throughout the Bronze Age, why should Minoans, who were not Greek, have written in a language not their own? This question raises the larger one of what the relationship was between Crete and the Greek mainland in the Bronze Age and leads us to an examination of mainland, or Helladic, culture.

The Mycenaeans

In the third millennium B.C.E.—the Early Helladic Period—most of the Greek mainland, including many of the sites of later Greek cities, was settled by people who used metal, built some impressive houses, and traded with Crete and the islands of the Aegean. The names they gave to places, names that were sometimes preserved by later invaders, make it clear that they were not Greeks and that they spoke a language that was not Indo-European (the language family to which Greek belongs).

Not long after the year 2000 B.C.E., many of the Early Helladic sites were destroyed by fire, some were abandoned, and still others appear to have yielded peacefully to an invading people. These signs of invasion probably signal the arrival of the Greeks.

All over Greece, there was a smooth transition between the Middle and Late Helladic periods. The invaders succeeded in establishing control of the entire mainland. The shaft graves cut into the rock at the royal palace–fortress of Mycenae show that they prospered and sometimes became very rich. At Mycenae, the richest finds come from the period after 1600 B.C.E. The city's wealth and power reached their peak during this time, and the culture of the whole mainland during the Late Helladic Period goes by the name *Mycenaean*.

The presence of the Greek Linear B tablets at Cnossus suggests that Greek invaders also established themselves in Crete, and there is good reason to believe that at the height of Mycenaean power (1400–1200 B.C.E.), Crete was part of the Mycenaean world. Although their dating is still controversial, the Linear B tablets at Cnossus seem to belong to Late Minoan III, so what is called the great "palace period" at Cnossus would have followed an invasion by Mycenaeans in 1400 B.C.E. These Greek invaders ruled Crete until the end of the Bronze Age.

MYCENAEAN CULTURE   The excavation of Mycenae, Pylos, and other Mycenaean sites reveals a culture influenced by, but very different from, the Minoan culture. Mycenae and Pylos, like Cnossus, were built some distance from the sea. It is plain, however, that defense against attack was foremost in the minds of the founders of the Mycenaean cities. Both Mycenae and Pylos were built on hills in a position commanding the neighboring territory. The Mycenaean people were warriors, as their art, architecture, and weapons reveal. The success of their campaigns and the defense of their territory required strong central authority, and all available evidence shows that the kings provided it. Their palaces, in which the royal family and its retainers lived, were located within the walls; most of the population lived outside the walls. Usually paintings covered the palace walls, as on Crete, but instead of peaceful scenery and games, the Mycenaean murals depicted scenes of war and boar hunting.

About 1500 B.C.E., the already impressive shaft graves were abandoned in favor of *tholos* tombs. These large, beehivelike chambers were built of enormous well-cut and fitted stones and were approached by an unroofed passage (*dromos*) cut horizontally into the side of the hill. The lintel block alone of one of these tombs weighs over one hundred tons. Only a strong king whose wealth was great, whose power was unquestioned, and who commanded the labor of many people could undertake such a project. His wealth probably came from plundering raids, piracy, and trade. Some of this trade went westward to Italy and Sicily, but most of it was with the islands of the Aegean, the coastal towns of Asia Minor, and the cities of Syria, Egypt, and Crete. The Mycenaeans sent pottery, olive oil, and animal hides in exchange for jewels and other luxuries.

Tablets containing the Mycenaean Linear B writing have been found all over the mainland; the largest and most useful collection was found at Pylos. These tablets reveal a world very similar to the one shown by the records at Cnossus. The king, whose title was *wanax*, held a royal domain, appointed officials, commanded servants, and kept a close record of what he owned and what was owed to him. This evidence confirms all the rest; the Mycenaean world was made up of several independent, powerful, and well-organized monarchies.

THE RISE AND FALL OF MYCENAEAN POWER   At the height of their power (1400–1200 B.C.E.), the Mycenaeans were prosperous and active. They enlarged their cities, expanded their trade, and even established commercial colonies in the East. They are mentioned in the archives of the Hittite kings of Asia Minor. They are named as marauders of the Nile Delta in Egyptian records. Sometime about 1250 B.C.E. they probably sacked Troy, on the coast of northwestern Asia Minor, giving rise to the epic poems of Homer—the *Iliad* and the *Odyssey*. (See Map 2–1.) Around 1200 B.C.E., however, the Mycenaean world showed signs of great trouble, and by 1100 B.C.E. it was gone. Its palaces were destroyed, many of its cities were abandoned, and its art, pattern of life, and system of writing were buried and forgotten.

What happened? Some recent scholars, noting evidence that the Aegean island of Thera (modern Santorini) suffered a massive volcanic explosion in the middle to late second millennium B.C.E., have suggested that this natural disaster was responsible. According to one version of this theory, the explosion occurred around 1400 B.C.E., blackening and poisoning the air for many miles around and sending a monstrous tidal wave that destroyed the great palace at Cnossus and, with it, Minoan culture. According to another version, the explosion took place about 1200 B.C.E., destroying Bronze Age culture throughout the Aegean. This second version conveniently accounts for the end of both Minoan and Mycenaean civilizations in a single blow, but the evidence does not support it. The Mycenaean towns were not destroyed all at once; many fell around 1200 B.C.E., but

MAP 2–1   THE AEGEAN AREA IN THE BRONZE AGE   *The Bronze Age in the Aegean area lasted from about 1900 to about 1100 B.C.E. Its culture on Crete is called Minoan and was at its height about 1900–1400 B.C.E. Bronze Age Helladic culture on the mainland flourished from about 1600–1200 B.C.E.*

some flourished for another century, and the Athens of the period was never destroyed or abandoned. No theory of natural disaster can account for this pattern, leaving us to seek less dramatic explanations for the end of Mycenaean civilization.

THE DORIAN INVASION   Some scholars have suggested that piratical sea raiders destroyed Pylos and, perhaps, other sites on the mainland. The Greeks themselves believed in a legend that told of the Dorians, a rude people from the north who spoke a Greek dialect different from that of the Mycenaean peoples. According to the legend, the Dorians joined with one of the Greek tribes, the Heraclidae, in an

attack on the southern Greek peninsula of Peloponnesus, which was repulsed. One hundred years later they returned and gained full control. Recent historians have identified this legend of "the return of the Heraclidae" with a Dorian invasion.

Archaeology has not provided material evidence of whether there was a single Dorian invasion or a series of them, and it is impossible as yet to say with any certainty what happened at the end of the Bronze Age in the Aegean. The chances are good, however, that Mycenaean civilization ended gradually over the century between 1200 B.C.E. and 1100 B.C.E. Its end may have been the result of internal conflicts among the Mycenaean kings combined with continuous pressure from outsiders, who raided, infiltrated, and eventually dominated Greece and its neighboring islands. There is reason to believe that Mycenaean society suffered internal weaknesses due to its organization around the centralized control of military force and agricultural production. This rigid organization may have deprived it of flexibility and vitality, leaving it vulnerable to outside challengers. In any case, Cnossus, Mycenae, and Pylos were abandoned, their secrets to be kept for over 3,000 years.

The Greek "Middle Ages" to about 750 B.C.E.

The immediate effects of the Dorian invasion were disastrous for the inhabitants of the Mycenaean world. The palaces and the kings and bureaucrats who managed them were destroyed. The wealth and organization that had supported the artists and merchants were likewise swept away by a barbarous people who did not have the knowledge or social organization to maintain them. Many villages were abandoned and never resettled. Some of their inhabitants probably turned to a nomadic life, and many perished. The chaos resulting from the collapse of the rigidly controlled palace culture produced severe depopulation and widespread poverty that lasted for a long time.

Greek Migrations

Another result of the invasion was the spread of the Greek people eastward from the mainland to the Aegean islands and the coast of Asia Minor. The Dorians themselves, after occupying most of the Peloponnesus, swept across the Aegean to occupy the southern islands and the southern part of the Anatolian coast.

These migrations made the Aegean a Greek lake. Trade with the old civilizations of the Near East, however, was virtually ended by the fall of the advanced Minoan and Mycenaean civilizations; nor was there much internal trade among the different parts of Greece. The Greeks were forced to turn inward, and each community was left largely to its own devices. The Near East was also in disarray at this time, and no great power arose to impose its ways and its will on the helpless people who lived about the Aegean. The Greeks were allowed time to recover from their disaster and to create their unique style of life.

Our knowledge of this period in Greek history rests on very limited sources. Writing disappeared after the fall of Mycenae, and no new script appeared until after 750 B.C.E., so we have no contemporary author to shed light on the period. Excavation reveals no architecture, sculpture, or painting until after 750 B.C.E.

The Age of Homer

For a picture of society in these "Dark Ages," the best source is Homer. His epic poems, the *Iliad* and the *Odyssey*, emerged from a tradition of oral poetry whose roots extend into the Mycenaean Age. Through the centuries bards had sung tales of the heroes who had fought at Troy, using verse arranged in rhythmic formulas to aid the memory. In this way some very old material was preserved into the eighth century B.C.E., when the poems attributed to Homer were finally written down. Although the poems tell of the deeds of Mycenaean Age heroes, the world they describe clearly differs from the Mycenaean world. Homer's heroes are not buried in *tholos* tombs, but are cremated; they worship gods in temples, whereas the Mycenaeans had no temples; they have chariots, but do not know their proper use in warfare. Certain aspects of the society described in the poems appear rather to resemble the world of the tenth and ninth centuries B.C.E., and other aspects appear to belong to the poet's own time, when population was growing at a swift pace and prosperity was returning, thanks to important changes in Greek agriculture, society, and government.

GOVERNMENT   In the Homeric poems, the power of the kings is much less than that of the Mycenaean rulers. Homeric kings were limited in their ability to make important decisions by the need to consult a council of nobles. The nobles felt free to discuss matters in vigorous language and in opposition to the king's wishes. In the *Iliad*, Achilles does not hesitate to address Agamemnon, the "most kingly" commander of the Trojan expedition, in these words: "you with a dog's face and a deer's heart." Such language may have been impolite, but it was not treasonous. The king, on the other hand, was free to ignore the council's advice, but it was risky for him to do so.

The right to speak in council was limited to noblemen, but the common people could not be ignored. If a king planned a war or a major change of policy during a campaign, he would not fail to call the common soldiers to an assembly; they could listen and express their feelings by acclamation, though they could not take part in the debate. Homer shows that even in these early times the Greeks, unlike their predecessors and contemporaries, practiced some forms of limited constitutional government.

maids and concubines. Some male slaves worked as shepherds. Few, if any, worked in agriculture, which depended on free labor throughout Greek history.

HOMERIC VALUES   The Homeric poems reflect an aristocratic code of values that powerfully influenced all future Greek thought. In classical times, Homer was the schoolbook of the Greeks. They memorized his texts, settled diplomatic disputes by citing passages in them, and emulated the behavior and cherished the values they found in them. Those values were physical prowess; courage; and fierce protection of one's family, friends, property, and, above all, personal honor and reputation. Speed of foot, strength, and, most of all, excellence at fighting make a man great, and all these attributes serve to promote personal honor. The great hero of the *Iliad*, Achilles, refuses to fight in battle, allowing his fellow Greeks to be slain and almost defeated, because Agamemnon has wounded his honor by taking away his battle prize. He returns not out of a sense of duty to the army, but to avenge the death of his dear friend Patroclus. Odysseus, the hero of the *Odyssey*, returning home after his wanderings, ruthlessly kills the many suitors who had, in his long absence, sought to marry his wife Penelope; they had dishonored him by consuming his wealth, wooing Penelope, and scorning his son.

The highest virtue in Homeric society was *arete*—manliness, courage in the most general sense, and the excellence proper to a hero. This quality was best revealed in a contest, or *agon*. Homeric battles are not primarily group combats, but a series of individual contests between great champions. One of the prime forms of entertainment is the athletic contest, and the funeral of Patroclus is celebrated by such a contest.

The central ethical idea in Homer can be found in the instructions that Achilles' father gives him when he sends him off to fight at Troy: "Always be the best and distinguished above others." The father of another Homeric hero has given his son exactly the same orders and has added to them the injunction: "Do not bring shame on the family of your fathers who were by far the best in Ephyre and in wide Lycia." Here in a nutshell we have the chief values of the aristocrats of Homer's world: to vie for individual supremacy in *arete* and to defend and increase the honor of the family. These would remain prominent aristocratic values long after Homeric society was only a memory.

WOMEN IN HOMERIC SOCIETY   In the world described by Homer the role of women was chiefly to bear and raise children, but the wives of the heroes also had a respected position, presiding over the household, overseeing the servants, and safeguarding the family property. (See "Husband and Wife in Homer's Troy.") They were prized for their beauty, constancy, and skill at

The *"Trojan Horse," depicted on a seventh-century B.C.E. Greek vase. According to legend, the Greeks finally defeated Troy by pretending to abandon their siege of the city, leaving a giant wooden horse behind. Soldiers hidden in the horse opened the gates of the city to their compatriots after the Trojans had brought it within their walls. Note the wheels on the horse and the Greek soldiers holding weapons and armor who are hiding inside it.*   Greek 10th–6th B.C.E. Trojan Horse and Greek Soldiers. Relief from neck of an earthenware amphora (640 B.C.E.) from Mykanos, overall ht. 120 cm. Archeological Museum, Mykonos, Greece. Photography by Erich Lessing

SOCIETY   Homeric society, nevertheless, was sharply divided into classes, the most important division being the one between nobles and everyone else. We do not know the origin of this distinction, but we cannot doubt that at this time Greek society was aristocratic. Birth determined noble status, and wealth usually accompanied it. Below the nobles were three other classes: *thetes*, landless laborers, and slaves. We do not know whether the *thetes* owned the land they worked outright (and so were free to sell it) or worked a hereditary plot that belonged to their clan (and was therefore not theirs to dispose of as they chose).

The worst condition was that of the free, but landless, hired agricultural laborer. The slave, at least, was attached to a family household and so was protected and fed. In a world where membership in a settled group gave the only security, the free laborers were desperately vulnerable. Slaves were few in number and were mostly women, who served as

Husband and Wife in Homer's Troy

Homer's poems provide a picture of early Greek ideas and institutions. In the Iliad, *the poet tells of the return from the battle of the Trojan hero Hector. He is greeted by his loving, "warm, generous wife," Andromache, who is carrying their baby son. Hector reaches for the boy, who is frightened to tears by the plume on his father's helmet. The father removes the helmet and prays that his son will grow up to be called "a better man than his father ... a joy to his mother's heart." The rest of the scene reveals the character of their marriage and the division of responsibility between men and women in their world.*

❖ *How does Homer depict the feelings of husband and wife toward one another? What are the tasks of the aristocratic woman revealed in this passage? What can be learned about the attitude towards death and duty?*

So Hector prayed and placed his son in the arms of his loving wife. Andromache pressed the child to her scented breast, smiling through her tears. Her husband noticed, and filled with pity now, Hector stroked her gently, trying to reassure her, repeating her name: "Andromache, dear one; why so desperate? Why so much grief for me? No man will hurl me down to Death, against my fate. And fate? No one alive has ever escaped it, neither brave man nor coward, I tell you—it's born with us the day that we are born. So please go home and tend to your own tasks, the distaff and the loom, and keep the women working hard as well. As for the fight-ing, men will see to that, all who were born in Troy but I most of all."

Hector aflash in arms took up his horsehair-crested helmet once again. And his loving wife went home, turning, glancing back again and again and weeping live warm tears. She quickly reached the sturdy house of Hector, man-killing Hector, and found her women gathered there inside and stirred them all to a high pitch of mourning. So in his house they raised the dirges for the dead, for Hector still alive, his people were so convinced that never again would he come home from battle, never escape the Argives' rage and bloody hands.

From *The Iliad* by Homer, translated by Robert Fagles, copyright © 1990 by Robert Fagles. Used by permission of Viking Penguin, a division of Penguin Putnam Inc.

weaving. All these fine qualities are combined in Penelope, the wife of Odysseus, probably the ideal Homeric woman. For the twenty years of her husband's absence, she put off the many suitors who sought to marry her and take his place, remained faithful to him, preserved his property, and protected the future of their son. Far different was the reputation of Agamemnon's wife, Clytemnestra who betrayed her husband while he was off fighting at Troy and murdered him on his return. Homer contrasts her with the virtuous Penelope in a passage that reveals a streak of hostility to women that can be found throughout the ancient history of the Greeks. (See "Hesiod Tells of the Creation of Woman.")

Not so did the daughter of Tyndareus fashion
　her evil
deeds, when she killed her wedded lord, and a
　song of loathing
will be hers among men, to make evil the reputation
of womankind, even for those whose acts are
　virtuous.[2]

Unlike Greek women in later centuries, the women of the higher class depicted in Homer are seen moving freely about their communities in town and country. They have a place alongside their husbands at the banquets in the great halls and take part in the conversation. In the *Odyssey*'s land of Phaeacia, admittedly a kind of fairyland, the wise queen Arete can decide the fate of suppliants and sometimes is asked to settle disputes even between men. A good marriage is seen as essential, admirable, and desirable. The shipwrecked Odysseus tries to win the sympathy of Arete's young daughter by wishing for her "all that you desire in your heart":

A husband and a home and the accompanying
　unity of mind and feeling
Which is so desirable, for there is nothing nobler
　or better than this,
When two people, who think alike, keep house
As man and wife; causing pain to their enemies,
And joy to their well-wishers, as they themselves
　know best.[3]

[2]*Odyssey* 24.199–202, trans. by Richmond Lattimore (Chicago: University of Chicago Press, 1965).

[3]Homer, *Odyssey*, 6.181–185, translated by M. Dillon and L. Garland, *Ancient Greece*, Routtledge, London and New York.

The *Polis*

The characteristic Greek institution was the *polis*. The common translation of that word as "city–state" is misleading, for it says both too much and too little. All Greek *poleis* began as little more than agricultural villages or towns, and many stayed that way, so the word "city" is inappropriate. All of them were states, in the sense of being independent political units, but they were much more than that. The *polis* was thought of as a community of relatives; all its citizens, who were theoretically descended from a common ancestor, belonged to subgroups, such as fighting brotherhoods or phratries, clans, and tribes, and worshiped the gods in common ceremonies.

Aristotle argued that the *polis* was a natural growth and that the human being was by nature "an animal who lives in a *polis*." Humans alone have the power of speech and from it derive the ability to distinguish good from bad and right from wrong, "and the sharing of these things is what makes a household and a *polis*." Therefore, humans who are incapable of sharing these things or who are so self-sufficient that they have no need of them are not humans at all, but either wild beasts or gods. Without law and justice, human beings are the worst and most dangerous of the animals. With them, humans can be the best, and justice exists only in the *polis*. These high claims were made in the fourth century B.C.E., hundreds of years after the *polis* came into existence, but they accurately reflect an attitude that was present from the first.

Development of the *Polis*

Originally the word *polis* referred only to a citadel—an elevated, defensible rock to which the farmers of the neighboring area could retreat in case of attack.

Hesiod Tells of the Creation of Woman

Hesiod was a farmer and a poet who lived in a village in central Greece about 700 B.C.E.. His poem Theogony *tells stories of how the gods came to be as they were. In one of these tales Zeus, as part of his conflict with the titan Prometheus, the divine benefactor who brought fire and other gifts to man, creates woman as a punishment. The story is an example of a hostile attitude towards women that is found in many early societies. Zeus orders the craftsman–god Hephaestus to create a woman out of clay and to have it made beautiful by the goddess Athena.*

❖ *What are the specific complaints Hesiod makes of women? What does he see as the advantages and disadvantages of marriage? What does this dark picture of women tell us about the society in which it emerged?*

Then the gods and mortal men were struck with amazement when they beheld this sheer inescapable snare for men. From her descend the race of women, the feminine sex; from her come the baneful race and types of women. Women, a great plague, make their abodes with mortal men, being ill-suited to Poverty's curse but suited to Plenty. Compare how the honey bees in the protected cells of the hives garner food for the drones, conspirers in evil works—all day long they are active until the sun goes down busily working and storing white honey during the daylight —while the drones keep within the protected cells of the hives and garner into their stomachs the food that others have worked for. Even so Zeus the Thunderer on High created women as an evil for men and conspirers in troublesome works. And in exchange for a good he gave a balancing evil. Whoever flees from marriage and women's mischievous works, being unwilling to wed, comes to baneful old age with no one to care for his needs, and though he has plenty to live on while he is living, collateral heirs divide his possessions when he is dead. As for the man who is fated to marry, if he obtains a virtuous wife, one endowed with good sense, throughout his life evil and good alternate endlessly. But that man who obtains a wife who is thoroughly bad lives having deep in his breast a pain which never subsides fixed in his innermost heart, and this is an evil incurable. Thus to deceive Zeus's mind is impossible or to get around it, for not even the son of Iapetos, crafty Prometheus, avoided his deep wrath, but in spite of his shrewdness suffers under compulsion great inescapable bondage.

The Acropolis in Athens and the hill called Acrocorinth in Corinth are examples. For some time, such high places and the adjacent farms made up the *polis*. The towns grew gradually and without planning, as their narrow, winding, and disorderly streets show. For centuries they had no walls. Unlike the city–states of the Near East, they were not placed for commercial convenience on rivers or the sea. Nor did they grow up around a temple to serve the needs of priests and to benefit from the needs of worshipers. The availability of farmland and of a natural fortress determined their location. They were placed either well inland or far enough away from the sea to avoid piratical raids. Only later and gradually did the *agora*—a marketplace and civic center—appear within the *polis*. The *agora* was to become the heart of the Greeks' remarkable social life, distinguished by conversation and argument carried on in the open air.

Some *poleis* probably came into existence early in the eighth century B.C.E. The institution was certainly common by the middle of the century, for all the colonies that were established by the Greeks in the years after 750 B.C.E. took the form of the *polis*. Once the new institution had been fully established, true monarchy disappeared. Vestigial kings survived in some places, but they were almost always only ceremonial figures without power. The original form of the *polis* was an aristocratic republic dominated by the nobility through its council of nobles and its monopoly of the magistracies.

Just as the *polis* emerged from sources within Greek society after the Bronze Age, striking changes also appeared in the creation and decoration of Greek pottery. A stunning example of the shift to the new Geometric style is the *Dipylon Vase*, discussed in "Art & the West" on p. 47.

About 750 B.C.E., coincident with the development of the *polis*, the Greeks borrowed a writing system from one of the Semitic scripts and added vowels to create the first true alphabet. This new Greek alphabet was easier to learn than any earlier writing system, leading to much wider literacy.

The Hoplite Phalanx

A new military technique was crucial to the development of the *polis*. In earlier times, the brunt of fighting had been carried on by small troops of cavalry and individual "champions" who first threw their spears and then came to close quarters with swords. Toward the end of the eighth century B.C.E., however, the hoplite phalanx came into being and remained the basis of Greek warfare thereafter.

The hoplite was a heavily armed infantryman who fought with a spear and a large shield. These soldiers were formed into a phalanx in close order, usually at least eight ranks deep. So long as the hoplites fought bravely and held their ground, there would be few casualties and no defeat; but if they gave way, the result was usually a rout. All depended on the discipline, strength, and courage of the individual soldier. At its best, the phalanx could withstand cavalry charges and defeat infantries not as well protected or disciplined. Until defeated by the Roman legion, it was the dominant military force in the eastern Mediterranean.

The usual hoplite battle in Greece was between the armies of two *poleis* quarreling over a piece of land. One army invaded the territory of the other when the crops were almost ready for harvest. The defending army had no choice but to protect its fields. If the army was beaten, its fields were captured or destroyed and its people might starve. In every way, the phalanx was a communal effort that relied not on the extraordinary actions of the individual, but on the courage of a considerable portion of the citizenry. This style of fighting produced a single decisive battle that reduced the time lost in fighting other kinds of warfare; it spared the houses, livestock, and other capital of the farmer–soldiers who made up the phalanx, and it reduced the number of casualties as well. It perfectly suited the farmer–soldier–citizen, who was the backbone of the *polis*, and, by keeping wars short and limiting their destructiveness and expense, it helped the *polis* prosper.

The phalanx and the *polis* arose together, and both heralded the decline of the kings. The phalanx, however, was not made up only of aristocrats. Most of the hoplites were farmers working small holdings. The immediate beneficiaries of the royal decline were the aristocrats, but because the existence of the *polis* depended on small farmers, their wishes could not long be wholly ignored. The rise of the hoplite phalanx created a bond between the aristocrats and the yeomen family farmers who fought in it. This bond helps explain why class conflicts were muted for some time. It also guaranteed, however, that the aristocrats, who dominated at first, would not always be unchallenged.

The Importance of the *Polis*

The Greeks looked to the *polis* for peace, order, prosperity, and honor in their lifetime. They counted on it to preserve their memory and to honor their de-

A Funeral Scene in Eighth-Century *B.C.E. Greece:* The Dipylon Vase

*H*ellenic civilization proper, as opposed to the more generally Mediterranean culture of the Minoan and Mycenaean periods of the Bronze Age, took shape in the four centuries from about 1100 to about 700 B.C.E. These are sometimes referred to as the Greek Dark Ages, chiefly because of how little is known about them, for there are no written sources for this period. There is better evidence for the history of art, for archaeology has turned up small sculptures in clay and bronze and a great deal of painted pottery that illuminate the development of the new culture.

Although the potters and vase painters of the early part of this period clearly learned much from their Mycenaean forerunners, their sharp break with the past is evident not only in the abandonment of older shapes and the development of new ones, but, most strikingly, in the style of their painting. The new style is called Geometric, from the dominant use of geometric forms—circles, rectangles and triangles—placed in parallel bands around the vases, instead of the freer forms favored by the Mycenaeans. The earliest and simplest examples are called Proto-Geometric. The next development was toward more complicated and fuller use of the geometric shapes and, finally, the appearance of human and animal figures alongside the geometric patterns.

The *Dipylon Vase* is a splendid example of the fully developed style. Its date is about 750 B.C.E., when the *polis*—the fully developed political community that would characterize Hellenic civilization—was just coming into being in a few places, when the Greeks were beginning to adapt the Phoenician alphabet to write their own language, and when Homer's great epic poems were taking shape. The vase, about 3½ feet tall, was found in the ancient cemetery outside the Dipylon gate to the ancient city of Athens. It is one of several large vases that served as burial monuments.

The painting depicts the funeral of an important person. At the center of the top band, or register, the body of the dead person is placed on a high platform. On either side, male and female mourners place their hands on the tops of their heads, as though tearing their hair in grief. In the lower register appears a funeral procession with horse-drawn chariots and soldiers carrying shields.

Although the bottom of the vase has holes that allow liquid offerings to pour through to the dead, the Greeks did not share the Egyptians' belief in an afterlife where the dead continue to engage in activities they enjoyed while alive. The Greek idea of death, on the contrary, was grim, and dark, and final.

Sources: Janson, *History of Art*, (New York: Prentice Hall and Harry N. Abrams, 1997), 110–112; Marilyn Stokstad, *Art History*, rev. ed. (Upper Saddle River, NJ: Prentice Hall, 1999), pp. 152–161.

The Dipylon Vase, c. 750 B.C.E. The Metropolitan Museum of Art, Rogers Fund, 1914. (14.130.14) Photograph © 1996 The Metropolitan Museum of Art.

scendants after death. Some of them came to see it not only as a ruler, but as the molder of its citizens. Knowing this, we can understand the pride and scorn that underlie the comparison made by the poet Phocylides between the Greek state and the capital of the great and powerful Assyrian Empire: "A little *polis* living orderly in a high place is stronger than a block-headed Nineveh."

Expansion of the Greek World

From the middle of the eighth century B.C.E. until well into the sixth century B.C.E., the Greeks vastly expanded the territory they controlled, their wealth, and their contacts with other peoples. A burst of colonizing activity placed *poleis* from Spain to the Black Sea. A century earlier, a few Greeks had established trading posts in Syria. There they had learned new techniques in the arts and crafts and much more from the older civilizations of the Near East.

Magna Graecia

Syria and its neighboring territory were too strong to penetrate, so the Greeks settled the southern coast of Macedonia and the Chalcidic peninsula. These regions were sparsely settled, and the natives were not well enough organized to resist the Greek colonists. Southern Italy and eastern Sicily were even more inviting areas. Before long, there were so many Greek colonies in Italy and Sicily that the Romans called the whole region *Magna Graecia*, "Great Greece." The Greeks also put colonies in Spain and southern France. In the seventh century B.C.E., Greek colonists settled the coasts of the northeastern Mediterranean, the Black Sea, and the straits connecting them. About the same time, they established settlements on the eastern part of the North African coast. The Greeks now had outposts throughout the Mediterranean world. (See Map 2–2.)

The Greek Colony

The Greeks did not lightly leave home to join a colony. The voyage by sea was dangerous and uncomfortable, and at the end of it were uncertainty and danger. Only powerful pressures like overpopulation and hunger for land drove thousands from their homes to establish new *poleis*.

The colony, although sponsored by the mother city, was established for the good of the colonists rather than for the benefit of those whom they left behind. The colonists tended to divide the land they settled into equal shares, reflecting an egalitarian tendency

MAP 2–2   GREEK COLONIZATION   *The height of Greek colonization was between about 750 and 550 B.C.E. Greek colonies stretched from the Mediterranean coasts of Spain and Gaul (modern France) in the west to the Black Sea and Asia Minor in the east.*

inherent in the ethical system of the yeoman farmers in the mother cities. They often copied their home constitution, worshiped the same gods as the people of the mother city at the same festivals in the same way, and carried on a busy trade with the mother city. Most colonies, though independent, were friendly with their mother cities. Each might ask the other for aid in time of trouble and expect to receive a friendly hearing, although neither was obligated to help the other.

The Athenians had colonies of this typical kind, but introduced innovations during their imperial period (478–404 B.C.E.). At one point they began to treat all the colonies of their empire as though they were Athenian settlements, requiring them to bring an offering of a cow and a suit of armor to the Great Panathenaic festival, just like true Athenian colonies. The goal may have been to cloak imperial rule in the more friendly garb of colonial family attachment.

The best known exception to the general rule of friendly relations between colony and mother city was the case of Corinth and its colony Corcyra, which quarreled and fought over more than two centuries. Thucydides tells of a fateful conflict between them that played a major role in causing the Peloponnesian War.

Colonization had a powerful influence on Greek life. By relieving the pressure of a growing population, it provided a safety valve that allowed the *poleis* to escape civil wars. By confronting the Greeks with the differences between themselves and the new peoples they met, colonization gave them a sense of cultural identity and fostered a Panhellenic ("all-Greek") spirit that led to the establishment of a number of common religious festivals. The most important ones were at Olympia, Delphi, Corinth, and Nemea.

Colonization also encouraged trade and industry. The influx of new wealth from abroad and the increased demand for goods from the homeland stimulated a more intensive use of the land and an emphasis on crops for export, chiefly the olive and the wine grape. The manufacture of pottery, tools, weapons, and fine artistic metalwork, as well as perfumed oil, the soap of the ancient Mediterranean world, was likewise encouraged. New opportunities allowed some men, sometimes outside the nobility, to become wealthy and important. The newly enriched became a troublesome element in the aristocratic *poleis*, for, although increasingly important in the life of their states, they were barred from political power, religious privileges, and social acceptance by the ruling aristocrats. These conditions soon created a crisis in many states.

The Tyrants (about 700–500 B.C.E.)

In some cities—perhaps only a small percentage of the more than 1,000 Greek *poleis*—the crisis produced by new economic and social conditions led to or intensified factional divisions within the ruling aristocracy. In the years between 700 and 500 B.C.E., the result was often the establishment of a tyranny.

THE RISE OF TYRANNY   A tyrant was a monarch who had gained power in an unorthodox or unconstitutional, but not necessarily wicked, way and who exercised a strong one-man rule that might well be beneficent and popular.

The founding tyrant was usually a member of the ruling aristocracy who either had a personal grievance or led an unsuccessful faction. He often rose to power because of his military ability and support from the hoplites. He generally had the support of the politically powerless group of the newly wealthy and of the poor farmers. When he took power, he often expelled many of his aristocratic opponents and divided at least some of their land among his supporters. He pleased his commercial and industrial supporters by destroying the privileges of the old aristocracy and by fostering trade and colonization.

The tyrants presided over a period of population growth that saw an increase especially in the number of city dwellers. They responded with a program of public works that included the improvement of drainage systems, care for the water supply, the construction and organization of marketplaces, the building and strengthening of city walls, and the erection of temples. They introduced new local festivals and elaborated the old ones. They were active in the patronage of the arts, supporting poets and artisans with gratifying results. All this activity contributed to the tyrant's popularity, to the prosperity of his city, and to his self-esteem.

In most cases, the tyrant's rule was secured by a personal bodyguard and by mercenary soldiers. An armed citizenry, necessary for an aggressive foreign policy, would have been dangerous, so the tyrants usually pursued a program of peaceful alliances with other tyrants abroad and avoided war.

THE END OF THE TYRANTS   By the end of the sixth century B.C.E., tyranny had disappeared from the Greek states and did not return in the same form or for the same reasons. The last tyrants were universally hated for the cruelty and repression they employed. They left bitter memories in their own states and became objects of fear and hatred everywhere.

Besides the outrages committed by individual tyrants, there was something about the very concept of tyranny that was inimical to the idea of the *polis*. The notion of the *polis* as a community to which every member must be responsible, the connection of justice with that community, and the natural aristocratic hatred of monarchy all made tyranny seem alien and offensive. The rule of a tyrant, however

---

beneficent, was arbitrary and unpredictable. Tyranny came into being in defiance of tradition and law, and the tyrant governed without either. He was not answerable in any way to his fellow citizens.

From a longer perspective, however, the tyrants made important contributions to the development of Greek civilization. They encouraged economic changes that helped secure the future prosperity of Greece. They increased communication with the rest of the Mediterranean world and cultivated the crafts and technology, as well as the arts and literature. Most important of all, they broke the grip of the aristocracy and put the productive powers of the most active and talented of its citizens fully at the service of the *polis*.

The Major States

Generalization about the *polis* becomes difficult not long after its appearance, for although the states had much in common, some of them developed in unique ways. Sparta and Athens, which became the two most powerful Greek states, had especially unusual histories.

Sparta

At first Sparta seems not to have been strikingly different from other *poleis*. About 725 B.C.E., however, the pressure of population and land hunger led the Spartans to launch a war of conquest against their western neighbor, Messenia. (See Map 2–3.) The First Messenian War gave the Spartans as much land as they would ever need. The reduction of the Messenians to the status of serfs, or Helots, meant that the Spartans did not even need to work the land that supported them.

The turning point in Spartan history came about 650 B.C.E., when, in the Second Messenian War, the Helots rebelled with the help of Argos and other Peloponnesian cities. The war was long and bitter and at one point threatened the existence of Sparta. After the revolt had been put down, the Spartans were forced to reconsider their way of life. They could not expect to keep down the Helots, who outnumbered them perhaps ten to one, and still maintain the old free and easy habits typical of most Greeks. Faced with the choice of making drastic changes and sacrifices or abandoning their control of Messenia, the Spartans chose to introduce fundamental reforms that turned their city forever after into a military academy and camp.

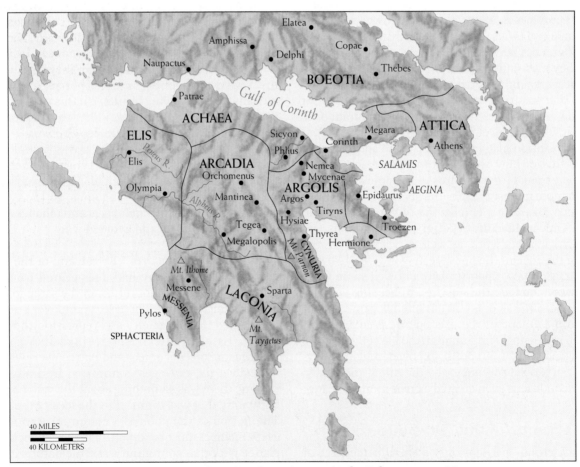

MAP 2–3   THE PELOPONNESUS   *Sparta's region, Laconia, was in the Peloponnesus. Nearby states were members of the Peloponnesian League under Sparta's leadership.*

Chronology of the Rise of Greece

ca. 2900–1150 B.C.E.	Minoan period
ca. 1900 B.C.E.	Probable date of the arrival of the Greeks on the mainland
ca. 1600–1150 B.C.E.	Mycenaean period
ca. 1250 B.C.E.	Sack of Troy (?)
ca. 1200–1150 B.C.E.	Destruction of Mycenaean centers in Greece
ca. 1100–750 B.C.E.	"Greek Dark Ages"
ca. 750–500 B.C.E.	Major period of Greek colonization
ca. 725 B.C.E.	Probable date when Homer flourished
ca. 700 B.C.E.	Probable date when Hesiod flourished
ca. 700–500 B.C.E.	Major period of Greek tyranny

SPARTAN SOCIETY   The new system that emerged late in the sixth century B.C.E. exerted control over each Spartan from birth, when officials of the state decided which infants were physically fit to survive. At the age of seven, the Spartan boy was taken from his mother and turned over to young instructors. He was trained in athletics and the military arts and taught to endure privation, to bear physical pain, and to live off the country, by theft if necessary. At twenty the Spartan youth was enrolled in the army, where he lived in barracks with his companions until the age of thirty. Marriage was permitted, but a strange sort of marriage it was, for the Spartan male could visit his wife only infrequently and by stealth. At thirty, he became a full citizen, an "equal." He took his meals at a public mess in the company of fifteen comrades. His food, a simple diet without much meat or wine, was provided by his own plot of land, worked by Helots. Military service was required until the age of sixty; only then could the Spartan retire to his home and family.

This educational program extended to women, too, although they were not given military training. Female infants were examined for fitness to survive in the same way as males. Girls were given gymnastic training, were permitted greater freedom of movement than among other Greeks, and were equally indoctrinated with the idea of service to Sparta.

The entire system was designed to change the natural feelings of devotion to family and children into a more powerful commitment to the *polis*. Privacy, luxury, and even comfort were sacrificed to the purpose of producing soldiers whose physical powers, training, and discipline made them the best in the world. Nothing that might turn the mind away from duty was permitted. The very use of coins was forbidden lest it corrupt the desires of Spartans. Neither family nor money were allowed to interfere with the only ambition permitted to a Spartan male: to win glory and the respect of his peers by bravery in war.

A large Spartan plate from the second quarter of the sixth century B.C.E. It shows traders weighing silphium, a medicinal plant from North Africa, before King Arcesilas of Cyrene, seated on the deck of a ship. Below them, workers pile cargo into the ship's hold. The monkey at the top of the scene and the lizard at the left suggest the location. Hirmer Fotoarchiv

The Greek and Persian Ways of War—Autocracy versus Freedom under the Law

The Greek historian Herodotus, who wrote his account of the wars between the Greeks and Persians more than half a century after they ended, was very interested in the differences between the ways of the Greeks and other peoples of the world. In the following passage he describes a conversation between Demaratus, an exiled king of Sparta, and Xerxes, the Great King of Persia. Demaratus had come to Xerxes' court after his exile. Xerxes received him kindly and made him a royal adviser.

❖ *On what does Xerxes rely for Persian military success? What is the source of Demaratus' confidence in the Spartans? Does the claim he makes hold for other Greeks as well as the Spartans? How is it possible to reconcile freedom with obedience to the laws?*

"How is it possible that a thousand men, or ten thousand, or fifty thousand, should stand up to an army as big as mine, especially if they were not under a single master, but all perfectly free to do as they pleased? Suppose them to have five thousand men: In that case we should be more than a thousand to one! If, like ours, their troops were subject to the control of a single man, then possibly for fear of him, in spite of the disparity in numbers, they might show some sort of factitious courage, or let themselves be whipped into battle; but, as every man is free to follow his fancy, it is not conceivable that they should do either. Indeed, my own opinion is that even on equal terms the Greeks could hardly face the Persians alone. We, too, have this thing that you were speaking of—I do not say it is common, but it does exist; for instance, amongst the Persians in my bodyguard there are men who would willingly fight with three Greeks together. But you know nothing of such things, or you could not talk such nonsense."

"My lord," Demaratus answered, "I knew before I began that if I spoke the truth you would not like it. But, as you demanded the plain truth and nothing less, I told you how things are with the Spartans. Yet you are well aware that I now feel but little affection for my countrymen, who robbed me of my hereditary power and privileges and made me a fugitive without a home—whereas your father welcomed me at his court and gave me the means of livelihood and somewhere to live. Surely it is unreasonable to reject kindness; any sensible man will cherish it. Personally I do not claim to be able to fight ten men—or two; indeed I should prefer not even to fight with one. But should it be necessary—should there be some great cause to urge me on—then nothing would give me more pleasure than to stand up to one of those men of yours who claim to be a match for three Greeks. So it is with the Spartans; fighting singly, they are as good as any, but fighting together they are the best soldiers in the world. They are free—yes—but not entirely free; for they have a master, and that master is Law, which they fear much more than your subjects fear you. Whatever this master commands they do; and his command never varies: it is never to retreat in battle, however great the odds, but always to stand firm, and to conquer or die. If, my lord, you think that what I have said is nonsense—very well; I am willing henceforward to hold my tongue. This time I spoke because you forced me to speak. In any case, I pray that all may turn out as you desire."

Xerxes burst out laughing at Demaratus' answer, and goodhumouredly let him go.

SPARTAN GOVERNMENT The Spartan constitution was mixed, containing elements of monarchy, oligarchy, and democracy. There were two kings, whose power was limited by law and also by the rivalry that usually existed between the two royal houses. The origins and explanation of this unusual dual kingship are unknown, but both kings ruled together in Sparta and exercised equal powers. Their functions were chiefly religious and military. A Spartan army rarely left home without a king in command.

The oligarchic element was represented by a council of elders consisting of twenty-eight men over the age of sixty, elected for life, and the kings. These elders had important judicial functions, sitting as a court in cases involving the kings. They also were consulted before any proposal was put before the assembly of Spartan citizens. In a traditional society like Sparta's, they must have had considerable influence.

The Spartan assembly consisted of all males over thirty. Theoretically, they were the final authority, but in practice, debate was carried on by magistrates, elders, and kings alone, and voting was usually by acclamation. Therefore, the assembly's real function was to ratify decisions already taken or to decide between positions favored by the leading figures. In addition, Sparta had a unique institution, the board of *ephors*. This consisted of five men elected annually by the assembly. Originally, boards of ephors appear to have been intended to check the power of the kings, but gradually they gained other important functions. They controlled foreign policy, oversaw the generalship of the kings on campaign, presided at the assembly, and guarded against rebellions by the Helots.

The whole system was remarkable both for the way in which it combined participation by the citizenry with significant checks on its power and for its unmatched stability. Most Greeks admired the Spartan state for these qualities and also for its ability to mold citizens so thoroughly to an ideal. Many political philosophers, from Plato to modern times, have based utopian schemes on a version of Sparta's constitution and educational system.

THE PELOPONNESIAN LEAGUE   By about 550 B.C.E. the Spartan system was well established, and its limitations were made plain. Suppression of the Helots required all the effort and energy that Sparta had. The Spartans could expand no further, but they could not allow unruly independent neighbors to cause unrest that might inflame the Helots.

When the Spartans defeated Tegea, their northern neighbor, they imposed an unusual peace. Instead of taking away land and subjugating the defeated state, Sparta left the Tegeans their land and their freedom. In exchange, they required the Tegeans to follow the Spartan lead in foreign affairs and to supply a fixed number of soldiers to Sparta on demand. This became the model for Spartan relations with the other states in the Peloponnesus. Soon Sparta was the leader of an alliance that included every Peloponnesian state but Argos; modern scholars have named this alliance the Peloponnesian League. It provided the Spartans with the security they needed, and it also made Sparta the most powerful *polis* in Hellenic history. By 500 B.C.E., Sparta and the league had given the Greeks a force capable of facing mighty threats from abroad. (See "The Greek and Persian Ways of War—Autocracy versus Freedom under the Law.")

Athens

Athens was slow to come into prominence and to join in the new activities that were changing the more advanced states. The reasons were several: Athens was not situated on the most favored trade routes of the eighth and seventh centuries B.C.E., its large area (about 1,000 square miles) allowed population growth without great pressure, and the unification of the many villages and districts within this territory into a single *polis* was not completed until the seventh century B.C.E. (See Map 2–4.)

ARISTOCRATIC RULE   In the seventh century B.C.E., Athens was a typical aristocratic *polis*. Its people were divided into four tribes and into several clans and brotherhoods (*phratries*). The aristocrats held the most land and the best land and dominated religious and political life. There was no written law, and decisions were rendered by powerful nobles on the basis of tradition and, most likely, self-interest. The state was governed by the Areopagus, a council of nobles deriving its name from the hill where it held its sessions. Annually the council elected nine magistrates, called *archons*, who joined the Areopagus after their year in office. Because the *archons* served for only a year, were checked by their colleagues, and looked forward to a lifetime as members of the Areopagus, it is plain that the aristocratic Areopagus, not the *archons*, was the true master of the state.

PRESSURE FOR CHANGE   In the seventh century B.C.E., the peaceful life of Athens experienced some disturbances, caused in part by quarrels within the nobility and in part by the beginnings of an agrarian crisis. In 632 B.C.E., a nobleman named Cylon attempted a coup to establish himself as tyrant. He was thwarted, but the unrest continued.

In 621 B.C.E., a man named Draco was given special authority to codify and publish laws for the first time. In later years Draco's penalties were thought to be harsh—hence the saying that his laws were written in blood. (We still speak of unusually harsh penalties as Draconian.) Draco's work was probably limited to laws concerning homicide and was aimed at ending blood feuds between clans, but it set an important precedent: The publication of laws strengthened the hand of the state against the local power of the nobles.

The root of Athens' troubles was agricultural. Many Athenians worked family farms, from which they obtained most of their living. It appears that they planted wheat, the staple crop, year after year without rotating fields or using enough fertilizer. Shifting to more intensive agricultural techniques and to the planting of trees and vines required capital, leading the less successful farmers to acquire excessive debt.

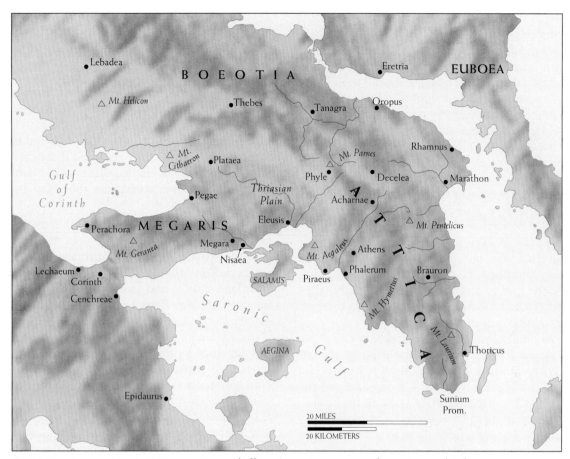

MAP 2–4   ATTICA AND VICINITY   *Citizens of all towns in Attica were also citizens of Athens.*

To survive, some farmers had to borrow from wealthy neighbors to get through the year. In return, they promised one-sixth of the next year's crop. The deposit of an inscribed stone on the entailed farms marked the arrangement. As their troubles persisted, debtors had to pledge their wives, their children, and themselves as surety for new loans. Inevitably, many Athenians defaulted and were enslaved. Some were even sold abroad. Revolutionary pressures grew among the poor, who began to demand the abolition of debt and a redistribution of the land.

REFORMS OF SOLON   In the year 594 B.C.E., as tradition has it, the Athenians elected Solon as the only *archon*, with extraordinary powers to legislate and revise the constitution. Immediately, he attacked the agrarian problem by canceling current debts and forbidding future loans secured by the person of the borrower. He helped bring back many Athenians enslaved abroad and freed those in Athens enslaved for debt. This program was called the "shaking off of burdens." It did not, however, solve the fundamental economic problem, and Solon did not redistribute the land.

In the short run, therefore, Solon did not put an end to the economic crisis, but his other econom-ic actions had profound success in the long run. He forbade the export of wheat and encouraged that of olive oil. This policy had the initial effect of making wheat more available in Attica and encouraging the cultivation of olive oil and wine as cash crops. By the fifth century B.C.E., the cultivation of cash crops had become so profitable that much Athenian land was diverted from grain production, and Athens became dependent on imported wheat. Solon also changed the Athenian standards of weights and measures to conform with those of Corinth and Euboea and the cities of the east. This change also encouraged commerce and turned Athens in the direction that would lead it to great prosperity in the fifth century B.C.E. Solon also encouraged industry by offering citizenship to foreign artisans, and his success is reflected in the development of the outstanding Attic pottery of the sixth century B.C.E.

Solon also significantly changed the constitution. Citizenship had previously been the privilege of all male adults whose fathers were citizens; to their number he added those immigrants who were tradesmen and merchants. All these Athenian citizens were divided into four classes on the basis of

The Rule of the Tyrant Pisistratus

Although tyranny came to have a bad reputation, the first tyrants were often popular because they broke the unchallenged domination of the aristocrats. Their careers were sometimes remembered fondly because their achievements contrasted favorably with those of their successors. So it was with the Athenian view of the reign of their first tyrant, Pisistratus, as suggested by this passage from Aristotle's Athenian Constitution, *written two centuries after the events described.*

❖ *What were the bases of Pisistratus' power? If he was a tyrant, why is his rule portrayed as a golden age? If it was a golden age, why did the Athenians after his death pass a law against the establishment of tyranny? What was the relation between the tyranny at Athens and the rule of law?*

Such was the origin and such the vicissitudes of the tyranny of Pisistratus. His administration was temperate, as has been said before, and more like constitutional government than a tyranny. Not only was he in every respect humane and mild and ready to forgive those who offended, but, in addition, he advanced money to the poorer people to help them in their labours, so that they might make their living by agriculture. In this he had two objects, first that they might not spend their time in the city but might be scattered over all the face of the country, and secondly that, being moderately well off and occupied with their own business, they might have neither the wish nor the time to attend to public affairs. At the same time his revenues were increased by the thorough cultivation of the country, since he imposed a tax of one-tenth on all the produce. For the same reasons he instituted the local justices, and often made expeditions in person into the country to inspect it and to settle disputes between individuals, that they might not come into the city and neglect their farms. It was in one of these progresses that, as the story goes, Pisistratus had his adventure with the man of Hymettus, who was cultivating the spot afterwards known as "Tax-free Farm." He saw a man digging and working at a very stony piece of ground, and being surprised he sent his attendant to ask what he got out of this plot of land. "Aches and pains," said the man; "and that's what Pisistratus ought to have his tenth of." The man spoke without knowing who his questioner was; but Pi-

sistratus was so pleased with his frank speech and his industry that he granted him exemption from all taxes. And so in matters in general he burdened the people as little as possible with his government, but always cultivated peace and kept them in all quietness. Hence the tyranny of Pisistratus was often spoken of proverbially as "the age of gold;" for when his sons succeeded him the government became much harsher. But most important of all in this respect was his popular and kindly disposition. In all things he was accustomed to observe the laws, without giving himself any exceptional privileges. Once he was summoned on a charge of homicide before the Areopagus, and he appeared in person to make his defense; but the prosecutor was afraid to present himself and abandoned the case. For these reasons he held power long, and whenever he was expelled he regained his position easily. The majority alike of the upper class and of the people were in his favour; the former he won by his social intercourse with them, the latter by the assistance which he gave to their private purses, and his nature fitted him to win the hearts of both. Moreover, the laws in reference to tyrants at that time in force at Athens were very mild, especially the one which applies more particularly to the establishment of a tyranny. The law ran as follows, "These are the ancestral statutes of the Athenians; if any persons shall make an attempt to establish a tyranny, or if any person shall join in setting up a tyranny, he shall lose his civic rights, both himself and his whole house."

Aristotle, Athenian Constitution, 16, from The Greek Historians by Francis R.B. Godolphin, editor. Copyright 1942 and renewed 1970 by Random House, Inc. Reprinted by permission of Random House, Inc.

wealth, measured by annual agricultural production. The two highest classes alone could hold the *archonship*, the chief magistracy in Athens, and sit on the Areopagus.

Men of the third class were allowed to serve as *hoplites*. They could be elected to a council of 400 chosen by all the citizens, 100 from each tribe. Solon seems to have meant this council to serve as a check on the Areopagus and to prepare any business that needed to be put before the traditional assembly of all adult male citizens. The *thetes* made up the last class. They voted in the assembly for the *archons* and the council members and on any other business brought before them by the *archons* and the council. They also sat on a new popular court established by Solon. This new court was recognized as a court of appeal, and by the fifth century B.C.E. almost all cases came before it. In Solon's Athens, as everywhere in the world before the twentieth century, women took no part in the political or judicial process.

PISISTRATUS THE TYRANT   Solon's efforts to avoid factional strife failed. Within a few years contention reached such a degree that no *archons* could be chosen. Out of this turmoil emerged the first Athenian tyranny. Pisistratus, a nobleman, leader of a faction, and military hero, briefly seized power in 560 B.C.E. and again in 556 B.C.E., but each time his support was inadequate and he was driven out. At last, in 546 B.C.E. he came back at the head of a mercenary army from abroad and established a successful tyranny. It lasted beyond his death, in 527 B.C.E., until the expulsion of his son Hippias in 510 B.C.E.

In many respects, Pisistratus resembled the other Greek tyrants. His rule rested on the force provided by mercenary soldiers. He engaged in great programs of public works, urban improvement, and religious piety. Temples were built and religious centers expanded and improved. Poets and artists were supported to add cultural luster to the court of the tyrant.

Pisistratus sought to increase the power of the central government at the expense of the nobles. The newly introduced festival of Dionysus and the improved and expanded Great Panathenaic festival helped fix attention on the capital city, as did the new temples and the reconstruction of the agora as the center of public life. Circuit judges were sent out into the country to hear cases, weakening the power of the local barons. All this time Pisistratus made no formal change in the Solonian constitution. Assembly, councils, and courts met; magistrates and councils were elected. Pisistratus merely saw to it that his supporters dominated these bodies. The intended effect was to blunt the sharp edge of tyranny with the appearance of constitutional government, and it worked. The rule of Pisistratus was remembered as popular and mild. The unintended effect was to give the Athenians more experience in the procedures of self-government and a growing taste for it. (See "The Rule of the Tyrant Pisistratus.")

Aristogeiton and Harmodius were Athenian aristocrats slain in 514 B.C.E. after assassinating Hipparchus, brother of the tyrant Hippias. After the overthrow of the Pisistratus in 510 B.C.E., the Athenians erected a statue to honor their memory. This is a Roman copy.
Scala/Art Resource, N.Y.

SPARTAN INTERVENTION   Pisistratus was succeeded by his oldest son, Hippias, who followed his father's ways at first. In 514 B.C.E., however, his brother Hipparchus was murdered as a result of a private quarrel. Hippias became nervous, suspicious, and harsh. The Alcmaeonids, one of the noble clans that Hippias and Hipparchus had exiled, won favor with the influential oracle at Delphi and used its support to persuade Sparta to attack the Athenian tyranny. Led by their ambitious king, Cleomenes I, the Spartans marched into Athenian territory in 510 B.C.E. and deposed Hippias, who went into exile to the Persian court. The tyranny was over.

The Spartans must have hoped to leave Athens in friendly hands, and indeed Cleomenes' friend Isagoras, a rival of the Alcmaeonids, held the leading position in Athens after the withdrawal of the Spartan army. Isagoras, however, faced competitors, chief among them Clisthenes of the restored Alcmaeonid clan. Clisthenes lost out in the initial political struggle among the noble factions. Isagoras seems then to have tried to restore a version of the pre-Solonian aristocratic state. As part of his plan, he carried through a purification of the citizen lists, removing those whom Solon or Pisistratus had enfranchised and any others thought to have a doubtful claim.

Clisthenes then took an unprecedented action—he turned to the people for political support and won it with a program of great popular appeal. In response, Isagoras called in the Spartans again; Cleomenes arrived and allowed Isagoras to expel Clisthenes and many of his supporters. But the fire of Athenian political consciousness, ignited by Solon and kept alive under Pisistratus, had been fanned into flames by the popular appeal of Clisthenes. The people refused to tolerate an aristocratic restoration and drove out the Spartans and Isagoras with them. Clisthenes and his allies returned, ready to put their program into effect.

CLISTHENES, THE FOUNDER OF DEMOCRACY A central aim of Clisthenes' reforms was to diminish the influence of traditional localities and regions in Athenian life, for these were an important source of power for the nobility and of factions in the state. He immediately restored to citizenship those Athenians who had supported him whom Isagoras had disenfranchised, and he added new citizens to the rolls. In 508 B.C.E. he made the *deme*, the equivalent of a small town in the country or a ward in the city, the basic unit of civic life. The *deme* was a purely political unit that elected its own officers. The distribution of *demes* in each tribe guaranteed that no region would dominate any of them. Because the tribes had common religious activities and fought as regimental units, the new organization also increased devotion to the *polis* and diminished regional divisions and personal loyalty to local barons.

A new council of 500 was invented to replace the Solonian council of 400. The council's main responsibility was to prepare legislation for discussion by the assembly, but it also had important financial duties and received foreign emissaries. Final authority in all things rested with the assembly of all adult male Athenian citizens. Debate in the assembly was free and open; any Athenian could submit legislation, offer amendments, or argue the merits of any question. In practice, political leaders did most of the talking. We may imagine that in the early days the

Key Events in the Early History of Sparta and Athens	
ca. 725–710 B.C.E.	First Messenian War
ca. 650–625 B.C.E.	Second Messenian War
632 B.C.E.	Cylon tries to establish a tyranny at Athens
621 B.C.E.	Draco publishes legal code at Athens
594 B.C.E.	Solon institutes reforms at Athens
ca. 560–550 B.C.E.	Sparta defeats Tegea: Beginning of Peloponnesian League
546–527 B.C.E.	Pisistratus reigns as tyrant at Athens (main period)
510 B.C.E.	Hippias, son of Pisistratus, deposed as tyrant of Athens
ca. 508–501 B.C.E.	Clisthenes institutes reforms at Athens

council had more authority than it did after the Athenians became more confident in their new self-government.

It is fair to call Clisthenes the father of Athenian democracy. He did not alter the property qualifications of Solon, but his enlargement of the citizen rolls, his diminution of the power of the aristocrats, and his elevation of the role of the assembly, with its effective and manageable council, all give him a firm claim to that title.

As a result of the work of Solon, Pisistratus, and Clisthenes, Athens entered the fifth century B.C.E. well on the way to prosperity and democracy. It was much more centralized and united than it had been, and it was ready to take its place among the major states that would lead the defense of Greece against the dangers that lay ahead.

Life in Archaic Greece

Society

As the "Dark Ages" ended, the features that would distinguish Greek society thereafter took shape. The roles of the artisan and the merchant grew more important as contact with the non-Hellenic world became easier. The great majority of people, however, continued to make their living from the land. Wealthy aristocrats with large estates, powerful households, families, and clans led very different lives from those of the poorer countryfolk and the independent farmers who had smaller and less fertile fields.

This terra-cotta figurine from Boeotia is a rare ancient Greek representation of the lives of ordinary people. It shows Boeotian women laundering clothes. Musée du Louvre, Paris

FARMERS   Ordinary country people rarely leave a written record of their thoughts or activities, and we have no such record from ancient Greece. The poet Hesiod (ca. 700 B.C.E.), however, was certainly no aristocrat. He presented himself as a small farmer, and his *Works and Days* gives some idea of the life of such a farmer. The crops included grain—chiefly barley, but also wheat; grapes for the making of wine; olives for food, but mainly for oil used for cooking, lighting, and washing; green vegetables, especially the bean; and some fruit. Sheep and goats provided milk and cheese. The Homeric heroes had great herds of cattle and ate lots of meat, but by Hesiod's time land fertile enough to provide fodder for cattle was needed to grow grain. He and small farmers like him tasted meat chiefly from sacrificial animals at festivals.

These farmers worked hard to make a living. Although Hesiod had the help of oxen and mules and one or two hired helpers for occasional labor, his life was one of continuous toil. The hardest work came in October, at the start of the rainy season, the time for the first plowing. The plow was light and easily broken, and the work of forcing the iron tip into the earth was backbreaking, even with the help of a team of oxen. For the less fortunate farmer, the cry of the crane that announced the time of year to plow "bites the heart of the man without oxen." Autumn and winter were the time for cutting wood, building wagons, and making tools. Late winter was the time to tend to the vines, May the time to harvest the grain, July to winnow and store it. Only at the height of summer's heat did Hesiod allow for rest, but when September came, it was time to harvest the grapes. No sooner was that task done than the cycle started again. The work went on under the burning sun and in the freezing cold.

Hesiod wrote nothing of pleasure or entertainment, but his poetry displays an excitement and pride that reveals the new hopes of a rural population more dynamic and confident than we know of anywhere else in the ancient world. Less austere farmers than Hesiod gathered at the blacksmith's shop for warmth and companionship in winter, and even he must have taken part in religious rites and festivals that were accompanied by some kind of entertainment. Nonetheless, the lives of yeoman farmers were certainly hard and their pleasures few. (See "Hesiod's *Farmer's Almanac*.")

ARISTOCRATS   Most aristocrats were rich enough to employ many hired laborers, sometimes sharecroppers, and sometimes even slaves, to work their extensive lands. They were therefore able to enjoy leisure for other activities. The center of aristocratic social life was the drinking party, or *symposium*. This activity was not a mere drinking bout, meant to remove inhibitions and produce oblivion. The Greeks, in fact, almost always mixed their wine with water, and one of the goals of the participants was to drink as much as the others without becoming drunk.

This scene on an Attic jar from late in the sixth century B.C.E. shows how olives, one of Athens' most important crops, were harvested. Courtesy of the Trustees of the British Museum. © The British Museum

Hesiod's *Farmer's Almanac*

Hesiod was a farmer and poet who lived in a village in Greece about 700 B.C.E. His poem Works and Days *contains wisdom on several subjects, but its final section amounts to a farmer's almanac, taking readers through the year and advising them on just when each activity is demanded. Hesiod painted a picture of a very hard life for Greek farmers, allowing rest only in the passage that follows.*

❖ *What might be Hesiod's purposes in writing this poem? What can be learned from this passage about the character of Greek farming? How did it differ from other modes of agriculture? What are the major virtues Hesiod associates with farming? How do they compare with the virtues celebrated by Homer?*

But when House-on-Back, the snail, crawls
    from the ground up
the plants, escaping the Pleiades, it's no longer
    time for vine-digging;
time rather to put an edge to your sickles, and
    rout out your helpers.
Keep away from sitting in the shade or lying in
    bed till the sun's up
in the time of the harvest, when the sunshine
    scorches your skin dry.
This is the season to push your work and bring
    home your harvest;
get up with the first light so you'll have enough
    to live on.
Dawn takes away from work a third part of the
    work's measure.
Dawn sets a man well along on his journey, in
    his work also,
dawn, who when she shows, has numerous
    people going their ways; dawn who puts the
    yoke upon many oxen.
But when the artichoke is in flower, and the
    clamorous cricket
sitting in his tree lets go his vociferous singing,
    that issues

from the beating of his wings, in the exhausting
    season of summer,
then is when goats are at their fattest, when the
    wine tastes best,
women are most lascivious, but the men's
    strength fails them
most, for the star Seirios shrivels them, knees
    and heads alike,
and the skin is all dried out in the heat; then, at
    that season,
one might have the shadow under the rock, and
    the wine of Biblis,
a curd cake, and all the milk that the goats can
    give you,
the meat of a heifer, bred in the woods, who has
    never borne a calf,
and of baby kids also. Then, too, one can sit in
    the shadow
and drink the bright-shining wine, his heart
    satiated with eating
and face turned in the direction where Zephyros
    blows briskly,
make three libations of water from a spring that
    keeps running forever
and has no mud in it; and pour wine for the
    fourth libation.

Hesiod, *Works and Days*, trans. by Richmond Lattimore © 1959 University of Michigan Press, pp. 87, 89. Reprinted by permission of University of Michigan Press.

The *symposium* was a carefully organized occasion, with a "king" chosen to set the order of events and to determine that night's mixture of wine and water. Only men took part; they ate and drank as they reclined on couches along the walls of the room. The sessions began with prayers and libations to the gods. Usually there were games, such as dice or *kottabos*, in which wine was flicked from the cups at different targets. Sometimes dancing girls or flute girls offered entertainment. Frequently the aristocratic participants provided their own amusements with songs, poetry, or even philosophical disputes. Characteristically, these took the form of contests, with some kind of prize for the winner, for aristocratic values continued to emphasize competition and the need to excel, whatever the arena.

This aspect of aristocratic life appears in the athletic contests that became widespread early in the sixth century. The games included running events; the long jump; the discus and javelin throws; the *pentathlon*, which included all of these; boxing; wrestling; and the chariot race. Only the rich could afford to raise, train, and race horses, so the chariot race was a special preserve of aristocracy. Wrestling, however, was also especially favored by the nobility, and the *palaestra*, or fields, where they practiced became an important social center for the aristocracy. The contrast between the hard, drab life of the farmers and the leisured and lively one of the aristocrats could hardly have been greater.

Religion

Like most ancient peoples, the Greeks were polytheists, and religion played an important part in their lives. A great part of Greek art and literature was closely connected with religion, as was the life of the *polis* in general.

OLYMPIAN GODS   The Greek pantheon consisted of the twelve gods who lived on Mount Olympus. These were

- Zeus, the father of the gods
- Hera, his wife

Zeus' siblings:

- Poseidon, his brother, god of the seas and earthquakes
- Hestia, his sister, goddess of the hearth
- Demeter, his sister, goddess of agriculture and marriage

and Zeus' children:

- Aphrodite, goddess of love and beauty
- Apollo, god of the sun, music, poetry, and prophecy
- Ares, god of war
- Artemis, goddess of the moon and the hunt
- Athena, goddess of wisdom and the arts
- Hephaestus, god of fire and metallurgy
- Hermes, messenger of the gods, connected with commerce and cunning

These gods were seen as behaving very much as mortals behaved, with all the foibles of humans, except that they were superhuman in these as well as in their strength and immortality. On the other hand, Zeus, at least, was seen as a source of human justice, and even the Olympians were understood to be subordinate to the Fates. Each *polis* had one of the Olympians as its guardian deity and worshiped that god in its own special way, but all the gods were Panhellenic. In the eighth and sev-

enth centuries B.C.E., common shrines were established at Olympia for the worship of Zeus, at Delphi for Apollo, at the Isthmus of Corinth for Poseidon, and at Nemea once again for Zeus. Each held athletic contests in honor of its deity, to which all Greeks were invited and for which a sacred truce was declared.

IMMORTALITY AND MORALITY   Besides the Olympians, the Greeks also worshiped countless lesser deities connected with local shrines. They even worshiped human heroes, real or legendary, who had accomplished great deeds and had earned immortality and divine status. The worship of these deities was not a very emotional experience. It was a matter of offering prayer, libations, and gifts in return for protection and favors from the god during the lifetime of the worshiper. There was no hope of immortality for the average human, and these devotions involved little moral teaching.

Most Greeks seem to have held to the common-sense notion that justice lay in paying one's debts. They thought that civic virtue consisted of worship-

This Attic cup from the fifth century B.C.E. *shows the two great poets from the island of Lesbos, Sappho (right) and Alcaeus.*   Hirmer Fotoarchiv

Sappho the Poet

Sappho was born at Mytilene on the island of Lesbos about 612 B.C.E. After a period of exile in Sicily, she returned and became a central figure in a thiastos, *a company of revelers who sang and danced in honor of a god. Sappho's group was made up of young girls who gave honor to Aphrodite and the Muses, the goddesses of the fine arts. They lived together intimately and affectionately. Sappho wrote poems to and about them and to celebrate their marriages. Her poems were highly admired in antiquity, winning her a position among the greatest lyric poets, but they are preserved only in fragments. The following selection illustrates one type of her poetry.*

❖ *How does the mood and style of the poem compare with the excerpts from Homer and Hesiod in this chapter? Since we have little reliable information about Sappho outside the fragments of her poems, what does the selection tell us about her life and activities?*

Fragment 94

"and honestly I want to die"
—so sobbing, many times, she left me
and she said this [to me]
"My god! what awful things are happening to us:
Sappho, I swear I am leaving you against my
   will."
And I replied to her in these words:
"Go with a light heart, and with memories
of me, for you know how we cherished you.
And if not, then I want to
remind you [   ]
[   ] and we had good times
For ma[ny garland]s of violets
and roses [   ] together

and [   ] you put on beside me
And many garlands
woven from flowers about your soft neck
[   ] fashioned
And with m[uch] myrrh
from rich flowers [   ]
and royal you rubbed your skin
And on soft beds
tender [   ]
you would satisfy desire [   ]
And there was no [   ] nothing
holy nor [   ]
from which [we] kept away
No grove [   ]
[   ] sound
[   ]"

From Sappho, *Fragment 94*, trans. by Ewen Bowie, in J. Boardman, J. Griffin, and O. Murray, *The Oxford History of the Classical World* (Oxford and New York: Oxford University Press, n.d.), p. 104.

ing the state deities in the traditional way, performing required public services, and fighting in defense of the state. To them, private morality meant to do good to one's friends and harm to one's enemies.

THE CULT OF DELPHIAN APOLLO   In the sixth century B.C.E., the influence of the cult of Apollo at Delphi and of his oracle there became very great. The oracle was the most important of several that helped satisfy the human craving for a clue to the future. The priests of Apollo preached moderation; their advice was exemplified in the two famous sayings identified with Apollo: "Know thyself" and "Nothing in excess." Humans needed self-control (*sophrosynē*). Its opposite was arrogance (*hubris*), brought on by excessive wealth or good fortune. *Hubris* led to moral blindness and, finally, to divine vengeance. This theme of moderation and the dire consequences of its absence was central to Greek popular morality and appears frequently in Greek literature.

THE CULT OF DIONYSUS AND THE ORPHIC CULT   The somewhat cold religion of the Olympian gods and of the cult of Apollo did little to assuage human fears or satisfy human hopes and passions. For these needs, the Greeks turned to other deities and rites. Of these deities, the most popular was Dionysus, a god of nature and fertility, of the grapevine, drunkenness, and sexual abandon. In some of his rites, this god was followed by *maenads*, female devotees who cavorted by night, ate raw flesh, and were reputed to tear to pieces any creature they came across.

The Orphic cult, named after its supposed founder, the mythical poet Orpheus, provided its followers with more hope than did the worship of the twelve Olympians. Cult followers are thought to

Theognis of Megara Gives Advice to a Young Aristocrat

Theognis was born about 580 B.C.E. and lived to see his native city Megara torn by social upheaval and civil war. His poems present the political and ethical ideas of the Greek aristocracy.

❖ *What does Theognis claim is the source of virtue among human beings? What role does he give to education in improving the character of people? What does he mean by "judgment"? What are the political and constitutional implications of his way of thinking?*

Do not consort with bad men, but always hold to the good. Eat and drink with them. You will learn good from good men, but if you mingle with the bad you will lose such wisdom as you already have. Therefore consort with the good and one day you will say that I give good advice to my friends.

We seek thoroughbred rams asses and horses, Cyrnus, and a man wants offspring of good breeding. But in marriage a good man does not decline to marry the bad daughter of a bad father, if he gives him much wealth. Nor does the wife of a bad man refuse to be his bedfellow if he be rich, preferring wealth to goodness. For they value possessions and a good man marries a woman of bad stock and the bad a woman of good. Wealth mixes the breed. So do not wonder, son of Polypaus, that the race of your citizens is obscured since bad things are mixed with good.

It is easier to beget and rear a man than to put good sense into him. No one has ever discovered a way to make a fool wise or a bad man good. If God had given the sons of Asclepius the knowledge to heal the evil nature and mischievous mind of man, great and frequent would be their pay. If thought could be made and put into a man, the son of a good man would never become bad, since he would obey good counsel. But you will never make the bad man good by teaching.

The best thing the gods give to men, Cyrnus, is judgment; judgment contains the ends of everything. O happy is the man who has it in his mind; it is much greater than destructive insolence and grievous satiety. There are no evils among mortals worse than these—for every evil, Cyrnus, comes out of them.

From *Sources in Greek Political Thought From Homer To Polybuis*, Donald Kagan, Editor. Copyright © 1965 by The Free Press, A Division of Simon & Schuster. Adapted with permission of the publisher.

have refused to kill animals or eat their flesh and to have believed in the transmigration of souls, which offered the prospect of some form of life after death.

Poetry

The great changes sweeping through the Greek world were also reflected in the poetry of the sixth century B.C.E. The lyric style—poetry meant to be sung, either by a chorus or by one person—predominated. Sappho of Lesbos, Anacreon of Teos, and Simonides of Cos composed personal poetry, often relating the pleasure and agony of love. (See "Sappho the Poet.") Alcaeus of Mytilene, an aristocrat driven from his city by a tyrant, wrote bitter invective.

Perhaps the most interesting poet of the century from a political point of view was Theognis of Megara. He was an aristocrat who lived through a tyranny, an unusually chaotic and violent democracy, and an oligarchy that restored order, but ended the rule of the old aristocracy. Theognis was the

spokesperson for the old, defeated aristocracy of birth. He divided everyone into two classes, the noble and the base; the former were the good, the latter bad. Those nobly born must associate only with others like themselves if they were to preserve their virtue; if they mingled with the base, they became base. Those born base, on the other hand, could never become noble. Only nobles could aspire to virtue, and only nobles possessed the critical moral and intellectual qualities—respect or honor and judgment. These qualities could not be taught; they were innate. Even so they had to be carefully guarded against corruption by wealth or by mingling with the base. Intermarriage between the noble and the base was especially condemned. These were the ideas of the unreconstructed nobility, whose power had been destroyed or reduced in most Greek states by this time. Such ideas remained alive in aristocratic hearts throughout the next century and greatly influenced later thinkers, Plato among them. (See "Theognis of Megara Gives Advice to a Young Aristocrat.")

	The Rise of Persia
559–530 B.C.E.	Reign of Cyrus the Great
546 B.C.E.	Persians conquer Lydia
530–522 B.C.E.	Reign of Cambyses
522–521 B.C.E.	Civil war in Persia
521–485 B.C.E.	Reign of Darius
485–465 B.C.E.	Reign of Xerxes

The Persian Wars

The Greeks' period of fortunate isolation and freedom ended in the sixth century B.C.E. They had established colonies along most of the coast of Asia Minor from as early as the eleventh century B.C.E. The colonies maintained friendly relations with the mainland but developed a flourishing economic and cultural life independent of their mother cities and of their eastern neighbors. In the middle of the sixth century B.C.E., however, these Greek cities of Asia Minor came under the control of Lydia and its king, Croesus (ca. 560–546 B.C.E.). Lydian rule seems not to have been very harsh, but the Persian conquest of Lydia in 546 B.C.E. brought a less pleasant subjugation.

The Persian Empire

The Persian Empire had been created in a single generation by Cyrus the Great, the founder of the Achaemenid dynasty. In 559 B.C.E. he came to the throne of Persia, then a small kingdom well to the east of the lower Mesopotamian Valley. He unified Persia under his rule, made an alliance with Babylonia, and led a successful rebellion toward the north against the Medes, the overlords of Persia. (See Map 2–5.) In succeeding years he expanded his empire in all directions, in the process defeating Croesus and occupying Lydia. Most of the Greek cities of Asia Minor sided with Croesus and resisted the Persians. By about 540 B.C.E., however, they had all been subdued. The western part of Asia Minor was divided into three provinces, each under its own *satrap*, or governor.

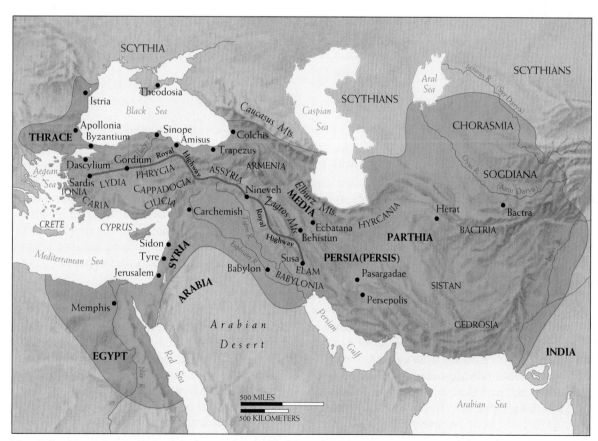

MAP 2–5   THE PERSIAN EMPIRE   *The empire created by Cyrus had reached its fullest extent under Darius when Persia attacked Greece in 490 B.C.E. It extended from India to the Aegean and even into Europe. It included the lands formerly ruled by Egyptians, Hittites, Babylonians, and Assyrians.*

Persian nobles pay homage to King Darius in this relief from the treasury at the Persian capital of Persepolis. Darius is seated on the throne; his son and successor Xerxes stands behind him. Darius and Xerxes are carved in larger scale to indicate their royal status.
Courtesy of the Oriental Institute of the University of Chicago

The Ionian Rebellion

The Ionian Greeks (those living on the central part of the west coast of Asia Minor and nearby islands) had been moving toward democracy and were not pleased to find themselves under the monarchical rule of Persia. That rule, however, was not overly burdensome at first. The Persians required their subjects to pay tribute and to serve in the Persian army. They ruled the Greek cities through local individuals, who governed their cities as "tyrants." Most of the "tyrants," however, were not harsh, the Persian tribute was not excessive, and the Greeks enjoyed general prosperity. Neither the death of Cyrus fighting on a distant frontier in 530 B.C.E. nor the suicide of his successor Cambyses, nor the civil war that followed it in 522–521 B.C.E. produced any disturbance in the Greek cities. When Darius emerged as Great King (as the Persian rulers styled themselves) in 521 B.C.E., he found Ionia perfectly obedient.

The private troubles of the ambitious tyrant of Miletus, Aristagoras, ended this calm. He had urged a Persian expedition against the island of Naxos; when it failed, he feared the consequences and organized the Ionian rebellion of 499 B.C.E. To gain support, he overthrew the tyrannies and proclaimed democratic constitutions. Then he turned to the mainland states for help, petitioning first Sparta, the most powerful Greek state. The Spartans, however, would have none of Aristagoras' promises of easy victory and great wealth. They had no close ties with the Ionians and no national interest in the re-

gion. Furthermore, they were terrified at the thought of leaving their homeland undefended against the Helots for a long time while their army was far off.

Aristagoras next sought help from the Athenians, who were related to the Ionians and had close ties of religion and tradition with them. Besides, Hippias, the deposed tyrant of Athens, was an honored guest at the court of Darius, and the Great King had already made it plain that he favored the tyrant's restoration. The Persians, moreover, controlled both sides of the Hellespont, the route to the grain fields beyond the Black Sea that were increasingly vital to Athens. Perhaps some Athenians already feared that a Persian attempt to conquer the Greek mainland was only a matter of time. The Athenian assembly agreed to send a fleet of twenty ships to help the rebels. The Athenian expedition was strengthened by five ships from Eretria in Euboea, which participated out of gratitude for past favors.

In 498 B.C.E. the Athenians and their allies made a surprise attack on Sardis, the old capital of Lydia and now the seat of the *satrap*, and burned it. This action caused the revolt to spread throughout the Greek cities of Asia Minor outside Ionia, but the Ionians could not follow it up. The Athenians withdrew and took no further part. Gradually the Persians reimposed their will. In 495 B.C.E. they defeated the Ionian fleet at Lade, and in the next year they wiped out Miletus. They killed many of the Miletan men, transported others to the Persian Gulf, and enslaved the women and children. The Ionian rebellion was over.

MAP 2–6   THE PERSIAN INVASION OF GREECE   *This map traces the route taken by the Persian king Xerxes in his invasion of Greece in 480 B.C.E. The gray arrows show movements of Xerxes' army, the purple arrows show movements of his navy, and the green arrows show movements of the Greek army and navy.*

The War in Greece

In 490 B.C.E. the Persians launched an expedition directly across the Aegean to punish Eretria and Athens, to restore Hippias, and to gain control of the Aegean Sea. (See Map 2–6.) They landed their infantry and cavalry forces first at Naxos, destroy-

ing it for its successful resistance in 499 B.C.E. Then they destroyed Eretria and deported its people deep into the interior of Persia.

MARATHON   Rather than submit and accept the restoration of the hated tyranny of Hippias, the Athenians chose to resist the Persian forces bearing

This bronze helmet was dedicated to Zeus by Miltiades to commemorate the Athenian victory over the Persians in 490 B.C.E.   Deutsche Archäologisches Institut, Athens

The Greek Wars against Persia	
ca. 560–546 B.C.E.	Greek cities of Asia Minor conquered by Croesus of Lydia
546 B.C.E.	Cyrus of Persia conquers Lydia and gains control of Greek cities
499–494 B.C.E.	Greek cities rebel (Ionian rebellion)
490 B.C.E.	Battle of Marathon
480–479 B.C.E.	Xerxes' invasion of Greece
480 B.C.E.	Battles of Thermopylae, Artemisium, and Salamis
479 B.C.E.	Battles of Plataea and Mycale

cian. During his *archonship* in 493 B.C.E., Athens had already taken the first step in that direction by building a fortified port at Piraeus. A decade later the Athenians came upon a rich vein of silver in the state mines, and Themistocles persuaded them to use the profits to increase their fleet. By 480 B.C.E. Athens had over 200 ships, the backbone of a navy that was to defeat the Persians.

Of the hundreds of Greek states, only thirty-one—led by Sparta, Athens, Corinth, and Aegina—were willing to fight as the Persian army gathered south of the Hellespont. In the spring of 480 B.C.E., Xerxes launched his invasion. The Persian strategy was to march into Greece, destroy Athens, defeat the Greek army, and add the Greeks to the number of Persian subjects. The huge Persian army needed to keep in touch with the fleet for supplies. If the Greeks could defeat the Persian navy, the army could not remain in Greece long. Themistocles knew that the Aegean was subject to sudden devastating storms. His strategy was to delay the Persian army and then to bring on the kind of naval battle he might hope to win.

The Greek League, founded specifically to resist this Persian invasion, met at Corinth as the Persians were ready to cross the Hellespont. They chose Sparta as leader on land and sea and first confronted the Persians at Thermopylae, the "hot gates," on land and off Artemisium at sea. The opening between the mountains and the sea at Thermopylae was so narrow that it might be held by a smaller army against a much larger one. The Spartans sent their king, Leonidas, with 300 of their own citizens and enough allies to make a total of about 9,000.

Severe storms wrecked many Persian ships while the Greek fleet waited safely in a protected harbor. Then Xerxes attacked Thermopylae, and for two days the Greeks butchered his best troops without serious loss to themselves. On the third day, how-

down on them and risk the same fate that had just befallen Eretria. Miltiades, an Athenian who had fled from Persian service, led the city's army to a confrontation with the Persians at Marathon.

A Persian victory at Marathon would have destroyed Athenian freedom and led to the conquest of all the mainland Greeks. The greatest achievements of Greek culture, most of which lay in the future, would never have occurred. But the Athenians won a decisive victory, instilling them with a sense of confidence and pride in their *polis*, their unique form of government, and themselves.

THE GREAT INVASION   Internal troubles prevented the Persians from taking swift revenge for their loss at Marathon. Almost ten years elapsed before Darius' successor, Xerxes, in 481 B.C.E., gathered an army of at least 150,000 men and a navy of more than 600 ships for the conquest of Greece. In Athens, Themistocles, who favored making Athens into a naval power, had become the leading politi-

A Greek hoplite *attacks a Persian soldier. The contrast between the Greek's metal body armor, large shield, and long spear and the Persian's cloth and leather garments indicates one reason the Greeks won. This Attic vase was found on Rhodes and dates from ca. 475 B.C.E.*
The Metropolitan Museum of Art, Rogers Fund, 1906

ever, a traitor showed the Persians a mountain trail that permitted them to come on the Greeks from behind. Many allies escaped, but Leonidas and his 300 Spartans all died fighting. At about the same time the Greek and Persian fleets fought an indecisive battle at Artemisium. The fall of Thermopylae, however, forced the Greek navy to withdraw.

After Thermopylae, the Persian army moved into Attica and burned Athens. If an inscription discovered in 1959 is authentic, Themistocles had foreseen this possibility before Thermopylae, and the Athenians had begun to evacuate their homeland before they sent their fleet north to fight at Artemisium.

DEFEATING THE PERSIANS The fate of Greece was decided in a sea battle in the narrow waters to the east of the island of Salamis, to which the Greek fleet withdrew after the battle at Artemisium. The Peloponnesians were reluctant to confront the Persian fleet at this spot, but Themistocles persuaded them to stay by threatening to remove all the Athenians from Greece and settle them anew in Italy. The Spartans knew that they and the other Greeks could not hope to win without the aid of the Athe-

nians. Because the Greek ships were fewer, slower, and less maneuverable than those of the Persians, the Greeks put soldiers on their ships and relied chiefly on hand-to-hand combat. In the ensuing battle the Persians lost more than half their ships and retreated to Asia with a good part of their army, but the danger was not over yet.

The Persian general Mardonius spent the winter in central Greece, and in the spring he unsuccessfully tried to win the Athenians away from the Greek League. The Spartan regent, Pausanias, then led the largest Greek army up to that time to confront Mardonius in Boeotia. At Plataea, in the summer of 479 B.C.E., the Persians suffered a decisive defeat. Mardonius died in battle and his army fled toward home.

Meanwhile the Ionian Greeks urged King Leotychidas, the Spartan commander of the fleet, to fight the Persian fleet at Samos. At Mycale, on the coast nearby, Leotychidas destroyed the Persian camp and its fleet offshore. The Persians fled the Aegean and Ionia. For the moment, at least, the Persian threat was gone.

In Perspective

Hellenic civilization, that unique cultural experience at the root of Western civilization, has powerfully influenced the peoples of the modern world. It was itself influenced by the great Bronze Age civilization of Crete called Minoan, and emerged from the collapse of the Bronze Age civilization on the Greek mainland called Mycenaean. These earlier Aegean civilizations more closely resembled other early civilizations in Egypt, Mesopotamia, Syria–Palestine, and elsewhere than the Hellenic civilization that sprang from them. They had highly developed cities; a system of writing; strong, centralized monarchical systems of government with tightly organized, large bureaucracies; hierarchical social systems; professional standing armies; and a regular system of taxation supporting all this. To a greater or lesser degree, these early civilizations tended toward cultural stability—changing little over time—and uniformity—all sharing many structural features. The striking thing about the emergence of Hellenic civilization is its sharp departure from this pattern.

The collapse of the Mycenaean world produced a harsh material and cultural decline for the Greeks. Cities were swept away and replaced by small farm villages. Trade all but ended, and communication among the Greeks themselves and between them and other peoples was sharply curtailed. The art of writing was lost for more than three centuries. During this "Dark Age," the Greeks—poor, small in number, isolated, and illiterate—were ignored by the rest of the world and left alone to develop their own society and the matrix of Hellenic civilization.

During the three-and-a-half centuries from about 1100 to 750 B.C.E., the Greeks set the foundations for their great achievements. The crucial unit in the new Greek way of life was the polis, *the Hellenic city-state. There were hundreds of them, and each evoked a kind of loyalty and attachment by its citizens that made the idea of dissolving one's own* polis *into a larger unit unthinkable. The result was a dynamic, many-faceted, competitive, sometimes chaotic world in which rivalry for excellence and victory had the highest value. This agonistic, or competitive, quality marks Greek life throughout its history. Its negative aspect was constant warfare among the states. Its positive side was an extraordinary achievement in literature and art; competition, sometimes formal and organized, spurred on poets and artists.*

Kings had been swept away with the Mycenaean world and the poleis *were republics. Since the Greeks were so poor, the difference in wealth among them was relatively small. Therefore, class distinctions were less marked and important than in other civilizations. The introduction of a new mode of fighting, the hoplite phalanx, had further leveling effects, for it placed the safety of the state in the hands of the average farmer. Armies were made up of citizen–soldiers, who were not paid and who returned to their farms after a campaign. As a result, political control was shared with a relatively large portion of the people, and participation in political life was highly valued. There was no bureaucracy, for there were no kings and not much economic surplus to support bureaucrats. Most states imposed no regular taxation. There was no separate caste of priests and little concern with any life after death. In this varied, dynamic, secular, and remarkably free context there arose speculative natural philosophy based on observation and reason, the root of modern natural science and philosophy.*

Contact with the rest of the world increased trade and wealth and brought in valuable new information and ideas. Greek art was powerfully shaped by Egyptian and Near Eastern models that were always adapted and changed rather than copied. Changes often produced social and economic strain, leading to the overthrow of traditional aristocratic regimes by tyrants. But monarchic rule was anathema to the Greeks, and these regimes were temporary. In Athens, the de-struction of the tyranny brought the world's first democracy. Sparta, on the other hand, developed a uniquely stable government that avoided tyranny and impressed the other Greeks.

The Greeks' time of independent development, untroubled by external forces, ended in the sixth century, when Persia's powerful Achaemenid dynasty conquered the Greek cities of Asia Minor. When the Persian kings tried to conquer the Greek mainland, however, the leading states managed to put their quarrels aside and unite against the common enemy. Their determination to preserve their freedom carried them to victory over tremendous odds.

REVIEW QUESTIONS

1. Describe the Minoan civilization of Crete. How did the later Bronze Age Mycenaean civilization differ from the Minoan civilization in political organization, art motifs, and military posture?
2. What are the most important historical sources for the Minoan and Mycenaean civilizations? Most particularly, what is Linear B, and what problems does it raise for the reconstruction of Bronze Age history? How valuable are the Homeric epics as sources of early Greek history?
3. Define the concept of a *polis*. What role did geography play in its development and why did the Greeks consider it a unique and valuable institution?
4. Compare the fundamental political, social, and economic institutions of Athens and Sparta about 500 B.C.E. Why did Sparta develop its unique form of government?
5. What were the main stages in the transformation of Athens from an aristocratic state to a democracy between 600 and 500 B.C.E.? In what ways did Draco, Solon, Pisistratus, and Clisthenes each contribute to the process?
6. Why did the Greeks and Persians go to war in 490 and 480 B.C.E.? What benefit could the Persians have derived from conquering Greece? Why were the Greeks able to defeat the Persians and how did they benefit from the victory?

SUGGESTED READINGS

A. ANDREWES, *Greek Tyrants* (1963). A clear and concise account of tyranny in early Greece.

A. R. BURN, *The Lyric Age of Greece* (1960). A discussion of early Greece that uses the evidence of poetry and archaeology to fill out the sparse historical record.

J. Chadwick, *The Mycenaean World* (1976). A readable account by an author who helped decipher Mycenaean writing.

J.M. Cook, *The Persian Empire* (1983). A valuable study of Persian history based on archeological and literary evidence.

O. Dickinson, *The Aegean Bronze Age* (1994). A fine survey of Bronze Age culture in the Aegean region.

R. Drews, *The End of the Bronze Age: Changes in Warfare and Catastrophes ca. 1200 B.C.* (1993). A scholarly and fascinating examination of the theories explaining the fall of the late Bronze Age civilizations.

V. Ehrenberg, *From Solon to Socrates* (1968). An interpretive history that makes good use of Greek literature to illuminate politics.

J. V. A. Fine, *The Ancient Greeks* (1983). An excellent survey that discusses historical problems and the evidence that gives rise to them.

M. I. Finley, *World of Odysseus*, 2d. ed. (1978). A fascinating attempt to reconstruct Homeric society.

W. G. Forrest, *The Emergence of Greek Democracy* (1966). A lively interpretation of Greek social and political developments in the archaic period.

P. Green, *The Greco–Persian Wars* (1998). A lively and stimulating history of the Persian wars.

V. D. Hanson, *The Western Way of War* (1989). A brilliant and lively discussion of the rise and character of the hoplite phalanx and its influence on Greek society.

V. D. Hanson, *The Other Greeks* (1995). A revolutionary account of the invention of the family farm by the Greeks and the central role of agrarianism in shaping the Greek city–state.

C. Hignett, *A History of the Athenian Constitution* (1952). A scholarly account, somewhat too skeptical of the ancient sources.

J. M. Hurwit, *The Art and Culture of Early Greece* (1985). A fascinating study of the art of early Greece in its literary and cultural context.

S. Isager and J. E. Skydsgaard, *Ancient Greek Agriculture: An Introduction* (1993). A new study of a fundamental subject.

D. Kagan, *The Great Dialogue: A History of Greek Political Thought from Homer to Polybius* (1965). A discussion of the relationship between the Greek historical experience and political theory.

H. D. F. Kitto, *The Greeks* (1951). A personal and illuminating interpretation of Greek culture.

W. K. Lacey, *The Family in Ancient Greece* (1984).

P. B. Manville, *The Origins of Citizenship in Ancient Athens* (1990). An examination of the origins of the concept of citizenship in the time of Solon of Athens.

L. G. Mitchell and P. J. Rhodes, eds., *The Development of the* Polis *in Archaic Greece* (1997). A collection of articles on the emergence and development of the Greek city–state.

I. Morris and B. Powell, eds., *A New Companion to Homer* (1997). A collection of articles treating Homeric questions in an accessible style.

O. Murray, *Early Greece* (1980). A lively and imaginative account of the early history of Greece to the end of the Persian War.

A. T. Olmstead, *History of the Persian Empire* (1960). A thorough survey.

C. Roebuck, *Ionian Trade and Colonization* (1959). An introduction to the history of the Greeks in the East.

R. Sallares, *The Ecology of the Ancient Greek World* (1991). A valuable study of the Greeks and their environment.

D. M. Schaps, *Economic Rights of Women in Ancient Greece* (1981).

A. M. Snodgrass, *The Dark Age of Greece* (1972). A good examination of the archaeological evidence.

C. G. Starr, *The Economic and Social Growth of Early Greece, 800–500 B.C.E.* (1977).

A. G. Woodhead, *Greeks in the West* (1962). An account of the Greek settlements in Italy and Sicily.

W. J. Woodhouse, *Solon the Liberator* (1965). A discussion of the great Athenian reformer.

D. C. Young, *The Olympic Myth of Greek Athletics* (1984). A lively challenge to the orthodox view that Greek athletes were amateurs.

Chapter 3

The Winged Victory of Samothrace. This is one of the great masterpieces of Hellenistic sculpture. It appears to be the work of the Rhodian sculptor Pythokritos, about 200 B.C.E. The statue stood in the sanctuary of the Great Gods on the Aegean island of Samothrace on a base made in the shape of a ship's prow. The goddess is seen as landing on the ship to crown its victorious commander and crew. Marble figure (190 B.C.E.) from Rhodos, Greece. Height 328 cm, MA 2369, Lourve, Dpt. des Antiquities Grecques/Romaines, Paris, France. © Photograph by Erich Lessing. Art Resource.

Classical and Hellenistic Greece

KEY TOPICS

- The Peloponnesian War and the struggle between Athens and Sparta
- Democracy and empire in fifth-century B.C.E. Athens
- Culture and society in Classical Greece
- The struggle for dominance in Greece after the Peloponnesian War
- The Hellenistic world

The Greeks' remarkable victory over the Persians in 480–479 B.C.E. won them another period of freedom and autonomy. They used this time to carry their political and cultural achievement to its height. In Athens, especially, it produced a great sense of confidence and ambition.

Spartan withdrawal from active leadership against the Persians left a vacuum that was filled by the Delian League, which soon turned into the Athenian Empire. At the same time as it tightened its hold over the Greek cities in and around the Aegean Sea, Athens developed an extraordinarily democratic constitution at home. Fears and jealousies of this new kind of state and empire created a split in the Greek world which led to a series of major wars that impoverished Greece and left it vulnerable to conquest. In 338 B.C.E. Philip of Macedon conquered the Greek states, putting an end to the age of the polis.

Aftermath of Victory

The unity of the Greeks had shown strain even in the life-and-death struggle against the Persians. Within two years of the Persian retreat it gave way almost completely and yielded to a division of the Greek world into two spheres of influence, dominated by Sparta and Athens. The need of the Ionian Greeks to obtain and defend their freedom from Persia and the desire of many Greeks to gain revenge and financial reparation for the Persian attack brought on the split.

The Delian League

Sparta had led the Greeks to victory, and it was natural to look to the Spartans to continue the campaign against Persia. But Sparta was ill-suited to the task, which required both a long-term commitment far from the Peloponnesus and continuous naval action.

Athens had become the leading naval power in Greece, and the same motives that led the Athenians to support the Ionian revolt prompted them to try to drive the Persians from the Aegean and the Hellespont. The Ionians were at least as eager for the Athenians to take the helm as the Athenians were to accept the responsibility and opportunity.

In the winter of 478–477 B.C.E., the islanders, the Greeks from the coast of Asia Minor and from some other Greek cities on the Aegean, met with the Athenians on the sacred island of Delos and swore oaths of alliance. As a symbol that the alliance was meant to be permanent, they dropped lumps of iron into the sea; the alliance was to hold until these lumps of iron rose to the surface. The aims of this new Delian League were to free those Greeks who were under Persian rule, to protect all against a Persian return, and to obtain compensation from the Persians by attacking their lands and taking booty. League policy was determined by a

MAP 3–1   CLASSICAL GREECE   *Greece in the Classical period (ca. 480–338 B.C.E.) centered on the Aegean Sea. Although there were important Greek settlements in Italy, Sicily, and all around the Black Sea, the area shown in this general reference map embraced the vast majority of Greek states.*

vote of an assembly in which each state, including Athens, had one vote. Athens, however, was clearly designated the leader.

From the first, the league was remarkably successful. The Persians were driven from Europe and the Hellespont, and the Aegean was cleared of pirates. Some states were forced into the league or were prevented from leaving. The members approved coercion because it was necessary for the common safety. In 467 B.C.E., a great victory over the Persians at the Eurymedon River in Asia Minor routed the Persians and added several cities to the league.

The Rise of Cimon

Cimon, son of Miltiades, the hero of Marathon, became the leading Athenian soldier and statesman soon after the war with Persia. Themistocles appears to have been driven from power by a coalition of his enemies. Ironically, the author of the Greek victory over Persia of 480 B.C.E. was exiled and ended his days at the court of the Persian king. Cimon, who was to dominate Athenian politics for almost two decades, pursued a policy of aggressive attacks on Persia and friendly relations with Sparta. In domestic affairs Cimon was conservative. He accepted the democratic constitution of Clisthenes, which appears to have become somewhat more limited after the Persian war. Defending this constitution and his interventionist foreign policy, Cimon led the Athenians and the Delian League to victory after victory, and his own popularity grew with his successes.

The First Peloponnesian War: Athens against Sparta

The Thasian Rebellion

In 465 B.C.E., the island of Thasos rebelled from the Delian League, and Cimon put it down after a siege of more than two years. The revolt of Thasos is the first recorded instance in which Athenian interests alone seemed to determine league policy, a significant step in the league's evolution into the Athenian Empire.

When Cimon returned to Athens from Thasos, he was charged with taking bribes for having refrained from conquering Macedonia, although conquering Macedonia had not been part of his assignment. He was acquitted; the trial was only a device by which his political opponents tried to reduce his influence. Their program at home was to undo the gains made by the Areopagus and to bring about further changes in the direction of democracy. In foreign policy, these enemies

of Cimon wanted to break with Sparta and to contest its claim to leadership over the Greeks. They intended at least to establish the independence of Athens and its alliance. The head of this faction was Ephialtes. His supporter, and the person chosen to be the public prosecutor of Cimon, was Pericles, a member of a distinguished Athenian family. He was still young, and his defeat in court did not do lasting damage to his career.

The Breach with Sparta

When the Thasians began their rebellion, they asked Sparta to invade Athens the next spring, and the *ephors*, the annual magistrates responsible for Sparta's foreign policy, agreed. An earthquake, however, accompanied by a rebellion of the Helots that threatened the survival of Sparta, prevented the invasion. The Spartans asked their allies, the Athenians among them, for help, and Cimon persuaded the Athenians to send it.

The results of this policy were disastrous for Cimon and his faction. While Cimon was in the Peloponnesus helping the Spartans, Ephialtes stripped the Areopagus of almost all its power. The Spartans, meanwhile, fearing "the boldness and revolutionary spirit of the Athenians," ultimately sent them home. In 462 B.C.E., Ephialtes was assassinated and Pericles replaced him as leader of the democratic faction. In the spring of 461 B.C.E. Cimon was ostracized, and Athens made an alliance with Argos, Sparta's traditional enemy. Almost overnight, Cimon's domestic and foreign policies had been overturned.

The Division of Greece

The new regime at Athens, led by Pericles and the democratic faction, was confident and ambitious. When Megara, getting the worst of a border dispute with Corinth, withdrew from the Peloponnesian League, the Athenians accepted the Megarians as allies. This alliance gave Athens a great strategic advantage, for Megara barred the way from the Peloponnesus to Athens. Sparta, however, resented the defection of Megara to Athens, leading to the outbreak of the First Peloponnesian War, the first phase in a protracted struggle between Athens and Sparta. The Athenians conquered Aegina and gained control of Boeotia. At this moment Athens was supreme and apparently invulnerable, controlling the states on its borders and dominating the sea. (See Map 3–2.)

About 455 B.C.E., however, the tide turned. A disastrous defeat met an Athenian fleet that had gone to aid an Egyptian rebellion against Persia. The great loss of men, ships, and prestige caused rebel-

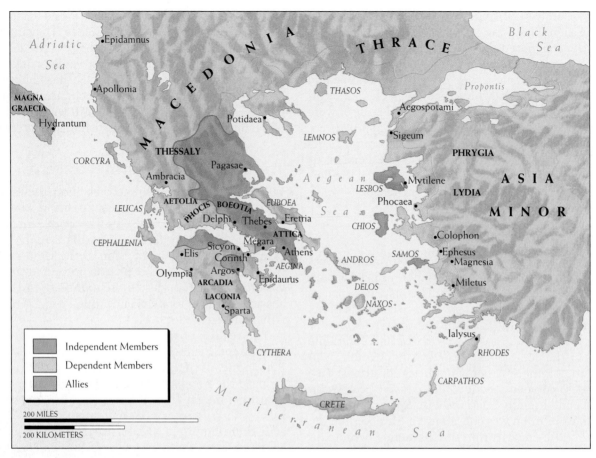

MAP 3–2   THE ATHENIAN EMPIRE ABOUT 450 B.C.E.   *The Athenian Empire at its fullest extent shortly before 450 B.C.E. We see Athens and the independent states that provided manned ships for the imperial fleet, but paid no tribute; dependent states that paid tribute; and states allied to, but not actually in, the empire.*

lions in the empire, forcing Athens to make a truce in Greece to subdue its allies in the Aegean. In 449 B.C.E., the Athenians ended the war against Persia.

In 446 B.C.E., the war on the Greek mainland broke out again. Rebellions in Boeotia and Megara removed Athens' land defenses and brought a Spartan invasion. Rather than fight, Pericles, the commander of the Athenian army, agreed to a peace of thirty years by the terms of which he abandoned all Athenian possessions on the Greek mainland outside of Attica. In return, the Spartans gave formal recognition to the Athenian Empire. From then on, Greece was divided into two power blocs: Sparta with its alliance on the mainland, and Athens ruling its empire in the Aegean.

Classical Greece

The Athenian Empire

After the Egyptian disaster, the Athenians moved the Delian League's treasury to Athens and began to keep one-sixtieth of the annual revenues for themselves. Because of the peace with Persia, there seemed no further reason for the allies to pay tribute, so the Athenians were compelled to find a new justification for their empire. (See "The Delian League Becomes the Athenian Empire.") They called for a Panhellenic congress to meet at Athens to discuss rebuilding the temples destroyed by the Persians and to consider how to maintain freedom of the seas. When Sparta's reluctance to participate prevented the congress, Athens felt free to continue to collect funds from the allies, both to maintain its navy and to rebuild the Athenian temples. Athenian propaganda suggested that henceforth the allies would be treated as colonies and Athens as their mother city, the whole to be held together by good feeling and common religious observances.

There is little reason, however, to believe that the allies were taken in or were truly content with their lot. Nothing could cloak the fact that Athens was becoming the master and its allies mere subjects. By 445 B.C.E., when the Thirty Years' Peace gave formal recognition to an Athenian Empire, only Chios, Les-

Key Events in Athenian History between the Persian War and the Great Peloponnesian War	
478–477 B.C.E.	Delian League founded
ca. 474–462 B.C.E.	Cimon leading politician
467 B.C.E.	Victory over Persians at Eurymedon River
465–463 B.C.E.	Rebellion of Thasos
462 B.C.E.	Ephialtes murdered; Pericles rises to leadership
461 B.C.E.	Cimon ostracized
461 B.C.E.	Reform of Areopagus
ca. 460 B.C.E.	First Peloponnesian War begins
454 B.C.E.	Athens defeated in Egypt; crisis in the Delian League
449 B.C.E.	Peace with Persia
445 B.C.E.	Thirty Years' Peace ends First Peloponnesian War

(a)

(b)

An Athenian silver four-drachma coin (tetradrachm) from the fifth century B.C.E. (440–430 B.C.E.). On the front (a) is the profile of Athena and on the back (b) is her symbol of wisdom, the owl. The silver from which the coins were struck came chiefly from the state mines at Sunium in southern Attica. Hirmer Foto archive

bos, and Samos were autonomous and provided ships. All the other states paid tribute. The change from alliance to empire came about because of the pressure of war and rebellion and largely because the allies were unwilling to see to their own defense. Although the empire had many friends among the lower classes and the democratic politicians in the subject cities, it came to be seen more and more as a tyranny. Athenian prosperity and security, however, had come to depend on the empire, and the Athenians were determined to defend it at any cost.

Athenian Democracy

Even as the Athenians were tightening their control over their empire, they were expanding democracy at home. Under the leadership of Pericles, they evolved the freest government the world had yet seen.

DEMOCRATIC LEGISLATION Legislation was passed making the *hoplite* class eligible for the *archonship*, and in practice no one was thereafter prevented from serving in this office on the basis of property class. Pericles himself proposed a law introducing pay for jury members, opening that important duty to the poor. Circuit judges were reintroduced, a policy making swift impartial justice available even to the poorest residents in the countryside.

Finally, Pericles himself introduced a bill limiting citizenship to those who had two citizen parents. From a modern perspective this measure might be seen as a step away from democracy, and, in fact, it would have barred Cimon and one of Pericles' ancestors. In Greek terms, however, it was quite natural. Democracy was defined as the privilege of those who held citizenship, making citizenship a valuable commodity. The decision to limit it would have increased its value. Thus, the bill must have won a large majority. Women, resident aliens, and slaves were also denied participation in government in all the Greek states.

HOW DID THE DEMOCRACY WORK? Within the citizen body, the extent of Athenian democracy was remarkable. Every decision of the state had to be approved by the popular assembly—a collection of the people, not their representatives. Every judicial decision was subject to appeal to a popular court of not fewer than 51, and as many as 1,501, citizens, chosen from an annual panel of jurors widely representative of the Athenian population. Most officials were selected by lot without regard to class. The main elected officials, such as the ten generals (the generalship was an office that had both political and military significance) and the imperial treasurers, were usually nobles and almost always rich men, but the people were free to choose otherwise. All public officials were subject to scrutiny before taking office and could be called to account and removed from office during their tenure. They were held to compulsory examination and accounting at the end of their term. There was no standing army, no police force, open or secret, and no way to coerce the people.

Pericles was elected to the generalship fifteen years in a row and thirty times in all, not because he was a dictator but because he was a persuasive speaker, a skillful politician, a respected military leader, an acknowledged patriot, and patently incorruptible. When he lost the people's confidence, they did not hesitate to depose him from office. In 443 B.C.E., however, he stood at the height of his power. The defeat of the Athenian fleet in the Egyptian campaign and the failure of Athens' continental campaigns had persuaded him to favor a conservative policy, seeking to retain the empire in the Aegean and live at peace with the Spartans. It was in this direction that he led Athens' imperial democracy in the years after the First Peloponnesian War. (See "Athenian Democracy: An Unfriendly View.")

The Women of Athens: Legal Status and Everyday Life

Greek society, like most societies all over the world throughout history, was dominated by men. This was true of the democratic city of Athens in the great days of Pericles, in the fifth century B.C.E., no less than of other Greek cities. The actual position of women in classical Athens, however, has been the subject of much controversy.

The bulk of the evidence, coming from the law, from philosophical and moral writings, and from information about the conditions of daily life and the organization of society, shows that women were excluded from most aspects of public life. They could not vote, could not take part in the political assemblies, could not hold public office, and could not take any direct part in politics. Since Athens was one of the few places in the ancient world where male citizens of all classes had these public responsibilities and opportunities, the exclusion of women was all the more significant.

The Acropolis was both the religious and civic center of Athens. In its final form it is the work of Pericles and his successors in the late fifth century B.C.E. This photograph shows the Parthenon and to its left the Erechtheum.   Meredith Pillon, Greek National Tourism Organization

The Delian League Becomes the Athenian Empire

In the years after its foundation in the winter of 478–477 B.C.E., the Delian League gradually underwent changes that finally justified calling it the Athenian Empire. In the following selection, the historian Thucydides explains why the organization changed its character.

❖ *Why did some allies choose to pay money rather than supply ships and men? Since membership in the league was originally voluntary, why did the allies refuse to meet their obligations? Who was responsible for converting a voluntary league of allies into the Athenian Empire?*

The causes which led to the defections of the allies were of different kinds, the principal being their neglect to pay the tribute or to furnish ships, and, in some cases, failure of military service. For the Athenians were exacting and oppressive, using coercive measures towards men who were neither willing nor accustomed to work hard. And for various reasons they soon began to prove less agreeable leaders than at first. They no longer fought upon an equality with the rest of the confederates, and they had no difficulty in reducing them when they revolted. Now the allies brought all this upon themselves; for the majority of them disliked military service and absence from home, and so they agreed to contribute a regular sum of money instead of ships. Whereby the Athenian navy was proportionally increased, while they themselves were always untrained and unprepared for war when they revolted.

Thucydides, *The Peloponnesian War*, Vol. 2, trans. by Benjamin Jowett, in *The Greek Historians*, ed. by F. R. B. Godolphin (New York: Random House, 1942), p. 609.

The same sources show that in the private aspects of life women were always under the control of a male guardian—a father, a husband, or some other male relative. Women married young, usually between the ages of twelve and eighteen, whereas their husbands were typically over thirty. In many ways, women's relationships with men were similar to father–daughter relationships. Marriages were arranged; women normally had no choice of husband, and their dowries were controlled by male relatives. Divorce was difficult for women to obtain, for they needed the approval of a male relative who was willing to serve as guardian after the dissolution of the marriage. In case of divorce, the dowry returned with the woman but was controlled by her father or the appropriate male relative.

The main function and responsibility of a respectable Athenian woman of a citizen family was to produce male heirs for the *oikos*, or household, of her husband. If, however, her father's *oikos* lacked a male heir, the daughter became an *epikleros*, the "heiress" to the family property. In that case, she was required by law to marry a relative on her father's side in order to produce the desired male offspring. In the Athenian way of thinking, women were "lent" by one household to another for bearing and raising a male heir to continue the existence of the *oikos*.

Because the pure and legitimate lineage of the offspring was important, women were carefully segregated from men outside the family and were confined to the women's quarters in the house. Men might seek sexual gratification outside the house with prostitutes of high or low style, frequently recruited from abroad. Respectable women stayed home to raise the children, cook, weave cloth, and oversee the management of the household. The only public function of women—an important one—was in the various rituals and festivals of the state religion. Apart from these activities, Athenian women were expected to remain at home out of sight, quiet and unnoticed. Pericles told the widows and mothers of the Athenian men who died in the first year of the Peloponnesian War only this: "Your great glory is not to fall short of your natural character, and the greatest glory of women is to be least talked about by men, whether for good or bad."

The picture of the legal status of women derived from these sources is largely accurate. It does not fit well, however, with other evidence from mythology, from pictorial art, and from the tragedies and comedies by the great Athenian dramatists. These often show women as central characters and powerful figures in both the public and the private spheres, suggesting that the role played by Athenian women may have been more complex than their legal status suggests. In

Athenian Democracy: An Unfriendly View

The following selection comes from an anonymous pamphlet thought to have been written in the midst of the Peloponnesian War. Because it has come down to us among the works of Xenophon, but cannot be his work, it is sometimes called "The Constitution of the Athenians" by Pseudo-Xenophon. It is also common to refer to the unknown author as "The Old Oligarch"—although neither his age nor his purpose is known—because of the obviously antidemocratic tone of the work. Such opinions were common among members of the upper classes in Athens late in the fifth century B.C.E. *and thereafter.*

❖ *What are the author's objections to democracy? Does he describe the workings of the Athenian democracy accurately? How would a defender of the Athenian constitution and way of life meet his complaints? Is there any merit in his criticisms?*

Now, in discussing the Athenian constitution, I cannot commend their present method of running the state, because in choosing it they preferred that the masses should do better than the respectable citizens; this, then, is my reason for not commending it. Since, however, they have made this choice, I will demonstrate how well they preserve their constitution and handle the other affairs for which the rest of the Greeks criticise them.

Again, some people are surprised at the fact that in all fields they give more power to the masses, the poor and the common people than they do to the respectable elements of society, but it will become clear that they preserve the democracy by doing precisely this. When the poor, the ordinary people and the lower classes flourish and increase in numbers, then the power of the democracy will be increased; if, however, the rich and the respectable flourish, the democrats increase the strength of their opponents. Throughout the world the aristocracy are opposed to democracy, for they are naturally least liable to loss of self control and injustice and most meticulous in their regard for what is respectable, whereas the masses display extreme ignorance, indiscipline and wickedness, for poverty gives them a tendency towards the ignoble, and in some cases lack of money leads to their being uneducated and ignorant.

It may be objected that they ought not to grant each and every man the right of speaking in the Ekklesia and serving on the Boule, but only the ablest and best of them; however, in this also they are acting in their own best interests by allowing the mob also a voice. If none but the respectable spoke in the Ekklesia and the Boule, the result would benefit that class and harm the masses; as it is, anyone who wishes rises and speaks, and as a member of the mob he discovers what is to his own advantage and that of those like him.

But someone may say: "How could such a man find out what was advantageous to himself and the common people?" The Athenians realise that this man, despite his ignorance and badness, brings them more advantage because he is well disposed to them than the ill-disposed respectable man would, despite his virtue and wisdom. Such practices do not produce the best city, but they are the best way of preserving democracy. For the common people do not wish to be deprived of their rights in an admirably governed city, but to be free and to rule the city; they are not disturbed by inferior laws, for the common people get their strength and freedom from what you define as inferior laws.

Aristotle and Xenophon on Democracy and Oligarchy, trans. with introductions and commentary by J. M. Moore (Berkeley and Los Angeles: University of California Press, 1975), pp. 37–38. Reprinted by permission of the University of California Press.

Aeschylus's tragedy *Agamemnon*, for example, Clytemnestra arranges the murder of her royal husband and establishes the tyranny of her lover, whom she dominates.

As a famous speech in Euripides' tragedy *Medea* makes clear, we are left with an apparent contradiction. In this speech, Medea paints a bleak picture of

the subjugation of women as dictated by their legal status. (See "Medea Bemoans the Condition of Women.") Yet Medea, as depicted by Euripides, is herself a powerful and terrifying figure who negotiates with kings. She is the central figure in a tragedy bearing her name, produced at state expense before most of the Athenian population and written by one of Athens'

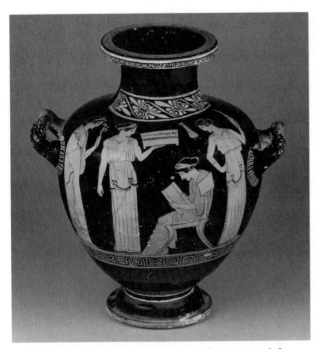

Greek Women at Leisure. Most Greek women of the upper classes appear to have led a secluded and confined existence, but there is some evidence that suggests a somewhat richer social and cultural life. The picture of these women comes from a water-jar of the mid-fifth century B.C.E. Women used them to bring water into the house from wells or fountains, where ancient comedies portray them as gathering and conversing. This scene, however, is indoors, in the women's quarters of the house. The seated woman reads from a scroll; another holds a chest containing other works of literature on scrolls while the remaining two listen attentively. The British Museum

ment. Socrates thought it worth his time to talk with her in the company of his followers and friends. In the dialogue *Menexenus*, Plato jokingly gives her credit for writing Pericles' speeches, including the *Funeral Oration*. There should be no doubt that she was taken seriously by both Pericles and the men in his circle.

In every way, Aspasia represented something very different from Athenian women. She was not a child, not a sheltered and repressed creature confined to the narrow world of slave women, children, and female relatives, but a beautiful, independent, brilliantly witty young woman capable of holding her own in conversation with the best minds in Greece and of discussing and illuminating any kind of question with her husband. There can be no doubt that he loved her dearly and passionately. He took her into his house, and whether or not they were formally and legally married, he treated her as his one and only beloved wife. Each morning when he left home and every evening when he returned, he embraced her and kissed her tenderly, by no means the ordinary greeting between an Athenian man and woman.

For an Athenian to consort with courtesans was normal—to take one into his house and treat her as a concubine, perhaps only a little less so. What was by no means normal, but was shocking and, to many, offensive, was to treat such a woman, a foreigner, as a wife, to lavish such affection on her as few Athenian wives enjoyed, to involve her regularly in conversation with other men, and to discuss important matters with her and treat her opinions with respect. The scandal was immense, and the comic poets made the most of it. Enemies claimed that Pericles was enslaved to a foreign woman who was using her hold over him for political purposes of her own. The Samian War, which arose over a quarrel between Aspasia's native Miletus and Samos, intensified these allegations, for the story spread that Pericles had launched the war at her bidding. After Pericles' death, Aristophanes would pick up these old charges and work them around comically to blame Aspasia for the Peloponnesian War as well.

To some degree, the reality of women's lives in Ancient Greece must have depended on their social and economic status. Poorer women necessarily worked hard at household as well as agricultural tasks and in shops. They also went out to the wells and fountains to fetch water, and both vase paintings and literature show women gathering and chatting at these places. Aristotle asks "How would it be possible to prevent the wives of the poor from going out of doors?"[1] Women of the better classes, however, had no such duties or opportunities. They were more easily and closely supervised. Our

greatest poets and dramatists. She is a cause of terror to the audience and, at the same time, an object of their pity and sympathy as a victim of injustice. She is certainly not, what Pericles recommended in his *Funeral Oration*, "least talked about by men, whether for good or for bad. At the same time, it is important to remember that she is a foreigner with magical powers, by no means a typical Athenian woman."

AN EXCEPTIONAL WOMAN: ASPASIA Pericles' life did not conform to his own prescription. After divorcing his first wife, he entered a liaison that was unique in his time, to a woman who was, in her own way, as remarkable as the great Athenian leader. His companion was Aspasia, a young woman who had left her native Miletus and come to live in Athens. The ancient writers refer to her as a *hetaira*, a kind of high-class courtesan who provided men with both erotic and other kinds of entertainment. She clearly had a keen and lively intellect and may well have been trained in the latest ideas and techniques of discussion in her native city, the home of the Greek enlighten-

[1] Aristotle, *Politics*, 1300a.

Medea Bemoans the Condition of Women

In 431 B.C.E., Euripides (ca. 485–406 B.C.E.) presented his play Medea *at the Festival of Dionysus in Athens. The heroine is a foreign woman who has unusual powers. Her description of the condition of women in the speech that follows, however, appears to be an accurate representation of the condition of women in fifth-century B.C.E. Athens.*

❖ *Apart from participation in politics, how did the lives of men and women differ in ancient Athens? How well or badly did that aspect of Athenian society suit the needs of the Athenian people and the state in the Classical Age? Since men had a dominant position in the state, and the presentation of tragedies was managed and financed by the state, how do you explain the sympathetic account of the condition of women Euripides puts into the mouth of Medea?*

Of all things which are living and can form a
    judgment
We women are the most unfortunate creatures.
Firstly, with an excess of wealth it is required
For us to buy a husband and take for our bodies
A master; for not to take one is even worse.
And now the question is serious whether we
    take
A good or bad one; for there is no easy escape
For a woman, nor can she say no to her mar-
    riage.
She arrives among new modes of behavior and
    manners,
And needs prophetic power, unless she has
    learned at home,
How best to manage him who shares the bed
    with her.
And if we work out all this well and carefully,

And the husband lives with us and lightly bears
    his yoke,
Then life is enviable. If not, I'd rather die.
A man, when he's tired of the company in his
    home,
Goes out of the house and puts an end to his
    boredom
And turns to a friend or companion of his
    own age.
But we are forced to keep our eyes on one alone.
What they say of us is that we have a peace-
    ful time
Living at home, while they do the fighting in
    war.
How wrong they are! I would very much
    rather stand
Three times in the front of battle than bear
    one child.

From Euripides, *Medea in Four Tragedies*, trans. by Rex Warner, copyright ©1955, The Bodley Head. Reprinted by permission of Random House Group, Ltd.

knowledge of the experience of women, however, comes from limited sources that do not always agree. Different scholars arrive at conflicting pictures by emphasizing one kind of a source rather than another. While the legal subordination of women cannot be doubted, the reality of their place in Greek society remains a lively topic of debate.

Slavery

The Greeks had some form of slavery from the earliest times, but true chattel slavery was initially rare. The most common forms of bondage were different kinds of serfdom in relatively backward areas such as Crete, Thessaly, and Sparta. As noted in Chapter 2, the Spartans conquered the natives of their region and reduced them to the status of Helots, subjects who belonged to the Spartan state and worked the land for the benefit of their Spartan masters. Another early form of bondage involving a severe, but rarely permanent, loss of freedom resulted from default in debt. In Athens, however, at about 600 B.C.E., such bondsmen, called *hektemoroi*, were sold outside their native land as true slaves until the reforms of Solon put an end to debt bondage entirely.

True chattel slavery began to increase about 500 B.C.E. and remained important to Greek society thereafter. The main sources of slaves were war captives and the captives of pirates. Like the Chinese, Egyptians, and many other peoples, the Greeks regarded foreigners as inferior, and most slaves working for the Greeks were foreigners. Greeks sometimes enslaved Greeks, but not to serve in their home territories.

The chief occupation of the Greeks, as of most of the world before our century, was agriculture. The great majority of Greek farmers worked small holdings too poor to support even one slave, but some had as many as one or two slaves to work alongside them. The upper classes had larger farms that were let out to free tenant farmers or worked by slaves, generally under an overseer who was himself a slave. Large landowners generally did not have a single great estate, but possessed several smaller farms scattered about the *polis*. This arrangement did not encourage the amassing of great numbers of agricultural slaves such as those who would later work the cotton and sugar plantations of the New World. Industry, however was different.

Larger numbers of slaves labored in industry, especially in mining. Nicias, a wealthy Athenian of the fifth century B.C.E., owned one thousand slaves whom he rented to a mining contractor for profit, but this is by far the largest number known. Most manufacturing was on a very small scale, with shops using one, two, or a handful of slaves. Slaves worked as craftsmen in almost every trade, and, like agricultural slaves on small farms, they worked alongside their masters. A significant proportion of slaves were domestic servants, and many were shepherds. Publicly held slaves served as policemen, prison attendants, clerks, and secretaries.

The number of slaves in ancient Greece and their importance to Greek society are the subjects of controversy. We have no useful figures of the absolute number of slaves or their percentage of the free population in the classical period (fifth and fourth centuries B.C.E.) that range from twenty thousand to one hundred thousand. Accepting the mean between the extremes, sixty thousand, and estimating the free population at its height at about forty thousand households, would yield a figure of fewer than two slaves per family. Estimates suggest that only a quarter to a third of free Athenians owned any slaves at all.

Some historians have noted that in the American South during the period before the Civil War—where slaves made up less than one-third of the total population and three-quarters of free Southerners had no slaves—the proportion of slaves to free citizens was similar to that of ancient Athens. Because slavery was so important to the economy of the South, these historians suggest, it may have been equally important and similarly oppressive in ancient Athens. This argument has several problems.[2] First, it is important to make a distinction between the cotton states of the American South before the Civil War, where a single cash crop, well suited for exploitation by large groups of slaves, dominated the economy and society, and Athens, where the economy was mixed, the

crops varied, and the land and its distribution were poorly suited to massive slavery.

Quite different, too, was the likelihood that a slave would become free. Americans rarely freed their slaves, but in Greece liberation was common. The most famous example is that of the Athenian slave Pasion, who began as a bank clerk, earned his freedom, became Athens' richest banker, and was awarded Athenian citizenship. Such cases were certainly rare, but gaining one's freedom was not.

It is important also to distinguish the American South, where skin color separated slaves from their masters, from the very different society of classical Athens. Southern masters were increasingly hostile to freeing slaves and afraid of slave rebellions, but in Athens slaves walked the streets with such ease that class-conscious Athenians were offended.

Even more remarkable, the Athenians sometimes considered freeing all their slaves. In 406 B.C.E., their city facing defeat in the Peloponnesian War, they freed all slaves of military age and granted citizenship to those who rowed the ships that won the battle of Arginusae. Twice more at crucial moments, similar proposals were made, although without success.

The Great Peloponnesian War

During the first decade after the Thirty Years' Peace of 445 B.C.E., the willingness of each side to respect the new arrangements was tested and not found wanting. About 435 B.C.E., however, a dispute in a remote and unimportant part of the Greek world ignited a long and disastrous war that shook the foundations of Greek civilization.

Causes

The spark that ignited the conflict was a civil war at Epidamnus, a Corcyraean colony on the Adriatic. This civil war caused a quarrel between Corcyra and her mother city and traditional enemy, Corinth, an ally of Sparta. The Corcyraean fleet was second in size only to that of Athens, and the Athenians feared that its capture by Corinth would change the balance of power at sea and seriously threaten Athenian security. As a result, they made an alliance with the previously neutral Corcyra, angering Corinth and leading to a series of crises in the years 433–432 B.C.E. that threatened to bring the Athenian Empire into conflict with the Peloponnesian League.

In the summer of 432 B.C.E., the Spartans met to consider the grievances of their allies. Persuaded, chiefly by the Corinthians, that Athens was an insatiably aggressive power seeking to enslave all the Greeks, they voted for war. The treaty of 445 B.C.E.

---

[2]M.I. Finley, "Was Greek Civilization Based on Slave Labor?," *Historia* 8 (1959): 151.

specifically provided that all differences be submitted to arbitration, and Athens repeatedly offered to arbitrate any question. Pericles insisted that the Athenians refuse to yield to threats or commands and that they uphold the treaty and the arbitration clause. Sparta refused to arbitrate, and in the spring of 431 B.C.E. its army marched into Attica, the Athenian homeland.

Strategic Stalemate

The Spartan strategy was traditional: to invade the enemy's country and threaten the crops, forcing the enemy to defend them in a *hoplite* battle. Such a battle the Spartans were sure to win because they had the better army and they outnumbered the Athenians at least two to one. Any ordinary *polis* would have yielded or fought and lost. Athens, however, had an enormous navy, an annual income from the empire, a vast reserve fund, and long walls that connected the fortified city with the fortified port of Piraeus.

The Athenians' strategy was to allow devastation of their own land to prove that Spartan invasions could not hurt Athens. At the same time, the Athenians launched seaborne raids on the Peloponnesian coast to show that Sparta's allies could be hurt. Pericles expected that within a year or two—three at most—the Peloponnesians would become discouraged and make peace, having learned their lesson. If the Peloponnesians held out, Athenian resources were inadequate to continue for more than four or five years without raising the tribute in the empire and running an unacceptable risk of rebellion.

The plan required restraint and the leadership only a Pericles could provide. In 429 B.C.E., however, in the wake of a devastating plague and a political crisis that had challenged his authority, Pericles died. After his death, no dominant leader emerged to hold the Athenians to a consistent policy. Two factions vied for influence: one, led by Nicias, wanted to continue the defensive policy, and the other, led by Cleon, preferred a more aggressive strategy. In 425 B.C.E., the aggressive faction was able to win a victory that changed the course of the war. Four hundred Spartans surrendered. Sparta offered peace at once to get them back. The great victory and the prestige it brought Athens made it safe to raise the imperial tribute, without which Athens could not continue to fight. The Athenians indeed wanted to continue, for the Spartan peace offer gave no adequate guarantee of Athenian security.

In 424 B.C.E., the Athenians undertook a more aggressive policy. They sought to make Athens safe by conquering Megara and Boeotia. Both attempts failed, and defeat helped discredit the aggressive policy, leading to a truce in 423 B.C.E. Meanwhile, Sparta's ablest

The Great Peloponnesian War	
435 B.C.E.	Civil war at Epidamnus
432 B.C.E.	Sparta declares war on Athens
431 B.C.E.	Peloponnesian invasion of Athens
421 B.C.E.	Peace of Nicias
415–413 B.C.E.	Athenian invasion of Sicily
405 B.C.E.	Battle of Aegospotami
404 B.C.E.	Athens surrenders

general, Brasidas, took a small army to Thrace and Macedonia. He captured Amphipolis, the most important Athenian colony in the region. Thucydides was in charge of the Athenian fleet in those waters and was held responsible for the city's loss. He was exiled and was thereby given the time and opportunity to write his famous history of the Great Peloponnesian War. In 422 B.C.E., Cleon led an expedition to undo the work of Brasidas. At Amphipolis, both he and Brasidas died in battle. The removal of these two leaders of the aggressive factions in their respective cities paved the way for the Peace of Nicias, named for its chief negotiator, which was ratified in the spring of 421 B.C.E.

The Fall of Athens

The peace, officially supposed to last fifty years and, with a few exceptions, guarantee the status quo, was in fact tenuous. Neither side carried out all its commitments, and several of Sparta's allies refused ratification. In 415 B.C.E., Alcibiades persuaded the Athenians to attack Sicily to bring it under Athenian control. This ambitious and unnecessary undertaking ended in disaster in 413 B.C.E. when the entire expedition was destroyed. The Athenians lost some two hundred ships, about 4,500 of their own men, and almost ten times as many allies. It shook Athenian prestige, reduced the power of Athens, provoked rebellions, and brought the wealth and power of Persia into the war on Sparta's side.

It is remarkable that the Athenians could continue fighting in spite of the disaster. They survived a brief oligarchic coup in 411 B.C.E. and won several important victories at sea as the war shifted to the Aegean. Their allies rebelled, however, and were sustained by fleets paid for by Persia. The Athenians saw their financial resources shrink and finally disappear. When their fleet was caught napping and was destroyed at Aegospotami in 405 B.C.E., they could not build another. The Spartans, under Lysander, a clever and ambitious general who was responsible for obtaining Persian support, cut off the food supply through the Hellespont, and the Athenians were starved into submission. In 404 B.C.E. they surrendered unconditionally; the city walls were dismantled, Athens was permitted no fleet, and the empire was gone. The Great Peloponnesian War was over.

Competition for Leadership in the Fourth Century B.C.E.

The defeat of Athens did not bring domination to the Spartans. Instead, the period from 404 B.C.E. until the Macedonian conquest of Greece in 338 B.C.E. was a time of intense rivalry among the Greek cities, each seeking to achieve leadership and control over some or all of the others. Sparta, a recovered Athens, and a newly powerful Thebes were the main competitors in a struggle that ultimately weakened all the Greeks and left them vulnerable to outside influence and control.

The Hegemony of Sparta

The collapse of the Athenian Empire created a vacuum of power in the Aegean and opened the way for Spartan leadership or hegemony. Fulfilling the contract that had brought them the funds to win the war, the Spartans handed the Greek cities of Asia Minor back to Persia. Under the leadership of Lysander, the Spartans went on to make a complete mockery of their promise to free the Greeks by stepping into the imperial role of Athens in the cities along the European coast and the islands of the Aegean. In most of the cities, Lysander installed a board of ten local oligarchs loyal to him and supported them with a Spartan garrison. Tribute brought in an annual revenue almost as great as that the Athenians had collected.

Limited population, the Helot problem, and traditional conservatism all made Sparta a less than ideal state to rule a maritime empire. The increasing arrogance of Sparta's policies alienated some of its allies, especially Thebes and Corinth. In 404 B.C.E. Lysander installed an oligarchic government in Athens, and the outrageous behavior of its leaders earned them the title "Thirty Tyrants." Democratic exiles took refuge in Thebes and Corinth and created an army to challenge the oligarchy. Sparta's conservative king, Pausanias, replaced Lysander, arranging a peaceful settlement and, ultimately, the restoration of democracy. Thereafter, Athenian foreign policy remained under Spartan control, but otherwise Athens was free.

In 405 B.C.E., Darius II of Persia died and was succeeded by Artaxerxes II. His younger brother, Cyrus, contested his rule and received Spartan help in recruiting a Greek mercenary army to help him win

the throne. The Greeks marched inland as far as Mesopotamia, where they defeated the Persians at Cunaxa in 401 B.C.E., but Cyrus was killed in the battle. The Greeks were able to march back to the Black Sea and safety; their success revealed the potential weakness of the Persian Empire.

The Greeks of Asia Minor had supported Cyrus and were now afraid of Artaxerxes' revenge. The Spartans accepted their request for aid and sent an army into Asia, attracted by the prospect of prestige, power, and money. In 396 B.C.E., the command of Sparta's army was given to a new king, Agesilaus. This leader dominated Sparta throughout its period of hegemony and until his death in 360 B.C.E. Some have argued that his consistent advocacy of aggressive policies that provided him with opportunities to display his bravery in battle may have been motivated by a psychological need to compensate for his physical lameness and his disputed claim to the throne.

Agesilaus collected much booty and frightened the Persians. They sent a messenger with money and promises of further support to friendly factions in all of the Greek states likely to help them against Sparta. By 395 B.C.E., Thebes was able to organize an alliance that included Argos, Corinth, and a resurgent Athens. The result was the Corinthian War (395–387 B.C.E.), which put an end to Sparta's Asian adventure. In 394 B.C.E., the Persian fleet destroyed Sparta's maritime empire. Meanwhile, the Athenians took advantage of events to rebuild their walls, to enlarge their navy, and even to recover some of their lost empire in the Aegean. The war ended when the exhausted Greek states accepted a peace dictated by the Great King of Persia.

The Persians, frightened now by the recovery of Athens, turned the management of Greece

The Spartan and Theban Hegemonies	
404–403 B.C.E.	"Thirty Tyrants" rule at Athens
401 B.C.E.	Expedition of Cyrus, rebellious prince of Persia; Battle of Cunaxa
400–387 B.C.E.	Spartan War against Persia
398–360 B.C.E.	Reign of Agesilaus at Sparta
395–387 B.C.E.	Corinthian War
382 B.C.E.	Sparta seizes Thebes
378 B.C.E.	Second Athenian Confederation founded
371 B.C.E.	Thebans defeat Sparta at Leuctra; end of Spartan hegemony
362 B.C.E.	Battle of Mantinea; end of Theban hegemony

Xenophon Recounts How Greece Brought Itself to Chaos

Confusion in Greece in the fourth century B.C.E. reached a climax with the inconclusive Battle of Mantinea in 362 B.C.E. The Theban leader Epaminondas was killed, and no other city or person emerged to provide the needed general leadership for Greece. Xenophon, a contemporary, pointed out the resulting near-chaos in Greek affairs—tempting ground for the soon-to-appear conquering Macedonians under their king Philip II.

❖ *What does this passage reveal about the nature of ancient Greek warfare and the customs surrounding it? How decisive were most battles in ancient Greece? Before the Macedonian conquest of Greece in 338 B.C.E., why was no state able to impose its rule over the others? Why was that possible elsewhere?*

The effective result of these achievements was the very opposite of that which the world at large anticipated. Here, where well-nigh the whole of Hellas was met together in one field, and the combatants stood rank against rank confronted, there was no one who doubted that, in the event of battle, the conquerors this day would rule; and that those who lost would be their subjects. But god so ordered it that both belligerents alike set up trophies as claiming victory, and neither interfered with the other in the act. Both parties alike gave back their enemy's dead under a truce, and in right of victory; both alike, in symbol of defeat, under a truce took back their dead. And though both claimed to have won the day, neither could show that he had thereby gained any accession of territory, or state, or empire, or was better situated than before the battle. Uncertainty and confusion, indeed, had gained ground, being tenfold greater throughout the length and breadth of Hellas after the battle than before.

Xenophon, *Hellenica*, trans. by H. G. Dakyns, in *The Greek Historians*, ed. by F. R. B. Godolphin (New York: Random House, 1942), p. 221.

over to Sparta. Agesilaus broke up all alliances except the Peloponnesian League. He used or threatened to use the Spartan army to interfere in other *poleis* and put friends of Sparta in power within them. Sparta reached a new level of lawless arrogance in 382 B.C.E., when it seized Thebes during peacetime without warning or pretext. In 379 B.C.E., a Spartan army made a similar attempt on Athens. That action persuaded the Athenians to join with Thebes, which had rebelled from Sparta a few months earlier, to wage war on the Spartans.

In 371 B.C.E., the Thebans, led by their great generals Pelopidas and Epaminondas, defeated the Spartans at Leuctra. The Thebans encouraged the Arcadian cities of the central Peloponnesus to form a league, freed the Helots, and helped them found a city of their own. They deprived Sparta of much of its farmland and of the people who worked it and hemmed it in with hostile neighbors. Sparta's population had shrunk so that it could put fewer than 2,000 men into the field at Leuctra. Sparta's aggressive policies had led to ruin. The Theban victory brought the end of Sparta as a power of the first rank.

The Hegemony of Thebes: The Second Athenian Empire

Thebes' power after the its victory at Leuctra lay in its democratic constitution, its control over Boeotia, and its two outstanding and popular generals. One of these generals, Pelopidas, died in a successful attempt to gain control of Thessaly. The other, Epaminondas, consolidated his work, making Thebes dominant over all Greece north of Athens and the Corinthian Gulf and challenging the reborn Athenian Empire in the Aegean. All this activity provoked resistance, and by 362 B.C.E. Thebes faced a Peloponnesian coalition as well as Athens. Epaminondas, once again leading a Boeotian army into the Peloponnesus, confronted this coalition at the Battle of Mantinea. His army was victorious, but Epaminondas himself was killed. With both its great leaders now dead, Theban dominance ended.

The Second Athenian Confederation, which Athens had organized in 378 B.C.E., was aimed at resisting Spartan aggression in the Aegean. Its constitution was careful to avoid the abuses of the Delian League, but the Athenians soon began to repeat them anyway. This time, however, they did not have the power to put down resistance. When the collapse of Sparta and Thebes and the restraint of Persia removed any reason for voluntary membership, Athens' allies revolted. By 355 B.C.E., Athens had to abandon most of the empire. After two centuries of almost continuous warfare, the Greeks returned to the chaotic disorganization that characterized the time before the founding of the Peloponnesian League. (See "Xenophon Recounts How Greece Brought Itself to Chaos.")

The Culture of Classical Greece

The repulse of the Persian invasion released a flood of creative activity in Greece that was rarely, if ever, matched anywhere at any time. The century and a half between the Persian retreat and the conquest of Greece by Philip of Macedon (479–338 B.C.E.) produced achievements of such quality as to justify the designation of that era as the Classical Period. (See "Art & the West.") Ironically, we often use the term "classical" to suggest calm and serenity, but the word that best describes the common element present in Greek life, thought, art, and literature in this period is "tension."

The Fifth Century B.C.E.

Two sources of tension contributed to the artistic outpouring of fifth-century B.C.E. Greece. One arose from the conflict between the Greeks' pride in their accomplishments and their concern that overreaching would bring retribution. Friction among the *poleis* intensified during this period as Athens and Sparta gathered most of them into two competing and menacing blocs. The victory over the Persians brought a sense of exultation in the capacity of humans to accomplish great things and a sense of confidence in the divine justice that had brought low the arrogant pride of Xerxes. But the Greeks recognized that the fate which had met Xerxes awaited all those who reached too far, creating a sense of unease. The second source of tension was the conflict between the soaring hopes and achievements of individuals and the claims and limits put on them by their fellow citizens in the *polis*. These tensions were felt throughout Greece. They had the most spectacular consequences, however, in Athens in its Golden Age, the time between the Persian and the Peloponnesian wars.

ATTIC TRAGEDY Nothing reflects Athens' concerns better than Attic tragedy, which emerged as a major form of Greek poetry in the fifth century B.C.E. The tragedies were presented in a contest as part of the public religious observations in honor of the god Dionysus. The festivals in which they were shown were civic occasions.

Each poet who wished to compete submitted his work to the *archon*. Each offered three tragedies (which might or might not have a common subject) and a satyr play, or comic choral dialogue with Dionysus, to close. The three best competitors were each awarded three actors and a chorus. The actors were paid by the state. The chorus was provided by a wealthy citizen selected by the state to perform this service as *choregos*, for the Athenians had no direct taxation to support such activities. Most of the tragedies were performed in the theater of Dionysus on the south side of the Acropolis, and as many as 30,000 Athenians could attend. Prizes and honors were awarded to the

The Theatre of Dionysus in Athens, seen from the Acropolis. It was here, in contests held in honor of Dionysus, that the great Attic tragedies and comedies were performed for the citizens of Athens.
Meredith Pillon, Greek National Tourism Organization

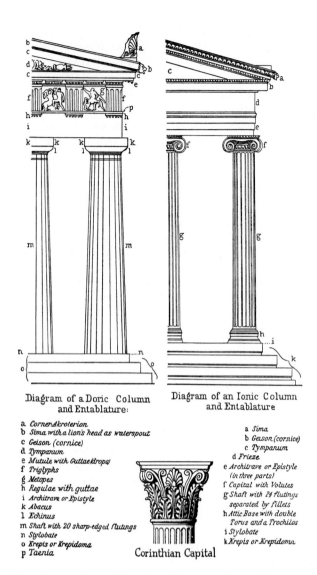

Diagram of a Doric Column and Entablature:

Diagram of an Ionic Column and Entablature

a *Corner Akroterion*
b *Sima with a lion's head as waterspout*
c *Geison (cornice)*
d *Tympanum*
e *Mutule with Guttae (trops)*
f *Triglyphs*
g *Metopes*
h *Regulae with guttae*
i *Architrave or Epistyle*
k *Abacus*
l *Echinus*
m *Shaft with 20 sharp-edged flutings*
n *Stylobate*
o *Krepis or Krepidoma*
p *Taenia*

a *Sima*
b *Geison (cornice)*
c *Tympanum*
d *Frieze*
e *Architrave or Epistyle (in three parts)*
f *Capital with Volutes*
g *Shaft with 24 flutings separated by fillets*
h *Attic Base with double Torus and a Trochilos*
i *Stylobate*
k *Krepis or Krepidoma*

Corinthian Capital

The three orders of Greek architecture, Doric, Ionic, and Corinthian, have had an enduring impact on Western architecture.

The porch of the maidens is part of the Erechtheum on the Athenian Acropolis near the Parthenon. Built between 421 and 409 B.C.E., the Erechtheum housed the shrines of three different gods. In place of the usual fluted columns, the porch uses the statues of young girls taking part in a religious festival. Meredith Pillon, Greek National Tourism Organization

author, the actor, and the *choragus* voted best by a jury of Athenians chosen by lot.

Attic tragedy served as a forum in which the poets raised vital issues of the day, enabling the Athenian audience to think about them in a serious, yet exciting, context. On rare occasions, the subject of a play might be a contemporary or historic event, but almost always it was chosen from mythology. Until late in the century, the tragedies always dealt solemnly with difficult questions of religion, politics, ethics, morality, or some combination of these. The plays of the dramatists Aeschylus and Sophocles, for example, follow this pattern. The plays of Euripides written toward the end of the century are less solemn and more concerned with individual psychology.

OLD COMEDY　Comedy was introduced into the Dionysian festival early in the fifth century B.C.E. Cratinus, Eupolis, and the great master of the genre called Old Comedy, Aristophanes (ca. 450–385 B.C.E.), the only one from whom we have complete plays, wrote political comedies. They were filled with scathing invective and satire against such contemporary figures as Pericles, Cleon, Socrates, and Euripides. (See "Lysistrata Ends the War.")

ARCHITECTURE AND SCULPTURE　The great architectural achievements of Periclean Athens, as much as Athenian tragedy, illustrate the magnificent results of the union and tension between religious and civic responsibilities on the one hand and the transcendent genius of the individual artist on the other. Beginning in 448 B.C.E. and continuing to the outbreak of the Great Peloponnesian War, Pericles undertook a great

Victory and Nobility in Bronze:
The Charioteer of Delphi

This freestanding statue of the *Charioteer of Delphi* is one of the few full-scale bronze sculptures that survive from the fifth century B.C.E. Polyzalus, the tyrant of the Greek city of Gela in Sicily, dedicated it after winning a victory in the chariot race in the Pythian games, either in 478 or 474. The games were held at the sacred shrine of the god Apollo at Delphi, and the statue was placed within the god's sanctuary, not far from Apollo's temple. (See p. 36.) Along with the Olympic games, the Isthmian games at Corinth and the Nemean games were great athletic contests, part of religious celebrations in honor of a god. The winners in these contests were frequently memorialized in poems inspired by their victories, often by the great poet Pindar.

The statue does not represent Polyzalas, who provided the horses, chariots, and equipment, but the professional charioteer whom he hired. It is all that remains of a group that included the chariot, horses, and a groom. It is possible that it also included a statue of Polyzalas himself, standing on the chariot next to the driver. The sculpture probably represented the scene after the race, when the winning chariot moved slowly in a victory procession.

The statue is made in what scholars call the "severe style" that emerged in Greece soon after the Persian invasion of 480–479. Compared with earlier statues from the Archaic period of Greek art, it is simple, without frills, serious, and austere. Unlike the earlier figures, which often wore a smile, the statues of the severe style wear a serious, even "moody," expression. Their sculptors seem to try to present what the Greeks called the *ethos*—the character—of the subject in their work.

One distinguished scholar makes the following observations: "It is easy to see how the charioteer could be taken as an embodiment, in the visual arts, of one of the odes of Pindar. Not only does it celebrate, like the Pythian Ode, a victory won at the festival games at Delphi, but the *ethos* which it conveys is a manifestation of Pindaric *arete*..., the 'innate excellence' of noble natures which gives them proficiency and pride in their human endeavors, but humility before the gods."[3]

[3] J. J. Politt, *Art and Experience in Classical Greece*, Cambridge University Press, Cambridge, 1972, p. 48.

Sources: J. J. Pollitt, *Art and Experience in Classical Greece* (Cambridge: Cambridge University Press, 1972), pp. 15–63. H. W. Janson and Anthony F. Janson, *History of Art*, 5th ed., rev. (Upper Saddle River, NJ: Prentice Hall, 1997), pp. 139–151.

The Charioteer of Delphi. c. 470 B.C.E. Nimatallah/Art Resource, NY

building program on the Acropolis. (See Map 3–3.) The funds were provided by the income from the empire. The new buildings included temples to honor the city's gods and a fitting gateway to the temples. Pericles' main purpose seems to have been to represent visually the greatness and power of Athens, but in such a way as to emphasize intellectual and artistic achievement—civilization rather than military and naval power. It was as though these buildings were tangible proof of Pericles' claim that Athens was "the school of Hellas"—that is, the intellectual center of all Greece.

PHILOSOPHY   The tragic dramas, architecture, and sculpture of the fifth century B.C.E. are all indications of an extraordinary concern with human beings—their capacities, their limits, their nature, and their place in the universe. The same concern is clear in the development of philosophy.

To be sure, some philosophers continued the speculation about the nature of the cosmos (as opposed to human nature) that began with Thales in the sixth century B.C.E. Parmenides of Elea and his pupil Zeno, in opposition to the earlier philosopher Heraclitus, argued that change was only an illusion of the senses. Reason and reflection showed that reality was fixed and unchanging, because it seemed evident that nothing could be created out of nothingness. Empedocles of Acragas further advanced such fundamental speculations by identifying four basic elements: fire, water, earth, and air. Like Parmenides, he thought that reality was permanent, but he thought it not immobile; the four elements, he contended, were moved by two primary forces: love and strife—or, as we might say, attraction and repulsion.

Empedocles' theory is clearly a step on the road to the atomic theory of Leucippus of Miletus and Democritus of Abdera. According to this theory, the world consists of innumerable tiny, solid, indivisible, and unchangeable particles—or "atoms"—that move about in the void. The size of the atoms and the arrangements they form when joined produce the secondary qualities that our senses perceive, such as color and shape. These secondary qualities are merely conventional—the result of human interpretation and agreement—unlike the atoms themselves, which are natural.

Previous to the atomists, Anaxagoras of Clazomenae, an older contemporary and a friend of Pericles, had spoken of tiny fundamental particles called seeds, which were put together on a rational basis by a force called *nous*, or "mind." Anaxagoras was thus suggesting a distinction between matter and mind. The atomists, however, regarded "soul," or mind, as material and believed that everything was guided by purely physical laws. In these conflicting positions,

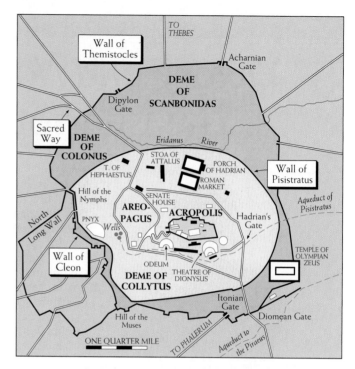

MAP 3–3   ANCIENT ATHENS   *This sketch locates some of the major features of the ancient city of Athens that have been excavated and are visible today. It includes monuments ranging in age from the earliest times to the period of the Roman Empire. The geographical relation of the Acropolis to the rest of the city is apparent, as is that of the Agora, the Areopagus (where the early council of aristocrats met), and the Pnyx (site of assembly for the larger, more democratic meetings of the entire people).*

we have the beginning of the enduring philosophical debate between materialism and idealism.

These speculations were of interest to very few people, and in fact, most Greeks were suspicious of them. A far more influential debate was begun by a group of professional teachers who emerged in the mid-fifth century B.C.E. Called *Sophists*, they traveled about and received pay for teaching such practical techniques of persuasion as rhetoric, dialectic, and argumentation. (Persuasive skills were much valued in democracies like Athens, where so many issues were resolved through open debate.) Some Sophists claimed to teach wisdom and even virtue. Reflecting the human focus characteristic of fifth-century thought, they refrained from speculations about the physical universe, instead applying reasoned analysis to human beliefs and institutions. In doing so, they identified a central problem of human social life and the life of the *polis*: the conflict between nature and custom, or law. The more traditional among them argued that law itself was in accord with nature and was of divine origin, a view that fortified the traditional beliefs of the *polis*.

Others argued, however, that laws were merely the result of convention—an agreement among people—and not in accord with nature. The laws could not pretend to be a positive moral force, but merely had the negative function of preventing people from harming each other. The most extreme Sophists argued that law was contrary to nature, a trick whereby the weak control the strong. Critias, an Athenian oligarch and one of the more extreme Sophists, went so far as to say that the gods themselves had been invented by some clever person to deter people from doing what they wished. Such ideas attacked the theoretical foundations of the *polis* and helped provoke the philosophical responses of Plato and Aristotle in the next century.

HISTORY The first prose literature in the form of history was an account of the Persian War written by Herodotus. "The father of history," as he has been deservedly called, was born shortly before the outbreak of the war. His account goes far beyond all previous chronicles, genealogies, and geographical studies and attempts to explain human actions and to draw instruction from them.

Although his work was completed about 425 B.C.E. and shows a few traces of Sophist influence, its spirit is that of an earlier time. Herodotus accepted the evidence of legends and oracles, although not uncritically, and often explained human events in terms of divine intervention. Human arrogance and divine vengeance are key forces that help explain the defeat of Croesus by Cyrus, as well as Xerxes' defeat by the Greeks. Yet the *History* is typical of its time in celebrating the crucial role of human intelligence as exemplified by Miltiades at Marathon and Themistocles at Salamis. Nor was Herodotus unaware of the importance of institutions. There is no mistaking his pride in the superiority of the Greek *polis* and the discipline it inspired in its citizen soldiers and his pride in the superiority of the Greeks' voluntary obedience to law over the Persians' fear of punishment.

Thucydides, the historian of the Peloponnesian War, was born about 460 B.C.E. and died a few years after the end of the Great Peloponnesian War. He was very much a product of the late fifth century B.C.E. His work, which was influenced by the secular, human-centered, skeptical rationalism of the Sophists, also reflects the scientific attitude of the school of medicine named for his contemporary, Hippocrates of Cos.

The Hippocratic school, known for its pioneering work in medicine and scientific theory, placed great emphasis on an approach to the understanding, diagnosis, and treatment of disease that combined careful observation with reason. In the same way, Thucydides took great pains to achieve factual accuracy and tried to use his evidence to discover meaningful patterns of human behavior. He believed that human nature was essentially unchanging, so that a wise person equipped with the understanding provided by history might accurately foresee events and thus help to guide them. He believed, however, that only a few had the ability to understand history and to put its lessons to good use. He thought that even the wisest could be foiled by the intervention of chance, which played a great role in human affairs. Thucydides focused his interest on politics, and in that area his assumptions about human nature do not seem unwarranted. His work has proved to be, as he hoped, "a possession forever." Its description of the terrible civil war between the two basic kinds of *poleis* is a final and fitting example of the tension that was the source of both the greatness and the decline of Classical Greece.

The Fourth Century B.C.E.

Historians often speak of the Peloponnesian War as the crisis of the *polis* and of the fourth century B.C.E. as the period of its decline. The war did bring powerfully important changes: the impoverishment of some Greek cities and, with it, an intensification of class conflict; the development of professionalism in the army; and demographic shifts that sometimes reduced the citizen population and increased the numbers of resident aliens. The Greeks of the fourth century B.C.E. did not know, however, that their traditional way of life was on the verge of destruction. Still, thinkers could not avoid recognizing that they lived in a time of troubles, and they responded in various ways. Some looked to the past and tried to shore up the weakened structure of the *polis*; others tended toward despair and looked for new solutions; and still others averted their gaze from the public arena altogether. All of these responses are apparent in the literature, philosophy, and art of the period.

DRAMA The tendency of some to turn away from the life of the *polis* and inward to everyday life, the family, and their own individuality is apparent in the poetry of the fourth century B.C.E. A new genre, called Middle Comedy, replaced the political subjects and personal invective of the Old Comedy with a comic–realistic depiction of daily life, plots of intrigue, and mild satire of domestic situations. Significantly, the role of the chorus, which in some way represented the *polis*, was very much diminished. These trends all continued and were carried even further in the New Comedy. Its leading playwright,

Lysistrata Ends the War

Aristophanes, the greatest of the Athenian comic poets, presented the play Lysistrata *in 411 B.C.E., two decades into the Great Peloponnesian War. The central idea of the plot is that the women of Athens, led by Lysistrata, tired of the privations imposed by the war, decide to take matters into their own hands and bring the war to an end. The device they employ is to get the women on both sides to deny their marital favors to their husbands, a kind of sexual strike that quickly achieves its purpose. Before the following passage, Lysistrata has set the terms the Spartans must accept. Next she turns to the Athenians. The play is a masterful example of Athenian Old Comedy, which was almost always full of contemporary and historical political satirical references and sexual and erotic puns and jokes. The references to "Peace" in the stage directions are to an actor playing the goddess Peace.*

❖ *To what historic event does the passage concerning "the Tyrant's days" refer? To what does the "Promontory of Pylos" refer? What was the real role of women in Athenian political life, and what does the play tell us about it? What is the relationship between humor and reality in this play?*

LYSISTRATA
(*Turning to the Athenians*)
—Men of Athens, do you think I'll let you off?
Have you forgotten the Tyrant's days, when you wore
the smock of slavery, when the Spartans turned to the spear,
cut down the pride of Thessaly, despatched the friends
of tyranny, and dispossessed your oppressors?
                                        Recall:
On that great day, your only allies were Spartans;
your liberty came at their hands, which stripped away
your servile garb and clothed you again in Freedom!

SPARTAN
(*Indicating Lysistrata*)
Hain't never seed no higher type of woman.
KINESIAS
(*Indicating Peace*)
Never saw one I wanted so much to top.
LYSISTRATA
(*Oblivious to the byplay, addressing both groups*)
With such a history of mutual benefits conferred
and received, why are you fighting? Stop this wickedness!
Come to terms with each other! What prevents you?
SPARTAN
We'd a heap sight druther make Peace, if we was indemnified with a plumb strategic location.
(*Pointing at Peace's rear*)
                                We'll take thet butte.

Menander (342–291 B.C.E.), completely abandoned mythological subjects in favor of domestic tragicomedy. His gentle satire of the foibles of ordinary people and his tales of lovers temporarily thwarted before a happy and proper ending would not be unfamiliar to viewers of modern situation comedies.

Tragedy faded as a robust and original form. It became common to revive the great plays of the previous century. No tragedies written in the fourth century B.C.E. have been preserved. The plays of Euripides, which rarely won first prize when first produced for Dionysian festival competitions, became increasingly popular in the fourth century and after. Euripides was less interested in

cosmic confrontations of conflicting principles than in the psychology and behavior of individual human beings. Some of his late plays, in fact, are less like the tragedies of Aeschylus and Sophocles than forerunners of later forms such as the New Comedy. Plays like *Helena*, *Andromeda*, and *Iphigenia in Tauris* are more like fairy tales, tales of adventure, or love stories than tragedies.

SCULPTURE   The same movement away from the grand, the ideal, and the general and toward the ordinary, the real, and the individual is apparent in the development of Greek sculpture. To see these developments, one has only to compare the statue of the

LYSISTRATA
Butte?
SPARTAN
The Promontory of Pylos—Sparta's Back Door.
We've missed it fer a turrible spell.
(*Reaching*)

Hev to keep our
hand in.
KINESIAS
(*Pushing him away*)
The price is too high—you'll never take that!
LYSISTRATA
Oh, let them have it.
KINESIAS

What room will we have left
for maneuvers?
LYSISTRATA

Demand another spot in exchange.
KINESIAS
(*Surveying Peace like a map as he addresses
the Spartan*)
Then you hand over to us—uh, let me see—
let's try Thessaly—
(*Indicating the relevant portions of Peace*)

First of all, Easy Mountain ...
then the Maniac Gulf behind it ...

and down to Megara for the legs ...
SPARTAN
You cain't take all of thet! Yore plumb
out of yore mind!
LYSISTRATA
(*To Kinesias*)

Don't argue. Let the legs go.
(*Kinesias nods. A pause, general smiles of
agreement*)

KINESIAS
(*Doffing his cloak*)
I feel an urgent desire to plow a few furrows.
SPARTAN
(*Doffing his cloak*)
Hit's time to work a few loads of fertilizer in.
LYSISTRATA
Conclude the treaty and the simple life is yours.
If such is your decision, convene your councils,
and then deliberate the matter with your allies.
KINESIAS
Deliberate? Allies?

We're over-extended already!
Wouldn't every ally approve of our position—
Union Now?
SPARTAN

I know I kin speak for ourn.
KINESIAS
And I for ours.

They're just a bunch of gigolos.
LYSISTRATA
I heartily approve.
Now first attend to your purification,
then we, the women, will welcome you to the
Citadel
and treat you to all the delights of a home-
cooked banquet.
Then you'll exchange your oaths and pledge
your faith,
and every man of you will take his wife
and depart for home.

Aristophanes, *Lysistrata*, trans. by Douglass Parker, in *Four Comedies by Aristophanes*, ed. by W. Arrowsmith (Ann Arbor: University of Michigan Press, 1969), pp. 79–81. Reprinted by permission of the University of Michigan Press.

Striding God of Artemisium (ca. 460 B.C.E.), thought to be either Zeus on the point of releasing a thunderbolt or Poseidon about to throw his trident, or the Doryphoros of Polycleitus (ca. 450–440 B.C.E.) with the Hermes of Praxiteles (ca. 340–330 B.C.E.) or the Apoxyomenos attributed to Lysippus (ca. 330 B.C.E.).

Philosophy and the Crisis of the *Polis*

SOCRATES   Probably the most complicated response to the crisis of the *polis* may be found in the life and teachings of Socrates (469–399 B.C.E.). Because he wrote nothing, our knowledge of him comes chiefly from his disciples Plato and Xenophon and from later tradition. Although as a young man he was interested in speculations about the physical world, he later turned to the investigation of ethics and morality; as Cicero put it, he brought philosophy down from the heavens. Socrates was committed to the search for truth and for the knowledge about human affairs that he believed could be discovered by reason. His method was to go among men, particularly those reputed to know something, such as craftsmen, poets, and politicians, in order to question and cross-examine them.

The result was always the same. Those Socrates questioned might have technical information and

The striding god from Artemisium is a bronze statue dating from about 460 B.C.E. It was found in the sea near Artemisium, the northern tip of the large Greek island of Euboea, and is now on display in the Athens archaeological museum. Exactly whom he represents is not known. Some have thought him to be Poseidon holding a trident; others believe that he is Zeus hurling a thunderbolt. In either case, he is a splendid representative of the early Classical period of Greek sculpture.
National Archaeological Museum, Athens

This is a Roman copy of the Apoxyomenos (the scraper) by Lysippus of Sicyon. It shows a young athlete scraping from his body the oil used for cleansing after exertion. The original was made about 330 B.C.E. Robert Miller

skills, but seldom had any knowledge of the fundamental principles of human behavior. It is understandable that Athenians so exposed should be angry with their examiner, and it is not surprising that they thought Socrates was undermining the beliefs and values of the *polis*. Socrates' unconcealed contempt for democracy, which seemingly relied on ignorant amateurs to make important political decisions without any certain knowledge, created further hostility. Moreover, his insistence on the primacy of his own individualism and his determination to pursue philosophy even against the wishes of his fellow citizens reinforced this hostility and the prejudice that went with it.

But Socrates, unlike the Sophists, did not accept pay for his teaching; he professed ignorance and denied that he taught at all. His individualism, moreover, was unlike the worldly hedonism of some of the Sophists. It was not wealth or pleasure or power that he urged people to seek, but "the greatest improvement of the soul." He differed also from the more radical Sophists in that he denied that the *polis* and its laws were mere-

ly conventional. He thought, on the contrary, that they had a legitimate claim on the citizen, and he proved it in the most convincing fashion.

In 399 B.C.E., he was condemned to death by an Athenian jury on the charges of bringing new gods into the city and of corrupting the youth. His dialectical inquiries had angered many important people. His criticism of democracy must have been viewed with suspicion, especially as Critias and Charmides, who were members of the Thirty Tyrants, and the traitor Alcibiades had been among his disciples. He was given a chance to escape but, as we are told in Plato's *Crito*, he refused to do so because of his veneration of the laws. Socrates' career set the stage for later responses to the travail of the *polis*. He recognized its difficulties and criticized its shortcomings, and he turned away from an active political life, but he did not abandon the idea of the *polis*. He fought as a soldier in its defense, obeyed its laws, and sought to put its values on a sound foundation by reason.

THE CYNICS One branch of Socratic thought—the concern with personal morality and one's own soul, the disdain of worldly pleasure and wealth, and the withdrawal from political life—was developed and then distorted almost beyond recognition by the Cynic school. Antisthenes (ca. 455–360 B.C.E.), a follower of Socrates, is said to have been its founder, but its most famous exemplar was Diogenes of Sinope (ca. 400–325 B.C.E.). Because Socrates disparaged wealth and worldly comfort, Diogenes wore rags and lived in a tub. He performed shameful acts in public and made his living by begging to show his rejection of convention. He believed that happiness lay in satisfying natural needs in the simplest and most direct way; because actions to this end, being natural, could not be indecent, they could and should be done publicly.

Socrates questioned the theoretical basis for popular religious beliefs; the Cynics, in contrast, ridiculed all religious observances. As Plato said, Diogenes was Socrates gone mad. Beyond that, the way of the Cynics contradicted important Socratic beliefs. Socrates, unlike traditional aristocrats such as Theognis, believed that virtue was a matter not of birth, but of knowledge and that people do wrong only through ignorance of what is virtuous. The Cynics, on the other hand, believed that "virtue is an affair of deeds and does not need a store of words and learning."[4] Wisdom and happiness come from pursuing the proper style of life, not from philosophy.

The Cynics moved even further away from Socrates by abandoning the concept of the *polis* entirely. When Diogenes was asked about his citizenship, he answered that he was *kosmopolites*, a citizen of the world. The Cynics plainly had turned away from the past, and their views anticipated those of the Hellenistic Age.

PLATO Plato (429–347 B.C.E.) was by far the most important of Socrates' associates and is a perfect example of the pupil who becomes greater than his master. He was the first systematic philosopher and therefore the first to place political ideas in their full philosophical context. He was also a writer of genius, leaving us twenty-six philosophical discussions. Almost all are in the form of dialogues, which

somehow make the examination of difficult and complicated philosophical problems seem dramatic and entertaining. Plato came from a noble Athenian family, and he looked forward to an active political career until the excesses of the Thirty Tyrants and the execution of Socrates discouraged him from that pursuit. Twice he made trips to Sicily in the hope of producing a model state at Syracuse under the tyrants Dionysius I and II, but without success.

In 386 B.C.E., he founded the Academy, a center of philosophical investigation and a school for training statesmen and citizens. It had a powerful impact on Greek thought and lasted until it was closed by the emperor Justinian in the sixth century C.E.

Like Socrates, Plato firmly believed in the *polis* and its values. Its virtues were order, harmony, and justice, and one of its main objects was to produce good people. Like his master, and unlike the radical Sophists, Plato thought that the *polis* was in accord with nature. He accepted Socrates' doctrine of the identity of virtue and knowledge. He made it plain what that knowledge was: *episteme*—science—a body of true and unchanging wisdom open to only a few philosophers, whose training, character, and intellect allowed them to see reality. Only such people were qualified to rule; they would prefer the life of pure contemplation, but would accept their responsibility and take their turn as philosopher kings. The training of such an individual required a specialization of function and a subordination of that individual to the community even greater than that at Sparta. This specialization would lead to Plato's definition of justice: that each person should do only that one thing to which his or her nature is best suited. (See "Plato on the Role of Women in His Utopian Republic.")

Plato saw quite well that the *polis* of his day suffered from terrible internal stress, class struggle, and factional divisions. His solution, however, was not that of some Greeks—that is, conquest and resulting economic prosperity. For Plato, the answer was in moral and political reform. The way to harmony was to destroy the causes of strife: private property, the family—anything, in short, that stood between the individual citizen and devotion to the *polis*.

Concern for the redemption of the polis was at the heart of Plato's system of philosophy. He began by asking the traditional questions: What is a good man, and how is he made? The goodness of a human being belonged to moral philosophy, and when goodness became a function of the state, it became political philosophy. Because goodness depended on knowledge of the good, it required a theory of knowledge and an investigation of what kind of knowledge was required for goodness. The answer must be metaphysical and so required a full examination of metaphysics. Even when the philosopher knew the good,

---

[4]Diogenes Laertius, *Life of Antisthenes*, 6.11.

however, the question remained how the state could bring its citizens to the necessary comprehension of that knowledge. The answer required a theory of education. Even purely logical and metaphysical questions, therefore, were subordinate to the overriding political questions. In this way, Plato's need to find a satisfactory foundation for the beleaguered polis contributed to the birth of systematic philosophy.

ARISTOTLE   Aristotle (384–322 B.C.E.) was a pupil of Plato's and owed much to the thought of his master, but his very different experience and cast of mind led him in some new directions. He was born at Stagirus in the Chalcidice, the son of the court doctor of neighboring Macedon. As a young man, he went to Athens to study at the Academy, where he stayed until Plato's death. Then he joined a Platonic colony at Assos in Asia Minor, and from there he moved to Mytilene. In both places he did research in marine biology, and biological interests played a large part in all his thoughts. In 342 B.C.E., Philip, the king of Macedon, appointed him tutor to his son, the young Alexander. (See the next section.)

In 336 B.C.E. Aristotle returned to Athens, where he founded his own school, the Lyceum, or the Peripatos, as it was also called because of the covered walk within it. In later years its members were called *Peripatetics*. On the death of Alexander in 323 B.C.E., the Athenians rebelled from Macedonian rule, and Aristotle found it wise to leave. He died at Chalcis in Euboea in the following year.

The Lyceum was a very different place from the Academy. Its members took little interest in mathematics and were concerned with gathering, ordering, and analyzing all human knowledge. Aristotle wrote dialogues on the Platonic model, but none survive. He and his students also prepared many collections of information to serve as the basis for scientific works. Of these, only the *Constitution of the Athenians*, one of 158 constitutional treatises, remains. Almost all of what we possess is in the form of philosophical and scientific studies, whose loose organization and style suggest that they were lecture notes. The range of subjects treated is astonishing, including logic, physics, astronomy, biology, ethics, rhetoric, literary criticism, and politics.

In each field, the method is the same. Aristotle began with observation of the empirical evidence, which in some cases was physical and in others was common opinion. To this body of information he applied reason and discovered inconsistencies or difficulties. To deal with these, he introduced metaphysical principles to explain the problems or to reconcile the inconsistencies.

Marble head of Aristotle. Louvre, Dept. des Antiquities Grecques/Romaines, Paris, France. © Photograph by Erich Lessing/ Art Resource, NY

His view on all subjects, like Plato's, was teleological; that is, both Plato and Aristotle recognized purposes apart from and greater than the will of the individual human being. Plato's purposes, however, were contained in ideas, or forms that were transcendental concepts outside the experience of most people. For Aristotle, the purposes of most things were easily inferred by observation of their behavior in the world. Aristotle's most striking characteristics are his moderation and his common sense. His epistemology finds room for both reason and experience; his metaphysics gives meaning and reality to both mind and body; his ethics aims at the good life, which is the contemplative life, but recognizes the necessity for moderate wealth, comfort, and pleasure.

All these qualities are evident in Aristotle's political thought. Like Plato, he opposed the Sophists' assertion that the *polis* was contrary to nature and the result of mere convention. His response was to apply the teleology he saw in all nature to politics as well. In his view, matter existed to achieve an end, and it developed until it achieved its form, which was its end. There was constant development from matter to form, from potential to actual. Therefore, human primitive instincts could be seen as the matter out of which the human's potential as a political being could be realized. The

Plato on the Role of Women in His Utopian Republic

The Greek invention of reasoned intellectual analysis of all things led the philosopher Plato to consider the problem of justice, which is the subject of his most famous dialogue, the Republic. *This leads him to sketch out a utopian state in which justice may be found and where the most radical arrangements may be necessary. These include the equality of the sexes and the destruction of the family in favor of the practice of men having wives and children in common. In the following excerpts, he argues for the fundamental equality of men and women and that women are no less appropriate as Guardians—leaders of the state— than men.*

❖ *What are Plato's reasons for treating men and women the same? What objections could be raised to that practice? Would that policy, even if appropriate in Plato's utopia, also be suitable to conditions in the real world of classical Athens? In the world of today?*

"If, then, we use the women for the same things as the men, they must also be taught the same things."

"Yes."

"Now music and gymnastics were given to the men."

"Yes."

"Then these two arts, and what has to do with war, must be assigned to the women also, and they must be used in the same ways."

"On the basis of what you say," he said, "it's likely."

"Perhaps," I said, "compared to what is habitual, many of the things now being said would look ridiculous if they were to be done as is said."

"Indeed they would," he said.

"Well," I said, "since we've started to speak, we mustn't be afraid of all the jokes—of whatever kind—the wits might make if such a change took place in gymnastic, in music and, not the least, in the bearing of arms and the riding of horses."

"Then," I said, "if either the class of men or that of women show its superiority in some art or other practice, then we'll say that that art must be assigned to it. But if they look as though they differ in this along, that the female bears and the male mounts, we'll assert that it has not thereby yet been proved that a woman differs from a man with respect to what we're talking about; rather, we'll still suppose that our guardians and their women must practice the same things."

"And rightly," he said.

"Therefore, my friend, there is no practice of a city's governors which belongs to woman because she's woman, or to man because he's man; but the natures are scattered alike among both animals; and woman participates according to nature in all practices, and man in all, but in all of them woman is weaker than man."

"Certainly."

"So, shall we assign all of them to men and none to women?"

"How could we?"

"For I suppose there is, as we shall assert, one woman apt at medicine and another not, one woman apt at music and another unmusical by nature."

"Of course."

"And isn't there then also one apt at gymnastic and at war, and another unwarlike and no lover of gymnastic?"

"I suppose so."

"And what about this? Is there a lover of wisdom and a hater of wisdom? And one who is spirited and another without spirit?"

"Yes, there are these too."

"There is, therefore one woman fit for guarding and another not, or wasn't it a nature of this sort we also selected for the men fit for guarding?"

"Certainly, that was it."

polis made individuals self-sufficient and allowed the full realization of their potentiality. It was therefore natural.

It was also the highest point in the evolution of the social institutions that serve the human need to continue the species—marriage, household, village, and, finally, *polis*. For Aristotle, the purpose of the *polis* was neither economic nor military, but moral. According to Aristotle, "The end of the state is the good life" (*Politics* 1280b), the life lived "for the sake of noble actions" (1281a), a life of virtue and morality.

Characteristically, Aristotle was less interested in the best state—the utopia that required philosophers to rule it—than in the best state that was practically possible, one that would combine justice with stability. The constitution for that state he called *politeia*, not the best constitution, but the next best, the one most suited to, and most possible for most states. Its quality was moderation, and it naturally gave power to neither the rich nor the poor, but to the middle class, which must also be the most numerous. The middle class possessed many virtues; because of its moderate wealth, it was free of the arrogance of the rich and the malice of the poor. For this reason, it was the most stable class.

The stability of the constitution also came from its being a mixed constitution, blending in some way the laws of democracy and of oligarchy. Aristotle's scheme was unique because of its realism and the breadth of its vision. All the political thinkers of the fourth century B.C.E. recognized that the *polis* was in danger, and all hoped to save it. All recognized the economic and social troubles that threatened it. Isocrates, a contemporary of Plato and Aristotle, urged a program of imperial conquest as a cure for poverty and revolution. Plato saw the folly of solving a political and moral problem by purely economic means and resorted to the creation of utopias. Aristotle combined the practical analysis of political and economic realities with the moral and political purposes of the traditional defenders of the *polis*. The result was a passionate confidence in the virtues of moderation and of the middle class and the proposal of a constitution that would give it power. It is ironic that the ablest defense of the *polis* came soon before its demise.

The Hellenistic World

The term "Hellenistic" was coined in the nineteenth century to describe the period of three centuries during which Greek culture spread far from its homeland to Egypt and far into Asia. The new civilization formed in this expansion was a mixture of Greek and Near Eastern elements, although the degree of mixture varied from time to time and place to place. The Hellenistic world was larger than the world of Classical Greece, and its major political units were much larger than the city–states, though these persisted in different forms. The new political and cultural order had its roots in the rise to power of a Macedonian dynasty that conquered Greece and the Persian Empire in the space of two generations.

The Macedonian Conquest

The quarrels among the Greeks brought on defeat and conquest by a new power that suddenly rose to eminence in the fourth century B.C.E.: the kingdom of Macedon. The Macedonians inhabited the land to the north of Thessaly (see Map 3–1), and through the centuries they had unknowingly served the vital purpose of protecting the Greek states from barbarian tribes further to the north.

By Greek standards, Macedon was a backward, semibarbaric land. It had no *poleis* and was ruled loosely by a king in a rather Homeric fashion. He was chosen partly on the basis of descent, but the acclamation of the army gathered in assembly was required to make him legitimate. Quarrels between pretenders to the throne and even murder to secure it were not uncommon. A council of nobles checked the royal power and could reject a weak or incompetent king. Hampered by constant wars with the barbarians, internal strife, loose organization, and lack of money, Macedon played no great part in Greek affairs up to the fourth century B.C.E.

The Macedonians were of the same stock as the Greeks and spoke a Greek dialect, and the nobles, at least, thought of themselves as Greeks. The kings claimed descent from Heracles and the royal house of Argos. They tried to bring Greek culture into their court and won acceptance at the Olympic games. If a king could be found to unify this nation, it was bound to play a greater part in Greek affairs.

PHILIP OF MACEDON   That king was Philip II (r. 359–336 B.C.E.), who, while still under thirty, took advantage of his appointment as regent to overthrow his infant nephew and make himself king. Like many of his predecessors, he admired Greek culture. Between 367 and 364 B.C.E. he had been a hostage in Thebes, where he learned much about Greek politics and warfare under the tutelage of Epaminondas. His talents for war and diplomacy and his boundless ambition made him the ablest king in Macedonian history. Using both diplomatic and military means, he was able to pacify the tribes on his frontiers and make his own hold on the throne firmer. Then he began to undermine Athenian control of the northern Aegean. He took Amphipolis, which gave him control of the Strymon Valley and of the gold and silver mines of Mount Pangaeus. The income allowed him to found new cities, to bribe politicians in foreign towns, and to reorganize his army into the finest fighting force in the world.

THE MACEDONIAN ARMY Philip put to good use what he had learned in Thebes and combined it with the advantages afforded by Macedonian society and tradition. His genius created a versatile and powerful army that was at once national and professional, unlike the amateur armies of citizen–soldiers who fought for the individual *poleis*.

The infantry was drawn from among Macedonian farmers and the frequently rebellious Macedonian hill people. In time, these two elements were integrated to form a loyal and effective national force. Infantrymen were armed with thirteen-foot pikes instead of the more common nine-foot pikes and stood in a more open phalanx formation than the

hoplite phalanx of the *poleis*. The effectiveness of this formation depended more on skillful use of the pike than the weight of the charge. In Macedonian tactics, the role of the phalanx was not to be the decisive force, but to hold the enemy until a massed cavalry charge could strike a winning blow on the flank or into a gap. The cavalry was made up of Macedonian nobles and clan leaders, called Companions, who lived closely with the king and developed a special loyalty to him.

Philip also employed mercenaries who knew the latest tactics used by mobile light-armed Greek troops and were familiar with the most sophisticated siege machinery known to the Greeks. With these mercenaries, and with draft forces from among his allies, he could expand on his native Macedonian army of as many as 40,000 men.

THE INVASION OF GREECE So armed, Philip turned south toward central Greece. Since 355 B.C.E., the Phocians had been fighting against Thebes and Thessaly. Philip gladly accepted the request of the Thessalians to be their general, defeated Phocis, and treacherously took control of Thessaly. Swiftly he

Demosthenes Denounces Philip of Macedon

Demosthenes (384–322 B.C.E.) was an Athenian statesman who urged his fellow citizens and other Greeks to resist the advance of Philip of Macedon (r. 359–336 B.C.E.). This passage is from the speech we call the First Philippic, *probably delivered in 351 B.C.E.*

❖ *Whom does Demosthenes blame for the danger facing Athens? What hope does he see of stopping Philip's advance? How important is Philip himself, according to Demosthenes, as a source of the menace to Athens and the rest of Greece?*

Do not imagine, that his empire is everlastingly secured to him as a god. There are those who hate and fear and envy him, Athenians, even among those that seem most friendly; and all feelings that are in other men belong, we may assume, to his confederates. But now they are cowed, having no refuge through your tardiness and indolence, which I say you must abandon forthwith. For you see, Athenians, the case, to what pitch of arrogance the man has advanced, who leaves you not even the choice of action or inaction, but threatens and uses (they say) outrageous language, and, unable to rest in possession of his conquests, continually widens their circle, and whilst we dally and delay, throws his net all around us.

When then, Athenians, when will ye act as becomes you? In what event? In that of necessity, I suppose. And how should we regard the events happening now? Methinks, to freemen the strongest necessity is the disgrace of their condition. Or tell me, do ye like walking about and asking one another:—is there any news? Why, could there be greater news than a man of Macedonia subduing Athenians, and directing the affairs of Greece? Is Philip dead? No, but he is sick. And what matters it to you? Should anything befall this man, you will soon create another Philip, if you attend to business thus. For even he has been exalted not so much by his own strength, as by our negligence.

Demosthenes, *The Olynthiac and Other Public Orations of Demosthenes* (London: George Bell and Sons, 1903), pp. 62–63.

turned northward again to Thrace and gained domination over the northern Aegean coast and the European side of the straits to the Black Sea. This conquest threatened the vital interests of Athens, which still had a formidable fleet of 300 ships.

The Athens of 350 B.C.E. was not the Athens of Pericles. It had neither imperial revenue nor allies to share the burden of war on land or sea, and its own population was smaller than in the fifth century B.C.E. The Athenians, therefore, were reluctant to go on expeditions themselves or even to send out mercenary armies under Athenian generals, for they had to be paid out of taxes or contributions from Athenian citizens.

The leading spokesman against these tendencies and the cautious foreign policy that went with them was Demosthenes (384–322 B.C.E.), one of the greatest orators in Greek history. He was convinced that Philip was a dangerous enemy to Athens and the other Greeks. He spent most of his career urging the Athenians to resist Philip's encroachments. (See "Demosthenes Denounces Philip of Macedon.") He was right, for beginning in 349 B.C.E., Philip attacked several cities in northern and central Greece and firmly planted Macedonian power in those regions. The king of "barbarian" Macedon was elected president of the Pythian Games at Delphi, and the Athenians were forced to concur in the election.

In these difficult times it was Athens' misfortune not to have the kind of consistent political leadership that Cimon or Pericles had offered a century earlier. Many, perhaps most, Athenians accepted Demosthenes' view of Philip, but few were willing to run the risks and make the sacrifices necessary to stop his advance. Others, like Eubulus, an outstanding financial official and conservative political leader, favored a cautious policy of cooperation with Philip in the hope that his aims were limited and were no real threat to Athens.

Not all Athenians feared Philip. Isocrates (436–338 B.C.E.), the head of an important rhetorical and philosophical school in Athens, looked to him to provide the unity and leadership needed for a Panhellenic campaign against Persia. He and other orators had been urging such a campaign for some years. They saw the conquest of Asia Minor as the solution to the economic, social, and political problems that had brought poverty and civil war to the Greek cities ever since the Peloponnesian War. Finally, there seem to have been some Athenians who were in the pay of Philip, for he used money lavishly to win support in all the cities.

The years between 346 B.C.E. and 340 B.C.E. were spent in diplomatic maneuvering, each side trying to win strategically useful allies. At last, Philip attacked Perinthus and Byzantium, the lifeline of Athenian commerce; in 340 B.C.E. he besieged both cities and declared war. The Athenian fleet saved both, and so in the following year Philip marched into Greece. Demosthenes performed wonders in rallying the Athenians and winning Thebes over to the Athenian side. In 338 B.C.E., however, Philip defeated the allied forces at Chaeronea in Boeotia. The decisive blow in this great battle was a cavalry charge led by the eighteen-year-old son of Philip, Alexander.

THE MACEDONIAN GOVERNMENT OF GREECE The Macedonian settlement of Greek affairs was not as harsh as many had feared, although in some cities the friends of Macedon came to power and killed or exiled their enemies. Demosthenes remained free to engage in politics. Athens was spared from attack on the condition that it give up what was left of its empire and follow the lead of Macedon. The rest of Greece was arranged in such a way as to remove all dangers to Philip's rule. To guarantee his security, Philip placed garrisons at Thebes, Chalcis, and Corinth.

In 338 B.C.E., Philip called a meeting of the Greek states to form the federal League of Corinth. The constitution of the league provided for autonomy, freedom from tribute and garrisons, and suppression of piracy and civil war. The league delegates would make foreign policy in theory without consulting their home governments or Philip. All this was a facade; not only was Philip of Macedon president of the league, but he was its ruler. The defeat at Chaeronea ended Greek freedom and autonomy. Although it maintained its form and way of life for some time, the *polis* had lost control of its own affairs and the special conditions that had made it unique.

Philip did not choose Corinth as the seat of his new confederacy simply from convenience or by accident. It was at Corinth that the Greeks had gathered to resist a Persian invasion almost 150 years earlier. And it was there in 337 B.C.E. that Philip announced his intention to invade Persia in a war of liberation and revenge as leader of the new league. In the spring of 336 B.C.E., however, as he prepared to begin the campaign, Philip was assassinated.

In 1977, a mound was excavated at the Macedonian village of Vergina. The structures that were revealed and the extraordinarily rich finds associated with them have led many scholars to conclude that this is the royal tomb of Philip II, and the evidence seems persuasive that they are right. Philip certainly deserved so distinguished a resting place. He found Macedon a disunited kingdom of semi-barbarians, despised and exploited by the Greeks. He left it a united kingdom, master and leader of the Greeks, rich, powerful, and ready to undertake the invasion of Asia.

Alexander the Great

Philip's first son, Alexander III (356–323 B.C.E.), later called Alexander the Great, succeeded his father at the age of twenty. Along with the throne, the young king inherited his father's daring plans for the conquest of Persia.

THE CONQUEST OF THE PERSIAN EMPIRE The Persian Empire was vast and its resources enormous. The usurper Cyrus and his Greek mercenaries, however, had shown it to be vulnerable when they penetrated deep into its interior in the fourth century B.C.E. Its size and disparate nature made it hard to control and exploit. Its rulers faced constant troubles on its far-flung frontiers and constant intrigues within the royal palace. Throughout the fourth century B.C.E. they had called on Greek mercenaries to suppress uprisings. At the time of Philip II's death in 336 B.C.E., Persia was ruled by a new and inexperienced king, Darius III. Yet with a navy that dominated the sea, a huge army, and vast wealth, it remained a formidable opponent.

In 334 B.C.E., Alexander crossed the Hellespont into Asia. His army consisted of about 30,000 infantry and 5,000 cavalry; he had no navy and little money. These facts determined his early strategy—he must seek quick and decisive battles to gain money and supplies from the conquered territory, and he must move along the coast to neutralize the Persian navy by depriving it of ports. Memnon, the commander of the Persian navy, recommended the perfect strategy against this plan: to retreat, to scorch the earth and deprive Alexander of supplies, to avoid battles, to use guerrilla tactics, and to stir up rebellion in Greece. He was ignored. The Persians preferred to stand and fight; their pride and courage were greater than their wisdom.

Alexander met the Persian forces of Asia Minor at the Granicus River, where he won a smashing victory in characteristic style. (See Map 3–4.) He led a cavalry charge across the river into the teeth of the enemy on the opposite bank. He almost lost his life in the process, but he won the devotion of his soldiers. That victory left the coast of Asia Minor open. Alexander captured the coastal cities, thus denying them to the Persian fleet.

In 333 B.C.E., Alexander marched inland to Syria, where he met the main Persian army under King Darius at Issus. Alexander himself led the cavalry charge that broke the Persian line and sent Darius fleeing into central Asia Minor. He continued along the coast and captured previously impregnable Tyre after a long and ingenious siege, putting an end to the threat of the Persian navy. He took Egypt with little trouble and was greeted as liberator, pharaoh, and son of Re (an Egyptian god whose Greek equivalent was Zeus).

At Tyre, Darius sent Alexander a peace offer, yielding his entire empire west of the Euphrates River and his daughter in exchange for an alliance and an end to the invasion. But Alexander aimed at conquering the whole empire and probably whatever lay beyond.

In the spring of 331 B.C.E., Alexander marched into Mesopotamia. At Gaugamela, near the ancient Assyrian city of Nineveh, he met Darius, ready for a last stand. Once again, Alexander's tactical genius and personal leadership carried the day. The Persians were broken, and Darius fled

This sculpture of Alexander the Great, king of Macedon and conqueror of the Persian Empire, was made in the second century B.C.E. and found at the ancient city of Magnesia in Asia Minor. Alexander's conquests spread Greek culture far from its homeland, laying the foundation of the Hellenistic world. Statue from Magnesia ad Sipylum. Archeological Museum, Istanbul, Turkey. Erich Lessing/Art Resource, N.Y.

once more. Alexander entered Babylon, again hailed as liberator and king.

In January of 330 B.C.E. he came to Persepolis, the Persian capital, which held splendid palaces and the royal treasury. This bonanza ended his financial troubles and put a vast sum of money into circulation, with economic consequences that lasted for centuries. After a stay of several months, Alexander burned Persepolis to dramatize the destruction of the native Persian dynasty and the completion of Hellenic revenge for the earlier Persian invasion of Greece.

The new regime could not be secure while Darius lived, so Alexander pursued him eastward. Just south of the Caspian Sea, he came upon the corpse of Darius, killed by his relative Bessus. The Persian nobles around Darius had lost faith in him and had joined in the plot. The murder removed Darius from Alexander's path, but now he had to catch Bessus, who proclaimed himself successor to Darius. The pursuit of Bessus (who was soon caught), combined with his own great curiosity and longing to go to the most distant places, took Alexander to the frontier of India.

Near Samarkand, in the land of the Scythians, he founded Alexandria Eschate ("Furthest Alexandria"), one of the many cities bearing his name that he founded as he traveled. As part of his grand scheme of amalgamation and conquest, he married the Bactrian princess Roxane and enrolled 30,000 young Bactrians into his army. These were to be trained and sent back to the center of the empire for later use.

In 327 B.C.E., Alexander took his army through the Khyber Pass in an attempt to conquer the lands around the Indus River (modern Pakistan). He reduced the king of these lands, Porus, to vassalage, but pushed on in the hope of reaching the river called Ocean that the Greeks believed encircled the world. Finally, his weary men refused to go on. By the spring of 324 B.C.E., the army was back at the Persian Gulf and celebrated in the Macedonian style, with a wild spree of drinking.

THE DEATH OF ALEXANDER   Alexander was filled with plans for the future: for the consolidation and organization of his empire; for geographical exploration; for building new cities, roads, and harbors; and perhaps even for further conquests in the west. There is even some evidence that he asked to be deified and worshiped as a god, although we cannot be sure if he really did so or why. In June of 323 B.C.E., however, he was overcome by a fever and died in Babylon at the age of thirty-three. His memory has never faded, and he soon became the subject of myth, legend, and romance. From the beginning, estimates of him have varied. Some have seen in him a man of grand and noble vision who transcended the narrow limits of Greek and Macedonian ethnocentrism and sought to realize the solidarity of hu-

mankind in a great world state. Others have seen him as a calculating despot, given to drunken brawls, brutality, and murder.

The truth is probably somewhere in between. Alexander was one of the greatest generals the world has seen; he never lost a battle or failed in a siege, and with a modest army he conquered a vast empire. He had rare organizational talents, and his plan for creating a multinational empire was the only intelligent way to consolidate his conquests. He established many new cities—seventy, according to tradition—mostly along trade routes. These cities had the effect of encouraging commerce and prosperity, as well as of introducing Hellenic civilization into new areas. It is hard to know if even Alexander could have held together the vast new empire he had created, but his death proved that only he would have had a chance to succeed.

The Successors

Nobody was prepared for Alexander's sudden death in 323 B.C.E., and affairs were further complicated by a weak succession: Roxane's unborn child and Alexander's weak-minded half-brother. His able and loyal Macedonian generals at first hoped to preserve the empire for the Macedonian royal house, and to this end they appointed themselves governors of the various provinces of the empire. The conflicting ambitions of these strong-willed men, however, led to prolonged warfare among various combinations of them. In these conflicts three of the original number were killed, and all of the direct members of the Macedonian royal house were either executed or murdered. With the murder of Roxane and her son in 310 B.C.E., there was no longer any focus for the enormous empire, and in 306 and 305 B.C.E. the surviving governors proclaimed themselves kings of their various holdings.

Three of these Macedonian generals founded dynasties of significance in the spread of Hellenistic culture:

- Ptolemy I, 367–283 B.C.E.; founder of the Thirty-First Dynasty in Egypt, the Ptolemies, of whom Cleopatra, who died in 30 B.C.E., was the last
- Seleucus I, 358–280 B.C.E.; founder of the Seleucid Dynasty in Mesopotamia
- Antigonus I, 382–301 B.C.E.; founder of the Antigonid Dynasty in Asia Minor and Macedon

For the first seventy-five years or so after the death of Alexander, the world ruled by his successors enjoyed considerable prosperity. The vast sums of money that he and they put into circulation greatly increased the level of economic activity. The opportunities for service and profit in the East attracted

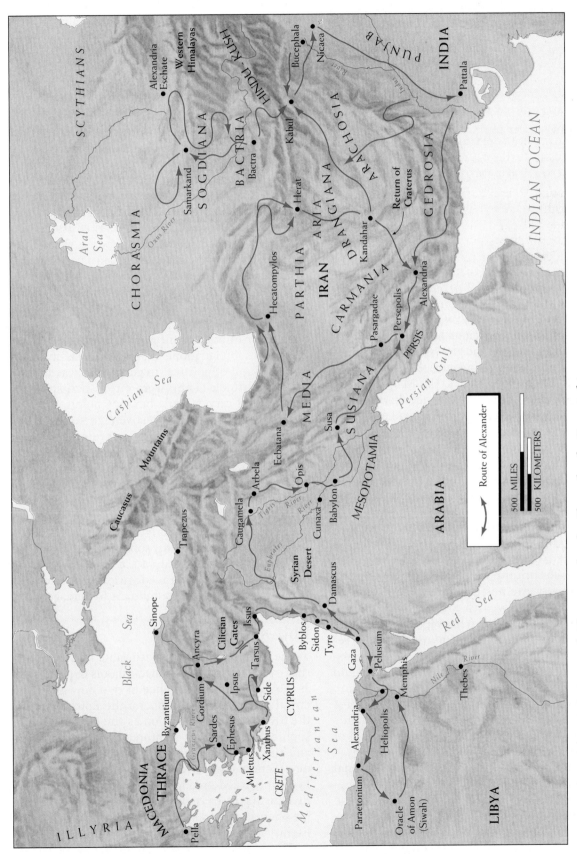

MAP 3–4 ALEXANDER'S CAMPAIGNS *The route taken by Alexander the Great in his conquest of the Persian Empire, 334–323 B.C.E. Starting from the Macedonian capital at Pella, he reached the Indus Valley before being turned back by his own restive troops. He died of fever in Mesopotamia.*

The Rise of Macedon	
359–336 B.C.E.	Reign of Philip II
338 B.C.E.	Battle of Chaeronea; Philip conquers Greece
338 B.C.E.	Founding of League of Corinth
336–323 B.C.E.	Reign of Alexander III, the Great
334 B.C.E.	Alexander invades Asia
333 B.C.E.	Battle of Issus
331 B.C.E.	Battle of Gaugamela
330 B.C.E.	Fall of Persepolis
327 B.C.E.	Alexander reaches Indus Valley
323 B.C.E.	Death of Alexander

many Greeks and relieved their native cities of some of the pressure of the poor. The opening of vast new territories to Greek trade, the increased demand for Greek products, and the new availability of desired goods, as well as the conscious policies of the Hellenistic kings, all helped the growth of commerce.

The new prosperity, however, was not evenly distributed. The urban Greeks, the Macedonians, and the Hellenized natives who made up the upper and middle classes lived in comfort and even luxury, but the rural native peasants did not. Unlike the independent men who owned and worked the relatively small and equal lots of the *polis* in earlier times, Hellenistic farmers were reduced to subordinate, dependent, peasant status, working on large plantations of decreasing efficiency. During prosperous times these distinctions were bearable, although even then there was tension between the two groups. After a while, however, the costs of continuing wars, inflation, and a gradual lessening of the positive effects of the introduction of Persian wealth all led to economic crisis. The kings bore down heavily on the middle classes, who were skilled at avoiding their responsibilities, however. The pressure on the peasants and the city laborers became great, too, and they responded by slowing down their work and even by striking. In Greece, economic pressures brought clashes between rich and poor, demands for the abolition of debt and the redistribution of land, and even, on occasion, civil war.

These internal divisions, along with international wars, weakened the capacity of the Hellenistic kingdoms to resist outside attack. By the middle of the second century B.C.E. they had all, except for Egypt, succumbed to an expanding Italian power, Rome. The two centuries between Alexander and the Roman conquest, however, were of great and lasting

importance. They saw the entire eastern Mediterranean coast, Greece, Egypt, Mesopotamia, and the old Persian Empire formed into a single political, economic, and cultural unit.

Hellenistic Culture

The career of Alexander the Great marked a significant turning point in Greek thought as it was represented in literature, philosophy, religion, and art. His conquests and the establishment of the successor kingdoms put an end to the central role of the *polis* in Greek life and thought. Some scholars disagree about the end of the *polis*, denying that Philip's victory at Chaeronea marked its demise. They point to the persistence of *poleis* throughout the Hellenistic period and even see a continuation of them in the Roman *municipia*. These were, however, only a shadow of the vital reality that had been the true *polis*.

Deprived of control of their foreign affairs, and with their important internal arrangements determined by a foreign monarch, the post-Classical cities lost the kind of political freedom that was basic to the old outlook. They were cities, perhaps—in a sense, even city–states—but not *poleis*. As time passed, they changed from sovereign states to municipal towns merged in military empires. Never again in antiquity would there be either a serious attack on or defense of the *polis*, for its importance was gone. For the most part, the Greeks after Alexander turned away from political solutions for their problems. Instead, they sought personal responses to their hopes and fears, particularly in religion, philosophy, and magic. The confident, sometimes arrogant, humanism of the fifth century B.C.E. gave way to a kind of resignation to fate, a recognition of helplessness before forces too great for humans to manage.

Philosophy

These developments are noticeable in the changes that overtook the established schools of philosophy as well as in the emergence of two new and influential groups of philosophers: the Epicureans and the Stoics. Athens' position as the center of philosophical studies was reinforced, for the Academy and the Lyceum continued in operation, and the new schools were also located in Athens. The Lyceum turned gradually away from the universal investigations of its founder, Aristotle, even from his scientific interests, to become a center chiefly of literary and especially historical studies.

The Academy turned even further away from its tradition. It adopted the systematic Skepticism of

Pyrrho of Elis. Under the leadership of Arcesilaus and Carneades, the Skeptics of the Academy became skilled at pointing out fallacies and weaknesses in the philosophies of the rival schools. They thought that nothing could be known and so consoled themselves and their followers by suggesting that nothing mattered. It was easy for them, therefore, to accept conventional morality and the world as it was. The Cynics, of course, continued to denounce convention and to advocate the crude life in accordance with nature, which some of them practiced publicly to the shock and outrage of respectable citizens. Neither Skepticism nor Cynicism had much appeal to the middle-class city dweller of the third century B.C.E., who sought some basis for choosing a way of life now that the *polis* no longer provided one ready made.

THE EPICUREANS   Epicurus of Athens (342–271 B.C.E.) formulated a new teaching, embodied in the school he founded in his native city in 306 B.C.E. His philosophy conformed to the mood of the times in that its goal was not knowledge, but human happiness, which he believed could be achieved if one followed a style of life based on reason. He took sense perception to be the basis of all human knowledge. The reality and reliability of sense perception rested on the acceptance of the physical universe described by the atomists, Democritus and Leucippus. The Epicureans proclaimed that atoms were continually falling through the void and giving off images that were in direct contact with the senses. These falling atoms could swerve in an arbitrary, unpredictable way to produce the combinations seen in the world.

Epicurus thereby removed an element of determinism that existed in the Democritean system. When a person died, the atoms that composed the body dispersed so that the person had no further existence or perception and therefore nothing to fear after death. Epicurus believed that the gods existed, but that they took no interest in human affairs. This belief amounted to a practical atheism, and Epicureans were often thought to be atheists.

The purpose of Epicurean physics was to liberate people from their fear of death, of the gods, and of all nonmaterial or supernatural powers. Epicurean ethics were hedonistic, that is, based on the acceptance of pleasure as true happiness. But pleasure for Epicurus was chiefly negative: the absence of pain and trouble. The goal of the Epicureans was *ataraxia*, the condition of being undisturbed, without trouble, pain, or responsibility. Ideally, a man should have enough means to allow him to withdraw from the world and

avoid business and public life. Epicurus even advised against marriage and children. He preached a life of genteel, restrained selfishness that might appeal to intellectual men of means, but was not calculated to be widely attractive.

THE STOICS   Soon after Epicurus began teaching in his garden in Athens, Zeno of Citium in Cyprus (335–263 B.C.E.) established the Stoic school. It derived its name from the *stoa poikile*, or painted portico, in the Athenian *agora*, where Zeno and his disciples walked and talked beginning about 300 B.C.E. From then until about the middle of the second century B.C.E., Zeno and his successors preached a philosophy that owed a good deal to Socrates, by way of the Cynics. It was fed also by a stream of Eastern thought. Zeno, of course, came from Phoenician Cyprus; Chrysippus, one of his successors, came from Cilicia; and other early Stoics came from such places as Carthage, Tarsus, and Babylon.

Like the Epicureans, the Stoics sought the happiness of the individual. Quite unlike them, the Stoics proposed a philosophy almost indistinguishable from religion. They believed that humans must live in harmony within themselves and in harmony with nature; for the Stoics, god and nature were the same. The guiding principle in nature was divine reason (*Logos*), or fire. Every human had a spark of this divinity, and after death it returned to the eternal divine spirit. From time to time the world was destroyed by fire, from which a new world arose.

The aim of humans, and the definition of human happiness, was the virtuous life: a life lived in accordance with natural law, "when all actions promote the harmony of the spirit dwelling in the individual man with the will of him who orders the universe."[5] To live such a life required the knowledge possessed only by the wise, who knew what was good, what was evil, and what was neither, but "indifferent." According to the Stoics, good and evil were dispositions of the mind or soul: prudence, justice, courage, temperance, and so on were good, whereas folly, injustice, cowardice, and the like were evil. Life, health, pleasure, beauty, strength, wealth, and so on, were neutral—morally indifferent—for they did not contribute either to happiness or to misery. Human misery came from an irrational mental contraction—from passion, which was a disease of the soul. The wise sought *apatheia*, or freedom from passion, because passion arose from things that were morally indifferent.

Politically, the Stoics fit well into the new world. They thought of it as a single *polis* in which

[5]Diogenes Laertius, Life of Antisthenes, 6 11.

Plutarch Cites Archimedes and Hellenistic Science

Archimedes (ca. 287–211 B.C.E.) was one of the great mathematicians and physicists of antiquity. He was a native of Syracuse in Sicily and a friend of its king. Plutarch discusses him in the following selection and reveals much about the ancient attitude toward applied science.

❖ *Was the attitude toward science and technology attributed to Archimedes by Plutarch common in the ancient world? How can that attitude be explained? If it was common, what were the consequences? Are distinctions between the importance of pure science and applied science made in the modern world? If so, are they the same as the ancient ones? How do you explain any similarities or differences?*

Archimedes, however, in writing to King Hiero, whose friend and near relation he was, had stated that given the force, any given weight might be moved, and even boasted, we are told, relying on the strength of demonstration, that if there were another earth, by going into it he could remove this. Hiero being struck with amazement at this, and entreating him to make good this problem by actual experiment, and show some great weight moved by a small engine, he fixed accordingly upon a ship of burden out of the king's arsenal, which could not be drawn out of the dock without great labour and many men; and, loading her with many passengers and a full freight, sitting himself the while far off, with no great endeavor, but only holding the head of the pulley in his hand and drawing the cords by degrees. ... Yet Archimedes possessed so high a spirit, so profound a soul, and such treasures of scientific knowledge, that though these inventions had now obtained him the renown of more than human sagacity, he yet would not deign to leave behind him any commentary or writing on such subjects; but, repudiating as sordid and ignoble the whole trade of engineering, and every sort of art that lends itself to mere use and profit, he placed his whole affection and ambition in those purer speculations where there can be no reference to the vulgar needs of life.

From Plutarch, "Marcellus," in *Lives of the Noble Grecians and Romans*, trans. by John Dryden, rev. by A. H. Clough (New York: Random House, n.d.), pp. 376–378.

all people were children of the same god. Although they did not forbid political activity, and many Stoics took part in political life, withdrawal was obviously preferable because the usual subjects of political argument were indifferent. Because the Stoics strove for inner harmony of the individual, their aim was a life lived in accordance with the divine will, their attitude fatalistic, and their goal a form of apathy. They fit in well with the reality of post-Alexandrian life. In fact, the spread of Stoicism facilitated the task of creating a new political system that relied not on the active participation of the governed, but merely on their docile submission.

Literature

The literature of the Hellenistic period reflects the new intellectual currents, the new conditions of literary life, and the new institutions created in that period. The center of literary production in the third and second centuries B.C.E. was the new city of Alexandria in Egypt. There the Ptolemies, the monarchs of Egypt during that time, founded the museum—a great research institute where royal funds supported scientists and scholars—and the library, which contained almost half a million volumes of papyrus scrolls.

The library contained much of the great body of past Greek literature, most of which has since been lost. The Alexandrian scholars saw to it that what they judged to be the best works were copied. They edited and criticized these works from the point of view of language, form, and content and wrote biographies of the authors. Their work is responsible for the preservation of most of what remains to us of ancient literature. Much of their work proved valuable, but some of it is dry, petty, quarrelsome, and simply foolish. At its best, however, it is full of learning and perception.

The scholarly atmosphere of Alexandria naturally gave rise to work in the field of history and its ancillary discipline, chronology. Eratosthenes (ca. 275–195 B.C.E.) established a chronology of important events dating from the Trojan War, and others undertook similar tasks. Contemporaries of Alexander, such as Ptolemy I, Aristobulus, and Nearchus, wrote what were apparently sober and essentially factual accounts of his career. Most of the work done by Hellenistic historians is known to us only in fragments cited by later writers. It seems in general to have emphasized sensational and biographical detail over the kind of rigorous impersonal analysis that marked the work of Thucydides.

Architecture and Sculpture

The advent of the Hellenistic monarchies greatly increased the opportunities open to architects and sculptors. Money was plentiful, rulers sought outlets for conspicuous display, new cities needed to be built and beautified, and the well-to-do created an increasing demand for objects of art. The new cities were usually laid out on the grid plan introduced in the fifth century B.C.E. by Hippodamus of Miletus. Temples were built on the classical model, and the covered portico, or stoa, became a very popular addition to the agoras of the Hellenistic towns.

Reflecting the cosmopolitan nature of the Hellenistic world, leading sculptors accepted commissions wherever they were attractive. The result was a certain uniformity of style, although Alexandria, Rhodes, and the kingdom of Pergamum in Asia Minor developed their own distinctive stylistic characteristics. For the most part, Hellenistic sculpture moved away from the balanced tension and idealism of the fifth century B.C.E. toward the sentimental, emotional, and realistic mode of the fourth century B.C.E. These qualities are readily apparent in the marble statue called the Laocoon, carved at Rhodes in the second century B.C.E. and afterward taken to Rome.

Mathematics and Science

Among the most spectacular and remarkable intellectual developments of the Hellenistic age were those that came in mathematics and science. The burst of activity in these subjects drew their in-

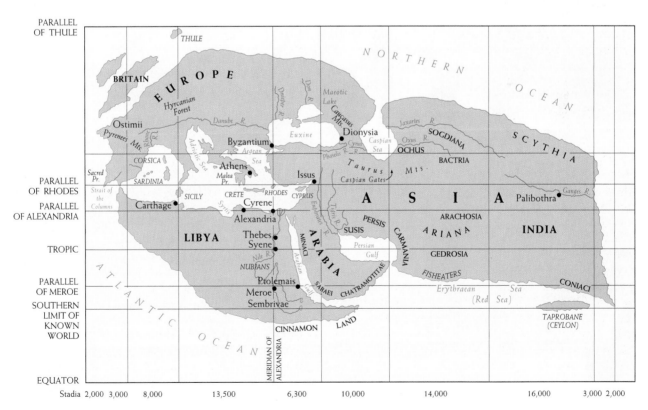

MAP 3–5   THE WORLD ACCORDING TO ERATOSTHENES   *Eratosthenes of Alexandria (ca. 275–195 B.C.E.) was a Hellenistic geographer. His map, reconstructed here, was remarkably accurate for its time. The world was divided by lines of "latitude" and "longitude," thus anticipating our global divisions.*

This is a Roman copy of one of the masterpieces of Hellenistic sculpture, the Laocoon. According to legend, Laocoon was a priest who warned the Trojans not to take the Greek's wooden horse within their city. This sculpture depicts his punishment. Great serpents sent by the goddess Athena, who was on the side of the Greeks, devoured Laocoon and his sons before the horrified people of Troy. Musei Vaticani

spiration from several sources. The stimulation and organization provided by the work of Plato and Aristotle should not be ignored. To these was added the impetus provided by Alexander's interest in science, evidenced by the scientists he took with him on his expedition and the aid he gave them in collecting data.

The expansion of Greek horizons geographically and the consequent contact with Egyptian and Babylonian knowledge were also helpful. Finally, the patronage of the Ptolemies and the opportunity for many scientists to work with one another at the museum at Alexandria provided a unique opportunity for scientific work. It is not too much to say that the work done by the Alexandrians formed the greater part of the scientific knowledge available to the Western world until the scientific revolution of the sixteenth and seventeenth centuries C.E.

Euclid's *Elements* (written early in the third century B.C.E.) remained the textbook of plane and solid geometry until recent times. Archimedes of Syracuse (ca. 287–212 B.C.E.) made further progress in geometry, established the theory of the lever in mechanics, and invented hydrostatics. (See "Plutarch Cites Archimedes and Hellenistic Science.")

These advances in mathematics, once applied to the Babylonian astronomical tables available to the Hellenistic world, spurred great progress in the field of astronomy. As early as the fourth century, Heraclides of Pontus (ca. 390–310 B.C.E.) had argued that Mercury and Venus circulate around the sun and not the Earth. He appears to have made other suggestions leading in the direction of a heliocentric theory of the universe. Most scholars, however, give credit for that theory to Aristarchus of Samos (ca. 310–230 B.C.E.), who asserted that the sun, along with the other fixed stars, did not move and that the Earth revolved around the sun in a circular orbit and rotated on its axis while doing so. The heliocentric theory ran contrary not only to the traditional view codified by Aristotle, but to what seemed to be common sense.

Hellenistic technology was not up to proving the theory, and, of course, the planetary orbits are not circular. The heliocentric theory did not, therefore, take hold. Hipparchus of Nicea (b. ca. 190 B.C.E.) constructed a model of the universe on the geocentric theory; his ingenious and complicated model did a very good job of accounting for the movements of the sun, the moon, and the planets. Ptolemy of Alexandria (second century C.E.) adopted Hipparchus' system with a few improvements. It remained dominant until the work of Copernicus, in the sixteenth century C.E.

A page from On Floating Bodies. *Archimedes' work was covered over by a tenth-century manuscript, but ultraviolet radiation reveals the original text and drawings underneath.* Christie's Images, Inc.

Hellenistic scientists made progress in mapping the Earth as well as the sky. Eratosthenes of Cyrene (ca. 275–195 B.C.E.) was able to calculate the circumference of the Earth to within about 200 miles. He wrote a treatise on geography based on mathematical and physical reasoning and the reports of travelers. In spite of the new data that were available to later geographers, Eratosthenes' map (see Map 3–5) was in many ways more accurate than the one constructed by Ptolemy of Alexandria, which became standard in the Middle Ages.

The Hellenistic Age contributed little to the life sciences, such as biology, zoology, and medicine. Even the sciences that had such impressive achievements to show in the third century B.C.E. made little progress thereafter. In fact, to some extent, there was a retreat from science. Astrology and magic became subjects of great interest as scientific advance lagged.

In Perspective

The Classical Age of Greece was a period of unparalleled achievement. While the rest of the world continued to be characterized by monarchical, hierarchical, command societies, in Athens democracy was carried as far as it would go before modern times. Although Athenian citizenship was limited to adult males of native parentage, citizens were granted full and active participation in every decision of the state without regard to wealth or class. Democracy disappeared late in the fourth century B.C.E. *with the end of Greek autonomy. When it returned in the modern world more than two millennia later, it was broader, but shallower. Democratic citizenship did not again imply the active direct participation of every citizen in the government of the state.*

It was in this democratic, imperial Athens that the greatest artistic, literary, and philosophical achievements of Classical Greece took place. Analytical, secular history, tragedy and comedy, the philosophical dialogue, an organized system of logic, and the logical philosophical treatise were among the achievements of the Classical Age. The tradition of rational, secular speculation in natural philosophy and science was carried forward, but more attention was devoted to human questions in medicine and ethical and political philosophy. A naturalistic style of art evolved that showed human beings first as they ideally might look and then as they really looked, an approach that dominated Greek and Roman art until the late stages of the Roman Empire. This naturalistic style had a powerful effect on the Italian Renaissance and, through it, the modern world.

These Hellenic developments, it should be clear, diverge sharply from the experience of previous cultures and of contemporary ones in the rest of the world. To a great degree, they sprang from the unique political experience of the Greeks, based on the independent city–states. That unique experience and the Classical period ended with the Macedonian conquest, which introduced the Hellenistic Age and ultimately made the Greeks subject to, or part of, some great national state or empire.

The Hellenistic Age speaks to us less fully and vividly than that of Classical Greece, chiefly because it had no historian to compare with Herodotus and Thucydides. We lack the clear picture that a continuous, rich, lively, and meaningful narrative provides. This deficiency should not obscure the great importance of the achievements of the age. The literature, art, scholarship, and science of the period deserve attention in their own right.

The Hellenistic Age did perform a vital civilizing function. It spread Greek culture over a remarkably wide area and made a significant and lasting impression on much of it. Greek culture also adjusted to its new surroundings to a degree, unifying and simplifying its cultural cargo to make it more accessible to outsiders. The various Greek dialects gave way to a version of the Attic tongue, the koine, *or common language.*

In the same way, the scholarship of Alexandria established canons of literary excellence and the scholarly tools with which to make the great treasures of Greek culture understandable to later generations. The syncretism of thought and belief introduced in this period also made understanding and accord more likely among peoples who were very different. When the Romans came into contact with Hellenism, they were powerfully impressed by it. When they conquered the Hellenistic world, they became, as Horace said, captives of its culture.

REVIEW QUESTIONS

1. How was the Delian League transformed into the Athenian Empire during the fifth century B.C.E.? Did the empire offer any advantages to its subjects? Why was there such resistance to Athenian efforts to unify the Greek world in the fifth and fourth centuries B.C.E.?

2. Why did Athens and Sparta come to blows in the Great Peloponnesian War? What was each side's strategy for victory? Why did Sparta win the war?

3. Give examples from art, literature, and philosophy of the tension that characterized Greek life and thought in the Classical Age. How does Hellenistic art differ from that of the Classical Age?

4. Between 431 and 362 B.C.E., Athens, Sparta, and Thebes each tried to impose hegemony over the city–states of Greece, but none succeeded except for short periods of time. Why did each state fail? What does your analysis tell you about the components of successful rule?

5. How and why did Philip II conquer Greece between 359 and 338 B.C.E.? How was he able to turn Macedon into a formidable military and political power? Why was Athens unable to defend itself against Macedon? Where does more of the credit for Philip's success lie; in Macedon's strength or in the weakness of the Greek city–states?

6. What were the major consequences of Alexander's death? Assess the achievement of Alexander. Was he a conscious promoter of Greek civilization or just an egomaniac drunk with the lust of conquest?

SUGGESTED READINGS

M. AUSTIN AND P. VIDAL-NAQUET, *The Economic and Social History of Classical Greece* (1977). A collection of documents with commentary.

A. B. BOSWORTH, *Conquest and Empire: The Reign of Alexander the Great* (1988). An excellent, tough-minded account.

J. BUCKLER, *The Theban Hegemony, 371–362* B.C.E. (1980). A study of Thebes at the height of its power.

W. BURKERT, *Greek Religion* (1985). A fine general study.

P. CARTLEDGE, *Agesilaus and the Crisis of Sparta* (1987). More than a biography of the Spartan king, this is a thorough study of Spartan society.

G. CAWKWELL, *Philip of Macedon* (1978). A brief, but learned, account of Philip's career.

W. R. CONNOR, *The New Politicians of Fifth-Century Athens* (1971). A study on changes in political style and their significance for Athenian society.

V. EHRENBERG, *The People of Aristophanes* (1962). A study of Athenian society as revealed by the comedies of Aristophanes.

J. R. ELLIS, *Philip II and Macedonian Imperialism* (1976). A study of the career of the founder of Macedonian power.

E. FANTHAM, H. FOLEY, N. KAMPEN, S. POMEROY, AND H. A. SHAPIRO, *Women in the Classical World* (1994). A valuable survey based on written and visual evidence.

J. R. L. FOX, *Alexander the Great* (1973). An imaginative account that does more justice to the Persian side of the problem than is usual.

Y. GARLAN, *Slavery in Ancient Greece* (1988). An up-to-date survey.

P. GREEN, *Alexander the Great* (1972). A lively biography.

P. GREEN, *From Alexander to Actium* (1990). A brilliant new synthesis of the Hellenistic period.

C. D. HAMILTON, *Agesilaus and the Failure of Spartan Hegemony* (1991). An excellent biography of the king who was the central figure in Sparta during its domination in the fourth century B.C.E.

N. G. L. HAMMOND AND G. T. GRIFFITH, *A History of Macedonia, Vol. 2, 550–336* B.C.E. (1979). A thorough account of Macedonian history that focuses on the careers of Philip and Alexander.

M.H. HANSEN, *The Athenian Democracy in the Age of Demosthenes* (1991). An analysis of the Athenian constitution and society in the fourth century B.C.E.

R. JUST, *Women in Athenian Law and Life* (1988). A good study of the place of women in Athenian life.

D. KAGAN, *Pericles of Athens and the Birth of Athenian Democracy* (1991). An account of the life and times of the great Athenian statesman.

D. KAGAN, *The Outbreak of the Peloponnesian War* (1969). A study of the period from the foundation of the Delian League to the coming of the Peloponnesian War that argues that war could have been avoided.

G. B. KERFERD, *The Sophistic Movement* (1981). A fine study of these worldly thinkers of the Classical period.

B. M. W. KNOX, *The Heroic Temper: Studies in Sophoclean Tragedy* (1964). A brilliant analysis of tragic heroism.

D. M. LEWIS, *Sparta and Persia* (1977). A valuable discussion of relations between Sparta and Persia in the fifth and fourth centuries B.C.E.

G. E. R. LLOYD, *Greek Science after Aristotle* (1974).

A. A. LONG, *Hellenistic Philosophy: Stoics, Epicureans, Skeptics* (1974). A solid study.

R. MEIGGS, *The Athenian Empire* (1972). A fine study of the rise and fall of the empire, making excellent use of inscriptions.

J. J. POLLITT, *Art and Experience in Classical Greece* (1972). A scholarly and entertaining study of the relationship between art and history in Classical Greece, with excellent illustrations.

J. J. POLLITT, *Art in the Hellenistic Age* (1986). An extraordinary analysis that places the art in its historical and intellectual context.

S. POMEROY, *Families in Classical and Hellenistic Greece* (1998). A valuable and thorough study of the Greek family.

M. I. ROSTOVTZEFF, *Social and Economic History of the Hellenistic World*, 3 vols. (1941). A masterpiece of synthesis by a great historian.

R. SEALEY, *Demosthenes and His Time* (1993). A learned and controversial study.

B. S. STRAUSS, *Athens after the Peloponnesian War* (1987). An excellent discussion of Athens' recovery and of the nature of Athenian society and politics in the fourth century B.C.E.

B. S. STRAUSS, *Fathers and Sons in Athens* (1993). A study of tension between the generations in Classical Athens.

V. TCHERIKOVER, *Hellenistic Civilization and the Jews* (1970). A fine study of the impact of Hellenism on the Jews.

G. VLASTOS, *Socrates: Ironist and Moral Philosopher* (1991). A study of the father of Western ethical philosophy.

G. VLASTOS, *Platonic Studies*, 2d ed. (1981). A valuable collection of essays on the philosophy of Plato.

F. W. WALBANK, *The Hellenistic World* (1981). A solid history.

A. E. ZIMMERN, *The Greek Commonwealth* (1961). A study of political, social, and economic conditions in fifth-century Athens.

Chapter 4

*This is a wall painting from a house in the provincial Roman town of Pompeii,
near the Bay of Naples. The house was buried, and thus preserved, in a rain of
ash and lava by the great eruption of Mt. Vesuvius in 79 C.E. The painting
shows a well-to-do couple, the wife wearing gold jewelry and holding a stylus
and wax tablet, the usual writing implements of the time. The picture seems to
emphasize her status as a wife, her personal attractiveness, and her literacy.*
Museo Nazionale, Napoli/Scala/Art Resource N.Y.

Rome: From Republic to Empire

KEY TOPICS

- The emergence of the Roman Republic
- The development of the republican constitution
- Roman expansion and imperialism
- The character of Roman society in the republican era
- The fall of the republic

The achievement of the Romans was one of the most remarkable in human history. The descendants of the inhabitants of a small village in central Italy, they came eventually to rule the entire Italian peninsula, then the entire Mediterranean coastline. They conquered most of the Near East and, finally, much of continental Europe. They ruled this vast empire under a single government that provided considerable peace and prosperity for centuries. Never before the Romans nor since has that area been united, and rarely, if ever, has it enjoyed a stable peace. But Rome's legacy was not merely military excellence and political organization. The Romans adopted and transformed the intellectual and cultural achievements of the Greeks and combined them with their own outlook and historical experience. The resulting Graeco-Roman tradition in literature, philosophy, and art provided the core of learning for the Middle Ages and pointed the way to the new paths taken in the Renaissance. It remains at the heart of Western civilization to this day.

Prehistoric Italy

The culture of Italy developed late. Paleolithic settlements gave way to the Neolithic mode of life only around 2500 B.C.E. The Bronze Age came around 1500 B.C.E. About 1000 B.C.E., bands of new arrivals—warlike peoples speaking a set of closely related languages we call Italic—began to infiltrate Italy from across the Adriatic Sea and around its northern end. These invaders cremated their dead and put the ashes in tombs stocked with weapons and armor. Their bronzework was of a higher quality than that of the people they displaced, and they were soon making weapons, armor, and tools of iron. By 800 B.C.E. they had occupied the highland pastures of the Apennines, and within a short time they began to challenge the earlier settlers for control of the tempting western plains. It would be the descendants of these tough mountain people—Umbrians, Sabines, Samnites, and Latins—together with others soon to arrive—Etruscans, Greeks, and Celts—who would shape the future of Italy.

The Etruscans

The Etruscans exerted the most powerful external influence on the Romans. Their civilization arose in Etruria (now Tuscany), west of the Apennines between the Arno and Tiber rivers, about 800 B.C.E. (See Map 4–1.) Their origin is far from clear, but their tomb architecture, resembling that of Asia Minor, and their practice of divining the future by inspecting the livers of sacrificial animals point to an eastern origin.

Government

The Etruscans brought civilization with them. Their settlements were self-governing, fortified city–states, of which twelve formed a loose religious confederation. At first, kings ruled these cities, but they were replaced by an aristocracy of the agrarian nobles. The latter ruled by means of a council and elected annual magistrates. The Etruscans were a military ruling class that dominated and exploited the native Italians (the predecessors of the later Italic speakers), who worked the Etruscans' land and mines and served as infantry in the Etruscan armies. This aristocracy accumulated considerable wealth through agriculture, industry, piracy, and a growing commerce with the Carthaginians and the Greeks.

Religion

The Etruscans' influence on the Romans was greatest in religion. They imagined a world filled with

MAP 4–1   ANCIENT ITALY   *This map of ancient Italy and its neighbors before the expansion of Rome shows major cities and towns as well as several geographical regions and the locations of some of the Italic and non-Italic peoples.*

gods and spirits, many of them evil. To deal with such demons, the Etruscans evolved complicated rituals and powerful priesthoods. Divination by sacrifice and omens in nature helped discover the divine will, and careful attention to precise rituals directed by priests helped please the gods. After a while the Etruscans, influenced by the Greeks, worshiped gods in the shape of humans and built temples for them.

Women

Etruscan women had a more significant role in family and society than did Greek women in the world of the *polis*. Etruscan wives appeared in public, in religious festivals, and at public banquets together with their husbands. Many of them were literate, and women both took part in athletic contests and watched them as spectators alongside of men. Inscriptions on tombs and paintings on coffins mention both father and mother of the deceased and

Much of what we know of the Etruscans comes from their funerary art. This sculpture of an Etruscan couple is part of a sarcophagus. Erich Lessing/Art Resource, N.Y.

often show husbands and wives together in respectful and loving attitudes.

Dominion

The Etruscan aristocracy remained aggressive and skillful in the use of horses and war chariots. In the seventh and sixth centuries B.C.E., they expanded their power in Italy and across the sea to Corsica and Elba. They conquered Latium (a region that included the small town of Rome) and Campania, where they became neighbors of the Greeks of Naples. In the north, they got as far as the Po Valley. These conquests were carried out by small bands led by Etruscan chieftains who did not work in concert and would not necessarily aid one another in distress. As a result, the conquests outside Etruria were not firmly based and did not last long.

Etruscan power reached its height some time before 500 B.C.E. and then rapidly declined. About 400 B.C.E., Celtic peoples from the area the Romans called Gaul (modern France) broke into the Po Valley and drove out the Etruscans. They settled this land so firmly that the Romans thereafter called it Cisalpine Gaul (Gaul on this side of the Alps). Eventually, even the Etruscan heartland in Etruria lost its independence and was incorporated into Roman Italy. The Etruscan language was forgotten, and Etruscan culture gradually became only a memory, but its influence on the Romans remained.

Royal Rome

Rome was an unimportant town in Latium until its conquest by the Etruscans, but its location—fifteen miles from the mouth of the Tiber River at the point

at which the hills made further navigation impossible—gave it several advantages over its Latin neighbors. The island in the Tiber southwest of the Capitoline Hill made the river fordable, so Rome was naturally a center for communication and trade, both east–west and north–south.

Government

In the sixth century B.C.E., Rome came under Etruscan control. Led by Etruscan kings, the Roman army, equipped and organized like the Greek phalanx, gained control of most of Latium. An effective political and social order that gave extraordinary power to the ruling figures in both public and private life made this success possible. To their kings the Romans gave the awesome power of *imperium*—the right to issue commands and to enforce them by fines, arrests, and corporal, or even capital, punishment. Although it tended apparently to remain in the same family, kingship was elective. The Roman Senate had to approve the candidate for the office, and a vote of the people gathered in an assembly formally granted the *imperium*. A basic characteristic of later Roman government—the granting of great power to executive officers contingent on the approval of the Senate and, ultimately, the people—was already apparent in this structure.

In theory and law, the king was the commander of the army, the chief priest, and the supreme judge. He could make decisions in foreign affairs, call out the army, lead it in battle, and impose discipline on his troops, all by virtue of his *imperium*. In practice, the royal power was much more limited.

The Senate was the second branch of the early Roman government. According to tradition, it originated when Romulus, Rome's legendary first king, chose 100 of Rome's leading men to advise him. The number of senators ultimately rose to 300, where it stayed through most of the history of the republic. Ostensibly, the Senate had neither executive nor legislative power; it met only when summoned by the king and then only to advise him. In reality its authority was great, for the senators, like the king, served for life. The Senate, therefore, had continuity and experience, and it was composed of the most powerful men in the state. It could not lightly be ignored.

The third branch of government, the curiate assembly, was made up of all citizens, as divided into thirty groups. (In early Rome, citizenship required descent from Roman parents on both sides.) The assembly met only when summoned by the king; he determined the agenda, made proposals, and recognized other speakers, if any. Usually, the assembly was called to listen and approve. Voting was not by head, but by group; a majority within each group determined its vote, and the decisions were made by majority vote of the groups. Group voting would be typical of all future forms of Roman assembly.

The Family

The center of Roman life was the family. At its head stood the father, whose power and authority within the family resembled those of the king within the state. Over his children, the father held broad powers analogous to *imperium* in the state; he had the right to sell his children into slavery, and he even had the power of life and death over them. Over his wife, he had less power; he could not sell or kill her. In practice, his power to dispose of his children was limited by consultation with the family, by public opinion, and, most of all, by tradition. A wife could not be divorced except for stated serious offenses, and even then she had to be convicted by a court made up of her male blood relatives. The Roman woman had a respected position and the main responsibility for managing the household. The father was the chief priest of the family. He led it in daily prayers to the dead, which reflected the ancestor worship central to the Roman family and state.

Women in Early Rome

Early Roman society was hierarchical and dominated by males. Throughout her life a woman was under the control of some adult male. Before her marriage it was her father, afterwards her husband or, when neither was available, a guardian chosen from one of their male relatives. Always her right to buy or sell property or make contracts required the approval of one of them. The Roman law gave control of a woman from father to husband by the right of *manus* (hand). This was conferred by one of two formal marriage ceremonies that were typical in early Rome. Over time, however, a third form of marriage became popular that left the power of *manus* in the hands of the woman's father, even after her marriage. This kind of union was similar to what we would call common-law marriage, in which a woman could stay out of her husband's control of her and her dowry by absenting herself from her husband's home for at least three consecutive nights each year. This gave her greater rights of inheritance in her father's family and greater independence in her marriage.

Busts of a Roman couple from the period of the Republic. Although some have identified the individuals as Cato the Younger and his daughter Porcia, no solid evidence confirms this claim. Roman sculpture. Vatican Museums, Vatican State. Scala/Art Resource N.Y.

In early Rome, marriage with *manus* was most common, but women of the upper classes had a position of influence and respect greater than the classical Greeks had and more like what appears to have been true of the Etruscans. Just as the husband was *paterfamilias*, the wife was *materfamilias*. She was mistress within the home, controlling access to the storerooms, keeping the accounts, and supervising the slaves and the raising of the children. She also was part of the family council and a respected adviser on all questions concerning the family. Divorce was difficult and rare, limited to a few specific transgressions by the wife, one of which was drunkenness. Even when divorced for cause, the wife retained her dowry.

Clientage

Clientage was one of Rome's most important institutions. The *client* was "an inferior entrusted, by custom or by himself, to the protection of a stranger more powerful than he, and rendering certain services and observances in return for this protection."[1] The Romans spoke of a client as being in the *fides*, or trust, of his patron, and so the relationship always had moral implications. The patron provided his client with protection, both physical and legal. He gave him economic assistance in the form of a land grant, the opportunity to work as a tenant farmer or a laborer on the patron's land, or simply handouts. In return, the client would fight for his patron, work his land, and support him politically. These mutual obligations were enforced by public opinion and tradition. When early custom was codified in the mid-fifth century B.C.E., one of the twelve tablets of laws announced, "Let the patron who has defrauded his client be accursed."

In the early history of Rome, patrons were rich and powerful whereas clients were poor and weak, but as time passed, it was not uncommon for rich and powerful members of the upper classes to become clients of even more powerful men, chiefly for political purposes. Because the client–patron relationship was hereditary and was sanctioned by religion and custom, it was to play a very important part in the life of the Roman Republic.

Patricians and Plebeians

In the royal period, Roman society was divided in two by a class distinction based on birth. The wealthy patrician upper class held a monopoly of power and influence. Its members alone could conduct state religious ceremonies, sit in the Senate, or hold office. They formed a closed caste by forbidding marriage outside their own group. (See "Art & the West.")

The plebeian lower class must have consisted originally of poor, dependent small farmers, laborers, and artisans, the clients of the nobility. As Rome and its population grew in various ways, families that were rich, but outside the charmed circle of patricians, grew wealthy. From very early times, therefore, there were rich plebeians, and incompetence and bad luck must have produced some poor patricians. The line between the classes and the monopoly of privileges remained firm, nevertheless, and the struggle of the plebeians to gain equality occupied more than two centuries of republican history.

The Republic

Roman tradition tells us that the outrageous behavior of the last kings led the noble families to revolt in 509 B.C.E., bringing the monarchy to a sudden close and leading to the creation of the Roman Republic.

Constitution

THE CONSULS The Roman constitution was an unwritten accumulation of laws and customs. The Romans were a conservative people and were never willing to deprive their chief magistrates of the great powers exercised by the monarchs. They elected two patricians to the office of consul and endowed them with *imperium*. They were assisted by two financial officials called *quaestors*, whose number ultimately reached eight. Like the kings, the consuls led the army, had religious duties, and served as judges. They retained the visible symbols of royalty—the purple robe, the ivory chair, and the *lictors* (minor officials), who accompanied them bearing rods and axe. The power of the consuls, however, was limited legally and institutionally as well as by custom.

The power of the consulship was granted not for life, but only for a year. Each consul could prevent any action by his colleague simply by saying no to his proposal, and the religious powers of the consuls were shared with others. Even the *imperium* was limited. Although the consuls had full powers of life and death while leading an army, within the sacred boundary of the city of Rome the citizens had the right to appeal all cases involving capital punishment to the popular assembly. Besides, after their one year in office, the consuls would spend the rest of their lives as members of the Senate. It was a most reckless consul who failed to ask the advice of the Senate or who failed to follow it when there was general agreement.

---

[1] E. Badian, *Foreign Clientelae* (264–70 B.C.E.) (Oxford, 1958), p. 1.

Family and Honor:
A Roman Patrician with the Busts of His Ancestors

*R*oman sculpture was heavily influenced by other cultures, first by the Etruscans and later by the Greeks of the Hellenistic period. No large sculptures remain from much before the first century B.C.E., but Roman writers reveal that from very early times it was the custom to honor leading generals and political leaders by setting up statues to them in public places. This practice continued and expanded throughout the history of Rome.

This statue of an unknown member of the Roman nobility, from late in the first century, illustrates an even more fundamental custom. He carries the images of two of his ancestors, probably his father and grandfather. The Greek historian Polybius, who lived among the leading aristocrats of Rome, tells of the funeral practice when an illustrious Roman of the upper class died. The body was placed on a platform in the Forum. If the deceased had a son, he would deliver a eulogy praising his father's virtues and achievements. After the funeral, writes Polybius, a wax image of the dead man would be placed "in the most conspicuous spot in his house, surmounted by a wooden canopy or shrine. This likeness consists of a mask made to represent the deceased with extraordinary fidelity both in shape and color. These likenesses they display at public sacrifices with much care. And when any illustrious member of the family dies, they carry these masks to the funeral, putting them on men whom they thought as like the originals as possible."[2]

At these funerals, after the speaker had praised the deceased, he went on to praise the others whose images were displayed. "The chief benefit of the ceremony is that it inspires young men to shrink from no exertion for the general welfare, in the hope of obtaining the glory which awaits the brave."[3]

The wax images, of course, did not last, so by the first century it was customary to make marble copies of them. Although the Romans admired, collected, and copied sculptures in the naturalistic style of the Hellenistic Greeks, these commemorative statues and masks had a severe and repetitive style that did not

A Roman Patrician with the busts of his ancestors. First century C.E. Musei Capitolini, Rome/Scala/Art Resource N.Y.

care about individual character and psychology. Instead, they represented a *type*—the stern and serious Roman aristocrat, the responsible father of his family, the dutiful and brave citizen and leader of his people.

[2]Polybius, *The Histories*, 6.53, translated by E. S. Shuckburgh (Bloomington, IN: Indiana University Press, 1962), pp. 503–504.
[3]Ibid.

Sources: Polybius 6.53; Janson, *Art History*, pp. 188–190. D. Kleiner, *Roman Sculpture*, (New Haven: Yale University Press, 1992).

The many checks on consular action tended to prevent initiative, swift action, and change, but this was just what a conservative, traditional, aristocratic republic wanted. Only in the military sphere did divided counsel and a short term of office create important problems. The Romans tried to get around the difficulties by sending only one consul into the field or, when this was impossible, allowing each consul sole command on alternate days. In really serious crises, the consuls, with the advice of the Senate, could appoint a single man, the *dictator*, to the command and could retire in his favor. The *dictator*'s term of office was limited to six months, but his own *imperium* was valid both inside and outside the city without appeal.

These devices worked well enough in the early years of the republic, when Rome's battles were near home. Longer wars and more sophisticated opponents, however, revealed the system's weaknesses and required significant changes. Long campaigns prompted the invention of the *proconsulship* in 325 B.C.E., whereby the term of a consul serving in the field was extended. This innovation contained the seeds of many troubles for the constitution.

The creation of the office of *praetor* also helped provide commanders for Rome's many campaigns. The basic function of the *praetors* was judicial, but they also had *imperium* and served as generals. *Praetors'* terms were also for one year. By the end of the republic, there were eight *praetors*, whose annual terms, like the consuls', could be extended for military commands when necessary.

The job of identifying citizens and classifying them according to age and property was at first the responsibility of the consuls. After the middle of the fifth century B.C.E., this job was delegated to a new office, that of *censor*. The Senate elected two *censors* every five years. They conducted a census and drew up the citizen rolls. Their task was not just clerical; the classification of the citizens fixed taxation and status, so the censors had to be men of fine reputation, former consuls. They soon acquired additional powers. By the fourth century B.C.E., they compiled the roll of senators and could strike senators from that roll not only for financial, but also for moral, reasons. As the prestige of the office grew, it came to be considered the ultimate prize of a Roman political career.

THE SENATE AND THE ASSEMBLY With the end of the monarchy, the Senate became the single continuous deliberative body in the Roman state, greatly increasing its influence and power. Its members were prominent patricians, often leaders of clans and patrons of many clients. The Senate soon gained

Lictors, pictured here, attended the chief Roman magistrates when they appeared in public. The axe carried by one of the lictors and the bound bundle of staffs carried by the others symbolize both the power of Roman magistrates to inflict corporal punishment on Roman citizens and the limits on that power. The bound staffs symbolize the right of citizens within the city of Rome not to be punished without a trial. The axe symbolizes the power of the magistrates, as commanders of the army, to put anyone to death without a trial outside the city walls.
Alinari/Art Resource, N.Y.

control of the state's finances and of foreign policy. Its formal advice was not lightly ignored either by magistrates or by popular assemblies.

The most important assembly in the early republic was the *centuriate assembly*, which was, in a sense, the Roman army acting in a political capacity. Its basic unit was the *century*, theoretically 100 fighting men classified according to their weapons, armor, and equipment. Because each man equipped himself, this meant that the organization was by classes according to wealth.

Voting was by century and proceeded in order of classification from the cavalry down. The assembly elected the consuls and several other magistrates, voted on bills put before it, made decisions of war and peace, and also served as the court of appeal against decisions of the magistrates affecting the life or property of a citizen. In theory, the assembly had final authority, but the Senate exercised great, if informal, influence.

THE STRUGGLE OF THE ORDERS The laws and constitution of the early republic gave to the patricians almost a monopoly of power and privilege. Plebeians were barred from public office, from priesthoods, and from other public religious offices. They could not serve as judges and could not even know the law, for there was no published legal code. The only law was traditional practice, and that existed only in the minds and actions of patrician magistrates. Plebeians were subject to the *imperium*, but could not exercise its power. They were not allowed to marry patricians. When Rome gained new land by conquest, patrician magistrates distributed it in a way that favored patricians. The patricians dominated the assemblies and the Senate. The plebeians undertook a campaign to achieve political, legal, and social equality, and this attempt, which succeeded after two centuries of intermittent effort, is called the Struggle of the Orders.

The most important source of plebeian success was the need for their military service. According to tradition, the plebeians, angered by patrician resistance to their demands, withdrew from the city and camped on the Sacred Mount. There they formed a plebeian tribal assembly and elected plebeian tribunes to protect them from the arbitrary power of the magistrates. They declared the tribune inviolate and sacrosanct; anyone laying violent hands on him was accursed and liable to death without trial. By extension of his right to protect the plebeians, the tribune gained the power to veto any action of a magistrate or any bill in a Roman assembly or the Senate. The plebeian assembly voted by tribe, and a vote of the assembly was binding on plebeians. They tried to make their decisions binding on all Romans, but could not do so until 287 B.C.E.

The next step was for the plebeians to obtain access to the laws, which they accomplished by 450 B.C.E., when early Roman custom in all its harshness and simplicity was codified in the Twelve Tables. In 445 B.C.E., plebeians gained the right to marry patricians. The main prize, the consulship, the patricians did not yield easily. Not until 367 B.C.E. did legislation—the Licinian–Sextian Laws—provide that at least one consul could be a plebeian.

The Rise of the Plebeians to Equality in Rome	
509 B.C.E.	Kings expelled; republic founded
450–449 B.C.E.	Laws of the Twelve Tables published
445 B.C.E.	Plebeians gain right of marriage with patricians
367 B.C.E.	Licinian–Sextian Laws open consulship to plebeians
300 B.C.E.	Plebeians attain chief priesthoods
287 B.C.E.	Laws passed by Plebeian Assembly made binding on all Romans

Before long, plebeians held other offices—even the dictatorship and the censorship. In 300 B.C.E. they were admitted to the most important priesthoods, the last religious barrier to equality. In 287 B.C.E., the plebeians completed their triumph. They once again withdrew from the city and secured the passage of a law whereby decisions of the plebeian assembly bound all Romans and did not require the approval of the Senate.

It might seem that the Roman aristocracy had given way under the pressure of the lower class. Yet the victory of the plebeians did not bring democracy. An aristocracy based strictly on birth had given way to an aristocracy more subtle, but no less restricted, based on a combination of wealth and birth. A relatively small group of rich and powerful families, both patrician and plebeian, known as *nobiles*, attained the highest offices in the state. The significant distinction was no longer between patrician and plebeian but between the *nobiles* and everyone else.

The absence of the secret ballot in the assemblies enabled the *nobiles* to control most decisions and elections by a combination of intimidation and bribery. The leading families were in constant competition with one another for office, power, and prestige, but they often combined in marriage and less formal alliances to keep the political plums within their own group. In the century from 233 to 133 B.C.E., for instance, twenty-six families provided 80 percent of the consuls, and only ten families accounted for almost 50 percent. These same families dominated the Senate, whose power became ever greater. Rome's success brought the Senate prestige, increased control of policy, and confidence in its capacity to rule. The end of the Struggle of the Orders brought domestic peace under a republican constitution dominated by a capable, if narrow, senatorial aristocracy. This outcome satisfied most Romans outside the ruling group, because Rome conquered Italy and brought many benefits to its citizens.

The Conquest of Italy

Not long after the fall of the monarchy in 509 B.C.E., a coalition of Romans, Latins, and Italian Greeks defeated the Etruscans and drove them out of Latium for good. Throughout the fifth century B.C.E., the powerful Etruscan city of Veii, only twelve miles north of the Tiber River, raided Roman territory. After a hard struggle and a long siege, the Romans took Veii in 392 B.C.E., more than doubling the size of Rome.

Roman policy toward defeated enemies used both the carrot and the stick. When the Romans made friendly alliances with some, they gained new soldiers for their army. When they treated others more harshly by annexing their land, they achieved a similar end. Service in the Roman army was based on property, and the distribution to poor Romans of conquered land made soldiers of previously useless men. It also gave the poor a stake in Rome and reduced the pressure against its aristocratic regime. The long siege of Veii kept soldiers from their farms during the campaign. From that time on, the Romans paid their soldiers, thus giving their army greater flexibility and a more professional quality.

GALLIC INVASION OF ITALY AND ROMAN REACTION At the beginning of the fourth century B.C.E., a disaster struck. In 387 B.C.E. the Gauls, barbaric Celtic tribes from across the Alps, defeated the Roman army and captured, looted, and burned Rome. The Gauls sought plunder, not conquest, so they extorted a ransom from the Romans and returned to their homes in the north. Rome's power appeared to be wiped out.

By about 350 B.C.E., however, the Romans were more dominant than ever. Their success in turning back new Gallic raids added still more to their power and prestige. As the Romans tightened their grip on Latium, the Latins became resentful. In 340 B.C.E., they demanded independence from Rome or full equality and launched a war of independence that lasted until 338 B.C.E. The victorious Romans dissolved the Latin League, and their treatment of the defeated opponents provided a model for the settlement of Italy.

ROMAN POLICY TOWARD THE CONQUERED The Romans did not destroy any of the Latin cities or their people, nor did they treat them all alike. Some near Rome received full Roman citizenship. Others farther away gained municipal status, which gave them the private rights of intermarriage and commerce with Romans, but not the public rights of voting and holding office in Rome. They retained the rights of local self-government and could obtain full Roman citizenship if they moved to Rome. They followed Rome in foreign policy and provided soldiers to serve in the Roman legions.

Still other states became allies of Rome on the basis of treaties, which differed from city to city. Some were given the private rights of intermarriage and commerce with Romans, and some were not; the allied states were always forbidden to exercise these rights with one another. Some, but not all, were allowed local autonomy. Land was taken from some, but not from others, nor was the percentage taken always the same. All the allies supplied troops to the army, in which they fought in auxiliary battalions under Roman officers, but they did not pay taxes to Rome.

Original Roman pavement of the Via Appia, part of the network of military roads that tied all Italy to Rome. These roads enabled Roman legions to move swiftly to enforce their control of Italy. The Via Appia dates from the fourth century B.C.E. Scala/Art Resource, N.Y.

On some of the conquered land the Romans placed colonies, permanent settlements of veteran soldiers in the territory of recently defeated enemies. The colonists retained their Roman citizenship and enjoyed home rule; in return for the land they had been given, they served as a kind of permanent garrison to deter or suppress rebellion. These colonies were usually connected to Rome by a network of military roads built as straight as possible and so durable that some are used even today. The roads guaranteed that a Roman army could swiftly reinforce an embattled colony or put down an uprising in any weather.

The Roman settlement of Latium reveals even more clearly than before the principles by which Rome was able to conquer and dominate Italy for many centuries. The excellent army and the diplomatic skill that allowed Rome to separate its enemies help to explain its conquests. The reputation for harsh punishment of rebels, and the sure promise that such punishment would be delivered was made unmistakably clear: Both the colonies and military roads help to explain the reluctance to revolt. But the positive side, represented by Rome's organization of the defeated states, is at least as important. The Romans did not regard the status given each newly conquered city as permanent. They held out to loyal allies the prospect of improving their status—even of achieving the ultimate prize, full Roman citizenship. In so doing, the Romans gave their allies a stake in Rome's future success and a sense of being colleagues, though subordinate ones, rather than subjects. The result, in general, was that most of Rome's allies remained loyal even when put to the severest test.

DEFEAT OF THE SAMNITES   The next great challenge to Roman arms came in a series of wars with a tough mountain people of the southern Apennines, the Samnites. Some of Rome's allies rebelled, and soon the Etruscans and Gauls joined in the war against Rome. But most of the allies remained loyal. In 295 B.C.E., at Sentinum, the Romans defeated an Italian coalition, and by 280 B.C.E. they were masters of central Italy. Their power extended from the Po Valley south to Apulia and Lucania.

Now the Romans were in direct contact with the Greek cities of southern Italy. Roman intervention in a quarrel between Greek cities brought them face to face with Pyrrhus, king of Epirus. Pyrrhus, probably the best general of his time, commanded a well-disciplined and experienced mercenary army, which he hired out for profit, and a new weapon: twenty war elephants. He defeated the Romans twice, but suffered many casualties. When one of his officers rejoiced at the victory, Pyrrhus told him, "If we win one more battle against the Romans we shall be completely ruined." This "Pyrrhic victory" led him to withdraw to Sicily in 275 B.C.E. The Greek cities that had hired him were forced to join the Roman confederation. By 265 B.C.E. Rome ruled all Italy as far north as the Po River, an area of 47,200 square miles. The year after the defeat of Pyrrhus, Ptolemy Philadelphus, king of Egypt, sent a message of congratulations to establish friendly relations with Rome. This act recognized Rome's new status as a power in the Hellenistic world.

Roman Expansion in Italy	
392 B.C.E.	Fall of Veii; Etruscans defeated
387 B.C.E.	Gauls burn Rome
338 B.C.E.	Latin League defeated
295 B.C.E.	Battle of Sentinum; Samnites and allies defeated
275 B.C.E.	Pyrrhus driven from Italy
265 B.C.E.	Rome rules Italy south of the Po River

Rome and Carthage

The conquest of southern Italy brought the Romans face to face with the great naval power of the western Mediterranean, Carthage. (See Map 4–2.) Late in the ninth century B.C.E., the Phoenician city of Tyre had planted a colony on the coast of northern Africa near modern Tunis, calling it the New City, or Carthage. In the sixth century B.C.E., the conquest of Phoenicia by the Assyrians and the Persians left Carthage independent and free to exploit its very advantageous situation. The city was located on a defensible site and commanded an excellent harbor that encouraged commerce. The coastal plain grew abundant grain, fruits, and vegetables. An inland plain allowed sheep herding. The Phoenician settlers conquered the native inhabitants and used them to work the land.

Beginning in the sixth century B.C.E., the Carthaginians expanded their domain to include the coast of northern Africa west beyond the Straits of Gibraltar and eastward into Libya. Overseas, they came to control the southern part of Spain, Sardinia, Corsica, Malta, the Balearic Islands, and western Sicily. The people of these territories, though originally allies, were all reduced to subjection like the natives of the Carthaginian home territory. They all served in the Carthaginian army or navy and paid tribute. Carthage also profited greatly from the mines of Spain and from an absolute monopoly of trade imposed on the western Mediterranean.

An attack by Hiero, tyrant of Syracuse, on the Sicilian city of Messana just across from Italy first caused trouble between Rome and Carthage. Messana had been seized by a group of Italian mercenary soldiers who called themselves *Mamertines*, the sons of the war god Mars. When Hiero defeated the Mamertines, some of them called on the Carthaginians to help save their city. Carthage agreed and sent a garrison, for the Carthaginians wanted to prevent Syracuse from dominating the straits. One Mamertine faction, however, fearing that Carthage might take undue advantage of the opportunity, asked Rome for help.

In 264 B.C.E., the request came to the Senate. Because a Punic garrison (the Romans called the Carthaginians *Phoenicians*; in Latin the word is *Poeni* or *Puni*—hence the adjective *Punic*) was in place at Messana, any intervention would be not against Syracuse, but against the mighty empire of Carthage. Unless Rome intervened, however, Carthage would gain control of all Sicily and the straits. The assembly voted to send an army to Messana and expelled the Punic garrison. The First Punic War was on.

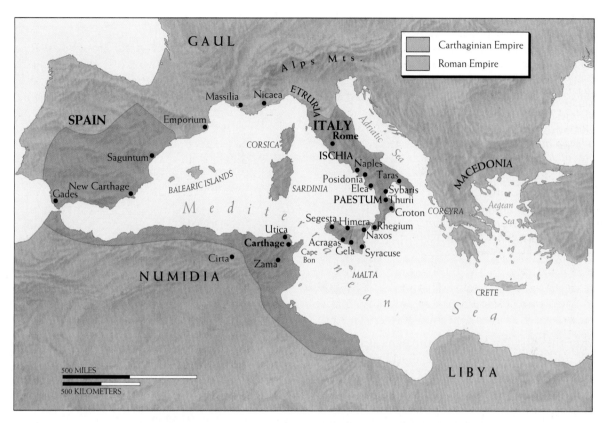

MAP 4–2   THE WESTERN MEDITERRANEAN AREA DURING THE RISE OF ROME   *This map covers the theater of conflict between the growing Roman dominions and those of Carthage in the third century* B.C.E. *The Carthaginian Empire stretched westward from the city (in modern Tunisia) along the North African coast and into southern Spain.*

THE FIRST PUNIC WAR (264–241 B.C.E.)   The war in Sicily soon settled into a stalemate until the Romans built a fleet to cut off supplies to the besieged Carthaginian cities at the western end of Sicily. When Carthage sent its own fleet to raise the siege, the Romans destroyed it. In 241 B.C.E. Carthage signed a treaty giving up Sicily and the islands between Italy and Sicily; it also agreed to pay a war indemnity in ten annual installments. Neither side was to attack the allies of the other. The peace was realistic and not unduly harsh; Rome had earned Sicily, and Carthage could well afford the indemnity. If it had been carried out in good faith, it might have brought lasting peace.

A rebellion, however, broke out in Carthage among the mercenaries, newly recruited from Sicily, who now demanded their pay. In 238 B.C.E., while Carthage was still preoccupied with the rebellion, Rome seized Sardinia and Corsica and demanded that Carthage pay an additional indemnity. This was a harsh and cynical action by the Romans; even the historian Polybius, a great champion of Rome, could find no justification for it. It undid the calming effects of the peace of 241 B.C.E. without preventing the Carthaginians from recovering their strength to seek vengeance in the future.

The conquest of overseas territory presented the Romans with new administrative problems. Instead of following the policy they had pursued in Italy, they made Sicily a province and Sardinia and Corsica another. It became common to extend the term of the governors of these provinces beyond a year. The governors were unchecked by colleagues and exercised full imperium. New magistracies, in effect, were thus created free of the limits put on the power of officials in Rome.

The new populations were neither Roman citizens nor allies; they were subjects who did not serve in the army, but paid tribute instead. The old practice of extending citizenship and, with it, loyalty to Rome thus stopped at the borders of Italy. Rome collected taxes on these subjects by "farming" them out at auction to the highest bidder. At first, the tax collectors were natives from the same province. Later they were Roman allies and, finally, Roman citizens below senatorial rank who could become powerful and wealthy by squeezing the provincials hard. These innovations were the basis for Rome's imperial organization in the future. In time, they strained the constitution and traditions to such a degree as to threaten the existence of the republic.

A Roman warship. Rome became a naval power late in its history, in the course of the First Punic War. Roman sailors initially lacked the skill and experience in sea warfare of their Carthaginian opponents, who could maneuver their oared ships to ram the enemy. To compensate for this disadvantage, the Romans sought to make a sea battle more like an encounter on land by devising ways to grapple enemy ships and board them with armed troops. In time, they also mastered the skillful use of the ram. This picture shows a Roman ship, propelled by oars, with both ram and soldiers, ready for either kind of fight. Direzione Generale Musei Vaticani.

After the First Punic War, campaigns against the Gauls and across the Adriatic distracted Rome. Meanwhile Hamilcar Barca, the Carthaginian governor of Spain from 237 B.C.E. until his death in 229 B.C.E., was leading Carthage on the road to recovery. Hamilcar sought to compensate for Carthaginian losses elsewhere by building a Punic Empire in Spain. He improved the ports and the commerce conducted in them, exploited the mines, gained control of the hinterland, won over many of the conquered tribes, and built a strong and disciplined army.

Hamilcar's successor, his son-in-law Hasdrubal, pursued the same policies. His success alarmed the Romans. They imposed a treaty in which he promised not to take an army north across the Ebro River in Spain, although Punic expansion in Spain was well south of that river at the time. Though the agreement appeared to put Rome in the position of giving orders to an inferior, it benefited both sides equally. If the Carthaginians accepted the limit of the Ebro on their expansion in Spain, the Romans would not interfere with that expansion.

THE SECOND PUNIC WAR (218–202 B.C.E.)   On Hasdrubal's assassination in 221 B.C.E., the army chose as his successor Hannibal, son of Hamilcar Barca. Hannibal was at that time twenty-five years old. He quickly consolidated and extended the Punic Empire in Spain. A few years before his accession, Rome had received an offer of alliance from the people of the Spanish town Saguntum (about one hundred miles south of the Ebro). The Romans accepted the friendship and the responsibilities it entailed, in the process violating at least the spirit of the Ebro treaty. At first, Hannibal was careful to avoid any action against Saguntum, but the Saguntines, con-

fident of Rome's protection, began to interfere with some of the Spanish tribes allied with Hannibal. When the Romans sent an embassy to Hannibal warning him to let Saguntum alone and repeating the injunction not to cross the Ebro, he ignored the warning and proceeded to besiege and capture the town. The Romans sent an ultimatum to Carthage demanding the surrender of Hannibal. Carthage refused, and Rome declared war in 218 B.C.E.

Between the close of the First Punic War and the outbreak of the Second, Rome had repeatedly provoked Carthage, taking Sardinia in 238 B.C.E. and interfering in Spain, but had taken no measures to prevent Carthage from building a powerful and dangerous empire or even to prepare defenses against a Punic attack in Spain. Hannibal saw to it that the Romans paid the price for these blunders. By September of 218 B.C.E. he was across the Alps, in Italy and among the friendly Gauls.

Hannibal defeated the Romans at the Ticinus River and crushed the joint consular armies at the Trebia River. In 217 B.C.E., he outmaneuvered and trapped another army at Lake Trasimene. The key to success, however, would be defection by Rome's allies. Hannibal released Italian prisoners without harm or ransom and moved his army south of Rome to encourage rebellion. But the allies remained firm.

Sobered by their defeats, the Romans elected Quintus Fabius Maximus dictator. His strategy was to avoid battle while following and harassing Hannibal's army. He would fight only when his army had recovered and then only on favorable ground.

In 216 B.C.E. Hannibal marched to Cannae in Apulia to tempt the Romans, under different generals, into another open fight. They sent off an army of some 80,000 men to meet him. Almost the entire

Roman army was killed or captured. It was the worst defeat in Roman history. Rome's prestige was shattered, and most of its allies in southern Italy, as well as Syracuse in Sicily, now went over to Hannibal. For more than a decade, no Roman army would dare face Hannibal in the open field.

Hannibal, however, had neither the numbers nor the supplies to besiege walled cities, nor did he have the equipment to take them by assault. To win the war in Spain, the Romans appointed Publius Cornelius Scipio (237–183 B.C.E.), later called Africanus, to the command in Spain with proconsular *imperium*. Scipio was not yet twenty-five and had held no high office. But he was a general almost as talented as Hannibal. Within a few years, young Scipio had conquered all Spain and had deprived Hannibal of hope of help from that region.

In 204 B.C.E. Scipio landed in Africa, defeated the Carthaginians, and forced them to accept a peace, the main clause of which was the withdrawal of Hannibal and his army from Italy. Hannibal had won every battle, but lost the war, for he had not counted on the determination of Rome and the loyalty of its allies. Hannibal's return inspired Carthage to break the peace and to risk all in battle. In 202 B.C.E., Scipio and Hannibal faced each other at the Battle of Zama. The generalship of Scipio and the desertion of Hannibal's mercenaries gave the victory to Rome. The new peace terms reduced Carthage to the status of a dependent ally of Rome. The Second Punic War ended the Carthaginian command of the western Mediterranean and Carthage's term as a great power. Rome ruled the seas and the entire Mediterranean coast from Italy westward.

The Republic's Conquest of the Hellenistic World

THE EAST By the middle of the third century B.C.E., the eastern Mediterranean had reached a condition of stability based on a balance of power among the three great Hellenistic kingdoms that allowed an established place even for lesser states. This equilibrium, however, was threatened by the activities of two aggressive monarchs: Philip V of Macedon (221–179 B.C.E.) and Antiochus III of the Seleucid kingdom (223–187 B.C.E.). Philip and Antiochus moved swiftly, the latter against Syria and Palestine, the former against cities in the Aegean, in the Hellespontine region, and on the coast of Asia Minor.

The threat that a more powerful Macedon might pose to Rome's friends and, perhaps, even to Italy was enough to persuade the Romans to intervene. Philip had already attempted to meddle in Roman affairs when he formed an alliance with

Carthage during the Second Punic War, provoking a conflict known as the First Macedonian War (215–205 B.C.E.). In 200 B.C.E., in an action that began the Second Macedonian War, the Romans sent an ultimatum to Philip ordering him not to attack any Greek city and to pay reparations to Pergamum. These orders were meant to provoke, not avoid, war, and Philip refused to obey. Two years later the Romans sent out a talented young general, Flamininus, who demanded that Philip withdraw from Greece entirely. In 197 B.C.E., with Greek support, Flamininus defeated Philip in the hills of Cynoscephalae in Thessaly, ending the war. The Greek cities freed from Philip were made autonomous, and in 196 B.C.E. Flamininus proclaimed the freedom of the Greeks.

Soon after the Romans withdrew from Greece, they came into conflict with Antiochus, who was expanding his power in Asia and on the European side of the Hellespont. On the pretext of freeing the Greeks from Roman domination, he landed an army on the Greek mainland. The Romans routed Antiochus at Thermopylae and quickly drove him from Greece. In 189 B.C.E., they crushed his army at Magnesia in Asia Minor. The peace of Apamia in the next year deprived Antiochus of his elephants and his navy and imposed a huge indemnity on him. Once again, the Romans took no territory for themselves and left several Greek cities in Asia free. They continued to regard Greece, and now Asia Minor, as a kind of protectorate in which they could intervene or not as they chose.

This relatively mild policy was destined to end as the stern and businesslike policies favored by the conservative censor Cato gained favor in Rome. A new harshness was to be applied to allies and bystanders, as well as to defeated opponents.

In 179 B.C.E., Perseus succeeded Philip V as king of Macedon. He tried to gain popularity in Greece

The Punic Wars	
264–241 B.C.E.	First Punic War
238 B.C.E.	Rome seizes Sardinia and Corsica
221 B.C.E.	Hannibal takes command of Punic army in Spain
218–202 B.C.E.	Second Punic War
216 B.C.E.	Battle of Cannae
209 B.C.E.	Scipio takes New Carthage
202 B.C.E.	Battle of Zama
149–146 B.C.E.	Third Punic War
146 B.C.E.	Destruction of Carthage

Plutarch Describes a Roman Triumph

In 168 B.C.E., L. Æmilius Paullus defeated King Perseus in the Battle of Pydna, bringing an end to the Third Macedonian War. For his great achievement, the Senate granted Paullus the right to celebrate a triumph, the great honorific procession granted only for extraordinary victories and eagerly sought by all Roman generals. Plutarch described the details of Paullus' triumph.

❖ *How do you explain the particular elements displayed on each day of the triumph? What purposes do you think a triumph served? What can be learned from this selection about the values celebrated by the Romans? How are they different from the values cherished by Americans in our day? Are there any similarities?*

The people erected scaffolds in the forum, in the circuses, as they call their buildings for horse races, and in all other parts of the city where they could best behold the show. The spectators were clad in white garments; all the temples were open, and full of garlands and perfumes; the ways were cleared and kept open by numerous officers, who drove back all who crowded into or ran across the main avenue. This triumph lasted three days. On the first, which was scarcely long enough for the sight, were to be seen the statues, pictures, and colossal images which were taken from the enemy, drawn upon two hundred and fifty chariots. On the second was carried in a great many wagons the finest and richest armour of the Macedonians, both of brass and steel, all newly polished and glittering; the pieces of which were piled up and arranged purposely with the greatest art, so as to seem to be tumbled in heaps carelessly and by chance.

On the third day, early in the morning, first came the trumpeters, who did not sound as they were wont in a procession or solemn entry, but such a charge as the Romans use when they encourage the soldiers to fight. Next followed young men wearing frocks with ornamented borders, who led to the sacrifice a hundred and twenty stalled oxen, with their horns gilded, and their heads adorned with ribbons and garlands; and with these were boys that carried basins for libation, of silver and gold.

After his children and their attendants came Perseus himself, clad all in black, and wearing the boots of his country, and looking like one altogether stunned and deprived of reason, through the greatness of his misfortunes. Next followed a great company of his friends and familiars, whose countenances were disfigured with grief, and who let the spectators see, by their tears and their continual looking upon Perseus, that it was his fortune they so much lamented, and that they were regardless of their own.

After these were carried four hundred crowns, all made of gold, sent from the cities by their respective deputations to Æmilius, in honour of his victory. Then he himself came, seated on a chariot magnificently adorned (a man well worthy to be looked at, even without these ensigns of power), dressed in a robe of purple, interwoven with gold, and holding a laurel branch in his right hand. All the army, in like manner, with boughs of laurel in their hands, divided into their bands and companies, followed the chariot of their commander; some singing verses, according to the usual custom, mingled with raillery; others, songs of triumph and the praise of Æmilius' deeds; who, indeed, was admired and accounted happy by all men, and unenvied by every one that was good; except so far as it seems the province of some god to lessen that happiness which is too great and inordinate, and so to mingle the affairs of human life that no one should be entirely free and exempt from calamities; but, as we read in Homer, that those should think themselves truly blessed whom fortune has given an equal share of good and evil.

From Plutarch, "Æemilius Paullus," in *Lives of the Noble Grecians and Romans*, trans. by John Dryden, rev. by A. H. Clough (New York: Random House, n.d.), pp. 340–341.

by favoring the democratic and revolutionary forces in the cities. The Romans, troubled by his threat to stability, launched the Third Macedonian War (172–168 B.C.E.), and in 168 B.C.E. Æmilius Paullus defeated Perseus at Pydna. (See "Plutarch Describes a Roman Triumph.") The peace that followed this war, reflecting the changed attitude at Rome, was harsh. It divided Macedon into four separate republics, whose citizens were forbidden to intermarry or even to do business across the new national boundaries. Leaders of anti-Roman factions in the Greek cities were punished severely.

When Æmilius Paullus returned from his victory, he celebrated for three days by parading the spoils of war, royal prisoners, and great wealth through the streets of Rome. The public treasury benefited to such a degree that the direct property tax on Roman citizens was abolished. Part of the booty went to the general and part to his soldiers. New motives were thereby introduced into Roman foreign policy, or, perhaps, old motives were given new prominence. Foreign campaigns could bring profit to the state, rewards to the army, and wealth, fame, honor, and political power to the general.

THE WEST   Harsh as the Romans had become toward the Greeks, they were even worse in their treatment of the people of the Iberian Peninsula, whom they considered barbarians. They committed dreadful atrocities, lied, cheated, and broke treaties to exploit and pacify the natives, who fought back fiercely in guerilla style. From 154 to 133 B.C.E. the fighting waxed, and it became hard to recruit Roman soldiers to participate in the increasingly ugly war. At last, in 134 B.C.E., Scipio Æmilianus took the key city of Numantia by siege and burned it to the ground. This put an end to the war in Spain.

Roman treatment of Carthage was no better. Although Carthage lived up to its treaty with Rome faithfully and posed no threat, some Romans refused to abandon their hatred and fear of the traditional enemy. Cato is said to have ended all his speeches in the Senate with the same sentence: "Ceterum censeo delendam esse Carthaginem" ("Besides, I think that Carthage must be destroyed"). At last the Romans took advantage of a technical breach of the peace to destroy Carthage. In 146 B.C.E. Scipio Æmilianus took

the city, plowed up its land, and put salt in the furrows as a symbol of the permanent abandonment of the site. The Romans incorporated it as the province of Africa, one of six Roman provinces, including Sicily, Sardinia–Corsica, Macedonia, Hither Spain, and Further Spain.

Civilization in the Early Roman Republic

Close and continued association with the Greeks of the Hellenistic world wrought important changes in the Roman style of life and thought. The Roman attitude toward the Greeks ranged from admiration for their culture and history to contempt for their constant squabbling, their commercial practices, and their weakness. Conservatives such as Cato might speak contemptuously of the Greeks as "Greeklings" (*Graeculi*), but even he learned Greek and absorbed Greek culture.

Before long, the education of the Roman upper classes was bilingual. In addition to the Twelve Tables, young Roman nobles studied Greek rhetoric, literature, and sometimes philosophy. These studies even had an effect on education and the Latin language. As early as the third century B.C.E. Livius Andronicus, a liberated Greek slave, translated the *Odyssey* into Latin. It became a primer for young Romans and put Latin on the road to becoming a literary language.

Religion

Roman religion was influenced by the Greeks almost from the beginning. The Romans identified their own gods with Greek equivalents and incorporated Greek mythology into their own. Mostly, however, Roman religious practice remained simple and Italian, until the third century B.C.E. brought important new influences from the East.

In 205 B.C.E. the Senate approved the public worship of Cybele, the Great Mother goddess from Phrygia. Hers was a fertility cult accompanied by ecstatic, frenzied, and sensual rites that shocked and outraged conservative Romans to such a degree that they soon banned the cult. Similarly, the Senate banned the worship of Dionysus, or Bacchus, in 186 B.C.E. In the second century B.C.E. interest in Babylonian astrology also grew, and the Senate's attempt in 139 B.C.E. to expel the "Chaldaeans," as the astrologers were called, did not prevent the continued influence of their superstition.

Roman Engagement Overseas	
215–205 B.C.E.	First Macedonian War
200–197 B.C.E.	Second Macedonian War
196 B.C.E.	Proclamation of Greek freedom by Flamininus at Corinth
189 B.C.E.	Battle of Magnesia; Antiochus defeated in Asia Minor
172–168 B.C.E.	Third Macedonian War
168 B.C.E.	Battle of Pydna
154–133 B.C.E.	Roman wars in Spain
134 B.C.E.	Numantia taken

Education

The education provided in the early centuries of the Roman Republic reflected the limited, conservative, and practical nature of that community of plain farmers and soldiers. Education was entirely the responsibility of the family, the father teaching his own son at home. It is not clear whether in these early times girls received any education, though they certainly did later on. The boys learned to read, write, and calculate, and they learned the skills of farming. They memorized the laws of the Twelve Tables, learned how to perform religious rites, heard stories of the great deeds of early Roman history and particularly those of their ancestors, and engaged in the physical training appropriate for potential soldiers. This course of study was practical, vocational, and moral; it aimed at making the boys moral, pious, patriotic, law abiding, and respectful of tradition.

HELLENIZED EDUCATION   In the third century B.C.E. the Romans came into contact with the Greeks of southern Italy, and this contact produced momentous changes in Roman education. Greek teachers introduced the study of language, literature, and philosophy, as well as the idea of a liberal education, or what the Romans called *humanitas*, the root of our concept of the humanities. The aim of education changed from the mastery of practical, vocational skills to an emphasis on broad intellectual training, critical thinking, an interest in ideas, and the development of a well-rounded person.

The new emphasis required students to learn Greek, for Rome did not yet have a literature of its own. Hereafter, educated Romans were expected to be bilingual. For this purpose, schools were established in which a teacher, called a *grammaticus*, taught students the Greek language and its literature, especially the poets and particularly Homer. After the completion of this elementary education, Roman boys of the upper classes studied rhetoric—the art of speaking and writing well. For the Greeks, rhetoric was a subject of less importance than philosophy. The more practical Romans took to it avidly, however, for it was of great use in legal disputes and was becoming ever more valuable in political life.

Some Romans were powerfully attracted to Greek literature and philosophy. The important and powerful Roman aristocrat, Scipio Æmilianus, the man who finally defeated and destroyed Carthage, surrounded himself and his friends with such Greek thinkers as the historian Polybius and the philosopher Panaetius.

Equally outstanding Romans, such as Cato the Elder, were more conservative and opposed the new learning on the grounds that it would weaken Roman moral fiber. (See "Cato Educates His Son.") They were able on more than one occasion to pass laws expelling philosophers and teachers of rhetoric. But these attempts to go back to older ways failed. The new education suited the needs of the Romans of the second century B.C.E. They found themselves changing from a rural to an urban society and were being thrust into the sophisticated world of Hellenistic Greeks.

By the last century of the Roman Republic, the new Hellenized education had become dominant. Latin literature had come into being, along with Latin translations of Greek poets, and these formed part of the course of study. But Roman gentlemen still were expected to be bilingual, and Greek language and literature were still central to the curriculum. Many schools were established. The number of educated people grew, extending beyond the senatorial class to the equestrians and outside Rome to the cities of Italy.

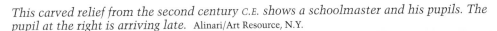

This carved relief from the second century C.E. shows a schoolmaster and his pupils. The pupil at the right is arriving late. Alinari/Art Resource, N.Y.

Cato Educates His Son

Marcus Porcius Cato (234–149 B.C.E.) was a remarkable Roman who rose from humble origins to the highest offices in the state. He stood as the firmest defender of the old Roman traditions at a time when Hellenic ideas were strongly influential. In the following passage, Plutarch tells how Cato attended to his son's education.

❖ *What was the curriculum prepared for Cato's son? Was it suitable for the kind of life he would lead? Was his education more or less helpful and appropriate in this way than that of the average American student today? Why did Cato teach his son himself? Why did he pay so much attention to Roman history? Was he wise in doing so?*

After the birth of his son, no business could be so urgent, unless it had a public character, as to prevent him from being present when his wife bathed and swaddled the babe. For the mother nursed it herself, and often gave suck also to the infants of her slaves, that so they might come to cherish a brotherly affection for her son. As soon as the boy showed signs of understanding, his father took him under his own charge and taught him to read, although he had an accomplished slave, Chilo by name, who was a school teacher, and taught many boys. Still, Cato thought it not right, as he tells us himself, that his son should be scolded by a slave, or have his ears tweaked when he was slow to learn, still less that he should be indebted to his slave for such a priceless thing as education. He was therefore himself not only the boy's reading teacher, but his tutor in law, and his athletic trainer, and he taught his son not merely to hurl the javelin and fight in armour and ride the horse, but also to box, to endure heat and cold, and to swim lustily through the eddies and billows of the Tiber. His *History of Rome*, as he tells us himself, he wrote out with his own hand and in large characters, that his son might have in his own home an aid to acquaintance with his country's ancient traditions.

Plutarch, *Cato Major*, 20, trans. by Bernadotte Perrin (London and New York: Loeb Classical Library, William Heinemann, 1914).

In the late republic, Roman education, though still entirely private, became more formal and organized. From the ages of seven to twelve, boys went to elementary school accompanied by a Greek slave called a *paedagogus* (whence our term *pedagogue*), who looked after their physical well-being and their manners, and who improved their ability in Greek conversation. At school the boys learned to read and write, using a wax tablet and a stylus, and to do simple arithmetic with an abacus and pebbles (*calculi*). Discipline was harsh and corporal punishment frequent. From twelve to sixteen, boys went to a higher school, where the *grammaticus* undertook to provide a liberal education, using Greek and Latin literature as his subject matter. In addition, he taught dialectic, arithmetic, geometry, astronomy, and music. Sometimes he included the elements of rhetoric, especially for those boys who would not go on to a higher education.

At sixteen, some boys went on to advanced study in rhetoric. The instructors were usually Greek. They trained their charges by studying models of fine speech of the past and by having them write, memorize, and declaim speeches suitable for different occasions. Sometimes the serious student attached himself to some famous public speaker and followed him about to learn what he could. Sometimes a rich and ambitious Roman would support a Greek philosopher in his own home. His son could converse with the philosopher and acquire the learning and polished thought necessary for the fully cultured gentleman. Some, like the great orator Cicero, undertook what we might call postgraduate study by traveling abroad to study with great teachers of rhetoric and philosophy in the Greek world.

One result of this whole style of education was to broaden the Romans' understanding through the careful study of a foreign language and culture. It made them a part of the older and wider culture of the Hellenistic world, a world that they had come to dominate and needed to understand.

EDUCATION FOR WOMEN   Though the evidence is limited, we can be sure that girls of the upper classes received an education equivalent at least to the early stages of a boy's education. They were probably taught by tutors at home rather than going to school, as was increasingly the fashion among boys in the late republic. Young women did not study with philosophers and rhetoricians, for they were usually married by the age at which the men were pursuing their higher edu-

This wall painting from the first century B.C.E. *comes from the villa of Publius Fannius Synistor at Pompeii and shows a woman playing a cithera.* Fresco on lime plaster. H. 6 ft. 1 1/2 in. W. 6 ft. 1 1/2 in. (187 x 187 cm.) The Metropolitan Museum of Art, Rogers Fund, 1903. (03.14.5) Photograph © 1986 The Metropolitan Museum of Art

cation. Still, some women found ways to continue their education. Some became prose writers and others poets. By the first century C.E., there were apparently enough learned women to provoke the complaints of a crotchety and conservative satirist:

Still more exasperating is the woman who begs as soon as she sits down to dinner, to discourse on poets and poetry, comparing Virgil with Homer; professors, critics, lawyers, auctioneers—even another woman—can't get a word in. She rattles on at such a rate that you'd think that all the pots and pans in the kitchen were crashing to the floor or that every bell in town was clanging. All by herself she makes as much noise as some primitive tribe chasing away an eclipse. She should learn the philosopher's lesson: "moderation is necessary even for intellectuals." And, if she still wants to appear educated and eloquent, let her dress as a man, sacrifice to men's gods and bathe in the men's baths. Wives shouldn't try to be public speakers; they shouldn't use rhetorical devices; they shouldn't read all the classics—there should be some things women don't understand. I myself cannot understand a woman who can quote the rules of grammar and never make a mistake and cites obscure, long-forgotten poets—as if men cared about such things. If she has to correct somebody let her correct her girl friends and leave her husband alone.[4]

(Also see "Women's Uprising in Republican Rome.")

[4]Juvenal, Satires 6.434–456, trans. by Roger Killian, Richard Lynch, Robert J. Rowland, and John Sims, cited by Sarah B. Pomeroy in *Goddesses, Whores, Wives, and Slaves* (New York: Schocken Books, 1975), p. 172.

Slavery

Like most ancient peoples, the Romans had slaves from very early in their history, but among the shepherds and family farmers of early Rome they were relatively few. Slavery became a basic element in the Roman economy and society only during the second century B.C.E., after the Romans had conquered most of the lands bordering the Mediterranean. In the time between the beginning of Rome's first war against Carthage (264 B.C.E.) and the conquest of Spain (133 B.C.E.), the Romans enslaved some 250,000 prisoners of war, greatly increasing the availability of slave labor and reducing its price. Many slaves worked as domestic servants, feeding the Roman upper class' growing appetite for luxury; at the other end of the spectrum, many worked in the mines of Spain and Sardinia. Some worked as artisans in small factories and shops or as public clerks. Slaves were permitted to marry, and they appear to have produced sizable families. As in Greece, domestic slaves and those used in crafts and commerce were permitted to earn money, to keep it, and, in some cases, to use it to purchase their own freedom. Manumission (the freeing of slaves) was very common among the Romans. After a time, a considerable proportion of the Roman people included freedmen who had been slaves themselves or whose ancestors had been bondsmen. It was not uncommon to see the son or grandson of a slave become wealthy as a freedman and the slave himself or his son become a Roman citizen.

The unique development in the Roman world was the emergence of an agricultural system that employed and depended on a vast number of slaves. By the time of Jesus there were between two and three million slaves in Italy, and about 35 to 40 percent of the total population, most of them part of great slave gangs that worked the vast plantations the Romans called *latifundia*. Turning from the grain that was the chief crop of the free Roman farmer, these large estates concentrated on such cash-producing products as wool, wine, and olive oil. The life of Rome's agricultural slaves appears to have been much harder than that of other Roman slaves and of slaves in other ancient societies, with the possible exception of slaves working in mines. *Latifundia* owners sought maximum profits and treated their slaves simply as means to that end. The slaves often worked in chains, were oppressed by brutal foremen, and lived in underground prisons.

Such harsh treatment led to a number of serious slave rebellions of a kind we do not hear of in other ancient societies. A rebellion in Sicily in 134 B.C.E.

Women's Uprising in Republican Rome

In 195 B.C.E., Roman women staged a rare public political protest when they demanded the repeal of a law passed two decades earlier during the Second Punic War, which they judged to limit their rights unfairly. Livy (59 B.C.E.–17 C.E.) describes the affair and the response of the traditionalist Marcus Porcius Cato (234–149 B.C.E.).

❖ *Of what did the women complain? How did they try to achieve their goals? Which of Cato's objections to their behavior do you think were most important? Since women did not vote or sit in assemblies, how can the outcome of the affair be explained?*

Amid the anxieties of great wars, either scarce finished or soon to come, an incident occurred, trivial to relate, but which, by reason of the passions it aroused, developed into a violent contention. [Two] tribunes of the people, proposed to the assembly the abrogation of the Oppian law. The tribune Gaius Oppius had carried this law in the heat of the Punic War,. . . that no woman should possess more than half an ounce of gold or wear a parti-coloured garment or ride in a carriage in the City or in a town within a mile thereof, except on the occasion of a religious festival. . . . [T]he Capitoline was filled with crowds of supporters and opponents of the bill. The matrons could not be kept at home by. . .their husbands' orders, but blocked all the streets and approaches to the Forum, begging the men as they came down to the Forum that, in the prosperous condition of the state, when the private fortunes of all men were daily increasing, they should allow the woman too to have their former distinctions restored. The crowd of women grew larger day by day; for they were now coming in from the towns and rural districts. Soon they dared even to approach and appeal to the consuls, the praetors, and the other officials, but one consul, at least, they found adamant, Marcus Porcius Cato, who spoke thus in favour of the law whose repeal was being urged:

"If each of us, citizens, had determined to assert his rights and dignity as a husband with 'respect to his own spouse, we should have less trouble with the sex as a whole; as it is, our liberty, destroyed at home by female violence, even here in the Forum is crushed and trodden underfoot, and because we have not kept them individually under control, we dread them collectively. . . . But from no class is there not the greatest danger if you permit them meetings. . . . and secret consultations.

"I should have said, 'What sort of practice is this, of running out into the streets and blocking the roads and speaking to other women's husbands? Could you not have made the same requests, each of your own husband, at home? And yet, not even at home, if modesty would keep matrons within the limits of their proper rights, did it become you to concern yourselves with the question of what laws should be adopted in this place or repealed.' Our ancestors permitted no woman to conduct even personal business without a guardian to intervene in her behalf; they wished them to be under the control of fathers, brothers, husbands; we (Heaven help us!) allow them now even to interfere in public affairs, yes, and to visit the Forum and our informal and formal sessions. Give loose rein to their uncontrollable nature and to this untamed creature and expect that they will themselves set bounds to their licence; unless you act, this is the least of the things enjoined upon women by custom or law and to which they submit with a feeling of injustice. It is complete liberty or, rather, if we wish to speak the truth, complete licence that they desire.

"If they win in this, what will they not attempt? Review all the laws with which your forefathers restrained their licence and made them subject to their husbands; even with all these bonds you can scarcely control them. What of this? If you suffer them to seize these bonds one by one and wrench themselves free and finally to be placed on a parity with their husbands, do you think that you will be able to endure them? The moment they begin to be your equals, they will be your superiors."

The next day an even greater crowd of women appeared in public, and all of them in a body beset the doors of those tribunes, who were vetoing their colleagues' proposal, and they did not desist until the threat of veto was withdrawn by the tribunes. After that there was no question that all the tribes would vote to repeal the law. The law was repealed twenty years after it was passed.

From *Livy*, trans. by Evan T. Stage (Cambridge, Mass.: Harvard University Press, 1935), XXXIV, i–iii; viii; pp. 413–419, 439.

kept the island in turmoil for more than two years, and the rebellion of the gladiators led by Spartacus in 73 B.C.E. produced an army of seventy thousand slaves that repeatedly defeated the Roman legions and overran all of southern Italy before it was brutally crushed.

Slavery retained its economic and social importance in the first century of the imperial period, but its centrality began to decline in the second. The institution was never abolished, nor did it disappear while the Roman Empire lasted, but over time it became less important. The reasons for this decline are rather obscure. A rise in the cost of slaves and a consequent reduction in their economic value seem to have been factors. More important, it appears, was a general economic decline that permitted increasing pressure on the free lower classes. More and more they were employed as *coloni*—tenant farmers—tied by imperial law to the land they worked, ostensibly free, but bonded and obligated. Over centuries, most agricultural slave labor was replaced by these increasingly serflike *coloni*. Pockets of slave labor remained as late as the time of Charlemagne, but the system of ancient slavery had essentially been replaced by the time the Roman Empire fell in the West.

Roman Imperialism: The Late Republic

Rome's expansion in Italy and overseas was accomplished without a grand general plan. (See Map 4–3.) The new territories were gained as a result of wars that the Romans believed were either defensive or preventive. Their foreign policy was aimed at providing security for Rome on Rome's terms, but these terms were often unacceptable to other nations and led to continued conflict. Whether intended or not, Rome's expansion brought the Romans an empire and, with it, power, wealth, and responsibilities. The need to govern an empire beyond the seas would severely test the republican constitution that had served Rome well during its years as a city–state and that had been well adapted to the mastery of Italy. Roman society and the Roman character had maintained their integrity through the period of expansion in Italy. But these would be tested by the temptations and strains presented by the wealth and the complicated problems of an overseas empire.

The Aftermath of Conquest

War and expansion changed the economic, social, and political life of Italy. Before the Punic wars most Italians owned their own farms, which provided the greater part of the family's needs. Some families owned larger holdings, but their lands chiefly grew grain, and they used the labor of clients, tenants, and hired workers rather than slaves. Fourteen years of fighting in the Second Punic War did terrible damage to much Italian farmland. Many veterans returning from the wars found it impossible or unprofitable to go back to their farms. Some moved to Rome, where they could find work as occasional laborers, but most stayed in the country to work as tenant farmers or hired hands. Often, the land they abandoned was gathered into large parcels by the wealthy. They converted these units, later called *latifundia*, into large plantations for growing cash crops—grain, olives, and grapes for wine—or into cattle ranches.

The upper classes had plenty of capital to stock and operate these estates because of profits from the war and from exploiting the provinces. Land was cheap, and slaves conquered in war provided cheap labor. By fair means and foul, large landholders obtained great quantities of public land and forced small farmers from it. These changes separated the people of Rome and Italy more sharply into rich and poor, landed and landless, privileged and deprived. The result was political, social, and, ultimately, constitutional conflict that threatened the existence of the republic.

The Gracchi

By the middle of the second century B.C.E., the problems caused by Rome's rapid expansion troubled perceptive Roman nobles. The fall in status of peasant farmers made it harder to recruit soldiers and came to present a political threat as well. The patron's traditional control over his clients was weakened by their flight from their land. Even those former landowners who worked on the land of their patrons as tenants or hired hands were less reliable. The introduction of the secret ballot in the 130s B.C.E. made them even more independent.

TIBERIUS GRACCHUS   In 133 B.C.E., Tiberius Gracchus tried to solve these problems. He became tribune for 133 B.C.E. on a program of land reform; some of the most powerful members of the Roman aristocracy helped him draft the bill. They meant it to be a moderate attempt at solving Rome's problems. The bill's target was public land that had been acquired and held illegally, some of it for many years. The bill allowed holders of this land to retain as many as 300 acres in clear title as private property, but the state would reclaim any-

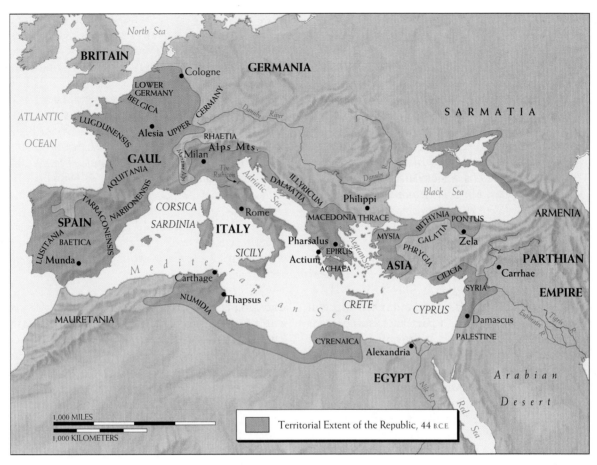

MAP 4–3 ROMAN DOMINIONS OF THE LATE ROMAN REPUBLIC *The Roman Republic's conquest of Mediterranean lands—and beyond—until the death of Julius Caesar is shown here. Areas conquered before Tiberius Gracchus (ca. 133 B.C.E.) are distinguished from later ones and from client areas owing allegiance to Rome.*

thing over that. The recovered land would be redistributed in small lots to the poor, who would pay a small rent to the state and could not sell what they had received.

The bill aroused great hostility. Many senators held vast estates and would be hurt by its passage. Others thought it would be a bad precedent to allow any interference with property rights, even ones so dubious as those pertaining to illegally held public land. Still others feared the political gains that Tiberius and his associates would make if the beneficiaries of their law were properly grateful to its drafters. (See "The Ruin of the Roman Family Farm and the Gracchan Reforms.")

When Tiberius put the bill before the tribal assembly, one of the tribunes, M. Octavius, interposed his veto. Tiberius went to the Senate to discuss his proposal, but the senators continued their opposition. Tiberius now had to choose between dropping the matter and undertaking a revolutionary course. Unwilling to give up, he put his bill before the trib-

al assembly again. Again Octavius vetoed. So Tiberius, strongly supported by the people, had Octavius removed from office, violating the constitution. The assembly's removal of a magistrate implied a fundamental shift of power from the Senate to the people. If the assembly could pass laws opposed by the Senate and vetoed by a tribune, if they could remove magistrates, then Rome would become a democracy like Athens instead of a traditional oligarchy. At this point many of Tiberius' powerful senatorial allies deserted him.

Tiberius proposed a second bill, harsher than the first and more appealing to the people, for he had given up hope of conciliating the Senate. This bill, which passed the assembly, provided for a commission to carry it out. When King Attalus of Pergamum died and left his kingdom to Rome, Tiberius proposed to use the Pergamene revenue to finance the commission. This proposal challenged the Senate's control both of finances and of foreign affairs. Hereafter there could be no compro-

The Ruin of the Roman Family Farm and the Gracchan Reforms

The independent family farm was the backbone both of the Greek polis *and of the early Roman Republic. Rome's conquests, the long wars that kept the citizen–soldier away from his farm, and the availability of great numbers of slaves at a low price, however, badly undercut the traditional way of farming and with it the foundations of republican society. In the following passage, Plutarch describes the process of agricultural change and the response to it of the reformer Tiberius Gracchus, tribune in 133* B.C.E.

❖ *What were the causes of the troubles faced by Roman farmers? What were the social and political consequences of the changes in agricultural life? What solution did Tiberius Gracchus propose? Can you think of any reasons, besides selfishness and greed, that people might oppose his plan?*

Of the territory which the Romans won in war from their neighbours, a part they sold, and a part they made common land, and assigned it for occupation to the poor and indigent among the citizens, on payment of a small rent into the public treasury. And when the rich began to offer larger rents and drove out the poor, a law was enacted forbidding the holding by one person of more than five hundred acres of land. For a short time this enactment gave a check to the rapacity of the rich, and was of assistance to the poor, who remained in their places on the land which they had rented and occupied the allotment which each had held from the outset. But later on the neighbouring rich men, by means of fictitious personages, transferred these rentals to themselves, and finally held most of the land openly in their own names. Then the poor, who had been ejected from their land, no longer showed themselves eager for military service, and neglected the bringing up of children, so that soon all Italy was conscious of a dearth of freemen, and was filled with gangs of foreign slaves, by whose aid the rich cultivated their estates, from which they had driven away the free citizens.

And it is thought that a law dealing with injustice and rapacity so great was never drawn up in milder and gentler terms. For men who ought to have been punished for their disobedience and to have surrendered with payment of a fine the land which they were illegally enjoying, these men it merely ordered to abandon their injust acquisitions upon being paid their value, and to admit into ownership of them such citizens as needed assistance. But although the rectification of the wrong was so considerate, the people were satisfied to let bygones be bygones if they could be secure from such wrong in the future; the men of wealth and substance, however, were led by their greed to hate the law, and by their wrath and contentiousness to hate the lawgiver, and tried to dissuade the people by alleging that Tiberius was introducing a re-distribution of land for the confusion of the body politic, and was stirring up a general revolution.

From Plutarch, "Tiberius Gracchus," in *Lives* 8–9, Vol. 10, trans. by Bernadotte Perrin and William Heinemann (London and New York: G. P. Putnam's Sons, 1921), pp. 159–167.

mise: Either Tiberius or the Roman constitution must go under.

Tiberius understood the danger that he would face if he stepped down from the tribunate, so he announced his candidacy for a second successive term, striking another blow at tradition. His opponents feared that he might go on to hold office indefinitely, to dominate Rome in what appeared to them a demagogic tyranny. They concentrated their fire on the constitutional issue, the deposition of the tribune. They appear to have had some success, for many of Tiberius' supporters did not come out to vote. At the elections a riot broke out, and a mob of senators and their clients killed Tiberius and some 300 of his followers and threw their bodies into the Tiber River. The Senate had put down the threat to its rule, but at the price of the first internal bloodshed in Roman political history.

The tribunate of Tiberius Gracchus brought a permanent change to Roman politics. Heretofore

Roman political struggles had generally been struggles for honor and reputation between great families or coalitions of such families. Fundamental issues were rarely at stake. The revolutionary proposals of Tiberius, however, and the senatorial resort to bloodshed created a new situation. Tiberius' use of the tribunate to challenge senatorial rule encouraged imitation in spite of his failure. From then on, Romans could pursue a political career that was not based solely on influence within the aristocracy; pressure from the people might be an effective substitute. In the last century of the republic, politicians who sought such backing were called *populares*, whereas those who supported the traditional role of the Senate were called *optimates* or "the best men."

These groups were not political parties with formal programs and party discipline, but they were more than merely vehicles for the political ambitions of unorthodox politicians. Fundamental questions—such as those about land reform, the treatment of the Italian allies, the power of the assemblies versus the power of the Senate, and other problems—divided the Roman people, from the time of Tiberius Gracchus to the fall of the republic. Some popular leaders, of course, were cynical self-seekers who used the issues only for their own ambitions. Some few may have been sincere advocates of a principled position. Most, no doubt, were a mixture of the two, like most politicians in most times. (See "Sallust on Factions and the Decline of the Republic.")

GAIUS GRACCHUS The tribunate of Gaius Gracchus (brother of Tiberius) was much more dangerous than that of Tiberius. All the tribunes of 123 B.C.E. were his supporters, so there could be no veto, and a recent law permitted the reelection of tribunes. Gaius developed a program of such breadth as to appeal to a variety of groups. First, he revived the agrarian commission, which had been allowed to lapse. Because there was not enough good public land left to meet the demand, he proposed to establish new colonies: two in Italy and one on the old site of Carthage. Among other popular acts, he put through a law stabilizing the price of grain in Rome, which involved building granaries to guarantee an adequate supply.

Gaius broke new ground in appealing to the equestrian order in his struggle against the Senate. The equestrians (so called because they served in the Roman cavalry) were neither peasants nor senators. A highly visible minority of them were businesspeople who supplied goods and services to the Roman state and collected its taxes. Almost continuous warfare and the need for tax collection in the provinces had made many of them rich. Most

of the time, these wealthy men had the same outlook as the Senate; generally, they used their profits to purchase land and to try to reach senatorial rank themselves. Still, they had a special interest in Roman expansion and in the exploitation of the provinces. Toward the latter part of the second century B.C.E., they came to have a clear sense of group interest and to exert political influence.

In 129 B.C.E., Pergamum became the new province of Asia. Gaius put through a law turning over to the equestrian order the privilege of collecting its revenue. He also barred senators from serving as jurors on the courts that tried provincial governors charged with extortion. The combination was a wonderful gift for wealthy equestrian businessmen, who were now free to squeeze profits out of the rich province of Asia without much fear of interference from the governors. The results for Roman provincial administration were bad, but the immediate political consequences for Gaius were excellent. The equestrians were now given reality as a class; as a political unit they might be set against the Senate or be formed into a coalition to serve Gaius's purposes.

Gaius easily won reelection as tribune for 122 B.C.E. He aimed at giving citizenship to the Italians, both to solve the problem that their dissatisfaction presented and to add them to his political coalition. But the common people did not want to share the advantages of Roman citizenship. The Senate seized on this proposal as a way of driving a wedge between Gaius and his supporters.

The Romans did not reelect Gaius for 121 B.C.E., leaving him vulnerable to his enemies. A hostile consul provoked an incident that led to violence. The Senate invented an extreme decree ordering the consuls to see to it that no harm came to the republic; in effect, this decree established martial law. Gaius was hunted down and killed, and a senatorial court condemned and put to death some 3,000 of his followers without any trial.

Marius and Sulla

For the moment, the senatorial oligarchy had fought off the challenge to its traditional position. Before long, it faced more serious dangers arising from troubles abroad. The first grew out of a dispute over the succession to the throne of Numidia, a client kingdom of Rome's near Carthage.

MARIUS AND THE JUGURTHINE WAR The victory of Jugurtha, who became king of Numidia, and his massacre of Roman and Italian businessmen in the province, gained Roman attention. Although the Senate was reluctant to become involved, pressure from the equestrians and the people forced the dec-

Sallust on Factions and the Decline of the Republic

Sallust (86–35 B.C.E.) was a supporter of Julius Caesar and of the political faction called populares, *translated here as "the democratic party," opponents of the* optimates, *translated here as "the nobility." In this selection from his monograph on the Jugurthine War, Sallust tries to explain Rome's troubles in the period after the destruction of Carthage in 146 B.C.E.*

❖ *Why did Sallust think that the destruction of Carthage marked the beginning of the decline of the Roman Republic? Does his account of events seem fair and dispassionate? How would a member of "the nobility" have evaluated the same events? Is the existence of factions or "parties" inevitably harmful to a republic?*

The division of the Roman state into warring factions, with all its attendant vices, had originated some years before, as a result of peace and of that material prosperity which men regard as the greatest blessing. Down to the destruction of Carthage, the people and Senate shared the government peaceably and with due restraint, and the citizens did not compete for glory or power; fear of its enemies preserved the good morals of the state. But when the people were relieved of this fear, the favourite vices of prosperity—licence and pride—appeared as a natural consequence. Thus the peace and quiet which they had longed for in time of adversity proved, when they obtained it, to be even more grievous and bitter than the adversity. For the nobles started to use their position, and the people their liberty, to gratify their selfish passions, every man snatching and seizing what he could for himself. So the whole community was split into parties, and the Republic, which hitherto had been the common interest of all, was torn asunder. The nobility had the advantage of being a close-knit body, whereas the democratic party was weakened by its loose organization, its supporters being dispersed among a huge multitude. One small group of oligarchs had everything in its control alike in peace and war—the treasury, the provinces, public offices, all distinctions and triumphs. The people were burdened with military services and poverty, while the spoils of war were snatched by the generals and shared with a handful of friends. Meantime, the soldiers' parents or young children, if they happened to have a powerful neighbour, might well be driven from their homes. Thus the possession of power gave unlimited scope to ruthless greed, which violated and plundered everything, respecting nothing and holding nothing sacred, till finally it brought about its own downfall. For the day came when noblemen rose to power who preferred true glory to unjust dominion: then the state was shaken to its foundations by civil strife, as by an earthquake.

Excerpt from *The Jugurthine War: The Conspiracy of Catiline* by Sallust, translated by S. A. Hanford (Penguin Classics, 1963) © S. A. Hanford, 1963.

laration of what became known as the Jugurthine War in 111 B.C.E.

As the war dragged on, the people, sometimes with good reason, suspected the Senate of taking bribes from Jugurtha. They elected C. Marius (157–86 B.C.E.) to the consulship for 107 B.C.E. The assembly, usurping the role of the Senate, assigned him to Numidia. This action was significant in several ways. Marius was a *novus homo*, a "new man"—that is, the first in the history of his family to reach the consulship. Although a wealthy equestrian, he had been born in the town of Arpinum and was outside the closed circle of the old Roman aristocracy. His earlier career had won him a reputation as an outstanding soldier and something of a political maverick.

Marius quickly defeated Jugurtha, but Jugurtha escaped and guerilla warfare continued. Finally, Marius's subordinate, L. Cornelius Sulla (138–78 B.C.E.), trapped Jugurtha and brought the war to an end. Marius celebrated the victory, but Sulla, an ambitious though impoverished descendant of an old Roman family, resented being cheated of the credit he thought he deserved. Soon rumors circulated crediting Sulla with the victory and diminishing Marius's role. Thus were the seeds planted for a personal rivalry and a mutual hostility that would last until Marius's death.

While the Romans were fighting Jugurtha, a far greater danger threatened Rome from the north. In 105 B.C.E. two barbaric tribes, the Cimbri and the Teutones, had come down the Rhone Valley and crushed a Roman army at Arausio (Orange). When these tribes threatened again, the Romans elected Marius to his second consulship to meet the danger. He served five consecutive terms until 100 B.C.E., when the crisis was over.

While the barbarians were occupied elsewhere, Marius used the time to make important changes in the army. He began using volunteers for the army, mostly the dispossessed farmers and rural proletarians whose problems had not been solved by the Gracchi. They enlisted for a long term of service and looked on the army not as an unwelcome duty, but as an opportunity and a career. They became semiprofessional clients of their general and sought guaranteed food, clothing, shelter, and booty from victories. They came to expect a piece of land as a form of mustering-out pay, or veteran's bonus, when they retired.

Volunteers were most likely to enlist with a man who was a capable soldier and influential enough to obtain what he needed for them. They looked to him rather than to the state for their rewards. He, on the other hand, had to obtain these favors from the Senate if he was to maintain his power and reputation. Marius' innovation created both the opportunity and the necessity for military leaders to gain enough power to challenge civilian authority. The promise of rewards won these leaders the personal loyalty of their troops, and that loyalty allowed them to frighten the Senate into granting their demands.

THE WAR AGAINST THE ITALIAN ALLIES (90–88 B.C.E.) For a decade Rome avoided serious troubles, but in that time the Senate took no action to deal with Italian discontent. The Italians were excluded from the land bill for Marius' veterans. Their discontent was serious enough to cause the Senate to expel all Italians from Rome in 95 B.C.E. Four years later, the tribune M. Livius Drusus put forward a bill to enfranchise the Italians. Drusus seems to have been a sincere aristocratic reformer, but he was assassinated in 90 B.C.E. Frustrated, the Italians revolted and established a separate confederation with its own capital and its own coinage.

Employing the traditional device of divide and conquer, the Romans immediately offered citizenship to those cities that remained loyal and soon made the same offer to the rebels if they laid down their arms. Even then, hard fighting was needed to put down the uprising, but by 88 B.C.E. the war against the allies was over. All the Italians became Roman citizens with the protections that citizenship offered. However, they re-

tained local self-government and a dedication to their own municipalities that made Italy flourish. The passage of time blurred the distinction between Romans and Italians and forged them into a single nation.

SULLA AND HIS DICTATORSHIP During the war against the allies, Sulla had performed well. He was elected consul for 88 B.C.E. and was given command of the war against Mithridates, who was leading a major rebellion in Asia. At this point, the seventy-year-old Marius emerged from obscurity and sought the command for himself. With popular and equestrian support, he got the assembly to transfer the command to him. Sulla, defending the rights of the Senate and his own interests, marched his army against Rome. This was the first time a Roman general had used his army against fellow citizens. Marius and his friends fled, and Sulla regained the command. No sooner had he left again for Asia, than Marius joined with the consul Cinna and reconquered Rome by force. He outlawed Sulla and launched a bloody massacre of the senatorial opposition. Marius died soon after his election to a seventh consulship, for 86 B.C.E.

Cinna now was the chief man at Rome. Supported by Marius's men, he held the consulship from 87

Mithridates the Great, king of Pontus. For two decades he opposed Rome's expansion. In this sculpture from the Louvre, he wears a lion's head in imitation of Hercules.
Giraudon/Art Resource, N.Y.

to 84 B.C.E. His future depended on Sulla's fortunes in the East.

By 85 B.C.E., Sulla had driven Mithridates from Greece and had crossed over to Asia Minor. Eager to regain control of Rome, he negotiated a compromise peace. In 83 B.C.E., he returned to Italy and fought a civil war that lasted for more than a year. Sulla won and drove the followers of Marius from Italy. He now held all power and had himself appointed dictator, not in the traditional sense, but for the express purpose of reconstituting the state.

Sulla's first step was to wipe out the opposition. The names of those proscribed were posted in public. As outlaws, they could be killed by anyone, and the killer received a reward. Sulla proscribed not only political opponents, but his personal enemies and men whose only crime was having wealth and property. With the proceeds from the confiscations, Sulla rewarded his veterans, perhaps as many as 100,000 men, and thereby built a solid base of support.

Sulla had enough power and influence to make himself the permanent ruler of Rome. He was traditional enough to want a restoration of senatorial government, but reformed so as to prevent the misfortunes of the past. To deal with the decimation of the Senate caused by the proscriptions and the civil war, he enrolled 300 new members, many of them from the equestrian order and the upper classes of the Italian cities. The

office of tribune, used by the Gracchi to attack senatorial rule, was made into a political dead end.

Sulla's most valuable reforms improved the quality of the courts and the entire legal system. He created new courts to deal with specified crimes, bringing the number of courts to eight. Because both judge and jurors were senators, the courts, too, enhanced senatorial power. These actions were the most permanent of Sulla's reforms, laying the foundation for Roman criminal law.

Sulla retired to a life of ease and luxury in 79 B.C.E. He could not, however, undo the effect of his own example—that of a general using the loyalty of his own troops to take power and to massacre his opponents, as well as innocent men. These actions proved to be more significant than his constitutional arrangements.

The Fall of the Republic

Pompey, Crassus, Caesar, and Cicero

Within a year of Sulla's death, his constitution came under assault. To deal with an armed threat to its powers, the Senate violated the very procedures meant to defend them. The Senate gave the command of the army to Pompey (106–48 B.C.E.), who was only twenty-eight and had never been elected to a magistracy. Then, when Sertorius, a Marian general, resisted senatorial control, the Senate appointed Pompey proconsul in Spain in 77 B.C.E. These actions ignored Sulla's rigid rules for office holding, which had been meant to guarantee experienced, loyal, and safe commanders. In 71 B.C.E. Pompey returned to Rome with new glory, having put down the rebellion of Sertorius. In 73 B.C.E., the Senate made another extraordinary appointment to put down a great slave rebellion led by the gladiator Spartacus. Marcus Licinius Crassus, a rich and ambitious senator (See "Plutarch Describes How Crassus Became a Millionnaire.") received powers that gave him command of almost all Italy. Together with the newly returned Pompey, he crushed the rebellion in 71 B.C.E. Extraordinary commands of this sort proved to be the ruin of the republic.

Crassus and Pompey were ambitious men whom the Senate feared. Both demanded special honors and election to the consulship for the year 70 B.C.E. Pompey was legally ineligible because he had never gone through the strict course of offices prescribed in Sulla's constitution, and Crassus needed Pompey's help. They joined forces, though they disliked and were jealous of each other. They gained popular support by promising to restore the full powers of

Pompey the Great (106–48 B.C.E.). He was successful in crushing rebellions against the Roman Republic.
Alinari/Art Resource, N.Y.

Plutarch Describes How Crassus Became a Millionaire

Marcus Licinius Crassus (ca. 112–53 B.C.E.) was a fine general, a powerful politician, and the richest person in Rome. There is no doubt that his wealth contributed greatly to his power. In the following selection, Plutarch describes how Crassus acquired his riches.

❖ *By what devices did Crassus become rich? Why is Plutarch critical of his techniques? How would they be described and evaluated in our own time? What does this passage tell us about the ways in which Roman society had changed since the days of the early republic?*

Most of [his wealth], if one must tell the scandalous truth, he gathered by fire and war, making the public calamities his greatest source of revenue. For when Sulla seized Rome and sold the property of those put to death by him, regarding and calling it booty, and wishing to make as many influential men as he could partners in the crime, Crassus refused neither to accept nor buy such property. Moreover, observing how natural and familiar at Rome were the burning and collapse of buildings, because of their massiveness and their closeness to one another, he bought slaves who were builders and architects. Then, when he had more than 500 of these, he would buy houses that were on fire and those adjoining the ones on fire. The owners would let them go for small sums, because of their fear and uncertainty, so that the greatest part of Rome came into his hands. But though he had so many artisans, he never built any house but the one he lived in, and used to say that those that were addicted to building would undo themselves without the help of other enemies. And though he had many silver mines, and very valuable land with laborers on it, yet one might consider all this as nothing compared with the value of his slaves, such a great number and variety did he possess—readers, amanuenses, silversmiths, stewards and table-servants. He himself directed their training, and took part in teaching them himself, accounting it, in a word, the chief duty of a master to care for his slaves as the living tools of household management.

Excerpt from Plutarch, *Life of Crassus*, trans. by N. Lewis and M. Reinhold, in *Roman Civilization*, Vol. 1, pp. 458–459. Copyright © 1955 Columbia University Press. Reprinted by permission of the publisher.

the tribunes, which Sulla had curtailed. And they gained equestrian backing by promising to restore equestrians to the extortion court juries. They both won election and repealed most of Sulla's constitution. This opened the way for further attacks on senatorial control and for collaboration between ambitious generals and demagogic tribunes.

In 67 B.C.E., a special law gave Pompey *imperium* for three years over the entire Mediterranean and fifty miles in from the coast. It also gave him the power to raise great quantities of troops and money to rid the area of pirates. The assembly passed the law over senatorial opposition, and in three months Pompey cleared the seas of piracy. Meanwhile, a new war had broken out with Mithridates. In 66 B.C.E. the assembly transferred the command to Pompey, giving him unprecedented powers. He held *imperium* over all Asia, with the right to make war and peace at will. His *imperium* was superior to that of any proconsul in the field.

Once again, Pompey justified his appointment. He defeated Mithridates and drove him to suicide. By 62 B.C.E., he had extended Rome's frontier to the Euphrates River and had organized the territories of Asia so well that his arrangements remained the basis of Roman rule well into the imperial period. When Pompey returned to Rome in 62 B.C.E., he had more power, prestige, and popular support than any Roman in history. The Senate and his personal enemies had reason to fear that he might emulate Sulla and establish his own rule.

Rome had not been quiet in Pompey's absence. Crassus was the foremost among those who had reason to fear Pompey's return. Although rich and influential, Crassus did not have the confidence of the Senate, a firm political base of his own, or the kind of military glory needed to rival Pompey. During the 60s B.C.E., therefore, he allied himself with various popular leaders.

The ablest of these men was Gaius Julius Caesar (100–44 B.C.E.). He was a descendant of an old, but politically obscure, patrician family that claimed descent from the kings and even from the goddess Venus. In spite of this noble lineage, Caesar was connected to the popular party through his aunt, the wife of Marius, and through his own wife, Cornelia, the daughter of Cinna. Caesar was an ambitious and determined young politician whose daring and rhetorical skill made him a valuable ally in winning the discontented of every class to the cause of the *populares*. Though Crassus was very much the senior partner, each needed the other to achieve what both wanted: significant military commands whereby they might build a reputation, a political following, and a military force to compete with Pompey's.

The chief opposition to Crassus' candidates for the consulship for 63 B.C.E. came from Cicero (106–43 B.C.E.), a *novus homo*, from Marius' home town of Arpinum. He had made a spectacular name as the leading lawyer in Rome. Cicero, though he came from outside the senatorial aristocracy, was no *popularis*. His program was to preserve the republic against demagogues and ambitious generals by making the government more liberal. He wanted to unite the stable elements of the state—the Senate and the equestrians—in a harmony of the orders. This program did not appeal to the senatorial oligarchy, but the Senate preferred Cicero to Catiline, a dangerous and popular politician thought to be linked with Crassus. Cicero and Antonius were elected consuls for 63 B.C.E., with Catiline running third.

Cicero soon learned of a plot hatched by Catiline. Catiline had run in the previous election on a platform of cancellation of debts; this appealed to discontented elements in general, but especially to the heavily indebted nobles and their many clients. Made desperate by defeat, Catiline planned to stir up rebellions around Italy, to cause confusion in the city, and to take it by force. Quick action by Cicero defeated Catiline.

Formation of the First Triumvirate

Toward the end of 62 B.C.E., Pompey landed at Brundisium. To general surprise, he disbanded his army, celebrated a great triumph, and returned to private life. He had delayed his return in the hope of finding Italy in such a state as to justify his keeping the army and dominating the scene. Cicero's quick suppression of Catiline prevented his plan. Pompey, therefore, had either to act illegally or to lay down his arms. Because he had not thought of monarchy or revolution, but

merely wanted to be recognized and treated as the greatest Roman, he chose the latter course.

Pompey had achieved amazing things for Rome and simply wanted the Senate to approve his excellent arrangements in the East and to make land allotments to his veterans. His demands were far from unreasonable, and a prudent Senate would have granted them and would have tried to employ his power in defense of the constitution. But the Senate was jealous and fearful of overmighty individuals and refused his requests. Pompey was driven to an alliance with his natural enemies, Crassus and Caesar, because all three found the Senate standing in the way of what they wanted.

In 60 B.C.E. Caesar returned to Rome from his governorship of Spain. He wanted the privilege of celebrating a triumph, the great victory procession that the Senate granted certain generals to honor especially great achievements, and of running for consul. The law did not allow him to do both, however, requiring him to stay outside the city with his army but demanding that he canvass for votes personally within the city. He asked for a special dispensation, but the Senate refused. Caesar then performed a political miracle. He reconciled Crassus with Pompey and gained the support of both for his own ambitions. So was born the First Triumvirate, an informal agreement among three Roman politicians, each seeking his private goals, which further undermined the future of the republic.

Julius Caesar and His Government of Rome

Though he was forced to forgo his triumph, Caesar's efforts were rewarded when he was elected to the consulship for 59 B.C.E. His fellow consul was M. Calpernius Bibulus, the son-in-law of Cato and a conservative hostile to Caesar and the other *populares*. Caesar did not hesitate to override his colleague. The triumvirs' program was quickly enacted. Caesar got the extraordinary command that would give him a chance to earn the glory and power with which to rival Pompey: the governorship of Illyricum and Gaul for five years. A land bill settled Pompey's veterans comfortably, and his eastern settlement was ratified. Crassus, much of whose influence came from his position as champion of the equestrians, won for them a great windfall by having the government renegotiate a tax contract in their favor. To guarantee themselves against any reversal of these actions, the triumvirs continued their informal but effective, collaboration, arranging for the election of friendly consuls and the departure of potential opponents.

Caesar was now free to seek the military success he craved. His province included Cisalpine Gaul in the Po Valley (by now occupied by many Italian settlers as well as Gauls) and Narbonese Gaul beyond the Alps (modern Provence).

Relying first on the excellent quality of his army and the experience of his officers and then on his own growing military ability, Caesar made great progress. By 56 B.C.E. he had conquered most of Gaul, but he had not yet consolidated his victories firmly. He therefore sought an extension of his command, but quarrels between Crassus and Pompey so weakened the Triumvirate that the Senate was prepared to order Caesar's recall.

To prevent the dissolution of his base of power, Caesar persuaded Crassus and Pompey to meet with him at Luca in northern Italy to renew the coalition. They agreed that Caesar would get another five-year command in Gaul, and Crassus and Pompey would be consuls again in 55 B.C.E. After that, they would each receive an army and a five-year command. Caesar was free to return to Gaul and finish the job. The capture of Alesia in 51 B.C.E. marked the end of the serious Gallic resistance and of Gallic liberty. For Caesar, it brought the wealth, fame, and military power he wanted. He commanded thirteen loyal legions, a match for his enemies as well as for his allies.

By the time Caesar was ready to return to Rome, the Triumvirate had dissolved and a crisis was at hand. At Carrhae, in 53 B.C.E., Crassus died trying to conquer the Parthians, successors to the Persian Empire. His death broke one link between Pompey and Caesar. The death of Caesar's daughter Julia, who had been Pompey's wife, dissolved another.

As Caesar's star rose, Pompey became jealous and fearful. He did not leave Rome but governed his province through a subordinate. In the late 50s B.C.E., political rioting at Rome caused the Senate to appoint Pompey sole consul. This grant of unprecedented power and responsibility brought Pompey closer to the senatorial aristocracy in mutual fear of, and hostility to, Caesar. The Senate wanted to bring Caesar back to Rome as a private citizen after his proconsular command expired. He would then be open to attack for past illegalities. Caesar tried to avoid the trap by asking permission to stand for the consulship in absentia.

Early in January of 49 B.C.E., the more extreme faction in the Senate had its way. It ordered Pompey to defend the state and Caesar to lay down his command by a specified day. For Caesar, this meant exile or death, so he ordered his legions to cross the Rubicon River, the boundary of his province. (See Map 4–4 and "Caesar Tells What Persuaded Him to Cross the Rubicon.") This action started a civil war. In 45 B.C.E. Caesar defeated the last forces of his enemies under Pompey's sons at Munda in Spain. The war was over, and Caesar, in Shakespeare's words, bestrode "the narrow world like a Colossus."

From the beginning of the civil war until his death in 44 B.C.E., Caesar spent less than a year and a half in Rome, and many of his actions were attempts to deal with immediate problems between campaigns. His innovations generally sought to make rational and orderly what was traditional and chaotic. An excellent example is Caesar's reform of the calendar. By 46 B.C.E. it was eighty days ahead of the proper season, because the official year was lunar, containing only 355 days. Using the best scientific advice, Caesar instituted a new calendar. With minor changes by Pope Gregory XIII in the sixteenth century, it is the calendar in use today.

Another general tendency of his reforms in the political area was the elevation of the role of Italians

A bust of Julius Caesar. Alinari/Art Resource, N.Y.

Caesar Tells What Persuaded Him to Cross the Rubicon

Julius Caesar competed with Pompey for the leading position in the Roman state. Complicated maneuvers failed to produce a compromise. In the following selection, Caesar gives his side of the story of the beginning of the Roman civil war. Note that Caesar writes about himself in the third person.

❖ *This selection, of course makes the case for Caesar's actions. From your reading in this book and from any other information you have, how do you think Pompey might have replied? On constitutional and legal grounds, who had the stronger case? On grounds of practical considerations and of the welfare of the Roman state, which party, if either, deserved support? If neither did, why not?*

These things being made known to Caesar, he harangued his soldiers; he reminded them of the wrongs done to him at all times by his enemies, and complained that Pompey had been alienated from him and led astray by them through envy and a malicious opposition to his glory, though he had always favored and promoted Pompey's honor and dignity. He complained that an innovation had been introduced into the republic, that the intercession of the tribunes, which had been restored a few years before by Sulla, was branded as a crime, and suppressed by force of arms; that Sulla, who had stripped the tribunes of every other power, had, nevertheless, left the privilege of intercession unrestrained; that Pompey, who pretended to restore what they had lost, had taken away the privileges which they formerly had; that whenever the senate decreed, "that the magistrates should take care that the republic sustained no injury" (by which words and decree the Roman people were obliged to repair to arms), it was only when pernicious laws were proposed; when the tribunes attempted violent measures; when the people seceded, and possessed themselves of the temples and eminences of the city; (and these instances of former times, he showed them were expiated by the fate of Saturninus and the Gracchi): that nothing of this kind was attempted now, nor even thought of: that no law was promulgated, no intrigue with the people going forward, no secession made; he exhorted them to defend from the malice of his enemies the reputation and honor of that general under whose command they had for nine years most successfully supported the state; fought many successful battles, and subdued all Gaul and Germany. The soldiers of the thirteenth legion, which was present (for in the beginning of the disturbances he had called it out, his other legions not having yet arrived), all cry out that they are ready to defend their general, and the tribunes of the commons, from all injuries.

Having made himself acquainted with the disposition of his soldiers, Caesar set off with that legion to Ariminum, and there met the tribunes, who had fled to him for protection.

Julius Caesar, *Commentaries*, trans. by W. A. McDevitte and W. S. Bosh (New York: Harper and Brothers, 1887), pp. 249–250.

and even provincials at the expense of the old Roman families, most of whom were his political enemies. He raised the number of senators to 900 and filled the Senate's depleted ranks with Italians and even Gauls. He was free with grants of Roman citizenship, giving the franchise to Cisalpine Gaul as a whole and to many individuals of various regions.

Caesar made few changes in the government of Rome. The Senate continued to play its role, in theory. But its increased size, its packing with supporters of Caesar, and his own monopoly of military power made the whole thing a sham. He treated the Senate as his creature, sometimes with disdain. His legal position rested on several powers. In 46 B.C.E. he was appointed dictator for ten years, and in the next year he was appointed for life. He also held the consulship, the immunity of a tribune (although, being a patrician, he had never been a tribune), the chief priesthood of the state, and a new position, prefect of morals, which gave him the censorial power. Usurping the elective power of the assemblies, he even named the magistrates for the next few years, because he expected to be away in the East.

The enemies of Caesar were quick to seize on every pretext to accuse him of aiming at monarchy. A senatorial conspiracy gathered strength under the leadership of Gaius Cassius Longinus and Marcus Junius Brutus and included some sixty senators in all. On March 15, 44 B.C.E., Caesar entered the Senate, characteristically without a bodyguard, and was stabbed to death. The assassins regarded themselves as heroic tyrannicides, but did not have a clear plan of action to follow the tyrant's death. No doubt they simply expected the republic to be restored in the old way, but things had gone too far for that. There followed instead thirteen more years of civil war, at the end of which the republic received its final burial. (See "Suetonius Describes Caesar's Dictatorship.")

The Second Triumvirate and the Emergence of Octavian

Caesar had had legions of followers, and he had a capable successor in Mark Antony. But the dictator had named his eighteen-year-old grandnephew, Gaius Octavius (63 B.C.E.–14 C.E.), as his heir and had left him three-quarters of his vast wealth. To everyone's surprise, the sickly and inexperienced young man came to Rome to claim his legacy. He gathered an army, won the support of many of Caesar's veterans, and became a figure of importance—the future Augustus.

At first, the Senate tried to use Octavius against Antony, but when the conservatives rejected his request for the consulship, Octavius broke with them. Following Sulla's grim precedent, he took his army and marched on Rome. There he finally assumed his adopted name, C. Julius Caesar Octavianus. Modern historians refer to him at this stage in his career as Octavian, although he insisted on being called Caesar. In August of 43 B.C.E., he became consul and declared the assassins of Caesar outlaws. Brutus and Cassius had an army of their own, so Octavian sought help on the Caesarean side. He made a pact with Mark Antony and M. Aemilius Lepidus, a Caesarean governor of the western provinces. They took control of Rome and had themselves appointed "triumvirs to put the republic in order," with great powers. This was the Second Triumvirate, and unlike the first, it was legally empowered to rule almost dictatorially.

The need to pay their troops, their own greed, and the passion that always emerges in civil wars led the triumvirs to start a wave of proscriptions that outdid even those of Sulla. In 42 B.C.E. the triumviral army defeated Brutus and Cassius at Philippi in Macedonia, and the last hope of republican restoration died with the tyrannicides. Each of the triumvirs received a command. The junior partner, Lepidus, was given Africa, Antony took the rich and inviting East, and Octavian got the West and the many troubles that went with it.

Octavian had to fight a war against Sextus, the son of Pompey, who held Sicily. He also had to settle 100,000 veterans in Italy, confiscating much property and making many enemies. Helped by his friend Agrippa, he defeated Sextus Pompey in 36 B.C.E. Among his close associates was Maecenas, who served him as adviser and diplomatic agent. Maecenas helped manage the delicate relations with Antony and Lepidus, but perhaps equally important was his role as a patron of the arts. Among his clients were Vergil and Horace, both of whom did important work for Octavian. They painted him as a restorer of traditional Roman values, as a man of ancient Roman lineage and of traditional Roman

A profile of Brutus, one of Caesar's assassins, appeared on this silver coin. The reverse shows a cap of liberty between two daggers and reads "Ides of March."
H. Roger-Viollet/Liason Agency, Inc.

Suetonius Describes Caesar's Dictatorship

Suetonius (ca. C.E. 69–ca. 140) wrote a series of biographies of the emperors from Julius Caesar to Domitian. In the following selection, he described some of Caesar's actions during his dictatorship in the years 46–44 B.C.E.

❖ *Why does Suetonius think Caesar deserved to be killed? To what group of Romans did his behavior give the greatest offense? How would other Romans view the pros and cons of Caesar's career?*

[Caesar's] other words and actions, however, so far outweigh all his good qualities, that it is thought he abused his power, and was justly cut off. For he not only obtained excessive honours, such as the consulship every year, the dictatorship for life, and the censorship, but also the title of emperor, and the surname of Father of His Country, besides having his statue amongst the kings, and a lofty couch in the theatre. He even suffered some honours to be decreed to him, which were unbefitting the most exalted of mankind; such as gilded chair of state in the senate-house and on his tribunal, a consecrated chariot, and banners in the Circensian procession, temples, altars, statues among the gods, a bed of state in the temples, a priest, and a college of priests dedicated to himself, like those of Pan; and that one of the months should be called by his name. There were, indeed, no honours which he did not either assume himself, or grant to others, at his will and pleasure. In his third and fourth consulship, he used only the title of the office, being content with the power of dictator, which was conferred upon him with the consulship; and in both years he substituted other consuls in his room, during the three last months; so that in the intervals he held no assemblies of the people, for the election of magistrates, excepting only tribunes and ediles of the people; and appointed officers, under the name of *praefects*, instead of the *praetors*, to administer the affairs of the city during his absence. The office of consul having become vacant, by the sudden death of one of the consuls the day before the calends of January [January 1], he conferred it on a person who requested it of him, for a few hours. Assuming the same licence, and regardless of the customs of his country, he appointed magistrates to hold their offices for terms of years. He granted the insignia of the consular dignity to ten persons of *praetorian* rank. He admitted into the senate some men who had been made free of the city, and even natives of Gaul, who were semi-barbarians. He likewise appointed to the management of the mint, and the public revenue of the state, some servants of his own household; and entrusted the command of three legions, which he left at Alexandria, to an old catamite of his, the son of his freed-man Rufinus.

He was guilty of the same extravagance in the language he publicly used, as Titus Ampius informs us; according to whom he said, "The republic is nothing but a name, without substance or reality. Sylla was an ignorant fellow to abdicate the dictatorship. Men ought to consider what is becoming when they talk with me, and look upon what I say as a law."

From Suetonius, *The Lives of the Twelve Caesars*, trans. by Alexander Thompson, revised by T. Forster, George Bell and Sons, 1903, pp. 45–47.

virtues, and as the culmination of Roman destiny. More and more he was identified with Italy and the West, as well as with order, justice, and virtue.

Meanwhile Antony was in the East, chiefly at Alexandria with Cleopatra, the queen of Egypt. In 36 B.C.E. he attacked Parthia, with disastrous results. Octavian had promised to send troops to support Antony's Parthian campaign, but never sent them. Antony was forced to depend on the East for support, and to some considerable degree, this meant reliance on Cleopatra. Octavian clearly understood the advantage of representing himself as the champion of the West, Italy, and Rome. Meanwhile he represented Antony as the man of the East and the dupe of Cleopatra, her tool in establishing Alexandria as the center of an empire and herself as its ruler. Such propaganda made it easier for Caesareans to abandon their veteran leader in favor of the young heir of Caesar. It did not help Antony's cause that he agreed to a public festival at Alexan-

MAP 4–4   THE CIVIL WARS OF THE LATE ROMAN REPUBLIC   *This map shows the extent of the territory controlled by Rome at the time of Caesar's death and the sites of the major battles of the civil wars of the late republic.*

dria in 34 B.C.E., where he and Cleopatra sat on golden thrones. She was proclaimed "Queen of Kings," her son by Julius Caesar was named "King of Kings," and parts of the Roman Empire were doled out to her various children.

By 32 B.C.E., all pretense of cooperation ended. Octavian and Antony each tried to put the best face on what was essentially a struggle for power. Lepidus had been put aside some years earlier. Antony sought senatorial support and promised to restore the republican constitution. Octavian seized and published what was alleged to be the will of Antony, revealing his gifts of provinces to the children of Cleopatra. This caused the conflict to take the form of East against West, Rome against Alexandria.

In 31 B.C.E., the matter was settled at Actium in western Greece. Agrippa, Octavian's best general, cut off the enemy by land and sea, forcing and winning a naval battle. Antony and Cleopatra escaped to Egypt, but Octavian pursued them to Alexandria, where both committed suicide. The civil wars were over, and at the age of thirty-two Octavian was absolute master of the Mediterranean world. His power was enormous, but so was the task before him. He had to restore peace, prosperity, and confidence. All of these required establishing a constitution that would reflect the new realities without offending unduly the traditional republican prejudices that still had so firm a grip on Rome and Italy.

In Perspective

The history of the Roman Republic was almost as sharp a departure from the common experiences of ancient civilizations as that of the Greek city–states. A monarchy in its earliest known form, Rome not long thereafter expelled its king, abandoned the institution of monarchy, and established an aristocratic republic somewhat like the poleis of the Greek "Dark Ages." But unlike the Greeks, the Romans continued to be in touch with foreign neighbors, including the far more civilized urban monarchies of the Etruscans. Nonetheless, the Romans clung faithfully to their republican institutions. For a long time the Romans remained a nation of farmers and herdsmen, to whom trade was relatively unimportant, especially outside Italy.

Over time, the caste distinctions between patricians and plebeians became unimportant. They were replaced by distinctions based on wealth and, even more important, aristocracy, wherein the significant distinction was between noble families,

The Fall of the Roman Republic

133 B.C.E.	Tribunate of Tiberius Gracchus
123–122 B.C.E.	Tribunate of Gaius Gracchus
111–105 B.C.E.	Jugurthine War
104–100 B.C.E.	Consecutive consulships of Marius
90–88 B.C.E.	War against the Italian allies
88 B.C.E.	Sulla's march on Rome
82 B.C.E.	Sulla assumes dictatorship
71 B.C.E.	Crassus crushes rebellion of Spartacus
71 B.C.E.	Pompey defeats Sertorius in Spain
70 B.C.E.	Consulship of Crassus and Pompey
60 B.C.E.	Formation of First Triumvirate
58–50 B.C.E.	Caesar in Gaul
53 B.C.E.	Crassus killed in Battle of Carrhae
49 B.C.E.	Caesar crosses Rubicon; civil war begins
48 B.C.E.	Pompey defeated at Pharsalus; killed in Egypt
46–44 B.C.E.	Caesar's dictatorship
45 B.C.E.	End of civil war
43 B.C.E.	Formation of Second Triumvirate
42 B.C.E.	Triumvirs defeat Brutus and Cassius at Philippi
31 B.C.E.	Octavian and Agrippa defeat Anthony at Actium

who held the highest elected offices in the state, and those outside the nobility. The Roman Republic from the first found itself engaged in almost continuous warfare with its neighbors—either in defense of its own territory, in fights over disputed territory, or in defense of other cities or states who were friends and allies of Rome.

Both internally and in their foreign relations, the Romans were a very legalistic people, placing great importance on traditional behavior encoded into laws. Although backed by the powerful authority of the magistrates at home and the potent Roman army abroad, the laws were based on experience, common sense, and equity. Roman law aimed at stability and fairness, and it succeeded well enough that few people who lived under it wanted to do away with it. It lived on and grew during the imperial period and beyond. During the European Middle Ages it played an important part in the revival of the West and continued to exert an influence into modern times.

The force of Roman arms, the high quality of Roman roads and bridges, and the pragmatic character of Roman law helped create something unique: an empire ruled by a republic, first a large one on land that included all of Italy and later one that commanded the shores of the entire Mediterranean and quite a distance inland in many places. Rome controlled an area that bears comparison with some of the empires of the East. It acquired that territory, wealth, and power in a state managed by annual magistrates elected by the male Roman citizens and by an aristocratic Senate, which had to take notice of popular assemblies and a published, impersonal code of law. It achieved its greatness with an army of citizens and allies, without a monarchy or a regular bureaucracy.

The temptations and responsibilities of governing a vast and rich empire, however, finally proved too much for the republican constitution. Trade grew, and with it a class of merchants and financiers—equestrians—that was neither aristocratic nor agricultural, but increasingly powerful. The influx of masses of slaves captured in war undermined the small farmers who had been the backbone of the Roman state and its army. As many of them were forced to leave their farms, they moved to the cities, chiefly to Rome, where they had no productive role. Conscripted armies of farmers serving relatively short terms gave way to volunteer armies of landless men serving as professionals and expecting to be rewarded for their services with gifts of land or money. The generals of these armies were not annual magistrates controlled by the Senate and the constitution, but ambitious military leaders seeking glory and political advantage.

The result was civil war and the destruction of the republic. The conquest of a vast empire moved the Romans away from their unusual historical traditions toward the more familiar path of empire trodden by older rulers in Egypt and Mesopotamia.

REVIEW QUESTIONS

1. In what ways did the institutions of family and clientage and the establishment of patrician and plebeian classes contribute to the stability of the early Roman Republic? How important were education and slavery to the success of the republic? the institution of slavery?

2. What was the Struggle of the Orders? What methods did plebeians use to get what they wanted? How was Roman society different after the struggle ended?

3. Discuss Rome's expansion to 265 B.C.E. How was Rome able to conquer and control Italy? In their relations with Greece and Asia Minor in the second century B.C.E., were the Romans looking for security? wealth? power? fame?

4. Explain the clash between the Romans and the Carthaginians in the First and Second Punic wars. Could the wars have been avoided? How did Rome benefit from its victory over Carthage? What problems were created by this victory?

5. What social, economic, and political problems did Italy have in the second century B.C.E.? What were the main proposals of Tiberius Gaius Gracchus? What questions about Roman society did they raise? Why did the proposals fail?

6. What were the problems that plagued the Roman Republic in the last century? What caused these problems and how did the Romans try to solve them? To what extent was the republic destroyed by ambitious generals who loved power more than Rome itself?

SUGGESTED READINGS

F. E. ADCOCK, *The Roman Art of War Under the Republic* (1940). A basic study of the subject.

E. BADIAN, *Foreign* Clientelae (1958). A brilliant study of the Roman idea of a client–patron relationship, extended to foreign affairs.

R. A. BAUMAN, *Women and Politics in Ancient Rome* (1992). A useful study of women's role in roman public life.

J. BOARDMAN, J. GRIFFIN, AND O. MURRAY, *The Oxford History of the Roman World* (1990). An encyclopedic approach to the varieties of the Roman experience.

P. A. BRUNT, *Social Conflicts in the Roman Republic* (1971). A fine study by a master of the subject.

T. J. CORNELL, *The Beginnings of Rome: Italy and Rome from the Bronze Age to the Punic Wars* (1995). A fine new study of early Rome.

T. CORNELL AND J. MATTHEWS, *Atlas of the Roman World* (1982). Much more than the title indicates, this book presents a comprehensive view of the Roman world in its physical and cultural setting.

M. GELZER, *Caesar: Politician and Statesman*, trans. by P. Needham (1968). The best biography of Caesar.

E. S. GRUEN, *The Last Generation of the Roman Republic* (1973). An interesting but controversial interpretation of the fall of the republic.

E. S. GRUEN, *The Hellenistic World and the Coming of Rome* (1984). A new interpretation of Rome's conquest of the eastern Mediterranean.

W. V. HARRIS, *War and Imperialism in Republican Rome, 327–70 B.C.E.* (1975). An analysis of Roman attitudes and intentions concerning imperial expansion and war.

KEAVENEY, *Lucullus: A Life* (1992). A biography of the famous Roman epicure.

S. LANCEL, *Carthage, a History.* (1995). A good account of Rome's great competitor.

J. F. LAZENBY, *Hannibal's War* (1978). An excellent military history of the Second Punic War.

F. B. MARSH, *A History of the Roman World from 146 to 30 B.C.E.*, 3d ed., rev. by H. H. Scullard (1963). An excellent narrative account.

T. N. MITCHELL, *Cicero, The Senior Statesman* (1991). An intelligent study of Cicero's later career.

C. NICOLET, *The World of the Citizen in Republican Rome* (1980). A valuable study of the meaning of Roman citizenship.

M. PALLOTTINO, *The Etruscans*, 6th ed. (1974). Makes especially good use of archaeological evidence.

J. RICH AND G. SHIPLEY, *War and Society in the Roman World* (1993). A useful collection of essays on military topics.

E. T. SALMON, *Roman Colonization under the Republic* (1970). An account of the character and importance of the Roman colony.

E. T. SALMON, *The Making of Roman Italy* (1980). The story of Roman expansion on the Italian peninsula.

H. H. SCULLARD, *A History of the Roman World 753–146 B.C.E.*, 4th ed. (1980). An unusually fine narrative history with useful critical notes.

D. STOCKTON, *Cicero: A Political Biography* (1971). A readable and interesting study.

G. WILLIAMS, *The Nature of Roman Poetry* (1970). An unusually graceful and perceptive literary study.

Chapter 5

***Hadrian's entry into Rome. This carved relief from the first half of the second
century*** C.E. ***shows the Emperor Hadrian at the city gates of Rome where he is
greeted by the guiding spirits of the Senate and the Roman people.*** Late Hadrianic–
early Autonine relief. Palazzo dei Conservatori, Rome, Italy. Nimatallah/Art Resource, N.Y.

The Roman Empire

KEY TOPICS

- The Augustan constitution
- The organization and government of the Roman Empire
- Culture and civilization from the late republic through the imperial period
- The early history of Christianity
- The decline and fall of Rome

The victory of Augustus put an end to the deadly period of civil strife that had begun with the murder of Tiberius Gracchus. The establishment of a monarchy, at first concealed in republican forms but gradually more obvious, brought a long period of peace. Rome's unquestioned control of the entire Mediterranean permitted the growth of trade and a prosperity in the first two centuries of the Roman Empire not to be equaled for more than a millennium.

Management of the empire outside Italy became more benign and efficient. With shared citizenship, the provinces usually accepted Roman rule readily and even enthusiastically. Latin became the official language of the western part of the empire and Greek the official language in the east. This permitted the growth and spread of a common culture, today called Classical Civilization, throughout the empire. The same conditions fostered a great outburst of ac-

tivity and excellence in the arts. The loss of political freedom, however, brought a decline in the vitality of the great Roman genre of rhetoric.

Christianity emerged in the first century C.E. as one of many competing Eastern cults. It continued to spread and attract converts, winning toleration and finally dominance in the fourth century. Christianity was powerfully shaped by the world of imperial Rome, absorbing and using classical culture even while fighting against it.

The third century C.E. brought serious attacks on several of Rome's frontiers, causing political and economic chaos. For a time, such emperors as Diocletian (r. 284–305) and Constantine (r. 306–337) instituted heroic measures to restore order. Their solutions involved increased centralization, militarization, and attempts to control closely every aspect of life. The emperors became more exalted and remote, the people increasingly burdened with heavy taxes even as the loss of economic freedom reduced their ability to pay. At last a new wave of barbarian attacks proved irresistible, and the Roman Empire in the west ended in the second half of the fifth century.

The Augustan Principate

If the problems facing Octavian after the Battle of Actium in 31 B.C.E. were great, so were his resources for addressing them. He was the master of a vast military force, the only one in the Roman world, and he had loyal and capable assistants. Of enormous importance was the rich treasury of Egypt, which Octavian treated as his personal property. He was helped by the great eagerness of the people of Italy for an end to civil war and a return to peace, order, and prosperity. In exchange for these, most people were prepared to accept a considerable abandonment of republican practices and to give significant power to an able ruler. The memory of Julius Caesar's fate, however, was still fresh in Octavian's mind. Its lesson was that it was dangerous to flaunt unprecedented powers and to disregard all republican traditions.

Octavian did not create his constitutional solution at a single stroke. It developed gradually as he tried new devices to fit his perception of changing conditions. Behind all the republican trappings and the apparent sharing of authority with the Senate, the government of Octavian, like that of his successors, was a monarchy. All real power, both civil and military, lay with the ruler—whether he was called by the unofficial title of *princeps*, or "first citizen," like Octavian, the founder of the regime, or *imperator*, "emperor," like those who followed. During the civil war Octavian's powers came from his triumviral status, whose dubious legality and unrepublican char-

acter were an embarrassment. From 31 B.C.E. on, he held the consulship each year, but this circumstance was neither strictly legal nor very satisfactory.

On January 13, 27 B.C.E., Octavian put forward a new plan in dramatic style, coming before the Senate to give up all his powers and provinces. In what was surely a rehearsed response, the Senate begged him to reconsider. At last he agreed to accept the provinces of Spain, Gaul, and Syria with proconsular power for military command and to retain the consulship in Rome. The other provinces would be governed by the Senate as before. Because the provinces he retained were border provinces that contained twenty of Rome's twenty-six legions, his true power was undiminished. The Senate, however, responded with almost hysterical gratitude, voting him many honors. Among them was the semireligious title "Augustus," which carried implications of veneration, majesty, and holiness. From this time on, historians speak of Rome's first emperor as Augustus and of his regime as the Principate. This would have pleased him, for it helps conceal the novel, unrepublican nature of the regime and the naked power on which it rested.

In 23 B.C.E., Augustus resigned his consulship and held that office only rarely thereafter. Instead, he was voted two powers that were to be the base of his rule thenceforth: the proconsular *imperium maius* and the tribunician power. The former made his proconsular power greater than that of any other proconsul and permitted him to exercise it even within the city of Rome. The latter gave him the right to conduct public business in the assemblies and the Senate, gave him the power of the veto, the tribunician sacrosanctity (immunity from arrest and punishment), and a connection with the Roman popular tradition. Thereafter, with only minor changes, Augustus' powers remained those conferred by the settlement of 23 B.C.E.

Administration

Augustus made important changes in the government of Rome, Italy, and the provinces. Most of his reforms reduced inefficiency and corruption, ended the danger to peace and order from ambitious individuals, and lessened the distinction between Romans and Italians, senators and equestrians. The assemblies lost their significance as a working part of the constitution, and the Senate took on most of the functions of the assemblies. Augustus purged the old Senate of undesirable members and fixed its number at 600. He recruited its members from wealthy men of good character, who entered after serving as lesser magistrates. Augustus controlled the elections and ensured that promising young men, whatever their origin, served the state as administrators and provincial governors. In this way, equestrians and Italians

This statue of Emperor Augustus (r. 27 B.C.E.–14 C.E.), now in the Vatican, stood in the villa of Augustus's wife Livia. The figures on the elaborate breastplate are all of symbolic significance. At the top, for example, Dawn in her chariot brings in a new day under the protective mantle of the sky god; in the center, Tiberius, Augustus' future successor, accepts the return of captured Roman army standards from a barbarian prince; and at the bottom, Mother Earth offers a horn of plenty.
Charitable Foundation/Gemeinnutzige Stiftung Leonard von Matt

who had no connection with the Roman aristocracy entered the Senate in great numbers. For all his power, Augustus was careful always to treat the Senate with respect and honor.

Augustus divided Rome into regions and wards with elected local officials. He gave the city, with its rickety wooden tenements, its first public fire department and rudimentary police force. Grain distribution to the poor was carefully controlled and limited, and organizations were created for providing an adequate water supply. The Augustan period was one of great prosperity, based on the wealth brought in by the conquest of Egypt, on the great increase in commerce and industry made possible by general peace and a vast program of public works, and on a strong return to successful small farming by Augustus's resettled veterans.

The union of political and military power in the hands of the *princeps* made it possible for him to install rational, efficient, and stable government in the provinces for the first time. The emperor, in effect, chose the governors, removed the incompetent or rapacious, and allowed the effective ones to keep their provinces for longer periods. Also, he provided for much greater local autonomy, giving considerable responsibility to the upper classes in the provincial cities and towns and to the tribal leaders in less civilized areas.

The Army and Defense

The main external problem facing Augustus—and one that haunted all his successors—was the northern frontier. (See Map 5–1.) Rome needed to pacify the regions to the north and the northeast of Italy and to find defensible frontiers against the recurring waves of barbarians. Augustus' plan was to push forward into central Europe to create the shortest possible defensive line. The eastern part of the plan succeeded, and the campaign in the west started well. In 9 C.E., however, there was a revolt led by the German tribal leader Herrmann, or Arminius, as the Romans called him. He ambushed and destroyed three Roman legions, and the aged Augustus abandoned the campaign, leaving a problem of border defense that caused great trouble for his successors.

Under Augustus, the armed forces achieved true professional status. Enlistment, chiefly by Italians, was for twenty years, but the pay was relatively good, with occasional bonuses and the promise of a pension on retirement in the form of money or a plot of land. Together with the auxiliaries from the provinces, these forces formed a frontier army of about 300,000 men. In normal times, this number was barely enough to hold the line.

The army permanently based in the provinces played a vital role in bringing Roman culture to the natives. The soldiers spread their language and customs, often marrying local women and settling down in the area of their service. They attracted merchants, who often became the nuclei of new towns and cities that grew into centers of Roman civilization. As time passed, the provincials on the frontiers became Roman citizens who helped strengthen Rome's defenses against the barbarians outside.

Religion and Morality

A century of political strife and civil war had undermined many of the foundations of traditional Roman society. Augustus thought it desirable to try to repair the damage. So he undertook a program aimed at preserving and restoring the traditional values of the family and religion in Rome and Italy. He introduced laws curbing adultery and divorce and encouraging early marriage and the procreation of legitimate children.

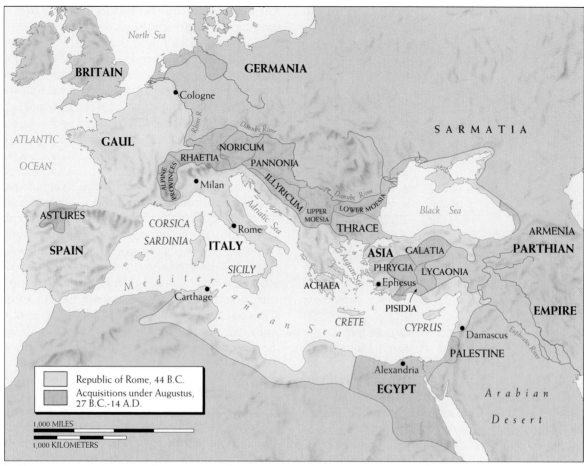

MAP 5–1   THE ROMAN EMPIRE, 14 C.E.   *This map shows the growth of the empire under Augustus and its extent at his death.*

He set an example of austere behavior in his own household and even banished his daughter, Julia, whose immoral behavior had become public knowledge.

Augustus worked at restoring the dignity of formal Roman religion, building many temples, reviving old cults, and reorganizing and invigorating the priestly colleges. He banned the worship of newly introduced foreign gods. Writers whom he patronized, such as Vergil, pointed out his family's legendary connection with Venus. During his lifetime he did not accept divine honors, though he was deified after his death. As with Julius Caesar, a state cult was dedicated to his worship.

Civilization of the Ciceronian and Augustan Ages

The high point of Roman culture came in the last century of the republic and during the principate of Augustus. Both periods reflected the dominant influence of Greek culture, especially its Hellenistic mode. Upper-class Romans were educated in Greek rhetoric, philosophy, and literature, which also served as the models for Roman writers and artists. Yet in spirit and sometimes in form, the art and writing of both periods show uniquely Roman qualities, though each in different ways.

The Late Republic

CICERO   The towering literary figure of the late republic was Cicero (106–43 B.C.E.). He is most famous for the orations he delivered in the law courts and in the Senate. Together with a considerable body of his private letters, these orations provide us with a clearer and fuller insight into his mind than into that of any other figure in antiquity. We see the political life of his period largely through his eyes. He also wrote treatises on rhetoric, ethics, and politics that put Greek philosophical ideas into Latin terminology and at the same time changed them to suit Roman conditions and values.

Cicero's own views provide support for his moderate and conservative practicality. He believed in a world governed by divine and natural law that human reason could perceive and human institutions reflect. He looked to law, custom, and tradition to produce both stability and liberty. His literary style, as well as his values and ideas, was an important legacy for the Middle Ages and, reinterpreted, for the Renaissance. He was killed at the order of Mark Antony, whose political opponent he had been during the civil wars after the death of Julius Caesar.

HISTORY   The last century of the republic produced some historical writing, much of which is lost to us. Sallust (86–35 B.C.E.) wrote a history of the years 78–67 B.C.E., but only a few fragments remain to remind us of his reputation as the greatest of republican historians. His surviving work consists of two pamphlets on the Jugurthine War and on the Catilinarian conspiracy of 63 B.C.E. They reveal his Caesarean and antisenatorial prejudices and the stylistic influence of Thucydides.

Julius Caesar wrote important treatises on the Gallic and civil wars. They are not fully rounded historical accounts, but chiefly military narratives written from Caesar's point of view and with propagandist intent. Their objective manner (Caesar always referred to himself in the third person) and their direct, simple, and vigorous style make them persuasive even today. They must have been most effective with their immediate audience.

LAW   The period from the Gracchi to the fall of the republic was important in the development of Roman law. Before that time, Roman law was essentially national and had developed chiefly by juridical decisions, case by case. Contact with foreign peoples and the influence of Greek ideas, however, forced a change. From the last century of the republic on, the edicts of the *praetors* had increasing importance in developing the Roman legal code. They interpreted and even changed and added to existing law. Quite early, the edicts of the magistrates who dealt with foreigners developed the idea of the *jus gentium*, or "law of peoples," as opposed to that arising strictly from the experience of the Romans. In the first century B.C.E., the influence of Greek thought made the idea of *jus gentium* identical with that of the *jus naturale*, or "natural law," taught by the Stoics. (See "Roman Law.") It was this view of a world ruled by divine reason that Cicero enshrined in his treatise on the law, *De Legibus*.

POETRY   The time of Cicero was also the period of two of Rome's greatest poets, Lucretius and Catullus, each representing a different aspect of Rome's poetic tradition. The Hellenistic poets and literary theorists saw two functions for the poet: entertainer and teacher. They thought the best poet combined both roles, and the Romans adopted the same view. When Naevius and Ennius wrote epics on Roman history, they combined historical and moral instruction with pleasure. Lucretius (ca. 99–55 B.C.E.) pursued a similar path in his epic poem *De Rerum Natura* (*On the Nature of the World*). In it, he set forth the scientific and philosophical ideas of Epicurus and Democritus with the zeal of a missionary trying to save society from fear and superstition. He knew that his doctrine might be bitter medicine to the reader: "That is why I have tried to administer it to you in the dulcet strain of poesy, coated with the sweet honey of the Muses."[1]

Catullus (ca. 84–54 B.C.E.) was a thoroughly different kind of poet. He wrote poems that were personal—even autobiographical. Imitating the Alexandrians, he wrote short poems filled with learned allusions to mythology, but he far surpassed his models in intensity of feeling. He wrote of the joys and pains of love, he hurled invective at important contemporaries like Julius Caesar, and he amused himself in witty poetic exchanges with others. He offered no moral lessons and was not interested in Rome's glorious history and in contemporary politics. In a sense, he is an example of the proud, independent, pleasure-seeking nobleman who characterized part of the aristocracy at the end of the republic.

The Age of Augustus

The spirit of the Augustan Age, the Golden Age of Roman literature, was quite different, reflecting the new conditions of society. The old aristocratic order, with its system of independent nobles following their own particular interests, was gone. So was the world of poets of the lower orders, receiving patronage from any of a number of individual aristocrats. Augustus replaced the complexity of republican patronage with a simple scheme in which all patronage flowed from the *princeps*, usually through his chief cultural adviser, Maecenas.

The major poets of this time, Vergil and Horace, had lost their property during the civil wars. The patronage of the *princeps* allowed them the leisure and the security to write poetry; at the same time, it made them dependent on him and limited their freedom of expression. They wrote on subjects that were useful for his policies and that glorified him and his family. These poets were not mere propagandists, however. It seems clear that mostly they were persuaded of the virtues of Augustus and his reign and sang its praises with some degree of sincerity. Because they were poets of genius, they were also able to maintain a measure of independence in their work.

VERGIL   Vergil (70–19 B.C.E.) was the most important of the Augustan poets. His first important works, the *Eclogues*, or *Bucolics*, are pastoral idylls

---

[1] Lucretius, *De Rerum Natura*, lines 931 ff.

Roman Law

One of the most important achievements of Roman civilization was the establishment over a wide area of a code of law derived from experience and custom but based on principles thought to apply universally and organized according to reason. It had a powerful influence in shaping the character of Western civilization long after the fall of the empire. The following selection, from the Digest, *compiled at the order of the emperor Justinian in the sixth century* C.E., *quotes the* Institutes, *a work by Ulpian, a leading jurist of the third century* C.E. *It discusses the fundamental issues underlying the Roman conception of law in the imperial period.*

❖ *According to this document, for what reason should a Roman citizen obey the law? How does this rationale compare with the rationale for obeying the law in Hammurabi's Mesopotamia or in democratic Athens? What is the importance of the concept of natural law? What are the consequences of rejecting such an idea?*

Justice and Law

(*Ulpian Institutes I*) When a man means to give his attention to law, he ought first to know whence the term law (*ius*) is derived. Now it is so called from justice (*iustitia*). In fact, as Celsus neatly defines it, *ius* is the art of the good and fair. Of this art we may deservedly be called the priests; we cherish justice and profess the knowledge of the good and the fair, separating the fair from the unfair, discriminating between the permitted and the forbidden, desiring to make men good, not only by the fear of penalties, but also by the incentives of rewards, affecting, if I mistake not, a true and not a simulated philosophy.

This subject comprises two categories, public law and private law. Public law is that which regards the constitution of the Roman state, private law that which looks to the interest of individuals; for some things are beneficial from the point of view of the state, and some with reference to private persons. Public law is concerned with sacred rites, with priests, with public officers. Private law is tripartite, being derived from the rules of natural law, or of the law of nations, or of civil law. Natural law is that which all animals have been taught by nature; this law is not peculiar to the human race, but is common to all animals which are produced on land or sea, and to the birds as well. From it comes the union of male and female, which we call matrimony, and the procreation and rearing of children; we find in fact that animals in general, even the wild beasts, are marked by acquaintance with this law. The law of nations is that which the various peoples of mankind observe. It is easy to see that it falls short of natural law, because the latter is common to all living creatures, whereas the former is common only to human beings in their mutual relations.

"Justice and Law" from Justinian, *Digest* I, i. iii–iv, trans. by Naphtali Lewis and Meyer Reinhold, in *Roman Civilization*, Vol. 2, p. 534. Copyright © 1955 Columbia University Press. Reprinted by permission of the publisher.

in a somewhat artificial mode. The subject of the *Georgics*, however, was suggested to Vergil by Maecenas. The model here was the early Greek poet Hesiod's *Works and Days*, but the mood and purpose of Vergil's poem are far different. It pays homage to the heroic human effort to forge order and social complexity out of an ever hostile and sometimes brutal natural environment. It was also a hymn to the cults, traditions, and greatness of Italy.

All this served the purpose of glorifying Augustus's resettlement of the veterans of the civil wars on Italian farms and his elevation of Italy to special status in the empire. Vergil's greatest work is the *Aeneid*, a long national epic that succeeded in placing the history of Rome in the great tradition of the Greeks and the Trojan War. Its hero, the Trojan war-

rior Aeneas, personifies the ideal Roman qualities of duty, responsibility, serious purpose, and patriotism. As the Romans' equivalent of Homer, Vergil glorified not the personal honor and excellence of the Greek epic heroes, but the civic greatness represented by Augustus and the peace and prosperity that he and the Julian family had given to imperial Rome.

HORACE   Horace (65–8 B.C.E.) was the son of a freeman and fought on the republican side until its defeat at Philippi. He was won over to the Augustan cause by the patronage of Maecenas and by the attractions of the Augustan reforms. His *Satires* are genial and humorous. His great skills as a lyric poet are best revealed in his *Odes*, which are ingenious in their adaptation of Greek meters to the requirements of Latin verse. Two of the *Odes* are directly in praise of Augustus, and many of them glorify the new Augustan order, the imperial family, and the empire.

PROPERTIUS Sextus Propertius lived in Rome in the second half of the first century B.C.E., a contemporary of Vergil and Horace. Like them, he was part of the poetic circle favored by Augustus' friend Maecenas. He wrote poetry in the form of elegies, appreciated for their grace and wit. (See "An Ideal Roman Woman.")

OVID The career of Ovid (43 B.C.E.–18 C.E.) reveals the darker side of Augustan influence on the arts. He wrote light and entertaining love elegies that reveal the sophistication and the loose sexual code of

a notorious sector of the Roman aristocracy whose values and way of life were contrary to the seriousness and family-centered life Augustus was trying to foster. Ovid's *Ars Amatoria*, a poetic textbook on the art of seduction, angered Augustus and was partly responsible for the poet's exile in 8 C.E. Ovid tried to recover favor, especially with his *Fasti*, a poetic treatment of Roman religious festivals, but to no avail. His most popular work is the *Metamorphoses*, a kind of mythological epic that turns Greek myths into charming stories in a graceful and lively style. Ovid's fame did not fade with his exile and death, but his fate was an effective warning to later poets.

HISTORY The achievements of Augustus, his emphasis on tradition, and the continuity of his regime with the glorious history of Rome encouraged both

An Ideal Roman Woman

Just after the fall of the Roman republic, late in the first century B.C.E., the poet Propertius wrote an elegy in honor of a woman of the Roman nobility, Cornelia, the stepdaughter of Augustus, the ruler of the newly established Principate. She was married to the aristocrat Paullus and was the mother of three children. Propertius presents her as defending herself before the last judgment of Hades, kind of the underworld. Her words were written by a man, but they seem to be an accurate representation of the values of the upper classes of Rome of both sexes.

❖ *In what achievements, associations and qualities did she take pride? What might a person of our time find absent? What limits are implied by what is missing?*

I was born to this, and when the wreath of
   marriage
Caught up my hair, and I was a woman grown,
it was your bed, my Paullus, that I came to
and now have left. The carving on the stone
says SHE WED BUT ONCE. O fathers long respected
victors in Africa, be my defense...
I asked no favours when Paullus was
   made censor:
no evil found its way within our walls.
I do not think I have disgraced my fathers:
I set a decent pattern in these halls.
Days had a quiet rhythm: no scandal touched us
from the wedding torch to the torch beside
   my bier.
A certain integrity is proof of breeding:
the love of virtue should not be born of fear.
Whatever the judge, whatever the lot fate
   gives me,

no woman needs to blush who sits at my side—...
For my children I wore the mother's robe
   of honor;
It was no empty house I left behind.
Lepidus, Paullus, still you bring me comfort
you closed my eyes when death had made
   me blind.
Twice in the curule chair I have seen my brother;
they cheered him as a consul the day before
   I died.
And you, my daughter, think of your censor-
   father,
choose one husband and live content at his side.
Our clan will rest on the children that you
   give it,
Secure in their promise I board the boat
   and rejoice.
Mine is the final triumph of any woman,
that her spirit earns the praise of a living voice.

From Propertius, *Elegies*, 4.11, translated by Constance Carrier, *The Poems of Propertius*, Indiana University Press, copyright © 1963, pp. 191–192. Reprinted by permission of Indiana University Press.

Ruins of the Roman Forum. From the earliest days of the city, the Forum was the center of Roman life. Augustus had it rebuilt, and it was frequently rebuilt and refurbished by his successors, so most of the surviving buildings date to the imperial period. Corbis

historical and antiquarian prose works. Some Augustan writers wrote scholarly treatises on history and geography in Greek. By far the most important and influential prose writer of the time, however, was Livy (59 B.C.E.–17 C.E.), an Italian from Padua. His *History of Rome* was written in Latin and treated the period from the legendary origins of Rome until 9 B.C.E. Only a fourth of his work is extant; of the rest we have only pitifully brief summaries. He based his history on earlier accounts and made no effort at original research. His great achievement was in telling the story of Rome in a continuous and impressive narrative. Its purpose was moral, and he set up historical models as examples of good and bad behavior and, above all, patriotism. He glorified Rome's greatness and connected it with Rome's past, as Augustus tried to do.

ARCHITECTURE AND SCULPTURE   Augustus was as great a patron of the visual arts as he was of literature. He embarked on a building program that beautified Rome, glorified his reign, and contributed to the general prosperity and his own popularity. He filled the Campus Martius with beautiful new buildings, theaters, baths, and basilicas; the Roman Forum was rebuilt; and Augustus built a forum of his own. At its heart was the temple of Mars the Avenger, which commemorated Augustus' victory and the greatness of his ancestors. On Rome's Palatine Hill he built a splendid temple to his patron god, Apollo, in pursuit of his religious policy.

Most of the building was influenced by the Greek classical style, which aimed at serenity and the ideal type. The same features were visible in the portrait sculpture of Augustus and his family. The greatest

A panel from the Ara Pacis (Altar of Peace). The altar was dedicated in 9 B.C.E. It was part of a propaganda campaign—involving poetry, architecture, myth, and history—that Augustus undertook to promote himself as the savior of Rome and the restorer of peace. This panel shows the goddess Earth and her children with cattle, sheep, and other symbols of agricultural wealth. Nimatallah/Art Resource, N.Y.

monument of the age is the *Ara Pacis*, or "Altar of Peace," dedicated in 9 B.C.E. Set originally in an open space in the Campus Martius, its walls still carry a relief. Part of it shows a procession in which Augustus and his family appear to move forward, followed in order by the magistrates, the Senate, and the people of Rome. There is no better symbol of the new order.

Imperial Rome, 14–180 C.E.

The central problem for Augustus's successors was the position of the ruler and his relationship to the ruled. Augustus tried to cloak the monarchical nature of his government, but his successors soon abandoned all pretense. The ruler came to be called *imperator*—from which comes our word "emperor"—as well as *Caesar*. The latter title signified connection with the imperial house, and the former indicated the military power on which everything was based.

The Emperors

Because Augustus was ostensibly only the "first citizen" of a restored republic and his powers were theoretically voted him by the Senate and the people, he could not legally name his successor. In actuality, however, he plainly designated his heirs by lavishing favors on them and by giving them a share in the imperial power and responsibility. Tiberius (r. 14–37 C.E.),[2] his immediate successor, was at first embarrassed by the ambiguity of his new role, but soon the monarchical and hereditary nature of the regime became patent. Gaius (Caligula, r. 37–41 C.E.), Claudius (r. 41–54 C.E.), and Nero (r. 54–68 C.E.) were all descended from either Augustus or his wife, Livia, and all were elevated because of that fact.

In 41 C.E., the naked military basis of imperial rule was revealed when the Praetorian Guard dragged the lame, stammering, and frightened Claudius from behind a curtain and made him emperor. In 68 C.E., the frontier legions learned what the historian Tacitus called "the secret of Empire…that an emperor could be made elsewhere than at Rome." Nero's incompetence and unpopularity, and especially his inability to control his armies, led to a serious rebellion in Gaul in 68 C.E. The year 69 saw four different emperors assume power in quick succession as different Roman armies took turns placing their commanders on the throne.

Vespasian (r. 69–79 C.E.) emerged victorious from the chaos, and his sons, Titus (r. 79–81 C.E.) and Domitian (r. 81–96 C.E.), carried forward his line, the Flavian dynasty. Vespasian was the first emperor who did not come from the old Roman nobility. He was a tough soldier who came from the Italian middle class. A good administrator and a hardheaded realist of rough wit, he resisted all attempts by flatterers to find noble ancestors for him. On his deathbed he is said to have ridiculed the practice of deifying emperors by saying, "Alas, I think I am becoming a god."

The assassination of Domitian put an end to the Flavian dynasty. Because Domitian had no close relative who had been designated as successor, the Senate put Nerva (r. 96–98 C.E.) on the throne to avoid chaos. He was the first of the five "good emperors," who included Trajan (r. 98–117 C.E.), Hadrian (r. 117–138 C.E.), Antoninus Pius (r. 138–161 C.E.), and Marcus Aurelius (r. 161–180 C.E.). Until Marcus Aurelius, none of these emperors had sons, so they each followed the example set by Nerva of adopting an able senator and establishing him as successor. This rare solution to the problem of monarchical succession was, therefore, only a historical accident. The result, nonetheless, was almost a century of peaceful succession and competent rule, which ended when Marcus Aurelius allowed his incompetent son, Commodus (r. 180–192 C.E.), to succeed him, with unfortunate results.

The genius of the Augustan settlement lay in its capacity to enlist the active cooperation of the upper classes and their effective organ, the Senate. The election of magistrates was taken from the assemblies and given to the Senate, which became the major center for legislation and exercised important judicial functions. This semblance of power persuaded some contemporaries and even some modern scholars that Augustus had established a "dyarchy,"—a system of joint rule by *princeps* and Senate. That was never true.

Rulers of the Early Empire	
27 B.C.E.–14 C.E.	Augustus
The Julio–Claudian Dynasty	
14–37 C.E.	Tiberius
37–41 C.E.	Gaius (Caligula)
41–54 C.E.	Claudius
54–68 C.E.	Nero
69 C.E.	Year of the Four Emperors
The Flavian Dynasty	
69–79 C.E.	Vespasian
79–81 C.E.	Titus
81–96 C.E.	Domitian
The "Good Emperors"	
96–98 C.E.	Nerva
98–117 C.E.	Trajan
117–138 C.E.	Hadrian
138–161 C.E.	Antoninus Pius
161–180 C.E.	Marcus Aurelius

---

[2] Dates for emperors give the years of their reigns, indicated by "r."

Spoils from the temple in Jerusalem were carried in triumphal procession by Roman troops. This relief from Titus's arch of victory in the Roman Forum celebrates his capture of Jerusalem after a two-year siege. The Jews found it difficult to reconcile their religion with Roman rule and frequently rebelled. Scala/Art Resource, N.Y.

The hollowness of the senatorial role became more apparent as time passed. Some emperors, like Vespasian, took pains to maintain, increase, and display the prestige and dignity of the Senate. Others, like Caligula, Nero, and Domitian, degraded the Senate and paraded their own despotic power. But from the first, the Senate's powers were illusory. Magisterial elections were, in fact, controlled by the emperors, and the Senate's legislative function quickly degenerated into mere assent to what the emperor or his representatives put before it. The true function of the Senate was to be a legislative and administrative extension of the emperor's rule.

There was, of course, some real opposition to the imperial rule. It sometimes took the form of plots against the life of the emperor. Plots and the suspicion of plots led to repression, the use of spies and paid informers, book burning, and executions. The opposition consisted chiefly of senators who looked back to republican liberty for their class and who found justification in the Greek and Roman traditions of tyrannicide as well as in the precepts of Stoicism. Plots and repression were most common under Nero and Domitian. From Nerva to Marcus Aurelius, however, the emperors, without yielding any power, again learned to enlist the cooperation of the upper class by courteous and modest deportment.

The Administration of the Empire

The provinces flourished economically and generally accepted Roman rule easily. (See Map 5–2.) In the eastern provinces, the emperor was worshiped as a god; even in Italy, most emperors were deified after their death as long as the imperial cult established by Augustus continued. Imperial policy usually combined an attempt to unify the empire and its various peoples with a respect for local customs and differences. Roman citizenship was spread ever more widely, and by 212 C.E. almost every inhabitant of the empire was a citizen. Latin became the language of the western provinces. Although the East remained essentially Greek in language and culture, even it adopted many aspects of Roman life. The spread of *Romanitis*, or "Roman-ness," was more than nominal, for senators and even emperors began to be drawn from provincial families.

LOCAL MUNICIPALITIES   From an administrative and cultural standpoint, the empire was a collection of cities and towns and had little to do with the countryside. Roman policy during the Principate was to raise urban centers to the status of Roman municipalities, with the rights and privileges attached to them. A typical municipal charter left

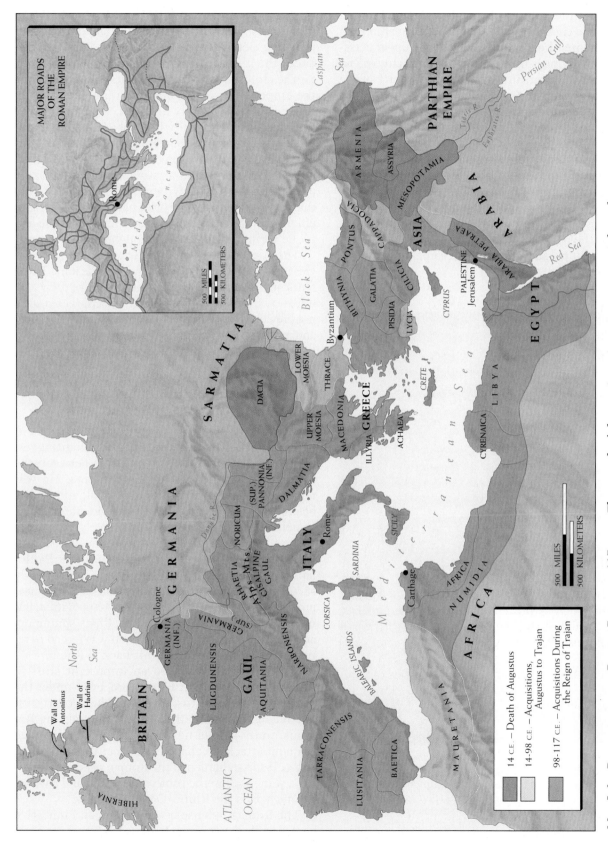

MAP 5–2   PROVINCES OF THE ROMAN EMPIRE TO 117 C.E.   *The growth of the empire to its greatest extent is here shown in three stages—at the death of Augustus in 14 C.E., at the death of Nerva in 98, and at the death of Trajan in 117. The division into provinces is also shown. The insert shows the main roads that tied the far-flung empire together.*

much responsibility in the hands of local councils and magistrates elected from the local aristocracy. Moreover, the holding of a magistracy, and later a seat on the council, carried Roman citizenship with it. Therefore, the Romans enlisted the upper classes of the provinces in their own government, spread Roman law and culture, and won the loyalty of the influential people. (For a glimpse into the lives of ordinary people see "Daily Life in a Roman Provincial Town: Graffiti from Pompeii.")

There were exceptions to this picture of success. The Jews found their religion incompatible with Roman demands and were savagely repressed when they rebelled in 66–70, 115–117, and 132–135 C.E. (See "The Bar-Kochba Rebellion: The Final Jewish Uprising against Rome.") In Egypt, the Romans exploited the peasants with exceptional ruthlessness and did not pursue a policy of urbanization.

Trajan's Column was erected at Rome about 110 C.E. to celebrate the emperor Trajan's (r. 98–117) victory over the Dacians beyond the Danube. Trajan pushed the boundaries of the Roman Empire to their farthest limits, defeating the Parthians in the east as well as the Dacians in the north. Carved in a spiraling relief, the column shows more than a thousand figures, accurately depicting people, buildings, flowers, animals, implements, and weapons. Scala/Art Resource, N.Y.

As the efficiency of the bureaucracy grew, so did the number and scope of its functions and therefore its size. The emperors came to take a broader view of their responsibilities for the welfare of their subjects than before. Nerva conceived and Trajan introduced the *alimenta*, a program of public assistance for the children of indigent parents. More and more the emperors intervened when municipalities got into difficulties, usually financial, sending imperial troubleshooters to deal with problems. The importance and autonomy of the municipalities shrank as the central administration took a greater part in local affairs. The provincial aristocracy came to regard public service in its own cities as a burden rather than an opportunity. The price paid for the increased efficiency offered by centralized control was the loss of the vitality of the cities throughout the empire.

The success of Roman civilization also came at great cost to the farmers who lived outside Italy. Taxes, rents, mandatory gifts, and military service drew capital away from the countryside to the cities on a scale not previously seen in the Graeco-Roman world. More and more the rich life of the urban elite came at the expense of millions of previously stable farmers.

FOREIGN POLICY Augustus' successors, for the most part, accepted his conservative and defensive foreign policy. Trajan was the first emperor to take the offensive in a sustained way. Between 101 and 106 C.E. he crossed the Danube and, after hard fighting, established the new province of Dacia between the Danube and the Carpathian Mountains. He was tempted, no doubt, by its important gold mines, but he probably was also pursuing a new general strategy: to defend the empire more aggressively by driving wedges into the territory of threatening barbarians. The same strategy dictated the invasion of the Parthian Empire in the east (113–117 C.E.). Trajan's early success was astonishing, and he established three new provinces in Armenia, Assyria, and Mesopotamia. But his lines were overextended. Rebellions sprang up, and the campaign crumbled. Trajan was forced to retreat, and he died before getting back to Rome.

Hadrian's reign marked an important shift in Rome's frontier policy. Heretofore, even under the successors of Augustus, Rome had been on the offensive against the barbarians. Although the Romans rarely gained new territory, they launched frequent attacks to chastise and pacify troublesome tribes. Hadrian hardened the Roman defenses, building a stone wall in the south of Scotland and a wooden one across the Rhine–Danube triangle.

The Roman defense became rigid, and initiative passed to the barbarians. Marcus Aurelius was compelled to spend most of his reign resisting dangerous attacks in the east and on the Danube frontier.

Daily Life in a Roman Provincial Town: Graffiti from Pompeii

On the walls of the houses of Pompeii, buried and preserved by the eruption of Mount Vesuvius in 79 C.E., are many scribblings that give us an idea of what the life of ordinary people was like.

✦ *How do these graffiti differ from those one sees in a modern American city? What do they reveal about the similarities and differences between the ordinary people of ancient Rome and the people of today? How would you account for the differences?*

I

Twenty pairs of gladiators of Decimus Lucretius Satrius Valens, lifetime flamen of Nero son of Caesar Augustus, and ten pairs of gladiators of Decimus Lucretius Valens, his son, will fight at Pompeii on April 8, 9, 10, 11, 12. There will be a full card of wild beast combats, and awnings [for the spectators]. Aemilius Celer [painted this sign], all alone in the moonlight.

II

Market days: Saturday in Pompeii, Sunday in Nuceria, Monday in Atella, Tuesday in Nola, Wednesday in Cumae, Thursday in Puteoli, Friday in Rome.

III

Pleasure says: "You can get a drink here for an as [a few cents], a better drink for two, Falernian for four."

IV

A copper pot is missing from this shop. 65 sesterces reward if anybody brings it back, 20 sesterces if he reveals the thief so we can get our property back.

V

The weaver Successus loves the innkeeper's slave girl, Iris by name. She doesn't care for him, but he begs her to take pity on him. Written by his rival. So long.

[Answer by the rival:] Just because you're bursting with envy, don't pick on a handsomer man, a lady-killer and a gallant.

[Answer by the first writer:] There's nothing more to say or write. You love Iris, who doesn't care for you.

VI

Take your lewd looks and flirting eyes off another man's wife, and show some decency on your face!

VII

Anybody in love, come here. I want to break Venus' ribs with a club and cripple the goddess' loins. If she can pierce my tender breast, why can't I break her head with a club?

VIII

I write at Love's dictation and Cupid's instruction;
  But damn it! I don't want to be a god without you.

IX

[A prostitute's sign:] I am yours for 2 asses cash.

Excerpt from *Roman Civilization*, by N. Lewis and M. Reinhold, Vol. 2, Columbia University Press, 1955. Reprinted by permission of Columbia University Press.

AGRICULTURE: THE DECLINE OF SLAVE LABOR AND THE RISE OF *COLONI* The defense of its frontiers put enormous pressure on the human and financial resources of the empire, but the effect of these pressures was not immediately felt. The empire generally experienced considerable economic growth well into the reigns of "good emperors." Internal peace and efficient administration benefited agriculture as well as trade and industry. Farming and trade developed together as political conditions made it easier to sell farm products at a distance.

Small farms continued to exist, but the large estate, managed by an absentee owner and growing cash crops, became the dominant form of agriculture. At first, as in the republican period, these estates were worked chiefly by slaves, but in the first century this began to change. Economic pressures on the free lower classes forced many of them to become tenant farmers, or *coloni*, and eventually the *coloni* replaced slaves as the mainstay of agricultural labor. Typically, these sharecroppers paid rent in labor or in kind, though sometimes they made

The Bar-Kochba Rebellion: The Final Jewish Uprising against Rome

Unlike most conquered peoples, the Jews found accommodation to Roman rule difficult. Their first rebellion was crushed by Vespasian's son, the future emperor Titus, in 70 C.E. At that time the Temple in Jerusalem was destroyed. A second revolt was put down in 117 C.E. Finally, when Hadrian ordered a Roman colony placed on the site of Jerusalem, Simon, who was called Bar-Kochba, or "Son of the Star," led a last uprising from 132 to 135. Dio Cassius describes the brutality of its suppression.

❖ *Did the Romans treat the Jews differently from other people under their control? What special problems did the Roman conquest pose to the Jews? What problems did the Jews present to the Romans?*

At Jerusalem Hadrian founded a city in place of the one which had been razed to the ground, naming it Aelia Capitolina, and on the site of the temple of the god he raised a new temple to Jupiter. This brought on a war of no slight importance nor of brief duration, for the Jews deemed it intolerable that foreign peoples should be settled in their city and foreign rites planted there....

At first the Romans took no account of them. Soon, however, all Judaea had been stirred up, and the Jews everywhere were showing signs of disturbance, were gathering together, and giving evidence of great hostility to the Romans, partly by secret and partly by overt acts; many outside peoples, too, were joining them through eagerness for gain, and the whole world, one might almost say, was being stirred up over the matter. Then, indeed, Hadrian sent his best generals against them. Foremost among these was Julius Severus, who was dispatched against the Jews from Britain, where he was governor....[In Judaea] he was able, rather slowly...but with comparatively little danger, to crush, exhaust, and exterminate them. Very few of them in fact survived. Fifty of their most important strongholds and 985 of their most famous villages were razed to the ground; 580,000 men were slain in the various raids and battles, and the number of those that perished by famine, disease, and fire was past finding out.

From Dio Cassius, *Roman History* 59.12–14, trans. by Ernest Cary (London: Loeb Classical Library and William Heinemann, 1916).

cash payments. Eventually, their movement was restricted, and they were tied to the land they worked, much as were the manorial serfs of the Middle Ages. Whatever its social costs, the system was economically efficient, however, and contributed to the general prosperity.

Although the economic importance of slavery began to decline in the second century with the rise of *coloni* labor, the institution was never abolished, nor did it disappear so long as the Roman Empire lasted. Pockets of slave labor remained as late as the time of Charlemagne. (See Chapter 6.)

Women of the Upper Classes

By the late years of the Roman republic, women of the upper classes had achieved a considerable degree of independence and influence. Some of them had become very wealthy through inheritance and very well educated. (See "Art & the West.") Women conducted literary salons and took part in literary groups. Marriage without the husband's right of *manus* became common, and some women conducted their sexual lives as freely as men. (See "Rome's Independent Women: Two Views.") The notorious Clodia, from one of Rome's noblest and most powerful families, is described as conducting many affairs, the most famous with the poet Catullus, who reviles her even as he describes the pangs of his love. Such women were reluctant to have children and increasingly employed contraception and abortion to avoid childbirth.

During the Principate, Augustus' daughter and granddaughter, both named Julia, were both the subject of scandal and punished for adultery. Augustus tried to restore Rome to an earlier ideal of decency and family integrity that reduced the power and sexual freedom of women. He also introduced legislation to encourage the procreation of children, but the new laws seem to have had little effect. In the

Portrait of a Young Woman from Pompeii

The Roman provincial city of Pompeii, near the Bay of Naples, was buried by an eruption of Mt. Vesuvius in 79 C.E. As a result, the town, together with its private houses and their contents, was remarkably well preserved until recovery in the eighteenth century. Among the discoveries were a number of works of art, including pictorial mosaics and paintings. This depiction of a young woman, on a round panel from a house in Pompeii, is part of a larger painting that includes her husband holding a volume of Plato's writings. The woman is holding a stylus and a booklet of wax tablets and is evidently in the process of writing. Her gold earrings and hair net show that she is a fashionable person of some means.

This painting comes from a modest two-story house from a residential district of the town. The main streets had shops where women went, accompanied by a slave. Pompeian remains show that women decorated themselves; among the remains are jewelry and cosmetic jars, as well as the earrings and golden net worn by the woman in this painting. She and her husband represent three significant concepts: the representation of the couple, a woman's attractiveness, and female literacy. "Such an image locates a woman in a world that combines the very old traditions—marriage and female beauty—as natural and necessary—with the notion of female competence; this last is hardly surprising as a motif in. . . Pompeii. . . , a place where women own property, do business, pay for construction, hold honorific and cultic office, and go about in public."[3] There must have been many such towns and many such women in the Roman Empire.

Young Woman Writing, detail of a wall painting from Pompeii. Late 1st century C.E. Diameter 14 ⅝" Museo Archeologico Nazionale, Naples, Italy/Art Resource. © Photograph by Erich Lessing.

Sources: Marilyn Stokstad, *Art History*, revised edition, Harry N. Abrams and Prentice Hall, New York, 1999, pp. 258–259; E. Fantham, H. P. Foley, N. B. Kampen, S. B. Pomeroy and H. A. Shapiro, *Women in the Classical World*, Oxford University Press, Oxford and New York, 1994, pages 340–341

[3] Fantham et. al., *Women in the Classical World*, p. 341.

Rome's Independent Women: Two Views

In the last years of the republic and into the transition to the empire, Roman writers begin to describe what might be called the "new woman." These women are pictured as wearing makeup, dressing and behaving shamelessly, and engaging in adulterous affairs. Perhaps the most shocking of their practices was to engage in sexual activity, but to refuse to have children. The following passages reveal two different approaches to the newly popular means of birth control. The first comes from the work of Soranus, a doctor who practiced in Rome late in the first century C.E. The second comes from the poet Ovid's poems about love.

❖ *What are the opinions of the doctors as to if and when abortion and contraception are appropriate? What reasons do they have for their opinions? What arguments does Ovid make against the use of abortion? How do these ancient arguments compare with modern ones?*

Soranus

For one party banishes abortives, citing the testimony of Hippocrates who says: "I will give to no one an abortive;" moreover, because it is the specific task of medicine to guard and preserve what has been engendered by nature. The other party prescribes abortives, but with discrimination, that is, they do not prescribe them when a person wishes to destroy the embryo because of adultery or out of consideration for youthful beauty; but only to prevent subsequent danger in parturition if the uterus is small and not capable of accommodating the complete development, or if the uterus at its orifice has knobbly swellings and fissures, of if some similar difficulty is involved. And they say the same about contraceptives as well, and we too agree with them.

Ovid

She who first began the practice of tearing out her tender progeny deserved to die in her own warfare. Can it be that, to be free of the flaw of stretchmarks, you have to scatter the tragic sands of carnage? Why will you subject your womb to the weapons of abortion and give dread piosons to the unborn? The tigress lurking in Armenia does no such thing, nor does the lioness dare destroy her young. Yet tender girls do so—though not with impunity; often she who kills what is in her womb dies herself.

Soranus, *Gynecology* 1.19.60 in O. Temkin, *Soranus: Gynecology* (Baltimore: 1956).
Ovid, *Amores* 2.14.5–9, 27–28, 35–38, translated by Natalie Kampen in E. Fantham, E. P. Foley, N. B. Kampen, S. B. Pomeroy and H. A. Shapiro, *Women in the Classical World* (New York: Oxford University Press 1994), pp. 301–302.

first imperial century several powerful women played an important, if unofficial, political role. Augustus' wife Livia had great influence during his reign, and he honored her with the title Augusta in his will. Even in the reign of her son (and Augustus' stepson) Tiberius, she exercised great influence. It was said that he fled Rome to live in Capri in order to escape her domination. The Emperor Claudius' wife Messalina took part in the plot to overthrow him. The Elder Agrippina, wife of the general Germanicus, was active in opposition to Tiberius, and her daughter, also called Agrippina, helped bring her son Nero to the throne. In later centuries, women's rights were expanded by permitting them to make wills and inherit from children. At the turn of the fourth century, the Emperor Domitian freed women from the need for guardianship.

Life in Imperial Rome: The Apartment House

The civilization of the Roman Empire depended on the vitality of its cities. The typical city had about 20,000 inhabitants, and perhaps only three or four had a population of more than 75,000. The population of Rome, however, was certainly greater than 500,000, perhaps more than a million. People coming to Rome for the first time found it overwhelming and were either thrilled or horrified by its size, bustle, and noise. The rich lived in elegant homes called *domūs*. These were single-storied houses with plenty of space, an open central courtyard, and several rooms designed for specific and different purposes, such as dining, sitting, or sleeping, in privacy and relative quiet. Though only a small portion of Rome's population lived in them, *domūs* took up as much as a third of the city's space. Public space for temples, markets, baths, gymnasiums, theaters, forums, and governmental buildings took up another quarter of Rome's territory.

This left less than half of Rome's area to house the mass of its inhabitants, who were squeezed into multiple dwellings that grew increasingly tall. Most Romans during the imperial period lived in apartment buildings called *insulae*, or "islands," that rose to a height of five or six stories and sometimes even more. The most famous of them, the Insula of Febiala, seems to have "towered above the Rome of the Antonines like a skyscraper."[4]

These buildings were divided into separate apartments (*cenicula*) of undifferentiated rooms, the same plan on each floor. The apartments were cramped and uncomfortable. They had neither central heating nor open fireplaces; heat and fire for cooking came from small, portable stoves. The apartments were hot in summer, cold in winter, and stuffy and smoky when the stoves were lit. There was no plumbing, so tenants needed to go into the streets to wells or fountains for water and to public baths and latrines, or to less regulated places. The higher up one lived, the more difficult were these trips, so chamber pots and commodes were kept in the rooms. These receptacles were emptied into vats on the staircase landings or in the alleys outside; on occasion, the contents, and even

[4] J. Carcopino, *Daily Life in Ancient Rome* (New Haven, CT: Yale University Press, 1940), p. 26.

the containers, were tossed out the window. Roman satirists complained of the discomforts and dangers of walking the streets beneath such windows. Roman law tried to find ways to assign responsibilities for the injuries done to dignity and person.

In spite of these difficulties, the attractions of the city and the shortage of space caused rents to rise, making life in the *insulae* buildings expensive as well as uncomfortable. It was also dangerous. The houses were lightly built of concrete and brick and were far too high for the limited area of their foundations, and so they often collapsed. Laws limiting the height of buildings were not always obeyed and did not, in any case, always prevent disaster. The satirist Juvenal did not exaggerate much when he wrote, "We inhabit a city held up chiefly by slats, for that is how the landlord patches up the cracks in the old wall, telling the tenants to sleep peacefully under the ruin that hangs over their heads." (See "Juvenal on Life in Rome.")

Even more serious was the threat of fire. Wooden beams supported the floors, and the rooms were lit by torches, candles, and oil lamps and heated by braziers. Fires broke out easily and, without running water, were not easily put out; once started, they usually led to disaster.

When we consider the character of these apartments and compare them with the attractive public places in the city, we can easily understand why the people of Rome spent most of their time out of doors.

This is a reconstruction of a typical Roman apartment house found at Ostia, Rome's port. The ground floor contained shops, and the stories above it held many apartments.
Museo della Civitá Romana, Rome, Italy. Scala/Art Resource, N.Y.

Juvenal on Life in Rome

The satirical poet Juvenal lived and worked in Rome in the late first and early second centuries C.E. His poems present a vivid picture of the material and cultural world of the Romans of his time. In the following passages, he tells of the discomforts and dangers of life in the city, both indoors and out.

❖ *According to Juvenal, what dangers awaited pedestrians in the Rome of his day? Who had responsibility for the condition of Rome? If the situation was as bad as he says, why was nothing done about it? Why did people choose to live in Rome at all and especially in the conditions he describes?*

Who, in Praeneste's cool, or the wooded Volsin-
    ian uplands,
Who, on Tivoli's heights, or a small town like
    Gabii, say,
Fears the collapse of his house? But Rome is
    supported on pipestems,
Matchsticks; it's cheaper, so, for the landlord to
    shore up his ruins,
Patch up the old cracked walls, and notify all
    the tenants
They can sleep secure, though the beams are in
    ruins above them.
No, the place to live is out there, where no cry
    of Fire!
Sounds the alarm of the night, with a neighbor
    yelling for water,
Moving his chattels and goods, and the whole
    third story is smoking.

Look at other things, the various dangers
    of nighttime.
How high it is to the cornice that breaks, and a
    chunk beats my brains out,
Or some slob heaves a jar, broken or cracked,
    from a window.
Bang! It comes down with a crash and proves
    its weight on the sidewalk.
You are a thoughtless fool, unmindful of
    sudden disaster,
If you don't make your will before you go out to
    have dinner.
There are as many deaths in the night as there
    are open windows
Where you pass by; if you're wise, you will
    pray, in your wretched devotions,
People may be content with no more than
    emptying slop jars.

....

From Juvenal, *The Satires of Juvenal*, trans. by Rolfe Humphries (Bloomington, IN: Indiana University Press, 1958), pp. 40, 43.

The Culture of the Early Empire

The years from 14 to 180 C.E. were a time of general prosperity and a flourishing material and artistic culture, but one not so brilliant and original as in the Age of Augustus.

LITERATURE   In Latin literature, the period between the death of Augustus and the time of Marcus Aurelius is known as the Silver Age. As the name implies, this age produced work of high quality although probably not of so high a quality as in the Augustan era. In contrast to the hopeful, positive optimists of the Augustans, the writers of the Silver Age were gloomy, negative, and pessimistic. In the works of the former period, praise of the emperor, his achievements, and the world abounds; in the latter, criticism and satire lurk everywhere. Some of the most important writers of the Silver

Age came from the Stoic opposition and reflected its hostility to the growing power and personal excesses of the emperors.

The writers of the second century C.E. appear to have turned away from contemporary affairs and even recent history. Historical writing was about remote periods so that there would be less danger of irritating imperial sensibilities. Scholarship was encouraged, but we hear little of poetry, especially that dealing with dangerous subjects. In the third century C.E., romances written in Greek became popular and offer further evidence of the tendency of writers of the time to seek and offer escape from contemporary realities.

ARCHITECTURE   The main contribution of the Romans lay in two new kinds of buildings—the great public bath and a new, freestanding kind of amphitheater—and in the advances in engineering that made these large structures possible. While keeping the basic post-and-lintel construction used by the Greeks, the Romans added to it the principle of the semicircular arch, borrowed from the Etruscans. They also made good use of concrete, a building material first used by the Hellenistic Greeks and fully developed by the Romans. The arch, combined with the post and lintel, produced the great Colosseum built by the Flavian emperors. When used internally in the form of vaults and domes, the arch permitted great buildings like the baths, of which the most famous and best preserved are those of the later emperors Caracalla and Diocletian. (See Map 5–3.)

One of Rome's most famous buildings, the Pantheon, begun by Augustus' friend Agrippa and rebuilt by Hadrian, combined all these elements. Its portico of Corinthian columns is of Greek origin, but its rotunda of brick-faced concrete with its domed ceiling and relieving arches is thoroughly Roman. The new engineering also made possible the construction of more mundane, but useful, structures like bridges and aqueducts.

SOCIETY　Seen from the harsh perspective of human history, the first two centuries of the Roman Empire deserve their reputation of a "golden age." One of the dark sides of Roman society, at least since the third century B.C.E., had been its increasing addiction to the brutal contests involving gladiators. By the end of the first century C.E., emperors regularly appealed to this barbaric entertainment as a way of winning the acclaim of their people (see "Seneca Describes Gladiatorial Shows.") On broader fronts in Roman society, by the second century C.E., troubles were brewing that foreshadowed the difficult times ahead. The literary efforts of the time reveal a flight from the present, from reality, and from the public realm to the past, to romance, and to private pursuits. Some of the same aspects may be seen in the more prosaic world of everyday life, especially in the decline of vitality in local government.

In the first century C.E., members of the upper classes vied with one another for election to municipal office and for the honor of doing service to their communities. By the second century C.E., it became necessary for the emperors to intervene to correct abuses in local affairs and even to force unwilling

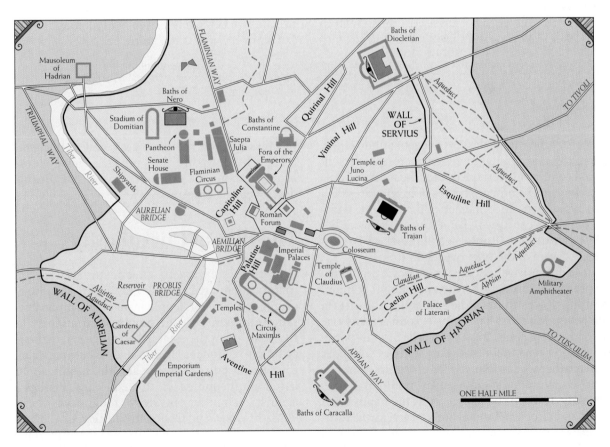

MAP 5–3　ANCIENT ROME　*This map of Rome during the late empire shows the seven hills on and around which the city was built, as well as the major walls, bridges, and other public sites and buildings.*

Seneca Describes Gladiatorial Shows

Roman society was never gentle, but by imperial times the public had become addicted to brutal public displays of violence in the form of combats involving gladiators. At first, gladiators were enslaved prisoners of war or condemned criminals, but later free men entered the combats, driven by poverty. They were all trained in schools by professional trainers. The following selection by Seneca gives an unfriendly account of the shows and of the spectators who watched them.

❖ *What does Seneca think of the gladiatorial contests? What does he think of the spectators? Who were the gladiators? What was the attitude of the spectators toward them? What do such entertainments say about the society in which they take place? Do they have any effect on the character of that society?*

I chanced to stop in at a midday show, expecting fun, wit, and some relaxation, when men's eyes take respite from the slaughter of their fellow men. It was just the reverse. The preceeding combats were merciful by comparison; now all trifling is put aside and it is pure murder. The men have no protective covering. Their entire bodies are exposed to the blows, and no blow is ever struck in vain....In the morning men are thrown to the lions and the bears, at noon they are thrown to their spectators. The spectators call for the slayer to be thrown to those who in turn will slay him, and they detain the victor for another butchering. The outcome for the combatants is death; the fight is waged with sword and fire. This goes on while the arena is free. "But one of them was a highway robber, he killed a man!" Because he killed he deserved to suffer this punishment, granted...."Kill him! Lash him! Burn him! Why does he meet the sword so timidly? Why doesn't he kill boldly? Why doesn't he die game? Whip him to meet his wounds! Let them trade blow for blow, chests bare and within reach!" And when the show stops for intermission, "Let's have men killed meanwhile! Let's not have nothing going on!"

"SenecaDescribes Gladiatorial Shows" from Seneca, *Moral Epistles*, in N. Lewis and M. Reinhold, *Roman Civilization*, Vol. 2, p. 230. Copyright © 1955 Columbia University Press. Reprinted by permission of the publisher.

members of the ruling classes to accept public office. Magistrates and council members were held personally and collectively responsible for the revenues due. There were even some instances of magistrates fleeing to avoid their office, a practice that became widespread in later centuries. (For a satirical view of life in first-century C.E. Rome, see "Dinner at Trimalchio's: A Satire of the Newly Rich at Rome.")

These difficulties reflected more basic problems. The prosperity brought by the end of civil war and the influx of wealth from the east could not sustain itself beyond the first half of the second century C.E. There also appears to have been a decline in population for reasons that remain mysterious. The cost of government kept rising. The emperors were required to maintain a standing army, minimal in size, but costly, to keep the people in Rome happy with "bread and circuses," to pay for an increasingly numerous bureaucracy, and to wage expensive wars to defend the frontiers against dangerous and determined barbarian enemies. The ever-increasing need for money compelled the emperors to raise taxes, to press hard on their subjects, and to bring on inflation by debasing the coinage. These elements brought about the desperate crises that ultimately destroyed the empire.

The Rise of Christianity

Christianity emerged, spread, survived, and ultimately conquered the Roman Empire in spite of its origin among poor people from an unimportant and remote province of the empire. Christianity faced the hostility of the established religious institutions of its native Judaea. It also had to compete against the official cults of Rome and the highly sophisticated philosophies of the educated classes and against such other "mystery" religions as the cults of Mithra, Isis, and Osiris. In addition to all this, the Christians faced the opposition of the imperial government and formal persecution. Yet Christianity achieved toleration and finally exclusive command as the official religion of the empire.

Jesus of Nazareth

An attempt to understand this amazing outcome must begin with the story of Jesus of Nazareth. The most important evidence about his life is in the Gospel accounts, all of them written well after his death. The earliest, by Mark, is dated about 70 C.E. and the latest, by John, about 100 C.E. They are not, moreover, attempts at simply describing the life of Jesus with historical accuracy. Rather, they are statements of faith by true believers. The authors of the Gospels believed that Jesus was the son of God and that he had come into the world to redeem humanity and to bring immortality to those who believed in him and followed his way. To the Gospel writers, Jesus' resurrection was striking proof of his teachings. At the same time, the Gospels regard Jesus as a figure in history, and they recount events in his life as well as his sayings.

There is no reason to doubt that Jesus was born in the province of Judaea in the time of Augustus and that he was a most effective teacher in the tra-dition of the prophets. This tradition promised the coming of a Messiah (in Greek, *christos*—so Jesus Christ means "Jesus the Messiah"), the redeemer who would make Israel triumph over its enemies and establish the kingdom of God on earth. In fact, Jesus seems to have insisted that the Messiah would not establish an earthly kingdom, but would bring an end to the world as human beings knew it at the Day of Judgment. On that day, God would reward the righteous with immortality and happiness in heaven and condemn the wicked to eternal suffer-ing in hell. Until then (a day that his followers be-lieved would come very soon), Jesus taught the faithful to abandon sin and worldly concerns; to fol-low him and his way; to follow the moral code de-scribed in the Sermon on the Mount, which preached love, charity, and humility; and to believe in him and his divine mission.

Jesus won a considerable following, especially among the poor, which caused great suspicion among the upper classes. His novel message and his criticism of the religious practices connected

Dinner at Trimalchio's: A Satire on the Newly Rich at Rome

The following selection is from Trimalchio's Feast, *part of a fragmentary satire called* The Satyricon, *by Petronius, a writer of the first century C.E. The speaker is a guest at a lavish dinner given by Trimalchio, a former slave risen to great wealth at Rome. In-cluded among the jibes and sneers is some useful information about life in this period.*

❖ *What is the source of Trimalchio's wealth? What sources of wealth were available at the time? What does this selection reveal about social mobility in the first cen-tury? What does it reveal about the range of commerce? How do you explain the tone of the narrator?*

"As for old Trimalchio, that man's got more farms than a kite could flap over. And there's more sil-ver plate stuffed in his porter's lodge than anoth-er man's got in his safe. As for slaves, whoosh! So help me, I'll bet not one in ten has ever seen his master. Your ordinary rich man is just peanuts compared to him; he could knock them all under a cabbage and you'd never know they were gone.

"And buy things? Not him. No sir, he raises everything right on his own estate. Wool, citron, pepper, you name it. By god, you'd find hen's milk if you looked around. Now take his wool. The home-grown strain wasn't good enough. So you know what he did? Imported rams from Taren-tum, bred them into the herd. Attic honey he rais-es at home. Ordered the bees special from Athens.

And the local bees are better for being crossbred too. And, you know, just the other day he sent off to India for some mushroom spawn. Every mule he owns had a wild ass for a daddy. And you see those pillows there? Every last one is stuffed with purple or scarlet wool. That boy's loaded!

"And don't sneer at his friends. They're all ex-slaves, but every one of them's rich. You see that guy down there on the next to last couch? He's worth a cool half-million. Came up from nowhere. Used to tote wood on his back. People say, but I don't know, he stole a cap off a hob-goblin's head and found a treasure. He's the god's fair-haired boy. That's luck for you, but I don't begrudge him. Not so long ago he was just a slave. Yes sir, he's doing all right."

From Petronius, *The Satyricon*, trans. by William Arrowsmith (Ann Arbor, MI: University of Michigan Press, 1959), pp. 35–36. Reprinted by permission of the University of Michgan Press.

Mark Describes the Resurrection of Jesus

Belief that Jesus rose from the dead after his Crucifixion (about 30 C.E.) was and is central to traditional Christian doctrine. The record of the Resurrection in the Gospel of Mark, written a generation later (toward 70 C.E.), is the earliest we have. The significance to most Christian groups revolves about the assurance given them that death and the grave are not final and that, instead, salvation for a future life is possible. The appeal of these views was to be nearly universal in the West during the Middle Ages. The church was commonly thought to be the means of implementing the promise of salvation—hence the enormous importance of the church's sacramental system, its rules, and its clergy.

❖ *Why are the stories of miracles such as the one described here important for the growth of Christianity? What is special and important about this miracle? Why is it important in the story that days passed between the death of Jesus and the opening of the tomb? Why might the early Christians believe this story? Why was belief in the resurrection important for Christianity in the centuries immediately after the life of Jesus? Is it still important today?*

And when evening had come, since it was the day of Preparation, that is, the day before the sabbath, Joseph of Arimathea, a respected member of the council, who was also himself looking for the kingdom of God, took courage and went to Pilate, and asked for the body of Jesus. And Pilate wondered if he were already dead; and summoning the centurion, he asked him whether he was already dead. And when he learned from the centurion that he was dead, he granted the body to Joseph. And he brought a linen shroud, and taking him down, wrapped him in the linen shroud, and laid him in a tomb which had been hewn out of the rock; and he rolled a stone against the door of the tomb. Mary Magdalene and Mary the mother of Jesus saw where he was laid.

And when the sabbath was past, Mary Magdalene, and Mary the mother of James, and Salome, bought spices, so that they might go and anoint him. And very early on the first day of the week they went to the tomb when the sun had risen. And they were saying to one another, "Who will roll away the stone for us from the door of the tomb?" And looking up, they saw that the stone was rolled back; for it was very large. And entering the tomb, they saw a young man sitting on the right side, dressed in a white robe; and they were amazed. And he said to them, "Do not be amazed; you seek Jesus of Nazareth, who was crucified. He has risen, he is not here, see the place where they laid him. But go, tell his disciples and Peter that he is going before you to Galilee; there you will see him, as he told you." And they went out and fled from the tomb; for trembling and astonishment had come upon them; and they said nothing to any one, for they were afraid.

Gospel of Mark 15:42–47; 16:1–8, *Revised Standard Version of the Bible* (New York: Thomas Nelson and Sons, 1946, 1952).

with the temple at Jerusalem and its priests provoked the hostility of the religious establishment. A misunderstanding of the movement made it easy to convince the Roman governor that Jesus and his followers might be dangerous revolutionaries. He was put to death in Jerusalem by the cruel and degrading device of crucifixion, probably in 30 C.E. His followers believed that he was resurrected on the third day after his death, and that belief became a critical element in the religion they propagated throughout the Roman Empire and beyond. (See "Mark Describes the Resurrection of Jesus.")

The new belief spread quickly to the Jewish communities of Syria and Asia Minor. There is reason to believe, however, that it might have had only a short life as a despised Jewish heresy were it not for the conversion and career of Saint Paul.

Paul of Tarsus

Paul was born Saul, a citizen of the Cilician city of Tarsus in Asia Minor. He had been trained in Hellenistic culture and was a Roman citizen. But he was also a zealous member of the Jewish sect known as the *Pharisees*, the group that was most strict in its insistence on adherence to the Jewish law. He took a vigorous part in the persecution of the early Christians until his own conversion outside Damascus about 35 C.E.

The great problem facing the early Christians was to resolve their relationship to Judaism. If the new faith was a version of Judaism, then it must adhere to the Jewish law and seek converts only among Jews. James, called the brother of Jesus, was a conservative who held to that view, whereas the Hellenist Jews tended to see Christianity as a new and universal religion. To force all converts to follow Jewish law would have been fatal to the growth of the new sect. Jewish law's many technicalities and dietary prohibitions were strange to gentiles, and the necessity of circumcision—a frightening, painful, and dangerous operation for adults—would have been a tremendous deterrent to conversion. Paul, converted and with his new name, supported the position of the Hellenists and soon won many converts among the gentiles. After some conflict within the sect, Paul won out. Consequently, the "apostle to the gentiles" deserves recognition as a crucial contributor to the success of Christianity.

Paul believed it important that the followers of Jesus be evangelists (messengers), to spread the gospel, or "good news," of God's gracious gift. He taught that Jesus would soon return for the Day of Judgment, and it was important that all who would should believe in him and accept his way. Faith in Jesus as the Christ was necessary, but not sufficient, for salvation, nor could good deeds alone achieve it. That final blessing of salvation was a gift of God's grace that would be granted to some, but not all.

Organization

Paul and the other apostles did their work well. The new religion spread throughout the Roman Empire and even beyond its borders. It had its greatest success in the cities and mostly among the poor and uneducated. The rites of the early communities appear to have been simple and few. Baptism by water removed original sin and permitted participation in the community and its activities. The central ritual was a common meal called the *agape*, or "love feast," followed by the ceremony of the *Eucharist*, or "thanksgiving," a celebration of the Lord's Supper in which unleavened bread was eaten and unfermented wine was drunk. There were also prayers, hymns, or readings from the Gospels.

Not all the early Christians were poor, and it became customary for the rich to provide for the poor at the common meals. The sense of common love fostered in these ways focused the community's attention on the needs of the weak, the sick, the unfortunate, and the unprotected. This concern gave the early Christian communities a warmth and a human appeal that stood in marked contrast to the coldness and impersonality of the pagan cults. No less attractive were the promise of salvation, the importance to God of each human soul, and the spiritual equality of all in the new faith. As Paul put it, "There is neither Jew nor Greek, there is neither slave nor free, there is neither male nor female; for you are all one in Christ Jesus."[5]

The future of Christianity depended on its communities' finding an organization that would preserve unity within the group and help protect it against enemies outside. At first, the churches had little formal organization. Soon, it appears, affairs were placed in the hands of boards of *presbyters*, or "elders," and *deacons*, or "those who serve." By the second century C.E., as their numbers grew, the Christians of each city tended to accept the authority and leadership of bishops (*episkopoi*, or "overseers"). Bishops were elected by the congregation to lead them in worship and to supervise funds. As time passed, the bishops extended their authority over the Christian communities in outlying towns and the countryside. The power and almost monarchical authority of the bishops were soon enhanced by the doctrine of Apostolic Succession, which asserted that the powers that Jesus had given his original disciples were passed on from bishop to bishop by ordination.

The bishops kept in touch with one another, maintained communications between different Christian communities, and prevented doctrinal and sectarian splintering, which would have destroyed Christian unity. They maintained internal discipline and dealt with the civil authorities. After a time they began the practice of coming together in councils to settle difficult questions, to establish orthodox opinion, and even to expel as heretics those who would not accept it. It is unlikely that Christianity could have survived the travails of its early years without such strong internal organization and government.

The Persecution of Christians

The new faith soon incurred the distrust of the pagan world and of the imperial government. At first, Christians were thought of as a Jewish sect and were therefore protected by Roman law. It soon became clear, however, that they were quite different, seeming both mysterious and dangerous. They denied the existence of the pagan gods and so were accused of atheism. Their refusal to worship the emperor was judged to be treason. Because they kept mostly to

---

[5] Galatians 3:28. *Revised Standard Version of the Bible.*

This is the Catacomb of the Jordani in Rome. The early Christians built miles of catacombs, or tunnels, in Rome. They were used as underground cemeteries and as refuges from persecution.   Charitable Foundation/Gemeinnutzige Stiftung Leonard von Matt

themselves, took no part in civic affairs, engaged in secret rites, and had an organized network of local associations, they were misunderstood and suspected. The love feasts were erroneously reported to be scenes of sexual scandal. The alarming doctrine of the actual presence of Jesus' body in the Eucharist was distorted into an accusation of cannibalism.

The privacy and secrecy of Christian life and worship ran counter to a traditional Roman dislike of any private association, especially any of a religious nature. Christians thus earned the reputation of being "haters of humanity." Claudius expelled them from Rome, and Nero tried to make them scapegoats for the great fire that struck the city in 64 C.E. By the end of the first century, "the name alone"— that is, simple membership in the Christian community—was a crime.

But, for the most part, the Roman government did not take the initiative in attacking Christians in the first two centuries. When one governor sought instructions for dealing with the Christians, the emperor Trajan urged moderation. Christians were not to be sought out, anonymous accusations were to be disregarded, and anyone denounced could be acquitted merely by renouncing Christ and sacrificing to the emperor. Unfortunately, no true Christian could meet the conditions, and so there were some martyrdoms.

Most persecutions in this period, however, were started not by the government, but by mob action. Though they lived quiet, inoffensive lives, some Christians must have seemed unbearably smug and self-righteous. Unlike the tolerant, easygoing pagans, who were generally willing to accept the new gods of foreign people and add them to the pantheon, the Christians denied the reality of the pagan gods. They proclaimed the unique rightness of their own way and looked forward to their own salvation and the damnation of nonbelievers. It is not surprising, therefore, that pagans disliked these strange and unsocial people, tended to blame misfortunes on them, and, in extreme cases, turned to violence. But even this adversity had its uses. It weeded out the weaklings among the Christians, and brought greater unity to those who remained faithful. It also provided the Church with martyrs around whom legends could grow that would inspire still greater devotion and dedication.

The Emergence of Catholicism

Division within the Christian Church may have been an even greater threat to its existence than persecution from outside. The great majority of Christians never accepted complex, intellectualized opinions, but held to what even then were traditional, simple, conservative beliefs. This body of majority opinion, considered to be universal, or "catholic," was enshrined by the church that came to be called *Catholic*. The Catholic Church's doctrines were deemed _orthodox_, that is, "holding the right opinions," whereas those holding contrary opinions were heretics.

The need to combat heretics, however, compelled the orthodox to formulate their own views more clearly and firmly. By the end of the second century C.E., an orthodox canon had been shaped that included the Old Testament, the Gospels, and the Epistles of Paul, among other writings. The process of creating a standard set of holy books was not completed for at least two more centuries, but a vitally important start had been made. The orthodox declared the Catholic Church itself to be the depository of Christian teaching and the bishops to be its receivers. They also drew up creeds, or brief statements of faith to which true Christians should adhere.

In the first century, all that was required of one to be a Christian was to be baptized, to partake of the Eucharist, and to call Jesus the Lord. By the end of the second century an orthodox Christian—that is, a member of the Catholic Church—was required to accept its creed, its canon of holy writings, and the authority of the bishops. The loose structure of the apostolic church had given way to an organized body with recognized leaders able to define its faith and to exclude those who did not accept it. Whatever the shortcomings of this development, there can be little doubt that it provided the clarity, unity, and discipline needed for survival.

Rome as a Center of the Early Church

During this same period, the church in Rome came to have special prominence. As the center of communications and the capital of the empire, Rome had natural advantages. After the Roman destruction of Jerusalem in 135 C.E., no other city had any convincing claim to primacy in the church. Besides having the largest single congregation of Christians, Rome also benefited from the tradition that Jesus' apostles Peter and Paul were martyred there.

Peter, moreover, was thought to be the first bishop of Rome. The Gospel of Matthew (16:18) reported Jesus' statement to Peter: "Thou art Peter [in Greek, *Petros*] and upon this rock [in Greek, *petra*] I will build my church." Eastern Christians might later point out that Peter had been leader of the Christian community at Antioch before he went to Rome. But in the second century the church at Antioch, along with the other Christian churches of Asia Minor, was fading in influence, and by 200 C.E. Rome was the most important center of Christianity. Because of the city's early influence and because of the Petrine doctrine derived from the Gospel of Matthew, later bishops of Rome claimed supremacy in the Catholic Church. But as the era of the "good emperors" came to a close, this controversy was far in the future.

The Crisis of the Third Century

Dio Cassius, a historian of the third century C.E., described the Roman Empire after the death of Marcus Aurelius as declining from "a kingdom of gold into one of iron and rust." Although we have seen that the gold contained more than a little impurity, there is no reason to quarrel with Dio's assessment of his own time. Commodus (r. 180–192 C.E.), the son of Marcus Aurelius, proved the wisdom of the "good emperors" in selecting their successors for their talents rather than for family ties. Commodus was incompetent and autocratic. He reduced the respect in which the imperial office was held, and his assassination brought the return of civil war.

Barbarian Invasions

The pressure on Rome's frontiers, already serious in the time of Marcus Aurelius, reached massive proportions in the third century. In the east, a new power arising in the old Persian Empire threatened the frontiers. In the third century B.C.E., the Parthians had made the Iranians independent of the Hellenistic kings and had established an empire of their own on the old foundations of the Persian Empire. Several Roman attempts to conquer them had failed, but as late as 198 C.E. the Romans could reach and destroy the Parthian capital and bring at least northern Mesopotamia under their rule.

In 224 C.E., however, a new Iranian dynasty, the Sassanians, seized control from the Parthians and brought new vitality to Persia. They soon recovered Mesopotamia and made raids deep into Roman provinces. In 260 C.E., they humiliated the Romans by actually taking the emperor Valerian prisoner; he died in captivity.

On the western and northern frontiers the pressure came not from a well-organized rival empire, but from an ever-increasing number of German tribes. Though they had been in contact with the Romans at least since the second century B.C.E., they had not been much affected by civilization. The men did no agricultural work, but confined their activities to hunting, drinking, and fighting. They were organized on a family basis by clans, hundreds, and tribes. They were led by chiefs, usually from a royal family, elected by the assembly of fighting men. The king was surrounded by a collection of warriors, whom the Romans called his *comitatus*. Always eager for plunder, these tough barbarians were attracted by the civilized delights they knew existed beyond the frontier of the Rhine and Danube rivers.

The most aggressive of the Germans in the third century C.E. were the Goths. Centuries earlier they had wandered from their ancestral home near the Baltic Sea into the area of southern Russia. In the 220s and 230s C.E., they began to put pressure on the Danube frontier. By about 250 C.E., they were able to penetrate the empire and overrun the Balkan provinces. The need to meet this threat and the one posed by the Persian Sassanids in the east made the Romans weaken their western frontiers, and other Germanic peoples—the Franks and the Alemanni—

broke through in those regions. There was considerable danger that Rome would be unable to meet this challenge.

Rome's perils were caused, no doubt, by the unprecedentedly numerous and simultaneous attacks, but its internal weakness encouraged these attacks. The Roman army was not what it had been in its best days. By the second century C.E., it was made up mostly of romanized provincials. The pressure on the frontiers and epidemics of plague in the time of Marcus Aurelius forced the emperor to resort to the conscription of slaves, gladiators, barbarians, and brigands. The training and discipline with which the Romans had conquered the Mediterranean world had declined. The Romans also failed to respond to the new conditions of constant pressure on all the frontiers. A strong, mobile reserve that could meet a threat in one place without causing a weakness elsewhere might have helped, but no such unit was created.

Septimius Severus (r. 193–211 C.E.) and his successors played a crucial role in the transformation of the character of the Roman army. Septimius was a military usurper who owed everything to the support of his soldiers. He meant to establish a family dynasty, in contrast to the policy of the "good emperors" of the second century. He was prepared to make Rome into an undisguised military monarchy. Septimius drew recruits for the army increasingly from peasants of the less civilized provinces.

Economic Difficulties

These changes were a response to the great financial needs caused by the barbarian attacks. Inflation had forced Commodus to raise the soldiers' pay. Yet the Severan emperors had to double it to keep up with prices, which increased the imperial budget by as much as 25 percent. To raise money, the emperors resorted to inventing new taxes, debasing the coinage, and even selling the palace furniture. But it was still hard to recruit troops. The new style of military life introduced by Septimius—with its laxer discipline, more pleasant duties, and greater opportunity for advancement, not only in the army but in Roman society—was needed to attract men into the army. The policy proved effective for a short time, but could not prevent the chaos of the late third century.

The same forces that caused problems for the army did great damage to society at large. The shortage of workers for the large farms, which had all but wiped out the independent family farm, reduced agricultural production. As external threats distracted the emperors, they were less able to preserve domestic peace. Piracy, brigandage, and the neglect of roads and harbors all hampered trade. So, too, did the debasement of the coinage and the inflation in general. Imperial taxation and confiscations of the property of the rich removed badly needed capital from productive use.

More and more, the government was required to demand services that had been given gladly in the past. Because the empire lived hand to mouth, with no significant reserve fund and no system of credit financing, the emperors were led to compel the people to provide food, supplies, money, and labor. The upper classes in the cities were made to serve as administrators without pay and to meet deficits in revenue out of their own pockets. Sometimes these demands caused provincial rebellions, as in Egypt and Gaul. More typically, they caused peasants and even town administrators to flee to escape their burdens. The result of all these difficulties was a weakening of Rome's economic strength when it was most needed.

The Social Order

The new conditions caused important changes in the social order. Direct attacks from hostile emperors and economic losses decimated the Senate and the traditional ruling class. Their ranks were filled by men coming up through the army. The whole state began to take on an increasingly military appearance. Distinctions among the classes by dress had been traditional since the republic; in the third and fourth centuries C.E., the people's everyday clothing had become a kind of uniform that precisely revealed status. Titles were assigned to ranks in society as to ranks in the army. The most important distinction was the one formally established by Septimius Severus, which drew a sharp line between the *honestiores* (senators, equestrians, the municipal aristocracy, and the soldiers) and the lower classes, or *humiliores*. Septimius gave the *honestiores* a privileged position before the law. They were given lighter punishments, could not be tortured, and alone had the right of appeal to the emperor.

As time passed, it became more difficult to move from the lower order to the higher, another example of the growing rigidity of the late Roman Empire. Peasants were tied to their lands, artisans to their crafts, soldiers to the army, merchants and shipowners to the needs of the state, and citizens of the municipal upper class to the collection and payment of increasingly burdensome taxes. Freedom and private initiative gave way before the needs of the state and its ever-expanding control of its citizens.

Civil Disorder

Commodus was killed on the last day of 192 C.E. The succeeding year was similar to the year 69. Three emperors ruled in swift succession, Septimius Severus emerging, as we have seen, to establish firm rule and a dynasty. The death of Alexander Severus, the last of the dynasty, in 235 C.E., brought on a half century of internal anarchy and foreign invasion.

The empire seemed on the point of collapse. But the two conspirators who overthrew and succeeded the emperor Gallienus proved to be able soldiers. Claudius II Gothicus (268–270 C.E.) and Aurelian (270–275 C.E.) drove back the barbarians and stamped out internal disorder. The soldiers who followed Aurelian on the throne were good fighters who made significant changes in Rome's system of defense. Around Rome, Athens, and other cities, they built heavy walls that could resist barbarian attack. They drew back their best troops from the frontiers, relying chiefly on a newly organized heavy cavalry and a mobile army near the emperor's own residence.

Hereafter, the army was composed largely of mercenaries who came from among the least civilized provincials and even from among the Germans. The officers gave personal loyalty to the emperor rather than to the empire. These officers became a foreign, hereditary caste of aristocrats that increasingly supplied high administrators and even emperors. In effect, the Roman people hired an army of mercenaries, who were only technically Roman, to protect them.

The Late Empire

During the fourth and fifth centuries the Romans strove to meet the many challenges, internal and external, that threatened the survival of their empire. Growing pressure from barbarian tribes pushing against its frontier intensified the empire's tendency to smother individuality, freedom, and initiative, in favor of an increasingly intrusive and autocratic centralized monarchy. Economic and military weakness increased, and it became even harder to keep the vast empire together. Hard and dangerous times may well have helped the rise of Christianity, encouraging people to turn away from the troubles and dangers of this world to concern about the next.

The Fourth Century and Imperial Reorganization

The period from Diocletian (r. 284–305 C.E.) to Constantine (r. 306–337 C.E.) was one of reconstruction

A mosaic from Carthage illustrating aspects of life on the manorial estate of a certain Julian in the province of Africa. His housing, provisions, and entertainment appear to have been opulent. Social boundaries hardened in the late empire, and large fortified estates like this increasingly dominated social and economic life. Musée Nationale du Bardo

and reorganization after a time of civil war and turmoil. Diocletian was from Illyria (the former Yugoslavia). He was a man of undistinguished birth who rose to the throne through the ranks of the army. He knew that he was not a great general and that the job of defending and governing the entire empire was too great for one individual.

Diocletian therefore decreed the introduction of the *tetrarchy*, the rule of the empire by four men with power divided territorially. (See Map 5–4.) He allotted the provinces of Thrace, Asia, and Egypt to himself. His co-emperor, Maximian, shared with him the title of Augustus and governed Italy, Africa, and Spain. In addition, two men were given the subordinate title of Caesar: Galerius, who was in charge of the Danube frontier and the Balkans, and Constantius, who governed Britain and Gaul. This arrangement not only afforded a good solution to the military problem, but also provided for a peaceful succession.

Diocletian was recognized as the senior Augustus, but each tetrarch was supreme in his own sphere. The Caesars were recognized as successors to each half of the empire, and their loyalty was enhanced by marriages to daughters of the Augusti. It was a return, in a way, to the precedent of the "good emperors" of 96–180 C.E., who chose their successors from the ranks of the ablest men. It seemed to promise orderly and peaceful transitions instead of assassinations, chaos, and civil war.

Each man established his residence and capital at a place convenient for frontier defense, and none chose Rome. The effective capital of Italy became the northern city of Milan. Diocletian beautified Rome by constructing his monumental baths, but he visited the city only once and made his own capital at Nicomedia in Bithynia. This was another step in the long leveling process that had reduced the eminence of Rome and Italy. It was also evidence of the growing importance of the east.

In 305 C.E., Diocletian retired and compelled his co-emperor to do the same. But his plan for a smooth succession failed completely. In 310 there were five Augusti and no Caesars. Out of this chaos, Constantine, son of Constantius, produced order. In 324 he defeated his last opponent and made himself sole emperor, uniting the empire once again; he reigned until 337. Mostly, Constantine carried forward the policies of Diocletian. He supported Christianity, however, which Diocletian had tried to suppress.

DEVELOPMENT OF AUTOCRACY   The development of the imperial office toward autocracy was carried to the extreme by Diocletian and Constantine. The emperor ruled by decree, consulting only a few high officials whom he himself appointed. The Senate had no role whatever, and its dignity was further diminished by the elimination of all distinctions between senator and equestrian.

The emperor was a remote figure surrounded by carefully chosen high officials. He lived in a great palace and was almost unapproachable. Those admitted to his presence had to prostrate themselves before him and kiss the hem of his robe, which was purple and had golden threads going through it. The emperor was addressed as *dominus*, or "lord," and his right to rule was not derived from the Roman people, but from heaven. All this remoteness and ceremony had a double purpose: to enhance the dignity of the emperor and to safeguard him against assassination.

Constantine erected the new city of Constantinople on the site of ancient Byzantium on the Bosporus, which leads to both the Aegean and Black Seas. He made it the new capital of the empire. Its strategic location was excellent for protecting the eastern and Danubian frontiers, and, surrounded on three sides by water, it was easily defended. This location also made it easier to carry forward the policies that fostered autocracy and Christianity. Rome was full of tradition, the center of senatorial and even republican memories and of pagan worship. Constantinople was free from both, and its dedication in 330 C.E. marked the beginning of a new era. Until its fall to the Turks in 1453, it served as a bas-

tion of civilization, the preserver of classical culture, a bulwark against barbarian attack, and the greatest city in Christendom.

The autocratic rule of the emperors was carried out by a civilian bureaucracy, carefully separated from the military to reduce the chances of rebellion by anyone combining the two kinds of power. Below the emperor's court the most important officials were the *praetorian* prefects, each of whom administered one of the four major areas into which the empire was divided: Gaul, Italy, Illyricum, and the Orient. The four prefectures were subdivided into twelve territorial units called *dioceses*, each under a vicar who was subordinate to the prefect. The dioceses were further divided into almost a hundred provinces, each under a provincial governor.

The operation of the entire system was supervised by a vast system of spies and secret police, without whom the increasingly rigid organization could not be trusted to perform. In spite of these efforts, the system was corrupt and inefficient.

The cost of maintaining a 400,000-man army as well as the vast civilian bureaucracy, the expensive imperial court, and the imperial taste for splendid buildings put a great strain on an already weak economy. Diocletian's attempts to establish a uniform and reliable currency failed, leading instead to increased inflation. To deal with it, he resorted to price control with his Edict of Maximum Prices in 301 C.E. For each product and each kind of labor, a maximum price was set, and violations were punishable by death. The edict failed despite the harshness of its provisions.

Peasants unable to pay their taxes and officials unable to collect them tried to escape. Diocletian resorted to stern regimentation to keep all in their places and at the service of the government. The terror of the third century forced many peasants to seek protection in the *villa*, or "country estate," of a large and powerful landowner and to become tenant farming *coloni*. As social boundaries hardened, these *coloni* and their descendants became increasingly tied to their estates.

DIVISION OF THE EMPIRE   The peace and unity established by Constantine did not last long. His death was followed by a struggle for succession that was won by Constantius II (r. 337–361 C.E.), whose death, in turn, left the empire to his young cousin Julian (r. 361–363 C.E.). Julian was called the Apostate by the Christians because of his attempt to stamp out Christianity and restore paganism. Julian undertook a campaign against Persia with the aim of putting a Roman on the throne of the Sassanids and ending the Persian menace once and for all. He penetrated deep into Persia, but was killed

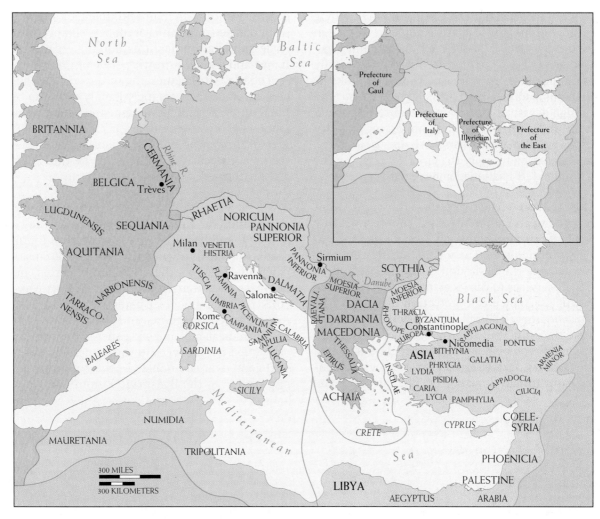

MAP 5–4 DIVISIONS OF THE ROMAN EMPIRE UNDER DIOCLETIAN *Diocletian divided the sprawling empire into four prefectures for more effective government and defense. The inset map shows their boundaries, and the larger map gives some details of regions and provinces. The major division between east and west was along the line running south between Pannonia and Moesia.*

in battle. His death put an end to the expedition and to the pagan revival.

The Germans in the West took advantage of the eastern campaign to attack along the Rhine and upper Danube rivers. And even greater trouble was brewing along the middle and upper Danube. (See Map 5–5.) That territory was occupied by the eastern Goths, known as the Ostrogoths. They were being pushed hard by their western cousins, the Visigoths, who in turn had been driven from their home in the Ukraine by the fierce Huns, a nomadic people from central Asia. (See "Ammianus Marcellinus Describes the People Called Huns.")

The emperor Valentinian (r. 364–375 C.E.) saw that he could not defend the empire alone and appointed his brother Valens (r. 364–378 C.E.) as coruler. Valentinian made his ... headquarters at Milan and spent the rest of his ... successfully against the

Franks and the Alemanni in the west. Valens was given control of the east. The empire was once again divided in two. The two emperors maintained their own courts, and the halves of the empire became increasingly separate and different. Latin was the language of the west and Greek of the east.

In 376 the Visigoths, pursued by the Huns, asked and received permission to enter the empire. Soon to be Christianized, they won rights of settlement and material assistance within the empire from the eastern emperor Valens (r. 364–378) in exchange for defending the eastern frontier as *foederati*, or special allies of the empire.

The Visigoths, however, did not keep their bargain with the Romans, retaining their weapons and plundering the Balkan provinces. Nor did the Romans comply: They treated the Visigoths cruelly, even forcing them to trade their children for dogs to eat. Valens attacked the Goths and died, along with most of his army, at Adrianople in Thrace in 378. Theodosius (r. 379–395 C.E.), an able and experienced general, was named coruler in the east. By a combination of military and diplomatic skills, Theodosius pacified the Goths, giving them land and a high degree of autonomy and enrolling many of them in his army. He made important military reforms, putting greater emphasis on the cavalry. Theodosius tried to unify the empire again, but his death in 395 left it divided and weak.

THE RURAL WEST   The two parts of the empire went their separate and different ways. The west became increasingly rural as barbarian invasions continued and grew in intensity. The *villa*, a fortified country estate, became the basic unit of life. There, *coloni* gave their services to the local magnate in return for economic assistance and protection from both barbarians and imperial officials. Many cities shrank to no more than tiny walled fortresses ruled by military commanders and bishops. The upper classes moved to the country and asserted ever greater independence from imperial authority. The failure of the

central authority to maintain the roads and the constant danger from bands of robbers sharply curtailed trade and communications, forcing greater self-reliance and a more primitive style of life.

The new world emerging in the west by the fifth century and after was increasingly made up of isolated units of rural aristocrats and their dependent laborers. The only institution providing a high degree of unity was the Christian Church. The pattern for the early Middle Ages in the west was already formed.

THE BYZANTINE EAST   In the east the situation was quite different. Constantinople became the center of a vital and flourishing culture we call Byzantine that lasted until the fifteenth century. Because of its defensible location, the skill of its emperors, and the firmness and strength of its base in Asia Minor, it could deflect and repulse barbarian attacks. A strong navy allowed commerce to flourish in the eastern Mediterranean and, in good times, far beyond. Cities continued to prosper, and the emperors made their will good over the nobles in the countryside. The civilization of the Byzantine Empire was a unique

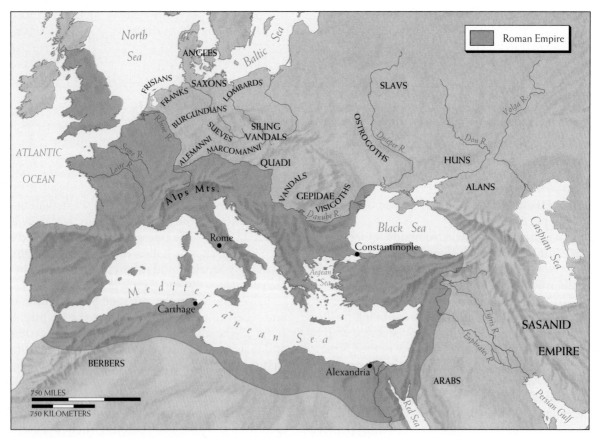

MAP 5–5   THE EMPIRE'S NEIGHBORS   *In the fourth century the Roman Empire was near-*
ly surrounded by ever more threatening neighbors. The map shows who these so-called
barbarians were and where they lived before their armed contact with the Romans.

Ammianus Marcellinus Describes the People Called Huns

Ammianus Marcellinus was born about 330 C.E. in Syria, where Greek was the language of his well-to-do family. After a military career and considerable travel, he lived in Rome and wrote an encyclopedic Latin history of the empire, covering the years 96 to 378 C.E. and giving special emphasis to the difficulties of the fourth century. Here he describes the Huns, one of the barbarous peoples pressing on the frontiers. Like most Romans, he was alarmed and appalled by the way of life of these nomadic peoples. His account is a combination of observation, hearsay, and prejudice, and it is not always easy to separate facts from fantasy.

❖ *In what ways did the culture of the Huns differ from that of the Romans? How did their way of life give them an advantage against Rome? How was it disadvantageous? Which of the writer's statements do you think are factual? Explain the reasons for your judgments.*

The people called Huns, barely mentioned in ancient records, live beyond the sea of Azof, on the border of the Frozen Ocean, and are a race savage beyond all parallel. At the very moment of birth the cheeks of their infant children are deeply marked by an iron, in order that the hair, instead of growing at the proper season on their faces, may be hindered by the scars; accordingly the Huns grow up without beards, and without any beauty. They all have closely knit and strong limbs and plump necks; they are of great size, and low legged, so that you might fancy them two-legged beasts or the stout figures which are hewn out in a rude manner with an ax on the posts at the end of bridges.

They are certainly in the shape of men, however uncouth, and are so hardy that they neither require fire nor well-flavored food, but live on the roots of such herbs as they get in the fields, or on the half-raw flesh of any animal, which they merely warm rapidly by placing it between their own thighs and the backs of their horses.

They never shelter themselves under roofed houses, but avoid them, as people ordinarily avoid sepulchers as things not fit for common use. Nor is there even to be found among them a cabin thatched with reeds; but they wander about, roaming over the mountains and the woods, and accustom themselves to bear frost and hunger and thirst from their very cradles....

There is not a person in the whole nation who cannot remain on his horse day and night. On horseback they buy and sell, they take their meat and drink, and there they recline on the narrow neck of their steed, and yield to sleep so deep as to indulge in every variety of dream.

And when any deliberation is to take place on any weighty matter, they all hold their common council on horseback. They are not under kingly authority, but are contented with the irregular government of their chiefs, and under their lead they force their way through all obstacles.

From Ammianus Marcellinus, *Res Gestae*, trans. by C. D. Yonge (London: George Bell and Son, 1862), pp. 312–314.

combination of classical culture, the Christian religion, Roman law, and eastern artistic influences.

While the west was being overrun by barbarians, the Roman Empire, in altered form, persisted in the east. While Rome shrank to an insignificant ecclesiastical town, Constantinople flourished as the seat of empire, the "New Rome." Indeed, the Byzantines even called themselves "Romans." When we contemplate the decline and fall of the Roman Empire in the fourth and fifth centuries, we are speaking only of the west. A form of classical culture persisted in the Byzantine East for a thousand years more.

The Triumph of Christianity

The rise of Christianity to dominance in the empire was closely connected with the political and cultural experience of the third and fourth centuries. Political chaos and decentralization had religious and cultural consequences.

RELIGIOUS CURRENTS IN THE EMPIRE   In some of the provinces, native languages replaced Latin and Greek, sometimes even for official purposes. The classical tradition that had been the basis of impe-

**Reigns of Selected Late Empire Rulers
(All dates are C.E.)**

180–192	Commodus
193–211	Septimius Severus
222–235	Alexander Severus
249–251	Decius
253–260	Valerian
253–268	Gallienus
268–270	Claudius II Gothicus
270–275	Aurelian
284–305	Diocletian
306–337	Constantine
324–337	Constantine sole emperor
337–361	Constantius II
361–363	Julian the Apostate
364–375	Valentinian
364–378	Valens
379–395	Theodosius

rial life became the exclusive possession of a small, educated aristocracy. In religion, the public cults had grown up in an urban environment and were largely political in character. As the importance of the cities diminished, so did the significance of their gods. People might still take comfort in the worship of the friendly, intimate deities of family, field, hearth, storehouse, and craft, but these gods were too petty to serve their needs in a confused and frightening world. The only universal worship was of the emperor, but he was far off, and obeisance to his cult was more a political than a religious act.

In the troubled times of the fourth and fifth centuries, people sought powerful, personal deities who would bring them safety and prosperity in this world and immortality in the next. Paganism was open and tolerant. It was by no means unusual for people to worship new deities alongside the old and even to intertwine elements of several to form a new amalgam by the device called *syncretism.*

Manichaeism was an especially potent rival of Christianity. Named for its founder, Mani, a Persian who lived in the third century C.E., this movement contained aspects of various religious traditions, including Zoroastrianism from Persia and both Judaism and Christianity. The Manichaeans pictured a world in which light and darkness, good and evil, were constantly at war. Good was spiritual and evil was material. Because human beings were made of matter, their bodies were a prison of evil and darkness, but they also contained an element of light and good. The "Father of Goodness" had sent Mani, among other prophets, to free humanity and gain its

salvation. To achieve salvation, humans must want to reach the realm of light and to abandon all physical desires. Manichaeans led an ascetic life and practiced a simple worship guided by a well-organized Church. The movement reached its greatest strength in the fourth and fifth centuries, and some of its central ideas persisted into the Middle Ages.

Christianity had something in common with these cults and answered many of the same needs felt by their devotees. None of them, however, attained Christianity's universality, and none appears to have given the early Christians and their leaders as much competition as the ancient philosophies or the state religion.

IMPERIAL PERSECUTION By the third century, Christianity had taken firm hold in the eastern provinces and in Italy. It had not made much headway in the west, however. (See Map 5–6.) Christian apologists pointed out that Christians were good citizens who differed from others only in not worshiping the public gods. Until the middle of the third century, the emperors tacitly accepted this view, without granting official toleration. As times became bad and the Christians became more numerous and visible, that policy changed. Popular opinion blamed disasters, natural and military, on the Christians.

About 250, the emperor Decius (r. 249–251 C.E.) invoked the aid of the gods in his war against the Goths and required that all citizens worship the state gods publicly. True Christians could not obey, and Decius started a major persecution. Many Christians—even some bishops—yielded to threats and torture, but others held out and were killed. Valerian (r. 253–260 C.E.) resumed the persecutions, partly to confiscate the wealth of rich Christians. His successors, however, found other matters more pressing, and the persecution lapsed until the end of the century.

By the time of Diocletian, the number of Christians had grown still greater and included some high state officials. At the same time, hostility to the Christians grew on every level. Diocletian was not generous toward unorthodox intellectual or religious movements. His own effort to bolster imperial power with the aura of divinity boded ill for the church, and in 303 he launched the most serious persecution inflicted on the Christians in the Roman Empire. He issued a series of edicts confiscating church property and destroying churches and their sacred books. He deprived upper-class Christians of public office and judicial rights, imprisoned clergy, and enslaved Christians of the lower classes. He placed heavy fines on anyone refusing to sacrifice to the public gods. A final decree required public sacrifices and libations. The persecution horrified many pagans, and the plight and the demeanor of the martyrs often aroused pity and sympathy.

Ancient states could not carry out a program of terror with the thoroughness of modern totalitarian governments, so the Christians and their church survived to enjoy what they must have considered a miraculous change of fortune. In 311 Galerius, who had been one of the most vigorous persecutors, was influenced, perhaps by his Christian wife, to issue the Edict of Toleration, permitting Christian worship.

The victory of Constantine and his emergence as sole ruler of the empire changed the condition of Christianity from a precariously tolerated sect to the religion favored by the emperor. This put it on the path to becoming the official and only legal religion in the empire.

EMERGENCE OF CHRISTIANITY AS THE STATE RELIGION
The sons of Constantine continued to favor the new religion, but the succession of Julian the Apostate posed a new threat. He was a devotee of traditional classical pagan culture and, as a believer in Neoplatonism, an opponent of Christianity. Neoplatonism was a religious philosophy, or a philosophical religion, whose connection with Platonic teachings was distant. Its chief formulator was Plotinus (205–270 C.E.), who tried to combine classical and rational philosophical speculation with the mystical spirit of his time. Plotinus's successors were bitter critics of Christianity, and their views influenced Julian. Though he refrained from persecution, he tried to undo the work of Constantine by withdrawing the privileges of the church, removing Christians from high offices, and introducing a new form of pagan worship. His reign, however, was short, and his work did not last.

In 394, Theodosius forbade the celebration of pagan cults and abolished the pagan religious calendar. At his death, Christianity was the official religion of the Roman Empire.

The establishment of Christianity as the state religion did not put an end to the troubles of the Christians and their church; instead, it created new ones and complicated some old ones. The favored position of the church attracted converts for the wrong reasons and diluted the moral excellence and spiritual fervor of its adherents. The problem of the relationship between church and state arose, presenting the possibility that religion would become subordinate to the state, as it had been in the classical world and in earlier civilizations. In the East, that is what happened to a considerable degree.

In the West, the weakness of the emperors prevented such a development and permitted church leaders to exercise remarkable independence. In 390 Ambrose, bishop of Milan, excommunicated Theodosius for a massacre he had carried out, and the emperor did humble penance. This act provided an important precedent for future assertions of the church's autonomy and authority, but it did not put an end to secular interference and influence in the church.

ARIANISM AND THE COUNCIL OF NICAEA Internal divisions proved to be even more troubling as new heresies emerged. Because they threatened the unity of an empire that was now Christian, they took on a political character and inevitably involved the emperor and the powers of the state. Before long, the world would view Christians persecuting other Christians with a zeal at least as great as had been displayed against them by the most fanatical pagans.

Among the many controversial views that arose, the most important and the most threatening was Arianism. It was founded by a priest named Arius of Alexandria (ca. 280–336 C.E.) in the fourth century. The issue creating difficulty was the relation of God the Father to God the Son. Arius argued that Jesus was a created being, unlike God the Father. He was, therefore, not made of the substance of God and was not eternal. "The Son has a beginning," he said, "but God is without beginning." For Arius, Jesus was neither fully man nor fully God, but something in between. Arius' view did away with the mysterious concept of the Trinity, the difficult doctrine that holds that God is three persons (the Father, the Son, and the Holy Spirit) and also one in substance and essence.

The Arian concept had the advantage of appearing to be simple, rational, and philosophically acceptable. To its ablest opponent, Athanasius, however, it had serious shortcomings. Athanasius (ca. 293–373 C.E.), later bishop of Alexandria, saw the Arian view as an impediment to any acceptable theory of salvation, to him the most important religious question. He adhered to the old Greek idea of salvation as involving the change of sinful mortality into divine immortality through the gift of "life." Only if Jesus were both fully human and fully God could the transformation of humanity to divinity have taken place in him and be transmitted by him to his disciples. "Christ was made man," he said, "that we might be made divine."

To deal with the growing controversy, Constantine called a council of Christian bishops at Nicaea, not far from Constantinople, in 325. For the emperor the question was essentially political, but for the disputants salvation was at stake. At Nicaea, the view expounded by Athanasius won out, became orthodox, and was embodied in the Nicene Creed. But Arianism persisted and spread. Some later emperors were either Arians or sympathetic to that view. Some of the most successful missionaries to the barbarians were Arians;

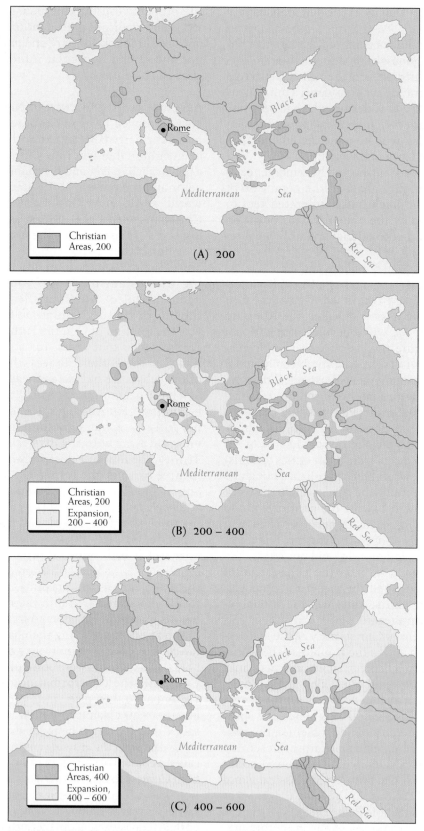

MAP 5–6   THE SPREAD OF CHRISTIANITY   *Christianity grew swiftly in the third, fourth, fifth, and sixth centuries—especially after the conversion of the emperors in the fourth century. By 600, on the eve of the birth of the new religion of Islam, Christianity was dominant throughout the Mediterranean world and most of western Europe.*

as a result, many of the German tribes that overran the empire were Arians. The Christian emperors hoped to bring unity to their increasingly decentralized realms by imposing the single religion. Over time it did prove to be a unifying force, but it also introduced divisions where none had existed before.

Arts and Letters in the Late Empire

The art and literature of the late empire reflect the confluence of pagan and Christian ideas and traditions as well as the conflict between them. Much of the literature is of a polemical nature and much of the art is propaganda.

The salvation of the empire from the chaos of the third century was accomplished by a military revolution based on and led by provincials whose origins were in the lower classes. They brought with them the fresh winds of cultural change, which blew out not only the dust of classical culture, but much of its substance as well. Yet the new ruling class was not interested in leveling; it wanted instead to establish itself as a new aristocracy. It thought of itself as effecting a great restoration rather than a revolution and sought to restore classical culture and absorb it. The confusion and uncertainty of the times were tempered in part, of course, by the comfort of Christianity. But the new ruling class sought order and stability—ethical, literary, and artistic—in the classical tradition as well.

The Preservation of Classical Culture

One of the main needs and accomplishments of this period was the preservation of classical culture. Ways were discovered to make it available and useful to the newly arrived ruling class. Works of the great classical authors were reproduced in many copies and were transferred from perishable and inconvenient papyrus rolls to sturdier codices, bound volumes that were as easy to use as modern books. Scholars also digested long works like Livy's *History of Rome* into shorter versions, wrote learned commentaries, and compiled grammars. Original works by pagan writers of the late empire were neither numerous nor especially distinguished.

Christian Writers

On the other hand, the late empire saw a great outpouring of Christian writings. There were many examples of Christian apologetics in poetry as well as in prose, and there were sermons, hymns, and biblical commentaries. Christianity could also boast important scholars. Jerome (348–420 C.E.), thoroughly trained

The Triumph of Christianity	
ca. 4 B.C.E.	Jesus of Nazareth born
ca. 30 C.E.	Crucifixion of Jesus
64 C.E.	Fire at Rome: persecution by Nero
ca. 70–100 C.E.	Gospels written
ca. 250–260 C.E.	Major persecutions by Decius and Valerian
303 C.E.	Persecution by Diocletian
311 C.E.	Galerius issues Edict of Toleration
312 C.E.	Battle of Milvian Bridge; conversion of Constantine to Christianity
325 C.E.	Council of Nicaea
395 C.E.	Christianity becomes official religion of Roman Empire

in both the east and the west in classical Latin literature and rhetoric, produced a revised version of the Bible in Latin. Commonly called the Vulgate, it became the Bible used by the Catholic Church. Probably the most important eastern scholar was Eusebius of Caesarea (ca. 260–340 C.E.). He wrote apologetics, an idealized biography of Constantine, and a valuable attempt to reconstruct the chronology of important events in the past. His most important contribution, however, was his *Ecclesiastical History*, an attempt to set forth the Christian view of history. He saw all of history as the working out of God's will. All of history, therefore, had a purpose and a direction, and Constantine's victory and the subsequent unity of empire and church were its culmination.

The closeness and also the complexity of the relationship between classical pagan culture and that of the Christianity of the late empire are nowhere better displayed than in the career and writings of Augustine (354–430 C.E.), bishop of Hippo in North Africa. He was born at Carthage and was trained as a teacher of rhetoric. His father was a pagan, but his mother was a Christian and hers was ultimately the stronger influence. He passed through several intellectual way stations—skepticism and Neoplatonism among others—before his conversion to Christianity. His training and skill in pagan rhetoric and philosophy made him peerless among his contemporaries as a defender of Christianity and as a theologian.

His greatest works are his *Confessions*, an autobiography describing the road to his conversion, and *The City of God*. The latter was a response to the pagan charge that Rome's sack by the Visigoths in 410 was caused by the abandonment of the

This late-Roman ivory plaque shows a scene from Christ's Passion. The art of the late empire was transitional between the classical past and the medieval future.
Crucifixion, carving, c. 420 A.D. (ivory). British Museum, London, UK/Bridgeman Art Library, London/New York

old gods and the advent of Christianity. The optimistic view held by some Christians that God's will worked its way in history and was easily comprehensible needed further support in the face of the Visigoths' sack of Rome. Augustine sought to separate the fate of Christianity from that of the Roman Empire. He contrasted the secular world, the City of Man, with the spiritual, the City of God. The former was selfish, the latter unselfish; the former evil, the latter good.

Augustine argued that history was moving forward, in the spiritual sense, to the Day of Judgment, but there was no reason to expect improvement before then in the secular sphere. The fall of Rome was neither surprising nor important. All states, even a Christian Rome, were part of the City of Man and were therefore corrupt and mortal. Only the City of God was immortal, and it, consisting of all the saints on earth and in heaven, was untouched by earthly calamities.

Though the *Confessions* and *The City of God* are Augustine's most famous works, they emphasize only a part of his thought. His treatises *On the Trin-*

ity and *On Christian Education* reveal the great skill with which he supported Christian belief with the learning, logic, and philosophy of the pagan classics. Augustine believed that faith is essential and primary (a thoroughly Christian view), but it is not a substitute for reason (the foundation of classical thought). Instead, faith is the starting point for, and liberator of, human reason, which continues to be the means by which people can understand what faith reveals. His writings constantly reveal the presence of both Christian faith and pagan reason, as well as the tension between them, a legacy he left to the Middle Ages.

The Problem of the Decline and Fall of the Empire in the West

Whether important to Augustine or not, the massive barbarian invasions of the fifth century put an end to effective imperial government in the west. For centuries people have speculated about the causes of the collapse of the ancient world. Every kind of reason has been put forward, and some suggestions seem to have nothing to do with reason at all. Exhaustion of the soil, plague, climatic change, and even poisoning caused by lead water pipes have been suggested as reasons for Rome's decline in population, vigor, and the capacity to defend itself. Some blame the institution of slavery and a resulting failure to make advances in science and technology. Others blame excessive government interference in the economic life of the empire and still others the destruction of the urban middle class, the carrier of classical culture.

Perhaps a simpler and more obvious explanation can be found. It might begin with the observation that the growth of so mighty an empire as Rome's was by no means inevitable. Rome's greatness had come from conquests that provided the Romans with the means to expand still further, until there were not enough Romans to conquer and govern any more peoples and territory. When pressure from outsiders grew, the Romans lacked the resources to advance and defeat the enemy as in the past. The tenacity and success of their resistance for so long were remarkable. Without new conquests to provide the immense wealth needed for the defense and maintenance of internal prosperity, the Romans finally yielded to unprecedented onslaughts by fierce and numerous attackers.

To blame the ancients and the institution of slavery for the failure to produce an industrial and economic revolution like that of the later Western world (one capable of producing wealth without taking it from another) is to stand the problem on its head. No one yet has a satisfactory explanation for those revolutions. So it is improper to blame any institution or society for not achieving what has been achieved only once in human history. Perhaps we would do well to think of the problem as Gibbon did:

The decline of Rome was the natural and inevitable effect of immoderate greatness. Prosperity ripened the principle of decay; the cause of the destruction multiplied with the extent of conquest; and, as soon as time or accident had removed the artificial supports, the stupendous fabric yielded to the pressure of its own weight. The story of the ruin is simple and obvious; and instead of inquiring why the Roman Empire was destroyed, we should rather be surprised that it had subsisted so long.[6]

[6] Edward Gibbon, *The History of the Decline and Fall of the Roman Empire*, 2d ed., Vol. 4, ed. by J. B. Bury (London: 1909), pp. 173–174.

In Perspective

Out of the civil wars and chaos that brought down the republic, Augustus brought unity, peace, order, and prosperity. As a result, he was regarded with almost religious awe and attained more military and political power than any Roman before him. He ruled firmly, but with moderation. He tried to limit military adventures and the costs they incurred. Augustus supported public works that encouraged trade and communication in the empire. He tried to restore and invigorate the old civic pride, and in this he had considerable success. He was less successful in promoting private morality based on family values. He patronized the arts so as to beautify Rome and glorify his reign. On his death, Augustus was able to pass on the regime to his family, the Julio-Claudians.

For almost two hundred years, with a few brief interruptions, the empire was generally prosperous, peaceful, and well run. But problems were growing. Management of the many responsibilities assumed by the government required the growth of a large bureaucracy that placed a heavy and increasing burden on the treasury, required higher taxes, and stifled both civic spirit and private enterprise. Pressure from barbarian tribes on the frontiers required a large standing army, which was also very costly and led to further rises in taxation.

In the late empire, Rome's rulers resorted to many devices for dealing with their problems. Policies came to include putting down internal military rebellions led by generals from different parts of the empire. More and more, the emperors' rule and their safety depended on the loyalty of the army, so they courted the soldiers' favor with gifts of various kinds. This only increased the burden of taxes; the rich and powerful found ways to avoid their obligations, making the load on everyone else all the heavier. The government's control over the lives of its people became ever greater and the society more rigid as people tried to flee to escape the crushing load of taxes. Expedients were tried, including inflating the currency, fixing farmers to the soil as serfs or coloni, building walls to keep the barbarians out, and bribing barbarian tribes to fight for Rome against other barbarians. Ultimately, all these measures failed. The Roman Empire in the west fell, leaving disunity, insecurity, disorder, and poverty. Like similar empires in the ancient world, it had been unable to sustain its "immoderate greatness."

REVIEW QUESTIONS

1. Discuss the Augustan constitution and government. What solutions did Augustus provide for the problems that had plagued the Roman Republic? Why was the Roman population willing to accept Augustus as head of the state?
2. How was the Roman Empire organized and why did it function smoothly? What role did the emperor play in the maintenance of political stability?
3. How did the literature in the Golden Age of Augustus differ from that of the Silver Age during the first and second centuries C.E.? How did the poetry of Vergil and Horace contribute to the stability of Augustus' rule?
4. In spite of unpromising beginnings, Christianity was enormously popular by the fourth century C.E. Why were Christians persecuted by Roman authorities? What were the more important reasons for Christianity's success?
5. What were the political, social, and economic problems that beset Rome in the third and fourth centuries C.E.? How did Diocletian and Constantine deal with them? Were they effective in stemming the tide of decline and disintegration in the Roman Empire? What problems were they unable to solve?
6. Discuss three theories that scholars have advanced to explain the decline and fall of the Roman Empire. What are the difficulties involved in explaining the fall? What explanation would you give?

SUGGESTED READINGS

T. Barnes, *The New Empire of Diocletian and Constantine* (1982). A study of the character of the late empire.

A. R. Birley, *Hadrian the Restless Emperor* (1997). A biography of an important emperor.

P. Brown, *Augustine of Hippo* (1967). A splendid biography.

P. Brown, *The World of Late Antiquity, C.E. 150–750* (1971). A brilliant and readable essay.

P. Brown, *Power and Persuasion in Late Antiquity: Towards a Christian Empire* (1992). A fine discussion of early Christianity and its complicated relationship with the Roman Empire.

A. Ferrill, *The Fall of the Roman Empire, The Military Explanation* (1986). An interpretation that emphasizes the decline in the quality of the Roman army.

A. Ferrill, *Caligula: Emperor of Rome* (1991). A biography of the monstrous young emperor.

E. Gibbon, *The History of the Decline and Fall of the Roman Empire*, 7 vols., ed. by J. B. Bury, 2d ed. (1909–1914). One of the masterworks of the English language.

M. Grant, *The Fall of the Roman Empire* (1990). A lively, well-written account.

A. H. M. Jones, *The Later Roman Empire*, 3 vols. (1964). A comprehensive study of the period.

D. Kagan, ed., *The End of the Roman Empire: Decline or Transformation?* 3d. ed. (1992). A collection of essays discussing the problem of the decline and fall of the Roman Empire.

M. L. W. Laistner, *The Greater Roman Historians* (1963). Essays on the major Roman historical writers.

J. Lebreton and J. Zeiller, *History of the Primitive Church*, 3 vols. (1962). The Catholic viewpoint.

H. Lietzmann, *History of the Early Church*, 2 vols. (1961). From the Protestant viewpoint.

E. N. Luttwak, *The Grand Strategy of the Roman Empire* (1976). An original and fascinating analysis by a keen student of modern strategy.

R. Macmullen, *Enemies of the Roman Order* (1966). An original and revealing examination of opposition to the emperors.

R. Macmullen, *Roman Social Relations, 50 B.C. to A.D. 284* (1981). An interesting study of social developments.

R. Macmullen, *Corruption and the Decline of Rome* (1988). A study that examines the importance of changes in ethical ideas and behavior.

R. W. Mathison, *Roman Aristocrats in Barbarian Gaul: Strategies for Survival* (1993). An unusual slant on the late empire.

F. G. B. Millar, *The Roman Empire and Its Neighbors* (1968). An analysis of Roman foreign relations in the imperial period.

F. G. B. Millar, *The Emperor in the Roman World, 31 B.C.–A.D. 337* (1977). A study of Roman imperial government.

F.G.B. Millar, *The Roman Near East, 31 B.C.–A.D. 337* (1993). A valuable study of Rome's relations with an important part of its empire.

A. Momigliano, ed., *The Conflict between Paganism and Christianity* (1963). A valuable collection of essays.

H. M. D. Parker, *A History of the Roman World from A.D. 138 to 337* (1969). A good survey.

M. I. Rostovtzeff, *Social and Economic History of the Roman Empire,* 2d. ed. (1957). A masterpiece whose main thesis has been much disputed.

V. Rudich, *Political Dissidence under Nero, the Price of Dissimulation* (1993). A brilliant exposition of the lives and thoughts of political dissidents in the early empire.

E. T. Salmon, *A History of the Roman World, 30 B.C. to 138 A.D.* (1968). A good survey.

G. E. M. de Ste. Croix, *The Class Struggle in the Ancient World* (1981). An ambitious interpretation of all of classical civilization from an idiosyncratic Marxist perspective.

R. Syme, *The Roman Revolution* (1960). A brilliant study of Augustus, his supporters, and their rise to power

Ancient Warfare

The Causes of War

War has been a persistent part of human experience since before the birth of civilization.[1] Organized warfare goes back to the Stone Age. There may be evidence of it as early as the late Paleolithic Age, but there can be no doubt that it was a significant human activity by the Neolithic Age. The earliest civilizations of Egypt and Mesopotamia added powerful new elements to the character of warfare and were from the first occupied with war, as were later Bronze and Iron Age cultures all over the world.

The earliest literary work in the Western tradition, Homer's *Iliad*, describes a long, bitter war and the men who fought it. The Rigvedic hymns of the ancient culture of India tell of the warrior god Indra, who smashes the fortifications of his enemies. The earliest civilizations of China were established by armies armed with spears, composite bows, and war chariots. The evidence is plentiful that war is one of the oldest and most continuous activities of the human species.

Ancient philosophers like Plato and Aristotle took all this for granted. They believed that men (they never thought of women in this context) were naturally acquisitive and aggressive and that governments and laws existed to curb those tendencies. The ancient Greeks, wracked as they were by perpetual war, were eager to investigate its causes. Thucydides, writing at the end of the fifth century B.C.E. set forth with great care the quarrels between the Athenians and the Peloponnesians and why they broke their treaty: "so that no one may ever have to seek the cause that led to the outbreak of so great a war among the Greeks." He provided a profound and helpful understanding of the causes of wars and of the motives of human beings in going to war. He understood war as the armed competition for power, but he thought that unusually wise and capable leaders could limit their own fears and desires and those of their people—could choose to gain and defend only so much power as was needed for their purposes.

In this struggle for power, whether for a rational sufficiency or in the insatiable drive for all the power there is, Thucydides found that people go to war out of "fear, honor, and interest."[2] That trio of motives is illuminating in understanding the origins of wars throughout history. That fear and interest move states to war will not surprise the modern reader, but that concern for honor should do so may seem strange. If we take honor to mean "fame," "glory," "renown," or "splendor," it may appear applicable to the premodern world alone. If, however, we understand its significance as "deference," "esteem," "just due," "regard," "respect," or "prestige," we will find it an important motive of nations in the modern world as well.

Wars are made by human beings who may choose different courses of action. Sometimes the decisions are made by a single individual or a small group, sometimes by a very large number. Their choices are always limited and affected by circumstances, and the closer they come to the outbreak of a war, the more limited the choices seem. Those who decide to make war always think they have good reason to fight. Although impersonal forces play a role and the reasons publicly given are not necessarily the true ones, the reasons must be taken seriously, for "the conflicts between states which have usually led to war have normally arisen, not from any irrational and emotional drives, but from almost a superabundance of analytic rationality....[I]n general men have fought during the past two hundred years neither because they are aggressive nor because they are acquisitive animals, but because they are reasoning ones: because they discern, or believe that they can discern, dangers before they become immediate, the possibility of threats before they are made."[3]

At any time in history, there has been widespread agreement that some things are desirable and worth fighting for. Liberty, autonomy, the freedom to ex-

---

[1]Arther Ferrill, *The Origins of War* (London, 1985), p. 13, says that "organized warfare appeared at least by the end of the Palaeolithic Age," but Richard A. Gabriel argues that true warfare did not come until the Bronze Age and the invention of the state and the social structure that came with it. No one, however, doubts that war is at least as old as civilization.

[2]1.75.3.

[3]*The Lessons of History* (New York, 1968), p. 81.

This mound marks the ancient city of Jericho. Thought by some to be the earliest Neolithic site in the Near East, it sprang up around an oasis about 7000 B.C.E. The thick stone walls and moat that surround it show that it was meant to be a fortress that could resist sieges, showing that warfare was common at least as early as the construction of this city. © Zev Radovan, Jerusalem, Israel

ercise one's religion, and the search for wealth have been among the most common through the ages. Fear of their opposites—slavery, subordination, religious suppression, and poverty—have probably been even greater causes of wars. All of them, however, depend on power, for the distribution of power determines who can and cannot impose his or her will on others. In one sense, there is no single cause of war, but a myriad. But in another sense, there is only one cause: Wars have rarely happened by accident or because of honest misunderstandings; most of them have resulted from calculations about power, which is valued because it can provide security, reputation, and material advantage.

In the sixth century B.C.E., the Greek philosopher Heracleitus observed that "war is the father of all things." In 1968 Will and Ariel Durant calculated that, in the previous 3,421 years, only 268 were free of war. There have been none since, suggesting that, in that respect, little has changed in more than three millennia. The reasons that have led to war in the past seem not to have disappeared. Human beings, organized into nations and states, continue to compete for a limited supply of desirable things, to seek honor and advantage, and to fear others. All too often, the result has been war.

War and Technology

The conduct of war is shaped at the deepest level by the character of the societies involved, their values, their needs, and their organization, but from the first, technology has played a vital role. Weapons and other necessities of war are the product of technological development, and war and technology have had a mutually stimulating effect from the earliest times as new technologies have helped shape the character of war and the needs of armies have provoked technological advance.

Fortress Walls
Jericho, built about 7000 B.C.E. in the Neolithic Age, already reveals the importance of warfare and the development of technology to deal with it. Jericho

This carving in low relief from the seventh century B.C.E. shows an Assyrian war-chariot and its charioteer. It comes from the palace of King Ashurbanipal at Nineveh, the capital of the mighty Assyrian Empire that dominated the Near East in his time. Erich Lessing/Art Resource, N.Y.

is surrounded by a stone wall 700 yards around, ten feet thick, and thirteen feet high, protected by a moat ten feet deep and thirty feet wide. This barrier made the town a powerful fortress that could be defeated only by an enemy who could besiege it long enough to starve it out. Nobody would have undertaken the expense and effort to build such a structure unless war was a relatively common danger. Not too many years after the rise of civilization in Mesoptamia (ca. 3000 B.C.E.) fortified Sumerian cities appeared in the south. A thousand years later, the pharaohs of the Twelfth Dynasty in Egypt devised a strategic defense system of fortresses on their southern frontier with Nubia. In early China the towns had no walls, because the surrounding plains lacked both trees and stone. During the Shang dynasty (ca.1766–1050 B.C.E.), however, towns with walls made of beaten earth appeared. Once the techniques needed to build fortresses strong enough to withstand attack were mastered, kingdoms could expand into empires that could defend their conquered lands.

The history of warfare and military technology is a story of continued change caused by a permanent competition between defense and offense. In time, construction of fortified stronghold provoked new devices and techniques for besieging them. Excavations in Egypt and Mesopotamia have uncovered scaling ladders, battering rams, siege towers (some of them mobile), and mines burrowing under fortress walls. Catapults capable of hurling stones against an enemy's walls appear in Greece in the fourth century B.C.E.; the weapon was brought to greater perfec-

tion and power by the Romans centuries later. Alexander the Great and some of his Hellenistic successors became skillful at storming fortified cities with the aid of such technology, but throughout ancient history, success against a fortified place usually came as a result of starvation and surrender after a long siege. Not until the invention of gunpowder and powerful canons did offensive technology overcome the defensive strength of fortification.

Army Against Army
A different kind of warfare, of army against army in the open field, appeared as early as the Stone Age. Scholars disagree as to whether it came in the Paleolithic Age or emerged in Neolithic times, but we know that warriors used such weapons as wooden or stone clubs, spears and axes with sharpened stone heads, and simple bows with stone-tipped arrows. The discovery of metallurgy brought the Bronze Age to Mesopotamia, perhaps as early as 3500 B.C.E., providing armies with weapons that were sharper and sturdier than stone and with body armor and helmets that brought greater safety to warriors. The Mesopotamian rulers already had wealth, a sizable population, a civilized organization, and substantial fortress walls. Now, with bronze weapons, Mesopotamian rulers could expand their empires far beyond their early frontiers. When, not much later, the Bronze Age came to Egypt, its rulers, too, used the new technology to expand and defend their wealthy kingdom.

The Chariot and the Bow
The next great revolution in warfare occurred with the inventions of the chariot and the composite bow. When these came together by about 1800 B.C.E. their users swept all before them, conquering both Egypt and Mesopotamia. The chariot was a light vehicle, a platform on two wheels pulled by a team of two or four horses that could move swiftly on a battlefield. It was strong enough to hold two men—a driver and a warrior—as it sped along on an open field. The wheels were of wood—not solid, but with spokes and a hub—and were attached to an axle; building them required great skill and experience. The warrior on the chariot wielded a new weapon: the composite bow, more powerful by far than anything that had come before it. Made of thin strips of wood glued together and fastened with animal tendons and horn, the bow was short and easy to use from a moving chariot. It could shoot a light arrow accu-

rately for 300 yards and penetrate the armor of the day at about 100. A man on a chariot on a flat enough field, using a composite bows with a quiver full of light arrows, could devastate an army of foot soldiers. "Circling at a distance of 100 or 200 yards from the herds of unarmoured foot soldiers, a chariot crew—one to drive, one to shoot—might have transfixed six men a minute. Ten minutes' work by ten chariots would cause 500 casualties or more."[4]

For several centuries, beginning about 1800 B.C.E., peoples from the north using such weapons smashed into Mesopotamia and conquered the kingdoms they attacked. In India, the Aryans, who also spoke an Indo-European language, smashed the indigenous Indus civilization. In Egypt, the Hyksos, speakers of a Semitic language, conquered the northern kingdom. In China, the chariot-riding Shang dynasty established an aristocratic rule based on the new weapons. In Europe, the Mycenaean Greeks used chariots, although it is not clear that they had the composite bow and used the tactics that had brought such great success elsewhere.

The most sophisticated users of ancient military technology before Alexander the Great were the Assyrians. They had a wide range of devices for siege warfare, and took them along on all their campaigns. As always, new weapons made of new materials with new techniques do not in themselves constitute a revolution in military affairs. To use them effectively, armies require organizations that can devise appropriate operational plans and train their soldiers in the needed skills and discipline. The Assyrian annals suggest that by the eighth century B.C.E. their kings had turned their chariot forces into "a weapon of shock and terror, manipulated by the driver to charge at breakneck speed behind a team of perfectly schooled horses and used by the archer as a platform from which to launch a hail of arrows; squadrons of chariots, their drivers trained to act in mutual support, might have clashed much as armoured vehicles have done in our time, success going to the side that could disable the larger opposing number, while the footmen unlucky or foolhardy enough to stand in their way would have been scattered like chaff."[5]

Mounted Cavalry

In 612 B.C.E., the great Assyrian empire fell before a coalition of opponents, but it had already been weakened by enemies who commanded a new military technique: mounted cavalry. Ironically, the Assyrians themselves may have been the first to develop the critical skills of riding astride a horse while keeping both hands free to shoot with a bow. The first peoples to use the new cavalry technology to great effect were nomads from the steppes of northern Eurasia. About 690 B.C.E., a people whom the Greeks called Cimmerians flooded into Asia Minor on their warhorses, shaking the established order. Later in that century they were followed by another group of steppe-nomads called the Scythians, who came from the Altai mountains in central Asia. The Scythians overthrew the Cimmerians and then joined with more settled peoples in the battles that destroyed the Assyrian empire. This was the beginning of a series of attacks by horse-riding nomads from the steppes against the settled lands to their south that lasted for two millennia. In China there is no clear evidence for such attacks before the fourth century B.C.E. but it is possible that attacks from Mongolia and nearby areas may have brought down the western Chou dynasty in 771 B.C.E.

In the Middle East the Babylonian Empire had succeeded the Assyrian, but was soon replaced by the Persian Empire. The Persians had no other way of preventing the nomads' devastating raids than to pay other nomads to defend their frontiers, and the Chinese emperors did the same. The Chinese also developed a cavalry that carried the crossbow, more powerful than the composite bow. Another device for defending against the invaders was the Great Wall of China, built during the Ch'in dynasty (256–206 B.C.E.) and designed to keep the ravaging horsemen out. But this, too, proved ineffective.

Despite endless perturbations of the political and military relationships between grassland and plowland, peoples of the steppe enjoyed a consistent advantage because of their superior mobility and the cheapness of their military equipment. This produced a pattern of recurrent nomad conquests of civilized lands.[6]

[4]John Keegan, *A History of Warfare* (New York: Vintage Books, 1993), p. 166.

[5]*Ibid*, pp. 176–177.

[6]William H. McNeill, *The Pursuit of Power* (Chicago: University of Chicago Press, 1982), p. 16.

The Great Wall of China was originally built during the Ch'in dynasty (256–206 B.C.E.), but what we see today is the wall as it was completely rebuilt during the Ming dynasty (1368–1644 C.E.). Paolo Koch/Photo Researchers, Inc.

Iron-wielding Warriors

Even as the chariot and the warhorse were having so great an impact on the nature of ancient warfare, a far more fundamental revolution in military affairs was underway. Bronze is an alloy of copper and tin, but the latter is a rather rare metal, so it was expensive. Horses also were costly to keep. So warfare that depended on bronze weapons and horses was necessarily limited to a relatively small number of men. About 1400 B.C.E., however, in Asia Minor, someone discovered the technique of working iron to give it an edge so hard and durable that tools and weapons made of it were clearly superior to those of bronze. Iron, moreover, is far more abundant than the components of bronze, is easier to work, and is much cheaper. For the first time, it became possible for common people to own and use metal. Now a much larger part of the population could own arms and armor, and "[o]rdinary farmers and herdsmen thereby achieved a new formidability in battle, and the narrowly aristocratic

structure of society characteristic of the chariot age altered abruptly. A more democratic era dawned as iron-wielding invaders overthrew ruling elites that had based their power on a monopoly of chariotry."[7]

Within two centuries, the new technology spread over the Middle East and into Europe. A new round of invasions by iron-wielding warriors swept away kingdoms and empires and brought new peoples to power. The Assyrians, combining the bureacratic organizational skills of Mesopotamian civilization with a warrior spirit and an ability to assimilate new techniques, achieved control of their own region with the aid of iron weapons, but many indigenous rulers of civilized lands were subdued or swept away. In Europe, a Greek-speaking people we call the Myceneans had ruled the Greek peninsula and the Aegean Sea with a Bronze Age civilization similar to those of the Middle East.

[7]*Ibid*, p. 12.

190

Between 1200 B.C.E. and 1100 B.C.E., however, the Mycenaeans were overthrown by a new wave of Greeks with iron weapons who obliterated the old civilization and brought a new culture based on new ways of fighting.

The Shield and the Phalanx

The heart of this new Greek civilization, which is called Hellenic, was the city state, or *polis*, hundreds of which came into being towards the end of the eighth century B.C.E. (See Chapter 2.) Their armies consisted of independent yeoman farmers who produced enough wealth to supply their own iron weapons and body armor, made cheap enough by the revolution in metallurgy. But again, these would have been of little value without organizational change. Now, a new way of warfare that made infantry the dominant fighting force on land for centuries, permitted an alliance of poor Greek states to defeat the mighty and wealthy Persian Empire. The soldiers, wearing helmets, body armor, and a heavy, large, round shield for protection, carried short iron swords, but used iron-tipped wooden pikes as their chief weapon. Arrayed in compact blocks called *phalanxes*, usually eight men deep, these freemen, well disciplined and highly motivated, defeated lesser infantries, archers, and cavalry. Adapted by the Macedonians under King Philip II and his son Alexander the Great, the hoplite phalanx remained the dominant infantry force until it was defeated by the Roman legion in the second century B.C.E.

Trireme Warfare

The Greeks also achieved supremacy at sea by improving an existing technological innovation and providing it with an effective operational plan. Oared galleys were known at Cyprus as early as about 1000 B.C.E. and the Phoenicians improved their speed and maneuverability by superimposing a second and then a third bank of rowers over the first to produce a ship that the Greeks called a *trireme*. The Greeks added outriggers for the top rowers, and it is possible that this permitted their rowers to use the full power of their strongest leg muscles by sliding back and forth as they rowed. At first, the main mode of trireme warfare was for one ship to come alongside another, grapple it, and send marines to board the enemy ship. In time, however, the Greeks placed a strong ram at the prow of each ship and learned how to row with great bursts of speed and to make sharp turns that allowed them to ram and disable their opponents by striking them in the side or rear. With such ships and tactics, the Greek triremes repeatedly sank fleets of the Egyptians and Phoenicians who rowed for the Persian Empire, thus gaining complete naval mastery.

The Macedonians came to dominate the Greek world, to conquer the Persian Empire, and to rule its successor states in the Hellenistic Period (323–31 B.C.E.), but technological innovation in military affairs played only a small part in their success. Military victories came chiefly from the quality of their leaders, the number, spirit, and discipline of their troops, and the ability to combine infantry, cavalry, and light-armed troops to win battles. Alexander's engineers also brought unprecedented skill to the use of siege weapons.

Roman Legions

The armies of the Roman Republic defeated Macedon in a series of wars in the third and second centuries B.C.E. and brought the entire Mediterranean world under Roman sway by the end of the second century. This conquest was achieved almost entirely by the power of the infantry. In time, the Roman army moved from the phalanx formation to a looser, more open order of battle based on the legion, which was divided into smaller, self-sufficient units. The Romans abandoned the pike as the chief infantry weapon, using instead the *pilum*, a heavy iron javelin that was thrown to cause disarray in the enemy line and permit the Romans to use their short, double-edged swords at close quarters. In the Imperial period, beginning especially in the third century of our era, nomadic barbarian tribes began applying the severe pressure on Rome's frontiers that would ultimately bring down the empire. Like the Chinese, the Romans built walls in some places to ease the burden of defending their extensive borders. In the empire's last years, the Romans began to use heavily armored horses ridden by knights in heavy armor, carrying lances and capable of charging an enemy with great force and effect. These armored cavalrymen, called *cataphracts* in Greek, would develop into a major new system of fighting in the Western Middle Ages, but they were too few to take a significant role in the final, futile defense of the empire.

❖ *How early is the evidence for warfare among human beings? What did Thucydides think that war was about? For what purposes did he think people went to war? Is war a rational or irrational action? Can you think of any good reason for fighting a war? How did war and technology affect one another in the ancient world?*

Part 2

476 C.E.–1300 C.E.

	POLITICS AND GOVERNMENT	SOCIETY AND ECONOMY	RELIGION AND CULTURE
300–500	315 Constantinople becomes new capital of Roman Empire 410 Visigoths sack Rome 451–453 Attila the Hun invades Italy 455 Vandals overrun Rome 476 Odovacer deposes the last Western emperor 489–493 Theodoric's Ostrogoth kingdom established in Italy	400 Cities and trade begin to decline in the West; Germanic (barbarian) tribes settle in the West	312 Constantine embraces Christianity 325 Council of Nicaea 380 Christianity becomes the official religion of the Roman Empire 413–426 Saint Augustine writes *City of God* 451 Council of Chalcedon 496 The Franks embrace Christianity
500–700	527–565 Reign of Justinian 568 Lombard invasion of Italy	533–534 *Corpus juris civilis* compiled by Justinian  Interior of Hagia Sophia	529 Saint Benedict founds monastery at Monte Cassino 537 Byzantine Church of Hagia Sophia completed 590–604 Pope Gregory the Great 622 Muhammad's flight from Mecca (Hegira)
700–900	632–733 Muslim expansion and conquests 734 Charles Martel defeats Muslims at Poitiers 768–814 Reign of Charlemagne 843 Treaty of Verdun partitions Carolingian empire	632–733 Muslims disrupt western Mediterranean trade 700 Agrarian society centered around the manor predominates in the west 700–800 Moldboard plow and three field system in use 700 Islam enters its Golden Age 800 Byzantium enters its Golden Age 800 Introduction of collar harness 850 Muslims occupy parts of Spain 880s Vikings penetrate central Europe	725–787 Iconoclastic Controversy in East ca. 775 *Donation of Constantine* 782 Alcuin of York runs Charlemagne's palace school 800 Pope Leo crowns Charlemagne emperor

THE MIDDLE AGES

476 C.E.–1300 C.E.

	POLITICS AND GOVERNMENT	SOCIETY AND ECONOMY	RELIGION AND CULTURE
900–1100	918 Saxon Henry I becomes first non-Frankish king, as Saxons succeed Carolingians in Germany	900 Introduction of the horseshoe	910 Benedictine monastery of Cluny founded
	987 Capetians succeed Carolingians in France	900–1100 Rise of towns, guilds, and urban culture in West	980s Orthodox Christianity penetrates Russia
	1066 Battle of Hastings (Norman Conquest of England)		1054 Schism between Eastern and Western churches
	 Harold's crowning. The Bayeux Tapestry		1075 Pope Gregory VII condemns lay investiture
		1086 *Domesday Book*	1095 Pope Urban II preaches the First Crusade
	1071 Seljuk Turks defeat Byzantine armies at Manzikert		
	1099 Jerusalem falls to Crusaders		
1100–1300	1152 Frederick I Barbarossa first Hohenstaufen emperor	1130 Gothic architecture begins to displace Romanesque	1122 Concordat of Worms ends Investiture Controversy
	1187 Saladin reconquers Jerusalem from West		1158 First European university founded in Bologna
	1204 Fourth Crusade captures Constantinople	1200 Shift from dues to rent tenancy on manors	
	1214 Philip II Augustus defeats English and German armies at Bouvines		1210 Franciscan order founded
	1215 Magna Carta		1216 Dominican order founded
	1240 Mongols dominate Russia		1265 Thomas Aquinas's *Summa Theologica* begun
	1250 Death of Frederick II (end of Hohenstaufen dynasty)		
	1257 German princes establish electoral college to elect emperor		ca. 1275 *Romance of the Rose*

Chapter 6

The story of Adam and Eve from Genesis 1–3. Here God creates Adam and then Eve from one of Adam's ribs, then blesses and gives them both dominion over the earth—but He forbids them to eat from the tree of the knowledge of good and evil in the garden of Eden. Eve and Adam disobey God and are cast out of the garden in shame, forever thereafter to do penance in toilsome lives—Eve by bearing children, Adam by hard labor. From the Moutier-Grandval Bible. By permission of the British Library

The Early Middle Ages:
Creating a New European Society and Culture (476–1000)

KEY TOPICS

- How the fusion of Germanic and Roman culture laid the foundation for a distinctively European society after the collapse of the western Roman Empire

- The Byzantine and Islamic empires and their impact on the West

- The role of the church in Western society during the early Middle Ages

- The political and economic features of Europe under the Franks

- The characteristics of feudal society

The early Middle Ages mark the birth of Europe. This period of recovery from the collapse of Roman civilization gave rise to forced experimentation with new ideas and institutions. Greco–Roman culture combined with the new Germanic culture and an evolving Christianity to create distinctive political and cultural forms within what had been the northern and western provinces of the Roman Empire. In government, religion, and language, as well as geography, these regions grew separate from the Eastern Byzantine world and the Islamic Arab world, which extended across North Africa from Spain to the eastern Mediterranean.

The early Middle Ages have been called, not with complete fairness, a "dark age," because during these centuries western Europe lost touch with classical, especially Greek, learning and science. People the Romans somewhat arrogantly called "barbarians"—because their origins were rural and they knew no Latin—intruded on the region from the north and east. German tribes that had been settling peacefully around the empire since the first century B.C.E.

began to migrate directly into it by the fourth century. During the fifth century, these tribes turned fiercely against their Roman hosts, largely because the Romans treated them so cruelly. To the south, Arab dominance transformed the Mediterranean into an often inhospitable "Islamic lake," greatly reducing (although by no means completely severing) Western trade with the East and isolating Western people more than they had been before. Thus surrounded and assailed from north, east, and south, Europe understandably became somewhat insular and even stagnant.

On the other hand, being forced to manage by themselves, western Europeans also learned to develop their native resources. The reign of Charlemagne saw a modest renaissance of antiquity. And the peculiar social and political forms that emerged during this period—manorialism and feudalism—not only were successful at coping with unprecedented chaos on local levels, but also proved to be fertile seedbeds for the growth of distinctive Western institutions.

On the Eve of the Frankish Ascendancy

As we have already seen, by the late third century the Roman Empire had become too large for a single sovereign to govern and was failing in many respects. The emperor Diocletian (r. 284–305) tried to strengthen the empire by dividing it between himself and a co-emperor, Maximian. The result was a dual empire with an eastern and a western half, each with its own emperor and, eventually, imperial bureaucracy. A critical shift of the empire's resources and orientation to the eastern half accompanied these changes. In 284 Diocletian moved to Nicomedia (in modern Turkey), where he remained until the last two years of his reign. As imperial rule weakened in the West and strengthened in the East, it also became increasingly autocratic.

In an attempt to end the factional strife that followed Diocletian's reign and to position himself better to meet the empire's new eastern enemies, Constantine the Great (r. 306–337) briefly reunited the empire by conquest (it would be redivided by his three sons and subsequent successors) and ruled as sole emperor of the eastern and western halves after 324. In that year, he moved the capital of the empire from Rome to Byzantium, an ancient city that stood at the crossroads of the major sea and land routes between Europe and Asia Minor. On the site of this ancient city, Constantine built the new city of Constantinople, dedicated in 330. Serving as the imperial residence and the new administrative center of

the empire, Constantinople gradually became a "new Rome." The "old" Rome, suffering from internal political quarrels and geographically distant from new military fronts in Syria and along the Danube River, declined in importance. The city and the western empire were actually on the wane in the late third and fourth centuries, well before the barbarian invasions in the West began. Milan had replaced Rome as the imperial residence in 286; in 402 the seat of Western government would be moved yet again, to Ravenna. When the barbarian invasions began in the late fourth century, the West was in political disarray, and imperial power and prestige had shifted decisively to Constantinople and the East.

Germanic Migrations

The German tribes did not burst in on the West all of a sudden. They were at first a token and benign presence on the fringes of the empire and even within it. Before the massive migrations from the north and the east, Roman and Germanic cultures had commingled peacefully for centuries. The Romans had "imported" barbarians as domestics, slaves, and soldiers. Barbarian soldiers rose to positions of high leadership and fame in Roman legions.

Beginning in 376 with a great influx of Visigoths, or "west Goths," into the empire, this peaceful coexistence ended. The Visigoths, accomplished horsemen and fierce warriors, were themselves pushed into the empire by the emergence of a notoriously violent people, the Huns, from the region of what is now Mongolia. The Visigoths ultimately reached southern Gaul and Spain. Soon to be Christianized, they won rights of settlement and material assistance within the empire from the eastern emperor Valens (r. 364–378) in exchange for defending the eastern frontier as *foederati*, or the emperor's "special allies."

Instead of the promised assistance, however, the Visigoths received harsh treatment from their new allies. They had arrived in the empire an impoverished people fleeing the Huns. So bad off were they that they traded their own children to the Romans for dogs to eat. The Romans, showing no mercy, charged them one child per dog. After repeated conflicts, the Visigoths rebelled and handily defeated Roman armies led by Valens at the Battle of Adrianople in 378.

After Adrianople, the Romans passively permitted the settlement of barbarians within the very heart of the western empire. The Vandals crossed the Rhine in 406 and within three decades gained control of northwest Africa and a sizable portion of the Mediterranean. The Burgundians, who came on the heels of the Vandals, settled in Gaul. Most important for subsequent Western history were the Franks, who settled northern and central Gaul,

A Contemporary Description of Attila the Hun

In 448 a Roman envoy, Priscus, visited the home of Attila in a Scythian village at the base of the Danube River, three years before Attila's famous invasion of Italy. Knowing Attila's reputation for savagery, he was surprised to find him a simple and cultured man.

❖ *How would you account for the discrepancy between this portrait of Attila and his reputation? Has history falsely portrayed this fiercest of warriors? What does it say about the Huns' system of justice that Attila dispensed judgments on the street as he walked?*

Attila's residence...was made of polished boards, and surrounded with wooden enclosures, designed not so much for protection as for appearance's sake....I entered the enclosure of Attila's palace, bearing gifts to his wife, whose name was Kreka....Having been admitted by the barbarians at the door, I found her reclining on a soft couch. The floor of the room was covered with woolen mats for walking on....Having approached, saluted her, and presented the gifts, I went out and walked to the other houses....Attila came forth from [one of] the house[s] with a dignified strut, looking round on this side and on that....Many persons who had lawsuits with one another came up and received his judgment. Then he returned into the house and received ambassadors of barbarous peoples....

[We were invited to a banquet with Attila at three o'clock.] The cupbearers gave us a cup, according to the national custom, that we might pray before we sat down. Having tasted the cup, we proceeded to take our seats, all the chairs being ranged along the walls of the room on either side. Attila sat in the middle on a couch; a second couch was set behind him, and from it steps led up to his bed, which was covered with linen sheets and wrought coverlets for ornament, such as Greeks and Romans used to deck bridal beds. The places on the right of Attila were held chief in honor; those on the left, where we sat, were only second....

The attendant of Attila first entered with a dish full of meat, and behind him came the other attendants with bread and viands [plates of food], which they laid on the tables. A luxurious meal, served on silver plate, had been made ready for us and the barbarian guests, but Attila ate nothing but meat on a wooden trencher [a wooden plate]. In everything else, too, he showed himself temperate; his cup was of wood, while to the guests were given goblets of gold and silver. His dress, too, was quite simple, affecting only to be clean. The sword he carried at his side, the latchets of his...shoes, the bridle of his horse were not adorned with gold or gems or anything costly...like those of the other Scythians.

[After two courses were eaten and] evening fell, torches were lit and two barbarians, coming forward in front of Attila, sang songs they had composed, celebrating his victories and deeds of valor in war.

From James Harvey Robinson, ed., *Readings in European History*, Vol. 1 (Boston: Athenaeum, 1904), pp. 47–48.

some along the seacoast (the Salian Franks) and others along the Rhine, Seine, and Loire Rivers (the Ripuarian Franks).

Why was there so little Roman resistance to these Germanic tribes, whose numbers—at most 100,000 people in the largest of them—were comparatively very small? The invaders were successful because they had come upon a badly overextended western empire divided politically by ambitious military commanders and weakened by decades of famine, pestilence, and overtaxation. By the second half of the fourth century, Roman frontiers had become too vast to manage. Efforts to do so by "barbarizing" the Roman army, that is, by recruiting many peasants into it and by making the Germanic tribes key Roman allies, only weakened it further. The eastern empire retained enough wealth and vitality to field new armies or to buy off the invaders. The western empire, in contrast, succumbed not only because of moral decay and materialism, but also because of a combination of military rivalry, political mismanagement, disease, and sheer poverty.

Fall of the Roman Empire

In the early fifth century, Italy and the "eternal city" of Rome suffered a series of devastating blows. In 410, the Visigoths, under Alaric (ca. 370–410), revolted and sacked Rome. In 452, the Huns, led by Attila—known to contemporaries as the "scourge

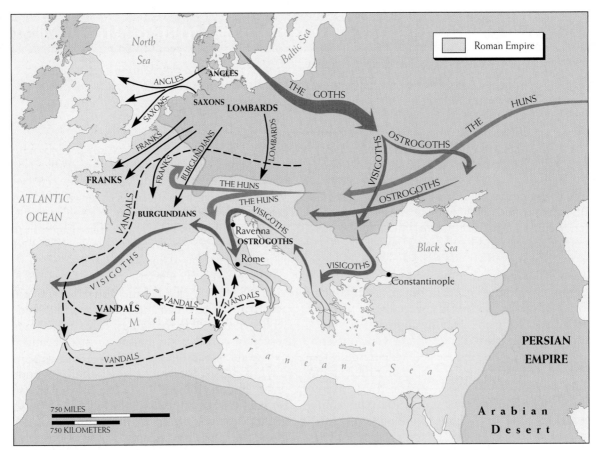

MAP 6–1   BARBARIAN MIGRATIONS INTO THE WEST IN THE FOURTH AND FIFTH CENTURIES   *The forceful intrusion of Germanic and non-Germanic barbarians into the Roman Empire from the last quarter of the fourth century through the fifth century made for a constantly changing pattern of movement and relations. The map shows the major routes taken by the usually unwelcome newcomers and the areas most deeply affected by main groups.*

of God"—invaded Italy. (See "A Contemporary Description of Attila the Hun.") And in 455 Rome was overrun yet again, this time by the Vandals.

By the mid-fifth century, power in western Europe had passed decisively from the hands of the Roman emperors to those of barbarian chieftains. In 476, the traditional date given for the fall of the Roman Empire, the barbarian Odovacer (ca. 434–493) deposed and replaced the western emperor Romulus Augustulus. The eastern emperor, Zeno (r. 474–491), recognized Odovacer's authority in the west, and Odovacer acknowledged Zeno as sole emperor, contenting himself to serve as Zeno's western viceroy. In a later coup in 493 manipulated by Zeno, Theodoric (ca. 454–526), king of the Ostrogoths, or "east Goths," replaced Odovacer. At least until the last part of his reign, Theodoric governed with the full acceptance of the Roman people and the Christian Church.

By the end of the fifth century, barbarians had thoroughly overrun the western empire. The Ostrogoths settled in Italy, the Franks in northern Gaul, the Burgundians in Provence, the Visigoths in southern Gaul and Spain, the Vandals in Africa and the western Mediterranean, and the Angles and Saxons in England. (See Map 6–1.)

Western Europe, however, was not transformed into a savage land. Its new masters were willing to learn from the people they had conquered; barbarian military victories did not result in a great defeat of Roman culture. Except in Britain and northern Gaul, Roman language, law, and government coexisted with the new Germanic institutions. In Italy under Theodoric, Roman law gradually replaced tribal custom. Only the Vandals and the Anglo-Saxons—and, after 466, the Visigoths—refused to profess at least titular obedience to the emperor in Constantinople.

That the Visigoths, the Ostrogoths, and the Vandals entered the West as Christianized people contributed to this accommodation of cultures. They were followers, however, of the Arian creed, considered heretical in the West. Arian Christians believed that Jesus Christ was not one identical being with God the Father—a point of view the Council of Nicaea had condemned in 325. (See Chapter 5.)

In spite of the hostility their Arian Christianity provoked, the Germans themselves admired Roman culture and had no desire to destroy it, although their rural lifestyle further weakened its urban foundations. Later, around 500, the Franks, under their strong king, Clovis, converted to the orthodox, or "Catholic," form of Christianity supported by the bishops of Rome. Then, as Roman Christians, the Franks helped conquer and convert the Goths and other barbarians in western Europe.

All things considered, rapprochement and a gradual interpenetration of two strong cultures—a creative tension—marked the period of the Germanic migrations. The stronger culture was the Roman, and it became dominant in a later fusion. Despite western military defeat, the Goths and the Franks became far more romanized than the Ro-

mans were germanized. The Latin language, Nicene Christianity, and eventually Roman law and government were to triumph in the West during the Middle Ages.

The Byzantine Empire

As western Europe succumbed to the Germanic invasions, imperial power shifted to the Byzantine Empire, that is, the eastern part of the Roman Empire. Emperor Constantine the Great began the rebuilding of Byzantium in 324, renaming the city Constantinople and dedicating it in 330. Constantinople became the sole capital of the empire and remained so until the successful revival of the western empire in the eighth century by Charlemagne.

Between 324 and 1453, the empire passed from an early period of expansion and splendor to a time of contraction and splintering and finally to

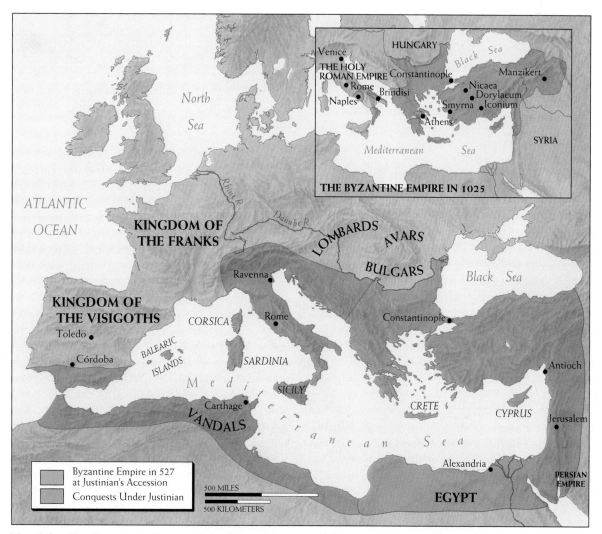

MAP 6–2   THE BYZANTINE EMPIRE AT THE TIME OF JUSTINIAN'S DEATH   *The inset shows the empire in 1025, before its losses to the Seljuk Turks.*

A sixth-century ivory panel depicting the Byzantine emperor Justinian as the champion of the Christian faith. From 500 to 1100, the Byzantine Empire was the center of Christian civilization. Giraudon/Art Resource, N.Y.

catastrophic defeat by the Ottoman Turks. Historians commonly divide the history of the empire into three distinct periods:

1. from the rebuilding of Byzantium as Constantinople in 324 to the beginning of the Arab expansion and the spread of Islam in 632
2. from 632 to the conquest of Asia Minor by the Seljuk Turks after the fall of Manzikert in 1071, or, as some prefer, to the fall of Constantinople to western Crusaders in 1204
3. from 1071 or 1204 to the fall of Constantinople to the Turks in 1453.

The Reign of Justinian

In terms of territory, political power, and culture, the first period of Byzantine history (324–632) was by far its greatest. The height of this period was the reign of the emperor Justinian (r. 527–565) and his brilliant wife, the empress Theodora (d. 548). (See Map 6–2.) The daughter of a bear trainer in the circus, the empress in her youth had fallen prey to the seedy side of sixth-century circus life. Her activities may have included prostitution, if the contro-

versial *Secret History* by Justinian's court historian, Procopius, is to be believed. Her background may have given her a toughness that fully matched and even exceeded her husband's. (See "The Character and 'Innovations' of Justinian and Theodora.")

An influential counselor, Theodora became a major figure in imperial government. In 532, Justinian contemplated abdication following riots against his rule that left much of Constantinople in ruins and thousands dead. Theodora stiffened his resolve, reportedly insisting that he crack down ruthlessly on the rioters and firmly reestablish his authority, which he most decisively did. In doctrinal matters, the empress clearly had a mind and will of her own. Whereas Justinian remained strictly orthodox in his Christian beliefs, Theodora lent her support to a Christian heresy known as Monophysitism, which taught that Jesus had only one nature, a composite divine–human one, not a fully human and fully divine dual nature, as orthodox doctrine taught. In the sixth century, the Monophysites formed a separate church that had a very strong influence in the eastern provinces of the empire. The imperial government persecuted them as heretics after Theodora's death, a policy that cost the empire dearly when, in the seventh century, Persian and Arab armies besieged its eastern frontiers. Bitter over their treatment, the Monophysites offered little resistance to the invaders.

LAW   The imperial goal in the East—as reflected in the policy "one God, one empire, one religion"—was to centralize government and impose legal and doctrinal conformity. To this end, Justinian collated and revised Roman law. This codification had become a pressing matter because of the enormous number of often contradictory legal decrees that had piled up since the mid-second century as the empire grew increasingly Christian and imperial rule increasingly autocratic.

Justinian's *Corpus juris civilis* or "body of civil law," was a fourfold compilation undertaken by a learned committee of lawyers. The first compilation, known as the *Code*, appeared in 533. It revised imperial edicts issued since the reign of Hadrian (r. 117–138). A second compilation, the *Novellae*, or "new things," contained the decrees issued by Justinian and his immediate successors after 534. The third compilation, the *Digest*, was a summary of the major opinions of the old legal experts. The fourth compilation, the *Institutes*, was a textbook for young scholars, which drew its lessons from the *Code* and the *Digest*. These works had little immediate effect on medieval common law, but, beginning with the Renaissance, they provided the foundation for most subsequent

The Character and 'Innovations' of Justinian and Theodora

According to Procopius, their court historian and biographer, Justinian and Theodora were tyrants, pure and simple. His Secret History *(sixth century), which some historians distrust as a source, had only criticism and condemnation for the two rulers. Procopius especially resented Theodora, and he did not believe that the rule of law was respected at the royal court.*

❖ *Is Procopius being fair to Justinian and Theodora? Is the* Secret History *an ancient tabloid? How does one know when a source is biased and self-serving and when it is telling the truth? What does Procopius most dislike about the queen? Was Theodora the last woman ruler to receive such criticism?*

Formerly, when the senate approached the Emperor, it paid homage in the following manner. Every patrician kissed him on the right breast; the Emperor [then] kissed the patrician on the head, and he was dismissed. Then the rest bent their right knee to the Emperor and withdrew. It was not customary to pay homage to the Queen.

But those who were admitted [in]to the presence of Justinian and Theodora, whether they were patricians or otherwise, fell on their faces on the floor, stretching their hands and feet out wide, kissed first one foot and then the other of the Augustus [i.e., the emperor], and then retired. Nor did Theodora refuse this honor; and she even received the ambassadors of the Persians and other barbarians and gave them presents, as if she were in command of the Roman Empire: a thing that had never happened in all previous time.

And formerly intimates of the Emperor called him Emperor and the Empress, Empress....But if anybody addressed either of these two as Emperor or Empress without adding "Your Majesty" or "Your Highness," or forgot to call himself their slave, he was considered either ignorant or insolent, and was dismissed in disgrace as if he had done some awful crime or committed some unpardonable sin.

And [whereas] before, only a few were sometimes admitted to the palace...when these two came to power, the magistrates and everybody else had no trouble in fairly living in the palace. This was because the magistrates of old had administered justice and the laws according to their conscience...but these two, taking control of everything to the misfortune of their subjects, forced everyone to come to them and beg like slaves. And almost any day one could see the law courts nearly deserted, while in the hall of the Emperor there was a jostling and pushing crowd that resembled nothing so much as a mob of slaves.

From *Secret History of Procopius* translated by Richard Atwater. Copyright © 1927 by Crown Publishers, Inc. Reprinted by permission of Crown Publishers, Inc.

European law down to the nineteenth century. They especially benefitted those rulers who aspired to centralize their states.

RELIGION Religion as well as law served imperial centralization. Since the fifth century, the patriarch of Constantinople had crowned emperors in that city. This practice reflected the close ties between rulers and the church. In 380 Christianity had been proclaimed the official religion of the eastern empire. All other religions and sects were denounced as "demented and insane."[1] Between the fourth and sixth centuries the patriarchs of Constantinople, Alexandria, Antioch, and Jerusalem acquired enormous wealth in the form of land and gold. The church, in turn, acted as the state's welfare agency, drawing on its generous endowments from pious rich donors to aid the poor and needy. The prestige and comfort of the clergy swelled the clerical ranks of the Eastern Church.

Orthodox Christianity was not, however, the only religion within the empire with a significant following. Nor did the rulers view religion as merely a political tool. At one time or another the Christian heresies of Arianism, Monophysitism, and Iconoclasm also received imperial support. Persecution and absorption into popular Christianity served to curtail many pagan religious practices.

The empire was also home, although at times a less than hospitable one, to large numbers of Jews. Non-Christian Romans saw Jews as narrow, dogmatic, and intolerant people in comparison with Christians, and

[1] Cyril Mango, *Byzantium: The Empire of New Rome* (New York: Charles Scribner's Sons, 1980) p. 88.

Hagia Sophia: A Temple Surpassing that of Solomon

Hagia Sophia, interior. Erich Lessing/Art Resource, N.Y.

One of the greatest achievements of Emperor Justinian's reign proved also to be one of the greatest in Byzantine art and architecture: Hagia Sophia (the Church of Holy Wisdom). It was built on the spot of another Christian church begun centuries earlier by Emperor Constantine (r. 306–337) and was completed in 360, later to be enhanced by Emperor Theodosius II (408–450), builder of Constantinople's fortified wall. In 532, the Nika riots (named after the rebels' cry of "victory" [nika]) completely destroyed this ancient church and almost toppled Justinian and Theodora.

One of Justinian's responses was Hagia Sophia, begun in the aftermath of the riots and completed in 537. Two of the age's great architects, Anthemius of Tralles and Isidore of Miletus, designed the building and oversaw its construction by a team of equally outstanding engineers, who employed one hundred master masons with crews of one hundred workers each, 10,000 in all. The sprawling new church rose 184 feet, its key feature a massive dome, 112 feet in diameter, made from five separate pieces from bottom (pendentive) to top (cupola). Circled with numerous windows, the dome flooded the nave with light and, together with the church's many other windows, glistening mosaics, and open spaces, gave the interior a remarkable airiness and luminosity.

A contemporary record of its construction, written two decades later by the royal biographer Pro-copius (probably under the constraint of the emperor and as propaganda) portrays Justinian as a knowledgeable engineer who conceived the building in a divine vision. (No mention is made of Theodora, whom Procopius appears to have intensely disliked.) In all probability, Justinian did little more than provide the funds, a reported 320,000 pounds of gold. Another retrospective account, written in the ninth century and largely fictional, has Justinian destroying the older church himself so that he might build a temple surpassing that of Solomon (possibly a criticism of the hubris of rulers past and present). Such accounts, while historically inaccurate, have been seen to reflect the popular view of contemporaries and not a few modern visitors to the church today: Hagia Sophia was too magnificent to have been the work of human minds and hands alone.

With the Turkish conquest of Constantinople in 1453, Hagia Sophia was transformed into a Muslim mosque with four prominent minarets; and as with the churches of many Protestants in Western Europe, its colorful mosaics were painted over in accordance with Muslim law, which deemed the depictions of God in Byzantine art idolatrous.

minaret – tower attached to a mosque

Sources: H. W. Janson & A. F. Janson, *History of Art*, 5th ed. (Upper Saddle River, NJ: Prentice Hall, 1997), pp. 252–254; Cyril Mango, "Byzantine Writers on the Fabric of Hagia Sophia," in *Hagia Sophia from the Age of Justinian to the Present*, ed. R. Mark and A. S. Cakmak (Cambridge, U.K.: Cambridge University Press, 1992), pp. 41–50.

idolatrous – worship idols

Empress Theodora and her attendants. The union of political and spiritual authority in the person of the empress is shown by the depiction on Theodora's mantle of three magi carrying gifts to the Virgin and Jesus.
Scala/Art Resource, N.Y.

they had little love for them. Under Roman law, Jews had legal protection so long as they did not proselytize among Christians, build new synagogues, or try to enter sensitive public offices or professions. Justinian (the emperor most intent on religious conformity within the empire) adopted a policy of encouraging Jews to convert voluntarily. Later emperors ordered all Jews to be baptized and granted tax breaks to those who voluntarily complied. But neither persuasion nor coercion succeeded in converting the empire's Jews.

CITIES During Justinian's reign the empire's strength was its more than 1,500 cities. The largest, with perhaps 350,000 inhabitants, was Constantinople, the cultural crossroads of the Asian and European civilizations. The large provincial cities had populations of 50,000. Between the fourth and fifth centuries, councils of about 200 members, all of whom were local wealthy landowners known as *decurions*, governed the cities. Decurions were the intellectual and economic elite of the empire. They were also heavily taxed, and for this reason they were not always the emperor's most docile or loyal servants. By the sixth century, special governors and bishops, appointed from the landholding classes, replaced the decurion councils and proved to be more reliable instruments of the emperor's will.

A fifth-century statistical record gives us some sense of the size and splendor of Constantinople at its peak. It lists five imperial and nine princely palaces; eight public and 153 private baths; four public forums; five granaries; two theaters; one hippodrome; 322 streets; 4,388 substantial houses; fifty-two porticoes; twenty public and 120 private bakeries; and

fourteen churches.[2] The most popular entertainments were the theater, frequently denounced by the clergy for nudity and immorality, and the races at the hippodrome. Many public taverns existed as well.

Eastern Influences

During the reign of Heraclius (r. 610–641) the empire took a decidedly Eastern, as opposed to Roman, direction. Heraclius spoke Greek, not Latin. He spent his entire reign resisting Persian and Islamic invasions, the former successfully, the latter in vain. Islamic armies progressively overran the empire after 632, directly attacking Constantinople for the first time in 677. Not until the reign of Leo III of the Isaurian dynasty (r. 717–740) were the Islamic armies repulsed and most of Asia Minor regained by the Byzantines.

Leo, however, offended Western Christians when he forbade the use of images in Eastern churches and tried to enforce the ban also in the West. This was an affront to Western Christianity, which had carefully nurtured the adoration of Jesus, Mary, and the saints in images and icons. Historians have speculated that Leo and his immediate successors pursued this policy under the influence of Islam, which condemned the veneration of images, perhaps hoping to placate the Muslims by joining them on this point of doctrine. Be that as it may, the banning of images was a major expression of eastern Caesaro-papism—the direct involvement of the emperor in religious dogma and practice as if he were both secular ruler and the head of the church—which, as we will see, the West-

[2]Mango, p. 76.

ern church always resisted. In addition to creating a new division within Christendom, the ban on images led to the destruction of much religious art until it was reversed in the late eighth century.

In 1071, the Byzantine Empire suffered a major defeat at the hands of the Muslim Seljuk Turks. Successful over Byzantine armies at Manzikert, the Turks rapidly overran the eastern provinces of the empire. This defeat was the beginning of the end of the empire, although the actual end—at the hands of the Seljuks' cousins, the Ottoman Turks—still lay centuries ahead. After two decades of steady Turkish advance, the eastern emperor Alexius I Comnenus (r. 1081–1118) invoked Western aid in 1092. Three years later, the West launched the first of the Crusades. A century later (1204), the Crusaders would inflict far more damage on Constantinople and Eastern Christendom than all previous non-Christian invaders had done.

Throughout the early Middle Ages, the Byzantine Empire remained a protective barrier between western Europe and hostile Persian, Arab, and Turkish armies. The Byzantines were also a major conduit of classical learning and science into the West down to the Renaissance. While western Europeans were fumbling to create a culture of their own, the cities of the Byzantine Empire provided them a model of a civilized society.

Islam and the Islamic World

A new drama began to unfold in the sixth century with the awakening of a rival far more dangerous to the West than the German tribes: the new faith of Islam. By the time of Muhammad's death (632), Islamic armies absorbed the attention and the resources of the emperors in Constantinople and rulers in the West.

At first, the Muslims were both open and cautious. They borrowed and integrated elements of Persian and Greek culture into their own. The new religion of Islam adopted elements of Christian, Jewish, and native pagan religious beliefs and practices. Muslims tolerated religious minorities within the territories they conquered, so long as these minorities recognized Islamic political rule, refrained from proselytizing among Muslims, and paid their taxes. Nonetheless, the Muslims were keen to protect the purity and integrity of Islamic religion, language, and law from any corrupting foreign influence. With the passage of time, and increased conflict with Eastern and Western Christians, this protective tendency grew stronger. Despite significant contacts and exchanges, Islamic culture would not penetrate the West as creatively as Germanic culture did, but would remain largely strange and threatening to Westerners.

Muhammad's Religion

Muhammad (570–632), an orphan, was raised by a family of modest means. As a youth, he worked as a merchant's assistant, traveling the major trade routes. When he was twenty-five, he married a wealthy Meccan widow. Thereafter, himself a wealthy man, he became a kind of social activist, criticizing Meccan materialism, paganism, and unjust treatment of the poor and needy. At about age forty, a deep religious experience heightened his commitment to reform and transformed his life. He began to receive revelations from the angel Gabriel, who recited God's word to him at irregular intervals. These revelations grew into the *Qur'an* (literally, a "reciting"), which his followers compiled between 650 and 651. The basic message Muhammad received was a summons to all Arabs to submit to God's will. Followers of Muhammad's religion came to be called *Muslim* ("submissive" or "surrendering"); the name applied to the religion itself, *Islam,* has the same derivation and means "submission."

The message was not a new one. It had been reiterated by a long line of Jewish prophets going back to Noah. According to Muslims, however, this line ended with Muhammad, who, as the last of God's chosen prophets, became "the Prophet." The *Qur'an* also recognized Jesus Christ as a prophet, but did not view him as God's coeternal and coequal son. Like Judaism, Islam was a monotheistic and theocentric religion, not a trinitarian one like Christianity.

Mecca was a major pagan pilgrimage site (the *Ka'ba*—a black meteorite that became Islam's holiest shrine—was originally a pagan object of worship). Muhammad's attacks on idolatry and immorality threatened the trade that flowed from the pilgrims, enraging the merchants of the city. Persecuted for their attacks on traditional religion, Muhammad and his followers fled in 622 to Medina, 240 miles to the north. This event came to be known as the *Hegira* and marks the beginning of the Islamic calendar.

In Medina, Muhammad organized his forces and drew throngs of devoted followers. He raided caravans going back and forth to Mecca. Also at this time he had his first conflicts with Medinan Jews, who were involved in Meccan trade. By 624 his army was powerful enough to conquer Mecca and make it the center of the new religion.

During these years the basic rules of Islamic practice evolved. True Muslims were expected (1) to be honest and modest in all their dealings and behavior; (2) to be unquestionably loyal to the Islamic community; (3) to abstain from pork and alcohol at all times; (4) to wash and pray facing Mecca five times a day; (5) to contribute to the support of the poor and needy; (6) to fast during daylight hours for one month each year; and (7) to make a pilgrimage to Mecca and visit the *Ka'ba* at least once in a lifetime. The last requirement reflects the degree to which Islam was an assimilationist religion; here it "Islamicized" a major pagan religious practice.

In another distinctive feature, Islam permitted Muslim men to have up to four wives—provided that they treated them all justly and gave each equal attention—and as many concubines as they wished. A husband could divorce a wife with a simple declaration, whereas a wife, to divorce her husband, had to have a very good reason and go before an official. A wife was expected to be totally loyal and devoted to her husband. She was allowed to show her face to no man but him.

In contrast to Christianity, Islam drew no rigid distinction between the clergy and the laity. A lay scholarly elite developed, however, that held moral authority within Islamic society and formed a kind of magisterium in moral and religious matters. This elite, known as the *ulema*, or "persons with correct knowledge," served a social function similar to that of a professional priesthood or rabbinate. Its members were men of great piety and obvious learning whose opinions came to have the force of law in Muslim society. They also kept a critical eye on Muslim rulers, seeing that they adhered to the letter of the *Qur'an*.

Islamic Diversity

The success of Islam lay in its ability to unify and inspire tribal Arabs and other non-Jewish and non-Christian people. In a world where Christianity and Judaism had reigned supreme among religions, Islam must also have appealed to Arab pride, for it made Muhammad history's major religious figure and his followers God's chosen people.

As early as the seventh century, however, disputes arose among Muslims over the shape of Islamic society that left permanent divisions within it. Disagreement over the true line of succession to Muhammad—the caliphate—was one source of discord. Another, tied to the first, was disagreement on doctrinal issues involving the extent to which Islam was meant to be an inclusive religion, open to the weak as well as to the strong. Several groups emerged from these disputes. The most radical was the Kharijites, whose leaders seceded from the camp of the caliph Ali (656-661) because Ali compromised with his enemies on a matter of principle. Righteous and judgmental, the Kharijites wanted to exclude all but rigorously virtuous Muslims from the community of the faithful. In 661 one of their members assassinated Ali.

Muslims are enjoined to live by the divine law, or Shari'a, *and have a right to have disputes settled by an arbiter of the* Shari'a. *Here we see a husband complaining about his wife before the state-appointed judge, or* qadi. *The wife, backed up by two other women, points an accusing finger at the husband. In such cases, the first duty of the* qadi, *who should be a learned person of faith, is to try to effect a reconciliation before the husband divorces his wife, or the wife herself seeks a divorce.* Cliché Bibliothèque Nationale de France, Paris

Another, more influential group was the Shi'a, or "partisans of Ali" (*Shi'at Ali*). The Shi'a looked on Ali and his descendants as the rightful successors of Muhammad not only by virtue of kinship, but also by the expressed will of the Prophet himself. To the Shi'a, Ali's assassination revealed the most basic truth of a devout Muslim life: a true *imam*, or "ruler," must expect to suffer unjustly even unto death in the world, and so, too, must his followers. A distinctive theology of martyrdom has ever since been a mark of Shi'a teaching. And the Shi'a, until modern times, have been an embattled minority within mainstream Islamic society.

A third group, which has been dominant for most of Islamic history, was the majority centrist Sunnis (followers of *sunna*, or "tradition"). Sunnis have always put loyalty to the community of Islam above all else and have spurned the exclusivism and purism of the Kharijites and the Shi'a.

Islamic Empires

Under Muhammad's first three successors—the caliphs Abu Bakr (r. 632–634), Umar (r. 634–644), and Uthman (r. 644–655)—Islam expanded by conquest throughout the southern and eastern Mediterranean, into territories mostly still held today by Islamic states. In the eighth century, Muslim armies occupied parts of Spain in the West and India in the East, producing a truly vast empire. (See Map 6–3.) The capital of this empire moved from Mecca to Damascus, and then, in 750, to Baghdad after a civil war in which the Abbasid dynasty replaced the Umayyad dynasty in the caliphate. Thereafter, the huge Muslim Empire broke up into separate states, each with its own line of caliphs, each claiming to be the true successor of Muhammad.

These conquests would not have been so rapid and thorough had the contemporary Byzantine and Persian empires not been exhausted after a long period of war. The Muslims struck at both empires shortly after the Byzantine emperor Heraclius (r. 610–641) had recovered Egypt, Palestine, Syria, and Asia Minor from the Persians. Before Heraclius died in 641, however, Arab armies had conquered Egypt, Palestine, and Syria; by 643 they had overrun most of the Persian Empire. Byzantine territory in North Africa fell by the end of the seventh century. Most of the inhabitants in the territory Heraclius had reconquered from the Persians, although Christian, were, like the Arabs, Semitic. Any religious unity they felt with the Byzantine Greeks may have been offset by hatred of the Byzantine Greek army of occupation. The Christian community was in any case badly divided. Heraclius's efforts to impose Greek "orthodox" beliefs on the Monophysitic churches of Egypt and Syria only increased the enmity between Greek and Semitic Christians. As a result, many Egyptian and Syrian Christians, hoping for deliverance from Byzantine oppression, may have welcomed the Islamic conquerors.

Although Islam gained converts from among the Christians in North Africa and Spain, its efforts to invade the heart of Christendom were in the end successfully rebuffed. In the West the ruler of the Franks, Charles Martel, defeated a raiding party of Arabs on the western frontier of Europe at Poitiers (today in central France) in 732. This victory ended any possible Arab effort to expand into western Europe by way of Spain. Beginning with Emperor Leo III (r. 717–740), the Isaurian dynasty of Byzantine rulers successfully defended Asia Minor from Islamic aggression. So effective were they that the subsequent Macedonian dynasty of

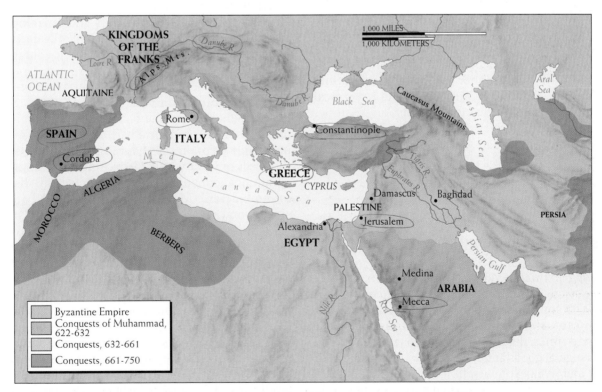

MAP 6–3   MUSLIM CONQUESTS AND DOMINATION OF THE MEDITERRANEAN TO ABOUT 750 C.E. *The rapid spread of Islam (both as a religion and as a politcal–military power) is shown here. Within 125 years of Muhammad's rise, Muslims came to dominate Spain and all areas south and east of the Mediterranean.*

Byzantine rulers (867–1057) expanded militarily and commercially into Arab lands. Muslim disunity after the tenth century greatly aided Byzantine success. The Byzantine Empire would ultimately fall to the Ottoman Turks, who would continue to strike terror into Christian hearts well into the sixteenth century, but after the Seljuk Turks took the Islamic capital of Baghdad in 1055 and the Christian Crusaders captured Jerusalem in 1099, the Muslims never again posed a serious threat to Western Christendom.

The Western Debt to Islamic Culture

Despite the hostility of the Christian West to the Islamic world, there was nonetheless much creative interchange between these two very different cultures, and the West profited greatly from it. The more advanced Arab civilization, which was enjoying its golden age during the West's early Middle Ages, taught Western farmers how to irrigate fields and Western artisans how to tan leather and refine silk. The West also gained from its contacts with Islamic scholars. Thanks to Arabic translators, major Greek works in astronomy, mathematics, and medicine became available in Latin to scholars in much of the West for the first time. And down to the sixteenth century, after the works of the famous ancient physicians Hippocrates and Galen, the basic gynecological and child-care manuals followed by Western midwives and physicians were compilations by the famed Baghdad physician Al-Razi (Rhazes), the philosopher and physician ibn-Sina (Avicenna) (980–1037), and ibn-Rushd (Averröes) (1126–1198), Islam's greatest authority on Aristotle. Jewish scholars also thrived amid the intellectual culture Islamic scholars created. The famed Spanish Jewish scholar Moses Maimonides (1135–1204) wrote in Arabic as well as in Hebrew.

Western Society and the Developing Christian Church

Facing barbarian invasions from the north and east and a strong Islamic presence in the Mediterranean, the West found itself in decline during the fifth and sixth centuries. As trade waned, cities rapidly fell on hard times, depriving the West of centers for the exchange of goods and ideas that would enable it to look and live beyond itself.

In the seventh century, the Byzantine emperors, their hands full with the Islamic threat in the East, were unable to assert themselves in the West, leaving most of the region in the control of the Franks

and the Lombards (a Germanic tribe that invaded Italy in the sixth century and settled in the Po Valley). Islamic dominance of the Mediterranean likewise closed the West to much trade or cultural influence from the East. As a result, western Europeans were forced to rely on their own resources and develop their Germanic and Greco-Roman heritage into their own distinctive culture.

As Western shipping declined in the Mediterranean, populations that would otherwise have been engaged in trade-related work in the cities moved in great numbers into interior regions. There they found the employment and protection they sought on the farms of the great landholders. The landholders, for their part, needed laborers and welcomed the new emigrants.

Peasants made up 90 percent of the population. Those who owned their own land were "free peasants." Some peasants became "serfs" by surrendering their land to a more powerful landholder in exchange for assistance in time of dire need, such as prolonged crop failure or foreign invasion. Basically, serfdom was a status of servitude to an economically and politically stronger person. Powerful landholders, after seizing all the agricultural land they could control, essentially reallocated it to the people who supplied labor and goods, offering them protection in return.

As the demand for agricultural products diminished in the great urban centers and as traffic between town and country declined, the farming belts became regionally insular and self-contained. Production and travel adjusted to local needs. There was little incentive for bold experimentation and exploration. The domains of the great landholders became the basic social and political units of society, and local barter economies sprang up within them. In these developments were sown the seeds of what would later come to be known as manorial and feudal society (which we will discuss in more detail). Manorial society involved a division of land and labor among lords, serfs, and other peasants for the profit of the lords and the protection of all. Feudal society involved the emergence of a special class of aristocratic warrior knights as guarantors of order.

While all of this was going on, one institution remained firmly entrenched within the cities: the Christian Church. The church had long modeled its own structure on that of the imperial Roman administration. Like the imperial government, church government was centralized and hierarchical. Strategically placed "generals" (bishops) in European cities looked for spiritual direction to their leader, the bishop of Rome. As the western empire crumbled, Roman governors withdrew, and populations emigrated to the countryside, the resulting vacuum of authority was filled by local bishops and cathedral chapters. The local cathedral became the center of urban life and the local bishop the highest authority for those who remained in the cities. In Rome, on a larger and more fateful scale, the pope took control of the city as the Western emperors gradually departed and died out. Left to its own devices, western Europe soon discovered that the Christian Church was its best repository of Roman administrative skills and classical culture.

The Christian Church had been graced with special privileges, great lands, and wealth by Emperor Constantine and his successors. In the first half of the fourth century, Christians gained legal standing and a favored status within the empire. In 391 Emperor Theodosius I (r. ca. 379–395) raised Christianity to the official religion of the empire. Both Theodosius and his predecessors acted as much for political effect as out of religious conviction. In 313 Christians made up about one-fifth of the population of the empire, and Christianity was unquestionably the strongest of the competing religions. Its main rivals were Mithraism, the religion popular among army officers and restricted to males, and the Egyptian cults of Isis and Serapis.

Challenged by Rome's decline to become a major political force, the Christian Church survived the period of Germanic and Islamic invasions a somewhat spiritually weakened and compromised institution. Yet it remained a potent civilizing and unifying force. It had a religious message of providential purpose and individual worth that could give solace and meaning to life at its worst. It had a ritual of baptism and a creedal confession that united people beyond the traditional barriers of social class, education, and gender. And alone in the West, the church retained an effective hierarchical administration, scattered throughout the old empire, staffed by the best-educated minds in Europe, and centered in emperorless Rome.

Writing after the fall of Rome, but before the emergence of Islam, Augustine (354–430) eloquently elaborated the Christian message and the force of its appeal in his chaotic times. In his *City of God*, he defended Christianity against those who held it responsible for the collapse of Roman civilization because it allegedly rejected the Roman gods and its message of love and forgiveness fostered weakness. He pointed out the empire's internal weaknesses and the constructive nature of Christian teaching, which he deemed superior to the ancient philosophies. He stressed in particular the discipline of the church and the power of its sacraments to heal and unite humankind in a new spiritual empire. The

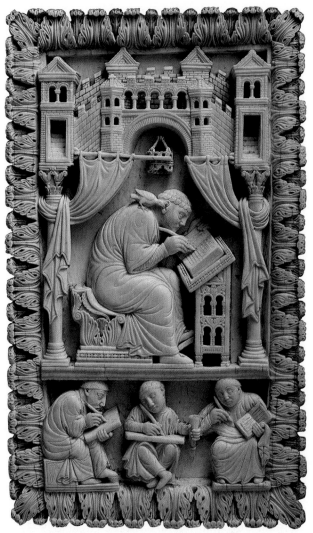

Saint Gregory the Great, shown in a monastic scriptorium, *or study, receiving the divine word from a dove perched on his shoulder. Below him three monks are writing. The middle monk holds an inkwell in his left hand.* Kunsthistorisches Museum, Vienna

book became a favorite of the Frankish king Charlemagne nearly 400 years later.

Monastic Culture

The church enjoyed the services of growing numbers of monks, who were not only loyal to its mission, but also objects of great popular respect. Monastic culture proved again and again to be the peculiar strength of the church during the Middle Ages.

The first monks were hermits who had withdrawn from society to pursue a more perfect way of life. They were inspired by the Christian ideal of a life of complete self-denial in imitation of Christ. The popularity of monasticism began to grow as Roman persecution of Christians waned and Christianity became the favored religion of the empire during the fourth century. Monasticism replaced martyrdom as the most perfect way to imitate Christ and to confess one's faith.

Christians came to view monastic life—embracing, as it did, the biblical "counsels of perfection" (chastity, poverty, and obedience)—as the purest form of religious practice, going beyond the baptism and creedal confession that identified ordinary believers. This view evolved during the Middle Ages into a belief in the general superiority of the clergy and in the church's mission over the laity and the state. That belief served the papacy in later confrontations with secular rulers.

Anthony of Egypt (ca. 251–356), the father of hermit monasticism, was inspired by Jesus' command to the rich young ruler: "If you will be perfect, sell all that you have, give it to the poor, and follow me" (Matthew 19:21). Anthony went into the desert to pray and work, setting an example followed by hundreds in Egypt, Syria, and Palestine in the fourth and fifth centuries.

Hermit monasticism was soon joined by the development of communal monasticism. In the first quarter of the fourth century, Pachomius (ca. 286–346) organized monks in southern Egypt into a highly regimented community in which hundreds shared a life of labor, order, and discipline enforced by a strict penal code. Such monastic communities grew to contain a thousand or more inhabitants. They were little "cities of God," trying to separate themselves from the collapsing Roman and the nominal Christian world. Basil the Great (329–379) popularized communal monasticism throughout the East, providing a rule that lessened the asceticism of Pachomius and directed monks beyond their segregated enclaves of perfection into such social worldly services as caring for orphans, widows, and the infirm in surrounding communities.

Athanasius (ca. 293–373) and Martin of Tours (ca. 315–399) introduced monasticism to the West. The teachings of John Cassian (ca. 360–435) and Jerome (ca. 340–420) then helped shape the basic values and practices of Western monasticism. The great organizer of Western monasticism, however, was Benedict of Nursia (ca. 480–547). In 529 he established a monastery at Monte Cassino, in Italy, founding the form of monasticism—Benedictine—that bears his name and that quickly came to dominate in the West. It eventually replaced an Irish, non-Benedictine monasticism that was common until the 600s in the British Isles and Gaul.

Benedict wrote *Rule for Monasteries*, a sophisticated and comprehensive plan for every activity of the monks, even detailing the manner in which they were to sleep. His *Rule* opposed the severities of earlier monasticism that tortured the body and anguished the mind. Benedict insisted on good food and even some wine, adequate clothing, and proper amounts of sleep and relaxation. Periods of devotion (about four hours each day) were set aside for the "work of God." That is, regular prayers, liturgical activities, and study alternated with manual labor (farming). This program permitted not a moment's idleness and carefully nurtured the religious, intellectual, and physical well-being of the cloistered monks. The monastery was directed by an abbot, whose command had to be obeyed unquestioningly.

Individual Benedictine monasteries remained autonomous until the later Middle Ages, when the Benedictines became a unified order of the church. During the early Middle Ages, Benedictine missionaries Christianized both England and Germany. Their disciplined organization and devotion to hard work made the Benedictines an economic and political power as well as a spiritual force wherever they settled.

The Doctrine of Papal Primacy

Constantine and his successors, especially the Eastern emperors, ruled religious life with an iron hand and consistently looked on the church as little more than a department of the state. Such political assumption of spiritual power involved the emperor directly in the church's affairs, even to the point of playing the theologian and imposing conciliar solutions on its doctrinal quarrels. State control of religion was the original church–state relation in the West. The bishops of Rome, however, never accepted such intervention and opposed it in every way they could. In the fifth and sixth centuries, taking advantage of imperial weakness and distraction, they developed for their own defense the weaponry of the doctrine of papal primacy. This doctrine raised the Roman pontiff to an unassailable supremacy within the church when it came to defining all other church doctrine. It also put him in a position to make important secular claims, leading to repeated conflicts between church and state and between pope and emperor throughout the Middle Ages.

Papal primacy was first asserted as a response to the decline of imperial Rome that accompanied the shift of the imperial residence in the West to Milan and, later, Ravenna. It was also a response to the concurrent claims of the patriarchs of the Eastern Church, who, after imperial power was transferred to Constantinople, looked on the bishop of Rome as a peer, not as a superior. In 381 the ecumenical Council of Constantinople declared the bishop of Constantinople to be of first rank after the bishop of Rome "because Constantinople is the new Rome."

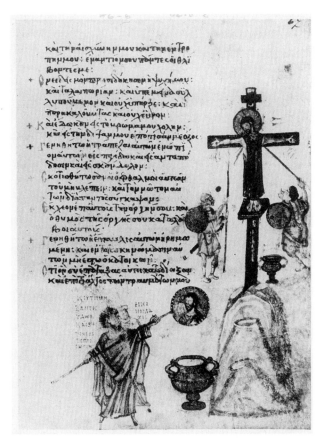

A ninth-century Byzantine manuscript shows an iconoclast whiting out an image of Christ. The Iconoclastic Controversy was an important factor in the division of Christendom into separate Latin and Greek branches. State Historical Museum, Moscow

In 451 the ecumenical Council of Chalcedon recognized Constantinople as having the same religious primacy in the East as Rome had traditionally possessed in the West. By the mid-sixth century, the bishop of Constantinople regularly described himself in correspondence as a "universal" patriarch.

Roman pontiffs, understandably jealous of such claims and resentful of the ecclesiastical interference of Eastern emperors, launched a counteroffensive. Pope Damasus I (r. 366–384)[3] took the first of several major steps in the rise of the Roman church when he declared a Roman "apostolic" primacy. Pointing to Jesus' words to Peter in the Gospel of Matthew (16:18) ("Thou art Peter, and upon this rock I will build my church"), he claimed himself and all other popes to be Peter's direct successors as the unique "rock" on which the Christian Church was built. Pope Leo I (r. 440–461) took still another fateful step by assuming the title *pontifex maximus*, or "supreme priest." He further proclaimed himself to

be endowed with a "plentitude of power," thereby establishing the supremacy of the bishop of Rome over all other bishops in the church. During Leo's reign, an imperial decree recognized his exclusive jurisdiction over the Western church. At the end of the fifth century, Pope Gelasius I (r. 492–496) proclaimed the authority of the clergy to be "more weighty" than the power of kings because priests had charge of divine affairs and the means of salvation.

Events, as well as ideology, favored the papacy. The Germanic and Islamic invasions, just as they had isolated the West by diverting the attention of the eastern empire, also prevented both emperors and eastern patriarchs from interfering in the affairs of the Western church. Islam may even be said to have "saved" the Western church from Eastern domination. At the same time, the emergent Lombards and Franks provided the church with new political allies. Eastern episcopal competition with Rome ended as bishopric after bishopric fell to Islamic armies in the East. The power of the exarch of Ravenna—the Byzantine emperor's viceroy in the West—was eclipsed by invading Lombards, who, thanks to Frankish prodding, became Nicene Christians loyal to Rome and, increasingly, a counterweight to Eastern power and influence in the West. In an unprecedented act, Pope Gregory I, "the Great" (r. 590–604), negotiated an independent peace treaty with the Lombards, completely ignoring the Eastern emperor and the imperial authorities in Ravenna, who were too weak to resist.

The Division of Christendom

As the events just discussed suggest, the division of Christendom into Eastern (Byzantine) and Western (Roman Catholic) churches has its roots in the early Middle Ages. The division was due in part to linguistic and cultural differences between the Greek East and the Roman, Latin-speaking West. A novel combination of Greek, Roman, and Asian elements shaped Byzantine culture, giving Eastern Christianity more of a mystical orientation than Western Christianity. Compared with their Western counterparts, Eastern Christians seemed to attribute less importance to life in this world and to be more concerned about questions affecting their eternal destiny. This strong mystical orientation toward the next world may also have permitted the Eastern patriarchs to submit more passively than Western popes could ever do to royal intervention in church affairs.

As in the West, Eastern Church organization closely followed that of the secular state. A patriarch ruled over metropolitans and archbishops in the cities and provinces; and they, in turn, ruled over

---

[3]Dates after popes' names are the years of each reign.

bishops, who stood as authorities over the local clergy. Except for the patriarch Michael Cerularius, who tried unsuccessfully in the eleventh century to free the church from its traditional tight state control, the patriarchs were normally carefully regulated by the emperor.

Contrary to the evolving Western tradition of universal clerical celibacy (which Western monastic culture encouraged), the Eastern Church permitted the marriage of parish priests (but not monks), while strictly forbidding bishops to marry. The Eastern Church also used leavened bread in the Eucharist, contrary to the Western custom of using unleavened bread, and rejected the Western doctrine of purgatory. Unlike the Roman Church, the Eastern Church accommodated the laity by recognizing divorce and by using vernacular liturgies. The Roman Church also objected to the tendency of the Eastern Church to compromise doctrinally with the politically powerful Arian and Monophysite Christians. Finally, in the background, the Eastern and Western churches both laid claim to jurisdiction over the newly converted areas in the North Balkans.

Beyond these issues, three major factors lay behind the religious break between East and West. The first revolved around questions of doctrinal authority. The Eastern Church put more stress on the authority of the Bible and the ecumenical councils of the church in the definition of Christian doctrine than on the counsel and decrees of the bishop of Rome. The claims of Roman popes to a special primacy of authority on the basis of the apostle Peter's commission from Jesus in the Gospel of Matthew were unacceptable to the East. In the East the independence and autonomy of national churches held sway. As Steven Runciman summarized, "The Byzantine ideal was a series of autocephalous state churches, linked by intercommunion and the faith of seven councils."[4] This basic issue of authority in matters of faith lay behind the mutual excommunication of Pope Nicholas I and Patriarch Photius in the ninth century and that of Pope Leo IX (through his ambassador to Constantinople, Cardinal Humbert) and Patriarch Michael Cerularius in 1054.

A second major factor in the separation of the two churches was the Western addition of the *filioque* clause to the Nicene–Constantinopolitan Creed. According to this anti-Arian clause, the Holy Spirit proceeds "also from the Son" (*filioque*) as well as from the Father. This addition made clear the Western belief that Christ was "fully substantial with God the Father" and not a lesser being.

The third factor dividing the Eastern and Western churches was the iconoclastic controversy of the first half of the eighth century. As noted in the discussion of the Byzantine Empire, after 725 the Eastern emperor, Leo III, banned the use of images in Eastern churches and attempted to enforce the ban in the West also. Images were greatly cherished in the West, and his actions met fierce official and popular resistance there. To punish the West for this disobedience, Leo confiscated papal lands in Sicily and Calabria (in southern Italy) and placed them under the jurisdiction of the subservient patriarch of Constantinople. Because these territories provided essential papal revenues, the Western church could not but view the emperor's action as a declaration of war. (Later Empress Irene made peace with the Roman Catholic Church on this issue and restored the use of images at the ecumenical Council of Nicaea in 787.)

Emperor Leo's direct challenge to the pope coincided with a renewed threat to Rome and the Western church from the Lombards of northern Italy. Assailed on two fronts, the Roman papacy seemed surely doomed. There has not, however, been a more resilient and enterprising institution in Western history than the papacy. Since Gregory the Great, who 150 years earlier had negotiated a treaty with the Lombards, popes had recognized the Franks of northern Gaul as Europe's ascendant power and had seen in them their surest protectors. In 754, Pope Stephen II (r. 752–757), initiating the most fruitful political alliance of the Middle Ages, enlisted the Franks and their ruler, Pepin III, to defend the church against the Lombards and as a Western counterweight to the Eastern emperor. This marriage of religion and politics created a new Western church and empire; it also determined much of the course of Western history into our time.

The Kingdom of the Franks

Merovingians and Carolingians: From Clovis to Charlemagne

A warrior chieftain, Clovis (ca. 466–511), who converted to orthodox Christianity around 496, founded the first Frankish dynasty, the Merovingians, named for Merovich, an early leader of one branch of the Franks. Clovis and his successors united the Salian and Ripuarian Franks, subdued the Arian Burgundians and Visigoths, and established the kingdom of the Franks within ancient Gaul, making the Franks and the Merovingian kings a significant force in western Europe. The Franks themselves occupied a broad belt of territory that extended throughout

[4]Steven Runciman, *Byzantine Civilization* (London: A. and C. Black, 1993), p. 128.

Major Political and Religious Developments of the Early Middle Ages

313	Emperor Constantine issues the *Edict of Milan*
325	Council of Nicaea defines Christian doctrine
410	Rome invaded by Visigoths under Alaric
413–426	Saint Augustine writes *City of God*
451	Council of Chalcedon further defines Christian doctrine
451–453	Europe invaded by the Huns under Attila
476	Barbarian Odovacer deposes Western emperor and rules as king of the Romans
489–493	Theodoric establishes kingdom of Ostrogoths in Italy
529	Saint Benedict founds monastery at Monte Cassino
533	Justinian codifies Roman law
622	Muhammad's flight from Mecca (*Hegira*)
732	Charles Martel defeats Muslims at Poitiers
754	Pope Stephen II and Pepin III ally

modern France, Belgium, the Netherlands, and western Germany, and their loyalties remained strictly tribal and local.

GOVERNING THE FRANKS In attempting to govern this sprawling kingdom, the Merovingians encountered what proved to be the most persistent problem of medieval political history—the competing claims of the "one" and the "many." On the one hand, the king struggled for a centralized government and transregional loyalty, and on the other, powerful local magnates strove to preserve their regional autonomy and traditions.

The Merovingian kings addressed this problem by making pacts with the landed nobility and by creating the royal office of *count*. The counts were men without possessions to whom the king gave great lands in the expectation that they would be, as the landed aristocrats often were not, loyal officers of the kingdom. But like local aristocrats, the Merovingian counts also let their immediate self-interest gain the upper hand. Once established in office for a period of time, they, too, became territorial rulers in their own right, so that the Frankish kingdom progressively fragmented into independent regions and tiny principalities. This centrifugal tendency was further aided by the Frankish custom of dividing the kingdom equally among the king's legitimate male heirs.

Rather than purchasing allegiance and unity within the kingdom, the Merovingian largess simply occasioned the rise of competing magnates and petty tyrants, who became laws unto themselves within their regions. By the seventh century, the Frankish king was king in title only and had no effective executive power. Real power came to be concentrated in the office of the *mayor of the palace*, spokesperson at the king's court for the great landowners of the three regions into which the Frankish kingdom was divided: Neustria, Austrasia, and Burgundy. Through this office, the Carolingian dynasty rose to power.

The Carolingians controlled the office of the mayor of the palace from the ascent to that post of Pepin I of Austrasia (d. 639) until 751, when, with the enterprising connivance of the pope, they simply expropriated the Frankish crown. Pepin II (d. 714) ruled in fact, if not in title, over the Frankish kingdom. His illegitimate son, Charles Martel ("the Hammer," d. 741), created a great cavalry by bestowing lands known as *benefices*, or *fiefs*, on powerful noblemen. In return, they agreed to be ready to serve as the king's army. It was such an army that checked the Islamic probings on the western front at Poitiers in 732—an important battle that helped to secure the borders of western Europe.

The fiefs so generously bestowed by Charles Martel to create his army came in large part from landed property that he usurped from the church. His alliance with the landed aristocracy in this grand manner permitted the Carolingians to have some measure of political success where the Merovingians had failed. The Carolingians created counts almost entirely out of the landed nobility from which the Carolingians themselves had risen. The Merovingians, in contrast, had tried to compete directly with these great aristocrats by raising landless men to power. By playing to strength rather than challenging it, the Carolingians strengthened themselves, at least for the short term. The church, by this time dependent on the protection of the Franks against the Eastern emperor and the Lombards, could only suffer in silence the usurpation of lands to which it held claim. Later, although they never returned them, the Franks partially compensated the church for these lands.

THE FRANKISH CHURCH The church came to play a large and enterprising role in the Frankish government. By Carolingian times, monasteries were a dominant force. Their intellectual achievements made them respected centers of culture. Their religious teaching and example imposed order on surrounding populations. Their relics and rituals made them magical shrines to which pilgrims came in great numbers. And, thanks to their many gifts and internal discipline and industry, many had become very profitable farms and landed estates, their abbots rich and powerful magnates. Already in Merovingian times, the higher clergy were employed in tandem with counts as royal agents.

It was the policy of the Carolingians, perfected by Charles Martel and his successor, Pepin III ("the Short," d. 768), to use the church to pacify conquered neighboring tribes—Frisians, Thüringians, Bavarians, and especially the Franks' archenemies, the Saxons. Conversion to Nicene Christianity became an integral part of the successful annexation of conquered lands and people. The cavalry broke their bodies, while the clergy won their hearts and minds. The Anglo–Saxon missionary Saint Boniface (born Wynfrith; 680?–754) was the most important cleric to serve Carolingian kings in this way. Christian bishops in missionary districts and elsewhere became lords, appointed by and subject to the king. In this ominous integration of secular and religious policy lay the seeds of the later Investiture Controversy of the eleventh and twelfth centuries. (See Chapter 7.)

The church served more than Carolingian territorial expansion. Pope Zacharias (r. 741–752) also sanctioned Pepin the Short's termination of the vestigial Merovingian dynasty and supported the Carolingian accession to outright kingship of the Franks. With the pope's public blessing, Pepin was proclaimed king by the nobility in council in 751, while the last of the Merovingians, the puppet king Childeric III, was hustled off to a monastery and dynastic oblivion. According to legend, Saint Boniface first anointed Pepin, thereby investing Frankish rule from the very start with a certain sacral character.

Zacharias's successor, Pope Stephen II (r. 752–757), did not let Pepin forget the favor of his predecessor. In 753, when the Lombards besieged Rome, Pope Stephen crossed the Alps and appealed directly to Pepin to cast out the invaders and to guarantee papal claims to central Italy, largely dominated at this time by the Eastern emperor. As already noted, in 754 the Franks and the church formed an alliance against the Lombards and the Eastern emperor. Carolingian kings became the protectors of the Catholic Church and thereby "kings by the grace of God." Pepin gained the title *patricius Romanorum*, "patrician of the Romans," a title first borne by the ruling families of Rome and heretofore applied to the representative of the Eastern emperor. In 755 the Franks defeated the Lombards and gave the pope the lands surrounding Rome, creating what came to be known as the *Papal States*.

In this period a fraudulent document appeared—the *Donation of Constantine* (written between 750 and 800)—that was enterprisingly designed to remind the Franks of the church's importance as the heir of Rome. Many believed it to be genuine until it was definitely exposed as a forgery in the fifteenth century by the humanist Lorenzo Valla.

The papacy had looked to the Franks for an ally strong enough to protect it from the Eastern emperors. It is an irony of history that the church found in the Carolingian dynasty a Western imperial government that drew almost as slight a boundary between state and church and between secular and religious policy as did eastern emperors. Although Carolingian patronage was eminently preferable to Eastern domination for the popes, it proved in its own way to be no less constraining.

The Reign of Charlemagne (768–814)

Charlemagne, the son of Pepin the Short, continued the role of his father as papal protector in Italy and his policy of territorial conquest in the north. After decisively defeating King Desiderius and the Lombards of northern Italy in 774, Charlemagne took upon himself the title "King of the Lombards" in Pavia. He widened the frontiers of his kingdom further by subjugating surrounding pagan tribes, foremost among them the Saxons, whom the Franks brutally Christianized and dispersed in small groups throughout Frankish lands. The Muslims were chased beyond the Pyrenees, and the Avars (a tribe related to the Huns) were practically annihilated, bringing the Danubian plains into the Frankish orbit. The defeat of the Avars was so complete that the expression "vanished like the Avars" came to be applied to anything that was irretrievably lost.

By the time of his death on January 28, 814, Charlemagne's kingdom embraced modern France, Belgium, Holland, Switzerland, almost the whole of western Germany, much of Italy, a portion of Spain, and the island of Corsica—an area about equal to that of the modern European Common Market. (See Map 6-4.)

THE NEW EMPIRE Encouraged by his ambitious advisers, Charlemagne came to harbor imperial designs. He desired to be not only king of all the Franks but a universal emperor as well. He had his sacred palace city, Aachen (in French, Aix-la-Chapelle), constructed in conscious imitation of the courts of the ancient Roman and contemporary Eastern emperors. Although he permitted the church its independence, he looked after it with a paternalism almost as great as that of any Eastern emperor. He used the church, above all, to promote social stability and hierarchical order throughout the kingdom—as an aid in the creation of a great

MAP 6–4   THE EMPIRE OF CHARLEMAGNE TO 814   *Building on the successes of his prede-cessors, Charlemagne greatly increased the Frankish domains. Such traditional enemies as the Saxons and the Lombards fell under his sway.*

Frankish Christian Empire. Frankish Christians were ceremoniously baptized, professed the Nicene Creed (with the *filioque* clause), and learned in church to revere Charlemagne.

The formation of a distinctive Carolingian Christendom was made clear in the 790s, when Charlemagne issued the so-called *Libri Carolini*. These documents attacked the ecumenical Council of Nicaea, which, in what was actually a friendly gesture to the West, had met in 787 to formulate a new, more accommodating position for the Eastern Church on the use of images.

Charlemagne fulfilled his imperial pretensions on Christmas Day, 800, when Pope Leo III (r.

795–816) crowned him emperor. This event began what would come to be known as the Holy Roman Empire, a revival of the old Roman Empire in the West, based in Germany after 870.

In 799, Pope Leo III had been imprisoned by the Roman aristocracy but escaped to the protection of Charlemagne, who restored him as pope. The fateful coronation of Charlemagne was thus in part an effort by the pope to enhance the church's stature and to gain some leverage over this powerful king. It was, however, no papal coup d'etat; Charlemagne's control over the church remained as strong after as before the event. If the coronation benefitted the church, as it certainly did, it also served Charlemagne's purposes.

Before his coronation, Charlemagne had been a minor Western potentate in the eyes of Eastern emperors. After the coronation, Eastern emperors reluctantly recognized his new imperial dignity, and Charlemagne even found it necessary to disclaim ambitions to rule as emperor over the East.

THE NEW EMPEROR Charlemagne stood a majestic six feet three and one half inches tall—a fact confirmed when his tomb was opened and exact measurements of his remains were taken in 1861. He was restless, ever ready for a hunt. Informal and gregarious, he insisted on the presence of friends even when he bathed. He was widely known for his practical jokes, lusty good humor, and warm hospitality. Aachen was a festive palace city to which people and gifts came from all over the world. In 802 Charlemagne even received from the caliph of Baghdad, Harun-al-Rashid, a white elephant, the transport of which across the Alps was as great a wonder as the creature itself.

Charlemagne had five official wives in succession, as well as many mistresses and concubines, and he sired numerous children. This connubial variety created special problems. His oldest son by his first marriage, Pepin, jealous of the attention shown by his father to the sons of his second wife and fearing the loss of paternal favor, joined with noble enemies in a conspiracy against his father. He spent the rest of his life in confinement in a monastery after the plot was exposed.

PROBLEMS OF GOVERNMENT Charlemagne governed his kingdom through counts, of whom there were perhaps as many as 250. They were strategically located within the administrative districts into which the kingdom was divided. In Carolingian practice the count tended to be a local magnate, one who already possessed the armed might and the self-interest to enforce the will of a generous king. He had three main duties: to maintain a local army loyal to the king, to collect tribute and dues, and to administer justice throughout his district.

This last responsibility he undertook through a district law court known as the *mallus*. The *mallus* received testimony from witnesses familiar with the parties involved in a dispute or criminal case, much as a modern court does. Through such testimony, it sought to discover the character and believability of each side. On occasion, in very difficult cases where the testimony was insufficient to determine guilt or innocence, recourse would be taken to judicial duels or to a variety of "divine" tests or ordeals. Among these was the length of time it took a defendant's hand to heal after immersion in boiling water. In an-

other, the ordeal by water, a defendant was thrown with his hands and feet bound into a river or pond that a priest had blessed. If he floated, he was pronounced guilty, because the pure water had obviously rejected him; if, however, the water received him and he sank, he was deemed innocent.

In such ordeals God was believed to render a verdict. Once guilt had been made clear to the *mallus*, either by testimony or by ordeal, it assessed a monetary compensation to be paid to the injured party. This most popular way of settling grievances usually ended hostilities between individuals and families.

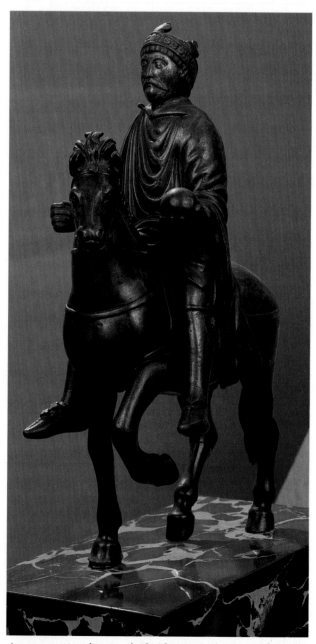

An equestrian figure of Charlemagne (or possibly one of his sons) from the early ninth century. Giraudon/Art Resource, N.Y.

As in Merovingian times, many counts used their official position and new judicial powers to their own advantage and became little despots within their districts. As the strong became stronger, they also became more independent. They began to look on the land grants with which they were paid as hereditary possessions rather than generous royal donations—a development that began to fragment Charlemagne's kingdom. Charlemagne tried to oversee his overseers and improve local justice by creating special royal envoys known as *missi dominici*. These were lay and clerical agents (counts and archbishops and bishops) who made annual visits to districts other than their own. But their impact was marginal. Permanent provincial governors, bearing the title of prefect, duke, or margrave, were created in what was still another attempt to supervise the counts and organize the outlying regions of the kingdom. But as these governors became established in their areas, they proved no less corruptible than the others.

Charlemagne never solved the problem of creating a loyal bureaucracy. Ecclesiastical agents proved no better than secular ones in this regard. Landowning bishops had not only the same responsibilities, but also the same secular lifestyles and aspirations as the royal counts. Save for their attendance to the liturgy and to church prayers, they were largely indistinguishable from the lay nobility. Capitularies, or royal decrees, discouraged the more outrageous behavior of the clergy. But Charlemagne also sensed, rightly, as the Gregorian reform of the eleventh century would prove, that the emergence of a distinctive, reform-minded class of ecclesiastical landowners would be a danger to royal government. He purposefully treated his bishops as he treated his counts, that is, as vassals who served at the king's pleasure.

To be a Christian in this period was more a matter of ritual and doctrine (being baptized and reciting the creed) than of following a prescription for ethical behavior and social service. Both clergy and laity were more concerned with contests over the most basic kinds of social protections than with more elevated ethical issues. An important legislative achievement of Charlemagne's reign, for example, was to give a free vassal the right to break his oath of loyalty to his lord if the lord tried to kill him, to reduce him to an unfree serf, to withhold promised protection in time of need, or to seduce his wife.

ALCUIN AND THE CAROLINGIAN RENAISSANCE
Charlemagne accumulated a great deal of wealth in the form of loot and land from conquered tribes. He used a substantial part of this booty to attract Europe's best scholars to Aachen, where they developed court culture and education. By making scholarship materially as well as intellectually rewarding, Charlemagne attracted such scholars as Theodulf of Orleans, Angilbert, his own biographer Einhard, and the renowned Anglo–Saxon master Alcuin of York (735–804). In 782, at almost fifty years of age, Alcuin became director of the king's palace school. He brought classical and Christian learning to Aachen in schools run by the monasteries. Alcuin was handsomely rewarded for his efforts with several monastic estates, including that of Saint Martin of Tours, the wealthiest in the kingdom.

Although Charlemagne also appreciated learning for its own sake, his grand palace school was not created simply for the love of antiquity. Charlemagne intended it to upgrade the administrative skills of the clerics and officials who staffed the royal bureaucracy. By preparing the sons of the nobility to run the religious and secular offices of the realm, court scholarship served kingdom building. The school provided basic instruction in the seven liberal arts, with special concentration on grammar, logic, rhetoric, and the basic mathematical arts. It therefore provided training in reading, writing, speaking, sound reasoning, and counting—the basic tools of bureaucracy.

Among the results of this intellectual activity was the appearance of a more accurate Latin in official documents and the development of a clear style of handwriting known as Carolingian minuscule, which was far more legible than Merovingian script. By making reading both easier and more pleasurable, Carolingian minuscule helped lay the foundations of subsequent Latin scholarship. It also increased lay literacy.

A modest renaissance of antiquity occurred in the palace school as scholars collected and preserved ancient manuscripts for a more curious posterity. Alcuin worked on a correct text of the Bible and made editions of the works of Gregory the Great and the monastic *Rule* of Saint Benedict. These scholarly activities aimed at concrete reforms and served official efforts to bring uniformity to church law and liturgy, to educate the clergy, and to improve moral life within the monasteries. Through personal correspondence and visitations, Alcuin created a genuine, if limited, community of scholars and clerics at court. He did much to infuse the highest administrative levels with a sense of comradeship and common purpose.

THE CAROLINGIAN MANOR The agrarian economy of the early Middle Ages was organized and controlled through village farms known as manors. (See "the Carolingian Manor.") On these, peasants labored as tenants for a lord, that is, a more powerful landowner who allotted them land and tenements in exchange for their services and a portion of their crops. The part of the land tended for the lord was the *demesne*, on average about one-quarter to one-

The Carolingian Manor

A capitulary from the reign of Charlemagne known as "De Villis" itemizes what the king received from his royal manors or village estates. It is a testimony both to Carolingian administrative ability and domination over the countryside.

❖ *What gave the lord the right to absolutely everything? (Has anything been overlooked?) How did the stewards and workers share in the manorial life? Was the arrangment a good deal for them as well as for the lord?*

That each steward shall make an annual statement of all our income: an account of our lands cultivated by the oxen which our ploughmen drive and of our lands which the tenants of farms ought to plough; an account of the pigs, of the rents, of the obligations and fines; of the game taken in our forests without our permission; of the various compositions; of the mills, of the forest, of the fields, of the bridges, and ships: of the free-men and the hundreds who are under obligations to our treasury; of markets, vineyards, and those who owe wine to us; of the hay, fire-wood, torches, planks, and other kinds of lumber; of the waste-lands; of the vegetables, millet, panic; of the wool, flax, and hemp; of the fruits of the trees, of the nut trees, larger and smaller; of the grafted trees of all kinds; of the gardens; of the turnips; of the fish-ponds; of the hides, skins, and horns; of the honey, wax; of the fat, tallow and soap; of the mulberry wine, cooked wine, mead, vinegar, beer, wine new and old; of the new grain and the old; of the hens and eggs; of the geese; the number of fishermen, smiths [workers in metal], swordmakers, and shoemakers; of the bins and boxes; of the turners and saddlers; of the forges and mines, that is iron and other mines; of the lead mines; of the tributaries; of the colts and fillies; they shall make all these known to us, set forth separately and in order, at Christmas, in order that we may know what and how much of each thing we have.

In each of our estates our stewards are to have as many cow-houses, piggeries, sheep-folds, stables for goats, as possible, and they ought never to be without these.

They must provide with the greatest care that whatever is prepared or made with the hands, that is, lard, smoked meat, salt meat, partially salted meat, wine, vinegar, mulberry wine, cooked wine, garns, mustard, cheese, butter, malt beer, mead, honey, wax, flour, all should be prepared and made with the greatest cleanliness.

That each steward on each of our domains shall always have, for the sake of ornament, swans, peacocks, pheasants, ducks, pigeons, partridges, turtle-doves.

That in each of our estates, the chambers shall be provided with counterpanes, cushions, pillows, bed-clothes, coverings for the tables and benches; vessels of brass, lead, iron and wood; andirons, chains, pothooks, adzes, axes, augers, cutlasses and all other kinds of tools, so that it shall never be necessary to go elsewhere for them, or to borrow them. And the weapons, which are carried against the enemy, shall be well cared for, so as to keep them in good condition.

For our women's work they are to give at the proper time, as has been ordered, the materials, that is the linen, wool, woad, vermilion, madder, wool-combs, teasels, soap grease, vessels and the other objects which are necessary.

Of the food-products other than meat, two-thirds shall be sent each year for our own use, that is of the vegetables, fish, cheese, butter, honey, mustard, vinegar, millet, panic, dried and green herbs, radishes, and in addition of the wax, soap and other small products.

That each steward shall have in his district good workmen, namely, blacksmiths, gold-smiths, silver-smiths, shoemakers, turners, carpenters, swordmakers, fishermen, foilers, soap-makers, men who know how to make beer cider, berry, and all the other kinds of beverages, bakers to make pastry for our table, net-makers who know how to make nets for hunting, fishing and fowling, and the other who are too numerous to be designated.

Translations and Reprints from the Original Sources of European History, Vol. 3 (Philadelphia: Department of History, University of Pennsylvania, 1909), pp. 2–4.

The invention of the moldboard plow greatly improved farming. The heavy plow cut deeply into the ground and furrowed it. This illustration from the Luttrell Psalter (ca. 1340) also shows that the traction harness, which lessened the strangulating effect of the yoke on the animals, had not yet been adopted. Indeed, one of the oxen seems to be on the verge of choking.
The British Library/E.T. Archive

third of the arable land. All crops grown there were harvested for the lord. The manor also included common meadows for grazing animals and forests reserved exclusively for the lord to hunt in.

Peasants were treated according to their personal status and the size of their tenements. A *freeman*, that is, a peasant with his own modest allodial, or hereditary, property (property free from the claims of an overlord), became a serf by surrendering his property to a greater landowner—a lord—in exchange for protection and assistance. The freeman received his land back from the lord with a clear definition of his economic and legal rights. Although the land was no longer his property, he had full possession and use of it and the number of services and amount of goods he was to supply to the lord were carefully spelled out.

Peasants who entered the service of a lord with little real property (perhaps only a few farm implements and animals) ended up as *unfree serfs*. Such serfs were much more vulnerable to the lord's demands, often spending up to three days a week working the lord's fields. Truly impoverished peasants, those who had nothing to offer a lord except their hands, had the lowest status and were the least protected from excessive demands on their labor.

All classes of serfs were subject to various dues in kind: firewood for cutting the lord's wood, sheep for being allowed to graze their sheep on the lord's land, and the like. Thus the lord, who, for his part, furnished shacks and small plots of land from his vast domain, had at his disposal an army of servants of varying status who provided him with everything from eggs to boots. Weak serfs often fled to monasteries rather than continue their servitude. That many serfs were discontented is reflected in the high number of recorded escapes. An astrological calendar from the period even marks the days most favorable for escaping. Escaped serfs roamed the land as beggars and vagabonds, searching for new and better masters.

By the time of Charlemagne, the moldboard plow and the three-field system of land cultivation were coming into use. These developments greatly improved agricultural productivity. The older "scratch" plow had crisscrossed the field with only slight penetration and required light, well-drained soils. The moldboard plow, by contrast, cut deep into the soil and turned it to form a ridge, providing a natural drainage system and permitting the deep planting of seeds. This new type of plow made cultivation possible in the regions north of the Mediterranean, where soils were dense and waterlogged from heavy precipitation.

Unlike the earlier two-field system of crop rotation, which simply alternated fallow with planted fields each year, the three-field system increased the amount of cultivated land by leaving only one third fallow in a given year. Indeed, the third field might be reclaimed from previously passed-over heavier soils now made workable by the moldboard plow, thus increasing the amount of land under cultivation in a dramatic fashion. It also better adjusted crops to seasons. In fall, one field was planted with winter crops of wheat or rye, to be harvested in early summer. In late spring, a second field was planted with summer crops of oats, barley, lentils, and legumes, which were harvested in August or September. The third field was left fallow, to be planted in its turn with winter and summer crops. The new summer crops, especially legumes, restored nitrogen to the soil and helped increase yields.

RELIGION AND THE CLERGY   The lower clergy lived among, and were drawn from, peasant ranks. They fared hardly better than peasants in Carolingian times. As owners of the churches on their lands, the lords had the right to raise chosen serfs to the post of parish priest, placing them in charge of the churches on the lords' estates. Church law directed a lord to set a serf free before he entered the clergy.

Lords, however, were reluctant to do this and risk thereby a possible later challenge to their jurisdiction over the ecclesiastical property with which the serf, as priest, was invested. Lords preferred a "serf priest," one who not only said the mass on Sundays and holidays, but who also continued to serve his lord during the week, waiting on the lord's table and tending his steeds. Like Charlemagne with his bishops, Frankish lords cultivated a docile parish clergy.

The ordinary people looked to religion for comfort and consolation. They especially associated religion with the major Christian holidays and festivals, such as Christmas and Easter. They baptized their children, attended mass, tried to learn the Lord's Prayer and the Apostles' Creed, and received the last rites from the priest as death approached. This was all probably done with more awe and simple faith than understanding. Because local priests on the manors were no better educated than their congregations, religious instruction in the meaning of Christian doctrine and practice remained at a bare minimum. The church sponsored street dramas in accordance with the church calendar. These were designed to impart the highlights of the Bible and church history and to instill basic Christian moral values.

People understandably became particularly attached in this period to the more tangible veneration of saints and relics. The Virgin Mary was also widely revered, although a true cult of Mary would not develop until the eleventh and twelfth centuries. Religious devotion to saints has been compared to subjection to powerful lords in the secular world. Both the saint and the lord were protectors whose honor the serfs were bound to defend and whose favor and help in time of need they hoped to receive. Veneration of saints also had strong points of contact with old tribal customs, from which the commonfolk were hardly detached. (Indeed, Charlemagne enforced laws against witchcraft, sorcery, and the ritual sacrifice of animals by monks.)

But religion also had an intrinsic appeal and special meaning to those masses of medieval men and women who found themselves burdened, fearful, and with little hope of material betterment on this side of eternity. Charlemagne shared many of the religious beliefs of his ordinary subjects. He collected and venerated relics, made pilgrimages to Rome, and frequented the Church of Saint Mary in Aachen several times a day. In his last will and testament, he directed that all but a fraction of his great treasure be spent to endow masses and prayers for his departed soul.

Breakup of the Carolingian Kingdom

In the last years of his life, an ailing Charlemagne knew that his empire was ungovernable. The seeds of dissolution lay in regionalism, that is, the de-

The tenth-century crown of the Holy Roman Emperor (the title applied to rulers who succeeded to the remains of Charlemagne's empire) reveals the close alliance between church and throne. The crown is surmounted by a cross, and it includes panels depicting the great kings of the Bible, David and Solomon. Kunsthistorisches Museum, Vienna

termination of each region, no matter how small, to look first—and often only—to its own self-interest. Despite his considerable skill and resolve, Charlemagne's realm became too fragmented among powerful regional magnates. Although they were his vassals, these same men were also landholders and lords in their own right. They knew that their sovereignty lessened as Charlemagne's increased and accordingly became reluctant royal servants. In feudal society, a direct relationship existed between physical proximity to authority and loyalty to authority. Local people obeyed local lords more readily than they obeyed a glorious, but distant king.

Charlemagne had been forced to recognize and even to enhance the power of regional magnates to win needed financial and military support. But as in the Merovingian kingdom, the tail came increasingly to wag the dog. Charlemagne's major attempt to enforce transregional discipline and the subordination of local interests to royal dictates was to create the institution of the *missi dominici*—royal overseers of the king's law and justice. But these new officials themselves fell prey to narrow, regional self-interest, and this effort also proved ultimately unsuccessful.

LOUIS THE PIOUS The Carolingian kings did not give up easily, however. Charlemagne's only surviving son and successor was Louis the Pious (r. 814–840), so-called because of his close alliance with the church and his promotion of puritanical reforms. Before his death, Charlemagne secured the imperial succession for Louis by raising him to "co-emperor" in a grand public ceremony. After Charlemagne's death, Louis no longer referred to himself as king of the Franks. He bore instead the single title of emperor. The assumption of this title reflected not only Carolingian pretense to an imperial dynasty, but also Louis' determination to unify his kingdom and raise its people above mere regional and tribal loyalties.

Unfortunately, Louis' own fertility joined with Salic, or Frankish, law and Frankish custom to prevent the attainment of this high goal. Louis had three sons by his first wife. According to Salic law, a ruler partitioned his kingdom equally among his surviving sons. (Salic law forbade women to inherit the throne.) Louis, who saw himself as an emperor and no mere king, recognized that a tripartite kingdom would hardly be an empire and acted early in his reign, in the year 817, to break this legal tradition. This he did by making his eldest son, Lothar (d. 855), co-regent and sole imperial heir. To Lothar's brothers he gave important, but much lesser, appanages, or assigned hereditary lands; Pepin (d. 838) became king of Aquitaine, and Louis "the German" (d. 876) became king of Bavaria, over the eastern Franks.

In 823 Louis's second wife, Judith of Bavaria, bore him a fourth son, Charles, later called "the Bald" (d. 877). Mindful of Frankish law and custom, and determined that her son should receive more than just a nominal inheritance, the queen incited the brothers Pepin and Louis against Lothar, who fled for refuge to the pope. More important, Judith was instrumental in persuading Louis to adhere to tradition and divide the kingdom equally among his four living sons. As their stepmother and the young Charles rose in their father's favor, the three brothers, fearing still further reversals, decided to act against their father. Supported by the pope, they joined forces and defeated their father in a battle near Colmar in 833.

As the bestower of crowns on emperors, the pope had an important stake in the preservation of the revived western empire and the imperial title. Louis' belated agreement to an equal partition of his kingdom threatened to weaken the pope as well as the royal family. Therefore, the pope condemned Louis and restored Lothar to his original inheritance. But Lothar's

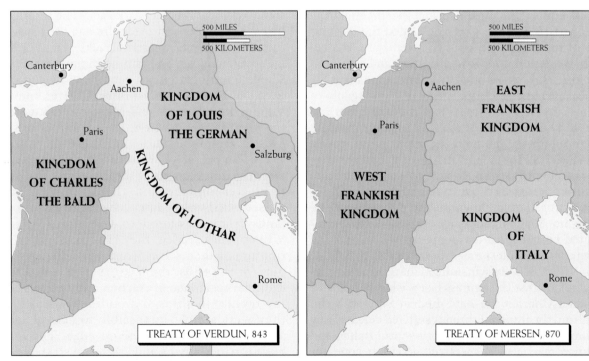

MAP 6–5 THE TREATY OF VERDUN, 843, AND THE TREATY OF MERSEN, 870 *The Treaty of Verdun divided the kingdom of Louis the Pious among his three feuding children: Charles the Bald, Lothar, and Louis the German. After Lothar's death in 855, his lands and titles were divided among his three sons: Louis, Charles, and Lothar II. When Lothar II, who had received his father's northern kingdom, died in 870, Charles the Bald and Louis the German claimed the middle kingdom and divided it between themselves in the Treaty of Mersen.*

regained imperial dignity only stirred anew the resentments of his brothers, including his stepbrother, Charles, who joined in renewed warfare against him.

THE TREATY OF VERDUN AND ITS AFTERMATH   In 843, with the Treaty of Verdun, peace finally came to the surviving heirs of Louis the Pious. (Pepin had died in 838.) But this agreement also brought about the disaster that Louis had originally feared. The great Carolingian Empire was partitioned into three equal parts. Lothar received a middle section, known as Lotharingia, which embraced roughly modern Holland, Belgium, Switzerland, Alsace–Lorraine, and Italy. Charles the Bald acquired the western part of the kingdom, or roughly modern France. And Louis the German took the eastern part, or roughly modern Germany. (See Map 6–5.)

Although Lothar retained the imperial title, the universal empire of Charlemagne and Louis the Pious ceased to exist after Verdun. Not until the sixteenth century, with the election in 1519 of Charles I of Spain as Holy Roman Emperor Charles V (see Chapter 11), would the Western world again see a kingdom so vast as Charlemagne's.

The Treaty of Verdun proved to be only the beginning of Carolingian fragmentation. When Lothar died in 855, his middle kingdom was divided equally among his three surviving sons, the eldest of whom, Louis II, retained Italy and the imperial title. This partition of the partition sealed the dissolution of the great empire of Charlemagne. Henceforth, western Europe saw an eastern and a western Frankish kingdom—roughly Germany and France—at war over the fractionalized middle kingdom, a contest that has continued into modern times.

In Italy the demise of the Carolingian emperors enhanced for the moment the power of the popes, who had become adept at filling vacuums. The popes were now strong enough to excommunicate weak emperors and override their wishes. In a major church crackdown on the polygyny of the Germans, Pope Nicholas I (r. 858–867) excommunicated Lothar II for divorcing his wife. After the death of the childless emperor Louis II in 875, Pope John VIII (r. 872–882) installed Charles the Bald as emperor against the express last wishes of Louis II.

When Charles the Bald died in 877, both the papal and the imperial thrones suffered defeat. They became pawns in the hands of powerful Italian and German magnates, respectively. Neither pope nor emperor knew dignity and power again until a new western imperial dynasty—the Saxons—attained dominance during the reign of Otto I (r. 962–973).

It is especially at this juncture in European history—the last quarter of the ninth and the first half of the tenth century—that one may speak with

The Carolingian Dynasty (751–987)

750–800	Donation of Constantine protests Frankish domination of church
751	Pepin III "the Short" becomes king of the Franks
755	Franks protect church against Lombards and create the Papal States
768–814	Charlemagne rules as king of the Franks
774	Charlemagne defeats Lombards in northern Italy
800	Pope Leo III crowns Charlemagne emperor
814–840	Louis the Pious succeeds Charlemagne as emperor
843	Treaty of Verdun partitions the Carolingian Empire
870	Treaty of Mersen allows eastern and western Frankish kingdoms to absorb the fragmented middle lands
962	Saxons under Otto I firmly established as successors to Carolingians in Germany
987	Capetian dynasty succeeds Carolingian in France

some justification of a "dark age." The internal political breakdown of the empire and the papacy coincided with new barbarian attacks, set off probably by overpopulation and famine in northern Europe. The late ninth and tenth centuries saw successive waves of Normans (North-men), better known as Vikings, from Scandinavia; Magyars, or Hungarians, the great horsemen from the eastern plains; and Muslims from the south. (See Map 6–6.)

For the people of western Europe, the Vikings were the most serious of these threats. They came in greater numbers and, thanks to their unsurpassed skills as seamen, swept over European lands from Novgorod to Gibraltar. Wherever Viking tribes settled, they brought conflict, warring among themselves when not with native peoples. In the 880s, the Vikings penetrated to the imperial residence of Aachen and to Paris. Moving rapidly in ships and raiding coastal towns, they were almost impossible to defend against and kept western Europe on edge. The Franks built fortified towns and castles in strategic locations, which served as refuges. When they could, they bought off the invaders with outright grants of land (for example, Normandy) and payments of silver. In the resulting political and social turmoil, local populations became more dependent than ever before on local strongmen for life, limb, and livelihood. This brutal reality provided the essential conditions for the maturation of feudal society in western Europe.

Feudal Society

The Middle Ages were characterized by a chronic absence of effective central government and the constant threat of famine, disease, and foreign invasion. In this state of affairs the weaker sought the protection of the stronger, and the true lords and masters became those who could guarantee immediate security from rapine and starvation. The term "feudal society" refers to the social, political, military, and economic system that emerged from these conditions.

The feudal society of the Middle Ages was a society dominated by warlords. What people needed most was the firm assurance that others could be depended on in time of dire need. Lesser men pledged themselves to powerful individuals— warlords or princes—recognizing them as personal superiors and promising them faithful service. Large

warrior groups of vassals sprang up and ultimately developed into a prominent professional military class with its own code of knightly conduct. The result was a network of relationships based on mutual loyalty that enabled warlords to acquire armies and to rule over territory, whether or not they owned land or had a legitimating royal title. The emergence of these extensive military organizations—warlords and their groups of professional military vassals—was an adaptation to the absence of strong central government and the predominance of a noncommercial, rural economy.

Origins

Following the modern authority on the subject, the late French historian Marc Bloch, historians distinguish the cruder forms of feudal government that evolved during the early Middle Ages from the sophisticated institutional arrangements by which princes and kings consolidated their territories and established royal rule during the High Middle Ages (the so-called second feudal age).

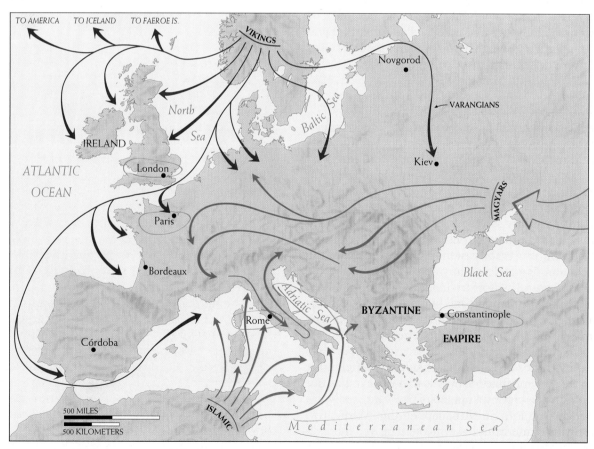

MAP 6–6   VIKING, ISLAMIC, AND MAGYAR INVASIONS TO THE ELEVENTH CENTURY   *Western Europe was sorely beset by new waves of outsiders from the ninth to the eleventh century. From north, east, and south, a stream of invading Vikings, Magyars, and Muslims brought the West at times to near collapse and, of course, gravely affected institutions within Europe.*

The origins of feudal government can be found in the divisions and conflicts of Merovingian society. In the sixth and seventh centuries it became customary for individual freemen who did not already belong to families or groups that could protect them to place themselves under the protection of more powerful freemen. In this way the latter built up armies and became local magnates, and the former solved the problem of simple survival. Freemen who so entrusted themselves to others were known as *ingenui in obsequio*, or "freemen in a contractual relation of dependence." Those who gave themselves to the king in this way were called *antrustiones*. All men of this type came to be described collectively as *vassi* or "those who serve," from which evolved the term *vassalage*, meaning the placement of oneself in the personal service of another who promises protection in return.

Landed nobles, like kings, tried to acquire as many such vassals as they could, because military strength in the early Middle Ages lay in numbers. Because it proved impossible to maintain these growing armies within the lord's own household (as was the original custom) or to support them by special monetary payments, the practice evolved of simply granting them land as a "tenement." Vassals were expected to dwell on these *benefices*, or *fiefs*, and maintain horses and other accouterments of war in good order. Originally, vassals therefore were little more than gangs-in-waiting.

Vassalage and the Fief

Vassalage involved "fealty" to the lord. To swear fealty was to promise to refrain from any action that might in any way threaten the lord's well-being and to perform personal services for him on his request. (See "Bishop Fulbert Describes the Obligations of Vassal and Lord.") Chief among the expected services was military duty as a mounted knight. This could involve a variety of activities: a short or long military expedition, escort duty, standing castle guard, or the placement of one's own fortress at the lord's disposal, if the vassal was of such stature as to have one. Continuous bargaining and bickering occurred over the terms of service. Limitations were placed on the number of days a lord could require services from a vassal. In France in the eleventh century, about forty days of service a year were considered sufficient. It also became possible for vassals to buy their way out of military service by a monetary payment, known as *scutage*. The lord, in turn, applied this payment to the hiring of mercenaries, who often proved more efficient than contract-conscious vassals.

Beyond his military duty, the vassal was also expected to give the lord advice when he requested it and to sit as a member of his court when the latter was in session. The vassal also owed his lord financial assistance when his lord was in obvious need or distress, for example, when he had been captured by his enemies and needed to be ransomed, or when he was outfitting himself for a crusade or a major military campaign. And gifts of money might also be expected when the lord's daughters married and his sons became knights.

Beginning with the reign of Louis the Pious (r. 814–840), bishops and abbots swore fealty to the king and received their offices from him as a benefice. The king formally "invested" these clerics in their offices during a special ceremony in which he presented them with a ring and a staff, the symbols of high spiritual office. Earlier, Louis' predecessors had confiscated church lands with only modest and belated compensation to the church in the form of a tithe required of all Frankish inhabitants. Long a sore point with the church, the

A seventh-century portrayal of a vassal, who kneels before his lord and inserts his hands between those of his lord in a gesture of mutual loyalty: the vassal promising to obey and serve his lord, the lord promising to support and protect his vassal. Spanish School (7th century). Lord and vassal, decorated page (vellum). Archivo de la Corona de Aragon, Barcelona, Spain. Index/Bridgeman Art Library

Bishop Fulbert Describes the Obligations of Vassal and Lord

Trust held the lord and vassal together. Their duties in this regard were carefully defined. Here are six general rules for vassal and lord, laid down by Bishop Fulbert of Chartres in a letter to William, Duke of Aquitaine, in 1020.

❖ *What are the respective obligations of vassal and lord? Do they seem fair for each side? Why might a vassal have more responsibilities and a lord fewer?*

He who swears fealty to his lord ought always to have these six things in memory: what is harmless, safe, honorable, useful, easy, practicable. Harmless, that is to say, that he should not injure his lord in his body; safe, that he should not injure him by betraying his secrets or the defenses upon which he relies for his safety; honorable, that he should not injure him in his possessions; easy and practicable, that that good which his lord is able to do easily he make not difficult, nor that which is practicable he make not impossible to him.

That the faithful vassal should avoid these injuries is certainly proper, but not for this alone does he deserve his holding; for it is not sufficient to abstain from evil, unless what is good is done also. It remains, therefore, that in the same six things mentioned above he should faithfully counsel and aid his lord, if he wishes to be looked upon as worthy of his benefice and to be safe concerning the fealty which he has sworn.

The lord also ought to act toward his faithful vassal reciprocally in all these things. And if he does not do this, he will be justly considered guilty of bad faith, just as the former, if he should be detected in avoiding or consenting to the avoidance of his duties, would be perfidious and perjured.

From James Harvey Robinson, ed., *Readings in European History*, Vol. 1 (Boston: Athenaeum, 1904), p. 184.

presumptuous practice of the lay investiture of the clergy provoked a serious confrontation of church and state in the late tenth and eleventh centuries. At that time, reform-minded clergy rebelled against what they then believed to be a kind of involuntary clerical vassalage. Even reform-minded clerics, however, welcomed the king's grants of land and power to the clergy.

The lord's obligations to his vassals were very specific. First, he was obligated to protect the vassal from physical harm and to stand as his advocate in public court. After fealty was sworn and homage paid, the lord provided for the vassal's physical maintenance by the bestowal of a *benefice*, or fief. The fief was simply the physical or material wherewithal to meet the vassal's military and other obligations. It could take the form of liquid wealth, as well as the more common grant of real property. There were so-called money fiefs, which empowered a vassal to receive regular payments from the lord's treasury. Such fiefs created potential conflicts because they made it possible for a nobleman in one land to acquire vassals among the nobility in another. Normally, the fief consisted of a landed estate of anywhere from a few to several thousand acres. But it could also take the form of a castle.

In Carolingian times a *benefice*, or fief, varied in size from one or more small villas to several *mansi*, agricultural holdings of twenty-five to forty-eight acres. The king's vassals are known to have received *benefices* of at least 30 and as many as 200 such *mansi*, truly a vast estate. Royal vassalage with a *benefice* understandably came to be widely sought by the highest classes of Carolingian society. As a royal policy, however, it ultimately proved deadly to the king. Although Carolingian kings jealously guarded their rights over property granted in *benefice* to vassals, resident vassals were still free to dispose of their *benefices* as they pleased. Vassals of the king, strengthened by his donations, in turn created their own vassals. These, in turn, created still further vassals of their own—vassals of vassals of vassals—in a pyramiding effect that had fragmented land and authority from the highest to the lowest levels by the late ninth century.

Fragmentation and Divided Loyalty

In addition to the fragmentation brought about by the multiplication of vassalage, effective occupation of land led gradually to claims of hereditary possession. Hereditary possession became a legally recognized principle in the ninth century and laid the basis for claims to real ownership. Fiefs given as royal donations became hereditary possessions and, with the passage of time, sometimes even the real property of the possessor.

Further, vassal engagements came to be multiplied in still another way as enterprising freemen sought to accumulate as much land as possible. One man could become a vassal to several different lords. This development led in the ninth century to the "liege lord"—that one master whom the vassal must obey even to the detriment of his other masters, should a direct conflict arise among them.

The problem of loyalty was reflected not only in the literature of the period, with its praise of the virtues of honor and fidelity, but also in the ceremonial development of the very act of "commendation" by which a freeman became a vassal. In the mid-eighth century, an "oath of fealty" highlighted the ceremony. A vassal reinforced his promise of fidelity to the lord by swearing a special oath with his hand on a sacred relic or the Bible. In the tenth and eleventh centuries, paying homage to the lord involved not only the swearing of such an oath, but also the placement of the vassal's hands between the lord's and the sealing of the ceremony with a kiss.

As the centuries passed, personal loyalty and service became quite secondary to the acquisition of property. In developments that signaled the waning of feudal society in the tenth century, the fief came to overshadow fealty, the *benefice* became more important than vassalage, and freemen proved themselves prepared to swear allegiance to the highest bidder.

Feudal arrangements nonetheless provided stability throughout the early Middle Ages and aided the difficult process of political centralization during the High Middle Ages. The genius of feudal government lay in its adaptability. Contracts of different kinds could be made with almost anybody, as circumstances required. The process embraced a wide spectrum of people, from the king at the top to the lowliest vassal in the remotest part of the kingdom. The foundations of the modern nation-state would emerge in France and England from the fine tuning of essentially feudal arrangements as kings sought to adapt their goal of centralized government to the reality of local power and control.

In Perspective

The centuries between 476 and 1000 saw both the decline of classical civilization and the birth of a new European civilization in the regions of what had been the western Roman Empire. Beginning in the fifth century, barbarian invasions separated western Europe culturally from much of its classical past. Although some important works and concepts survived from antiquity and the Christian Church preserved major features of Roman government, the West would be recovering its classical heritage for centuries in "renaissances" that stretched into the sixteenth century. Out of the mixture of barbarian and surviving or recovered classical culture, a distinct Western culture was born. Aided and abetted by the Christian Church, the Franks created a new imperial tradition and shaped basic Western political and social institutions for centuries to come.

The early Middle Ages also saw the emergence of a rift in Christendom between the Eastern and Western branches of the church. Evolving from the initial division of the Roman Empire into eastern and western parts, this rift widened, resulting in bitter conflict between popes and patriarchs.

During this period, the capital of the Byzantine Empire, Constantinople, far exceeded in population and culture any city of the West. Serving both as a buffer against Persian, Arab, and Turkish invasions of the West and as a major repository of classical learning and science for western scholars, the Byzantine Empire did much to make possible the development of western Europe as a distinctive political and cultural entity. Another cultural and religious rival of the West, Islam, also saw its golden age during these same centuries. Like the Byzantine world, the Muslim world preserved ancient scholarship and, especially through Muslim Spain, provided a conduit for retransmitting it to the West. But despite examples of coexistence and even friendship, the cultures of the Western and Muslim worlds were too different and their people too estranged and suspicious of one another for them to become good neighbors.

The early Middle Ages were not centuries of great ambition in the West. It was a time when modest foundations were being laid. Despite a certain common religious culture, Western society remained primitive and fragmented, probably more so than anywhere else in the contemporary world. Two distinctive social institutions developed in response to these conditions: manorialism and feudalism. Manorialism ensured that all would be fed and cared for; feudalism provided protection from outside predators. Western people were concerned primarily to satisfy basic needs; great cultural ambition would come later.

REVIEW QUESTIONS

1. Trace the history of Christianity to the coronation of the emperor Charlemagne in 800. What distinctive features characterized the early church? What role did the church play in the world after the fall of the western Roman Empire?

2. Discuss the growth of the Frankish kingdom, including its relationship with the church, through the reign of Charlemagne. What were the characteristics of Charlemagne's rule? Why did Charlemagne encourage learning at his court? How could the Carolingian renaissance have been dangerous to Charlemagne's rule? Why did his empire break apart?

3. How and why was the history of the eastern half of the Roman empire so different from that of the western half? How would you assess the rule of Justinian over the Byzantine empire? How would you compare Justinian to Charlemagne?

4. What were the tenets of Islam, and how were the Muslims suddenly able to build an empire? Assess the importance of the Muslim invasions for the development of western Europe.

5. How and why did feudal society begin? What were the essential ingredients of feudalism? How easy do you think it would be for modern society to "slip back" into a feudal pattern?

SUGGESTED READINGS

G. BARRACLOUGH, *The Crucible of Europe: The Ninth and Tenth Centuries* (1976). Sweeping survey of political history.

R. BARTLETT, *Trial by Fire and Water: The Medieval Judicial Ordeal* (1986). Makes sense of these seemingly bizarre ways of letting God decide guilt or innocence.

M. BLOCH, *Feudal Society*, vols. 1 and 2, trans. by L. A. Manyon (1971). A classic on the topic and an example of historical study.

P. BROWN, *Augustine of Hippo: A Biography* (1967). Late antiquity seen through the biography of its greatest Christian thinker.

H. CHADWICK, *The Early Church* (1967). Among the best treatments of early Christianity.

R. H. C. DAVIS, *A History of Medieval Europe: From Constantine to St. Louis* (1972). Unsurpassed in clarity.

K. F. DREW (ED.), *The Barbarian Invasions: Catalyst of a New Order* (1970). Collection of essays that focuses the issues.

G. DUBY, *The Early Growth of the European Economy: Warriors and Peasants from the Seventh to the Twelfth Century* (1974). Readable, authoritative account of rural society.

H. FICHTENAU, *The Carolingian Empire: The Age of Charlemagne*, trans. by Peter Munz (1964). Strongest on political history of the era.

J. V. A. FINE, *The Early Medieval Balkans: Sixth–Twelfth Centuries* (1983). Insight into the ethnic divisions that form the background to modern conflict in the region.

F. L. GANSHOF, *Feudalism*, trans. by Philip Grierson (1964). The most profound brief analysis of the subject.

R. HODGES AND D. WHITEHOUSE, *Mohammed, Charlemagne and the Origins of Europe* (1982). Account of the social and economic history of early medieval Europe.

A. HOURANI, *A History of the Arab Peoples* (1991). A comprehensive text that includes an excellent overview of the origins and early history of Islam.

D. KNOWLES, *Christian Monasticism* (1969). Sweeping survey with helpful photographs.

M. L. W. LAISTNER, *Thought and Letters in Western Europe, 500 to 900* (1957). Among the best surveys of early medieval intellectual history.

J. LECLERCQ, *The Love of Learning and the Desire for God: A Study of Monastic Culture*, trans. by Catherine Misrahi (1962). Lucid, delightful, absorbing account of the ideals of monks.

B. LEWIS, *The Muslim Discovery of Europe* (1982). Authoritative account from the Muslim perspective.

C. MANGO, *Byzantium: The Empire of New Rome* (1980). Perhaps the most readable account of the subject.

R. MCKITTERICK, *The Frankish Kingdoms under the Carolingians, 751–987* (1983). The fate of Carolingian government.

P. MUNZ, *The Age of Charlemagne* (1971). Penetrating social history of the period.

S. RUNCIMAN, *Byzantine Civilization* (1970). Succinct, comprehensive account by a master.

P. SAWYER, *The Age of the Vikings* (1962). Among the best accounts.

R. W. SOUTHERN, *The Making of the Middle Ages* (1973). Originally published in 1953, but still a fresh account by an imaginative historian.

C. STEPHENSON, *Medieval Feudalism* (1969). Excellent short summary and introduction.

A. A. VASILIEV, *History of the Byzantine Empire 324–1453* (1952). The most comprehensive treatment in English.

W. WALTHER, *Woman in Islam* (1981). One hour spent with this book teaches more about the social import of Islam than days spent with others.

S. WEMPLE, *Women in Frankish Society: Marriage and the Cloister 500–900* (1981). What marriage and the cloister meant to women in these early centuries.

L. WHITE, JR., *Medieval Technology and Social Change* (1962). Often fascinating account of the way primitive technology changed life.

Chapter 7

The central nave of the Romanesque abbey of St. Faith (Foy) in Conques, France, where the female saint's relics lie. Roasted alive and beheaded in the third century Gaul, she became widely revered in France, England, Italy, and Spain, and was later a popular South American saint. The interior of the abbey reveals bulky and tightly built pillars, uniform rounded arches, and the restricted lighting that are characteristic of classic Romanesque architecture. Compare and contrast the abbey of St. Faith with the Gothic cathedral of Salisbury, England on pages 248–249. Scala/Art Resource, N.Y.

The High Middle Ages:
The Rise of European Empires and States (1000–1300)

KEY TOPICS

- The revival of the Holy Roman Empire by a new German dynasty, the Saxons

- The emergence of a great reform movement in the church and the church's successful challenge to political domination by kings and emperors

- The development of strong national monarchies in England and France

- The fragmentation of Germany in the wake of a centuries-long struggle between the emperors of the Hohenstaufen dynasty and the papacy

The High Middle Ages mark a period of political expansion and consolidation and of intellectual flowering and synthesis. The noted medievalist Joseph Strayer called it the age that saw "the full development of all the potentialities of medieval civilization."[1] Some even argue that as far as the development of Western institutions is concerned, this was a more creative period than the later Italian Renaissance and the German Reformation.

The High Middle Ages saw the borders of western Europe largely secured against foreign invaders. Although intermittent Muslim aggression continued well into the sixteenth century, fear of assault from without diminished. On the contrary, a striking change occurred during the late eleventh century and the twelfth century: western Europe, which had for so long been the prey of foreign powers, became, through the Crusades and foreign trade, the feared hunter within both the eastern Byzantine world and the Muslim world.

[1]*Western History in the Middle Ages—A Short History* (New York: Appleton-Century-Crofts, 1955), pp. 9, 127.

During the High Middle Ages, "national" monarchies emerged. Rulers in England and France successfully adapted feudal principles of government to create newly centralized political realms. At the same time, parliaments and popular assemblies emerged to secure the rights and customs of the privileged many—the nobility, the clergy, and propertied townspeople—against the desires of kings. In the process, the foundations of modern European states were laid. The Holy Roman Empire, however, proved the great exception to this centralizing trend: Despite a revival of the empire under the Ottonians (Otto I, the most powerful member of the Saxon imperial dynasty, and his immediate successors, Otto II and Otto III), the events of these centuries left it weak and fragmented until modern times.

The High Middle Ages also saw the Latin, or Western, church establish itself in concept and law as a spiritual authority independent of monarchical secular government, thus sowing the seeds of the distinctive Western separation of church and state. During the Investiture Controversy, the confrontation between popes and emperors that began in the late eleventh century and lasted through the twelfth, a reformed papacy overcame its long subservience to the Carolingian and Ottonian kings. In this struggle over the authority of rulers to designate bishops and other high clergy and to invest them with their symbols of authority, the papacy, under Gregory II and his immediate successors, won out. It did so, however, by becoming itself a monarchy among the world's emerging monarchies, preparing the way for still more dangerous confrontations between popes and emperors in the later Middle Ages. Some religious reformers later saw in the Gregorian papacy of the High Middle Ages the fall of the church from its spiritual mission as well as a declaration of its independence from secular power.

Otto I and the Revival of the Empire

The fortunes of both the old empire and the papacy began to revive after the dark period of the late ninth century and the early tenth century. In 918 the Saxon Henry I ("the Fowler," d. 936), the strongest of the German dukes, became the first non-Frankish king of Germany.

Unifying Germany

Henry rebuilt royal power by forcibly combining the duchies of Swabia, Bavaria, Saxony, Franconia, and Lotharingia. He secured imperial borders by checking the invasions of the Hungarians and the

Danes. Although much smaller than Charlemagne's empire, the German kingdom Henry created placed his son and successor Otto I (r. 936–973) in a strong territorial position.

The very able Otto maneuvered his own kin into positions of power in Bavaria, Swabia, and Franconia. He refused to recognize each duchy as an independent hereditary entity, as the nobility increasingly expected, dealing with each instead as a subordinate member of a unified kingdom. In a truly imperial gesture in 951, he invaded Italy and proclaimed himself its king. In 955 he won his most magnificent victory when he defeated the Hungarians at Lechfeld. This victory secured German borders against new barbarian attack, further unified the German duchies, and earned Otto the well-deserved title "the Great." In defining the boundaries of western Europe, Otto's conquest was comparable with Charles Martel's earlier triumph over the Saracens at Poitiers in 732.

Embracing the Church

As part of a careful rebuilding program, Otto, following the example of his predecessors, enlisted the church. Bishops and abbots—men who possessed a sense of universal empire, yet because they did not marry, could not found competitive dynasties—were made royal princes and agents of the king. Because these clergy, as royal bureaucrats, received great land holdings and immunity from local counts and dukes, they also found such vassalage to the king very attractive. The medieval church did not become a great territorial power reluctantly. It appreciated the blessings of receiving, while teaching the blessedness of giving.

In 961 Otto, who had long aspired to the imperial crown, responded to a call for help from Pope John XII (955–964), who was then being bullied by an Italian enemy of the German king, Berengar of Friuli. In recompense for this rescue, Pope John crowned Otto emperor on February 2, 962. Otto, for his part, recognized the existence of the Papal States and proclaimed himself their special protector. The church was now more than ever under royal control. Its bishops and abbots were Otto's appointees and bureaucrats, and the pope reigned in Rome only by the power of the emperor's sword.

Pope John, belatedly recognizing the royal web in which the church had become entangled, joined in Italian opposition to the new emperor. This turnabout brought Otto's swift revenge. An ecclesiastical synod over which Otto presided deposed Pope John and proclaimed that henceforth no pope could take office without first swearing an oath of allegiance to the emperor. Under Otto I, popes ruled at the emperor's pleasure.

As these events reflect, Otto had shifted the royal focus from Germany to Italy. His successors—Otto II (r. 973–983) and Otto III (r. 983–1002)—became so preoccupied with running the affairs of Italy that their German base began to disintegrate, sacrificed to imperial dreams. They might have learned a lesson from the contemporary Capetian kings, the successor dynasty to the Carolingians in France. These kings, perhaps more by circumstance than by design, pursued a very different course than the Ottonians. They mended local fences and concentrated their limited resources to secure a tight grip on their immediate royal domain, never neglecting it for the sake of foreign adventure.

The Ottonians, in contrast, reached far beyond their grasp when they tried to subdue Italy. As the briefly revived empire began to crumble in the first quarter of the eleventh century, the church, long unhappy with Carolingian and Ottonian domination, prepared to declare its independence and exact its own vengeance.

The Reviving Catholic Church

During the late ninth and early tenth centuries the clergy had become tools of kings and magnates and the papacy a toy of Italian nobles. The Ottonians made bishops their servile princes and likewise dominated the papacy. The church was about to gain renewed respect and authority, however, thanks not only to the failing fortunes of the overextended empire, but also to a new, determined force for reform within the church itself.

The Cluny Reform Movement

The great monastery in Cluny in east-central France gave birth to a monastic reform movement that progressively won the support of secular lords and German kings. In doing so, this movement enabled the church to challenge its domination by royal authority at both the episcopal and papal levels.

The reformers of Cluny were aided by widespread popular respect for the church that found expression in lay religious fervor and generous baronial patronage of religious houses. One reason so many people admired clerics and monks was that the church was medieval society's most democratic institution as far as lay participation was concerned. In the Middle Ages any man could theoretically rise to the position of pope, who was supposed to be elected by "the people and the clergy." All people were candidates for the church's grace and salvation. The church promised a better life to come to the great mass of ordinary people, who found the present one brutish and without hope.

Benedictine monks at choir. The reform movement that began at the Benedictine monastery at Cluny in northern France in the tenth century spread throughout the church and was ultimately responsible for the reassertion of papal authority. Courtesy of the Trustees of the British Library

Since the fall of the Roman Empire, popular support for the church had been especially inspired by the example set by monks. Monasteries provided an important alternative way of life for the religiously earnest in an age when most people had very few options. Monks remained the least secularized and most spiritual of the church's clergy. Their cultural achievements were widely admired, their relics and rituals were considered magical, and their high religious ideals and sacrifices were imitated by the laity.

The tenth and eleventh centuries saw an unprecedented boom in the construction of monasteries. William the Pious, duke of Aquitaine, founded Cluny in 910. It was a Benedictine monastery devoted to the strictest observance of Saint Benedict's *Rule for Monasteries*, with a special emphasis on liturgical purity. Although the reformers who emerged at Cluny were loosely organized and their demands not always consistent, they shared a determination to maintain a spiritual church. They absolutely rejected the subservience of the clergy, especially that of the German bishops, to royal authority. They taught that the pope in Rome was sole ruler over all the clergy.

No local secular rulers, the Cluniacs asserted, could have any control over their monasteries. They further denounced the transgression of ascetic piety by "secular" parish clergy, who maintained concubines in a relationship akin to marriage. (Later a distinction would be formalized between the *secular* clergy, who lived and ministered in the world [*saeculum*] and the *regular* clergy, monks and nuns withdrawn from the world and living according to a special rule [*regula*].)

The Cluny reformers resolved to free the clergy from both kings and "wives"—to create an independent and chaste clergy. The church alone was to be the clergy's lord and spouse. Thus, the distinctive Western separation of church and state and the celibacy of the Catholic clergy, both of which continue today, had their definitive origins in the Cluny reform movement.

Cluny rapidly became a center from which reformers were dispatched to other monasteries throughout France and Italy. Under its aggressive abbots, especially Saint Odo (r. 926–946), it grew to embrace almost 1,500 dependent cloisters, each devoted to monastic and church reform. In the latter half of the eleventh century, the Cluny reformers reached the summit of their influence when the papacy itself embraced their reform program.

The proclamation of a series of church decrees called the Peace of God in the late ninth and early tenth centuries reflected the influence of the Cluny movement. Emerging from a cooperative venture between the clergy and the higher nobility, these decrees tried to lessen the endemic warfare of medieval society by threatening excommunication for all who, at any time, harmed members of such vulnerable groups as women, peasants, merchants, and the clergy. The Peace of God was subsequently reinforced by the Truce of God, a church order proclaiming that all men must abstain from every form of violence and warfare during a certain part of each week (eventually from Wednesday night to Monday morning) and in all holy seasons.

Popes devoted to reforms like those urged by Cluny came to power during the reign of Emperor Henry III (r. 1039–1056). Pope Leo IX (r. 1049–1054) promoted regional synods to oppose simony (the selling of spiritual things, especially as church offices) and clerical marriage (celibacy was not strictly enforced among the secular clergy until after the eleventh century). He also placed Cluniacs in key administrative posts in Rome. Imperial influence over the papacy, however,

was still strong during Henry III's reign and provided a counterweight to the great aristocratic families that manipulated the elections of popes for their own gain. Before Leo IX's papacy, Henry had deposed three such popes, each a pawn of a Roman noble faction, and had installed a German bishop of his own choosing who ruled as Pope Clement II (r. 1046–1047).

Such high-handed practices ended soon after Henry III's death. During the turbulent minority of his successor, Henry IV (r. 1056–1106), reform popes began to assert themselves more openly. Pope Stephen IX (1057–1058) reigned without imperial ratification, contrary to the earlier declaration of Otto I. To prevent local factional control of papal elections, Pope Nicholas II (1059–1061) decreed in 1059 that a body of high church officials and advisers known as the College of Cardinals would henceforth choose the pope, establishing the procedures for papal succession that the Catholic Church still follows. With this action, the papacy declared its full independence from both local Italian and distant royal interference. Rulers continued nevertheless to have considerable indirect influence on the election of popes.

Pope Nicholas II also embraced Cluny's strictures against simony and clerical concubinage and even struck his own political alliances with the Normans in Sicily and with France and Tuscany. His successor, Pope Alexander II (r. 1061–1073), was elected solely by the College of Cardinals, although not without a struggle.

The Investiture Struggle: Gregory VII and Henry IV

Alexander's successor was Pope Gregory VII (r. 1073–1085), a fierce advocate of Cluny's reforms who had entered the papal bureaucracy a quarter century earlier during the pontificate of Leo IX. (See "Pope Gregory VII Asserts the Power of the Pope.") It was he who put the church's declaration of independence to the test. Cluniacs had repeatedly inveighed against simony. Cardinal Humbert, a prominent reformer, argued that lay investiture of the clergy—that is, the appointment of bishops and other church officials by secular officials and rulers—was the worst form of this evil practice. In 1075 Pope Gregory embraced these arguments and condemned, under penalty of excommunication, lay investiture of clergy at any level. He had primarily in mind the emperor's well-established custom of installing bishops by presenting them with the ring and staff that symbolized episcopal office.

After Gregory's ruling, emperors were no more able to install bishops than they were to install popes. As popes were elected by the College of Cardinals and were not raised up by kings or nobles,

Pope Gregory VII Asserts the Power of the Pope

Church reformers of the high Middle Ages vigorously asserted the power of the pope within the church and his rights against emperors and all others who might encroach on the papal sphere of jurisdiction. Here is a statement of the basic principles of the Gregorian reformers, known as the **Dictatus Papae** *("The Sayings of the Pope"), which is attributed to Pope Gregory VII (1073–1085).*

❖ *In defining his powers as pope, on what authority does Pope Gregory base his authority? How many of his assertions are historically verifiable by actual events in church history? Can any of them be illustrated from Chapters 6 and 7? Compare Gregory's statements on papal power with those of Marsilius of Padua on pp. 307.*

That the Roman Church was founded by God alone.

That the Roman Pontiff alone is rightly to be called universal.

That the Pope may depose the absent.

That for him alone it is lawful to enact new laws according to the needs of the time, to assemble together new congregations, to make an abbey of a canonry; and...to divide a rich bishopric and unite the poor ones.

That he alone may use the imperial insignia.

That the Pope is the only one whose feet are to be kissed by all princes.

That his name alone is to be recited in churches.

That his title is unique in the world.

That he may depose emperors.

That he may transfer bishops, if necessary, from one See to another.

That no synod may be called a general one without his order.

That no chapter or book may be regarded as canonical without his authority.

That no sentence of his may be retracted by any one; and that he, alone of all, can retract it.

That he himself may be judged by no one.

That the Roman Church has never erred, nor ever, by the witness of Scripture, shall err to all eternity.

That the Pope may absolve subjects of unjust men from their fealty.

From *Church and State through the Centuries: A Collection of Historic Documents*, trans. and ed. by S. Z. Ehler and John B. Morrall (New York: Biblo and Tannen, 1967), pp. 43–44. Reprinted by permission of Biblio–Moser Book Publishers.

so bishops would henceforth be installed in their offices by high ecclesiastical authority empowered by the pope. The spiritual origins and allegiance of episcopal office would thereby be made clear.

Gregory's prohibition came as a jolt to royal authority. Since the days of Charlemagne, emperors had routinely passed out bishoprics to favored clergy. Bishops, who received royal estates, were the emperors' appointees and servants of the state. Henry IV's Carolingian and Ottonian predecessors had carefully nurtured the theocratic character of the empire in both concept and administrative bureaucracy. The church and religion had become integral parts of government.

Now the emperor, Henry IV, suddenly found himself ordered to secularize the empire by drawing a distinct line between the spheres of temporal and spiritual—royal and ecclesiastical—authority and jurisdiction. But if his key administrators were no longer to be his own carefully chosen and sworn servants, then was not his kingdom in jeopardy? Henry considered Gregory's action a direct challenge to his authority. The territorial princes, on the other hand,

ever tending away from the center and eager to see the emperor weakened, were quick to see the advantages of Gregory's ruling. If a weak emperor could not gain a bishop's ear, then a strong prince might, thus bringing the offices of the church into his orbit of power. In the hope of gaining an advantage over both the emperor and the clergy in their territory, the princes fully supported Gregory's edict.

The lines of battle were quickly drawn. Henry assembled his loyal German bishops at Worms in January 1076 and had them proclaim their independence from Gregory. Gregory promptly responded with the church's heavy artillery: He excommunicated Henry and absolved all Henry's subjects from loyalty to him. This turn of events delighted the German princes, and Henry found himself facing a general revolt led by the duchy of Saxony. He had no recourse but to come to terms with Gregory. In a famous scene, Henry prostrated himself outside Gregory's castle retreat at Canossa on January 25, 1077. There he reportedly stood barefoot in the snow off and on for three days before the pope agreed to absolve him.

A twelfth-century German manuscript portrays the struggle between Emperor Henry IV and Pope Gregory VII. In the top panel, Henry installs the puppet pope Clement III and drives Gregory from Rome. Below, Gregory dies in exile. The artist was a monk; his sympathies were with Gregory, not Henry.
Thuringer Universitäts- und Landesbibliothek Jena: Ms. Bos. q. 6, Blatt 79r.

Papal power had at this moment reached a pinnacle (it would attain even greater heights during the papacy of Innocent III [r. 1198–1216], who also had rulers at his mercy). But such peaks must also be descended. Gregory's power, as he must have known when he restored Henry to power, was soon to be challenged.

Henry regrouped his forces, regained much of his power within the empire, and soon acted as if the humiliation at Canossa had never occurred. In March 1080 Gregory excommunicated Henry once again, but this time the action was ineffectual. (Historically, repeated excommunications of the same individual have proved to have diminishing returns.) In 1084 Henry, absolutely dominant, installed his own antipope, Clement III, and forced Gregory into exile, where he died the following year. It appeared as if the old practice of kings controlling popes had been restored—with a vengeance. Clement, however, was never recognized within the church, and Gregory's followers, who retained wide popular support, regained power during the pontificates of Victor III (r. 1086–1087) and Urban II (r. 1088–1099).

The settlement of the investiture controversy came in 1122 with the Concordat of Worms. Emperor Henry V (r. 1106–1125), having early abandoned his predecessors' practice of nominating popes and raising up antipopes, formally renounced his power to invest bishops with ring and staff. In exchange, Pope Calixtus II (r. 1119–1124) recognized the emperor's right to be present and to invest bishops with fiefs before and after their investment with ring and staff by the church. The old church–state "back-scratching" in this way continued, but now on very different terms. The clergy received their offices and attendant religious powers solely from ecclesiastical authority and no longer from kings and emperors. Rulers continued to bestow lands and worldly goods on high clergy in the hope of influencing them. The Concordat of Worms thus made the clergy more independent, but not necessarily less worldly.

The Gregorian party may have won the independence of the clergy, but the price it paid was to encourage division among the feudal forces within the empire. The pope made himself strong by making imperial authority weak. In the end, those who profited most from the investiture controversy were the German princes.

The new Gregorian fence between temporal and spiritual power did not prevent kings and popes from being good neighbors if each was willing. Succeeding centuries, however, proved that the aspirations of kings were too often in conflict with those of popes for peaceful coexistence to endure. The most bitter clash between church and state was still to come. It would occur during the late thirteenth century and early fourteenth century in the confrontation between Pope Boniface VIII and King Philip IV of France. (See Chapter 9.)

The First Crusades

If an index of popular piety and support for the pope in the High Middle Ages is needed, the Crusades amply provide it. What the Cluny reform was to the clergy, the first Crusades to the Holy Land were to the laity: an outlet for the heightened religious zeal of the late eleventh and twelfth centuries, Europe's most religious period before the Protestant Reformation.

Late in the eleventh century, the Byzantine Empire was under severe pressure from the Seljuk Turks, and the eastern emperor, Alexius I Comnenus, appealed for Western aid. At the Council of Clermont in 1095, Pope Urban II responded positively to this appeal, setting the First Crusade in motion. (See "Pope Urban II [r. 1088–1099] Preaches the First Crusade.") This event has puzzled some historians, because the First Crusade was a risky venture. But the pope, the nobility, and western society at large had much to gain by removing large numbers of nobility temporarily from Europe. Too many idle, restless noble youths were spending a great part of their lives feuding with each other and raiding other people's land. The pope recognized that peace and tranquility might be gained at home by sending factious aristocrats abroad with their accouterments of war (100,000 went with the First Crusade). And the nobility recognized that there were fortunes to be made in foreign wars. This was especially true of the younger sons of noblemen, who, in an age of growing population and shrinking landed wealth, saw the Crusades as an opportunity to become landowners. Pope Urban may also have envisioned the Crusade leading to a reconciliation and possible reunion with the Eastern Church.

Religion was not the only motive inspiring the Crusaders; hot blood and greed were equally influential. But unlike the later Crusades, undertaken for patently mercenary reasons, the early Crusades were to a very high degree inspired by genuine religious piety and were carefully orchestrated by the revived papacy. Popes promised participants in the First Crusade a plenary indulgence should they die in battle, that is, a complete remission of any outstanding temporal punishment for their unrepented mortal sins and hence release from suffering for them in purgatory. In addition to this direct spiritual reward, the Crusaders were also impelled by their enthusiasm for a Holy War against the hated infidel and the romance of a pilgrimage to the Holy Land. All these elements combined to make the First Crusade a rousing success, at least from the Christian point of view.

With the journeys to Jerusalem came a cleansing of European Christendom en route that would inten-

sify in the thirteenth century under Pope Innocent III and the new mendicant orders of Dominicans and Franciscans. Jewish communities along the Crusaders' routes, particularly in the lands along the Rhine, became the objects of pogroms, as Christian knights attempted to rid Europe of Jews as well as Muslims.

THE FIRST VICTORY   The eastern emperor welcomed any aid against advancing Islamic armies. The Crusaders did not, however, assemble to defend Europe's borders against aggression. They freely took the offensive to rescue the holy city of Jerusalem, which had been in non-Christian hands since the seventh century, from the Seljuk Turks. To this end, three great armies—tens of thousands of Crusaders—gathered in France, Germany, and Italy. Following different routes, they reassembled in Constantinople in 1097. (See Map 7–1.)

The convergence of these spirited soldiers on the eastern capital was a cultural shock that only deepened antipathy toward the West. The eastern emperor suspected their true motives, and the common people, whom they pillaged and suppressed, hardly considered them Christian brothers in a common cause. Nonetheless these fanatical Crusaders accomplished what no eastern army had been able to do. They soundly defeated one Seljuk army after another in a steady advance toward Jerusalem, which fell to them on July 15, 1099. The Crusaders' success resulted from their superior military discipline and weaponry. It also helped that they had descended upon a politically divided and factious Islamic world that initially lacked the unity to organize an effective resistance.

The victorious Crusaders divided the conquered territory into the feudal states of Jerusalem, Edessa, and Antioch, which they held as alleged fiefs from the pope. Godfrey of Bouillon, leader of the French–German army (and after him, his brother Baldwin), ruled over the kingdom of Jerusalem. The Crusaders, however, remained only small islands within a great sea of Muslims, who looked on the Western invaders as hardly more than savages. And once settled in the Holy Land, the Crusaders found themselves increasingly on the defensive. Now an occupying rather than a conquering army, they became obsessed with fortifying their position. They built castles throughout the Holy Land, the ruins of many of which are still visible today.

Once secure within their castle enclaves, the Crusaders ceased to live off the land, as they had done since leaving Europe, and relied more and more on imports from home. The once fierce warriors became international businesspeople as they developed the economic resources of their new possessions. The Knights Templars, originally a military–religious order, became castle stewards and escorts of Western

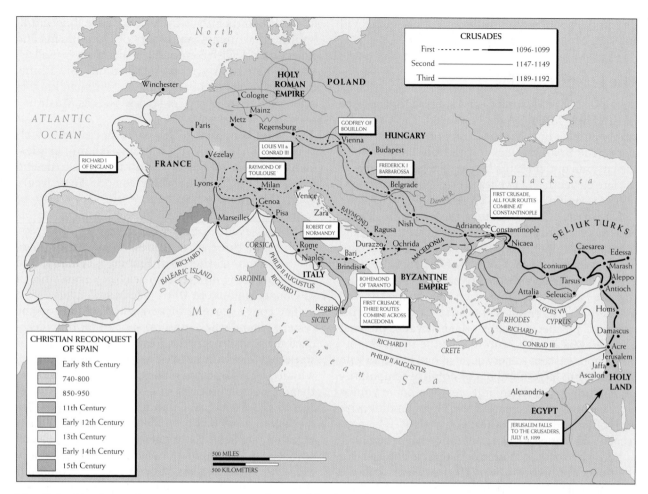

MAP 7–1   THE EARLY CRUSADES   *Routes and several leaders of the Crusades during the first century of the move-*
ment are shown. The names on this map do not exhaust the list of great nobles who went on the First Crusade. The
even showier array of monarchs of the Second and Third Crusades still left the Crusades, on balance, ineffective in
achieving their goals.

pilgrims to and from the Holy Land, in the process accumulating great wealth and becoming important bankers and moneylenders.

THE SECOND CRUSADE   Native resistance finally broke the Crusaders around midcentury, and the forty-odd-year Latin presence in the East began to crumble. Edessa fell to Islamic armies in 1144. A Second Crusade, preached by the eminent Bernard of Clairvaux (1091–1153), Christendom's most powerful monastic leader, attempted a rescue, but it met with dismal failure. In October 1187, Saladin (r. 1138–1193), king of Egypt and Syria, reconquered Jerusalem itself. Save for a brief interlude in the thirteenth century, it remained thereafter in Islamic hands until modern times.

THE THIRD CRUSADE   A Third Crusade in the twelfth century (1189–1192) attempted yet another rescue, enlisting as its leaders the most powerful western rulers: Emperor Frederick Barbarossa; Richard the

Lion-Hearted, king of England; and Philip Augustus, king of France. But the Third Crusade proved a tragicomic commentary on the passing of the original crusading spirit. Frederick Barbarossa accidentally drowned while fording the Saleph River, a small stream, near the end of his journey across Asia Minor. Richard the Lion-Hearted and Philip Augustus reached the outskirts of Jerusalem, but their intense personal rivalry shattered the Crusaders' unity and chances of victory. Philip Augustus returned to France and made war on Richard's continental territories. Richard fell captive to the Emperor Henry VI as he was returning to England. (Henry VI suspected Richard of plotting against him with Henry's mortal enemy, Henry the Lion, the duke of Saxony, who happened also to be Richard's brother-in-law.)

The English paid a handsome ransom for their adventurous king's release. Popular resentment of taxes levied for this ransom became part of the background of the revolt against the English monarchy

Pope Urban II (r. 1088–1099) Preaches the First Crusade

When Pope Urban II summoned the First Crusade in a sermon at the Council of Clermont on November 26, 1095, he painted a most savage picture of the Muslims who controlled Jerusalem. Urban also promised the Crusaders, who responded by the tens of thousands, remission of their unrepented sins and assurance of heaven. Robert the Monk is one of four witnesses who has left us a summary of the sermon.

❖ *Is the pope engaging in a propaganda and smear campaign? What are the images he creates of the enemy and how accurate and fair are they? Did the Christian Church have a greater claim to Jerusalem than the people then living there? Does a religious connection with the past entitle one group to confiscate the land of another?*

From the confines of Jerusalem and the city of Constantinople a horrible tale has gone forth and very frequently has been brought to our ears, namely, that a race from the kingdom of the Persians [that is, the Seljuk Turks], an accursed race, a race utterly alienated from God, a generation forsooth which has not directed its heart and has not entrusted its spirit to God, has invaded the lands of those Christians and has depopulated them by the sword, pillage and fire; it has led away a part of the captives into its own country, and a part it has destroyed by cruel tortures; it has either entirely destroyed the churches of God or appropriated them for the rites of its own religion. They destroy the altars, after having defiled them with their uncleanness. They circumcise the Christians, and the blood of the circumcision they either spread upon the altars or pour into the vases of the baptismal font. When they wish to torture people by a base death, they perforate their navels, and dragging forth the extremity of the intestines, bind it to a stake; then with flogging they lead the victim around until the viscera having gushed forth the victim falls prostrate upon the ground. Others they bind to a post and pierce with arrows. Others they compel to extend their necks and then, attack-

ing them with naked swords, attempt to cut through the neck with a single blow. What shall I say of the abominable rape of the women? The kingdom of the Greeks is now dismembered by them and deprived of territory so vast in extent that it can not be traversed in a march of two months. On whom therefore is the labor of avenging these wrongs and of recovering this territory incumbent, if not upon you? ...

Jerusalem is the navel of the world; the land is fruitful above others, like another paradise of delights. This the Redeemer of the human race has made illustrious by His advent, has beautified by residence, has consecrated by suffering, has redeemed by death, has glorified by burial. This royal city, therefore, situated at the centre of the world, is now held captive by His enemies, and is in subjection to those who do not know God, to the worship of the heathens. She seeks therefore and desires to be liberated, and does not cease to implore you to come to her aid. From you especially she asks succor, because, as we have already said, God has conferred upon you above all nations great glory in arms. Accordingly undertake this journey for the remission of your sins, with the assurance of the imperishable glory of the kingdom of heaven.

Translations and reprints from *Original Sources of European History*, Vol. 1 (Philadelphia: Department of History, University of Pennsylvania, 1910), pp. 5–7.

that led to the royal recognition of Magna Carta in 1215 (discussed later in the chapter).

The long-term results of the first three Crusades had little to do with their original purpose. Politically and religiously they were a failure, and the Holy Land reverted as firmly as ever to Muslim hands. The Crusades did, however, act for centuries as a safety valve for violence-prone Europe. More importantly, they stimulated Western trade with the East. The merchants of Venice, Pisa, and Genoa followed the Cru-

saders across to lucrative new markets. The need to resupply the new Christian settlements in the Near East reopened old trade routes that had long been closed by Islamic domination of the Mediterranean and established important new ones as well.

It is a commentary on both the degeneration of the original crusading ideal and the Crusaders' true historical importance that the Fourth Crusade turned into a large commercial venture manipulated by the Venetians. And wherever new trading centers sprang up along the Crusader routes, cultural as well as economic commerce occurred. Western Christians learned firsthand about Islamic culture and Muslims about the Christian West.

The Pontificate of Innocent III (r. 1198–1216)

Pope Innocent III was a papal monarch in the Gregorian tradition of papal independence from secular domination. He proclaimed and practiced as none before him the doctrine of the plenitude of papal power. In a famous statement, he likened the relationship of the pope to the emperor—or the church to the state—to that of the sun to the moon. As the moon received its light from the sun, so the emperor received his brilliance (that is, his crown) from the hand of the pope—an allusion to the famous precedent set on Christmas Day, 800, when Pope Leo III crowned Charlemagne.

Although this pretentious theory greatly exceeded Innocent's ability to practice it, he and his successors did not hesitate to act on the ambitions it reflected. When Philip II, the king of France, tried unlawfully to annul his marriage, Innocent placed France under interdict, suspending all church services save baptism and the last rites. The same punishment befell England with even greater force when King John refused to accept Innocent's nominee for archbishop of Canterbury. And as we will see later in the chapter, Innocent intervened frequently and forcefully in the affairs of the Holy Roman Empire.

THE NEW PAPAL MONARCHY Innocent made the papacy a great secular power, with financial resources and a bureaucracy equal to those of contemporary monarchs. During his reign the papacy transformed itself, in effect, into an efficient ecclesio-commercial complex, which would be attacked by reformers throughout the later Middle Ages. Innocent consolidated and expanded ecclesiastical taxes on the laity, the chief of which was "Peter's pence." In England, that tax, long a levy on all but the poorest houses, became a lump-sum payment by the English crown during Innocent's reign. Innocent also imposed an income tax of 2.5 percent on the clergy. Annates (the payment of a portion or all of the first year's income received by the holder of a new *benefice*) and fees for the *pallium* (an archbishop's symbol of office) became especially favored revenue-gathering devices.

Innocent also reserved to the pope the absolution of many sins and religious crimes, forcing those desirous of pardons or exemptions to bargain directly with Rome. It was a measure of the degree to which the papacy had embraced the new money

The crusaders capture the city of Antioch in 1098 during the First Crusade. From Le Miroir Historial *(fifteenth century) by Vincent de Beauvais.* Musée Conde Chantilly. E. T. Archive, London

economy that it employed Lombard merchants and bankers to collect the growing papal revenues.

CRUSADES IN FRANCE AND THE EAST Innocent's predilection for power politics also expressed itself in his use of the Crusade, the traditional weapon of the church against Islam, to suppress internal dissent and heresy. Heresy had grown under the influence of native religious reform movements that tried, often naïvely, to disassociate the church from the growing materialism of the age and to keep it pure of political scheming. A good deal of heresy also stemmed from anticlericalism fed by real abuses of the clergy witnessed directly by the laity, such as immorality, greed, and poor pastoral service.

The idealism of these movements was too extreme for the papacy. In 1209 Innocent launched a Crusade against the Albigensians, also known as Cathars, or "pure ones." These advocates of an ascetic, dualist religion were concentrated in the area of Albi in Languedoc in southern France, but Catharism also had adherents among the laity in Italy and Spain. The Albigensians generally sought a pure and simple religious life, following the model of the apostles of Jesus in the New Testament. They opposed Christian teaching on several points. They denied the Old Testament and its God of wrath, as well as the Christian belief in God's incarnation in Jesus Christ. They conceived of the church as an invisible, spiritual force, and resisted it as a legal, financial, and dogmatic institution.

The more radical Cathars opposed human procreation, because to reproduce corporeal bodies was to prolong the imprisonment of immortal souls in dying matter. They avoided it either through extreme sexual asceticism or the use of contraceptives (sponges and acidic ointments) and even abortion. On the other hand, the Cathars' strong dualism justified latitude in sexual behavior on the part of ordinary believers, in the belief that the flesh and the spirit were so fundamentally different that it mattered little what the former did. It was in opposition to such beliefs that the church developed its social teachings condemning contraception and abortion.

The Crusades against the Albigensians were carried out by powerful noblemen from northern France. These great magnates, led by Simon de Montfort, were as much attracted by the great wealth of the area of Languedoc as they were moved by Christian conscience to stamp out heresy. The Crusades also allowed the northerners to extend their political power into the south. They resulted in a succession of massacres and ended with a special Crusade led by King Louis VIII of France from 1225 to 1226, which destroyed the Albigensians as a political entity. Pope Gregory IX (r. 1227–1241) introduced the Inquisition into the region to complete the work of the Crusaders. This institution, a formal tribunal for the detection and punishment of heresy, had been in use by the church since the mid-twelfth century as a way for bishops to maintain diocesan discipline. During Innocent's pontificate it became centralized in the papacy. Papal legates were dispatched to chosen regions to conduct interrogations and the subsequent trials and executions.

THE FOURTH CRUSADE   It was also during Innocent's pontificate that the Fourth Crusade to the Holy Land was launched. In 1202, some 30,000 Crusaders arrived in Venice to set sail for Egypt. When they were unable to pay the price of transport, the Venetians negotiated an alternative to payment: conquest of Zara, a rival Christian port city on the Adriatic. To the shock of Pope Innocent III, the Crusaders obliged. This digression of the Crusaders from their original goal proved to be only their first. They soon besieged Constantinople itself, which was completely in Western hands by 1204.

This stunning event brought Venice new lands and maritime rights that assured its domination of the eastern Mediterranean. Constantinople now became the center for Western trade throughout the Near East. Although its capture had been an embarrassment to the pope, the papacy soon adjusted to this unforeseen turn of events and shared in the spoils. The Western church had a unique opportunity to extend its presence into the East. A confidant of Innocent's became patriarch of Constantinople and launched a mission to win the Greeks and the Slavs to the Roman Church. Western control of Constantinople continued until 1261, when the Eastern emperor Michael Paleologus, helped by the Genoese, who envied Venetian prosperity in the East, finally recaptured the city. The more than fifty-year occupation of Constantinople did nothing to heal the political and religious divisions between East and West. When Constantinople returned to eastern hands, East–West relations were at a new low.

THE FOURTH LATERAN COUNCIL   Under Innocent's direction, the Fourth Lateran Council met in 1215 to formalize church discipline throughout the hierarchy, from pope to parish priest. Many important landmarks in ecclesiastical legislation issued from this council. It gave full dogmatic sanction to the controversial doctrine of transubstantiation, according to which the bread and wine of the Lord's Supper become the true body and blood of Christ when consecrated by a priest in the sacrament of the Eucharist. This doctrine has been part of Catholic teaching ever since. It reflects the influence of the Cluniac monks and those of a new order, the Cistercians. During the twelfth century, these orders made the adoration of the Virgin Mary (the patron saint of the Cistercians) and the worship of Christ in the Eucharist the centerpieces of a reformed, christocentric piety. The doctrine of transubstantiation is an expression of the popularity of this piety. It also enhanced the power and authority of the clergy, because it specified that only they could perform the miracle of the Eucharist.

In addition, the council made annual confession and Easter communion mandatory for every adult Christian. This legislation formalized the sacrament of penance as the church's key instrument of religious education and discipline in the later Middle Ages.

FRANCISCANS AND DOMINICANS   During his reign, Pope Innocent gave official sanction to two new monastic orders: the Franciscans and the Dominicans. No other action of the pope had more of an effect on spiritual life. Unlike other regular clergy, the members of these mendicant orders, known as friars, did not confine themselves to the cloister. They went out into the world to preach the church's mission and to combat heresy, begging or working to support themselves (hence the term "mendicant").

Lay interest in spiritual devotion, especially among urban women, was particularly intense at the turn of the twelfth century. In addition to the heretical Albigensians, there were movements of Waldensians, Beguines, and Beghards, each of which stressed biblical simplicity in religion and a life of poverty in imitation of Christ. Such movements were especially active in Italy and France. Their heterodox teachings—teachings that, although not necessarily heretical, nonetheless challenged church orthodoxy—and the critical frame of mind they promoted caused the pope deep concern. Innocent feared they would inspire lay piety to turn militantly against the church. The Franciscan and Dominican orders, however, emerged from the same background of intense religiosity. By sanctioning them and thus keeping their followers within the confines of church organization, the pope provided a response to heterodox piety as well as an answer to lay criticism of the worldliness of the papal monarchy.

The Franciscan order was founded by Saint Francis of Assisi (1182–1226), the son of a rich Italian cloth merchant, who became disaffected with wealth and urged his followers to live a life of extreme poverty. Pope Innocent recognized the order in 1210, and its official rule was approved in 1223. The Dominican order, the Order of Preachers, was founded by Saint Dominic (1170–1221), a well-educated Spanish cleric, and was sanctioned in 1216. Both orders received special privileges from the pope and were solely under his jurisdiction. This special relationship with Rome gave the friars an independence from local clerical authority that bred resentment among some secular clergy.

Pope Gregory IX (r. 1227–1241) canonized Saint Francis only two years after Francis's death—a fitting honor for Francis and a stroke of genius on the part of the pope. By bringing the age's most popular religious figure, one who had even miraculously received the stigmata (bleeding wounds like those of the crucified Jesus), so emphatically within the confines of the church, he enhanced papal authority over lay piety.

Two years after the canonization, however, Gregory canceled Saint Francis's own *Testament* as an authoritative rule for the Franciscan order. He did so because he found it to be an impractical guide for the order and because the unconventional nomadic life of strict poverty it advocated conflicted with papal plans to enlist the order as an arm of church policy. (See "Saint Francis of Assisi Sets Out His Religious Ideals.") Most Franciscans themselves, under the leadership of moderates like Saint Bonaventure, general of the order between 1257 and 1274, also came to doubt the wisdom of extreme asceticism. During the thirteenth century the main branch of the order progressively complied with papal wishes. In the fourteenth century the pope condemned a radical branch, the Spiritual Franciscans, extreme followers of Saint Francis who considered him almost a new Messiah. In his condemnation, the pope declared absolute poverty a fictitious ideal that not even Christ endorsed.

The Dominicans, a less factious order, combated doctrinal error through visitations and preaching. They conformed convents of Beguines to the church's teaching, led the church's campaign against heretics in southern France, and staffed the offices of the Inquisition after its centralization by Pope Gregory IX in 1223. The great Dominican theologian Thomas Aquinas (d. 1274) was canonized in 1322. His efforts to synthesize faith and reason resulted in a definitive and enduring statement of Catholic belief. (See Chapter 8.)

The Dominicans and the Franciscans strengthened the church among the laity. Through the institution of so-called Third orders, they provided ordinary men and women the opportunity to affiliate with the monastic life and pursue the high religious ideals of poverty, obedience, and chastity, while remaining laypeople. Laity who joined such orders were known as tertiaries. Such organizations helped keep lay piety orthodox and within the church during a period of heightened religiosity.

England and France: Hastings (1066) to Bouvines (1214)

In 1066 the death of the childless Anglo–Saxon ruler Edward the Confessor (so named because of his reputation for piety) occasioned the most important change in English political life. Edward's mother was a Norman, giving the duke of Normandy a hereditary claim to the English throne. Before his death, Edward, who was not a strong ruler, acknowledged the duke's claim and even directed that his throne be given to William, the reigning duke of Normandy (d. 1087). But the Anglo–Saxon assembly, which customarily bestowed the royal power, had a mind of its own and vetoed Edward's last wishes, choosing instead Harold Godwinsson. This defiant action triggered the swift conquest of England by the powerful Normans. William's forces defeated Harold's army at Hastings on October 14, 1066. (See "How William the Conqueror Won the Battle of Hastings.") Within weeks of the invasion William was crowned king of England in Westminster Abbey, both by right of heredity and by right of conquest.

Dominicans (left), and Franciscans (right). Unlike the other religious orders, the Do-minicans and Franciscans did not live in cloisters, but wandered about preaching and combating heresy. They depended for support on their own labor and the kindness of the laity. Cliche Bibliothèque Nationale de France–Paris

William the Conqueror

Thereafter, William embarked on a twenty-year conquest that eventually made all of England his domain. Every landholder, whether large or small, was henceforth his vassal, holding land legally as a fief from the king. William organized his new English nation shrewdly. He established a strong monarchy whose power was not fragmented by independent territorial princes. He kept the Anglo–Saxon tax system and the practice of court writs (legal warnings) as a flexible form of central control over localities. And he took care not to destroy the Anglo–Saxon quasi-democratic tradition of frequent "parleying"—that is, the holding of conferences between the king and lesser powers who had vested interests in royal decisions.

The practice of parleying had been initially nurtured by Alfred the Great (r. 871–899). A strong and willful king who had forcibly unified England, Alfred cherished the advice of his councilors in the making of laws. His example was respected and emulated by Canute (r. 1016–1035), the Dane who restored order and brought unity to England after the civil wars that engulfed the land during the reign of the incompetent Ethelred II (r. 978–1016). The new Norman king, William, although he thoroughly subjugated his noble vassals to the crown, maintained the tradition of parleying by consulting with them regularly about decisions of state. The result was a unique blending of the "one" and the "many," a balance between monarchical and parliamentary elements that has ever since been a feature of English government—although the English Parliament as we know it today

did not formally develop as an institution until the late thirteenth century.

For administration and taxation purposes William commissioned a county-by-county survey of his new realm, a detailed accounting known as the *Domesday Book* (1080–1086). The title of the book may reflect the thoroughness and finality of the survey. As none would escape the doomsday judgment of God, so none was overlooked by William's assessors.

Henry II

William's son, Henry I (r. 1100–1135), died without a male heir, throwing England into virtual anarchy until the accession of Henry II (r. 1154–1189). Son of the duke of Anjou and Matilda, daughter of Henry I, Henry mounted the throne as head of the new Plantagenet dynasty, the family name of the Angevin (or Anjouan) line of kings who ruled England until the death of Richard III in 1485. Henry tried to recapture the efficiency and stability of his grandfather's regime, but in the process he steered the English monarchy rapidly toward an oppressive rule. Partly by inheritance from his father (Anjou) and partly by his marriage to Eleanor of Aquitaine (ca. 1122–1204), Henry brought to the throne greatly expanded French holdings, virtually the entire west coast of France.

The union with Eleanor created the so-called Angevin, or English–French, Empire. Eleanor married Henry while he was still the count of Anjou and not yet king of England. The marriage occurred only eight weeks after the annulment of Eleanor's fifteen-year marriage to the ascetic French king Louis VII in March

Saint Francis of Assisi Sets Out His Religious Ideals

Saint Francis of Assisi (1182–1226) was the founder of the Franciscan order of friars. The religious principles by which he required his followers to live were stated in the Rule of the Order, *which Pope Honorius III approved in 1223. The chief principle was to lead a life of poverty. The ideal of poverty caused conflict between the order and the pope, who feared that some Franciscans carried it too far.*

❖ *Can ideals be so high that they threaten the well-being of an institution? What would have happened to the church if all clergy, including the pope, had lived a life of poverty, begging, and working with their hands, as the* Rule *of Saint Francis instructs? What provisions are there in the* Rule *to assure the pope of the order's loyalty?*

This is the rule and way of living of the Minorite brothers, namely, to observe the holy Gospel of our Lord Jesus Christ, living in obedience, without personal possessions, and in chastity. Brother Francis promises obedience and reverence to our lord Pope Honorius, and to his successors who canonically enter upon their office, and to the Roman Church. And the other brothers shall be bound to obey Brother Francis and his successors.

I firmly command all the brothers by no means to receive coin or money, of themselves or through an intervening person. But for the needs of the sick and for clothing the other brothers, the ministers alone and the guardians shall provide through spiritual friends, as it may seem to them that necessity demands, according to time, place, and the coldness of the temperature. This one thing being always borne in mind, that, as has been said, they receive neither coin nor money.

Those brothers to whom God has given the ability to labor shall do so faithfully and devoutly, but in such manner that idleness, the enemy of the soul, being averted, they may not extinguish the spirit of holy prayer and devotion, to which other temporal things should be subservient. As a reward, moreover, for their labor, they may receive for themselves and their brothers the necessities of life, but not coin or money; and this humbly, as becomes the servants of God and the followers of most holy poverty.

The brothers shall appropriate nothing to themselves, neither a house, nor a place, nor anything; but as pilgrims and strangers in this world, in poverty and humility serving God, they shall confidently go seeking for alms. Nor need they be ashamed, for the Lord made Himself poor for us in this world.

From Frederic Austin Ogg, ed., *A Source Book of Mediaeval History: Documents Illustrative of European Life and Institutions from the German Invasions to the Renaissance* (New York: Telegraph Books, 1908), pp. 375–376.

1152. Although the annulment was granted on grounds of consanguinity (blood relationship), the true reason for the dissolution of the marriage was Louis's suspicion of infidelity. (According to rumor, Eleanor had been intimate with a cousin.) The annulment was very costly to Louis, who lost Aquitaine along with his wife. Eleanor and Henry had eight children, five of them sons, among them the future kings Richard the Lion-Hearted and John.

In addition to gaining control of most of the coast of France, Henry also conquered a part of Ireland and made the king of Scotland his vassal. Louis VII saw a mortal threat to France in this English expansion. He responded by adopting what came to be a permanent French policy of containment and expulsion of the English from their continental holdings in France. This policy was not finally successful until the mid-fifteenth

century, when English power on the continent collapsed after the Hundred Years' War.

Eleanor of Aquitaine and Court Culture

Eleanor of Aquitaine was a powerful influence on both politics and culture in twelfth-century France and England. She had accompanied her first husband, King Louis VII, on the Second Crusade, becoming an example for women of lesser stature, who were also then venturing in increasing numbers into war and business and other areas previously considered the province of men. After marrying Henry, she settled in Angers, the chief town of Anjou, where she sponsored troubadours and poets at her lively court. There the troubadour Bernart de Ventadorn composed in Eleanor's honor many of the most popular love songs of high medieval aristo-

The Growing Power and Influence of the Church

910	Cluny founded by William the Pious
1059	Pope Nicholas II establishes College of Cardinals
1075	Pope Gregory VII condemns lay investiture of clergy under penalty of excommunication
1076	Emperor Henry IV excommunicated by Pope Gregory VII for defying ban on lay investiture
1077	Henry IV begs for and receives papal absolution in Canossa
1084	Henry IV installs an antipope and forces Gregory VII into exile
1095	Pope Urban II preaches the First Crusade at the Council of Clermont
1099	Jerusalem falls to the Crusaders; forty-five years of Western rule in the Holy Land begins
1122	Concordat of Worms between Emperor Henry V and Pope Calixtus II ends Investiture Controversy
1144	Islamic armies reconquer Edessa
1187	Jerusalem reconquered by Saladin, King of Egypt and Syria
1189–1192	Third Crusade fails to recover the Holy Land from Islamic armies
1202	Fourth Crusade launched; captures Constantinople instead of going to Holy Land
1209	Pope Innocent III launches Albigensian Crusade in southern France; excommunicates King John of England
1210	Pope Innocent III recognizes the Franciscan order
1215	Fourth Lateran Council sanctions doctrine of transubstantiation and mandates annual confession by all adult Christians

After her separation from Henry in 1170 and until Henry confined her in England, Eleanor lived in Poitiers with her daughter Marie, the countess of Champagne; the two made the court of Poitiers a famous center for the literature of courtly love. This genre, with its thinly veiled eroticism, has been viewed as an attack on medieval ascetic values. Be that as it may, it was certainly a commentary on contemporary domestic life within the aristocracy. The troubadours hardly promoted promiscuity at court—the code of chivalry that guided relations between lords and their vassals condemned the seduction of the wife of one's lord as the most heinous of offenses, punishable, in some places, by castration or execution (or both). Rather, the troubadours presented in a frank and entertaining way stories that satirized carnal love or depicted it with tragic irony while glorifying the ennobling power of friendly, or "courteous," love. The most famous courtly literature was that of Chrétien de Troyes, whose stories of King Arthur and the Knights of the Round Table contained the tragic story of Sir Lancelot's secret and illicit love for Arthur's wife, Guinevere.

Popular Rebellion and Magna Carta

As Henry II acquired new lands abroad, he became more autocratic at home. He forced his will on the clergy in the Constitutions of Clarendon (1164). These measures placed limitations on judicial appeals to Rome, subjected the clergy to the civil courts, and gave the king control over the election of bishops. The result was strong political resistance from both the nobility and the clergy. The archbishop of Canterbury, Thomas à Becket (1118?–1170), once Henry's compliant chancellor, broke openly with the king and fled to Louis VII. Becket's subsequent assassination in 1170 and his canonization by Pope Alexander III in 1172 helped focus popular resentment against the king's heavy-handed tactics. (Two hundred years later, Geoffrey Chaucer, writing in an age made cynical by the Black Death and the Hundred Years' War, had the pilgrims of his *Canterbury Tales* journey to the shrine of Thomas à Becket.)

Under Henry's successors, the brothers Richard the Lion-Hearted (r. 1189–1199) and John (r. 1199–1216), burdensome taxation in support of unnecessary foreign Crusades and a failing war with France turned resistance into outright rebellion. Richard had to be ransomed at a high price from the Holy Roman emperor Henry VI, who had taken him prisoner during his return from the ill-fated Third Crusade. In 1209 Pope Innocent III, in a dispute with King John over the pope's choice for archbishop of Canterbury, ex-

cratic society. Eleanor spent the years 1154 to 1170 as Henry's queen in England. She separated from Henry in 1170, partly because of his public philandering and cruel treatment of her, and took revenge on him by joining Louis VII in provoking Henry's three surviving sons, who were unhappy with the terms of their inheritance, into unsuccessful rebellion against their father in 1173. From 1179 until his death in 1189, Henry kept Eleanor under mild house arrest to prevent any further such mischief from her.

William the Conqueror on horseback urging his troops into combat with the English at the Battle of Hastings (October 14, 1066). Detail from the Bayeux Tapestry, scene 51, about 1073–1083. Musée de la Tapisserie, Bayeux, France. Giraudon/Art Resource, N.Y.

communicated the king and placed England under interdict. To extricate himself and keep his throne, John had to make humiliating concessions, even declaring his country a fief of the pope. The last straw for the English, however, was the defeat of the king's forces by the French at Bouvines in 1214. With the full support of the clergy and the townspeople, English barons revolted against John. The popular rebellion ended with the king's grudging recognition of Magna Carta, or "Great Charter" in 1215.

The Magna Carta put limits on autocratic behavior of the kind exhibited by Norman kings and their successors, the Angevin or Plantagenet kings. It also secured the rights of the many—at least, the privileged many—against the monarchy. In Magna Carta the privileged preserved their right to be represented at the highest levels of government in important matters like taxation. But the monarchy was also preserved and left strong. Some argue that just such a balancing of the one and the many, the stronger and the comparatively weaker—preserving both sides and giving real power to each—was precisely the goal of feudal government. (See "The English Nobility Imposes Restraints on King John.")

Political accident clearly had more to do with Magna Carta than political genius. Nevertheless, the English did manage to avoid both a dissolution of the monarchy by the nobility and the abridgment of the rights of the nobility by the monarchy. Although King John continued to resist the Magna Carta in every way, and succeeding kings ignored it, Magna Carta nonetheless became a cornerstone of modern English law.

Philip II Augustus

The English struggle in the High Middle Ages was to secure the rights of the many, not the authority of the king. The French, on the other hand, faced the opposite problem. In 987, noblemen chose Hugh Capet to succeed the last Carolingian ruler, replacing the Carolingian dynasty with the Capetian dynasty. For two centuries thereafter, until the reign of Philip II Augustus (r. 1180–1223), powerful feudal princes dominated France.

During this period, after a rash initial attempt to challenge the more powerful French nobility before they had enough strength to do so, the Capetian kings concentrated their limited resources on securing the royal domain, their uncontested territory around Paris and the Île-de-France to the northeast. Aggressively exercising their feudal rights, French kings, especially after 1100, gained near absolute obedience from the noblemen in this area, and in the process established a solid base of power. By the reign of Philip II, Paris had become the center of French government and culture and the Capetian dynasty a secure hereditary monarchy. Thereafter, the kings of France could impose their will on the French nobles, who were always in law, if not in political fact, the king's sworn vassals.

In an indirect way the Norman conquest of England helped stir France to unity and made it possible for the Capetian kings to establish a truly national monarchy. The duke of Normandy, who after 1066 was master of the whole of England, was also among the vassals of the French king in Paris. Capetian kings understandably watched with alarm as the power of their Norman vassal grew. Other powerful vassals of the king also watched with alarm. King Louis VI, the Fat (r. 1108–1137), entered an alliance with Flanders, traditionally a Norman enemy. King Louis VII (r. 1137–1180), assisted by a brilliant minister, Suger, the abbot of St. Denis and famous for his patronage of Gothic architecture (see "Art & the West"), found allies in the great northern French cities and used their wealth to build a royal army.

How William the Conqueror Won the Battle of Hastings

This account of the Battle of Hastings appears in the Chronicle *of the kings of* England, *written by a Benedictine monk, William of Malmesbury, the son of a Norman father and an English mother. Although William wrote over a half century after the Battle of Hastings, his chronicle is our fullest account of these events.*

❖ *Where does Brother William think the winning difference lay between the two sides (Norman and English)? Might the fact that he was half Norman and a monk as well prejudice his account in favor of William the Conqueror? Are there statements in the document that suggest or deny this?*

The courageous leaders mutually prepared for battle, each according to his national custom. The English passed the night without sleep, in drinking and singing, and in the morning proceeded without delay against the enemy. All on foot, armed with battle-axes, and covering themselves in front by joining their shields, they formed an impenetrable body.... King Harold himself, on foot, stood with his brothers near the standard in order that, so long as all shared equal danger, none could think of retreating....

The Normans passed the whole night in confessing their sins, and received the communion of the Lord's body in the morning. Their infantry, with bows and arrows, formed the vanguard, while their cavalry, divided into wings, was placed in the rear. The duke [of Normandy], with serene countenance, declaring aloud that God would favor his...side, called for his arms... Then starting the song of Roland, in order that...the example of that [early French war] hero might stimulate the soldiers, and calling on God for assistance, the battle commenced on both sides...neither side yielding ground during the greater part of the day.

Observing this, William gave a signal to his troops, that, pretending flight, they should withdraw from the field. By means of this device the solid phalanx of the English opened for the purpose of cutting down the fleeing enemy and thus brought upon itself swift destruction; for the Normans, facing about, attacked them, thus disordered, and compelled them to fly....

[The English were not] without their own revenge, for, by frequently making a stand, they slaughtered their pursuers in heaps... [Such] alternating victory, first by one side and then by the other, continued as long as Harold lived to check the retreat; but when he fell, his brain pierced by an arrow, the flight of the English ceased not until night.

From Frederic Austin Ogg (ed.), *A Source Book of Mediaeval History: Documents Illustrative of European Life and Institutions from the German Invasions to the Renaissance* (New York: Telegraph Books, 1908), pp. 235–237.

When he succeeded Louis VII as king, Philip II Augustus inherited financial resources and a skilled bureaucracy that put him in a strong position. He was able to resist the competition of the French nobility and the clergy and to focus on the contest with the English king. Confronted at the same time with an internal and an international struggle, he proved successful in both. His armies occupied all the English king's territories on the French coast except for Aquitaine. As a showdown with the English neared on the continent, however, Holy Roman Emperor Otto IV (r. 1198–1215) entered the fray on the side of the English, and the French found themselves assailed from both east and west. But when the international armies finally clashed at Bouvines in Flanders on July 27, 1214, in what history records as the first great European battle, the French won handily over the opposing Anglo–Flemish–German army. This victory unified France politically around the monarchy and thereby laid the foundation for French ascendancy in the later Middle Ages. The defeat so weakened Otto IV that he fell from power in Germany. (It also, as we have seen, sparked the rebellion in England that forced King John to accept Magna Carta.)

France in the Thirteenth Century: The Reign of Louis IX

If Innocent III realized the fondest ambitions of medieval popes, Louis IX (r. 1226–1270), the grandson of Philip Augustus, embodied the medieval view of the perfect ruler. Coming to power in the wake of the French victory at Bouvines (1214), Louis inherited a unified and secure kingdom. Although he was endowed with a moral character that far exceeded that of his royal and papal contemporaries, he was also at times prey to naïveté. Not beset by the problems of sheer survival, and a reformer at heart, Louis found himself free to concentrate on what medieval people believed to be the business of civilization.

Generosity Abroad

Magnanimity in politics is not always a sign of strength, and Louis could be very magnanimous. Although in a strong position during negotiations for the Treaty of Paris (1259), which momentarily settled the dispute between France and England, he refused to take advantage of it to drive the English from their French possessions. Had he done so and ruthlessly confiscated English territories on the French coast, he might have lessened, if not averted altogether, the conflict underlying the Hundred Years' War, which began in the fourteenth century. Instead he surrendered disputed territory on the borders of Gascony to the English king, Henry

A depiction of the murder of Saint Thomas à Becket in Canterbury cathedral. From the Playfair Book of Hours. Victoria and Albert Museum/Art Resource, N.Y., Ms. L 475–1918

III, and confirmed Henry's possession of the duchy of Aquitaine.

Although he occasionally chastised popes for their crude political ambitions, Louis remained neutral during the long struggle between the German Hohenstaufen emperor Frederick II and the papacy (discussed later in the chapter); and his neutrality redounded very much to the pope's advantage. Louis also remained neutral when his brother, Charles of Anjou, intervened in Italy and Sicily against the Hohenstaufens, again to the pope's advantage. Urged on by the pope and his noble supporters, Charles was crowned king of Sicily in Rome, and his subsequent defeat of the son and grandson of Frederick II ended the Hohenstaufen dynasty. For such service to the church, both by action and by inaction, the Capetian kings of the thirteenth century became the objects of many papal favors.

Order and Excellence at Home

Louis's greatest achievements lay at home. The efficient French bureaucracy, which his predecessors had used to exploit their subjects, became under Louis an instrument of order and fair play in local government. He sent forth royal commissioners (*enquêteurs*), reminiscent of Charlemagne's far less successful *missi dominici*. Their mission was to monitor the royal officials responsible for local governmental administration (especially the *baillis* and *prévôts*, whose offices had been created by his predecessor, Philip Augustus) and to ensure that justice would truly be meted out to all. These royal ambassadors were received as genuine tribunes of the people. Louis further abolished private wars and serfdom within his royal domain. He gave his subjects the judicial right of appeal from local to higher courts and made the tax system, by medieval standards, more equitable. The French people came to associate their king with justice; consequently, national feeling, the glue of nationhood, grew very strong during his reign.

Respected by the kings of Europe and possessed of far greater moral authority than the pope, Louis became an arbiter among the world's powers. During his reign French society and culture became an example to all of Europe, a pattern that would continue into the modern period. Northern France became the showcase of monastic reform, chivalry, and Gothic art and architecture. Louis's reign also coincided with the golden age of Scholasticism, which saw the convergence of Europe's greatest thinkers on Paris, among them Saint Thomas Aquinas and Saint Bonaventure. (See Chapter 8.)

Louis' perfection remained, however, that of a medieval king. Like his father, Louis VIII (r. 1223–

The English Nobility Imposes Restraints on King John

The gradual building of a sound English constitutional monarchy in the Middle Ages required the king's willingness to share power. He had to be strong, but could not act as a despot or rule by fiat. The danger of despotism became acute in England under the rule of King John. In 1215 the English nobility forced him to recognize Magna Carta, which reaffirmed traditional rights and personal liberties that are still enshrined in English law.

❖ *Does the Magna Carta protect basic rights or special privileges? Does this protection suggest that there was a sense of fairness in the past? Does the granting of such protection in any way weaken the king?*

A free man shall not be fined for a small offense, except in proportion to the gravity of the offense; and for a great offense he shall be fined in proportion to the magnitude of the offense, saving his freehold [property]; and a merchant in the same way, saving his merchandise; and the villein [a free serf, bound only to his lord] shall be fined in the same way, saving his wainage [wagon], if he shall be at [the king's] mercy. And none of the above fines shall be imposed except by the oaths of honest men of the neighborhood....

No constable or other bailiff of [the king] shall take anyone's grain or other chattels without immediately paying for them in money, unless he is able to obtain a postponement at the good will of the seller.

No constable shall require any knight to give money in place of his ward of a castle [i.e., standing guard], if he is willing to furnish that ward in his own person, or through another honest man, if he himself is not able to do it for a reasonable cause; and if we shall lead or send him into the army, he shall be free from ward in proportion to the amount of time which he has been in the army through us.

No sheriff or bailiff of [the king], or any one else, shall take horses or wagons of any free man, for carrying purposes, except on the permission of that free man.

Neither we nor our bailiffs will take the wood of another man for castles, or for anything else which we are doing, except by the permission of him to whom the wood belongs....

No free man shall be taken, or imprisoned, or dispossessed, or outlawed, or banished, or in any way injured, nor will we go upon him, nor send upon him, except by the legal judgment of his peers, or by the law of the land.

To no one will we sell, to no one will we deny or delay, right or justice.

From James Harvey Robinson, ed., *Readings in European History*, Vol. 1 (Boston: Athenaeum, 1904), pp. 236–237.

1226), who had taken part in the Albigensian Crusade, Louis was something of a religious fanatic. He sponsored the French Inquisition. He led two French Crusades against the Muslims, which, although inspired by the purest religious motives, proved to be personal disasters. During the first (1248–1254), Louis was captured and had to be ransomed out of Egypt. He died of a fever during the second in 1270. It was especially for this selfless, but also useless, service on behalf of the church that Louis later received the rare honor of sainthood. Probably not coincidentally, the church bestowed this honor when it was under pressure from a more powerful and less than "most Christian" French king, the ruthless Philip IV, "the Fair" (r. 1285–1314). (See Chapter 9.)

The Hohenstaufen Empire (1152–1272)

During the twelfth and thirteenth centuries, stable governments developed in both England and France. In England Magna Carta balanced the rights of the nobility against the authority of the kings, and in France the reign of Philip II Augustus secured the authority of the king over the competitive claims of the nobility. During the reign of Louis IX, the French exercised international influence over politics and culture. The story within the Holy Roman Empire, which embraced Germany, Burgundy, and northern Italy by the mid-thirteenth century, was very different. (See Map 7–2.) There, primarily be-

Salisbury Cathedral:
A Church Filled with Light

Salisbury Cathedral, England. © Christopher Cormack/Corbis

Between 1050 and 1150 Christian churches and abbeys had been built predominately in the Romanesque style. Fortress-like, with thick stone walls and heavy rounded arches, Romanesque architecture expressed the Church's role as a refuge for the faithful and its status as a newly emerging worldy power. But beginning in France around 1140, Gothic architecture replaced Romanesque as the dominant style across most of Europe. During the next 100 years—the Age of the Great Cathedrals—numerous magnificent churches were built in England, Germany Spain, Poland and Italy.

The architects of the great Gothic cathedrals had two main goals: to give mathematical harmony to the church (an expression of divine law and a source of true beauty), and to bring more light into it than had ever been possible. By contrast with Romanesque churches, Gothic churches soared to towering heights and were filled with light. This was achieved through a new technical design. Architects and builders used ribbed, criss-crossed vaulting on the ceiling to create Gothic architecture's soaring pointed arches without having to support the arches by widening their base. Supports known today as "flying buttresses" were built into the exterior walls to shift much of the building's weight off of the walls themselves, which thus could become thinner. Because the exterior walls no longer had to carry so much weight, they could be pierced with wide expanses of stained glass windows that flooded the churches with colored light. These windows displayed both biblical and historical figures, including the church's saintly and lay patrons.

Salisbury Cathedral, shown here, is a prime example of early English Gothic architecture. Built between 1220 and 1226, the cathedral required 60,000 tons of stone, which arrived in 10 cartloads daily from March to October for 46 years, hauled by workers from a quarry 12 miles away. Note the soaring arches and the ribbed vaulting on the ceiling of the cathedral's interior. The exterior view shows the flying buttresses placed symmetrically between the arched windows on the sides of the cathedral and the intricately decorated west facade with ornamental carvings and statuary spaced evenly across the wall.

Salisbury Cathedral, England. The Image Works.

cause of the efforts of the Hohenstaufen dynasty to extend imperial power into southern Italy, disunity and blood feuding remained the order of the day for two centuries. It left as a legacy the fragmentation of Germany until the nineteenth century.

Frederick I Barbarossa

The investiture struggle had earlier weakened imperial authority. After the Concordat of Worms, the German princes were the supreme lay powers within the rich ecclesiastical territories and held a dominant influence over the appointment of the Church's bishops.

The power of the emperor promised to recuperate, however, with the accession to the throne of Frederick I Barbarossa (r. 1152–1190) of the Hohenstaufen dynasty, the most powerful line of emperors yet to succeed the Ottonians. This new dynasty not only reestablished imperial authority, but also started a new, deadlier phase in the contest between popes and emperors. Never have kings and popes despised and persecuted one another more than during the Hohenstaufen dynasty. (See "Hildegard of Binge Advises Frederick I Barbarossa.)

Frederick I confronted powerful feudal princes in Germany and Lombardy and a pope in Rome who still looked on the emperor as his creature. However, the incessant strife among the princes and the turmoil caused by the papacy's pretensions to great political power alienated many people. Such popular sentiment presented Frederick with an opportunity to recover imperial authority, and he was shrewd enough to take advantage of it. Frederick especially took advantage of the contemporary revival of Roman law, which served him on two fronts. On one hand, it praised centralized authority, that of king or emperor, against the nobility; on the other, it stressed the secular origins of imperial power against the tradition of Roman election of the emperor and papal coronation of him, thus reducing papal involvement to a minimum.

From his base of operation in Switzerland Frederick attempted to hold his empire together by invoking feudal bonds. He was relatively successful in Germany, thanks largely to the fall from power and exile in 1180 of his strongest German rival, Henry the Lion (d. 1195), the duke of Saxony. While he could not defeat the many German duchies, Frederick never missed an opportunity to remind each German ruler of his prescribed duties as one who held his land legally as a fief of the emperor. The same tactic had also been successfully employed by the Capetian kings of France when they faced superior forces of the nobility.

Italian popes proved to be the greatest obstacle to Frederick's plans to revive his empire. In 1155 he restored Pope Adrian IV (r. 1154–1159) to power in Rome

after a religious revolutionary had taken control of the city. For his efforts, Frederick won a coveted papal coronation—and strictly on his terms, not on those of the pope. Despite fierce resistance to him in Italy, led by Milan, the door to Italy had opened, and an imperial assembly sanctioned his claims to Italian lands.

As this challenge to royal authority was occurring, Cardinal Roland, a skilled lawyer, became Pope Alexander III (r. 1159–1181). In a clever effort to strengthen the papacy against growing imperial influence, the new pope had, while still a cardinal, negotiated an alliance between the papacy and the Norman kingdom of Sicily. Knowing him to be a very capable foe, Frederick opposed his election as pope and backed a rival candidate after the election in a futile effort to undo it. Frederick now found himself at war with the pope, Milan, and Sicily.

By 1167 the combined forces of the north Italian communes had driven Frederick back into Germany, and a decade later, in 1176, Italian forces soundly defeated his armies at Legnano. In the Peace of Constance in 1183, which ended the hostilities, Frederick recognized the claims of the Lombard cities to full rights of self-rule, a great blow to his imperial plans.

Henry VI and the Sicilian Connection

Frederick's reign thus ended with stalemate in Germany and defeat in Italy. At his death in 1190 he was not a ruler equal in stature to the kings of England and France. After the Peace of Constance, he seems to have accepted the reality of the empire's division among the feudal princes of Germany.

King Louis IX (1226–1270) giving justice. Louis, who was canonized in 1297, was the medieval ideal of a perfect ruler. From "Justiniani in Fortiatum," fol. 34. France, 14th C. Bibliotica Real, El Escorial, Madrid, Spain. Giraudon/Art Resource, NY

However, in the last years of his reign he seized an opportunity to gain control of Sicily, then still a papal ally, and form a new territorial base of power for future emperors. The opportunity arose when the Norman ruler of the kingdom of Sicily, William II (r. 1166–1189), sought an alliance with Frederick that would free him to pursue a scheme to conquer Constantinople. In 1186 a most fateful marriage occurred between Frederick's son, the future Henry VI (r. 1190–1197), and Constance, the heiress to the kingdom of Sicily, which promised to change the balance of imperial–papal power.

It proved, however, to be but another well-laid plan that went astray. The Sicilian kingdom became a fatal distraction for succeeding Hohenstaufen kings, tempting them to sacrifice their traditional territorial base in northern Europe to dreams of imperialism. Equally disastrous for the Hohenstaufens, the union of the empire with Sicily left Rome encircled, ensuring even greater emmity from a papacy already thoroughly distrustful of the emperor.

When Henry VI became emperor in 1190, he faced a hostile papacy, German princes more defiant than ever of the emperor, and an England whose adventurous king, Richard the Lion-Hearted, plotted against Henry VI with the old Hohenstaufen enemy, the exiled duke of Saxony, Henry the Lion.

It was into these circumstances that the future Emperor Frederick II was born in 1194. Heretofore the German princes had not recognized birth alone as qualifying one for the imperial throne, although the offspring of the emperor did have the inside track. To ensure baby Frederick's succession and stabilize his monarchy, Henry campaigned vigorously for recognition of the principle of hereditary succession. He won many German princes to his side by granting them what he asked for himself and his son: full hereditary rights to their own fiefs. Not surprisingly, the encircled papacy strongly opposed hereditary succession and joined dissident German princes against Henry.

Otto IV and the Welf Interregnum

Henry died in September 1197, leaving his son Frederick a ward of the pope. Henry's brother succeeded him as German king, but the Welf family, who were German rivals of the Hohenstaufens, put forth their own candidate, whom the English supported, while the French, beginning a series of interventions in German affairs, stuck with the Hohenstaufens. The papacy supported first one side and then the other, depending on which seemed most to threaten it. The new struggle for power soon threw Germany into anarchy and civil war.

The Welf candidate, Otto of Brunswick, outlasted his rival and was crowned Otto IV by his followers in Aachen in 1198, thereafter winning general recognition in Germany. In October 1209, Pope Innocent III (r. 1198–1216) boldly meddled in German politics by crowning Otto emperor in Rome. Playing one German dynasty against the other in an evident attempt to curb imperial power in Italy, while fully restoring papal power there, the pope had badly underestimated the ambition of the new German emperor. After his papal coronation, Otto proceeded to attack Sicily, an old imperial policy threatening to Rome. Four months after crowning Otto emperor, Pope Innocent excommunicated him.

Frederick II

Casting about for a counterweight to the treacherous Otto, the pope joined with the French, who had remained loyal to the Hohenstaufens. His new ally, French king Philip Augustus, impressed on Innocent that a solution to their mutual problem with Otto IV lay near at hand in the person of Innocent's ward, Frederick of Sicily, son of the late Hohenstaufen Emperor Henry VI, who had now come of age. Unlike Otto, the young Frederick had an immediate hereditary claim to the imperial throne. In December 1212, with papal, French, and German support, Frederick was crowned king of the Romans, in the German city of Mainz. Within a year and a half, Philip Augustus ended the reign of Otto IV on the battlefield of Bouvines, and three years later (1215), Frederick II was crowned emperor again, this time in the sacred imperial city of Aachen.

During his reign, Frederick effectively turned dreams of a unified Germany into a nightmare of disunity, assuring German fragmentation until modern times. Raised Sicilian and dreading travel beyond the Alps, Frederick spent only nine of his thirty-eight years as emperor in Germany, and six of those were before 1218. Although he pursued his royal interests in Germany, he did so mostly through representatives, seeming to desire only the imperial title for himself and his sons and willing to give the German princes whatever they wanted to secure it. It was this eager compliance with their demands that laid the foundation for six centuries of German division. In 1220 he recognized the jurisdictional claims of the ecclesiastical princes of Germany, and twelve years later (1232) he extended the same recognition to the secular princes.

Frederick's concessions were tantamount to an abdication of imperial power in Germany. Some view them as a kind of German Magna Carta in that they secured the rights of the German nobility for the forseeable future. But unlike the king of England with-

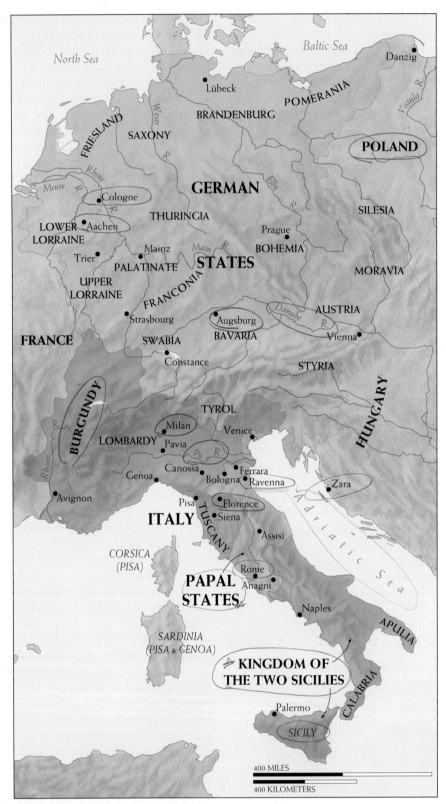

MAP 7–2   GERMANY AND ITALY IN THE MIDDLE AGES *Medieval Germany and Italy were divided lands. The Holy Roman Empire (Germany) embraced hundreds of independent territories that the emperor ruled only in name. The papacy controlled the Rome area and tried to enforce its will on Romagna. Under the Hohenstaufens (mid-twelfth to mid-thirteenth century), internal German divisions and papal conflict reached new heights; German rulers sought to extend their power to southern Italy and Sicily.*

Hildegard of Bingen Advises Frederick I Barbarrossa

Hildegard of Bingen (1098–1179) would have been a remarkable and highly accomplished woman in any century. Sought out by contemporaries for her mystical visions, which she recorded and illustrated, she was also a recognized authority on the natural sciences and herbal medicine, composed her own original musical scores, and had a wide circle of correspondents that included many of her centuries' leading rulers and churchmen.

Born in Mainz, Germany, the tenth child of a wealthy knight, she had her first vision at six. When she was eight, her parents sent her to a local Benedictine cloister in Disibodenber, named after St. Disibod, a local seventh-century Celtic missionary to Germany. There she gained proficiency in Latin and as good an education as any woman of her time. She became a nun at fifteen, and at thirty-eight assumed the position of abbess in the cloister in which she had grown up. Declaring her visions to be divinely inspired, the archbishop of Mainz recorded them for posterity. Together with her scientific and medical writings they attracted to the cloister many who sought career advice and cures.

So many came that Hildegard left Disobodenberg to found a new convent near Bingen in 1147, where she lived out the rest of her life writing and conducting a far-flung correspondence with the admiring powerful and influential people of her age.

The following letter is one of four she wrote to Frederick I Barbarossa, the first Hohenstaufen emperor, apparently shortly after his coronation as emperor in 1152. Frederick, on the other hand, wrote only one to her.

❖ *Why might Hildegard have written more often to Frederick than he to her? Is there anything in the letter that suggests a woman or a gifted visionary has written it? Why would a famous and powerful emperor want the advice of such a person? Did he follow her advice (see text)?*

Now, O king, pay careful attention! All lands are clouded by the plots of the many people who through the blackness of their souls put out the light of justice. Robbers and vagrants destroy the way of the Lord. O king, control with the sceptre of compassion the slothful, changeable, and wild habits of men. For you have a name of renown, since you are the king in Israel [that is, a divine king in the line of kings stemming from Old Testament times]. For your name is of high repute. Make sure, then, when the highest Judge looks at you, you will not be charged with not having rightly grasped your office, for then you must indeed blush with shame. May this be far from you! It is a well-known truth that it is right that the ruler imitate his predecessors in all that is good. For the idle morals of the princes are black indeed, since they run about in negligence and filth. Flee from this, O king! Be rather an armed fighter who bravely withstands the Devil, so that God doesn't strike you down and thereby scandal come over your earthly kingdom. God protect you from eternal destruction. May your times not be dry [that is, may they be times of growth and progress]. God guard you and may you live in eternity! So cast off all greed and choose moderation. For that is what the highest King loves.

Sources: *Hildegard of Bingen's Book of Divine Works with Letters and Songs*, ed. by Matthew Fox (Bear & Company, Santa Fe, 1987), pp. 289–290; Hildegard of Bingen, *The Book of the Rewards of Life*, trans. by Bruce W. Hozeski (Garland Publishing, Inc., New York, 1994), pp. xi–xiii.

in his realm, Frederick did little to secure the rights of the emperor in Germany. Whereas Magna Carta had the long-term consequence of promoting a balance of power between king and parliament, Frederick simply made the German princes little emperors within their respective realms. Centuries of petty absolutism, not parliamentary government, were the result.

Frederick's relations with the pope were equally disastrous, leading to his excommunication on four different occasions—the first in 1227 for refusing to

955	Otto I defeats Hungarians at Lechfeld, securing Europe's eastern border
1066	Normans win the Battle of Hastings and assume English rule
1152	Frederick I Barbarossa becomes first Hohenstaufen emperor; reestablishes imperial authority
1154	Henry II assumes the English throne as the first Plantagenet or Angevin king
1164	Henry II forces the Constitutions of Clarendon on the English clergy
1170	Henry II's defiant archbishop, Thomas à Becket, assassinated
1176	Papal and other Italian armies defeat Frederick I at Legnano
1194	Birth of future Hohenstaufen ruler Frederick II, who becomes a ward of the pope
1198	Welf interregnum in the empire begins under Otto IV
1212	Frederick II crowned emperor in Mainz with papal, French, and German support
1214	French armies under Philip II Augustus defeat combined English and German forces at Bouvines in the first major European battle
1215	English barons revolt against King John and force the king's recognition of Magna Carta
1227	Frederick II excommunicated for the first of four times by the pope; conflict between Hohenstaufen dynasty and papacy begins
1250	Frederick II dies, having been defeated by the German princes with papal support
1257	German princes establish their own electoral college to elect future emperors

finish a crusade he had begun at the pope's request. He was also determined to control Lombardy and Sicily, a policy that was anathema to the pope. The papacy came to view Frederick as the Antichrist, the biblical beast of the Apocalypse, whose persecution of the faithful signaled the end of the world.

The papacy won the long struggle that ensued, although its victory was arguably a Pyrrhic one. During this bitter contest, Pope Innocent IV (r. 1243–1254) launched the church into European politics on a massive scale, a policy that left the church highly vulnerable to criticism from both religious reformers and royal apologists. Pope Innocent organized the German princes against Frederick, who—thanks to Frederick's grand con-

cessions—were a superior force and able to gain full control of Germany by the 1240s.

When Frederick died in 1250, the German monarchy died with him. The princes established their own informal electoral college in 1257, which thereafter controlled the succession. Through this institution, which the emperor recognized in 1356, the "king of the Romans" became a puppet of the princes, and one with firmly attached strings. The princes elected him directly, and his offspring had no hereditary right to succeed him.

Between 1250 and 1272 the Hohenstaufen dynasty slowly faded into oblivion. Independent princes henceforth controlled Germany, while the imperial kingdon in Italy fell to local Italian magnates. The connection between Germany and Sicily ended forever, and the papal monarchy emerged as one of Europe's most formidable powers, soon to enter its most costly conflict of the Middle Ages with the new French and English monarchies. Internal division and the absence of a representative system of government persisted in Germany for six centuries. Even after Chancellor Bismarck created a new German empire in 1871, the legacy of the Hohenstaufen dynasty's defeat was still visible until the end of World War I.

In Perspective

With its borders finally secured, western Europe was free to develop its political institutions and cultural forms during the High Middle Ages. The map of Europe as we know it today began to take shape. England and France can be seen forming into modern nation–states, but within Germany and the Holy Roman Empire the story was different. There, imperial rule first revived (under the Ottonians) and then collapsed totally (under the Hohenstaufen dynasty). The consequences for Germany were ominous: thereafter, it became Europe's most fractured land. On a local level, however, an effective organization of society from noble to serf emerged throughout western Europe.

The major disruption of the period was an unprecedented conflict between former allies, church and state. During the Investiture Struggle and the period of the Crusades, the church became a powerful monarchy in its own right. For the first time it competed with secular states on the latter's own terms, dethroning emperors, kings, and princes by excommunication and interdict. In doing so, it inadvertently laid the foundation for the Western doctrine of the separation of church and state.

Having succeeded so brilliantly in defending its spiritual authority against rulers, popes ventured boldly into the realm of secular politics as well, especially during the pontificates of Innocent III and Innocent IV. As the sad story of the Hohenstaufen dynasty attests, the popes had remarkable, if short-lived, success there also. But the Church was to pay dearly for its successes, both spiritually and politically. Secularization of the papacy during the High Middle Ages left it vulnerable to the attacks of a new breed of unforgiving religious reformers, and the powerful monarchs of the later Middle Ages were to subject it to bold and vengeful bullying.

REVIEW QUESTIONS

1. Discuss the rise of the German Empire and the accomplishments of the Saxon king, Otto I. How was he able to consolidate political rule over the various German duchies and use the church to his advantage? Does he deserve the title "the Great"?

2. What were the main reasons for the Cluny reform movement? How do you account for its success? How important was the impact of this reform movement on the subsequent history of the medieval church?

3. Discuss the conflict between Pope Gregory VII and King Henry IV over the issue of lay investiture. What were the causes of the controversy, the actions of the contending parties, and the outcome of the struggle? What was at stake for each of the disputants, and what were the ramifications of the struggle?

4. The eighteenth-century French intellectual Voltaire said that the Holy Roman Empire was neither holy nor Roman. What did he mean? Do you agree with him?

5. What major development in western and eastern Europe encouraged the emergence of the Crusades? Why were the Crusaders unsuccessful in establishing lasting political and religious control over the Holy Land? What were the political, religious, and economic results of the Crusades? Which do you consider most important and why?

6. Hohenstaufen rule proved disastrous for Germany's development as a nation. What were some of the factors preventing German consolidation during that era? Why did Germany remain in feudal chaos while France and England eventually coalesced into reasonably strong states?

SUGGESTED READINGS

J. W. BALDWIN, *The Government of Philip Augustus* (1986). An important scholarly work.

G. BARRACLOUGH, *The Origins of Modern Germany* (1946). Dated, but penetrating, political narrative setting modern Germany in the perspective of the Middle Ages.

A. CAPELLANUS, *The Art of Courtly Love*, trans. by J. J. Parry (1941). Documents from the court of Marie de Champagne.

H. E. J. COWDREY, *Popes, Monks, and Crusaders* (1984). Re-creation of the atmosphere that gave birth to the Crusades.

R. H. C. DAVIS, *A History of Medieval Europe: From Constantine to St. Louis* (1972), Part 2. Succinct, lucid survey.

E. M. HALLAM, *Capetian France 987–1328* (1980). Very good on politics and heretics.

J. C. HOLT, *Magna Carta*, 2d ed. (1992). The famous document and its interpretation by succeeding generations.

E. H. KANTOROWICZ, *The King's Two Bodies* (1957). Controversial analysis of political concepts in the High Middle Ages.

K. LEYSER, *Rule and Conflict in Early Medieval Society: Ottonian Saxony* (1979). Basic and authoritative.

K. LEYSER, *Medieval Germany and Its Neighbors, 900–1250* (1982). Basic and authoritative.

P. MANDONNET, *St. Dominic and His Work* (1944). On the origins of the Dominican order.

H. E. MAYER, *The Crusades*, trans. by John Gilligham (1972). Extremely detailed; the best one-volume account.

J. B. MORRALL, *Political Thought in Medieval Times* (1962). Readable and illuminating account.

C. PETIT-DUTAILLIS, *The Feudal Monarchy in France and England from the Tenth to the Thirteenth Century*, trans. by E. D. Hunt (1964). Political narrative in great detail.

S. REYNOLDS, *Kingdoms and Communities in Western Europe 900–1300* (1984). For the medieval origins of Western political and cultural traditions.

J. RILEY-SMITH, *The Crusades: A Short History* (1987). Up-to-date, lucid, and readable.

W. ROESENER, *Peasants in the Middle Ages* (1992) Up to date overview.

JOSEPH SCHATAZMILLER, *Jews, Medicine, and Medieval Society* (1994). Information on Jewish women physicians.

B. TIERNEY, *The Crisis of Church and State* (1964). Extremely useful collection of key documents.

Chapter 8

A depiction of court and countryside in thirteenth-century Italy. The oldest of three parts of Castle Buonconsiglio in Trent, Italy was built in the mid-thirteenth century (1239–1255) between the city's north and east gates, through which workers can be seen hauling wood into the city by ox cart, while royals of both sexes ride out on horseback. Scala/Art Resource, N.Y.

Medieval Society:
Hierarchies, Towns, Universities, and Families (1000–1300)

The Traditional Order of Life
Nobles
Clergy
Peasants

Towns and Townspeople
The Chartering of Towns
The Rise of Merchants
Challenging the Old Lords
New Models of Government
Towns and Kings
Jews in Christian Society

Schools and Universities
University of Bologna
Cathedral Schools
University of Paris
The Curriculum
Philosophy and Theology

Women in Medieval Society

The Lives of Children

KEY TOPICS

- The major groups composing medieval society
- The rise of towns and a new merchant class
- The founding of universities and educational curricula
- How women and children fared in the Middle Ages

Between the tenth and twelfth centuries, European agricultural production steadily improved, due to a warming climate and improved technology. With increased food supplies came something of a population explosion by the eleventh century. The recovery of the countryside in turn stimulated new migration into and trade with the long-dormant towns. A revival of old towns and the creation of new ones resulted. A rich and complex fabric of life developed, closely integrating town and countryside and allowing civilization to flourish in the twelfth and thirteenth centuries as it had not done in the West since the Roman Empire. Beginning with the Crusades, trade with distant towns and foreign lands also revived. With the rise of towns, a new merchant class, the ancestors of modern capitalists, came into being. Enormous numbers of skilled artisans and day workers, especially in the clothmaking industries, were the foundation of the new urban wealth.

Urban culture and education also flourished. The revival of trade with the East and contacts with Muslim intellectuals, particularly in Spain, made possible the recovery of ancient scholarship and science. Unlike the comparative dabbling in antiquity during Carolingian times, the twelfth century enjoyed a true renaissance of classical learning. Schools and curricula also broadened beyond the clergy during the twelfth century to educate laity, thereby greatly increasing lay literacy and the role of the laity in government and culture.

In the mid-twelfth century in France, Gothic architecture began to replace the plain and ponderous Romanesque preferred by fortress Europe during the early Middle Ages. Its new grace and beauty—soaring arches, bold flying buttresses, dazzling light, and stained glass—were a testament to the vitality of humankind as well as to the glory of God in this unique period of human achievement.

The Traditional Order of Life

In the art and literature of the Middle Ages, three basic social groups were represented: those who fought as mounted knights (the landed nobility), those who prayed (the clergy), and those who labored in fields and shops (the peasantry and village artisans). After the revival of towns in the eleventh century, there emerged a fourth social group: the long-distance traders and merchants. Like the peasantry, they also labored, but in ways strange to the traditional groups. They were freemen who often possessed great wealth, yet unlike the nobility and the clergy, they owned no land, and unlike the peasantry, they did not toil in fields and shops. Their rise to power caused an important crack in the old social order, for they drew behind them the leadership of the urban artisan groups created by the new urban industries that grew up in the wake of the revival of trade. During the late Middle Ages these new "middling classes" firmly established themselves, and their numbers have been enlarging ever since.

Nobles

As a distinctive social group, not all nobles were originally great men with large hereditary lands. Many rose from the ranks of feudal vassals or warrior knights. The successful vassal attained a special social and legal status based on his landed wealth (accumulated fiefs), his exercise of authority over others, and his distinctive social customs—all of which set him apart from others in medieval society. By the late Middle Ages, there had evolved a distinguishable higher and lower nobility living in both town and country. The higher were the great landowners and territorial magnates, long the dominant powers in their regions; the lower comprised petty landlords, the descendants of minor knights, newly rich merchants who could buy country estates, and wealthy farmers patiently risen from ancestral serfdom.

It was a special mark of the nobility that they lived off the labor of others. Basically lords of manors, the nobility of the early and High Middle Ages neither tilled the soil like the peasantry nor engaged in the commerce of merchants—activities considered beneath their dignity. The nobleman resided in a country mansion or, if he were particularly wealthy, a castle. Personal preference drew him to the countryside as much as the fact that his fiefs were usually rural manors. (See "Art & the West.")

WARRIORS Arms were the nobleman's profession; to wage war was his sole occupation and reason for living. In the eighth century the adoption of stirrups made mounted warriors, or cavalry, the key ingredient of a successful army. (Stirrups had the advantage of permitting the rider to strike a blow without falling to the ground.) Good horses (and a warrior needed several) and the accompanying armor and weaponry of horse warfare were expensive. Only those with means could pursue the life of a cavalryman. The nobleman's fief provided the means to acquire the expensive military equipment that his rank required. He maintained his enviable position as he had gained it, by fighting for his chief.

The nobility accordingly celebrated the physical strength, courage, and constant activity of warfare. Warring gave them both new riches and an opportunity to gain honor and glory. Knights were paid a share in the plunder of victory, and in time of war everything became fair game. Special war wagons, designed for the collection and transport of booty, followed them into battle. Sadness greeted periods of peace, as they meant economic stagnation and boredom. Whereas the peasants and the townspeople counted peace the condition of their occupational success, the nobility despised it as unnatural to their profession.

They looked down on the peasantry as cowards who ran and hid in time of war. Urban merchants, who amassed wealth by business methods strange to feudal society, were held in equal contempt, which increased as the affluence and political power of the townspeople grew. The nobility possessed as strong a sense of superiority over these "unwarlike" people as the clergy did over the general run of laity.

KNIGHTHOOD The nobleman nurtured his sense of distinctiveness within medieval society by the chivalric ritual of dubbing to knighthood. This ceremonial entrance into the noble class became almost a religious sacrament. The ceremony was preceded by a bath of purification, confession, communion, and a prayer vigil. Thereafter, the priest blessed the knight's standard, lance, and sword. As prayers were chanted, the priest girded the knight with his sword and presented him his shield, enlisting him as much in the defense of the church as in the service of his lord. Dubbing raised the nobleman to a state as sacred in his sphere as clerical ordination made the priest in his. The comparison is legitimate: The clergy and the nobility were medieval society's privileged estates. The appointment of noblemen to high ecclesiastical office and their eager participation in the church's Crusades had strong ideological and social underpinnings as well as economic and political motives.

In the twelfth century, knighthood was legally restricted to men of high birth. This circumscription of noble ranks came in reaction to the growing wealth, political power, and successful social climbing of newly rich townspeople (mostly merchants), who formed a new urban patriciate that was increasingly competitive with the lower nobility. Kings remained free, however, to raise up knights at will and did not shrink from increasing royal revenues by selling noble titles to wealthy merchants. But the law was building fences—fortunately, not without gates—between town and countryside in the High Middle Ages.

SPORTSMEN In peacetime, the nobility had two favorite amusements: hunting and tournaments. Where they could, noblemen progressively monopolized the rights to game, forbidding the commoners from hunting in "lords'" forests. This practice built resentment among common people to the level of revolt. Free game, fishing, and access to wood were basic demands in the petitions of grievance and the revolts of the peasantry throughout the High and later Middle Ages.

The pastime of tournaments also sowed seeds of social disruption, but more within the ranks of the nobility itself. Tournaments were designed not only to keep men fit for war, but also to provide the excitement of war without the useless maiming and killing of prized vassals. But as regions competed fiercely with one another for victory and glory, even mock battles with blunted weapons proved to be deadly. Often, tournaments got out of hand, ending with bloodshed and animosity among the combatants. (The intense emotions and occasional violence that accompany interregional soccer in Europe today may be seen as a survival of this kind of rivalry.) The church came to oppose tournaments as occasions of pagan revelry and senseless violence. Kings and princes also turned against them as sources of division within their realms. Henry II of England proscribed them in the twelfth century. They did not end in France until the mid-sixteenth century, after Henry II of France was mortally wounded by a shaft through his visor during a tournament celebrating his daughter's marriage.

COURTLY LOVE From the repeated assemblies in the courts of barons and kings, set codes of social conduct, or "courtesy," developed in noble circles. With the French leading the way, mannered behavior and court etiquette became almost as important as expertise in the battlefield. Knights became literate gentlemen, and lyric poets sang and moralized at court. The cultivation of a code of behavior and a special literature to eulogize it was not unrelated to problems within the social life of the nobility. Noblemen were notorious philanderers; their illegitimate children mingled openly with their legitimate offspring in their houses. The advent of courtesy was in part an effort to reform this situation.

Although the poetry of courtly love was sprinkled with frank eroticism and the beloved in these epics

Noblewomen watch a tournament. These mock battles were designed to provide the excitement of war without its mayhem. However, they tended to get out of hand, resulting in bloodshed and even death. University of Heidelberg

were married women pursued by those to whom they were not married, the love recommended by the poet was usually love at a distance, unconsummated by sexual intercourse. It was love without touching, a kind of sex without physical contact, and only as such was it considered ennobling. Court poets depicted those who succumbed to illicit carnal love as reaping at least as much suffering as joy from it.

SOCIAL DIVISIONS No medieval social group was absolutely uniform—not the nobility, the clergy, the townspeople, or even the peasantry. Not only was the nobility a class apart; it also had strong social divisions within its own ranks. Noblemen formed a broad spectrum—from minor vassals without subordinate vassals to mighty barons, the principal vassals of a king or prince, who had many vassals of their own. Dignity and status within the nobility were directly related to the exercise of authority over others; a chief with many vassals obviously far excelled the small country nobleman who served another and was lord over none but himself.

Illuminated Manuscripts:
The Luttrell Psalter

Sir Geoffrey Luttrell on Horseback. From *The Luttrell Psalter,* by permission of The British Library.

In the Middle Ages, religious devotion could be a very personal affair. Often, that devotion was linked to more secular interests and concerns. The illustrations on the right show a knight and his family at dinner while servants carry in the feast. The same man appears above with his wife and daughter-in-law, and, although aging, he carries the full armor of the newest fashion, the joust.

The manuscript depicts an English knight, Sir Geoffrey Luttrell, who was born in the last part of the thirteenth century. Although Sir Geoffrey bears the trappings of a knight from a medieval romance,

this image was actually painted as an illustration for a religious book known as a "Psalter," a collection of the Psalms and other religious texts for personal devotion.

The Psalter was one of the more common types of medieval illuminated manuscripts. A manuscript was made from parchment—animal skin, which when properly prepared, allowed for writing and decoration. The process required soaking the skin of a cow, goat, or sheep in different solutions and repeatedly scraping it to remove the hair. The best manuscripts came from the thinnest, whitest parchment, which took the most labor to produce. Once the parchment was prepared, it was taken to a workshop to be written upon and decorated. Manuscript workshops varied over the centuries of the Middle Ages. Manuscripts from sixth- or seventh-century monasteries might even be written outdoors, where the light was best, while later manuscripts might be copied in a well-lit room within the monastery.

In the thirteenth century, the type of person commissioning a manuscript began to change, and with that change came others, even in the kind of manuscripts produced. Lay people—not just monks and priests—wanted to own manuscripts. In cities like Paris and Oxford, workshops grew outside monasteries, and from the thirteenth to the fifteenth centuries, the number of people manufacturing and owning manuscripts steadily increased. Topics changed as well: although many were religious, there were also romances and other stories, texts for law and medicine, and genealogocal and ceremonial scrolls. Illuminated manuscripts might have real gold leaf applied to letters or pictures, the glittering reflection from which rendered them full of light, or "illuminated." Gold leaf, expensive pigments, elaborate patterns, and creative designs in the margins combined to make these illuminated manuscripts among the most expensive and desirable.

Throughout the Middle Ages almost all manuscripts were made for a specific client or patron: monastery, church, king, or member of the land-owning gentry, such as Sir Geoffrey Luttrell. In Paris, students might enter a workshop, choose the texts they desired, and have a special "economy" copy made to order. A king might commission a devotional book for his bride with illuminations on every page, perhaps even with certain pages depicting the young girl herself praying to the Virgin Mary. It is unclear exactly why Sir Geoffrey ordered his Pslater, but we can be sure that one of the most personal and most telling objects a medieval person might own was an illuminated manuscript.

When the printing press came into use for making illustrated books in the 1480s, the illuminated manuscript lost its prominence. More people could afford printed books, whose variety and number were now greater than ever before.

Sources: Alexander, J. J. G. *Medieval Illuminators and Their Methods of Work*. New Haven: Yale University Press, 1992. Backhouse, Janet. *The Luttrell Psalter*. London: British Library, 1989. Camille, M. *Mirror in Parchment: The Luttrell Psalter and the Making of Medieval England*. Chicago: University of Chicago Press, 1998. De Hamel, C. *A History of Illuminated Manuscripts*. (7th–16th centuries) London: Phaidon, 1986. Sandler, L. F. *Gothic Manuscripts, 1285–1385* (A Survey of Manuscripts Illuminated in the British Isles, General editor J. J. G. Alexander, Vol. 6), 2 vols. (London: University of Toronto Press, 1996).

[Top] *The Lord of the Manor Dining.* From *The Luttrell Psalter,* by permission of The British Library. [Bottom] *Kitchen Scene; Chopping Meat.* From *The Luttrell Psalter,* by permission of The British Library.

261

A lady and her knight going hunting. Bildarchiv Preussischer
Kulturbesitz

Even among the domestic servants of the nobility,
a social hierarchy developed according to assigned
manorial duties. Although they were peasants in the
eyes of the law, the chief stewards—charged with overseeing the operation of the lord's manor and entrusted with the care and education of the noble
children—became powerful "lords" within their "domains." Some freemen found the status of the steward enviable enough to surrender their own freedom
and become domestic servants in the hope of attaining it. In time, the social superiority of the higher ranks
of domestic servants won legal recognition as medieval law adjusted to acknowledge the privileges of
wealth and power at whatever level they appeared.

By the late Middle Ages, several factors forced the
landed nobility into a steep economic and political decline from which it never recovered. Climatic changes
and agricultural failures created large famines, while
the great plague (see Chapter 9) brought about unprecedented population losses. Changing military tactics occasioned by the use of infantry and heavy
artillery during the Hundred Years' War made the noble
cavalry nearly obsolete. And the alliance of wealthy
towns with the king weakened the nobility within

their very own domains. One can speak of a waning of
the landed nobility after the fourteenth century. Thereafter, the effective possession of land and wealth counted far more than parentage and lineage as a
qualification for entrance into the highest social class.

Clergy

Unlike the nobility and the peasantry, the clergy
was an open estate. Although the clerical hierarchy reflected the social classes from which the clergy came, one was still a cleric by religious training
and ordination, not by the circumstances of birth or
military prowess.

REGULAR AND SECULAR CLERICS   There were two
basic types of clerical vocation: the regular clergy and
the secular clergy. The regular clergy was made up of
the orders of monks who lived according to a special
ascetic rule (*regula*) in cloisters separated from the
world. They were the spiritual elite among the clergy, and theirs was not a way of life lightly entered.
Canon law required that one be at least twenty-one
years of age before making a final profession of the
monastic vows of poverty, chastity, and obedience.
The monks' personal sacrifices and high religious
ideals made them much respected in high medieval
society. This popularity was a major factor in the success of the Cluny reform movement and of the Crusades of the eleventh and twelfth centuries. The
Crusades provided laypeople with a way to participate in the admired life of asceticism and prayer; in
these holy pilgrimages they had the opportunity to
imitate the suffering and perhaps even the death of
Jesus, as the monks imitated his suffering and death
by retreat from the world and severe self-denial.

Many monks (and also nuns, who increasingly
embraced the vows of poverty, obedience, and
chastity without a clerical rank) secluded themselves altogether. The regular clergy, however, were
never completely cut off from the secular world.
They maintained frequent contact with the laity
through such charitable activities as feeding the des-
titute and tending the sick, through liberal arts instruction in monastic schools, through special
pastoral commissions from the pope, and as sup-
plemental preachers and confessors in parish
churches during Lent and other peak religious seasons. It became the mark of the Dominican and
Franciscan friars to live a common life according to
a special rule and still to be active in a worldly ministry. Some monks, because of their learning and
rhetorical skills, even rose to prominence as secretaries and private confessors to kings and queens.

The secular clergy, those who lived and worked
directly among the laity in the world (*saeculum*),

formed a vast hierarchy. At the top were the high prelates—the wealthy cardinals, archbishops, and bishops, who were drawn almost exclusively from the nobility—and below them the urban priests, the cathedral canons, and the court clerks. Finally, there was the great mass of poor parish priests, who were neither financially nor intellectually very far above the common people they served. (The basic educational requirement was an ability to say the mass.) Until the Gregorian reform in the eleventh century, parish priests lived with women in a relationship akin to marriage, and their concubines and children were accepted within the communities they served. Because of their relative poverty, it was not unusual for priests to "moonlight" as teachers, artisans, or farmers. Their parishioners also accepted and even admired this practice.

NEW ORDERS One of the results of the Gregorian reform was the creation of new religious orders aspiring to a life of poverty and self-sacrifice in imitation of Christ and the first apostles. The more important were the Canons Regular (founded 1050–1100), the Carthusians (founded 1084), the Cistercians (founded 1098), and the Praemonstratensians (founded 1121). Carthusians, Cistercians, and Praemonstratensians practiced extreme austerity in their quest to recapture the pure religious life of the early Church.

Strictest of them all were the Carthusians. Members lived in isolation and fasted three days a week. They also devoted themselves to long periods of silence and even self-flagellation in their quest for perfect self-denial and conformity to Christ.

The Cistercians (from Citeaux in Burgundy) were a reform wing of the Benedictine order and were known as the "white monks," a reference to their all-white attire, symbolic of apostolic purity. (The Praemonstratensians also wore white.) They hoped to avoid the materialistic influences of urban society and maintain uncorrupted the original *Rule* of Saint Benedict, which their leaders believed Cluny was compromising. The Cistercians accordingly stressed anew the inner life and spiritual goals of monasticism. They located their houses in remote areas and denied themselves worldly comforts and distractions. Remarkably successful, the order could count 300 chapter houses within a century of its founding, and many others imitated its more austere spirituality.

The Canons Regular were independent groups of secular clergy (and also earnest laity) who, in addition to serving laity in the world, adopted the *Rule* of Saint Augustine (a monastic guide dating from around the year 500) and practiced the ascetic virtues of regular clerics. There were monks who renounced exclusive withdrawal from the world. There were also priests who renounced exclusive involvement in it. By merg-

ing the life of the cloister with traditional clerical duties, the Canons Regular foreshadowed the mendicant friars of the thirteenth century—the Dominicans and the Franciscans, who combined the ascetic ideals of the cloister with a very active ministry in the world.

The monasteries and nunneries of the established orders recruited candidates from among the wealthiest social groups. Crowding in the convents and the absence of patronage gave rise in the thirteenth century to lay satellite convents known as Beguine houses. These convents housed religiously earnest unmarried women from the upper and middle social strata. Cologne established 100 such houses between 1250 and 1350, each containing eight to twelve women. Several of these convents, in Cologne and elsewhere, became heterodox in religious doctrine and practice, falling prey to heresy. Among the responsibilities of the new religious orders of Dominicans and Franciscans was the "regularization" of such convents.

PROMINENCE OF THE CLERGY The clergy constituted a far greater proportion of medieval society than modern society. Estimates suggest that 1.5 percent of fourteenth-century Europe was in clerical garb. The clergy were concentrated in urban areas, especially in towns with universities and cathedrals, where, in addition to studying, they found work in a wide variety of religious services. In late fourteenth-century England there was one cleric for every seventy laypeople, and in counties with a cathedral or a university the proportion rose to one cleric for every fifty laypeople.[1] In large university towns, the clergy might exceed 10 percent of the population.

Despite the moonlighting of poorer parish priests, the clergy as a whole, like the nobility, lived on the labor of others. Their income came from the regular collection of tithes and church taxes according to an elaborate system that evolved in the High and later Middle Ages. The church was, of course, a major landowner and regularly collected rents and fees. Monastic communities and high prelates amassed great fortunes; there was a popular saying that the granaries were always full in the monasteries. The immense secular power attached to high clerical posts can be seen in the intensity of the investiture struggle. The loss of the right to present chosen clergy with the ring and staff of episcopal office was a direct threat to the emperor's control of his realm. The bishops had become royal agents and were ingratiated to that purpose with royal lands that the emperor could ill afford to have slip from his control.

---

[1] Denys Hay, *Europe in the Fourteenth and Fifteenth Centuries,* 2d ed. (New York: Holt, Rinehart, 1966), pp. 58–59.

During the greater part of the Middle Ages, the clergy were the "first estate," and theology was the queen of the sciences. How did the clergy come into such prominence? A lot of it was self-proclaimed. However, there was also popular respect and reverence for the clergy's role as mediator between God and humanity. The priest brought the very Son of God down to earth when he celebrated the sacrament of the Eucharist; his absolution released penitents from punishment for mortal sin. It was declared improper for mere laypeople to sit in judgment on such a priest.

Theologians elaborated the distinction between the clergy and the laity very much to the clergy's benefit. The belief in the superior status of the clergy underlay the evolution of clerical privileges and immunities in both person and property. As holy persons, the clergy were not supposed to be taxed by secular rulers without special permission from the proper ecclesiastical authorities. Clerical crimes were under the jurisdiction of special ecclesiastical courts, not the secular courts. Because churches and monasteries were deemed holy places, they, too, were free from secular taxation and legal jurisdiction. Hunted criminals, lay and clerical, regularly sought asylum within them, disrupting the normal processes of law and order. When city officials violated this privilege of asylum, ecclesiastical authorities threatened excommunication and interdict. People feared this suspension of the church's sacraments, including Christian burial, almost as much as they feared the criminals to whom the church gave asylum.

By the late Middle Ages, townspeople came increasingly to resent the special immunities of the clergy. They complained that it was not proper for the clergy to have greater privileges, yet far fewer responsibilities, than all others who lived within the town walls. An early sixteenth-century lampoon reflected what had by then become a widespread sentiment:

Priests, monks, and nuns
Are but a burden to the earth.
They have decided
That they will not become citizens.
That's why they're so greedy—
They stand firm against our city
And will swear no allegiance to it.
And we hear their fine excuses:
"It would cause us much toil and trouble
Should we pledge our troth as burghers."[2]

The separation of church and state and the distinction between the clergy and the laity have persisted into modern times. After the fifteenth century, however, the clergy ceased to be the superior class they had been for so much of the Middle Ages. In both Protestant and Catholic lands, governments progressively subjected them to the basic responsibilities of citizenship.

Peasants

The largest and lowest social group in medieval society was the one on whose labor the welfare of all the others depended: the agrarian peasantry. Many peasants lived on and worked the manors of the nobility, the primitive cells of rural social life. All were to one degree or another dependent on their lords and were considered their property. The manor in Frankish times was a plot of land within a village, ranging from twelve to seventy-five acres in size, assigned to a certain member by a settled tribe or clan. This member and his family became lords of the land, and those who came to dwell there formed a smaller, self-sufficient community within a larger village community. In the early Middle Ages such manors consisted of the dwellings of the lord and his family, the cottages of the peasant workers, agricultural sheds, and fields.

THE DUTIES OF TENANCY The landowner or lord of the manor required a certain amount of produce (grain, eggs, and the like) and a certain number of services from the peasant families that came to dwell on and farm his land. The tenants were free to divide the labor as they wished, and what goods remained after the lord's levies were met were their own. A powerful lord might own many such manors. Kings later based their military and tax assessments on the number of manors owned by a vassal landlord. No set rules governed the size of manors. There were manors of a hundred acres or less and some of several thousand or more.

There were both servile and free manors. The tenants of the latter had originally been freemen known as *coloni*. Original inhabitants of the territory and petty landowners, they swapped their small possessions for a guarantee of security from a more powerful lord, who came in this way to possess their land. Unlike the pure serfdom of the servile manors, whose tenants had no original claim to a part of the land, the tenancy obligations on free manors tended to be limited and the tenants' rights more carefully defined. It was a milder serfdom. Tenants of servile manors were by comparison far more vulnerable to the whims of their landlords. These two types of manors tended, however, to merge. The most common situation was the manor on which tenants of greater and lesser degrees of servitude dwelt together, their services to the lord defined by their personal status and local custom. In many regions free, self-governing peasant communities existed without any overlords and tenancy obligations.

[2] Cited by S. Ozment, *The Reformation in the Cities* (New Haven, CT: Yale University Press, 1975), p. 36.

The livelihood of towns and castles depended on the labor of peasants. Here a peasant family collects the September grape harvest outside a fortified castle in France, most likely for the making of wine. From Les Tres Riches heures du duc de Berry, Chateau de Saumur, Musée Condé, Chantilly, France. Giraudon/Art Resource, N.Y.

The lord held both judicial and police powers. He owned and operated the machines that processed crops into food and drink. Marc Bloch, the modern authority on manorial society, has vividly depicted the duties of tenancy:

On certain days the tenant brings the lord's steward perhaps a few small silver coins or, more often, sheaves of grain harvested on his fields, chickens from his farmyard, cakes of wax from his beehives or from the swarms of the neighboring forest. At other times he works on the arable or the meadows of the demesne [the lord's plot of land in the manorial fields, between one-third and one-half of that available]. Or else we find him carting casks of wine or sacks of grain on behalf of the master to distant residences. His is the labour which repairs the walls or moats of the castle. If the master has guests the peasant strips his own bed to provide the necessary extra bed-clothes. When the hunting season comes round he feeds the pack. If war breaks out he does duty as a footsoldier or orderly, under the leadership of the reeve of the village.[3]

[3] Marc Bloch, *Feudal Society*, trans. by L. A. Manyon (Chicago: University of Chicago Press, 1968), p. 250.

The lord also had the right to subject his tenants to exactions known as banalities. He could, for example, force them to breed their cows with his bull and to pay for the privilege, to grind their bread grains in his mill, to bake their bread in his oven, to make their wine in his wine press, to buy their beer from his brewery, and even to surrender to him the tongues or other choice parts of all animals slaughtered on his lands. The lord also collected a serf's best animal as an inheritance tax. Without the lord's permission, serfs could neither travel nor marry outside the manor in which they served.

THE LIFE OF A SERF   Exploited as the serfs may appear to have been from a modern point of view, their status was far from chattel slavery. It was to the lord's advantage to keep his serfs healthy and happy; his welfare, like theirs, depended on a successful harvest. Serfs had their own dwellings and modest strips of land and lived by the produce of their own labor and organization. They were permitted to market for their own profit what surpluses might remain after the harvest. They were free to choose their spouses within the local village, although the lord's permission was required if a wife or husband was sought from another village. And serfs could pass their property (their dwellings and field strips) and worldly goods on to their children.

Peasants lived in timber-framed huts. Except for the higher domestic servants, they seldom ventured far beyond their own villages. The local priest often was their window on the world, and church festivals were their major communal entertainment. Their religiosity was based in large part on the church being the only show in town, although their religious beliefs were by no means unambiguously Christian.

Despite the social distinctions between free and servile serfs—and, within these groups, between those who owned ploughs and oxen and those who possessed only hoes—the common dependence on the soil forced close cooperation. The ratio of seed to grain yield was consistently poor; about two bushels of seed were required to produce six to ten bushels of grain in good times. There was rarely an abundance of bread and ale, the staple peasant foods. Two important American crops, potatoes and corn (maize), were unknown in Europe until the sixteenth century. Pork was the major source of protein, and every peasant household had its pigs. At slaughter time a family might also receive a little tough beef. But basically, everyone depended on the grain crops. When they failed or fell short, the peasantry simply went hungry unless the lord had surplus stores that he was willing to share.

CHANGES IN THE MANOR Two basic changes occurred in the evolution of the manor from the early to the later Middle Ages. The first was the fragmentation of the manor and the rise to dominance of the single-family holding. This development was aided by such technological advances as the collar harness (ca. 800), the horseshoe (ca. 900), and the three-field system of crop rotation, which made it easier for smaller familial units to support themselves. As the lords parceled out their land to new tenants, their own plots became progressively smaller. The increase in tenants and the decrease in the lord's fields brought about a corresponding reduction in the labor services exacted from the tenants. Also, the bringing of new fields into production increased individual holdings and modified labor services. In France, by the reign of Louis IX (r. 1226–1270), only a few days of labor a year were required, whereas in the time of Charlemagne peasants had worked the lords' fields several days a week.

As the single-family unit replaced the clan as the basic nuclear group, assessments of goods and services fell on individual fields and households, no longer on manors as a whole. Family farms replaced manorial units. The peasants' carefully nurtured communal life made possible a family's retention of its land and dwelling after the death of the head of the household. In this way, land and property remained in the possession of a single family from generation to generation.

The second change in the evolution of the manor was the conversion of the serf's dues into money payments, a change made possible by the revival of trade and the rise of the towns. This development, completed by the thirteenth century, permitted serfs to hold their land as rent-paying tenants and to overcome their servile status. Although tenants thereby gained greater freedom, they were not necessarily better off materially. Whereas servile workers could have counted on the benevolent assistance of their landlords in hard times, rent-paying workers were left, by and large, to their own devices. Their independence caused some landlords to treat them with indifference and even resentment.

Lands and properties that had been occupied by generations of peasants and were recognized as their own were always under the threat of the lord's claim to a prior right of inheritance and even outright usurpation. As their demesnes declined, the lords were increasingly tempted to encroach on such traditionally common lands. The peasantry fiercely resisted such efforts, instinctively clinging to the little they had. In many regions they successfully organized to gain a voice in the choice of petty rural officials.

By the mid-fourteenth century a declining nobility in England and France, faced with the ravages of the great plague and the Hundred Years' War, tried to turn back the historical clock by increasing taxes on the peasantry and passing laws to restrict their migration into the cities. The peasantry responded with armed revolts in the countryside. These revolts became the rural equivalents of the organization of medieval cities in sworn communes to protect their self-interests against powerful territorial rulers. The revolts of the agrarian peasantry, like those of the urban proletariat, were brutally crushed. They stand out at the end of the Middle Ages as violent testimony to the breakup of medieval society. As growing national sentiment would break its political unity and heretical movements end its nominal religious unity, the peasantry's revolts revealed the absence of medieval social unity.

Towns and Townspeople

In the eleventh and twelfth centuries, towns held only about 5 percent of western Europe's population. By comparison to modern towns, they were not very large. Of Germany's 3,000 towns, for example, 2,800 had populations under 1,000. Only fifteen German towns exceeded 10,000. The largest, Cologne, had 30,000. In England, only London had more than 10,000. Paris was larger than London, but not by much. The largest European towns were in Italy; Florence approached 100,000 and Milan was not far behind. Despite their comparatively small size, towns then, as now, were where the action was. In the town, one could find the whole of medieval society and its most creative segments.

The Chartering of Towns

Towns were originally dominated by feudal lords, both lay and clerical. The lords created the towns by granting charters to those who would agree to live and work within them. The charters guaranteed their safety and gave inhabitants a degree of independence unknown on the land. The purpose was originally to concentrate skilled laborers who could manufacture the finished goods desired by lords and bishops. In this way, manorial society may be seen actually creating its urban challenger and weakening itself. Because they longed for finished goods and for the luxuries that came from faraway places, noblemen had urged their serfs to become skilled at making such things. The new skills required to do this in turn gave serfs a new importance and power. By the eleventh century, skilled serfs began to pay their manorial dues in manufactured goods, rather than in field labor, eggs, chickens, and beans, as they had earlier. In return for a fixed rent and proper sub-servience, serfs were also encouraged to settle and work in towns. There they gained special rights and privileges by way of the charters.

As towns grew and beckoned, many serfs fled the countryside with their skills and went directly to the new urban centers. There they found the freedom and profits that could lift an industrious craftsperson into higher social ranks. As this migration of serfs to the towns accelerated, the lords in the countryside offered them more favorable terms of tenure to keep them on the land. In that way, the growth of towns improved the lot of serfs generally. But serfs could not easily be kept down on the farms after they had discovered the opportunities of town life.

The Rise of Merchants

Not only did rural society give the towns their crafts-people and day laborers, but the first merchants themselves may also have been enterprising serfs. Certainly, some of the long-distance traders were men who had nothing to lose and everything to gain by the enormous risks of foreign trade. They traveled together in armed caravans and convoys, buying goods and products as cheaply as possible at the source, and selling them for all they could get in Western ports. (See Map 8–1.) More than anything else, it was the greed and daring of these rough-hewn men that created Western urban life as we know it today.

At first the merchants were not liked by the traditional social groups—nobility, clergy, and peasantry—who considered them an oddity. As late as the fifteenth century, we find the landed nobility still snubbing the urban patriciate. Such snobbery probably never died out among the older landed nobility, who looked down on the traders as men with poor breeding, little character, and money they did not properly earn or deserve. Over time, however, the powerful grew to respect the merchants, and the weak always tried to imitate them, because wherever the merchants went, they left a trail of wealth behind.

Challenging the Old Lords

As the traders established themselves in towns, they grew in wealth and numbers, formed their own protective associations, and soon found themselves able to challenge traditional seigneurial authority. Merchants especially wanted to end the arbitrary tolls and tariffs imposed by regional magnates over the surrounding countryside. Such regulations hampered the flow of commerce on which both merchant and craftsperson in the growing urban export industries depended. Wherever merchants settled in large numbers, they opposed the tolls, tariffs, and

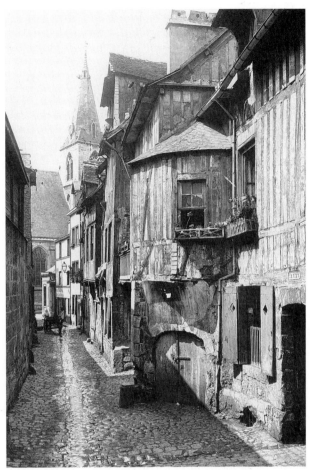

The Rue du Matelas, a French street in Rouen, Normandy, was preserved intact from the Middle Ages to World War II. Note the narrowness of the street and the open sewer running down its center. The houses were built of rough cast stone, mud, and timber. H. Roger Viollet/Liaison Agency, Inc.

other petty restrictions that discouraged the flow of trade. Merchant guilds or protective associations sprang up in the eleventh century, followed in the twelfth by guilds of craftspeople (drapers, haberdashers, furriers, hosiers, goldsmiths, and so on), who worked to advance the business interests of both merchants and craftspeople, as well as to enhance the personal well-being of their members. This quickly brought them into conflict with the norms of comparatively static agricultural society.

Townspeople needed simple and uniform laws and a government sympathetic to their new forms of business activity, not the fortress mentality of the lords of the countryside. Such a need could not but create a struggle with the old nobility within and outside the towns. This conflict led towns in the High and later Middle Ages to form their own independent communes and to ally themselves with kings against the nobility in the countryside, a development that would eventually rearrange the centers of power in medieval Europe and dissolve classic feudal government.

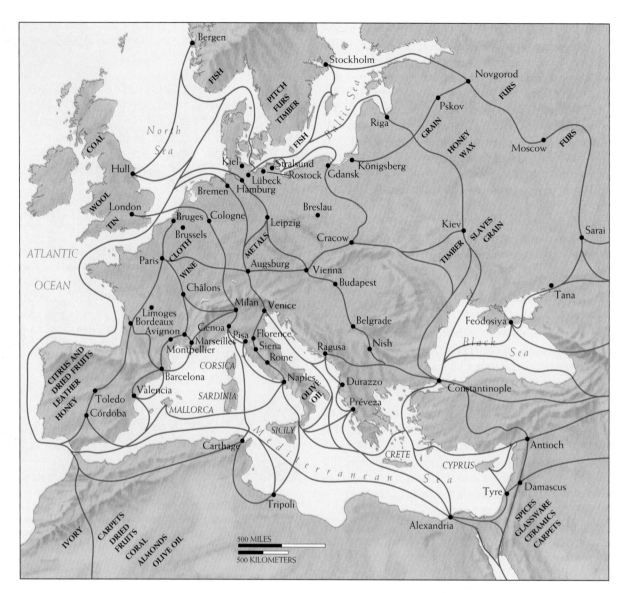

MAP 8–1   SOME MEDIEVAL TRADE ROUTES AND REGIONAL PRODUCTS   *The map shows some of the channels that came to be used in interregional commerce and what was traded in a particular region.*

Because the merchants were so clearly the engine of the urban economy, small shopkeepers and artisans identified far more with them than with the aloof lords and bishops who were a town's original masters. Most townspeople found their own interests best served by the development of urban life in the direction the merchants wanted it to go. That is, they wanted greater commercial freedom, fewer barriers to trade and business, and a freer secular life—in sum, a less closed urban life. The lesser nobility (the small knights) outside the towns also recognized the new mercantile economy to be the wave of the future. During the eleventh and twelfth centuries, the burgher upper class increased its economic strength and successfully challenged the old urban lords for control of the towns.

New Models of Government

With urban autonomy came new models of self-government. Around 1100 the old urban nobility and the new burgher upper class merged. It was a marriage between those wealthy by birth (inherited property) and those who made their fortunes in long-distance trade. From this new ruling class was born the aristocratic town council, which henceforth came to govern towns.

Enriching and complicating the situation even more, small artisans and craftspeople also slowly developed their own protective associations or guilds and began to gain a voice in government. The towns' ability to provide opportunities for the "little person" had created the slogan, "Town air brings freedom." In the countryside the air one breathed still belonged to the lord of the land; but in the towns residents were treated as freemen. Within town walls, people thought of themselves as citizens with basic rights, not subjects liable to their masters' whim. Economic hardship certainly continued to exist among the lower urban groups despite their basic legal and political freedoms. But social mobility was at least a possibility in the towns.

KEEPING PEOPLE IN THEIR PLACES   Traditional measures of success had great appeal within the towns. Despite their economic independence, the wealthiest urban groups admired and imitated the lifestyle of the old landed nobility. Although the latter treated the urban patriciate with disdain, successful merchants longed to live the noble, knightly life. They wanted coats of arms, castles, country estates, and the life of a gentleman or a lady on a great manor. This became particularly true in the later Middle Ages, when reliable bills of exchange and international regulation of trade, together with the maturation of merchant firms, allowed merchants to conduct their business by mail. Then only the young apprentices did a lot of traveling, to learn the business from the ground up. When merchants became rich enough to do so, they took their fortunes to the countryside.

Such social climbing disturbed city councils, and when merchants departed for the countryside, towns often lost out economically. A need to be socially distinguished and distinct pervaded urban society. The merchants were just the tip of the iceberg. Towns tried to control this need by defining grades of luxury in dress and residence for the various social groups and vocations. Overly conspicuous consumption was a kind of indecent exposure punishable by law. Such sumptuary laws restricted the types and amount of clothing one might wear (the length and width of fur pieces, for example) and how one might decorate one's dwelling architecturally. In this way, people were forced to dress and live according to their station in life. The intention of such laws was positive: to maintain social order and dampen social conflict by keeping everyone clearly and peacefully in their place. (See "The Laws and Customs of Chester.")

The Laws and Customs of Chester

The following laws and customs appear in the Domesday Book *(1080–1086). They were included there because the English town of Chester was among the forty or so towns in which the king had a financial interest. The town paid a portion of the fines it collected for criminal behavior to the king's representative.*

❖ *In terms of fines and financial loss, what were the most serious crimes? Was simple negligence punished? Did religion play a role in the setting of any of these fines? Do the fines suggest vigilance or pettiness?*

If any free man of the king broke the peace which had been granted and killed a man in his house, all his land and money came to the king, and he himself became an outlaw.

He who shed blood between Monday morning and the ninth hour of Saturday compounded for it with [i.e., paid a fine of] ten shillings. From the ninth hour of Saturday to Monday morning bloodshed was compounded for with twenty shillings. Similarly any one paid twenty shillings who shed blood in the twelve days after Christmas, on the day of the Purification of the Blessed Mary, on the first day after Easter, the first day of Pentecost, Ascension day, on the Assumption or Nativity of the Blessed Mary, and on the day of All Saints.... He who committed theft or robbery, or exercised violence upon a woman in a house, compounded for each of these with forty shillings....

If fire burned the city, he from whose house it started compounded for it with three oras [about two shillings worth] of pennies, and gave to his next neighbor two shillings. Of all these forfeitures, two parts belonged to the king and the third to the earl.

A man or a woman making false measure in the city, and being arrested, compounded for it with four shillings. Similarly a person making bad ale was either placed in the ducking stool or gave four shillings to the reeve [the bailiff]. This forfeiture the officer of the king and of the earl received in the city, in whosesoever land it has been done, either of the bishop or of another man. Similarly also, if any one held the toll back beyond three nights, he compounded for it with forty shillings.

From James Harvey Robinson, ed., *Readings in European History*, Vol. 1 (Boston: Athenaeum, 1904), pp. 406–407.

Skilled workers were an integral component of the commerce of medieval towns. This scene shows the manufacture of cannons in a foundry in Florence. Scala/Art Resource, N.Y.

SOCIAL CONFLICT AND PROTECTIVE ASSOCIATIONS (GUILDS) Despite unified resistance to external domination, medieval towns were not internally harmonious social units. They were a collection of many selfish and competitive communities, each seeking to advance its own business and family interests. Conflict between "haves" and "have-nots" was inevitable, especially because medieval towns had little concept of social and economic equality. Theoretically, poor artisans could work their way up from lower social and vocational levels, and some lucky ones did. But so long as they had not done so, they were excluded from the city council. Only families of long standing in the town who owned property had full rights of citizenship and a direct say in the town's government at the highest levels. Government, in other words, was inbred and aristocratic.

Conflict also existed between the poorest workers in the export trades (usually the weavers and woolcombers) and the economically better off and socially ascending independent workers and small shopkeepers. The better-off workers also had their differences with the merchants, whose export trade often brought competitive foreign goods into the city. So independent workers and small shopkeepers organized to restrict foreign trade to a minimum and corner the local market in certain items.

Over time, the formation of artisan guilds gave workers in the trades a direct voice in government. Ironically, a long-term effect of this gain was to limit the social mobility of the poorest artisans. The guilds gained representation on city councils, where, to discourage imports, they used their power to enforce quality standards and fair prices on local businesses. These actions created tight restrictions on guild membership, squeezing out poorer artisans and tradesmen. As a result, lesser merchants and artisans found their opportunities progressively limited. So rigid and exclusive did the dominant guilds become that they often stifled their own creativity and inflamed the journeymen whom they excluded from their ranks. Unrepresented artisans and craftspeople constituted a true urban proletariat prevented by law from forming their own guilds or entering existing ones. The efforts by guild-dominated governments to protect local craftspeople and industries tended to narrow trade and depress the economy for all.

Towns and Kings

By providing kings with the resources they needed to curb factious noblemen, towns became a major force in the transition from feudal societies to national governments. In many places kings and towns formally allied against the traditional lords of the land. A notable exception to this general development is England, where the towns joined with the barons against the oppressive monarchy of King John (r. 1199–1216), becoming part of the parliamentary opposition to the crown. But by the fifteenth century, kings and towns had also joined forces in England, so much so that by century's end Henry Tudor (r. 1485–1509) was known as the "burgher king."

Towns attracted kings and emperors for obvious reasons. Towns were a ready source of educated bureaucrats and lawyers who knew Roman law, the tool for running kingdoms and empires. Money was also to be found in the towns in great quantity, enabling kings to hire their own armies and free themselves from dependence on the nobility. Towns had the human, financial, and technological resources to empower kings. By such alliances, towns won royal political recognition and had their constitutions guaranteed. This proved somewhat easier to do in the stronger coastal areas than in interior areas, where urban life remained less vigorous and territorial government was on the rise. In France, towns became integrated early into royal government. In Germany, they fell under ever tighter control by the princes. In Italy, uniquely, towns expanded to dominate the surrounding countryside, becoming genuine city–states during the Renaissance.

It was also in the towns' interest to have a strong monarch as their protector against despotic local lords and princes, who were always eager to integrate or engulf the towns within their expanding territories. Unlike a local magnate, a king tended to remain at a distance, allowing towns to exercise their precious autonomy. A king was thus the more desirable overlord. It was also an advantage to a town to have its long-distance trade conducted in the name of a known powerful monarch. This gave predators pause and improved official cooperation along the way. Both sides—kings and towns—gained from such alliances.

Between the eleventh and fourteenth centuries, towns had considerable freedom and autonomy. As in Roman times, they again became the flourishing centers of Western civilization. But after the fourteenth century, and even earlier in France and England, the towns, like the church before them, were steadily bent to the political will of kings and princes in most places. By the seventeenth century few would be truly autonomous, the vast majority integrated thoroughly into the larger purposes of the "state."

Jews in Christian Society

Towns also attracted large numbers of Jews. It was within the major urban centers, particularly in France and Germany, that Jews gathered between the late twelfth and thirteenth centuries. They did so both by choice and for safety in the increasingly hostile Christian world. Mutually wary of one another, Christians and Jews sought to limit their contacts with each other to exchanges between merchants and scholars. The church expressly forbade Jews from hiring Christians in their businesses and from holding any public authority over them. In the cities, Jews plied trades in their own small businesses, and many became wealthy bankers to kings and popes, as well as having private business clients among both Christians and Jews. Jewish intellectual and religious culture had always been very elaborate and sophisticated, both dazzling and threatening to Christians who viewed it from outside. These various factors—the separateness of Jews, their economic power, and their cultural strength—contributed to suspicion and distrust among Christians, whose religious teaching held Jews responsible for the death of Christ.

Between the late twelfth and early fourteenth centuries, Jews were exiled from France and persecuted elsewhere as well. Two factors were behind this unprecedented surge in anti-Jewish sentiment. The first was a desire on the part of kings to confiscate Jewish wealth and property and eliminate the Jews as economic competitors with the monarchy. (French kings acted similarly in the fourteenth century against a wealthy Christian military order known as the Knights Templars; see Chapters 7 and 9.) The other factor behind the surge in anti-Jewish sentiment was the church's increasing political vulnerability to the new dynastic monarchies. Faced with the loss of its political power, the church became more determined than ever to maintain its spiritual hegemony. With the beginning of the Crusades and the creation of new mendicant orders, the church powerfully reasserted claims to spiritual sovereignty over Europe and beyond, instigating major campaigns against dissenters, heretics, witches, and Jews at home as well as against the infidel abroad. (See "The Massacre of Jews during the First Crusade (1096).")

Schools and Universities

In the twelfth century, Byzantine and Spanish Islamic scholars made it possible for the works of Aristotle on logic, the writings of Euclid and Ptolemy, the basic works of Greek physicians and Arab mathematicians, and the larger texts of Roman law to circulate among Western scholars. Islamic scholars especially preserved these works. They also wrote extensive, thought-provoking commentaries on Greek texts, which were translated into Latin and made available to Western scholars and students. The result of this renaissance of ancient knowledge was an intellectual ferment that gave rise to Western universities.

University of Bologna

The first important Western university, established by Emperor Frederick I Barbarossa in 1158, was in Bologna. There we find the first formal organizations of students and masters and the first degree programs—the institutional foundations of the modern university. Originally, the term "university" meant simply a corporation of individuals (students and masters) who joined for their mutual protection from overarching episcopal authority (the local bishop oversaw the university) and from the local townspeople. Because townspeople then looked on students as foreigners without civil rights, such protective unions were necessary. They followed the model of an urban trade guild.

Bolognese students also "unionized" to guarantee fair rents and prices from their often reluctant hosts. And students demanded regular, high-quality teaching from their masters. In Italy, students actually hired their own teachers, set pay scales, and drew up desired lecture topics. Masters who did not keep their promises or live up to student expectations were boycotted. Price gouging by townspeople was met with the threat to move the university to another town. This could rather easily be done because the university was not yet tied to a fixed physical plant. Students and masters moved freely from town to town as they chose. Such mobility gave them a unique independence from their surroundings.

Masters also formed their own protective associations and established procedures and standards for certification to teach within their ranks. The first academic degree was a certificate that licensed one to teach, a *licentia docendi*. It granted graduates in the liberal arts program, the program basic to all higher learning, as well as those in the higher professional sciences of medicine, theology, and law, "the right to teach anywhere" (*ius ibique docendi*).

Bologna was famous for the revival of Roman law. During the Frankish era and later, from the seventh to the eleventh centuries, only the most rudimentary manuals of Roman law had survived. With the growth of trade and towns in the late eleventh century, Western scholars had come into contact with the larger and more important parts of the *Corpus juris civilis* of Justinian, which had been lost during the intervening centuries. The study and dissemination of this recovered material was now undertaken in Bologna under the direction of a learned man

The Massacre of Jews during the First Crusade (1096)

Crusades embraced the full social spectrum. Already before the First Crusade, itinerant preachers like Peter the Hermit (1050–1115) inspired popular crusades by urging peasants and artisans to seek a better life and perhaps also heaven by marching to the Holy Land along familiar pilgrim routes. So-called people's crusades both preceded and followed the First Crusade, also pillaging Jewish towns en route. The following description recounts the pillaging of the Jewish community of Speyer during the First Crusade.

❖ *How did the Crusaders justify killing Jews in Speyer? Was it Christian law or doctrine to kill Jews who refused to be baptized? Why didn't the Jews defend themselves in more aggressive ways? Is this an example of a Crusade turned mob?*

It came to pass that, when [the crusaders] traversed towns where there were Jews, they said..."Behold we journey a long way to seek the idolatrous shrine and to take vengeance upon the Muslims. But here are the Jews dwelling among us, whose ancestors killed [Jesus Christ]....Let us take vengeance first upon them. Let us wipe them out as a nation; Israel's name will be mentioned no more. Or else let them be like us and acknowledge the son born of menstruation."

Now when the [Jewish] communities heard their words, they reverted to...repentance, prayer and charity. The hands of the holy people [Jews] fell weak and their hearts melted and their strength flagged. They hid themselves in innermost chambers before the ever turning sword....They fasted three consecutive days, both day and night, in addition to daily fasts....They cried out and gave forth a loud and bitter shriek. But their Father did not answer them...

That year Passover fell on Thursday and the new moon of Iyyar on Friday. On the eight of Iyyar, on the Sabbath, the enemy [the Crusaders] arose against the Jewish community of Speyer and killed eleven [holy] souls who sanctified their Creator on the holy Sabbath day and refused to be baptised [at the hands of the Crusaders].

The University of Bologna in central Italy was distinguished as the center for the revival of Roman law. This carving on the tomb of a Bologna professor of law shows students attending one of his lectures.
Scala/Art Resource, N.Y.

named Irnerius, who flourished in the early twelfth century. He and his students made authoritative commentaries, or glosses, on existing laws based on their newly broadened knowledge of the *Corpus juris civilis*. They thereby expanded legal knowledge. Around 1140, a monk named Gratian, also resident in Bologna, created the standard legal text in church, or canon, law, the *Concordance of Discordant Canons*, known simply as Gratian's *Decretum*.

As Bologna was the model for southern European universities (that is, those of Spain, Italy, and southern France) and the study of law, so Paris became the model for northern European universities and the study of theology. Oxford, Cambridge, and (much later) Heidelberg were among its imitators. All these universities required a foundation in the liberal arts for advanced study in the higher sciences of medicine, theology, and law. The arts program consisted of the *trivium* (grammar, rhetoric, and logic) and the *quadrivium* (arithmetic, geometry, astronomy, and music), or, more simply, the language arts and the mathematical arts.

Cathedral Schools

Before the emergence of universities, the liberal arts had been taught in cathedral and monastery schools. The purpose of these schools was to train the clergy, and their curricula tended understandably to be narrowly restricted to this goal. But by the late eleventh and twelfth centuries, cathedral schools

also began to provide lectures for nonclerical students and they broadened their curricula to include some training for purely secular vocations. In 1179, a papal decree obliged cathedrals to provide teachers gratis for laity who wanted to learn.

After 1200, increasing numbers of future notaries and merchants who had no particular interest in becoming priests, but who needed Latin and related intellectual disciplines to fill their secular positions, studied side by side with aspiring priests in cathedral and monastery schools. By the thirteenth century, the demand for secretaries and notaries in the growing urban and territorial governments and for literate personnel in the expanding merchant firms gave rise to special schools for strictly secular vocational preparation. With the appearance of these schools, the church began for the first time to lose some of its monopoly on higher education.

The most famous of the cathedral schools were those of Rheims and Chartres. Chartres won fame under the direction of such distinguished teachers as Fulbert, Saint Ivo, and Saint Bernard of Chartres (not to be confused with the more famous Saint Bernard of Clairvaux). Gerbert, who later became Pope Sylvester II (r. 999–1003), guided Rheims to greatness in the last quarter of the tenth century. Gerbert was filled with enthusiasm for knowledge and promoted both logical and rhetorical studies. He did much to raise the study of logic to preeminence within the liberal arts, despite his personal belief in the greater relevance of rhetoric to the promotion of Christianity.

University of Paris

The University of Paris grew institutionally out of the cathedral school of Notre Dame, among others. King Philip Augustus and Pope Innocent III gave the new university its charter in 1200. At Paris the college, or house system, originated. At first, a college was just a hospice providing room and board for poor students who could not afford to rent rooms in town. But the educational life of the university quickly expanded into fixed structures and began to thrive on their sure endowments. University-run colleges made the overseeing and protection of students easier and gave the university a new prominence as a permanent urban institution.

In Paris, the most famous college was the Sorbonne, founded around 1257 by Robert de Sorbon, chaplain to the king, for the housing of theology students. In Oxford and Cambridge, the colleges became the basic unit of student life and were indistinguishable from the university proper. By the end of the Middle Ages such colleges had tied universities to physical plants and fixed foundations.

In this engraving, a teacher at the University of Paris leads fellow scholars in a discussion. As shown here, all of the students wore the scholar's cap and gown. Corbis

Their mobility was forevermore restricted, as was, compared with earlier times, their autonomy and freedom.

As a group, students at Paris had power and prestige. They enjoyed royal protections and privileges denied ordinary citizens. Many Parisian students were well to do, and not a few were spoiled and petulant. (See "Student Life at the University of Paris.") They did not endear themselves to the townspeople, whom they considered to be inferior. That townspeople sometimes let their resentments of such students lead to violence against them is made clear from the city's ordinances, which were highly protective of students. For example, city law forbade the beating of students. Only those students who had clearly committed serious crimes could be imprisoned. Only in self-defense might a citizen strike a student. All citizens were obligated to testify against anyone seen abusing a student. University laws also required all teachers to be carefully examined before being licensed to teach Parisian students. The law thus recognized students as both a valuable and a vulnerable resource.

The Curriculum

Before the so-called renaissance of the twelfth century, when many Greek and Arabic texts became available to Western scholars and students in Latin translations, the education available within the cathedral and monastery schools had been quite limited. Students learned grammar, rhetoric, and some elementary geometry and astronomy. They had the classical Latin grammars of Donatus and Priscian, Saint Augustine's treatise, *On Christian Doctrine*, and Cassiodorus's treatise, *On Divine and Secular Learning*. The writings of Boethius provided instruction in arithmetic and music and preserved the small body of Aristotle's works on logic then known in the West. After the textual finds of the early twelfth century, Western scholars recovered the whole of Aristotle's logic, the astronomy of Ptolemy, the writings of Euclid, and many Latin classics. By the mid-thirteenth century, almost all of Aristotle's works circulated in the West.

In the High Middle Ages, the learning process remained very basic. The assumption was that truth already existed; it was not something that one had to go out and find. It was there, requiring only to be properly organized, elucidated, and defended. Such conviction made logic and dialectic the focus of education. Students wrote commentaries on authoritative texts, especially those of Aristotle and the Church Fathers. Teachers did not encourage students to strive independently for undiscovered truth. Students rather learned to organize and harmonize the accepted truths of tradition, which were drilled into them.

Student Life at the University of Paris

As the following account by Jacques de Vitry makes clear, not all students at the University of Paris in the thirteenth century were there to gain knowledge. Students fought constantly and subjected each other to ethnic insults and slurs.

❖ *Why were students from different lands so prejudiced against one another? Does the rivalry of faculty members appear to have been as intense as that among students? What are the student criticisms of the faculty? Do they sound credible?*

Almost all the students at Paris, foreigners and natives, did absolutely nothing except learn or hear something new. Some studied merely to acquire knowledge, which is curiosity; others to acquire fame, which is vanity; others still for the sake of gain, which is cupidity and the vice of simony. Very few studied for their own edification, or that of others. They wrangled and disputed not merely about the various sects or about some discussions; but the differences between the countries also caused dissensions, hatreds and virulent animosities among them, and they impudently uttered all kinds of affronts and insults against one another.

They affirmed that the English were drunkards and had tails; the sons of France proud, effeminate and carefully adorned like women. They said that the Germans were furious and obscene at their feasts; the Normans, vain and boastful; the Poitevins, traitors and always adventurers. The Burgundians they considered vulgar and stupid. The Bretons were reputed to be fickle and changeable, and were often reproached for the death of Arthur. The Lombards were called avaricious, vicious and cowardly; the Romans, seditious, turbulent and slanderous; the Sicilians, tyrannical and cruel; the inhabitants of Brabant, men of blood, incendiaries, brigands and ravishers; the Flemish, fickle, prodigal, gluttonous, yielding as butter, and slothful. After such insults from words they often came to blows.

I will not speak of those logicians [professors of logic and dialectic] before whose eyes flitted constantly "the lice of Egypt," that is to say, all the sophistical subtleties, so that no one could comprehend their eloquent discourses in which, as says Isaiah, "there is no wisdom." As to the doctors of theology, "seated in Moses' seat," they were swollen with learning, but their charity was not edifying. Teaching and not practicing, they have "become as sounding brass or a tinkling cymbal," or like a canal of stone, always dry, which ought to carry water to "the bed of spices." They not only hated one another, but by their flatteries they enticed away the students of others; each one seeking his own glory, but caring not a whit about the welfare of souls.

Translations and Reprints from the Original Sources of European History, Vol. 2 (Philadelphia: Department of History, University of Pennsylvania, 1902), pp. 19–20.

This method of study, based on logic and dialectic, was known as *Scholasticism*. It reigned supreme in all the faculties—in law and medicine as well as in philosophy and theology. Students read the traditional authorities in their field, formed short summaries of their teaching, disputed them with their peers by elaborating traditional arguments pro and con, and then drew conclusions. Logic and dialectic dominated training in the arts because they were the tools that could discipline knowledge and thought. *Dialectic* is a negative logical inquiry, the art of discovering a truth by finding the contradictions in arguments against it. Astonishingly, medical students did no practical work; they studied and debated the authoritative texts just as law and theology students did.

Few books existed for students, and because printing with movable type did not yet exist, those available were expensive hand-copied works. So students could not leisurely master a subject in the quiet of their studies. They had rather to learn it in discussion, lecture, and debate. There was a lot of memorizing, and the ability to think on one's feet was stressed. Rhetoric, or persuasive argument, was the ultimate goal, that is, the ability to make an eloquent defense of the knowledge one had clarified by logic and dialectic. Successful students became virtual walking encyclopedias; their education both filled their heads with knowledge and gave them the ability to recite it impressively.

THE SUMMA The twelfth century saw the rise of the *summa*, an authoritative summary of allegedly all that was known about a particular subject. The summa's main purpose was to conciliate traditional authorities and heap up clarified truth. In canon law, there was Gratian's *Concordance of Discordant Canons* (around 1142), whose very title embodies the scholastic method. In theology, there was Peter Lombard's *Four Books of Sentences* (1155–1157). Embracing traditional teaching on God, the creation, Christ, and the sacraments, it was destined to become the standard theological textbook until the Protestant reformers declared it unbiblical. It had evolved from Peter Abelard's *Sic et Non* (around 1122), a much smaller work that juxtaposed seemingly contradictory statements on the same subject by revered authorities. Out of this same tradition came Saint Thomas Aquinas's magnificent *Summa Theologiae* (begun in 1265), to many the last word on theology, which the medieval summa was always intended to be. (See "Thomas Aquinas Proves the Existence of God.")

University study normally began between the ages of twelve and fifteen. Students coming to university were expected to bring with them a good knowledge of Latin gained in local schools or from a private tutor. Once there, students spent four years perfecting their Latin (particularly in the study of the *trivium*) before attaining the bachelor-of-arts degree. A master's degree thereafter might take three or four years, during which time students studied mathematics, natural science, and philosophy by way of classical texts. A degree in theology at Paris might take more than twenty years of study from beginning to end.

CRITICS OF SCHOLASTICISM   Even in the heyday of Scholasticism, this kind of education had its strong critics. Prominent among them were John of Salis-

Thomas Aquinas Proves the Existence of God

People in the Middle Ages saw continuity between Earth and heaven, the world of the living and the world of the dead. For intellectuals, reason and revelation, while different, were also believed to be connected, so that reasoned argument could prove some of what the Bible revealed to faith. Thomas Aquinas, perhaps the greatest medieval theologian, here states his famous five arguments for the existence of God, which he believed any rational person would agree with.

❖ *Are these arguments persuasive? Which is the most persuasive, which the least? Are they basically the same argument?*

Is there a God?

REPLY: There are five ways in which one can prove that there is a God.

The FIRST...is based on change. Some things...are certainly in process of change: this we plainly see. Now anything in the process of change is being changed by something else....Hence one is bound to arrive at some first cause of change not itself being changed by anything, and this is what everybody understands by God.

The SECOND way is based on the nature of causation. In the observable world causes are found to be ordered in series....Such a series must however stop somewhere....One is therefore forced to suppose some first cause, to which everyone gives the name "God."

The THIRD way is based on what need not be and on what must be....Some...things...can be, but need not be for we find them springing up and dying away....Now everything cannot be like this [for then we must conclude that] once upon a time there was nothing. But if that were true there would be noth-

ing even now, because some thing that does not exist can only be brought into being by something already existing....One is forced therefore to suppose something which must be...[and] is itself the cause that other things must be.

The FOURTH way is based on the gradation observed in things. Some things are found to be more good, more true, more noble...and other things less [so]. But such comparative terms describe varying degrees of approximation to a superlative...[something that is] the truest and best and most noble of things....There is something, therefore, which causes in all other things their being, their goodness, and whatever other perfection they have. And this we call "God."

The FIFTH way is based on the guidedness of nature. An orderedness of actions to an end is observed in all bodies obeying natural laws...; they truly tend to a goal and do not merely hit it by accident....Everything in nature, therefore, is directed to its goal by someone with intelligence, and this we call "God."

Thomas Aquinas, *Summa Theologiae, I*, ed. by Thomas Gilby (Image Books, New York: 1969), pp. 67–70.

bury (ca. 1120–1180) and Saint Bernard of Clairvaux (1090–1153), who thought the scholastic method was a heartless and presumptuous way to train minds and a threat to the church.

There were critics also within the ordinary faculty ranks, the so-called *dictatores*. These professional grammarians and rhetoricians, the forerunners of later humanists, gave students practical instruction in the composition of letters and documents. They taught good writing and speaking, and in contrast to the highly abstract logic and dialectic of scholastic education, they stressed practice over theory. (The difference might be compared with that between a modern expository writing program, in which execution is the focus, and a modern English department, wherein theory is the focus.) Later humanists, establishing an approach still favored in modern liberal arts education, would urge scholars to go directly to sources in their original languages and draw their own conclusions.

Philosophy and Theology

Scholastics quarreled over the proper relationship between philosophy (which, for them, meant almost exclusively the writings of Aristotle) and theology (which they believed to be a special "science" based on divine revelation). The problem between philosophy and theology arose because, in Christian eyes, there was a lot of heresy in Aristotle's writings, especially as his teaching was interpreted by certain Islamic commentators. These commentators did not treat his work as a handmaiden to Christianity. For example, Aristotle believed in the eternality of the world (that the world had always been). This plainly called into question the Judeo–Christian teaching that the world had been created in time, as stressed in the book of Genesis. Aristotle also taught that intellect, or mind, was ultimately one, a seeming denial of individuality and hence of Christian teaching about individual responsibility and personal immortality.

When theologians took the logic and metaphysics of Aristotle over into their theologies, some critics believed that it posed a threat to biblical teaching and traditional church authority. Berengar of Tours (d. 1088), for example, was a Scholastic who applied logic to the sacrament of the Eucharist; and before long he found himself questioning the church's teaching on transubstantiation (which was not yet official dogma). Peter Abelard (1079–1142) tried to subject the Trinity to logical examination. He found that, by Aristotle's logic, three could not be one nor one three, in contrast to the church's teachings about the unity of God the Father, Son, and Holy Ghost.

The boldness of these new logicians shocked conservatives. Monastic leaders especially wondered whether the liberal arts course of study, dominated by Aristotle's writings, was more foe than ally of theological study. The love of learning had clearly gotten in the way of the love of God as far as the critics of Scholasticism were concerned.

A century of such suspicion and criticism of Aristotle's alleged undermining of Christian theology culminated in 1277 when the bishop of Paris condemned 219 philosophical propositions. The condemnation was directed against scholars who seemed to the authorities to be more interested in secular philosophy than in Christian truth. It chilled the relationship between learning and religion. Reason and revelation thereafter became two very different spheres of knowledge, much as church and state were then also being forced apart in the world of secular politics. William of Ockham (d. 1349) represented conservative opinion on the issue and signaled its future direction when he denied that essential matters of theology could be addressed as if they were empirical. To know God's mind, Christians must content themselves with biblical revelation; reason could not know God directly.

Women in Medieval Society

The image and the reality of medieval women are two very different things. The image, both for contemporaries and for us today, was strongly influenced by the views of male Christian clergy, whose ideal was the celibate life of chastity, poverty, and obedience. Drawing on classical medical, philosophical, and legal traditions that predated Christianity, as well as on ancient biblical theology, Christian theologians depicted women as physically, mentally, and morally weaker than men.

On the basis of such assumptions, medieval church and society sanctioned the coercive treatment of women, including corrective wife beating in extreme cases. Christian clergy generally considered marriage a debased state by comparison with the religious life, and in their writings they praised virgins and celibate widows over wives. Women, as the Bible clearly taught, were the "weaker vessel." In marriage, their role was to be subject and obedient to their husbands, who, as the stronger, had a duty to protect and discipline them.

This image of the medieval woman suggests that she had two basic options in life: to become either a subjugated housewife or a confined nun. In reality, the vast majority of medieval women were neither.

IMAGE AND STATUS Both within and outside Christianity, this image of women—not yet to speak of the reality of their lives—was contradicted. In chivalric romances and courtly love literature of

A fifteenth-century rendering of an eleventh- or twelfth-century marketplace. Medieval women were active in all trades, but especially in the food and clothing industries.
Scala/Art Resource, N.Y.

the twelfth and thirteenth centuries, as in the contemporaneous cult of the Virgin Mary, women were presented as objects of service and devotion to be praised and admired—even put on pedestals and treated as superior to men. If the church shared traditional misogynist sentiments, it also condemned them, as in the case of the *Romance of the Rose* (late thirteenth century) and other popular "bawdy" literature.

The learned churchman Peter Lombard (1100–1169) sanctioned an image of women that didactic Christian literature often invoked. Why, he asked, was Eve created from Adam's rib and not instead taken from his head or his feet? The answer was clear: God took Eve from Adam's side because he wanted woman neither to rule over nor to be enslaved by man, but to stand squarely at his side, as his companion and partner in mutual aid and trust. By so insisting on the spiritual equality of men and women and their shared responsibility to one another within marriage, the church also helped to raise the dignity of women.

Germanic law treated women better than Roman law had done. Women had basic rights under law that prevented their being treated as

chattels. And there was far greater equality between the sexes: Unlike Roman women, who as teens married men much older than themselves, German women married as adults and their husbands were of similar age. Another practice unknown to the Romans was the groom's conveyance of a marriage portion, or dowry, to his bride to have and to hold as her own in the event of widowhood. All the major Germanic law codes recognized the economic freedom of women, that is, their right to inherit, administer, dispose of, and confer on their children family property and wealth. They could also press charges in court against men for bodily injury and rape. Depending on the country in question, punishments for rape ranged from fines, flogging, and banishment to blinding, castration, and death.

LIFE CHOICES   The nunnery was an option for only a very few unmarried women from the higher social classes. Entrance required a dowry (*dos*) and could be almost as expensive as a wedding, although usually it was less. Within the nunnery, a woman could rise to a position of leadership as abbess or mother superior and could exercise an organizational and administrative authority denied her in much of secular life. The nunneries of the established religious orders were under male supervision, however, so that even abbesses had finally to answer to higher male authority.

Nunneries also provided women an escape from the debilitating effects of multiple pregnancies. In the ninth century, under the influence of Christianity, the Carolingians made monogamous marriage their official policy. Heretofore they had practiced polygyny and concubinage and had permitted divorce. The result was both a boon and a burden to women. On one hand, the selection of a wife now became a very special event, and wives gained greater dignity and legal security. On the other hand, a woman's labor as household manager and bearer of children greatly increased.

The aristocratic wife not only ran a large household, but was also the agent of her husband during his absence. In addition to these responsibilities, one wife now had sole responsibility for the propagation of heirs. The Carolingian wife also became the sole object of her husband's wrath and displeasure. Such demands clearly took

their toll. The mortality rates of Frankish women increased and their longevity decreased after the ninth century.

Under such conditions, the cloister could serve as a welcome refuge to women. The number of women in cloisters was never very great, however. In late medieval England, for example, it is estimated that there were no more than 3,500 cloistered women. (See "The Regulation of Prostitutes in London (1393).")

The vast majority of medieval women were neither aristocratic housewives nor nuns, but working women. Much evidence suggests that they were respected and loved by their husbands, perhaps because they worked shoulder by shoulder and hour by hour with them. Between the ages of ten and fifteen, girls were apprenticed in a trade much as were boys, and they learned to be skilled workers. If they married, they might continue their particular trade, operating their bakeshops or dress shops next to their husbands' business, or become assistants and partners in the shops of their husbands. Women appeared in virtually every "blue-collar" trade, from butcher to goldsmith, although they were especially

The Regulation of Prostitutes in London (1393)

As with the nunnery, the brothel was also a recognized special place for women, and, again like the nunnery, the women's activities were carefully regulated by male authority, only now for social rather than theological reasons. Prostitution was deemed to be both morally repugnant and socially necessary—an outlet for single men (married men were not supposed to frequent brothels) and thereby protection for young maidens, whose virginity was important on the marriage market. A magnet for brawling and, after the fifteenth century, a known source of venereal disease (syphilis), prostitution was subjected to strict controls in medieval towns. An ordinance of 1393 describes the concerns of London authorities and their determination to restrict prostitutes to well-monitored brothels.

❖ *Why can prostitutes not have free run of the city? Is this sensible legislation or is it gender bias? What exactly does a prostitute lose if she breaks the law?*

Whereas many...broils and dissensions have arisen in times past, and many men have been slain and murdered by reason of the frequent...consorting with common harlots, at taverns, brewhouses of [peddlars], and other places of ill-fame, within the said city and the suburbs thereof...Hence we do by our command forbid, on behalf of our Lord the King, and the Mayor and Alderman of the City of London, that any such women shall go about or lodge in the said city, or in the suburbs thereof, by night or by day; but they are to keep themselves to the places thereunto assigned, that is to say, the [bathhouses] on the other side of [the River] Thames, and Cokkeslane; on pain of losing and forfeiting the upper garment that she shall be wearing, together with her hood [the striped clothing required of all legal prostitutes, indicating their profession]..."

prominent in the food and clothing industries. Women belonged to guilds, just like men, and they became craftmasters. In the later Middle Ages, townswomen increasingly had the opportunity to go to school and to gain vernacular literacy.

It is also true that women did not have as wide a range of vocations as men, although the vocational destinies of the vast majority of men were as fixed as those of women. Women were excluded from the learned professions of scholarship, medicine, and law. They often found their freedom of movement within a profession more carefully regulated than a man's. Usually, women performed the same work as men for a wage 25 percent lower. And, as is still true today, women filled the ranks of domestic servants in urban households in disproportionate numbers. Still, women remained as prominent and as creative a part of workaday medieval society as men.

The Lives of Children

The image of medieval children and the reality of their lives seem also to have been two very different things. Until recently, historians were inclined to believe that parents were emotionally distant from their children during the Middle Ages. Evidence of low esteem for children comes from a variety of sources.

Depicted are two children's pastimes: catching butterflies with a net (center child) and spinning tops (lower left). The third child is using a walker, despite his appearance of being too old to need it. All three indicate contemporary recognition of children and the stages of life they go through. The Bridgeman Art Library International

CHILDREN AS "LITTLE ADULTS" Some historians maintain that children are rarely portrayed as different from adults in medieval art and sculpture. If, pictorially, children and adults look alike, were people in the Middle Ages aware of childhood as a separate period of life requiring special care and treatment? There was also high infant and child mortality, which, it seems, could only have discouraged parents from making a high emotional investment in their children. How could a parent dare to have a deep emotional attachment to a child who had a 30–50 percent chance of dying before age five?

During the Middle Ages, children assumed adult responsibilities early in life. The children of peasants labored in the fields alongside their parents as soon as they could physically manage the work. Urban artisans and burghers sent their children out of their homes into apprenticeships in various crafts and trades between the ages of eight and twelve. Can such early removal of children from their homes be taken for anything but low affection for children? That children were expected to grow up fast is attested to by the canonical ages for marriage, twelve for girls and fourteen for boys (although few actually married at these ages).

The practice of infanticide is an even more striking suggestion of low esteem for children in ancient and early medieval times. According to Tacitus, the Romans exposed unwanted children, especially girls, at birth. In this way, they regulated family size. The surviving children appear to have been given plenty of attention and affection. The Germanic tribes of medieval Europe, by contrast, had large families, but tended to neglect their children in comparison with the Romans. Infanticide, particularly of girls, continued to be practiced in the early Middle Ages, as shown by its condemnation in penance books and by church synods. Parents were forbidden to sleep with infants and small children to prevent them from being suffocated, either by accident or by design.

Among the German tribes, one paid a much lower *wergild*, or compensatory fine, for injury to a child than for injury to an adult. The *wergild* for injuring a child was only one-fifth that for injuring an adult. That paid for injury to a female child under fifteen was one-half that for injury to a male child—a strong indication that female children were the least esteemed members of German tribal society. Mothers appear also to have nursed boys longer than they did girls, which favored boys' health and survival. A woman's *wergild*, however, increased a full eightfold between infancy and her childbearing years, at which time she had obviously become highly prized.[4]

[4] David Herlihy, "Medieval Children," in *Essays on Medieval Civilization*, ed. by B. K. Lackner and K. R. Phelp (Austin, TX: University of Texas Press, 1978), pp. 109–131.

CHILDHOOD AS A SPECIAL STAGE Despite such varied evidence of parental distance and neglect, there is another side to the story. Since the early Middle Ages, physicians and theologians, at least, had understood childhood to be a distinct and special stage of life. Isidore (560–636), the metropolitan of Seville and a leading intellectual authority throughout the Middle Ages, carefully distinguished six ages of life, the first four of which were infancy (between one and seven years of age), childhood (seven to fourteen), adolescence, and youth.

According to the medical authorities, infancy proper extended from birth to anywhere between six months and two years (depending on the authority) and covered the period of speechlessness and suckling. The period thereafter, until age seven, was considered a higher level of infancy, marked by the beginning of a child's ability to speak and his or her weaning. At age seven, when a child could think and act decisively and speak clearly, childhood proper began. After this point, a child could be reasoned with, could profit from regular discipline, and could begin to train for a lifelong vocation. At seven a child was ready for schooling, private tutoring, or apprenticeship in a chosen craft or trade. Until physical growth was completed, however—and that could extend to twenty-one years of age—the child or youth was legally under the guardianship of parents or a surrogate authority.

There is evidence that high infant and child mortality, rather than distancing parents from children, actually made parents look on children as all the more precious. The medical authorities respected during the Middle Ages—Hippocrates, Galen, and Soranus of Ephesus—dealt at length with postnatal care and childhood diseases. Both in learned and in popular medicine, sensible as well as fanciful cures can be found for the leading killers of children (diarrhea, worms, pneumonia, and fever). When infants and children died, medieval parents grieved as pitiably as modern parents do. In the art and literature of the Middle Ages, we find mothers baptizing dead infants and children or carrying them to pilgrim shrines in the hope of reviving them. There are also examples of mental illness and suicide brought on by the death of a child.[5]

Clear evidence of special attention being paid to children is also found in the great variety of children's toys and even devices like walkers and potty chairs, which existed in the Middle Ages. The medieval authorities on child rearing widely condemned child abuse and urged moderation in the disciplining of children. In church art and drama, parents were urged to love their children as Mary loved Jesus. And early apprenticeships may also be interpreted as an expression of parental love and concern rather than indifference and low esteem. For in the Middle Ages, no parental responsibility was thought greater than that of equipping a child for useful and gainful work. Certainly, by the High Middle Ages if not earlier, children were widely viewed as special creatures with their own needs and rights.

In Perspective

During the High Middle Ages, the growth of Mediterranean trade revived old cities and caused the creation of new ones. The Crusades aided and abetted this development. Italian cities especially flourished during the late eleventh and twelfth centuries. Venice dominated Mediterranean trade and extended its political and economic influence throughout the Near East. It had its own safe ports as far away as Syria. As cities grew in population and became rich with successful trade, a new social group, the long-distance traders, rose to prominence. By marriage and political organization, these merchant families organized themselves into an unstoppable force. They successfully challenged the old nobility in and around the cities. A new elite of merchants gained control of city governments almost everywhere. They brought with them a policy of open trade and the blessings and problems of nascent capitalism. Artisans and small shopkeepers at the lower end of the economic spectrum aspired to follow their example, as new opportunities opened for all. The seeds of social conflict and of urban class struggle had been sown.

One very positive result of the new wealth of towns was the patronage of education and culture. These matters were given an emphasis not experienced since Roman times. Western Europe's first universities appeared in the eleventh century and universities steadily expanded over the next four centuries. There were twenty by 1300. Not only did Scholasticism flourish, but a new literature, art, and architecture developed as well, reflecting both a new human vitality and the reshaping of society and politics. For all of this, western Europeans had no one to thank so much as the new class of merchants, whose greed, daring, and ambition made it all possible.

[5] Klaus Arnold, *Kind und Gesellschaft im Mittelalter und Renaissance* (Paderborn, Germany: 1980), pp. 31, 37.

REVIEW QUESTIONS

1. How did the responsibilities of the nobility differ from those of the clergy and the peasantry during the High Middle Ages? In what ways did each social class contribute to the stability of society?
2. What led to the revival of trade and the growth of towns in the twelfth century? What political and social conditions were essential for a revival of trade? How did towns change medieval society?
3. From your understanding of the functions of the medieval university, assess the strengths and weaknesses of higher education in that period. Comment especially on the curriculum.
4. How would you define Scholasticism? What was the Scholastic program and method of study? Who were the main critics of Scholasticism and what were their complaints?
5. How would you assess the position of women in Germanic law and Roman law? What were the options and responsibilities for women in each social class? What are the differing theories regarding the image of children in the Middle Ages?

SUGGESTED READINGS

E. Amt (Ed.), *Women's Lives in Medieval Europe: A Sourcebook* (1993). Outstanding collection of sources.

P. Ariès, *Centuries of Childhood: A Social History of Family Life* (1962). Pioneer effort on the subject.

J. W. Baldwin, *The Scholastic Culture of the Middle Ages: 1000–1300* (1971). Best brief synthesis available.

M. Bloch, *French Rural History*, trans. by J. Sondheimer (1966). A classic by a great modern historian.

J. Brundage, *Law, Sex and Christian Society in Medieval Europe* (1987). The Church's conception and regulation of sexuality.

G. Duby, *The Three Orders: Feudal Society Imagined*, trans. by A. Goldhammer (1981). Large, comprehensive, authoritative.

E. Gilson, *Heloise and Abelard* (1968). Analysis and defense of medieval scholarly and gender values.

J. Goody, *The Development of the Family and Marriage in Europe* (1983). Interesting effort to explain the Church's stake in the regulation of family and marriage.

B. A. Hanawalt, *The Ties That Bound: Peasant Families in Medieval England* (1986). Illuminating demographic and economic study of rural life.

B. A. Hanawalt, *Growing Up in Medieval London* (1993). Excellent, positive portrayal of parental and societal treatment of children.

C. H. Haskins, *The Renaissance of the Twelfth Century* (1927). Still the standard account.

C. H. Haskins, *The Rise of Universities* (1972). A short, minor classic.

D. Herlihy, *Medieval Households* (1985). Bread-and-butter account of household structure in antiquity and the Middle Ages.

G. Künstler, *Romanesque Art in Europe* (1973). Standard survey.

G. Leff, *Paris and Oxford Universities in the Thirteenth and Fourteenth Centuries: An Institutional and Intellectual History (1968).* Very good on Scholastic debates.

R. S. Loomis (Ed.), *The Development of Arthurian Romance* (1963). Essays debating its meaning and significance.

R. Lopez, *The Commercial Revolution of the Middle Ages 900–1350* (1971). A master's brief survey.

E. Mâle, *The Gothic Image: Religious Art in France in the Thirteenth Century* (1913). An enduring classic.

L. de Mause (Ed.), *The History of Childhood* (1974). Very substantive and provocative essays with an interest in the inner as well as the material lives of children.

R. I. Moore, *The Formation of a Persecuting Society: Power and Deviance in Western Europe, 950–1250* (1987). A sympathetic look at heresy and dissent.

A. Murray, *Reason and Society in the Middle Ages* (1978). A view of the Middle Ages as an age of reason as well as of faith.

J. T. Noonan, *Contraception: A History of Its Treatment by the Catholic Theologians and Canonists* (1967). Fascinating account of medieval theological attitudes toward sexuality and sex-related problems.

E. Panofsky, *Gothic Architecture and Scholasticism* (1951). A controversial classic.

H. Pirenne, *Medieval Cities: Their Origins and the Revival of Trade*, trans. by F. D. Halsey (1970). A minor classic.

H. Rashdall, *The Universities of Europe in the Middle Ages*, vols. 1–3 (1936). Dated, but still extremely useful for documents of the period.

I. S. ROBINSON, *The Papacy, 1073–1198: Continuity and Innovation* (1990). A fresh look at the papacy in this period of its reform and independence.

S. SHAHAR, *The Fourth Estate: A History of Women in the Middle Ages* (1983). A comprehensive survey, making clear the great variety of women's work.

B. STOCK, *The Implications of Literacy* (1983). How the ability to read changed medieval society.

L. THORNDIKE, *University Records and Life in the Middle Ages* (1975). Rich primary sources for both curricular and extracurricular life.

The Invention of Printing in China and Europe

The ability to put information and ideas on paper and to circulate them widely in multiple identical copies has been credited in the West with the rise of Humanism, the Protestant Reformation, the modern state, and the Scientific Revolution. In truth, the message preceded the machinery: It was a preexisting desire to rule more effectively, to shape and control the course of events that brought the printing press into existence in both China and Europe. Before there was printing, there were rulers, religious leaders, and merchants eager to disperse their laws, scriptures, and wares more widely and efficiently among their subjects, followers, and customers.

To create the needed skilled agents and bureaucrats, leaders of state, church, and business cooperated in the sponsorship of schools and education, which spurred the growth of reading and writing among the middle and upper urban classes. Literacy, in turn, fueled the desire for easily accessible and reliable information. Literacy came more slowly to the lower social classes, as authorities feared too much knowledge in the hands of the uneducated or poorly educated would only fan the fires of discontent. To the many who remained illiterate after the invention of printing, information was conveyed carefully in oral and pictorial form. Printed official statements were designed to be read to as well as read by people, and religious leaders put images and pictures in the hands of simple folk, hoping to content them with saints and charms.

Resources and Technology: Paper and Ink

Among the indispensable materials of the print revolution were sizable supplies of durable, inexpensive paper and a reliable ink. As early as the Shang period (1766–1122 B.C.E.) a water-based soot and gum ink was used across Asia. (Europe would not have such an ink until the early Middle Ages.) Also in the Shang period, official seals and stamps used to authenticate documents were made by carving bronze, jade, ivory, gold, and stone in a reverse direction (that is, in a mirror form, to prevent the print from appearing backwards).

Similar seals appeared in ancient Mesopotamia and Egypt but only for religious use, not for the affairs of daily secular life. Later, more easily carved clay or wax seals reproduced characters on silk or bamboo surfaces.

Silk in the East and parchment in the West had been early, but very expensive, print media. Bamboo and wood were cheaper, but neither was suited to large-scale printing.

A step forward occurred in the second century B.C.E, when the Chinese invented a crude paper from hemp fibers, which was used only for wrappings. Three centuries later (105 C.E.), an imperial eunuch named Ts'ia Lun combined tree bark, hemp, rags, and old fish nets into a superior paper on which one could reliably write. A better blend of mulberry bark, fish nets, and natural fibers became the standard paper mixture. By the Tang period (618–907), high-quality paper manufacturing had become a major industry.

In the eighth century, the improved Chinese recipe began to make its way west, after Chinese prisoners taught their Arab captors how to make paper. By the ninth century, Samarkand in Russian Turkestan had become the leading supplier of paper in the East. A century later, Baghdad and Damascus shipped fine paper to Egypt and Europe. Italy became a major Western manufacturer in the thirteenth century followed by Nuremberg, Germany, in the late fourteenth.

Early Printing Techniques

By the seventh century C.E., multiple copies of the Confucian Scriptures were made by taking paper rubbings from stone and metal engravings, a direct prelude to block printing. At this time in the West, the arts of engraving, and particularly of coin-casting (by hammering hot alloy on an anvil that bore a carved design), took the first steps toward printing with movable type.

The invention of printing occurred much earlier in the East than in the West. The Chinese invented "block printing" (that is, printing with carved wooden blocks) in the eighth century, almost six hundred years before the technique appeared in Europe (1395). The Chinese also far outpaced the West in printing with "movable type" (that is, with individual char-

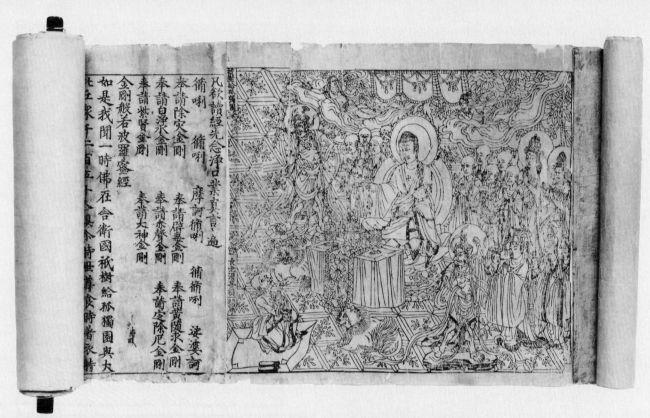

*The Diamond Sutra. This Chinese translation of a Sanskrit Buddhist work was printed in
868 and found at Tunhuang. It is the earliest dated piece of block printing yet discovered.*
The Granger Collection

acters or letters that could be arranged by hand to
make a page)—a technique invented by Pi Scheng in
the 1040s, four hundred years before Johann Gutenberg set up the first Western press in Mainz, Germany (around 1450).

Block printing used hard wood (preferably from
pear or jujube trees), whose surface was glazed with
a filler (glue, wax, or clay). A paper copy of what one
wanted to duplicate (be it a drawn image, a written
sentence, or both) was placed face down on a wet
glaze covering the block and the characters cut into
it. The process accommodated any artistic style
while allowing text and illustration to coexist harmoniously on a page. Once carved, the block was
inked and mild pressure applied, allowing a great
many copies to be made before it wore out.

The first movable type was ceramic. The printer
set each character or piece in an iron form and
arranged them on an iron baking plate filled with
heated resin and wax which, when cooled, created
a tight page. After the print run was finished, the
plate was heated again to melt the wax and free the
type for new settings. Ceramic and later metal type
were fragile and left uneven impressions, and metal
type was expensive as well and did not hold water-
based Chinese inks.

Carved wooden type did not have these problems
and therefore became the preferred tool. Set in a
wooden frame and tightened with wooden wedges,
the readied page was inked up and an impression
made, just as in printing with carved wooden blocks.
Cutting a complete set of type or font required much
time and effort because of the complexity and enor-
mity of Chinese script. To do the latter justice, a
busy press required 10,000 individual characters,
and that number could increase several-fold, depending on the project.

Printing Comes of Age
In 952, after a quarter century of preparation, a standardized Chinese text, unblemished by any scribal
errors, was printed for the first time on a large scale.

That text, the Confucian Classics, was an epochal event in the history of printing. The main reading of the elite, these famous scrolls became the basis of the entry exam for a government office. In awakening people to the power of printing, the Confucian Classics may be compared to the publication of Gutenberg's Latin Bible.

The Sung period (960–1278) saw the first sustained flowering of block printing. Still today among the Chinese the phrase "Sung style" connotes high quality. Three monumental publications stand out: the Standard Histories of previous Chinese dynasties, serially appearing between 994 and 1063; the Buddhist Scriptures in scrolls up to sixty feet and longer, requiring 130,000 carved wooden blocks (971–983); and the Taoist Scriptures (early eleventh century). For the literate, but not necessarily highly educated, numerous how-to books on medical, botanical, and agricultural topics became available. Printed paper money also appeared for the first time in copper-poor Szechwan during the Sung.

There is no certain evidence that printing was a complete gift of the Far East to the West. Although some scholars believe that Chinese block printing accompanied playing cards through the Islamic world and into Europe, the actual connecting links have not yet been demonstrated. So while there was a definite "paper trail" from East to West, Europe appears to have developed its own inks and invented its own block and movable type printing presses independently.[1]

Indeed in East and West, different writing systems would favor distinct forms of printing: In China, carved wood blocks suited an ideographic script that required a seemingly boundless number of characters. Each ideograph, or character, expressed a complete concept. In contrast, European writing was based on a very small phonetic alphabet. Each letter could express meaning only when connected to other letters, forming words. For such a system, movable metal type worked far better than carved wood blocks. So while China mastered movable type printing earlier than the West, the enormous number of characters required by the Chinese language made movable type impractical.

A European Printshop. This 1568 woodcut by Hans Sachs shows typesetting (rear) and printing (front) underway in an early printshop. Printing made it possible to reproduce exactly and in quantity both text and illustrations, leading to the distribution of scientific and technical information on a scale unimaginable in the pre-print world. Houghton Library, Harvard University

Ironically, the simpler machinery of block printing did greater justice to China's more intricate and complex script, while Europe's far simpler script required the more complex machinery of movable type. Today the Chinese still face the problem of storing and retrieving their rich language in digitized form, "the space-age equivalent of movable type." In telecommunications, they prefer faxes, "the modern-day equivalent of the block print."[2]

Society and Printing

In neither East nor West do the availability of essential material resources (wood, ink, and paper) and the development of new technologies sufficiently

[1]Carter, *The Invention of Printing in China and Its Spread Westward*, pp. 143, 150, 182.

[2]Twitchett, *Printing and Publishing in Medieval China*, p. 86.

explain the advent of printing. Cultural and emotional factors played an equally large role. In China, the religious and moral demands of Buddhists, Taoists, and Confucians lay behind the invention of block printing. For Buddhists, copying and disseminating their sacred writings had always been a traditional path of salvation. Taoists wanted to hang protective charms or seals around their necks, printed sacred messages blessed by their priests that were up to four inches wide. These were apparently the first block prints. Confucianists, too, lobbied for standardized printed copies of their texts, which they had for centuries duplicated by crude rubbings from stone-carved originals.

In Europe, the major religious orders (Augustinians, Dominicans, and Franciscans) and popular lay religious movements (Waldensians, Lollards, and Hussites) joined with Humanists to promote the printing of standardized, orthodox editions of the Bible and other religious writings. As the numbers of literate laity steadily grew, the demand for cheap, practical reading material (calendars, newssheets, and how-to pamphlets) also rapidly increased. By 1500, fifty years after Gutenberg's invention, two hundred printing presses operated throughout Europe, sixty of them in German cities. And just as in China, the large print runs of the new presses tended to be religious or moral subjects in the early years: Latin Bibles and religious books, indulgences and Protestant pamphlets, along with decorated playing cards often bearing moral messages.

With the printing press came the first copyright laws. Knowledge had previously been considered to be "free." The great majority of medieval scholars and writers were clergy, who lived by church or other patronage and whose knowledge was deemed a gift of God to be shared freely with all. After the printing press, however, a new sense of intellectual property emerged. In Europe, primitive protective laws took the form of a ruler's "privilege," by which a ruler pledged to punish the pirating of a particular work within his or her realm over a limited period of time. Such measures had clear limits: More than half of the books published during the first century of print in the West were pirated editions, a situation that would not change significantly until the eighteenth century.

Government censorship laws also ran apace with the growth of printing. The clergy of Cologne, Germany, issued the first prohibition of heretical books in 1479. In 1485 the church banned the works of the heretics John Wycliffe and John Huss Europe-wide, and two years later the pope promulgated the first bull against any and all books "harmful to the faith." In 1521 Emperor Charles V banned Martin Luther's works throughout the Holy Roman Empire, along with their author. In 1527 the first publisher was hanged for printing a banned book of Luther's. And in 1559 the pope established the Index of Forbidden Books, which still exists.

Printing stimulated numerous new ancillary trades. In addition to the proliferation of bookstores and the rise of traveling booksellers, who carried flyers from town to town promoting particular works, there were new speciality stationery shops, ink and inkstone stores, bookshelf and reading-table makers, and businesses manufacturing brushes and other printing tools. The new print industry also brought social and economic upheaval to city and countryside when, like modern corporations relocating factories to underdeveloped countries, it went in search of cheaper labor by moving presses out of guild-dominated cities and into the freer marketplace of the countryside.

For society's authorities, the new numbers of literate citizens and subjects made changes and reforms both easier and more difficult. As a tool of propaganda, the printing press remained a two-edged sword. On the one hand, it gave authorities the means to propagandize more effectively than ever. On the other hand, the new literate public found itself in an unprecedented position to recognize deceit, challenge tradition, and expose injustice.

❖ Why did the invention of printing occur earlier in the East than in the West? Did the West inherit all of its knowledge of printing from the East? What are the differences between Chinese and European writing systems? What problems do these systems create for printing? Why might one Chinese scholar prefer to send another Chinese scholar a fax rather than an e-mail? What was the impact of printing on Chinese and European societies?

Sources: Thomas F. Carter, *The Invention of Printing in China and Its Spread Westward* (1925). Elisabeth L. Eisensrein, *The Printing Press as an Agent of Change*, I–II (1979). Rudolf Hirsch, *Printing, Selling and Reading 1450–1550* (1967). Constance R. Miller, *Technical and Cultural Prerequisites for the Invention of Printing in China and the West* (1983). Denis Twitchett, *Printing and Publishing in Medieval China* (1983).

Part 3
1300–1750

	POLITICS AND GOVERNMENT	SOCIETY AND ECONOMY	RELIGION AND CULTURE
1300–1400	1309–1377 Pope resides in Avignon 1337–1453 Hundred Years' War 1356 *Golden Bull* creates German electoral college	1315–1317 Greatest famine of the Middle Ages 1347–1350 Black Death peaks 1358 *Jacquerie* shakes France 1378 Ciompi Revolt in Florence 1381 English peasants' revolt	1300–1325 Dante Alighieri writes *Divine Comedy* 1302 Boniface VIII issues bull *Unam Sanctam* 1350 Boccaccio, *Decameron* 1375–1527 The Renaissance in Italy 1378–1417 The Great Schism 1380–1395 Chaucer writes *Canterbury Tales* 1390–1430 Christine de Pisan writes in defense of women 1414–1417 The Council of Constance
1400–1500	1415–1433 Hussite revolt in Bohemia 1428–1519 Aztecs expand in central Mexico 1429 Joan of Arc leads French to victory in Orleans 1434 Medici rule begins in Florence 1453–1471 Wars of the Roses in England 1469 Marriage of Ferdinand and Isabella 1487 Henry Tudor creates Court of Star Chamber	1450 Johann Gutenberg invents printing with movable type 1492 Christopher Columbus encounters the Americas 1498 Vasco da Gama reaches India	1425–1450 Lorenzo Valla exposes the *Donation of Constantine* 1450 Thomas à Kempis, *Imitation of Christ* 1492 Expulsion of Jews from Spain
1500–1600	1519 Charles V crowned Holy Roman emperor 1530 *Augsburg Confession* defines Lutheranism 1547 Ivan the Terrible becomes tsar of Russia 1555 *Peace of Augsburg* recognizes the legal principle, *cuius regio, eius religio* 1568–1603 Reign of Elizabeth I of England 1572 Saint Bartholomew's Day Massacre 1588 English defeat of Spanish Armada 1598 Edict of Nantes gives Huguenots religious and civil rights	1519 Hernan Cortes lands in Mexico 1519–1522 Ferdinand Magellan circumnavigates the Earth 1525 German Peasants' Revolt 1531–1533 Francisco Pizarro conquers the Incas 1540 Spanish open silver mines in Peru, Bolivia, and Mexico 1550–1600 The great witch panics  Elizabeth I, The Armada Portrait	1513 Niccolo Machiavelli, *The Prince* 1516 Erasmus compiles a Greek New Testament 1516 Thomas More, *Utopia* 1517 Martin Luther's Ninety-five theses 1534 Henry VIII declared head of English Church 1540 Jesuit order founded 1541 John Calvin becomes Geneva's reformer 1543 Copernicus, *On the Revolutions of the Heavenly Spheres* 1545–1563 Council of Trent 1549 English *Book of Common Prayer*

EUROPE IN TRANSITION

1300–1750

	POLITICS AND GOVERNMENT	SOCIETY AND ECONOMY	RELIGION AND CULTURE
1600–1700	1624–1642 Era of Richelieu in France	1600–1700 Period of greatest Dutch economic prosperity	1605 Bacon, *The Advancement of Learning*; Shakespeare, *King Lear*; Cervantes, *Don Quixote*
	1629–1640 Charles I's years of personal rule	1600–early 1700s Spain maintains commercial monopoly in Latin America	1609 Kepler, *The New Astronomy*
	1640 Long Parliament convenes	1607 English settle Jamestown, Virginia	1611 King James Version of the English Bible
	1642 Outbreak of civil war in England	1608 French settle Quebec	1632 Galileo, *Dialogues on the Two Chief Systems of the World*
	1643–1661 Cardinal Mazarin regent for Louis XIV	1618–1648 Thirty Years' War devastates German economy	1637 Descartes, *Discourse on Method*
	1648 Peace of Westphalia	1619 African slaves first bought at Jamestown, Virginia	1651 Hobbes, *Leviathan*
	1649–1652 The *Fronde* in France	1650s–1670s Commercial rivalry between Dutch and English	
	1649 Charles I executed		
	1660 Charles II restored to the English throne	1661–1683 Colbert seeks to stimulate French economic growth	1687 Newton, *Principia Mathematica*
	1661–1715 Louis XIV's years of personal rule		1689 English Toleration Act
	1682–1725 Reign of Peter the Great		
	1685 James II becomes king of England		
	Louis XIV revokes Edict of Nantes	1690 Paris Foundling Hospital established	1690 Locke, *Essay Concerning Human Understanding*
	1688 "Glorious Revolution" in Britain		
1700–1789	1700–1721 Great Northern War between Sweden and Russia	1715–1763 Era of major colonial rivalry in the Caribbean	1739 Wesley begins field preaching
	1702–1714 War of Spanish Succession	1719 Mississippi Bubble in France	1748 Montesquieu, *Spirit of the Laws*
	1713 Peace of Utrecht	1733 James Kay's flying shuttle	1750 Rousseau, *Discourse on the Moral Effects of the Arts and Sciences*
	1720–1740 Age of Walpole in England and Fleury in France	1750s Agricultural Revolution in Britain	1751 First volume Diderot's *Encyclopedia*
	1740 Maria Theresa succeeds to the Habsburg throne	1750–1840 Growth of new cities	
		1763 Britain becomes dominant in India	1762 Rousseau, *Social Contract* and *Émile*
	1740–1748 War of the Austrian Succession	1763–1789 Enlightened absolutist rulers seek to spur economic growth	1763 Voltaire, Treatise on Tolerance
	1756–1763 Seven Years' War		
	1767 Legislative Commission in Russia	1765 James Hargreaves's spinning jenny	
	1772 First Partition of Poland	1769 Richard Arkwright's waterframe	1774 Goethe, *Sorrow of Young Werther*
	1776 American Declaration of Independence	1771–1775 Pugachev's Rebellion	1776 Smith, *Wealth of Nations*
			1781 Kant, *Critique of Pure Reason*
			Joseph II adopts policy of toleration in Austria

Declaration of Independence

1778 France aids the American colonies

Chapter 9

***The apparition of the Knight of Death, an allegory of the plague approaching
a city, whose defenses against it are all too unsure.*** From the *Tres Riches Heures du
Duc de Berry* (1284), Limbourg Brothers. Ms. 65/1284, fol. 90v. Musée Conde, Chantilly, France.
Giraudon/Art Resource, N.Y.

The Late Middle Ages:
Social and Political Breakdown
(1300–1527)

KEY TOPICS

- The Hundred Years' War between England and France
- The effects of the bubonic plague on population and society
- The growing power of secular rulers over the papacy
- Schism, heresy, and reform of the church

The late Middle Ages saw almost unprecedented political, social, and ecclesiastical calamity. France and England grappled with each other in a bitter conflict known as the Hundred Years' War (1337–1453), an exercise in seemingly willful self-destruction that was made even more terrible in its later stages by the introduction of gunpowder and the invention of heavy artillery. Bubonic plague, known to contemporaries as the "Black Death," swept over almost all of Europe, killing as much as one-third of the population in many regions between 1348 and 1350 and transforming many pious Christians into believers in the omnipotence of death. A schism emerged within the church, which lasted thirty-nine years (1378–1417) and led, by 1409, to the election of no fewer than three competing popes and colleges of cardinals. In 1453, the Turks marched seemingly invincibly through Constantinople and toward the West. As their political and religious institutions buckled, as disease, bandits, and wolves ravaged their cities in the wake of war, and as Islamic armies gathered at their borders, Europeans beheld what seemed to be the imminent total collapse of Western civilization.

It was in this period that such scholars as Marsilius of Padua, William of Ockham, and Lorenzo Valla produced lasting criticisms of medieval assumptions about the nature of God, humankind, and society. Kings worked through parliaments and clergy through councils to place lasting limits on the pope's temporal power. The notion, derived from Roman law, that a secular ruler is accountable to the body of which he or she is head had already found expression in documents like the Magna Carta. It came increasingly to carry the force of accepted principle, and conciliarists (advocates of the judicial superiority of a church council over a pope) sought to extend it to establish papal accountability to the church.

But viewed in terms of their three great calamities—war, plague, and schism—the fourteenth and fifteenth centuries were years in which politics resisted wisdom, nature strained mercy, and the church was less than faithful to its mandate.

The Hundred Years' War and the Rise of National Sentiment

Medieval governments were by no means all-powerful and secure. The rivalry of petty lords kept localities in turmoil, and dynastic rivalries could plunge entire lands into war, especially when power was being transferred to a new ruler, and woe to the ruling dynasty that failed to produce a male heir.

To field the armies and collect the revenues that made their existence possible, late medieval rulers depended on carefully negotiated alliances among a wide range of lesser powers. Like kings and queens in earlier centuries, they, too, practiced the art of feudal government, but on a grander scale and with greater sophistication. To maintain the order they required, the Norman kings of England and the Capetian kings of France finetuned traditional feudal relationships, stressing the duties of lesser to higher power and the unquestioning loyalty noble vassals owed the king. The result was a degree of centralized royal power unseen before in these lands and a nascent "national" consciousness that equipped both France and England for international warfare.

The Causes of the War

The conflict that came to be known as the Hundred Years' War began in May 1337 and lasted until October 1453. The English king Edward III (r. 1327–1377), the grandson of Philip the Fair of France (r. 1285–1314), may be said to have started the war by asserting a claim to the French throne when the French king Charles IV (r. 1322–1328), the last of Philip the Fair's surviving sons, died without a male heir. The French barons had no intention of placing the then fifteen-year-old Edward on the French throne, choosing instead the first cousin of Charles IV, Philip VI of Valois (r. 1328–1350), the first of a new French dynasty that ruled into the sixteenth century.

But there was more to the war than just an English king's assertion of a claim to the French throne. England and France were then emergent territorial powers in too close proximity to one another. Edward was actually a vassal of Philip's, holding several sizable French territories as fiefs from the king of France, a relationship that went back to the days of the Norman conquest. English possession of any French land was repugnant to the French because it threatened the royal policy of centralization. England and France also quarreled over control of Flanders, which, although a French fief, was subject to political influence from England because its principal industry, the manufacture of cloth, depended on supplies of imported English wool. Compounding these frictions was a long history of prejudice and animosity between the French and English people, who constantly confronted one another on the high seas and in port towns. Taken together, these various factors made the Hundred Years' War a struggle for national identity as well as for control of territory.

FRENCH WEAKNESS   France had three times the population of England, was far the wealthier of the two countries, and fought on its own soil. Yet, for the greater part of the conflict, until after 1415, the major battles ended in often stunning English victories. (See Map 9–1.) The primary reason for these French failures was internal disunity caused by endemic social conflicts. Unlike England,

Edward III pays homage to his feudal lord Philip VI of France. Legally, Edward was a vassal of the king of France. Archives Snark International/Art Resource, N.Y.

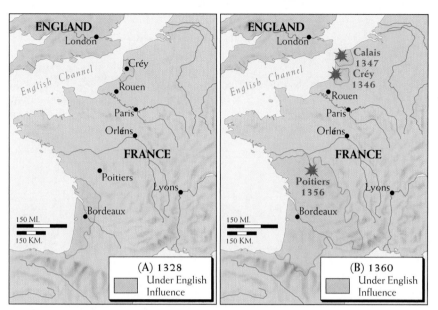

MAP 9–1 THE HUNDRED YEARS' WAR *The Hundred Years' War went on intermittently from the late 1330s until 1453. These maps show the remarkable English territorial gains up to the sudden and decisive turning of the tide of battle in favor of the French by the forces of Joan of Arc in 1429.*

Scene from an encamped army, surrounded by a barricade of wagons, some of which contain artillery pointed outward. 15th-century Germany. Kunstammlungen der Frusten zu Waldburg-Wolfegg, fol. 54r

France was still struggling in the fourteenth century to make the transition from a fragmented feudal society to a centralized "modern" state.

Desperate to raise money for the war, French kings resorted to such financial policies as depreciating the currency and borrowing heavily from Italian bankers, which aggravated internal conflicts. In 1355, in a bid to secure funds, the king convened a representative council of townspeople and nobles that came to be known as the Estates General. Although it levied taxes at the king's request, its members also used the king's plight to enhance their own regional rights and privileges, thereby deepening territorial divisions.

France's defeats also reflected English military superiority. The English infantry was more disciplined than the French, and English archers carried a formidable weapon, the longbow, capable of firing six arrows a minute with enough force to pierce an inch of wood or the armor of a knight at two hundred yards.

Finally, French weakness during the Hundred Years' War was due in no small degree to the comparative mediocrity of its royal leadership. English kings were far the shrewder.

Progress of the War

The war had three major stages of development, each ending with a seemingly decisive victory by one or the other side.

THE CONFLICT DURING THE REIGN OF EDWARD III   In the first stage of the war, Edward embargoed English wool to Flanders, sparking urban rebellions by merchants and the trade guilds. Inspired by a rich merchant, Jacob van Artevelde, the Flemish cities, led by Ghent, revolted against the French and in 1340 signed an alliance with England acknowledging Edward as king of France. On June 23 of that same year, in the first great battle of the war, Edward defeated the French fleet in the Bay of Sluys, but his subsequent effort to invade France by way of Flanders failed.

In 1346 Edward attacked Normandy and, after a series of easy victories that culminated at the Battle of Crécy, seized Calais. Exhaustion of both sides and the onset of the Black Death forced a truce in late 1347, and the war entered a brief lull. In 1356, near Poitiers, the English won their greatest victory, rout-

This miniature illustrates two scenes from the English peasant revolt of 1381. On the left, Wat Tyler, one of the leaders of the revolt, is executed in the presence of King Richard II. On the right, King Richard urges armed peasants to end their rebellion. Arthur Hacker, *The Cloister of the World*. The Bridgeman Art Library.

ing France's noble cavalry and taking the French king, John II the Good (r. 1350–1364), captive back to England. The defeat brought a complete breakdown of political order to France.

Power in France now lay with the Estates General. Led by the powerful merchants of Paris under Étienne Marcel, that body took advantage of royal weakness, demanding and receiving rights similar to those granted the English privileged classes in the Magna Carta. But unlike the English Parliament, which represented the interests of a comparatively unified English nobility, the French Estates General was too divided to be an instrument for effective government.

To secure their rights, the French privileged classes forced the peasantry to pay ever-increasing taxes and to repair their war-damaged properties without compensation. This bullying became more than the peasants could bear, and they rose up in several regions in a series of bloody rebellions known as the *Jacquerie* in 1358 (after the peasant revolutionary popularly known as *Jacques Bonhomme*, or "simple Jack"). The nobility quickly put down the revolt, matching the rebels atrocity for atrocity.

On May 9, 1360, another milestone of the war was reached when England forced the Peace of Brétigny on the French. This agreement declared an end to Edward's vassalage to the king of France and affirmed his sovereignty over English territories in France (including Gascony, Guyenne, Poitou, and Calais). France also agreed to pay a ransom of three

million gold crowns to win King John the Good's release. In return, Edward simply renounced his claim to the French throne.

Such a partition of French territorial control was completely unrealistic, and sober observers on both sides knew that it could not last long. France struck back in the late 1360s and by the time of Edward's death in 1377 had beaten the English back to coastal enclaves and the territory of Bordeaux.

FRENCH DEFEAT AND THE TREATY OF TROYES After Edward's death the English war effort lessened, partly because of domestic problems within England. During the reign of Richard II (r. 1377–1399), England had its own version of the *Jacquerie*. In June 1381, long-oppressed peasants and artisans joined in a great revolt of the unprivileged classes under the leadership of John Ball, a secular priest, and Wat Tyler, a journeyman. As in France, the revolt was brutally crushed within the year, but it left the country divided for decades.

The war intensified under Henry V (r. 1413–1422), who took advantage of internal French turmoil created by the rise to power of the duchy of Burgundy. With France deeply divided, Henry V struck hard in Normandy. Happy to see the rest of France besieged, the Burgundians foolishly watched from the sidelines while Henry's army routed the opposition led by the count of Armagnac, who had picked up the royal banner at Agincourt on October 25, 1415. In the years thereafter, belatedly recognizing that the defeat of

France would leave them easy prey for the English, the Burgundians closed ranks with French royal forces. The renewed French unity, loose as it was, promised to bring eventual victory over the English, but it was shattered in September 1419 when the duke of Burgundy was assassinated. In the aftermath of this shocking event, the duke's son and heir, determined to avenge his father's death, joined forces with the English.

France now became Henry V's for the taking—at least in the short run. The Treaty of Troyes in 1420 disinherited the legitimate heir to the French throne and proclaimed Henry V the successor to the French king, Charles VI. When Henry and Charles died within months of one another in 1422, the infant Henry VI of England was proclaimed in Paris to be king of both France and England. The dream of Edward III that had set the war in motion—to make the ruler of England the ruler also of France—had been realized, at least for the moment.

The son of Charles VI went into retreat in Bourges, where, on the death of his father, he became Charles VII to most of the French people, who ignored the Treaty of Troyes. Displaying unprecedented national feeling inspired by the remarkable Joan of Arc, they soon rallied to his cause and came together in an ultimately victorious coalition.

A contemporary portrait of Joan of Arc (1412–1431) in the National Archives in Paris. 15th c. Franco-Flemish miniature. Archives Nationales, Paris, France. Giraudon/Art Resource, N.Y.

The Hundred Years' War (1337–1443)	
1340	English victory at Bay of Sluys
1346	English victory at Crécy and seizure of Calais
1347	Black Death strikes
1356	English victory at Poitiers
1358	*Jacquerie* disrupts France
1360	Peace of Brétigny recognizes English holdings in France
1381	English peasants revolt
1415	English victory at Agincourt
1422	Treaty of Troyes proclaims Henry VI ruler of both England and France
1429	Joan of Arc leads French to victory at Orléans
1431	Joan of Arc executed as a heretic
1453	War ends; English retain only coastal town of Calais

JOAN OF ARC AND THE WAR'S CONCLUSION   Joan of Arc (1412–1431), a peasant from Domrémy, presented herself to Charles VII in March 1429, declaring that the King of Heaven had called her to deliver besieged Orléans from the English. The king was understandably skeptical, but being in retreat from what seemed to be a hopeless war, he was willing to try anything to reverse French fortunes. And the deliverance of Orléans, a city strategic to the control of the territory south of the Loire, would be a godsend. Charles's desperation overcame his skepticism, and he gave Joan his leave.

Circumstances worked perfectly to her advantage. The English force, already exhausted by a six-month siege of Orléans, was at the point of withdrawal when Joan arrived with fresh French troops. After repulsing the English from Orléans, the French enjoyed a succession of victories they popularly attributed to Joan. She deserved much of this credit, but not because she was a military genius. She provided the French with something military experts could not: inspiration and a sense of national identity and self-confidence. Within a few months of the liberation of Orléans, Charles VII received his crown in Rheims and ended the nine-year "disinheritance" prescribed by the Treaty of Troyes.

Charles forgot his liberator as quickly as he had embraced her. When the Burgundians captured Joan in May 1430, he was in a position to secure her release, but did little for her. The Burgundians and the English wanted her publicly discredited, believing this would also discredit Charles VII and demoralize French resistance. She was turned

Joan of Arc Refuses to Recant Her Beliefs

Joan of Arc, threatened with torture, refused to recant her beliefs and instead defended the instructions she had received from the voices that spoke to her.

❖ *In the following excerpt from her self-defense, do you get the impression that the judges have made up their minds about Joan in advance? How does this judicial process, which was based on intensive interrogation of the accused, differ from a trial today? Why was Joan deemed heretical and not insane when she acknowledged hearing voices?*

On Wednesday, May 9th of the same year [1431], Joan was brought into the great tower of the castle of Rouen before us the said judges. And [she] was required and admonished to speak the truth on many different points contained in her trial which she had denied or to which she had given false replies, whereas we possessed certain information, proofs, and vehement presumptions upon them. Many of the points were read and explained to her, and she was told that if she did not confess them truthfully she would be put to the torture, the instruments of which were shown to her all ready in the tower. There were also present by our instruction men ready to put her to the torture in order to restore her to the way and knowledge of truth, and by this means to procure the salvation of her body and soul which by her lying inventions she exposed to such grave perils.

To which the said Joan answered in this manner: "Truly if you were to tear me limb from limb and separate my soul from my body, I would not tell you anything more: and if I did say anything, I should afterwards declare that you had compelled me to say it by force." Then she said that on Holy Cross Day last she received comfort from St. Gabriel; she firmly believes it was St. Gabriel. She knew by her voices whether she should submit to the Church, since the clergy were pressing her hard to submit. Her voices told her that if she desired Our Lord to aid her she must wait upon Him in all her doings. She said that Our Lord has always been the master of her doings, and the Enemy never had power over them. She asked her voices if she would be burned and they answered that she must wait upon God, and He would aid her.

From *The Trial of Jeanne D'Arc*, trans. by W. P. Barrett (New York: Gotham House, 1932), pp. 303–304.

over to the Inquisition in English-held Rouen. The inquisitors broke the courageous "Maid of Orléans" after ten weeks of interrogation, and she was executed as a relapsed heretic on May 30, 1431. (See "Joan of Arc Refuses to Recant Her Beliefs.") Twenty-five years later (1456) Charles reopened her trial, and she was declared innocent of all the charges. In 1920 the church declared her a saint.

In 1435, the duke of Burgundy made peace with Charles. France, now unified and at peace with Burgundy, continued progressively to force the English back. By 1453, the date of the war's end, the English held only their coastal enclave of Calais.

The Hundred Years' War, with sixty-eight years of at least nominal peace and forty-four of hot war, had lasting political and social consequences. It devastated France, but it also awakened French nationalism and hastened the transition there from a feudal monarchy to a centralized state. It saw Burgundy become a major European political power. And it encouraged the English, in response to the seesawing allegiance of the Netherlands throughout the conflict, to develop their own clothing industry and foreign markets. In both France and England the burden of the on-again, off-again war fell most heavily on the peasantry, who were forced to support it with taxes and services.

The Black Death

Preconditions and Causes

In the late Middle Ages, nine-tenths of the population worked the land. The three-field system, in use in most areas since well before the fourteenth century, had increased the amount of arable land and thereby the food supply. The growth of cities and trade had also stimulated agricultural science and productivity. But as the food supply grew, so did the population. It is estimated that Europe's population

A Renaissance portrayal of the sixth-century (590) procession of St. Gregory to St. Peter's, an effort to end a plague. From the Soane Book of Hours *(c. 1500).*
Sir John Soane's Museum. E.T. Archive, London

doubled between the years 1000 and 1300 and by 1300 had begun to outstrip food production. There were now more people than there was food available to feed them or jobs to employ them, and the average European faced the probability of extreme hunger at least once during his or her expected thirty-five-year life span.

Between 1315 and 1317, crop failures produced the greatest famine of the Middle Ages. Densely populated urban areas such as the industrial towns of the Netherlands experienced great suffering. Decades of overpopulation, economic depression, famine, and bad health progressively weakened Europe's population and made it highly vulnerable to a virulent bubonic plague that struck with full force in 1348.

This "Black Death," so called by contemporaries because of the way it discolored the body, was probably introduced by seaborne rats from Black Sea areas and followed the trade routes from Asia into Europe. Appearing in Sicily in late 1347, it entered Europe through the port cities of Venice, Genoa, and Pisa in 1348, and from there it swept

rapidly through Spain and southern France and into northern Europe. Areas that lay outside the major trade routes, like Bohemia, appear to have remained virtually unaffected.

Bubonic plague made numerous reappearances in succeeding decades. By the early fifteenth century, it is estimated that western Europe as a whole had lost as much as two-fifths of its population. A full recovery did not occur until the sixteenth century. (See Map 9–2.)

Popular Remedies

The plague, transmitted by rat- or human-borne fleas, often reached a victim's lungs during the course of the disease. From the lungs, it could be spread from person to person by the victim's sneezing and wheezing. Contemporary physicians had no understanding of these processes, so even the most rudimentary prophylaxis against the disease was lacking. To the people of the time, the Black Death was a catastrophe with no apparent explanation and against which there was no known defense. Throughout much of western

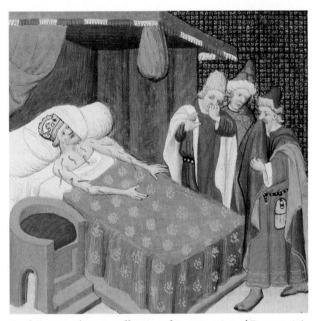

In this scene from an illustrated manuscript of Boccaccio's Decameron, *physicians apply leeches to an emperor. The text says he suffered from a disease that caused a terrible stench, which is why the physicians are holding their noses. Bleeding was the agreed-upon best way to prevent and cure illness and was practiced as late as the nineteenth century. Its popularity was rooted in the belief that a build-up of foul matter in the body caused illness by disrupting the body's four humors (blood, phlegm, yellow bile, and black bile). Bleeding released the foul matter and restored equilibrium among the humors, thus preserving good health by strengthening resistance to disease.*
Jean-Loup Charmet/Science Photo Library

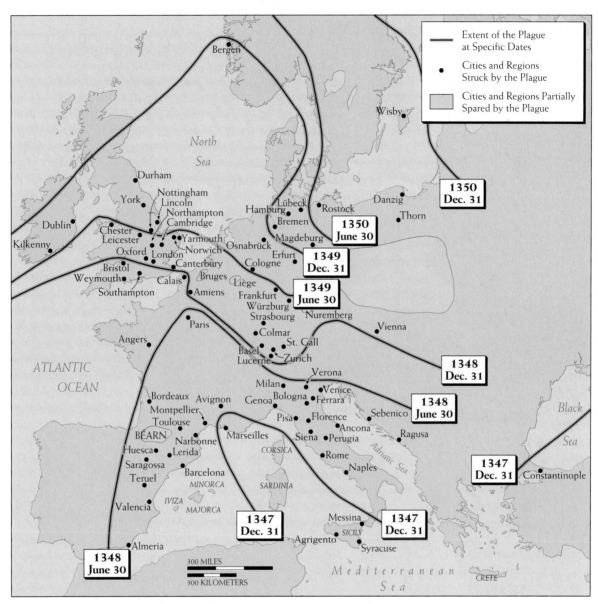

MAP 9–2   SPREAD OF THE BLACK DEATH   *Apparently introduced by seaborne rats from Black Sea areas where plague-infested rodents have long been known, the Black Death brought huge human, social, and economic consequences. One of the lower estimates of Europeans dying is 25,000,000. The map charts the plague's spread in the mid-fourteenth century. Generally following trade routes, the plague reached Scandinavia by 1350, and some believe it then went on to Iceland and even Greenland. Areas off the main trade routes were largely spared.*

Europe it inspired an obsession with death and dying and a deep pessimism that endured for decades after the plague years. (See "Art & the West.")

Popular wisdom held that a corruption in the atmosphere caused the disease. Some blamed poisonous fumes released by earthquakes. Many adopted aromatic amulets as a remedy. According to the contemporary observations of Boccaccio, who recorded the varied reactions to the plague in the *Decameron* (1353), some sought a remedy in moderation and a temperate life; others gave them-

selves over entirely to their passions (sexual promiscuity within the stricken areas apparently ran high); and still others, "the most sound, perhaps, in judgment," chose flight and seclusion as the best medicine. (See "Boccaccio Describes the Black Death in Florence.")

Among the most extreme social reactions were processions of flagellants. These religious fanatics beat themselves in ritual penance until they bled, believing that such action would bring divine intervention. The terror created by the flagellants (whose

Images of Death
in the Late Middle Ages

The Prince of the World in the Church of St. Sebald, Nürnberg, 1320–1330. Germnisches
Nationalmuseum, Nürnberg.

hroughout the Middle Ages, people perceived, and artists portrayed death both realistically and religiously: on the one hand, as a terrible, inescapable fate, and on the other, as the beginning of a new, eternal life, either in heaven or in hell. That life is death (transitory) and death is life (the afterlife) were two urgent and ironic teachings of the Christian Church. Many laity, finding the present world undesirable and death no sure release into a better one, understandably resisted. Graphic and sermonic instruction in the "Art of Dying" became the Church's response. Shown here, a sandstone sculpture, *The Prince of the World*, carries a vivid warning. When viewers looked behind this young, attractive prince, they discovered that beauty is only skin deep: His body, like everyone else's, is filled with worms and flesh-eating frogs. A serpent spirals up his left leg and enters his back—an allusion to the biblical teaching that the wages of sin are death. To drive home human mortality, the Church instructed laity to think often about the inevitability of death by visiting dying relatives and friends, watching them die and being buried, and thereafter visiting their graves often. This, in turn, would move them to resist the devil's temptations, obey the Church, avoid sin, and become eligible for heaven in the afterlife.

During the late Middle Ages, in both literature and art, the "Dance of Death" became a new reminder of human mortality and the need for Christian living and Church instruction. (It was first painted in 1424, on the wall of the Church of the Holy Innocents in Paris.) Death appeared as a living skeleton in lively conversation with mortal representatives—from pope to friar in the religious world, from emperor to laborer in the secular—none of whom, no matter how mighty, can elude Death's grasp. Even the Son of God, as an incarnate man, died a dreadful death. Although emerging in the late Middle Ages, the "Dance of Death" conveyed an old message, apparently urgently needed at the time because of the indiscipline and self-indulgence occasioned by the new horrors of the Black Death and the Hundred Years' War.

The Church's last word on death, however, was resplendently positive: Mortal men and women of true faith, like the crucified Son of God, might look forward to eternal life as shown in *The Resurrection*, from the *Isenheim Altarpiece*, 1509/10–1515.

Sources: Alberto Tenenti, "Death in History," in *Life and Death in Fifteenth Century Florence*, ed. M. Tetel et al. (Durham, NC: Duke University Press, 1989); Donald Weinstein, "The Art of Dying Well and Popular Piety in the Preaching and Thought of Girolamo Savonarola," in *ibid.*, 88–104; and James M. Clark, *The Dance of Death in the Middle Ages and the Renaissance* (Glasgow: Jackson, Son, and Col, 1950), pp. 1–4, 22–24, 106–110. Joseph L. Koerner, *The Moment of Self-Portraiture in German Renaissance Art* (Chicago, University of Chicago Press, 1993), pp. 199–200. H. W. Janson et al., *History of Art* (Upper Saddle River, NJ: Prentice Hall, 1997), p. 528.

Gruenwald, Mathias (1460–1528), *The Resurrection*. A panel from the Isenheim Altar. Limewood (around 1515), 250 × 650 cm. Musée d'Unterlinden, Colmar, France.

Boccaccio Describes the Ravages of the Black Death in Florence

The Black Death provided an excuse to the poet, humanist, and storyteller Giovanni Boccaccio (1313–1375) to assemble his great collection of tales, the Decameron. *Ten congenial men and women flee Florence to escape the plague and while away the time telling stories. In one of the stories, Boccaccio embeds a fine clinical description of plague symptoms as seen in Florence in 1348 and of the powerlessness of physicians and the lack of remedies.*

❖ *What did people do to escape the plague? Was any of it sound medical practice? What does the study of calamities like the Black Death tell us about the people of the past?*

In Florence, despite all that human wisdom and forethought could devise to avert it, even as the cleansing of the city from many impurities by officials appointed for the purpose, the refusal of entrance to all sick folk, and the adoption of many precautions for the preservation of health; despite also humble supplications addressed to God, and often repeated both in public procession and otherwise, by the devout; towards the beginning of the spring of the said year [1348] the doleful effects of the pestilence began to be horribly apparent by symptoms that [appeared] as if miraculous.

Not such were these symptoms as in the East, where an issue of blood from the nose was a manifest sign of inevitable death; but in men and women alike it first betrayed itself by the emergence of certain tumours in the groin or the armpits, some of which grew as large as a common apple, others as an egg, some more, some less, which the common folk called *gavoccioli*. From the two said parts of the body this deadly *gavoccioli* soon began to propagate and spread itself in all directions indifferently; after which the form of the malady began to change, spots black or livid making their appearance in many cases on the arm or the thigh or elsewhere, now few and large, now minute and numerous. And as the *gavoccioli* had been and still were an infallible token of approaching death, such also were these spots on whomsoever they shewed themselves. Which maladies seemed to set entirely at naught both the art of the physician and the virtues of physic; indeed, whether it was that the disorder was of a nature to defy such treatment, or that the physicians were at fault... and, being in ignorance of its source, failed to apply the proper remedies; in either case, not merely were those that recovered few, but almost all died within three days of the appearance of the said symptoms...and in most cases without any fever or other attendant malady.

From *The Decameron of Giovanni Boccaccio*, trans. by J. M. Rigg (London: J. M. Dent & Sons, 1930), p. 5.

dirty bodies may actually have served to transport the disease) became so socially disruptive and threatening even to established authority, that the church finally outlawed their processions.

Jews were cast as scapegoats for the plague. Centuries of Christian propaganda had bred hatred toward them, as had their role as society's moneylenders. Pogroms occurred in several cities, sometimes incited by the arrival of flagellants.

Social and Economic Consequences

Whole villages vanished in the wake of the plague. Among the social and economic consequences of this depopulation were a shrunken labor supply and a decline in the value of the estates of the nobility.

FARMS DECLINE   As the number of farm laborers decreased, their wages increased and those of skilled artisans soared. Many serfs now chose to commute their labor services by money payments or to abandon the farm altogether and pursue more interesting and rewarding jobs in skilled craft industries in the cities. Agricultural prices fell because of lowered demand, and the price of luxury and manufactured goods—the work of skilled artisans—rose. The noble landholders suffered the greatest decline in power

A caricature of physicians (early sixteenth century). In the Middle Ages and later, people recognized the shortcomings of physicians and surgeons and visited them only as a last resort. Here a physician carries a uroscope (for collecting and examining urine); cloudy or discolored urine signaled an immediate need for bleeding. The physician/surgeon wears surgical shoes and his assistant carries a flail—a comment on the risks of medical services. Hacker Art Books Inc.

from this new state of affairs. They were forced to pay more for finished products and for farm labor, but received a smaller return on their agricultural produce. Everywhere their rents were in steady decline after the plague.

PEASANTS REVOLT To recoup their losses, some landowners converted arable land to sheep pasture, substituting more profitable wool production for labor-intensive grain crops. Others abandoned the effort to farm their land and simply leased it to the highest bidder. Landowners also sought simply to reverse their misfortune—to close off the new economic opportunities opened for the peasantry by the demographic crisis—through repressive legislation that forced peasants to stay on their farms and froze their wages at low levels. In France the direct tax on the peasantry, the *taille*, was increased, and opposition to it was prominent among the grievances behind the *Jacquerie*. In 1351, the English Parliament passed a Statute of Laborers,

which limited wages to preplague levels and restricted the ability of peasants to leave the land of their traditional masters. Opposition to such legislation was also a prominent factor in the English peasants' revolt in 1381.

CITIES REBOUND Although the plague hit urban populations especially hard, the cities and their skilled industries came, in time, to prosper from its effects. Cities had always been careful to protect their interests; as they grew, they passed legislation to regulate competition from rural areas and to control immigration. After the plague, the reach of such laws was progressively extended beyond the cities to include surrounding lands belonging to impoverished nobles and feudal landlords, many of whom were peacefully integrated into urban life.

The omnipresence of death whetted the appetite for goods that only skilled urban industries could produce. Expensive cloths and jewelry, furs from the north, and silks from the south were in great demand in the second half of the fourteenth century. Faced with life at its worst, people insisted on having the very best. Initially, this new demand could not be met. The basic unit of urban industry was the master and apprentices (usually one or two), whose numbers were purposely kept low and whose privileges were jealously guarded. The craft of the skilled artisan was passed from master to apprentice only very slowly. The first wave of plague transformed this already restricted supply of skilled artisans into a shortage almost overnight. As a result, the prices of manufactured and luxury items rose to new heights, and this in turn encouraged workers to migrate from the countryside to the city and learn the skills of artisans. Townspeople in effect profited coming and going from the forces that impoverished the landed nobility. As wealth poured into the cities and per capita income rose, the cost to urban dwellers of agricultural products from the countryside, now less in demand, declined.

There was also gain, as well as loss, for the church. Although it suffered losses as a great landholder and was politically weakened, it had received new revenues from the vastly increased demand for religious services for the dead and the dying and from the multiplication of gifts and bequests.

New Conflicts and Opportunities

By increasing the importance of skilled artisans, the plague contributed to new conflicts within the cities. The economic and political power of local artisans and trade guilds grew steadily in the late Middle Ages, along with the demand for their goods and services. The merchant and patrician classes found it increasingly difficult to maintain their traditional dominance and grudgingly gave guild masters a voice in city government. As the guilds won political power, they encouraged restrictive legislation to protect local industries. These restrictions, in turn, brought confrontations between master artisans, who wanted to keep their numbers low and expand their industries at a snail's pace, and the many journeymen, who were eager to rise to the rank of master. To the long-existing conflict between the guilds and the urban patriciate was now added a conflict within the guilds themselves.

After 1350 the two traditional "containers" of monarchy—the landed nobility and the church—were politically on the defensive, to no small degree as a consequence of the plague. Kings took full advantage of the new situation, drawing on growing national sentiment to centralize their governments and economies. As already noted, the plague reduced the economic power of the landed nobility. In the same period, the battles of the Hundred Years' War demonstrated the military superiority of paid professional armies over the traditional noble cavalry, thus bringing into question the role of the nobility. The plague also killed many members of the clergy—perhaps one-third of the German clergy fell victim to it as they dutifully ministered to the sick and dying. The reduction in clerical ranks occurred in the same century in which the residence of the pope in Avignon (1309–1377) and the Great Schism (1378–1415) were undermining much of the church's popular support.

Ecclesiastical Breakdown and Revival: The Late Medieval Church

At first glance, the popes may appear to have been in a very favorable position in the latter half of the thirteenth century. Frederick II had been vanquished and imperial pressure on Rome had been removed. The French king, Louis IX, was an enthusiastic supporter of the church, as evidenced by his two disastrous Crusades, which won him sainthood. Although it lasted only seven years, a reunion of the Eastern church with Rome was proclaimed by the Council of Lyons in 1274, when the Western church took advantage of Emperor Michael Palaeologus's request for aid against the Turks. But despite these positive events, the church was not really in as favorable a position as it appeared.

The Thirteenth-Century Papacy

As early as the reign of Pope Innocent III (r. 1198–1216), when papal power reached its height, there were ominous developments. Innocent had elaborated the doctrine of papal plenitude of power and on that authority had declared saints, disposed of *benefices*, and created a centralized papal monarchy with a clearly political mission. Innocent's transformation of the papacy into a great secular power weakened the church spiritually even as it strengthened it politically. Thereafter, the church as a papal monarchy and the church as the "body of the faithful" came increasingly to be differentiated. It was against the "papal church" and in the name of the "true Christian Church" that both reformers and heretics raised their voices in protest until the Protestant Reformation.

What Innocent began his successors perfected. Under Urban IV (r. 1261–1264), the papacy established its own law court, the *Rota Romana*, which tightened and centralized the church's legal proceedings. The latter half of the thirteenth century saw an elaboration of the system of clerical taxation; what had begun in the twelfth century as an emergency measure to raise funds for the Crusades became a fixed institution. In the same period, papal power to determine appointments to many major and minor church offices—the "reservation of *benefices*"—was greatly broadened. The thirteenth-century papacy became a powerful political institution governed by its own law and courts, serviced by an efficient international bureaucracy, and preoccupied with secular goals.

Papal centralization of the church undermined both diocesan authority and popular support. Rome's interests, not local needs, came to control church appointments, policies, and discipline. Discontented lower clergy appealed to the higher authority of Rome against the disciplinary measures of local bishops. In the second half of the thirteenth century, bishops and abbots protested such undercutting of their power. To its critics, the church in Rome was hardly more than a legalized, "fiscalized," bureaucratic institution. As early as the late twelfth century, heretical movements of Cathars and Waldensians had appealed to the biblical ideal of simplicity and separation from the world. Other reformers who were unquestionably loyal to the church, such as Saint Francis of Assisi, would also protest a perceived materialism in official religion.

Political Fragmentation The church of the thirteenth century was being undermined by more than internal religious disunity. The demise of imperial power meant that the papacy in Rome was no longer the leader of anti-imperial (Guelf, or propapal) sentiment in Italy. Instead of being the center of Italian resistance to the emperor, popes now found themselves on the defensive against their old allies. That was the ironic price paid by the papacy to vanquish the Hohenstaufens.

Rulers with a stake in Italian politics now directed the intrigue formerly aimed at the emperor toward the College of Cardinals. For example, Charles of Anjou, king of Sicily, managed to create a French–Sicilian faction within the college. Such efforts to control the decisions of the college led Pope Gregory X (r. 1271– 1276) to establish the practice of sequestering the cardinals immediately on the death of the pope. The purpose of this so-called conclave of cardinals was to minimize extraneous political influence on the election of new popes, but the college had become so politicized that it proved to be of little avail.

In 1294 such a conclave, in frustration after a deadlock of more than two years, chose a saintly, but inept, Calabrian hermit as Pope Celestine V. Celestine abdicated under suspicious circumstances after only a few weeks in office. He also died under suspicious circumstances; his successor's critics later argued that he had been murdered for political reasons by the powers behind the papal throne to ensure the survival of the papal office. His tragicomic reign shocked a majority of the College of Cardinals into unified action. He was quickly replaced by his very opposite, Pope Boniface VIII (r. 1294–1303), a nobleman and a skilled politician. His pontificate, however, would augur the beginning of the end of papal pretensions to great-power status.

Boniface VIII and Philip the Fair

Boniface came to rule when England and France were maturing as nation–states. In England, a long tradition of consultation between the king and powerful members of English society evolved into formal "parliaments" during the reigns of Henry III (r. 1216–1272) and Edward I (r. 1272–1307), and these meetings helped to create a unified kingdom. The reign of the French king Philip IV the Fair (1285–1314) saw France become an efficient, centralized monarchy. Philip was no Saint Louis, but a ruthless politician. He was determined to end England's continental holdings, control wealthy Flanders, and establish French hegemony within the Holy Roman Empire.

Boniface had the further misfortune of bringing to the papal throne memories of the way earlier popes had brought kings and emperors to their knees. Very painfully he was to discover that the papal monarchy

Pope Boniface VIII (r. 1294–1303), depicted here, opposed the taxation of the clergy by the kings of France and England and issued one of the strongest declarations of papal authority over rulers, the bull Unam Sanctam. This statue is in the Museo Civico, Bologna, Italy. Scala/Art Resource, N.Y.

of the early thirteenth century was no match for the new political powers of the late thirteenth century.

THE ROYAL CHALLENGE TO PAPAL AUTHORITY France and England were on the brink of all-out war when Boniface became pope in 1294. Only Edward I's preoccupation with rebellion in Scotland, which the

Boniface VIII Reasserts the Church's Claim to Temporal Power

Defied by the French and the English, Pope Boniface VIII (r. 1294–1303) boldly reasserted the temporal power of the church in the bull Unam Sanctam *(November 1302). This document claimed that both spiritual and temporal power on earth were under the pope's jurisdiction, because in the hierarchy of the universe spiritual power both preceded and sat in judgment on temporal power.*

❖ *On what does the pope base his claims to supremacy? Is his argument logical, or does he beg the question? On what basis did secular rulers attack his arguments?*

We are taught by the words of the Gospel that in this church and in her power there are two swords, a spiritual one and a temporal one....Certainly anyone who denies that the temporal sword is in the power of Peter has not paid heed to the words of the Lord when he said, "Put up thy sword into its sheath" (Matthew 26:52). Both then are in the power of the church, the material sword and the spiritual. But the one is exercised for the church, the other by the church, the one by the hand of the priest, the other by the hand of kings and soldiers, though at the will and suffrance of the authority subject to the spiritual power....For, according to the blessed Dionysius, it is the law of divinity for the lowest to be led to the highest through intermediaries. In the order of the universe all things are not kept in order in the same fashion and immediately but the lowest are ordered by the intermediate and inferiors by superiors. But that the spiritual power excels any earthly one in dignity and nobility we ought the more openly to confess in proportion as spiritual things excel temporal ones. Moreover we clearly perceive this from the giving of tithes, from benediction and sanctification, from the acceptance of this power and from the very government of things. For, the truth bearing witness, the spiritual power has to institute the earthly power and to judge it if it has not been good. So it is verified the prophecy of Jeremiah (1:10) concerning the church and the power of the church, "Lo, I have set thee this day over the nations and over kingdoms."

Reprinted with the permission of Simon & Schuster from *The Crisis of Church and State, 1050–1300* by Brian Tierney. Copyright © 1964 by Prentice-Hall, Inc., renewed 1992 by Brian Tierney.

French encouraged, prevented him from invading France and starting the Hundred Years' War a half century earlier than it did start. As both countries mobilized for war, they used the pretext of preparing for a Crusade to tax the clergy heavily. In 1215 Pope Innocent III had decreed that the clergy were to pay no taxes to rulers without prior papal consent. Viewing English and French taxation of the clergy as an assault on traditional clerical rights, Boniface took a strong stand against it. On February 5, 1296, he issued a bull, *Clericis laicos*, which forbade lay taxation of the clergy without prior papal approval and took back all previous papal dispensations in this regard.

In England, Edward I retaliated by denying the clergy the right to be heard in royal court, in effect removing from them the protection of the king. But it was Philip the Fair who struck back with a vengeance: In August 1296 he forbade the exportation of money from France to Rome, thereby denying the papacy revenues it needed to operate. Boniface had no choice but to come quickly to terms

with Philip. He conceded Philip the right to tax the French clergy "during an emergency," and, not coincidentally, he canonized Louis IX in the same year.

Boniface was then also under siege by powerful Italian enemies, whom Philip did not fail to patronize. A noble family (the Colonnas), rivals of Boniface's family (the Gaetani) and radical followers of Saint Francis of Assisi (the Spiritual Franciscans), were at this time seeking to invalidate Boniface's election as pope on the grounds that Celestine V had resigned the office under coercion. Charges of heresy, simony, and even the murder of Celestine were hurled against Boniface.

Boniface's fortunes appeared to revive in 1300, a "Jubilee year." During such a year, all Catholics who visited Rome and fulfilled certain conditions had the penalties for their unrepented sins remitted. Tens of thousands of pilgrims flocked to Rome in that year, and Boniface, heady with this display of popular religiosity, reinserted himself into international politics. He championed Scottish resistance to England, for which he received a firm rebuke from an outraged Edward I and from Parliament.

But once again a confrontation with the king of France proved the more costly. Philip seemed to be eager for another fight with the pope. He arrested Boniface's Parisian legate, Bernard Saisset, the bishop of Pamiers and also a powerful secular lord, whose independence Philip had opposed. Accused of heresy and treason, Saisset was tried and convicted in the king's court. Thereafter, Philip demanded that Boniface recognize the process against Saisset, something that Boniface could do only if he was prepared to surrender his jurisdiction over the French episcopate. This challenge could not be sidestepped, and Boniface acted swiftly to champion Saisset as a defender of clerical political independence within France. He demanded Saisset's unconditional release, revoked all previous agreements with Philip in the matter of clerical taxation, and ordered the French bishops to convene in Rome within a year. A bull, *Ausculta fili*, or "Listen, My Son," was sent to Philip in December 1301, pointedly informing him that "God has set popes over kings and kingdoms."

UNAM SANCTAM (1302) Philip unleashed a ruthless antipapal campaign. Two royal apologists, Pierre Dubois and John of Paris, refuted papal claims to the right to intervene in temporal matters. Increasingly placed on the defensive, Boniface made a last-ditch stand against state control of national churches. On November 18, 1302, he issued the bull *Unam Sanctam*. This famous statement of papal power declared that temporal authority was "subject" to the spiritual power of the church. On its face a bold assertion, *Unam Sanctam* was in truth the desperate act of a besieged papacy. (See "Boniface VIII Reasserts the Church's Claim to Temporal Power.")

After *Unam Sanctam*, the French and the Colonnas moved against Boniface with force. Guillaume de Nogaret, Philip's chief minister, denounced Boniface to the French clergy as a common heretic and criminal. An army, led by Nogaret and Sciarra Colonna, surprised the pope in mid-August 1303 at his retreat in Anagni. Boniface was badly beaten and almost executed before an aroused populace liberated and returned him safely

Marsilius of Padua Denies Coercive Power to the Clergy

According to Marsilius, the Bible gave the pope no right to pronounce and execute sentences on any person. The clergy held a strictly moral and spiritual rule, their judgments to be executed only in the afterlife, not in the present one. Here, on earth, they should be obedient to secular authority. Marsilius argued this point by appealing to the example of Jesus.

❖ *How do Marsilius's arguments compare with those of Pope Boniface in the preceding document? Does Marsilius's argument, if accepted, destroy the worldly authority of the church? Why was his teaching condemned as heretical?*

We now wish...to adduce the truths of the holy Scripture...which explicitly command or counsel that neither the Roman bishop called pope, nor any other bishop or priest, or deacon, has or ought to have any rulership or coercive judgment or jurisdiction over any priest or nonpriest, ruler, community, group, or individual of whatever condition....Christ himself came into the world not to dominate men, nor to judge them [coercively]...not to wield temporal rule, but rather to be subject as regards the...present life; and moreover, he wanted to and did exclude himself, his apostles and disciples, and their successors, the bishops or priests, from all coercive authority or worldly rule, both by his example and by his word of counsel or command....When he was brought before Pontius Pilate...and accused of having called himself king of the Jews, and [Pilate] asked him whether he had said this...[his] reply included these words...."My kingdom is not of this world," that is, I have not come to reign by temporal rule or dominion, in the way...worldly kings reign.... This, then, is the kingdom concerning which he came to teach and order, a kingdom which consists in the acts whereby the eternal kingdom is attained, that is, the acts of faith and the other theological virtues; not however, by coercing anyone thereto.

Excerpt from *Marsilius of Padua: The Defender of Peace:* The Defensor Pacis, trans. by Alan Gewirth. Copyright © 1967 by Columbia University Press, pp. 113–116. Reprinted by permission of the publisher.

A book illustration of the Palace of the Popes in Avignon in 1409, the year in which Christendom found itself confronted by three duly elected popes. The "keys" to the kingdom of God, which the pope held on earth as the vicar of Christ, decorate the three turret flags of the palace. In the foreground, the French poet Pierre Salmon, then journeying via Avignon to Rome, commiserates with a monk over the sad state of the Church and France, then at war with England. Book illustration, French, 1409. Paris, Bibliotheque Nationale. AKG Photo.

to Rome. But the ordeal proved too much for him and he died a few months later, in October 1303.

Boniface's immediate successor, Benedict XI (r. 1303–1304), excommunicated Nogaret for his deed, but there was to be no lasting papal retaliation. Benedict's successor, Clement V (r. 1305–1314), was forced into French subservience. A former archbishop of Bordeaux, Clement declared that *Unam Sanctam* should not be understood as in any way diminishing French royal authority. He released Nogaret from excommunication and pliantly condemned the Knights Templars, whose treasure Philip thereafter forcibly expropriated.

In 1309 Clement moved the papal court to Avignon, an imperial city on the southeastern border of France. Situated on land that belonged to the pope, the city maintained its independence from the king. In 1311 Clement made it his permanent residence, to escape both a Rome ridden with strife after the confrontation between Boniface and Philip and

further pressure from Philip. There the papacy was to remain until 1377.

After Boniface's humiliation, popes never again seriously threatened kings and emperors, despite continuing papal excommunications and political intrigue. In the future, the relation between church and state would tilt in favor of the state and the control of religion by powerful monarchies. Ecclesiastical authority would become subordinate to larger secular political purposes.

The Avignon Papacy (1309–1377)

The Avignon papacy was in appearance, although not always in fact, under strong French influence. During Clement V's pontificate the French came to dominate the College of Cardinals, testing the papacy's agility both politically and economically. Finding itself cut off from its Roman estates, the papacy had to innovate to get needed funds. Clement expanded papal taxes, especially the practice of collecting annates, the first year's revenue of a church office, or *benefices* bestowed by the pope. Clement VI (r. 1342–1352) began the practice of selling indulgences, or pardons for unrepented sins. To make the purchase of indulgences more compelling, church doctrine on purgatory—a place of punishment where souls would atone for venial sins—also developed during this period. By the fifteenth century the church had extended indulgences to cover the souls of people already dead, allowing the living to buy a reduced sentence in purgatory for their deceased loved ones. Such practices contributed to the Avignon papacy's reputation for materialism and political scheming and gave reformers new ammunition.

POPE JOHN XXII Pope John XXII (r. 1316–1334), the most powerful Avignon pope, tried to restore papal independence and to return to Italy. This goal led him into war with the Visconti, the most powerful ruling family of Milan, and a costly contest with Emperor Louis IV. John had challenged Louis's election as emperor in 1314 in favor of the rival Habsburg candidate. The result was a minor replay of the confrontation between Philip the Fair and Boniface VIII. When John obstinately and without legal justification refused to recognize Louis's election, the emperor retaliated by declaring John deposed and putting in his place an antipope. As Philip the Fair had also done, Louis enlisted the support of the Spiritual Franciscans, whose views on absolute poverty had been condemned by John as heretical. Two outstanding pamphleteers wrote lasting tracts for the royal cause: William of Ockham, whom John excommunicated in 1328, and Marsilius of Padua (ca. 1290–1342), whose teaching John declared heretical in 1327.

In his *Defender of Peace* (1324), Marsilius of Padua stressed the independent origins and autonomy of secular government. Clergy were subjected to the strictest apostolic ideals and confined to purely spiritual functions, and all power of coercive judgment was denied the pope. Marsilius argued that spiritual crimes must await an eternal punishment. Transgressions of divine law, over which the pope had jurisdiction, were to be punished in the next life, not in the present one, unless the secular ruler declared a divine law also a secular law. This assertion was a direct challenge to the power of the pope to excommunicate rulers and place countries under interdict. The *Defender of Peace* depicted the pope as a subordinate member of a society over which the emperor ruled supreme and in which temporal peace was the highest good. (See "Marsilius of Padua Denies Coercive Power to the Clergy.")

John XXII made the papacy a sophisticated international agency and adroitly adjusted it to the growing European money economy. The more the *Curia*, or papal court, mastered the latter, however, the more vulnerable it became to criticism. Under John's successor, Benedict XII (r. 1334–1342), the papacy became entrenched in Avignon. Seemingly forgetting Rome altogether, Benedict began construction of the great Palace of the Popes and attempted to reform both papal government and the religious life. His high-living French successor, Clement VI, placed papal policy in lockstep with the French. In this period the cardinals became barely more than lobbyists for policies favorable to their secular patrons.

NATIONAL OPPOSITION TO THE AVIGNON PAPACY As Avignon's fiscal tentacles probed new areas, monarchies took strong action to protect their interests. The latter half of the fourteenth century saw legislation restricting papal jurisdiction and taxation in France, England, and Germany. In England, where the Avignon papacy was identified with the French enemy after the outbreak of the Hundred Years' War, statutes that restricted payments and appeals to Rome and the pope's power to make high ecclesiastical appointments were passed by Parliament several times between 1351 and 1393.

In France, ecclesiastical appointments and taxation were regulated by the so-called Gallican liberties. These national rights over religion had long been exercised in fact and were legally acknowledged by the church in the *Pragmatic Sanction of Bourges*, published by Charles VII (r. 1422–1461) in 1438. This agreement recognized the right of the French church to elect its own clergy without papal

A portrayal of John Huss as he was led to the stake at Constance. After his execution, his bones and ashes were scattered in the Rhine River to prevent his followers from claiming them as relics. This pen-and-ink drawing is from Ulrich von Richenthal's Chronicle of the Council of Constance (ca. 1450). The Bettman Archive

interference, prohibited the payment of annates to Rome, and limited the right of appeals from French courts to the *Curia* in Rome. In German and Swiss cities in the fourteenth and fifteenth centuries, local governments also took the initiative to limit and even to overturn traditional clerical privileges and immunities.

JOHN WYCLIFFE AND JOHN HUSS The popular lay religious movements that most successfully assailed the late medieval church were the Lollards in England and the Hussites in Bohemia. The Lollards looked to the writings of John Wycliffe (d. 1384) to justify their demands, and both moderate and extreme Hussites to the writings of John Huss (d. 1415), although both Wycliffe and Huss would have disclaimed the extremists who revolted in their names.

Wycliffe was an Oxford theologian and a philosopher of high standing. His work initially served the anticlerical policies of the English government. He became within England what William of Ockham and Marsilius of Padua had been at the Bavarian court of Emperor Louis IV: a major intellectual spokesman for the rights of royalty against the secular pretensions of popes. After 1350 English kings greatly reduced the power of the Avignon papacy to make ecclesiastical appointments and collect taxes within England, a position that Wycliffe strongly

The Ruin of the Church during the Schism

Nicholas of Clamanges, a theologian writing around 1400, viewed the decades-long division of the papacy and the continuing growth of two separate papal courts, one in Avignon, another in Rome, as proof that the high clergy had become thoroughly corrupt. Popes and bishops had so lost face, that their threats of excommunication now fell on deaf ears. Only by ending the Schism could the church begin to restore its authority.

❖ *What incentive did either pope have to end the Schism? Did the loss of efficacy of papal disciplinary actions such as excommunication provide such an incentive? Which, if either, of the papal courts seemed to have greater validity?*

After the great increase of worldly goods...boundless avarice and blind ambition invaded the hearts of churchmen...Carried away by the glory of their position and the extent of their power [they] soon gave way to the[ir] degrading effects....Three most exacting and troublesome masters had now to be satisfied. *Luxury* demanded sundry gratifications—wine, sleep, banquets, music, debasing sports, and courtesans....*Display* required fine houses, castles, towers, palaces, rich and varied furniture, expensive clothes, horses, servants and the pomp of luxury....*Avarice*...carefully brought together vast treasures to supply the demands of the above vices....

For carrying on exactions and gathering their gains...the popes appointed their collectors in every province, those namely whom they knew to be most skillful in extracting money, owing to [their]

energy, diligence, or harshness of temper....To these the popes granted the power of anathematizing anyone, even prelates, and of expelling from the communion of the faithful everyone who did not...satisfy their demands for money....Hence came suspensions from divine service, interdicts from entering a church, and anathemas a thousandfold intensified in severity.

Such things were resorted to in the rarest instances by the [Church] Fathers, and then only for the most horrible of crimes; for by these penalties a man is separated from the companionship of the faithful and turned over to Satan. But nowadays these inflictions have so fallen in esteem that they are used for the lightest offense, often for no offense at all, so that they no longer bring terror but are objects of contempt.

From James Harvey Robinson, ed., *Readings in European History*, Vol. I (Boston: Athenaeum, 1904), pp. 508–509.

supported. His views on clerical poverty followed original Franciscan ideals and, more by accident than by design, gave justification to government restriction and even confiscation of church properties within England. Wycliffe argued that the clergy "ought to be content with food and clothing."

Wycliffe also maintained that personal merit, not rank and office, was the only basis of religious authority. This was a dangerous teaching, because it raised allegedly pious laypeople above allegedly corrupt ecclesiastics, regardless of the latter's official stature. There was a threat in such teaching to secular as well as ecclesiastical dominion and jurisdiction. At his posthumous condemnation by the pope, Wycliffe was accused of the ancient heresy of Donatism—the teaching that the efficacy of the church's sacraments did not lie in their true performance, but also depended on the moral character of the clergy who administered them. Wycliffe also

anticipated certain Protestant criticisms of the medieval church by challenging papal infallibility, the sale of indulgences, the authority of scripture, and the dogma of transubstantiation.

The Lollards, English advocates of Wycliffe's teaching, like the Waldensians, preached in the vernacular, disseminated translations of Holy Scripture, and championed clerical poverty. At first, they came from every social class. Lollards were especially prominent among the groups that had something tangible to gain from the confiscation of clerical properties (the nobility and the gentry) or that had suffered most under the current church system (the lower clergy and the poor people). After the English peasants' revolt in 1381, an uprising filled with egalitarian notions that could find support in Wycliffe's teaching, Lollardy was officially viewed as subversive. Opposed by an alliance of church and crown, it became a capital offense in England by 1401.

Heresy was not so easily brought to heel in Bohemia, where it coalesced with a strong national movement. The University of Prague, founded in 1348, became the center for both Czech nationalism and a native religious reform movement. The latter began within the bounds of orthodoxy. It was led by local intellectuals and preachers, the most famous of whom was John Huss, the rector of the university after 1403.

The Czech reformers supported vernacular translations of the Bible and were critical of traditional ceremonies and allegedly superstitious practices, particularly those relating to the sacrament of the Eucharist. They advocated lay communion with cup as well as bread, which was traditionally reserved only for the clergy as a sign of the clergy's spiritual superiority over the laity. Hussites taught that bread and wine remained bread and wine after priestly consecration, and they questioned the validity of sacraments performed by priests in mortal sin.

Wycliffe's teaching appears to have influenced the movement very early. Regular traffic between England and Bohemia had existed for decades, ever since the marriage in 1381 of Anne of Bohemia to King Richard II. Czech students studied at Oxford, and many returned with copies of Wycliffe's writings.

Huss became the leader of the pro-Wycliffe faction at the University of Prague. In 1410 his activities brought about his excommunication and the placement of Prague under papal interdict. In 1414 Huss won an audience with the newly assembled Council of Constance. He journeyed to the council eagerly, armed with a safe-conduct pass from Emperor Sigismund, naïvely believing that he would convince his strongest critics of the truth of his teaching. Within weeks of his arrival in early November 1414, he was formally accused of heresy and imprisoned. He died at the stake on July 6, 1415, and was followed there less than a year later by his colleague Jerome of Prague.

The reaction in Bohemia to the execution of these national heroes was fierce revolt. Militant Hussites, the Taborites, set out to transform Bohemia by force into a religious and social paradise under the military leadership of John Ziska. After a decade of belligerent protest, the Hussites won significant religious reforms and control over the Bohemian church from the Council of Basel.

The Great Schism (1378–1417) and the Conciliar Movement to 1449

Pope Gregory XI (r. 1370–1378) reestablished the papacy in Rome in January 1377, ending what had come to be known as the "Babylonian Captivity" of the church in Avignon, a reference to the biblical bondage of the Israelites. The return to Rome proved to be short lived, however.

URBAN VI AND CLEMENT VII   On Gregory's death, the cardinals, in Rome, elected an Italian archbishop as Pope Urban VI (r. 1378–1389), who immediately announced his intention to reform the *Curia*. This was an unexpected challenge to the cardinals, most of whom were French, and they responded by calling for the return of the papacy to Avignon. The French king, Charles V, wanting to keep the papacy within the sphere of French influence, lent his support to a schism, which came to be known as the "Great Schism."

On September 20, 1378, five months after Urban's election, thirteen cardinals, all but one of whom was French, formed their own conclave and elected Pope Clement VII (r. 1378–1397), a cousin of the French king. They insisted that they had voted for Urban in fear of their lives, surrounded by a Roman mob demanding the election of an Italian pope. Be that as it may, the papacy now became a "two-headed thing" and a scandal to Christendom. (See "The Ruin of the Church during the Schism.") Allegiance to the two papal courts divided along political lines. England and its allies (the Holy Roman Empire, Hungary, Bohemia, and Poland) acknowledged Urban VI, whereas France and those in its orbit (Naples, Scotland, Castile, and Aragon) supported Clement VII. The Roman line of popes has, however, been recognized de facto in subsequent church history.

Two approaches were initially taken to end the schism. One tried to win the mutual cession of both popes, thereby clearing the way for the election of a new pope. The other sought to secure the resignation of the one in favor of the other. Both approaches proved completely fruitless. Each pope considered himself fully legitimate, and too much was at stake for a magnanimous concession on the part of either. One way remained: the forced deposition of both popes by a special council of the church.

CONCILIAR THEORY OF CHURCH GOVERNMENT   Legally, a church council could be convened only by a pope, but the competing popes were not inclined to summon a council they knew would depose them. Also, the deposition of a legitimate pope against his will by a council of the church was as serious a matter then as the forced deposition of a monarch by a representative assembly.

The correctness of a conciliar deposition of a pope was thus debated a full thirty years before any direct action was taken. Advocates sought to fashion a church in which a representative council could effectively regulate the actions of the pope. The con-

Genghis Khan holding an audience. This Persian miniature shows the great conqueror and founder of the Mongol empire with members of his army and entourage as well as an apparent supplicant (lower right). E.T. Archive

ciliarists defined the church as the whole body of the faithful, of which the elected head, the pope, was only one part. And the pope's sole purpose was to maintain the unity and well-being of the church—something that the schismatic popes were far from doing. The conciliarists further argued that a council of the church acted with greater authority than the pope alone. In the eyes of the pope(s), such a concept of the church threatened both its political and its religious unity.

THE COUNCIL OF PISA (1409–1410)   On the basis of the arguments of the conciliarists, cardinals representing both popes convened a council on their own authority in Pisa in 1409, deposed both the Roman and the Avignon popes, and elected a new pope, Alexander V. To the council's consternation, neither pope accepted its action, and Christendom suddenly faced the spectacle of three contending popes. Although the vast majority of Latin Christendom accepted Alexander and his Pisan successor John XXIII (r. 1410–1415), the popes of Rome and Avignon refused to step down.

THE COUNCIL OF CONSTANCE (1414–1417)   The intolerable situation ended when Emperor Sigismund

prevailed on John XXIII to summon a new council in Constance in 1414, which the Roman pope Gregory XII also recognized. In a famous declaration entitled *Sacrosancta*, the council asserted its supremacy and proceeded to elect a new pope, Martin V (r. 1417–1431), after the three contending popes had either resigned or been deposed. The council then made provisions for regular meetings of church councils, within five, then seven, and thereafter every ten years.

Despite the role of the council of Constance in ending the Great Schism, in the official eyes of the church it was not a legitimate council. Nor have the schismatic popes of Avignon and Pisa been recognized as legitimate. (For this reason, another pope could take the name John XXIII in 1958.)

THE COUNCIL OF BASEL (R. 1431–1449)   Conciliar government of the church peaked at the Council of Basel, when the council negotiated church doctrine with heretics. In 1432 the Hussites of Bohemia presented the *Four Articles of Prague* to the council as a basis for the negotiations. This document contained requests for (1) giving the laity the Eucharist with cup as well as bread; (2) free, itinerant preaching; (3) the exclusion of the clergy from holding secular offices and owning property; and (4) just punishment of clergy who commit mortal sins.

In November 1433 an agreement was reached between the emperor, the council, and the Hussites, giving the Bohemians jurisdiction over their church similar to that held by the French and the English. Three of the four Prague articles were conceded: communion with cup, free preaching by ordained clergy, and like punishment of clergy and laity for mortal sins.

The end of the Hussite wars and the reform legislation curtailing the papal power of appointment and taxation were the high points of the Council of Basel. The exercise of such power by a council did not please the pope, and in 1438 he gained the opportunity to upstage the Council of Basel by negotiating a reunion with the Eastern Church. The agreement, signed in Florence in 1439, was short lived, but it restored papal prestige and signaled the demise of the Conciliar Movement. The Council of Basel collapsed in 1449. A decade later Pope Pius II (r. 1458–1464) issued the papal bull *Execrabilis* (1460) condemning appeals to councils as "erroneous and abominable" and "completely null and void."

Although many who had worked for reform now despaired of ever attaining it, the Conciliar Movement was not a total failure. It planted deep within the conscience of all Western peoples the conviction that the role of a leader of an institution is to provide for the well-being of its members, not just for that of the leader.

A second consequence of the Conciliar Movement was the devolving of religious responsibility onto the laity and secular government. Without papal leadership, secular control of national or territorial churches increased. Kings asserted power over the church in England and France. In German, Swiss, and Italian cities magistrates and city councils reformed and regulated religious life. This development could not be reversed by the powerful popes of the High Renaissance. On the contrary, as the papacy became a limited territorial regime, national control of the church ran apace. Perceived as just one among several Italian states, the Papal States could now be opposed as much on the grounds of "national" policy as for religious reasons.

Medieval Russia

In the late tenth century, Prince Vladimir of Kiev (972–1015), at that time Russia's dominant city, received delegations of Muslims, Roman Catholics, Jews, and Greek Orthodox Christians, each of which hoped to see Russians embrace their religion. Vladimir chose Greek Orthodoxy, which became the religion of Russia, adding strong cultural bonds to the close commercial ties that had long linked Russia to the Byzantine Empire.

Politics and Society

Vladimir's successor, Yaroslav the Wise (1016–1054), developed Kiev into a magnificent political and cultural center, with architecture rivaling that of Constantinople. He also sought contacts with the West in an unsuccessful effort to counter the political influence of the Byzantine emperors. After his death, rivalry among their princes slowly divided Russians into three cultural groups: the Great Russians, the White Russians, and the Little Russians (Ukrainians). Autonomous principalities also challenged Kiev's dominance, and it became just one of several national centers. Government in the principalities combined monarchy (the prince), aristocracy (the prince's council of noblemen), and democracy (a popular assembly of all adult males). The broadest social division was between freemen and slaves. Freemen included the clergy, army officers, *boyars* (wealthy landowners), townspeople, and peasants. Slaves were mostly prisoners of war. Debtors working off their debts made up a large, semifree, intermediate group.

Mongol Rule (1243–1480)

In the thirteenth century, Mongol, or Tatar, armies swept over China, much of the Islamic world, and Russia. Ghengis Khan (1155–1227) invaded Russia in 1223, and Kiev fell to Batu Khan in 1240. Russian cities became dependent, tribute-paying principalities of the segment of the Mongol Empire called the Golden Horde (a phrase derived from the Tatar words for the color of Batu Khan's tent), which included the steppe region of what is now southern Russia and had its capital at Sarai, on the lower Volga. The Golden Horde stationed officials in all the principal Russian towns to oversee taxation and the conscription of soldiers into Tatar armies. Mongol rule created further cultural divisions between Russia and the West. The Mongols intermarried with the Russians and also created harems filled with Russian women. Russians who resisted were sold into slavery in foreign lands. Russian women— under the influence of Islam, which had become the religion of the Golden Horde—began to wear veils and to lead more secluded lives. The Mongols, however, left Russian political and religious institutions largely intact and, thanks to their far-flung trade, brought most Russians greater peace and prosperity than they had enjoyed before.

Liberation

The princes of Moscow cooperated with their overlords in the collection of tribute and grew wealthy under the Mongols. As Mongol rule weakened, the princes took control of the territory surrounding the city. In a process that has come to be known as "the gathering of the Russian Land," they then gradually expanded the principality of Moscow through land purchases, colonization, and conquest. In 1380, Grand Duke Dimitri of Moscow (1350–1389) defeated Tatar forces at Kulikov Meadow in a victory that marks the beginning of the decline of Mongol hegemony. Another century would pass before Ivan III, called Ivan the Great (d. 1505), would bring all of northern Russia under Moscow's control and end Mongol rule (1480). By the last quarter of the fourteenth century, however, Moscow had become the political and religious center of Russia, replacing Kiev. In Russian eyes, it was destined to become the "third Rome" after the fall of Constantinople to the Turks in 1453.

In Perspective

War, plague, and schism convulsed much of late medieval Europe throughout the fourteenth and into the fifteenth century. Two-fifths of the population, particularly along the major trade routes, died from plague in the fourteenth century. War and famine continued to take untold numbers after the plague had passed. The introduction of gunpowder and heavy artillery during the long years of warfare between England and France resulted in new forms of human destruction. Periodic revolts erupted in town and countryside as ordinary people attempted to defend their traditional communal rights and privileges against the new autocratic territorial regimes. Even God's house seemed to be in shambles in 1409, when no fewer than three popes came to rule simultaneously.

There is, however, another side to the late Middle Ages. By the end of the fifteenth century the population losses were rapidly being made up. Between 1300 and 1500, education had become far more accessible, especially to laypeople. The number of universities increased 250 percent, from twenty to seventy, and the rise in the number of residential colleges was even more impressive, especially in France, where sixty-three were built. The fourteenth century saw the birth of humanism, and the fifteenth century gave us the printing press. Most impressive were the artistic and cultural achievements of the Italian Renaissance during the fifteenth century. The later Middle Ages were thus a period of growth and creativity, as well as one of waning and decline.

REVIEW QUESTIONS

1. What were the underlying and precipitating causes of the Hundred Years' War? What advantages did each side have? Why were the French finally able to drive the English almost entirely out of France?
2. What were the causes of the Black Death, and why did it spread so quickly throughout western Europe? Where was it most virulent? What were its effects on European society? How important do you think disease is in changing the course of history?
3. Discuss the struggle between Pope Boniface VIII and King Philip the Fair. Why was Boniface so impotent in the conflict? How had political conditions changed since the reign of Pope Innocent III in the late twelfth century, and what did that mean for the papacy?
4. Briefly trace the history of the church from 1200 to 1450. How did it respond to political threats from the growing power of monarchs? How great an influence did the church have on secular events?
5. What was the Avignon papacy, and why did it occur? What effect did it have on the state of the papacy? What relation does it have to the Great Schism? How did the church become divided and how was it reunited? Why was the Conciliar Movement a setback for the papacy?
6. Why were kings in the late thirteenth and early fourteenth centuries able to control the church more than the church could control the kings? How did kings attack the church during this period? Contrast these events with earlier ones in which the pope dominated rulers.

SUGGESTED READINGS

C. ALLMAND, *The Hundred Years' War: England and France at War, c. 1300–c. 1450* (1988). Good overview of the war's development and consequences.

P. ARIÈS, *The Hour of Our Death* (1983). People's familiarity with, and philosophy of, death in the Middle Ages.

R. Barber (Ed.), *The Pastons: Letters of a Family in the War of the Roses* (1984). Revelations of English family life in an age of crisis.

J. le Goff, *The Birth of Purgatory*, trans. by A. Goldhammer (1984). Cultural impact of the idea.

J. Huizinga, *The Waning of the Middle Ages: A Study of the Forms of Life, Thought, and Art in France and the Netherlands in the Dawn of the Renaissance* (1924). A classic study of "mentality" at the end of the Middle Ages; exaggerated, but engrossing.

W. H. McNeill, *Plagues and Peoples* (1976). The Black Death in a broader context.

D. N. Nicol, *The Byzantine Lady: Ten Portraits, 1250–1500* (1994)

F. Oakley, *The Western Church in the Later Middle Ages* (1979). Eloquent, sympathetic survey.

S. Ozment, *The Age of Reform, 1250–1550* (1980). Highlights of late medieval intellectual and religious history.

E. Perroy, *The Hundred Years' War*, trans. by W. B. Wells (1965). Still the most comprehensive one-volume account.

Y. Renovard, *The Avignon Papacy, 1305–1403*, trans. by D. Bethell (1970). The standard narrative account.

M. Spinka, *John Huss's Concept of the Church* (1966). Lucid and authoritative account of Hussite theology.

B. Tierney, *The Crisis of Church and State, 1050–1300* (1964). Part IV provides the major documents in the clash between Boniface VIII and Philip the Fair.

C. T. Wood, *Philip the Fair and Boniface VIII* (1967). Excerpts from the scholarly debate over the significance of this confrontation.

P. Ziegler, *The Black Death* (1969). Highly readable account.

Chapter 10

A map of America in 1596 with representations of the great Western explorers Columbus, Vespucci, Magellan, and Pizarro. Etching by Theodor de Bry, National Museum, Berlin. Bildarchiv Preussischer Kulturbesitz.

Renaissance and Discovery

KEY TOPICS

- The politics, culture, and art of the Italian Renaissance
- Political struggle and foreign intervention in Italy
- The powerful new monarchies of northern Europe
- The thought and culture of the northern Renaissance

If the late Middle Ages saw unprecedented chaos, it also witnessed a rebirth that would continue into the seventeenth century. Two modern Dutch scholars have employed the same word (Herfsttij, or "harvesttide") with different connotations to describe the period. Johan Huizinga has used the word to mean a "waning" or "decline," and Heiko Oberman has used it to mean "harvest." If something was dying away, some ripe fruit was being gathered and seed grain was sown. The late Middle Ages was a time of creative fragmentation.

By the late fifteenth century, Europe was recovering well from two of the three crises of the late Middle Ages: the demographic and the political. The great losses in population were being recaptured, and increasingly able monarchs and rulers were imposing a new political order. A solution to the religious crisis, however, would have to await the Reformation and Counter-Reformation of the sixteenth century.

Although the opposite would be true in the sixteenth and seventeenth centuries, the city–states of Italy survived the century and a half between 1300 and 1450 better than the territorial states of northern Europe. This was due to Italy's strategic location between East and West and its lucrative Eurasian trade. Great wealth gave rulers and merchants the ability to *work their will on both society and culture. They became patrons of government, education, and the arts, always as much for self-aggrandizement as out of benevolence, for whether a patron was a family, a firm, a government, or the church, their endowments enhanced their reputation and power. The result of such patronage was a cultural Renaissance in Italian cities unmatched elsewhere.*

With the fall of Constantinople to the Turks in 1453, the shrinkage of Italy's once unlimited trading empire began. City–state soon turned against city–state, and by the 1490s the armies of France invaded Italy. Within a quarter century, Italy's great Renaissance had peaked.

The fifteenth century also saw an unprecedented scholarly renaissance. Italian and northern humanists made a full recovery of classical knowledge and languages and set in motion educational reforms and cultural changes that would spread throughout Europe in the fifteenth and sixteenth centuries. In the process the Italian humanists invented, for all practical purposes, critical historical scholarship and exploited a new fifteenth-century invention, the "divine art" of printing with movable type.

In this period the vernacular—the local language—began to take its place alongside Latin, the international language, as a widely used literary and political means of communication. And European lands progressively superseded the universal Church as the community of highest allegiance, as patriotism and incipient nationalism seized hearts and minds as strongly as religion. Nations henceforth "transcended" themselves not by journeys to Rome, but by competitive voyages to the Far East and the Americas, as the age of global exploration opened.

For Europe, the late fifteenth and sixteenth centuries were a period of unprecedented territorial expansion and ideological experimentation. Permanent colonies were established within the Americas, and the exploitation of the New World's human and mineral resources was begun. Imported American gold and silver spurred scientific invention and a new weapons industry and touched off an inflationary spiral that produced an escalation in prices by the century's end. The new bullion also helped create an international traffic in African slaves as rival African tribes sold their captives to the Portuguese. These slaves were brought in ever-increasing numbers to work the mines and the plantations of the New World as replacements for faltering American natives. The period also saw social engineering and political planning on a large scale. Newly centralized governments began to put long-range economic policies into practice, a development that came to be known as mercantilism.

The Renaissance in Italy (1375–1527)

A historian has described the Renaissance as the "prototype of the modern world." In his *Civilization of the Renaissance in Italy* (1860), Jacob Burckhardt argues that in fourteenth- and fifteenth-century Italy, through the revival of ancient learning, new secular and scientific values began to supplant traditional religious beliefs. This was the period in which people began to adopt a rational, objective, and statistical approach to reality and to rediscover the importance of the individual and his or her artistic creativity. The result, in Burckhardt's words, was a release of the "full, whole nature of man."

Other scholars have found Burckhardt's description far too modernizing an interpretation of the Renaissance and have accused him of overlooking the continuity between the Middle Ages and the Renaissance. His critics especially stress the still strongly Christian character of Renaissance humanism. They point out that earlier "renaissances," especially that of the twelfth century, also saw the revival of the ancient classics, interest in the Latin language and Greek science, and an appreciation of the worth and creativity of individuals.

Despite the exaggeration and bias of Burckhardt's portrayal, most scholars agree that the Renaissance was a time of transition from the medieval to the modern world. Medieval Europe, especially before the twelfth century, had been a fragmented feudal society with an agricultural economy, and its thought and culture were largely dominated by the church. Renaissance Europe, especially after the fourteenth century, was characterized by growing national consciousness and political centralization, an urban economy based on organized commerce and capitalism, and ever-greater lay and secular control of thought and culture, including religion.

The distinctive features and achievements of the Renaissance are most strikingly revealed in Italy from roughly 1375 to 1527, the year of the infamous sack of Rome by imperial soldiers. What was achieved in Italy during the late fourteenth to the early sixteenth centuries also deeply influenced northern Europe. (See "Art & the West.")

The Italian City–State

Renaissance society was no simple cultural transformation. It first took distinctive shape within the cities of late medieval Italy. Italy had always had a cultural advantage over the rest of Europe because its geography made it the natural gateway between East and West. Venice, Genoa, and Pisa traded uninterruptedly with the Near East throughout the Middle Ages

Art & the West

An Unprecedented Self-Portrait

Albrecht Dürer (1471–1528), the greatest German painter of the Renaissance, was the son of a Nuremberg goldsmith and the apprentice of the city's then most famous painter, Michael Wolgemut. Naturally gifted and trained from childhood, Dürer at thirteen could draw so lifelike a reflection of himself in a mirror, that senior artists already then recognized his genius. A dowry from his marriage at twenty-two (his wife, Agnes Frey, was nineteen) permitted him to travel to Venice, where he acquired the skills of the great Italian artists. His ability to paint realistically led contemporaries to compare him to the legendary ancient Greek painter Apelles and won him many humanistic and princely patrons. According to one story, his dog, passing by a just finished painting his master had put outside to dry, mistook the work for the master himself and gave it a loving lick, leaving a permanent mark on the painting that Dürer proudly pointed out.

The *Self-Portrait* of 1500 was one of perhaps thirty self-portraits over Dürer's lifetime. (No previous artist painted himself as often or as provocatively.) For some scholars this painting signals a change from the medieval toward a more modern worldview. The individual becomes the primary focus, supplanting God and king. Exalting the power of art and the artist, Dürer presents himself as Christ-like and full faced, a pose traditionally reserved for members of the Holy Trinity. His own autograph, placed at eye level, backs up the portrait's bold proclamation: "I, Albrecht Dürer, divinely inspired artist."

The portrait's powerful effect is achieved by strict adherence to the rules of geometric proportionality (a subject on which Dürer wrote a major book) and by painstaking attention to detail. It is a work of perfect symmetry, and each hair of his head—even the fur on his coat—seems to have been drawn individually with great care. What the viewer beholds is neither Christ nor Everyman, but the gifted individual as many Renaissance thinkers dreamed him to be: a divinely endowed person capable of great achievement.

Dürer, Albrecht (1471–1528). *Self-portrait at Age 28 with Fur Coat*. 1500. Oil on wood, 67 × 49 cm. Alte Pinakothek, Munich, Germany. Scala/Art Resource, N.Y.

Sources: Jane Campbell Hutchison, *Albrecht Dürer: A Biography* (Princeton: Princeton University Press, 1990); Joseph Leo Koerner, *The Moment of Self-Portraiture in German Renaissance Art* (Chicago, 1993), esp. pp. xviii, 8–9, 40–42.

and maintained vibrant urban societies. When commerce revived on a large scale in the eleventh century, Italian merchants quickly mastered the business skills of organization, bookkeeping, scouting new markets, and securing monopolies. During the thirteenth and fourteenth centuries, trade-rich cities expanded to become powerful city–states, dominating the political and economic life of the surrounding countryside. By the fifteenth century, the great Italian cities had become the bankers of much of Europe.

GROWTH OF CITY–STATES   The growth of Italian cities and urban culture was assisted by the endemic warfare between the emperor and the pope and the Guelf (propapal) and Ghibelline (proimperial) factions that this warfare had created. Either of these might have successfully challenged the cities had they permitted each other to concentrate on that. Instead, they chose to weaken one another and thus strengthened the merchant oligarchies of the cities. Unlike those of northern Europe, which tended to be dominated by kings and territorial princes, the great Italian cities were left free to expand. They became independent states, absorbing the surrounding countryside and assimilating the area's nobility in a unique urban meld of old and new rich. There were five such major, competitive states in Italy: the duchy of Milan; the republics of Florence and Venice; the Papal States; and the kingdom of Naples. (See Map 10–1.)

Social strife and competition for political power were so intense within the cities that most had evolved into despotisms by the fifteenth century just to survive. Venice was a notable exception. It was ruled by a successful merchant oligarchy with power located in a patrician senate of 300 members and a ruthless judicial body, the Council of Ten, which anticipated and suppressed rival groups. Elsewhere, the new social classes and divisions within society produced by rapid urban growth fueled chronic, near-anarchic conflict.

SOCIAL CLASS AND CONFLICT   Florence was the most striking example. There were four distinguishable social groups within the city. The first was the old rich, or *grandi*, the nobles and merchants who traditionally ruled the city. The second group was the emergent newly rich merchant class—capitalists and bankers known as the *popolo grosso*, or "fat people." They began to challenge the old rich for political power in the late thirteenth and early fourteenth centuries. Then there were the middle-burgher ranks of guild masters, shop owners, and professionals—those smaller businesspeople who, in Florence as elsewhere, tended to take the side of the new rich against the conservative policies of the old rich. Finally, there was the *popolo minuto*, or the "little people," the lower economic classes. In 1457 one-third of the population of Florence, about 30,000 people, were officially listed as paupers, that is, having no wealth at all.

These social divisions produced conflict at every level of society, to which was added the ever-present fear of foreign intrigue. In 1378 there was a great revolt of the poor known as the Ciompi Revolt. It resulted from a combination of three factors that made life unbearable for those at the bottom of society: the feuding between the old and the new rich; the social anarchy that had resulted from the Black Death, which cut the city's population almost in half; and the collapse of the banking houses of Bardi and Peruzzi, which left the poor more economically vulnerable than ever. The successful revolt established a chaotic four-year reign of power by the lower Florentine classes. True stability did not return to Florence until the ascent to power of Cosimo de' Medici (1389–1464) in 1434.

Duchy of Milan	Republic of Venice
Republic of Genoa	Papal States
Republic of Florence	Kingdom of Naples

MAP 10–1   RENAISSANCE ITALY   *The city–states of Renaissance Italy were self-contained principalities whose internal strife was monitored by their despots and whose external aggression was long successfully controlled by treaty.*

Florentine women doing needlework, spinning, and weaving. These activities took up much of a woman's time and contributed to the elegance of dress for which Florentine men and women were famed.
Alinari/Art Resource

DESPOTISM AND DIPLOMACY The wealthiest Florentine, Cosimo de' Medici, was an astute statesman. He controlled the city internally from behind the scenes, skillfully manipulating the constitution and influencing elections. Florence was governed by a council, first of six and later of eight members, known as the *Signoria*. These men were chosen from the most powerful guilds—those representing the major clothing industries (cloth, wool, fur, and silk) and such other groups as bankers, judges, and doctors. Through his informal, cordial relations with the electoral committee, Cosimo was able to keep councillors loyal to him in the *Signoria*. As head of the Office of Public Debt, he was able to favor congenial factions. His grandson Lorenzo the Magnificent (1449–1492, r. 1478–1492) ruled Florence in almost totalitarian fashion during the last quarter of the fifteenth century. The assassination of his brother in 1478 by a rival family, the Pazzi, who plotted with the pope against Medici rule, made Lorenzo a cautious and determined ruler.

Despotism was less subtle elsewhere. To prevent internal social conflict and foreign intrigue from paralyzing their cities, the dominant groups cooperated to install a hired strongman. Known as a *podestà*, his purpose was to maintain law and order. He was given executive, military, and judicial authority. His mandate was direct and simple: to permit, by whatever means required, the normal flow of business activity without which neither the old rich, the new rich, nor the poor of a city could long survive. Because these despots could not depend on the divided populace, they operated through mercenary armies, which they obtained through military brokers known as *condottieri*.

It was a hazardous job. Not only were despots subject to dismissal by the oligarchies that hired them, but they were also popular objects of assassination attempts. The spoils of success, however, were very great. In Milan, it was as despots that the Visconti family came to power in 1278 and the Sforza family in 1450. Both ruled without constitutional restraints or serious political competition. The latter produced one of Machiavelli's heroes, Ludovico il Moro.

Political turbulence and warfare gave birth to diplomacy. Consequently, the various city–states could stay abreast of foreign military developments and, if shrewd enough, gain power and advantage short of actually going to war. Most city–states established resident embassies in the fifteenth century. Their ambassadors not only represented them in ceremonies and as negotiators, but also became their watchful eyes and ears at rival courts.

Whether within the comparatively tranquil republic of Venice, the strong-arm democracy of Florence, or the undisguised despotism of Milan, the disciplined Italian city proved a most congenial climate for an unprecedented flowering of thought and culture. Italian Renaissance culture was promoted as vigorously by despots as by republicans and as enthusiastically by secularized popes as by the more spiritually minded.

Cosimo de' Medici (1389–1464), Florentine banker and statesman, in his lifetime the city's wealthiest man and most successful politician. This portrait is by Pontormo.
Erich Lessing, Art Resource, N.Y.

Such widespread support occurred because the main requirement for patronage of the arts and letters was the one thing that Italian cities of the High Renaissance had in abundance: great wealth.

Humanism

Several schools of thought exist on the meaning of "humanism." There are those who see the Italian Renaissance as the birth of modernity, characterized by an un-Christian philosophy that stressed the dignity of humankind and championed individualism and secular values. (These are the followers of the nineteenth-century historian Jacob Burckhardt.) Others argue that humanists were the very champions of authentic Catholic Christianity, who opposed the pagan teaching of Aristotle and the ineloquent Scholasticism that his writings nurtured. Still others see humanism as a form of scholarship consciously designed to promote a sense of civic responsibility and political liberty.

An authoritative modern commentator on humanism, Paul O. Kristeller, has accused all these views of dealing more with the secondary effects than with the essence of humanism. Humanism, he believes, was no particular philosophy or value system, but simply an educational program that concentrated on rhetoric and sound scholarship for their own sake.

There is truth in each of these definitions. Humanism was the scholarly study of the Latin and Greek classics and of the ancient Church Fathers both for its own sake and in the hope of a rebirth of ancient norms and values. Humanists advocated the *studia humanitatis*, a liberal arts program of study that embraced grammar, rhetoric, poetry, history, politics, and moral philosophy. Not only were these subjects considered a joy in themselves, but they were also seen as celebrating the dignity of humankind and preparing people for a life of virtuous action. The Florentine Leonardo Bruni (ca. 1370–1444) first gave the name *humanitas*, or "humanity," to the learning that resulted from such scholarly pursuits. Bruni was a student of Manuel Chrysoloras, a Byzantine scholar who opened the world of Greek scholarship to a generation of young Italian humanists when he taught at Florence between 1397 and 1403.

The first humanists were orators and poets. They wrote original literature in both the classical and the vernacular languages, inspired by and modeled on the newly discovered works of the ancients. They also taught rhetoric within the universities. When humanists were not employed as teachers of rhetoric, their talents were sought as secretaries, speechwriters, and diplomats in princely and papal courts.

The study of classical and Christian antiquity existed before the Italian Renaissance. There were recoveries of ancient civilization during the Carolingian renaissance of the ninth century, within the cathedral school of Chartres in the twelfth century, during the great Aristotelian revival in Paris in the thirteenth century, and among the Augustinians in the early fourteenth century. These precedents, however, only partially compare with the grand achievements of the Italian Renaissance of the late Middle Ages. The latter was far more secular and lay dominated, had much broader interests, was blessed with far more recovered manuscripts, and possessed far superior technical skills than had been the case in the earlier "rebirths" of antiquity.

Unlike their Scholastic rivals, humanists were less bound to recent tradition; they did not focus all their attention on summarizing and comparing the views of recognized authorities on a text or question, but went directly to the original sources themselves. And their most respected sources were classical and biblical, not the medieval philosophers and theologians. Avidly searching out manuscript collections, Italian humanists made the full sources of Greek and Latin antiquity available to scholars during the fourteenth and fifteenth centuries. Mastery of Latin and Greek was the surgeon's tool of the humanist. There is a kernel of truth—but only a kernel—in the humanists' arrogant assertion that the period between themselves and classical civilization was a "dark middle age."

PETRARCH, DANTE, AND BOCCACCIO Francesco Petrarch (1304–1374) was the "father of humanism." (See "Petrarch's Letter to Posterity.") He left the legal profession to pursue letters and poetry. Most of his life was spent in and around Avignon. He was involved in Cola di Rienzo's popular revolt and two-year reign (1347–1349) in Rome as "tribune" of the Roman people. Petrarch also served the Visconti family in Milan in his later years.

Petrarch celebrated ancient Rome in his *Letters to the Ancient Dead*, fancied personal letters to Cicero, Livy, Vergil, and Horace. He also wrote a Latin epic poem (*Africa*, a poetic historical tribute to the Roman general Scipio Africanus) and a set of biographies of famous Roman men (*Lives of Illustrious Men*). Petrarch's most famous contemporary work was a collection of highly introspective love sonnets to a certain Laura, a married woman whom he romantically admired from a safe distance.

His critical textual studies, elitism, and contempt for the allegedly useless learning of the Scholastics were features that many later humanists also shared. Classical and Christian values coexist, not always harmoniously, in his work, an uneasy coexistence that is seen in many later humanists. Medieval Christian values can be seen in Petrarch's imagined dialogues with Saint Augustine and in tracts written to defend the personal immortality of the soul against the Aristotelians.

Petrarch was, however, far more secular in orientation than his famous near-contemporary Dante Alighieri (1265–1321), whose *Vita Nuova* and *Divine Comedy* form, with Petrarch's sonnets, the cornerstones of Italian vernacular literature. Petrarch's student and friend Giovanni Boccaccio (1313–1375) was also a pioneer of humanist studies. His *Decameron*—one hundred often bawdy tales told by three men and seven women in a country retreat from the plague that ravaged Florence in 1348—is both a stinging social commentary (especially in its exposé of sexual and economic misconduct) and a sympathetic look at human behavior. An avid collector of manuscripts, Boccaccio also assembled an encyclopedia of Greek and Roman mythology.

Petrarch's Letter to Posterity

In old age Petrarch wrote a highly personal letter to posterity in which he summarized the lessons he had learned during his lifetime. The letter also summarizes the original values of Renaissance humanists: their suspicion of purely materialistic pleasure, the importance they attached to friendship, and their utter devotion to and love of antiquity.

❖ *Does Petrarch's letter give equal weight to classical and Christian values? Why would he have preferred to live in another age?*

I have always possessed extreme contempt for wealth; not that riches are not desirable in themselves, but because I hate the anxiety and care which are invariably associated with them....I have, on the contrary, led a happier existence with plain living and ordinary fare....

The pleasure of dining with one's friends is so great that nothing has ever given me more delight than their unexpected arrival, nor have I ever willingly sat down to table without a companion....

The greatest kings of this age have loved and courted me....I have fled, however, from many...to whom I was greatly attached; and such was my innate longing for liberty that I studiously avoided those whose very name seemed incompatible with the freedom I loved.

I possess a well-balanced rather than a keen intellect—one prone to all kinds of good and wholesome study, but especially to moral philosophy and the art of poetry. The latter I neglected as time went on, and took delight in sacred literature....Among the many subjects that interested me, I dwelt especially upon antiquity, for our own age has always repelled me, so that, had it not been for the love of those dear to me, I should have preferred to have been born in any other period than our own. In order to forget my own time, I have constantly striven to place myself in spirit in other ages, and consequently I delighted in history....

If only I have lived well, it matter little to me how I have talked. Mere elegance of language can produce at best but an empty fame.

Frederick Austen Ogg, ed., *A Source Book of Mediaeval History: Documents Illustrative of European Life and Institutions from the German Invasions to the Renaissance* (New York: American Book Company, 1908), pp. 470–473.

Dante Alighieri (1265–1321) portrayed with scenes of hell, purgatory, and paradise from the Divine Comedy, *his classic epic poem.* Scala/Art Resource, N.Y.

EDUCATIONAL REFORMS AND GOALS Humanists were not bashful scholars. They delighted in going directly to primary sources and refused to be slaves to tradition. Such an attitude not only made them innovative educators, but also kept them constantly in search of new sources of information. Magnificent manuscript collections were assembled with great care, as if they were potent medicines for the ills of contemporary society.

The goal of humanist studies was to be wise and to speak eloquently, to know what is good, and to practice virtue. Learning was not to remain abstract and unpracticed. "It is better to will the good than to know the truth," Petrarch had taught, and this became a motto of many later humanists, who, like Petrarch, believed that learning ennobled people. Pietro Paolo Vergerio (1349–1420), the author of the most influential Renaissance tract on education, *On the Morals That Befit a Free Man*, left a classic summary of the humanist concept of a liberal education:

We call those studies liberal which are worthy of a free man; those studies by which we attain and practice virtue and wisdom; that education which calls forth, trains, and develops those highest gifts of body and mind which ennoble men and which are rightly judged to rank next in dignity to virtue only, for to a vulgar temper, gain and pleasure are the one aim of existence, to a lofty nature, moral worth and fame.[1]

The ideal of a useful education and well-rounded people inspired far-reaching reforms in traditional education. Quintilian's *Education of the Orator*, the

complete text of which was discovered in 1416, became the basic classical guide for the humanist revision of the traditional curriculum. Vittorino da Feltre (d. 1446) exemplified the ideals of humanist teaching. He not only had his students read the difficult works of Pliny, Ptolemy, Terence, Plautus, Livy, and Plutarch, but also subjected them to vigorous physical exercise and games. Another famous educator, Guarino da Verona (d. 1460), rector of the new University of Ferrara and a student of the age's most renowned Greek scholar, Manuel Chrysoloras, streamlined the study of classical languages and gave it systematic form.

Humanist learning was not confined to the classroom, as Baldassare Castiglione's (1478–1529) famous *Book of the Courtier* illustrates. Written as a practical guide for the nobility at the court of Urbino, it embodies the highest ideals of Italian humanism. It depicts the successful courtier as one who knew how to integrate knowledge of ancient languages and history with athletic, military, and musical skills, while practicing good manners and exhibiting a high moral character.

Noblewomen also played a role at court in education and culture, among them none more so than Christine de Pisan (1363?–1434). The Italian-born daughter of the physician and astrologer of the French king Charles V, she received as fine an education at the French court as anyone could have. She became expert in classical, French, and Italian languages and literature. Married at fifteen and the widowed mother of three at twenty-seven, she turned to writing lyric poetry to support herself. She soon became a well-known woman of letters who was much read throughout the courts of Europe. Her most famous

---

[1] Cited by De Lamar Jensen, *Renaissance Europe: Age of Recovery and Reconciliation* (Lexington, MA: D. C. Health, 1981), p. 111.

work, *The City of Ladies*, is a chronicle of the accomplishments of the great women of history. (See "Christine de Pisan Instructs Women on How to Handle Their Husbands.")

THE FLORENTINE "ACADEMY" AND THE REVIVAL OF PLATONISM Of all the important recoveries of the past made during the Italian Renaissance, none stands out more than the revival of Greek studies, especially the works of Plato, in fifteenth-century Florence. Many factors combined to bring this revival about. An important foundation was laid in 1397 when the city invited Manuel Chrysoloras to come from Constantinople to promote Greek learning. A half century later (1439), the ecumenical Council of Ferrara–Florence, having convened to negotiate the reunion of the Eastern and Western churches, opened the door for many Greek scholars and manuscripts to enter the West.

After the fall of Constantinople to the Turks in 1453, Greek scholars fled to Florence for refuge. This was the background against which the Florentine Platonic Academy evolved under the patronage of Cosimo de' Medici and the supervision of Marsilio Ficino (1433–1499) and Pico della Mirandola (1463–1494).

The thinkers of the Renaissance were interested in every variety of ancient wisdom. They were especially attracted, however, to the Platonic tradition and to those Church Fathers who tried to synthesize Platonic philosophy with Christian teaching. The "Florentine Academy" was actually not a formal school, but an informal gathering of influential Florentine humanists devoted to the revival of the works of Plato and the Neoplatonists: Plotinus, Proclus, Porphyry, and Dionysius the Areopagite. To this end, Ficino edited and published the complete works of Plato.

Christine de Pisan Instructs Women on How to Handle Their Husbands

Renowned Renaissance noblewoman Christine de Pisan has the modern reputation of being perhaps the first feminist, and her book, The Treasure of the City of Ladies *(also known as* The Book of Three Virtues*), has been described as the Renaissance woman's survival manual. Here she gives advice to the wives of artisans.*

❖ *How does Christine de Pisan's image of husband and wife compare with other medieval views? Would the church take issue with her advice in any way? As a noblewoman commenting on the married life of artisans, does her high social standing influence her advice? Would she give similar advice to women of her own social class?*

All wives of artisans should be very painstaking and diligent if they wish to have the necessities of life. They should encourage their husbands or their workmen to get to work early in the morning and work until late....[And] the wife herself should [also] be involved in the work to the extent that she knows all about it, so that she may know how to oversee his workers if her husband is absent, and to reprove them if they do not do well....And when customers come to her husband and try to drive a hard bargain, she ought to warn him solicitously to take care that he does not make a bad deal. She should advise him to be chary of giving too much credit if he does not know precisely where and to whom it is going, for in this way many come to poverty....

In addition, she ought to keep her husband's love as much as she can, to this end: that he will stay at home more willingly and that he may not have any reason to join the foolish crowds of other young men in taverns and indulge in unnecessary and extravagant expense, as many tradesmen do, especially in Paris. By treating him kindly she should protect him as well as she can from this. It is said that three things drive a man from his home: a quarrelsome wife, a smoking fireplace, and a leaking roof. She too ought to stay at home gladly and not go off every day traipsing hither and yon gossiping with the neighbours and visiting her chums to find out what everyone is doing. That is done by slovenly housewives roaming about the town in groups. Nor should she go off on these pilgrimages got up for no good reason and involving a lot of needless expense.

Excerpt from *The Treasure of the City of Ladies* or *The Book of the Three Virtues*, by Christine de Pisan, trans. by Sarah Lawson (Penguin Classics, 1985), this translation copyright © Sarah Lawson, 1985. Reprinted by permission of Penguin Books Ltd.

The appeal of Platonism lay in its flattering view of human nature. It distinguished between an eternal sphere of being and the perishable world in which humans actually lived. Human reason was believed to belong to the former—indeed, to have preexisted in this pristine world and to continue to commune with it, to which the present knowledge of mathematical and moral truth bore witness.

Strong Platonic influence can be seen in Pico's *Oration on the Dignity of Man*, perhaps the most famous Renaissance statement on the nature of humankind. Pico wrote the *Oration* as an introduction to a pretentious collection of 900 theses. Published in Rome in December 1486, the theses were intended to serve as the basis for a public debate on all of life's important topics. The *Oration* drew on Platonic teaching to depict humans as the only creatures in the world who possessed the freedom to be whatever they chose, able at will to rise to the height of angels or to descend to the level of pigs.

CRITICAL WORK OF THE HUMANISTS: LORENZO VALLA
Because they were guided by a scholarly ideal of philological accuracy and historical truthfulness, the humanists could become critics of tradition even when that was not their intention. Dispassionate critical scholarship shook long-standing foundations, not the least of which were those of the medieval church.

The work of Lorenzo Valla (1406–1457), author of the standard Renaissance text on Latin philology, the *Elegances of the Latin Language* (1444), reveals the explosive character of the new learning. Although a good Catholic, Valla became a hero to later Protestants. His popularity among Protestants stemmed from his defense of predestination against the advocates of free will, and especially from his exposé of the *Donation of Constantine*. (See Chapter 6.)

The fraudulent *Donation*, written in the eighth century, purported to be a grant of vast territories made by the fourth-century Roman emperor Constantine to the pope. Valla did not intend the exposé of the *Donation* to have the devastating force that Protestants later attributed to it. He only proved in a careful, scholarly way what others had long suspected. Using the most rudimentary textual analysis and historical logic, Valla demonstrated that the document was filled with such anachronistic terms as *fief* and that it contained material that could not be in a genuine fourth-century document. In the same dispassionate way, Valla also pointed out errors in the Latin Vulgate, still the authorized version of the Bible for the Western church.

Such discoveries did not make Valla any less loyal to the church, nor did they prevent his faithful fulfillment of the office of apostolic secretary in Rome under Pope Nicholas V. Nonetheless, historical criticism of this type served those less loyal to the medieval church. It was no accident that young humanists formed the first identifiable group of Martin Luther's supporters.

CIVIC HUMANISM Italian humanists were exponents of applied knowledge; their basic criticism of traditional education was that much of it was useless. Education, they believed, should promote individual virtue and public service. This ideal inspired what has been called civic humanism, by which is meant examples of humanist leadership of the political and cultural life. The most striking instance is to be found in Florence. There three humanists served as chancellors: Colluccio Salutati (1331–1406), Leonardo Bruni (ca. 1370–1444), and Poggio Bracciolini (1380–1459). Each used his rhetorical skills to rally the Florentines against the aggression of Naples and Milan. Bruni and Poggio also wrote adulatory histories of the city. Another accomplished humanist scholar, Leon Battista Alberti (1402–1472), was a noted architect and builder in the city. Whether it was humanism that accounted for such civic activity or just a desire to exercise great power remains a debated issue.

On the other hand, many humanists became cliquish and snobbish, an intellectual elite concerned only with pursuing narrow, antiquarian interests and writing pure, classical Latin in the quiet of their studies. It was in reaction to this elitist trend that the humanist historians Niccolò Machiavelli (1469–1527) and Francesco Guicciardini (1483–1540) adopted the vernacular and made contemporary history their primary source and subject matter.

Renaissance Art

In Renaissance Italy, as in Reformation Europe, the values and interests of the laity were no longer subordinated to those of the clergy. In education, culture, and religion, the laity assumed a leading role and established models for the clergy to imitate. This was a development due in part to the church's loss of international power during the great crises of the late Middle Ages. It was also encouraged by the rise of national sentiment, the creation of competent national bureaucracies staffed by the laity rather than by clerics, and the rapid growth of lay education during the fourteenth and fifteenth centuries. Medieval Christian values were adjusting to a more this-worldly spirit. Men and women began again to appreciate

Giotto's portrayal of the funeral of Saint Francis of Assisi. The saint is surrounded by his admiring brothers and a knight of Assisi (first on the right). Giotto's (1266–1336) work signals the evolution toward Renaissance art. The damaged areas on this fresco resulted from the removal of nineteenth-century restorations. Scala/Art Resource, N.Y.

and even glorify the secular world, secular learning, and purely human pursuits as ends in themselves.

This new perspective on life is prominent in the painting and sculpture of the High Renaissance—the late fifteenth and early sixteenth centuries, when Renaissance art reached its full maturity. Whereas medieval art tended to be abstract and formulaic, Renaissance art was emphatically concerned with the observation of the natural world and the communication of human emotions. Renaissance artists also tried to give their works a greater rational (chiefly mathematical) order—a symmetry and proportionality that reflected pictorially their deeply held belief in the harmony of the universe. The interest of Renaissance artists in ancient Roman art was closely allied to an independent interest in humanity and nature.

Renaissance artists had the advantage of new technical skills developed during the fifteenth century. In addition to the availability of oil paints, two special techniques were perfected: that of using shading to enhance naturalness (*chiaroscuro*) and that of adjusting the size of figures to give the viewer a feeling of continuity with the painting (linear perspective). These techniques permitted the artist to "rationalize" space and paint a more natural world. The result was that, compared to their flat Byzantine and Gothic counterparts, Renaissance paintings were filled with energy and life and stood out from the canvas in three dimensions.

The new direction was signaled by Giotto (1266–1336), the father of Renaissance painting. An admirer of Saint Francis of Assisi, whose love of nature he shared, Giotto painted a more natural world than his Byzantine and Gothic predecessors. Though still filled with religious seriousness, his work was no longer so abstract and unnatural a depiction of

the world. The painter Masaccio (1401–1428) and the sculptor Donatello (1386–1466) continued to portray the world around them more literally and naturally. The heights were reached by the great masters of the High Renaissance: Leonardo da Vinci (1452–1519), Raphael (1483–1520), and Michelangelo Buonarroti (1475–1564).

LEONARDO DA VINCI More than any other person in the period, Leonardo exhibited the Renaissance ideal of the universal person. He was a true mas-

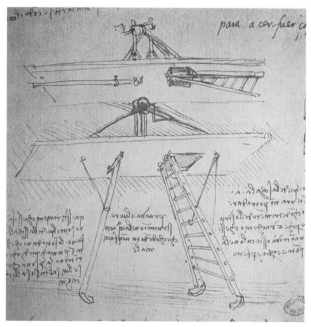

Aviation drawings by Leonardo da Vinci (1452–1519), who imagined a possible flying machine with a retractable ladder for boarding. David Forbert/SuperStock, Inc.

ter of many skills. One of the greatest painters of all time, he was also a military engineer for Ludovico il Moro in Milan, Cesare Borgia in Romagna, and the French king Francis I. Leonardo advocated scientific experimentation, dissected corpses to learn anatomy, and was an accomplished, self-taught botanist. His inventive mind foresaw such modern machines as airplanes and submarines. Indeed, the variety of his interests was so great that it could shorten his attention span, so that he was constantly moving from one activity to another. His great skill in conveying inner moods through complex facial features can be seen in the most famous of his paintings, the *Mona Lisa*, as well as in his self-portrait.

RAPHAEL   A man of great sensitivity and kindness, Raphael was apparently loved by contemporaries as much for his person as for his work. His premature death at thirty-seven cut short his artistic career. He is famous for his tender madonnas, the best known of which graced the monastery of San Sisto in Piacenza and is now in Dresden. Art historians praise his fresco *The School of Athens*,

a grandly conceived portrayal of the great masters of Western philosophy, as a virtually perfect example of Renaissance technique. It depicts Plato and Aristotle surrounded by the great philosophers and scientists of antiquity, who are portrayed with features of Raphael's famous contemporaries, including Leonardo and Michelangelo.

MICHELANGELO   The melancholy genius Michelangelo also excelled in a variety of arts and crafts. His eighteen-foot godlike sculpture David, which long stood majestically in the great square of Florence, is a perfect example of the Renaissance artist's devotion to harmony, symmetry, and proportion, as well as the extreme glorification of the human form. Four different popes commissioned works by Michelangelo. The most famous of these works are the frescoes for the Sistine Chapel, painted during the pontificate of Pope Julius II (r. 1503–1513), who

Commissioned in 1501, when the artist was 26, Michelangelo's David *became the symbol of the Florentine republic and was displayed in front of the Palazzo Vecchio. The detail shown here highlights the restrained emotion and dignity for which the statue is famous.* Michelangelo (1475–1564) David-p. (testa di profilo.) Accademia Firenze. Scala/Art Resource

Portrait by Raphael of Baldassare Castiglione (1748–1529), author of the Cortegiano. Portrait (c. 1515) now in the Louvre. Cliche des Musées Nationaux

These two works by Donatello, sculpted fifteen years apart, reveal the psychological complexity of Renaissance artists and their work. On the left is a youthful, sexy David, standing awkwardly and seemingly puzzled on the head of the slain Goliath. Created in 1440, it is the earliest free-standing nude made in the West since Roman times. Art Resource, N.Y *On the right, sculpted in 1454–1455 from poplar wood, is Mary Magdalen returned from her desert retreat; she is a frightful, toothless old woman, shorn of all dignity.* Scala/Art Resource, N.Y.

The frescoes of Michelangelo on the west wall ceiling of the Sistine Chapel in the Vatican Palace. Above the altar is his Last Judgment. Brett Froomer/The Image Bank

also set Michelangelo to work on the pope's own magnificent tomb. (See "Michaelangelo and Pope Julius II.") The Sistine frescoes originally covered 10,000 square feet and involved 343 figures, over half of which exceeded 10 feet in height. But it is their originality and perfection as works of art that impress most. This labor of love and piety took four years to complete. A person of incredible energy and endurance who lived to be almost ninety, Michelangelo insisted on doing almost everything himself and permitted his assistants only a few of the many chores involved in his work.

His later works are more complex and suggest deep personal changes. They mark, artistically and philosophically, the passing of High Renaissance painting and the advent of a new style known as mannerism, which reached its peak in the late sixteenth and early seventeenth centuries. A reaction against the simplicity and symmetry of High Renaissance art (which also found expression in music and literature), mannerism made room for the strange and even the abnormal and gave freer reign to the subjectivity of the artist. Mannerism acquired its name because the

artist was permitted to express his or her own individual perceptions and feelings, to paint, compose, or write in a "mannered," or "affected," way. Tintoretto (d. 1594) and especially El Greco (d. 1614) became mannerism's supreme representatives.

Slavery in the Renaissance

Throughout Renaissance Italy, slavery flourished as extravagantly as art and culture. A thriving western slave market existed as early as the twelfth century, when the Spanish sold Muslim slaves captured in raids and war to wealthy Italians and other interested buyers. Contemporaries looked on such slavery as a merciful act, since these captives would otherwise have been killed. In addition to widespread household or domestic slavery, collective plantation slavery, following East Asian models, also developed during the High Middle Ages in the eastern Mediterranean. In the savannas of Sudan and on Venetian estates on the islands of Cyprus and Crete, gangs of slaves worked sugar cane plantations, the model for later western Mediterranean and New World slavery.

After the Black Death (1348–1350) had reduced the supply of laborers everywhere in western Europe, the demand for slaves soared. Slaves now began to be imported from Africa, the Balkans, Constantinople, Cyprus, Crete, and the lands surrounding the Black Sea. Because slaves were taken randomly from conquered people, they consisted of many races: Tatars, Circassians, Greeks, Russians, Georgians, and Iranians as well as Asians and Africans. According to one source, "By the end of the fourteenth century, there was hardly a well-to-do household in Tuscany without at least one slave: brides brought them [to their marriages] as part of their dowry, doctors accepted them from their patients in lieu of fees—and it was not unusual to find them even in the service of a priest."[2]

Owners had complete dominion over their slaves; in Italian law, this meant the "[power] to have, hold, sell, alienate, exchange, enjoy, rent or unrent, dispose of in [their] will[s], judge soul and body, and do with in perpetuity whatsoever may please [them] and [their] heirs and no man may gainsay [them]."[3] A strong, young, healthy slave cost the equivalent of the wages paid a free servant over several years. Considering the lifetime of free service thereafter, slaves could be well worth the cost.

The Tatars and Africans appear to have been the worst treated. But as in ancient Greece and Rome, slaves at this time were generally accepted as family members and were integrated into households. Not a few women slaves became mothers of their masters' children. Quite a few children of such

[2] Iris Origo, *The Merchant of Prato: Francesco di Marco Datini, 1335–1410* (New York: David Godine, 1986), pp. 90–91.

[3] *Ibid.*, p. 209.

Michelangelo and Pope Julius II

Vasari here describes how Pope Julius, the most fearsome and worldly of the Renaissance popes, forced Michelangelo to complete the Sistine Chapel before Michelangelo was ready to do so.

❖ *Did Michelangelo hold his own with the pope? What does this interchange suggest about the relationship of patrons and artists in the Renaissance? Were great artists like Michelangelo so revered that they could do virtually as they pleased?*

[The pope was very anxious to see the decoration of the Sistine Chapel completed and constantly inquired when it would be finished.] On one occasion, therefore, Michelangelo replied, "It will be finished when I shall have done all that I believe is required to satisfy Art." "And we command," rejoined the pontiff, "that you satisfy our wish to have it done quickly," adding that if it were not at once completed, he would have Michelangelo thrown headlong from the scaffolding. Hearing this, our artist, who feared the fury of the pope, and with good cause, without taking time to add what was wanting, took down the remainder of the scaffolding to the great satisfaction of the whole city on All Saints' day, when Pope Julius went into that chapel to sing mass. But Michelangelo had much desired to retouch some portions of the work *a secco* [that is, after the damp plaster upon which the paint had been originally laid *al fresco* had dried], as had been done by the older masters who had painted the stories on the walls. He would also have gladly added a little ultramarine to the draperies and gilded other parts, to the end that the whole might have a richer and more striking effect.

The pope, too, hearing that these things were still wanting, and finding that all who beheld the chapel praised it highly, would now fain have had the additions made. But as Michelangelo thought reconstructing the scaffold too long an affair, the pictures remained as they were, although the pope, who often saw Michelangelo, would sometimes say, "Let the chapel be enriched with bright colors and gold; it looks poor." When Michelangelo would reply familiarly, "Holy Father, the men of those days did not adorn themselves with gold; those who are painted here less than any, for they were none too rich; besides which they were holy men, and must have despised riches and ornaments."

From James Harvey Robinson, ed., *Readings in European History*, Vol. 1 (Boston: Athenaeum, 1904), pp. 538–539.

This portrait of Katharina, by Albrecht Dürer, provides evidence of African slavery in Europe during the sixteenth century. Katharina was in the service of one João Bradao, a Portuguese economic minister living in Antwerp, then the financial center of Europe. Dürer became friends with Bradao during his stay in the Low Countries in the winter of 1520–1521. Albrecht Dürer, Portrait of the Moorish Woman Katharina. Uffizi Florence, Italy. Foto Marburg/Art Resource, NY

unions were adopted and raised as legitimate heirs of their fathers. It was clearly in the interest of their owners to keep slaves healthy and happy; otherwise they were of little use and could even become a threat. Still, slaves remained a foreign and suspected presence in Italian society; they were, as all knew, uprooted and resentful people.

Italy's Political Decline: The French Invasions (1494–1527)

The Treaty of Lodi

As a land of autonomous city–states, Italy had always relied on internal cooperation for its peace and safety from foreign invasion—especially by the Turks. Such cooperation had been maintained during the latter half of the fifteenth century thanks to a carefully constructed political alliance known as the Treaty of Lodi (1454–1455). The terms of the treaty brought Milan and Naples, long traditional enemies, into alliance with Florence. These three stood together for decades against Venice, which was frequently joined by the Papal States, to create an internal balance of power. When a foreign enemy threatened Italy, however, the five formed a united front.

Around 1490, following the rise to power of the Milanese despot Ludovico il Moro, hostilities between Milan and Naples resumed. The peace made possible by the Treaty of Lodi ended in 1494 when Naples, supported by Florence and the Borgia Pope Alexander VI (r. 1492–1503), prepared to attack Milan. Ludovico made what proved to be a fatal response in these new political alignments: He appealed for aid to the French. French kings had ruled Naples from 1266 to 1435, before they were driven out by Duke Alfonso of Sicily. Breaking a wise Italian rule, Ludovico invited the French to reenter Italy and revive their dynastic claim to Naples. In his haste to check his rival Naples, Ludovico did not recognize sufficiently that France also had dynastic claims to Milan. Nor did he foresee how insatiable the French appetite for Italian territory would become once French armies had crossed the Alps.

Charles VIII's March through Italy

The French king Louis XI had resisted the temptation to invade Italy, while nonetheless keeping French dynastic claims in Italy alive. His successor, Charles VIII (r. 1483–1498), an eager youth in his twenties, responded to Ludovico's call with lightning speed. Within five months, he had crossed the Alps (August 1495) and raced as conqueror through Florence and the Papal States into Naples. As Charles approached Florence, the Florentine ruler, Piero dé Medici, who had allied with Naples against Milan, tried to placate the French king by handing over Pisa and other Florentine possessions. Such appeasement only brought about Piero's forced exile by a population that was revolutionized then by the radical Dominican preacher Girolamo Savonarola (1452–1498). Savonarola convinced most of the fearful Florentines that the French king's arrival was a long-delayed and fully justified divine vengeance on their immorality.

Charles entered Florence without resistance. Thanks to Savonarola's flattery and the payment of a large ransom, the city was spared a threatened destruction. Savonarola continued to exercise virtual rule over Florence for four years after Charles's departure. The Florentines proved, however, not to be the stuff theocracies are made of. Savonarola's moral rigor and antipapal policies made it impossible for him to survive indefinitely. This became especially true after the Italian cities reunited and the ouster of the French invader, whom Savonarola had praised as a godsend, became national policy. Savonarola was imprisoned and executed in May 1498.

Charles's lightning march through Italy also struck terror in non-Italian hearts. Ferdinand of Aragon, who hoped to expand his own possessions in Italy from his kingdom of Sicily, now found himself vulnerable to a French–Italian axis. He took the initiative to create a counteralliance—the League of Venice, formed in March 1495—in which he joined with Venice, the Papal States, and Emperor Maximilian I against the French. The alliance set the stage for a conflict between France and Spain that would not end until 1559.

Ludovico il Moro meanwhile recognized that he had sown the wind; having desired a French invasion only so long as it weakened his enemies, he now saw Milan threatened by the whirlwind of events that he had himself created. In reaction, he joined the League of Venice, and this alliance was able to send Charles into retreat by May. Charles remained thereafter on the defensive until his death in April 1498.

Pope Alexander VI and the Borgia Family

The French returned to Italy under Charles's successor, Louis XII (r. 1498–1515). This time they were assisted by a new Italian ally, the Borgia pope, Alexander VI. Alexander was probably the most corrupt pope who ever sat on the papal throne. He openly promoted the political careers of Cesare and Lucrezia Borgia, the children he had had before he became pope, and he placed papal policy in tandem with the efforts of his powerful family to secure a political base in Romagna.

In Romagna, several principalities had fallen away from the church during the Avignon papacy. And Venice, the pope's ally within the League of Venice, continued to contest the Papal States for their loyalty. Seeing that a French alliance could give him the opportunity to reestablish control over the region, Alexander took steps to secure French favor. He annulled Louis XII's marriage to Charles VIII's sister so that Louis could marry Charles's widow, Anne of Brittany—a popular political move designed to keep Brittany French. The pope also bestowed a cardinal's hat on the archbishop of Rouen, Louis's favorite cleric. Most important, Alexander agreed to abandon the League of Venice; this withdrawal of support made the league too weak to resist a French reconquest of Milan. In exchange, Cesare Borgia received the sister of the king of

Navarre, Charlotte d'Albret, in marriage, a union that greatly enhanced Borgia military strength. Cesare also received land grants from Louis XII and the promise of French military aid in Romagna.

All in all it was a scandalous trade-off, but one that made it possible for both the French king and the pope to realize their ambitions within Italy. Louis successfully invaded Milan in August 1499. Ludovico il Moro, who had originally opened the Pandora's box of French invasion, spent his last years languishing in a French prison. In 1500 Louis and Ferdinand of Aragon divided Naples between them, while the pope and Cesare Borgia conquered the cities of Romagna without opposition. Alexander awarded his victorious son the title "duke of Romagna."

Pope Julius II

Cardinal Giuliano della Rovere, a strong opponent of the Borgia family, succeeded Alexander VI as Pope Julius II (r. 1503–1513). He suppressed the Borgias and placed their newly conquered lands in Romagna under papal jurisdiction. Julius came to be known as the "warrior pope," because he brought the Renaissance papacy to a peak of military prowess and diplomatic intrigue. Shocked, as were other contemporaries, by this thoroughly secular papacy, the

Major Political Events of the Italian Renaissance (1375–1527)	
1378–1382	The Ciompi Revolt in Florence
1434	Medici rule in Florence established by Cosimo de' Medici
1454–1455	Treaty of Lodi allies Milan, Naples, and Florence (in effect until 1494)
1494	Charles VIII of France invades Italy
1494–1498	Savonarola controls Florence
1495	League of Venice unites Venice, Milan, the Papal States, the Holy Roman Empire, and Spain against France
1499	Louis XII invades Milan (the second French invasion of Italy)
1500	The Borgias conquer Romagna
1512–1513	The Holy League (Pope Julius II, Ferdinand of Aragon, Emperor Maximilian, and Venice) defeats the French
1513	Machiavelli writes *The Prince*
1515	Francis I leads the third French invasion of Italy
1516	Concordat of Bologna between France and the papacy
1527	Sack of Rome by imperial soldiers

humanist Erasmus (1466?–1536), who had witnessed in disbelief a bullfight in the papal palace during a visit to Rome, wrote a popular anonymous satire entitled *Julius Excluded from Heaven*. This humorous account purported to describe the pope's unsuccessful efforts to convince Saint Peter that he was worthy of admission to heaven.

Assisted by his powerful allies, Pope Julius succeeded in driving the Venetians out of Romagna in 1509. Thus, he ended Venetian claims in the region and fully secured the Papal States. Having realized this long-sought papal goal, Julius turned to the second major undertaking of his pontificate: ridding Italy of his former ally, the French invader. Julius, Ferdinand of Aragon, and Venice formed a second Holy League in October 1511, and within a short period Emperor Maximilian I and the Swiss joined them. By 1512 the league had the French in full retreat, and they were soundly defeated by the Swiss in 1513 at Novara.

The French were nothing if not persistent. They invaded Italy a third time under Louis's successor, Francis I (r. 1515–1547). French armies massacred Swiss soldiers of the Holy League at Marignano in September 1515, avenging the earlier defeat at Novara. The victory won the Concordat of Bologna from the people in August 1516. The agreement gave the French king control over the French clergy in exchange for French recognition of the pope's superiority over church councils and his right to collect annates in France. This was an important compromise that helped keep France Catholic after the outbreak of the Protestant Reformation. But the new French entry into Italy also led to the first of four major wars with Spain in the first half of the sixteenth century: the Habsburg–Valois wars, none of which France won.

Niccolò Machiavelli

The period of foreign invasions made a shambles of Italy. The same period that saw Italy's cultural peak in the work of Leonardo, Raphael, and Michelangelo also witnessed Italy's political tragedy. One who watched as French, Spanish, and German armies wreaked havoc on Italy was Niccolò Machiavelli (1469–1527). The more he saw, the more convinced he became that Italian political unity and independence were ends that justified any means.

A humanist and a careful student of ancient Rome, Machiavelli was impressed by the way Roman rulers and citizens had then defended their homeland. They possessed *virtù*, the ability to act decisively and heroically for the good of their country. Stories of ancient Roman patriotism and self-sacrifice were Machiavelli's favorites, and he lamented the absence of such traits among his compatriots. Such romanticizing of the Roman past caused some exaggeration of both ancient virtue and contemporary failings. His Florentine contemporary, Francesco Guicciardini, a more sober historian less given to idealizing antiquity, wrote truer chronicles of Florentine and Italian history.

Machiavelli also held deep republican ideals, which he did not want to see vanish from Italy. He believed that a strong and determined people could struggle successfully with fortune. He scolded the Italian people for the self-destruction their own internal feuding was causing. He wanted an end to that behavior above all, so that a reunited Italy could drive all foreign armies out.

But were his fellow citizens up to such a challenge? The juxtaposition of what Machiavelli believed the ancient Romans had been with the failure of his contemporaries to attain such high ideals made him the famous cynic whose name—in the epithet "Machiavellian"—has become synonymous with ruthless political expediency. Only a strongman, he concluded in the end, could impose order on so divided and selfish a people; the salvation of Italy required, for the present, a cunning dictator. (See "Machiavelli Discusses the Most Important Trait for a Ruler.")

It has been argued that Machiavelli wrote *The Prince* in 1513 as a cynical satire on the way rulers actually did behave and not as a serious recommendation of unprincipled despotic rule. To take his advocacy of tyranny literally, it is argued, contradicts both his earlier works and his own strong family tradition of republican service. But Machiavelli seems to have been in earnest when he advised rulers to discover the advantages of fraud and brutality, at least as a temporary means to the higher end of a unified Italy. He apparently hoped to see a strong ruler emerge from the Medici family, which had captured the papacy in 1513 with the pontificate of Leo X (r. 1513–1521). At the same time, the Medici family retained control over the powerful territorial state of Florence. The situation was similar to that of Machiavelli's hero Cesare Borgia and his father Pope Alexander VI, who had earlier brought factious Romagna to heel by placing secular family goals and religious policy in tandem. The Prince was pointedly dedicated to Lorenzo de' Medici, duke of Urbino and grandson of Lorenzo the Magnificent.

Whatever Machiavelli's hopes may have been, the Medicis were not destined to be Italy's deliverers. The second Medici pope, Clement VII (r. 1523–1534), watched helplessly as Rome was sacked by the army of Emperor Charles V in 1527, also the year of Machiavelli's death.

Machiavelli Discusses the Most Important Trait for a Ruler

Machiavelli believed that the most important personality trait of a successful ruler was the ability to instill fear in his subjects.

❖ *Why did Machiavelli maintain that rulers must be feared? Do American politicians of today appear to embrace Machiavelli's theory?*

Here the question arises; whether it is better to be loved than feared or feared than loved. The answer is that it would be desirable to be both but, since that is difficult, it is much safer to be feared than to be loved, if one must choose. For on men in general this observation may be made: they are ungrateful, fickle, and deceitful, eager to avoid dangers, and avid for gain, and while you are useful to them they are all with you, offering you their blood, their property, their lives, and their sons so long as danger is remote, as we noted above, but when it approaches they turn on you. Any prince, trusting only in their words and having no other preparations made, will fall to his ruin, for friendships that are bought at a price and not by greatness and nobility of soul are paid for indeed, but they are not owned and cannot be called upon in time of need. Men have less hesitation in offending a man who is loved than one who is feared, for love is held by a bond of obligation which, as men are wicked, is broken whenever personal advantage suggests it, but fear is accompanied by the dread of punishment which never relaxes.

From Niccolò Machiavelli, *The Prince* (1513), trans. and ed. by Thomas G. Bergin (New York: Appleton-Century-Crofts, 1947), p. 48.

Revival of Monarchy in Northern Europe

After 1450, there was a progressive shift from divided feudal to unified national monarchies as "sovereign" rulers emerged. This is not to say that the dynastic and chivalric ideals of feudal monarchy vanished. Territorial princes did not pass from the scene; representative bodies persisted and in some areas even grew in influence. But in the late fifteenth and early sixteenth centuries, the old problem of the one and the many was decided in favor of the interests of monarchy.

The feudal monarchy of the High Middle Ages was characterized by the division of the basic powers of government between the king and his semiautonomous vassals. The nobility and the towns had acted with varying degrees of unity and success through evolving representative assemblies such as the English Parliament, the French Estates General, and the Spanish *Cortés* to thwart the centralization of royal power. Because of the Hundred Years' War and the Great Schism in the church, the nobility and the clergy were in decline by the late Middle Ages and less able to contain expanding monarchies.

The increasingly important towns began to ally with the king. Loyal, business-wise townspeople, not the nobility and the clergy, increasingly staffed the royal offices and became the king's lawyers, bookkeepers, military tacticians, and foreign diplomats. This new alliance between king and town broke the bonds of feudal society and made possible the rise of sovereign states.

In a sovereign state, the powers of taxation, war making, and law enforcement no longer belong to semiautonomous vassals, but are concentrated in the monarch and are exercised by his or her chosen agents. Taxes, wars, and laws become national, rather than merely regional, matters. Only as monarchs became able to act independently of the nobility and representative assemblies could they overcome the decentralization that had been the basic obstacle to nation building. Ferdinand and Isabella of Spain rarely called the *Cortés* into session. The French Estates General did not meet at all from 1484 to 1560. Henry VII (r. 1485–1509) of England managed to raise revenues without going begging to Parliament after Parliament voted him customs revenues for life in 1485. Monarchs were also assisted by brilliant theorists, from Marsilius of Padua in the fourteenth century to Machiavelli to Jean Bodin in the sixteenth, who eloquently argued the sovereign rights of monarchy.

The many were, of course, never totally subjugated to the one. But in the last half of the fifteenth century, rulers demonstrated that the law was their creature. They appointed civil servants whose vision was no longer merely local or regional. In Castile they were the *corregidores*, in England the justices of the peace, and in France bailiffs operating through well-drilled lieutenants. These royal ministers and agents could become closely attached to the localities they administered in the ruler's name. And regions were able to secure congenial royal appointments. Throughout England, for example, local magnates served as representatives of the Tudors. Nonetheless, these new executives remained royal executives, bureaucrats whose outlook was "national" and whose loyalty was to the "state."

Monarchies also began to create standing national armies in the fifteenth century. The noble cavalry receded as the infantry and the artillery became the backbone of royal armies. Mercenary soldiers were recruited from Switzerland and Germany to form the major part of the "king's army." Professional soldiers who fought for pay and booty proved far more efficient than feudal vassals who fought simply for honor's sake. Monarchs who failed to meet their payrolls, however, faced a new danger of mutiny and banditry on the part of foreign troops.

The growing cost of warfare in the fifteenth and sixteenth centuries increased the need of monarchs for new national sources of income, but their efforts to expand royal revenues were hampered by the stubborn belief among the highest classes that they were immune from government taxation. The nobility guarded their properties and traditional rights and despised taxation as an insult and a humiliation. Royal revenues accordingly grew at the expense of those least able to resist and least able to pay.

The monarchs had several options when it came to raising money. As feudal lords, they could collect rents from their royal domains. They could also levy national taxes on basic food and clothing, such as the *gabelle*, or "salt tax," in France and the *alcabala*, or 10-percent sales tax on commercial transactions, in Spain. The rulers could also levy direct taxes on the peasantry, which they did through agreeable representative assemblies of the privileged classes in which the peasantry did not sit. The *taille*, which the French kings independently determined from year to year after the Estates General was suspended in 1484, was such a tax. Innovative fund-raising devices in the fifteenth century included the sale of public offices and the issuance of high-interest government bonds. But rulers did not levy taxes on the powerful nobility. Rather, they borrowed from rich nobles and the great bankers of Italy and Germany. In money matters, the privileged classes remained as much the kings' creditors and competitors as their subjects.

France

Charles VII (r. 1422–1461) was a king made great by those who served him. His ministers created a permanent professional army, which—thanks initially to the inspiration of Joan of Arc—drove the English out of France. And largely because of the enterprise of an independent merchant banker named Jacques Coeur, the French also developed a strong economy, diplomatic corps, and national administration during Charles's reign. These were the sturdy tools with which Charles's son and successor, the ruthless Louis XI (r. 1461–1483), made France a great power.

There were two cornerstones of French nation building in the fifteenth century. The first was the collapse of the English Empire in France following the Hundred Years' War. The second was the defeat of Charles the Bold and his duchy of Burgundy. Perhaps Europe's strongest political power in the mid-fifteenth century, Burgundy aspired to dwarf both France and the Holy Roman Empire as the leader of a dominant middle kingdom. It might have done so had not the continental powers joined in opposition.

When Charles the Bold died in defeat in a battle at Nancy in 1477, the dream of Burgundian Empire died with him. Louis XI and Habsburg emperor Maximilian I divided the conquered Burgundian lands between them, with the treaty-wise Habsburgs getting the better part. The dissolution of Burgundy ended its constant intrigue against the French king and left Louis XI free to secure the monarchy. The newly acquired Burgundian lands and his own Angevin inheritance permitted the king to end his reign with a kingdom almost twice the size of that with which he had started. Louis successfully harnessed the nobility, expanded the trade and industry so carefully nurtured by Jacques Coeur, created a national postal system, and even established a lucrative silk industry at Lyons (later transferred to Tours).

A strong nation is a two-edged sword. Because Louis's successors inherited a secure and efficient government, they felt free to pursue what proved ultimately to be a debilitating foreign policy. Conquests in Italy in the 1490s and a long series of losing wars with the Habsburgs in the first half of the sixteenth century left France by the mid-sixteenth century again a defeated nation almost as divided internally as during the Hundred Years' War.

Spain

Spain, too, became a strong country in the late fifteenth century. Both Castile and Aragon had been poorly ruled and divided kingdoms in the mid-fifteenth century. The union of Isabella of Castile (r. 1474–1504) and Ferdinand of Aragon (r. 1479–1516) changed that situation. The two future sovereigns married in 1469, despite strong protests from neighboring Portugal and France, both of whom foresaw the formidable European power the marriage would create. Castile was by far the richer and more populous of the two, having an estimated five million inhabitants to Aragon's population of under one million. Castile was also distinguished by its lucrative sheep-farming industry, run by a government-backed organization called the *Mesta*, another example of a developing centralized economic planning. Although the marriage of Ferdinand and Isabella dynastically united the two kingdoms, they remained constitutionally separated. Each retained its respective government agencies—separate laws, armies, coinage, and taxation—and cultural traditions.

Ferdinand and Isabella could do together what neither was able to accomplish alone: subdue their realms, secure their borders, venture abroad militarily, and Christianize the whole of Spain. Between 1482 and 1492 they conquered the Moors in Granada. Naples became a Spanish possession in 1504. By 1512 Ferdinand had secured his northern borders by conquering the kingdom of Navarre. Internally, Ferdinand and Isabella won the allegiance of the *Hermandad*, a powerful league of cities and towns that served them against stubborn landowners. Townspeople allied themselves with the crown and progressively replaced the nobility within the royal administration. The crown also extended its authority over the wealthy chivalric orders, a further circumscription of the power of the nobility.

Spain had long been remarkable among European lands as a place where three religions—Islam, Judaism, and Christianity—coexisted with a certain degree of toleration. This toleration was to end dramatically under Ferdinand and Isabella, who made Spain the prime exemplar of state-controlled religion.

Ferdinand and Isabella exercised almost total control over the Spanish church as they placed religion in the service of national unity. They appointed the higher clergy and the officers of the Inquisition. The latter, run by Tomás de Torquemada (d. 1498), Isabella's confessor, was a key national agency established in 1479 to monitor the activity of converted Jews (*conversos*) and Muslims (*Moriscos*) in Spain. In 1492 the Jews were exiled and their properties were confiscated. In 1502 nonconverting Moors in Granada were driven into exile by Cardinal Francisco Jiménez de Cisneros (1437–1517), under whom Spanish spiritual life remained largely uniform and successfully controlled. This was a major reason Spain remained a loyal Catholic country throughout the sixteenth century and provided a base of operation for the European Counter-Reformation.

Despite a certain internal narrowness, Ferdinand and Isabella were rulers with wide horizons. They contracted anti-French marriage alliances that came to determine a large part of European history in the sixteenth century. In 1496 their eldest daughter, Joanna, later known as "the Mad," married Archduke Philip, the son of Emperor Maximilian I. The fruit of this union, Charles I, was the first ruler over a united Spain; by his inheritance and election as emperor in 1519, he came to rule over a European kingdom almost equal in size to that of Charlemagne. A second daughter, Catherine of Aragon, wed Arthur, the son of the English king Henry VII. After Arthur's premature death, she was betrothed to his brother, the future King Henry VIII (r. 1509–1547), whom she married eight years later, in 1509. The failure of this marriage became the key factor in the emergence of the Anglican church and the English Reformation.

The new power of Spain was also revealed in Ferdinand and Isabella's promotion of overseas exploration. They sponsored the Genoese adventurer Christopher Columbus (1451–1506), who arrived at the islands of the Caribbean while sailing west in search of a shorter route to the spice markets of the Far East. This patronage led to the creation of the Spanish Empire in Mexico and Peru, whose gold and silver mines helped to make Spain Europe's dominant power in the sixteenth century.

England

The latter half of the fifteenth century was a period of especially difficult political trial for the English. Following the Hundred Years' War, a defeated England was subjected to internal warfare between two rival branches of the royal family: the House of York and the House of Lancaster. This conflict, known to us today as the Wars of the Roses (because York's symbol, according to legend, was a white rose and Lancaster's a red rose), kept England in turmoil from 1455 to 1485.

The Lancastrian monarchy of Henry VI (r. 1422–1461) was consistently challenged by the duke of York and his supporters in the prosperous southern towns. In 1461 Edward IV (r. 1461–1483), son of the duke of York, successfully seized power and instituted a strong-arm rule that lasted more than twenty years; it was only briefly interrupted, in 1470–1471, by Henry VI's short-lived restoration. Assisted by loyal and able ministers, Edward effectively increased the power and finances of the monarchy.

His brother, Richard III (r. 1483–1485), usurped the throne from Edward's son, and after Richard's death, the new Tudor dynasty portrayed him as an unprincipled villain who had also murdered Edward's sons in the Tower of London to secure his hold on the throne. The best-known version of this characterization—unjust according to some—is found in Shakespeare's *Richard III*. Be that as it may, Richard's reign saw the growth of support for the exiled Lancastrian Henry Tudor, who returned to England to defeat Richard on Bosworth Field in August 1485.

Henry Tudor ruled as Henry VII (r. 1485–1509), the first of the new Tudor dynasty that would dominate England throughout the sixteenth century. To bring the rival royal families together and to make the hereditary claim of his offspring to the throne uncontestable, Henry married Edward IV's daughter, Elizabeth of York. He succeeded in disciplining the English nobility through a special instrument of the royal will known as the Court of Star Chamber. Created with the sanction of Parliament in 1487, the court was intended to end the perversion of English justice by "over-mighty subjects," that is, powerful nobles who used intimidation and bribery to win favorable verdicts in court cases. In the Court of Star Chamber, the king's councillors sat as judges and were not swayed by such tactics. The result was a more equitable court system.

It was also a court more amenable to the royal will. Henry shrewdly construed legal precedents to the advantage of the crown, using English law to further the ends of monarchy. He managed to confiscate lands and fortunes of nobles with such success that he was able to govern without dependence on Parliament for royal funds, always a cornerstone of strong monarchy. In these ways, Henry began to shape a monarchy that would develop into one of early modern Europe's most exemplary governments during the reign of his granddaughter, Elizabeth I.

The Holy Roman Empire

Germany and Italy were the striking exceptions to the steady development of politically centralized lands in the last half of the fifteenth century. Unlike England, France, and Spain, the Holy Roman Empire saw the many thoroughly repulse the one. In Germany, territorial rulers and cities resisted every effort at national consolidation and unity. As in Carolingian times, rulers continued to partition their kingdoms, however small, among their sons. By the late fifteenth century, Germany was hopelessly divided into some 300 autonomous political entities.

The princes and the cities did work together to create the machinery of law and order, if not of union, within the divided empire. The emperor and the major German territorial rulers reached an agreement in 1356, the *Golden Bull*. It established a seven-member electoral college consisting of the archbishops of Mainz, Trier, and Cologne; the duke of Saxony; the margrave of Brandenburg; the count Palatine; and the king of Bohemia. This group also functioned as an administrative body. They elected the emperor and, in cooperation with him, provided what transregional unity and administration existed.

The figure of the emperor gave the empire a single ruler in law if not in fact. The conditions of his rule and the extent of his powers over his subjects, especially the seven electors, were renegotiated with every imperial election. Therefore, the rights of the many (the princes) were always balanced against the power of the one (the emperor).

In the fifteenth century, an effort was made to control incessant feuding by the creation of an imperial diet known as the *Reichstag*. This was a national assembly of the seven electors, the nonelectoral princes, and representatives from the sixty-five imperial free cities. The cities were the weakest of the three bodies represented in the diet. During such an assembly in Worms in 1495, the members won from Emperor Maximilian I (r. 1493–1519) an imperial ban on private warfare, the creation of a Supreme Court of Justice to enforce internal peace, and an imperial Council of Regency to coordinate imperial and internal German policy. The latter was only grudgingly conceded by the emperor because it gave the princes a share in executive power.

Although important, these reforms were still a poor substitute for true national unity. In the sixteenth and seventeenth centuries, the territorial princes became virtually sovereign rulers in their various domains. Such disunity aided religious dissent and conflict. It was in the cities and territories of still-feudal, fractionalized, backward Germany that the Protestant Reformation broke out in the sixteenth century.

The Northern Renaissance

The scholarly works of northern humanists created a climate favorable to religious and educational reforms on the eve of the Reformation. Northern humanism was initially stimulated by the importation of Italian learning through such varied intermediaries as students who had studied in Italy, merchants who traded there, and the Brothers of the Common Life. This last was an influential lay religious movement that began in the Netherlands and permitted men and women to live a shared religious life without making formal vows of poverty, chastity, and obedience.

The northern humanists, however, developed their own distinctive culture. They tended to come from more diverse social backgrounds and to be more devoted to religious reforms than their Italian counterparts. They were also more willing to write for lay audiences as well as for a narrow intelligentsia. Thanks to the invention of printing with movable type, it became possible for humanists to convey their educational ideals to laypeople and clerics alike. Printing gave new power and influence to elites in both church and state, who now could popularize their viewpoints freely and widely.

The Printing Press

A variety of forces converged in the fourteenth and fifteenth centuries to give rise to the invention of the printing press. Since the days of Charlemagne, kings and princes had encouraged schools and literacy, to help provide educated bureaucrats to staff the offices of their kingdoms. Without people who could read, think critically, and write reliable reports, no kingdom, large or small, could be properly governed. By the fifteenth century, a new literate lay public had been created, thanks to the enormous expansion of schools and universities during the late Middle Ages. (The number of universities more than tripled between 1300 and 1500, growing from twenty to seventy.)

The invention of a cheap way to manufacture paper also helped to make books economical and to broaden their content. Manuscript books had been inscribed on vellum, a cumbersome and expensive medium. (It required 170 calfskins or 300 sheepskins to make a single vellum Bible.) Single-sheet woodcuts had long been printed. This in-

volved carving a block of wood, inking it, and then stamping out as many copies as one could make before the wood deteriorated. The end product was much like a modern poster.

In response to the demand for books created by the expansion of lay literacy, Johann Gutenberg (d. 1468) invented printing with movable type in the mid-fifteenth century in the German city of Mainz, the center of printing for the whole of western Europe. Thereafter, books were rapidly and handsomely produced on topics both profound and practical and were intended for ordinary lay readers, scholars, and clerics alike. Especially popular in the early decades of print were books of piety and religion, calendars and almanacs, and "how-to" books (for example, on child rearing, making brandies and liquors, curing animals, and farming successfully).

The new technology proved enormously profitable to printers, whose numbers exploded. By 1500, within a scant fifty years of Gutenberg's press, printing presses operated in at least sixty German cities and in more than 200 cities throughout Europe. The printing press was a boon to the careers of humanists, who now gained international audiences.

Literacy deeply affected people everywhere, nurturing self-esteem and a critical frame of mind. By standardizing texts, the print revolution made anyone who could read an instant authority. Rulers in church and state now had to deal with a less credulous and less docile laity. Print was a powerful tool for political and religious propaganda as well. Kings could now indoctrinate people as never be-

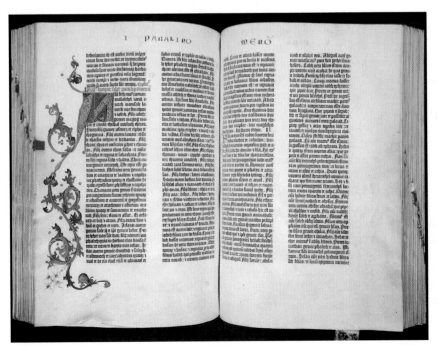

The printing press made possible the diffusion of Renaissance learning. But no book stimulated thought more at this time than did the Bible. With Gutenberg's publication of a printed Bible in 1454, scholars gained access to a dependable, standardized text, so that Scripture could be discussed and debated as never before. Reproduced by permission of The Huntington Library, San Marino, California

fore, and clergymen found themselves able to mass-produce both indulgences and pamphlets. (See "The West & the World," p. 284.)

Erasmus

The far-reaching influence of Desiderius Erasmus (1466?–1536), the most famous of the northern humanists and the "prince of the humanists," illustrates the impact of the printing press. Erasmus gained fame both as an educational and as a religious reformer. His life and work make clear that many loyal Catholics wanted major reforms long before the Reformation made them a reality.

Erasmus earned his living by tutoring when patrons were scarce. He prepared short Latin dialogues for his students that were intended to teach them how to speak and live well, inculcating good manners and language by encouraging them to imitate what they read.

These dialogues were published under the title *Colloquies*; they grew in number and length in consecutive editions, coming also to embrace anticlerical dialogues and satires on popular religious superstition. Erasmus collected ancient and contemporary proverbs as well, which he published under the title *Adages*. Beginning with about 800 examples, he increased his collection to more than 5,000 in the final edition of the work. Among the locutions that the *Adages* popularized are the common modern expression "to leave no stone unturned" and the saying "Where there is smoke, there is fire."

Erasmus aspired to unite the classical ideals of humanity and civic virtue with the Christian ideals of love and piety. He believed that disciplined study of the classics and the Bible, if begun early enough, was the best way to reform both individuals and society. He summarized his own beliefs with the phrase *philosophia Christi*, a simple, ethical piety in imitation of Christ. He set this ideal in starkest contrast to what he believed to be the dogmatic, ceremonial, and factious religious practice of the later Middle Ages. What most offended him about the Scholastics, both those of the late Middle Ages and, increasingly, the new Lutheran ones, was their letting doctrine and disputation overshadow humble piety and Christian practice.

To promote his own religious beliefs, Erasmus labored to make the ancient Christian sources available in their original versions. He believed that only as people drank from the pure, unadulterated sources could moral and religious health result. He edited the works of the Church fathers and produced a Greek edition of the New Testament (1516), which became the basis for his new, more accurate Latin translation (1519).

These various enterprises did not please church authorities. They were unhappy with both Erasmus's "improvements" on the Vulgate, Christendom's Bible for over a thousand years, and his popular anticlerical satires. At one point in the mid-sixteenth century, all of Erasmus's works were placed on the *Index of Forbidden Books*. Erasmus also received Luther's unqualified condemnation for his views on the freedom of human will. Still, Erasmus's works became basic tools of reform in the hands of both Protestant and Catholic reformers.

Humanism and Reform

In Germany, England, France, and Spain, humanism stirred both educational and religious reform.

GERMANY   Rudolf Agricola (1443–1485), the "father of German humanism," spent ten years in Italy and introduced Italian learning to Germany when he returned. Conrad Celtis (d. 1508), the first German poet laureate, and Ulrich von Hutten (1488–1523), a fiery knight, gave German humanism a nationalist coloring hostile to non-German cultures, particularly Roman culture. Von Hutten especially illustrates the union of humanism, German nationalism, and Luther's religious reform. A poet who admired Erasmus, he attacked indulgences and published an edition of Valla's exposé of the Donation of Constantine. He died in 1523, the victim of a hopeless knights' revolt against the princes.

The *cause célèbre* that brought von Hutten onto the historical stage and unified reform-minded German humanists was the Reuchlin affair. Johann Reuchlin (1455–1522) was Europe's foremost Christian authority on Hebrew and Jewish learning. He wrote the first reliable Hebrew grammar by a Christian scholar and was personally attracted to Jewish mysticism. Around 1506, supported by the Dominican order in Cologne, a Christian who had converted from Judaism began a movement to suppress Jewish writings. When this man, whose name was Pfefferkorn, attacked Reuchlin, many German humanists, in the name of academic freedom and good scholarship—not for any pro-Jewish sentiment—rushed to Reuchlin's defense. The controversy lasted several years and produced one of the great satires of the period, the *Letters of Obscure Men* (1515), a merciless satire of monks and Scholastics to which von Hutten contributed. When Martin Luther came under attack in 1517 for his famous ninety-five theses against indulgences, many German humanists saw a repetition of the Scholastic attack on Reuchlin and rushed to his side.

ENGLAND   Italian learning came to England by way of English scholars and merchants and visiting Italian prelates. Lectures by William Grocyn (d. 1519) and Thomas Linacre (d. 1524) at Oxford

Thomas More (1478–1535), painted by Hans Holbein the Younger in 1527. The English statesman and author was beheaded by Henry VIII for his refusal to recognize the king's sovereignty over the English church.
The Frick Collection, New York

and those of Erasmus at Cambridge marked the scholarly maturation of English humanism. John Colet (1467–1519), dean of Saint Paul's Cathedral, patronized humanist studies for the young and promoted religious reform as well.

Thomas More (1478–1535), a close friend of Erasmus, is the best known English humanist. His *Utopia* (1516), a conservative criticism of contemporary society, rivals the plays of Shakespeare as the most-read sixteenth-century English work. *Utopia* depicted an imaginary society based on reason and tolerance that overcame social and political injustice by holding all property and goods in common and requiring everyone to earn their bread by their own work.

More became one of Henry VIII's most trusted diplomats. But his repudiation of the Act of Supremacy (1534), which made the king of England head of the English church in place of the pope (see Chapter 11), and his refusal to recognize the king's marriage to Anne Boleyn led to his execution in July 1535. Although More remained Catholic, humanism in England, as also in Germany, played an important role in preparing the way for the English Reformation.

FRANCE The French invasions of Italy made it possible for Italian learning to penetrate France, stirring both educational and religious reform. Guillaume Budé (1468–1540), an accomplished Greek scholar, and Jacques Lefèvre d'Étaples (1454–1536), a biblical authority, were the leaders of French humanism. Lefèvre's scholarly works exemplified the new critical scholarship and influenced Martin Luther. Guillaume Briçonnet (1470–1533), the bishop of Meaux, and Marguerite d'Angoulême (1492–1549), sister of King Francis I, the future queen of Navarre, and a successful spiritual writer in her own right, cultivated a generation of young reform-minded humanists. The future Protestant reformer John Calvin was a product of this native reform circle.

SPAIN Whereas in England, France, and Germany, humanism prepared the way for Protestant reforms, in Spain it entered the service of the Catholic Church. Here the key figure was Francisco Jiménez de Cisneros (1437–1517), a confessor to Queen Isabella and, after 1508, the "Grand Inquisitor"—a position that allowed him to enforce the strictest religious orthodoxy. Jiménez founded the University of Alcalá near Madrid in 1509, printed a Greek edition of the New Testament, and translated many religious tracts designed to reform clerical life and better direct lay piety. His great achievement, taking fifteen years to complete, was the *Complutensian Polyglot Bible*, a six-volume work that placed the Hebrew, Greek, and Latin versions of the Bible in parallel columns. Such scholarly projects and internal church reforms joined with the repressive measures of Ferdinand and Isabella to keep Spain strictly Catholic throughout the Age of Reformation.

Voyages of Discovery and the New Empire in the West

On the eve of the Reformation, the geographical as well as the intellectual horizons of Western people were changing. The fifteenth century saw the beginning of western Europe's global expansion and the transference of commercial supremacy from the Mediterranean and the Baltic to the Atlantic seaboard.

Gold and Spices

Mercenary motives, reinforced by traditional missionary ideals, inspired the Portuguese prince Henry the Navigator (1394–1460) to sponsor the Portuguese exploration of the African coast. His

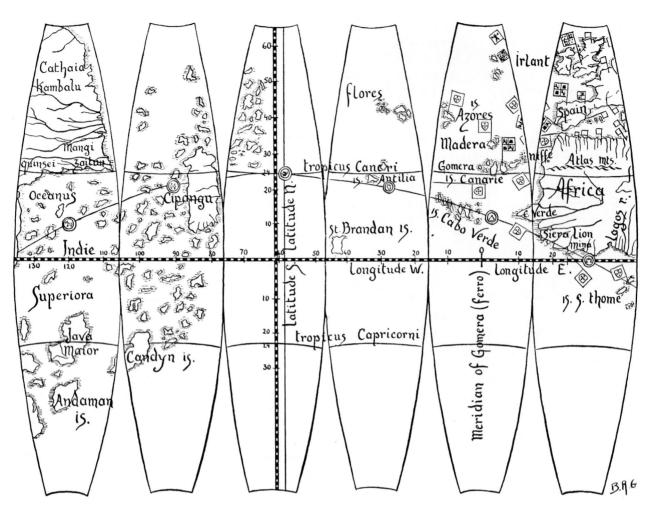

What Columbus knew of the world in 1492 was contained in this map by the Nuremberg geographer Martin Behaim, creator of the first spherical globe of the Earth. The ocean section of Behaim's globe is reproduced here. Departing the Canary Islands (in the second section from the right), Columbus expected his first major landfall to be Japan (Cipangu, in the second section from the left). When he landed at San Salvador, he thought he was on the outer island of Japan. And when he arrived in Cuba, he thought he was in Japan. Reprinted from *Admiral of the Ocean Sea* by Samuel Eliot Morison. Copyright 1942 by Samuel Eliot Morison; renewed 1970 by Samuel Eliot Morison. By permission of Little, Brown and Company, Boston, Massachusetts

main object was the gold trade, which Muslims had monopolized for centuries. By the last decades of the fifteenth century, gold from Guinea was entering Europe by way of Portuguese ships calling at the port cities of Lisbon and Antwerp, rather than by the traditional Arab land routes. Antwerp became the financial center of Europe, a commercial crossroads where the enterprise and derring-do of the Portuguese, the Spanish, and especially the Flemish met the capital funds of the German banking houses of Fugger and Welser.

The rush for gold quickly expanded into a rush for the spice markets of India. In the fifteenth century the diet of most Europeans was a dull combination of bread and gruel, cabbage, turnips, peas,

lentils, and onions, together with what meat became available during seasonal periods of slaughter. Spices, especially pepper and cloves, were in great demand, both to preserve and to enhance the taste of food.

Bartholomeu Dias (d. 1500) opened the Portuguese Empire in the East when he rounded the Cape of Good Hope at the tip of Africa in 1487. A decade later, in 1498, Vasco da Gama (d. 1524) reached the coast of India. When he returned to Portugal, he brought with him a cargo worth sixty times the cost of the voyage. Later, the Portuguese established themselves firmly on the Malabar Coast with colonies in Goa and Calcutta and successfully challenged the Arabs and the Venetians for control of the European spice trade.

While the Portuguese concentrated on the Indian Ocean, the Spanish set sail across the Atlantic. They did so in the hope of establishing a shorter route to the rich spice markets of the East Indies. But rather than beating the Portuguese at their own game, Christopher Columbus (1451–1506) came upon the Americas instead.

Amerigo Vespucci (1451–1512) and Ferdinand Magellan (1480–1521) showed that these new lands were not the outermost territory of the Far East, as Columbus died believing. Their travels proved the lands to be an entirely new continent that opened on the still greater Pacific Ocean. Magellan, in search of a westward route to the East Indies, died in the Philippines. (See Map 10–2.)

The Spanish Empire in the New World

Columbus's voyage of 1492 marked, unknowingly to those who undertook and financed it, the beginning of more than three centuries of Spanish conquest, exploitation, and administration of a vast American empire. That imperial venture produced important results for the cultures of both the European and the American

continents. The gold and silver extracted from its American possessions financed Spain's major role in the religious and political conflicts of the age and contributed to European inflation in the sixteenth century.

In large expanses of both South and North America, Spanish government set an imprint of Roman Catholicism, economic dependence, and hierarchical social structure that has endured to the present day. Such influence was already clear with Columbus. On October 12, 1492, after a thirty-three day voyage from the Canary Islands, Columbus landed in San Salvador (Watlings Island) in the eastern Bahamas. He thought that he was on an outer island of Japan (or what he called Cipangu); he had undertaken his journey in the mistaken notion that the island of Japan would be the first land mass he would reach as he sailed west. This belief was based on Marco Polo's accounts of his years in China in the thirteenth century and the first globe map of the world, by Martin Behaim. That map, published in 1492, showed only ocean between the west coast of Europe and the east coast of Asia. Not until his third voyage to the Caribbean did Columbus realize that the island of Cuba was not Japan and that the South American continent beyond it was not China.

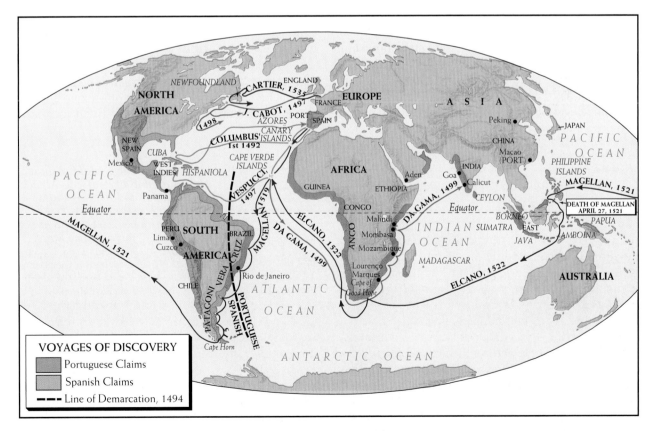

MAP 10–2 EUROPEAN VOYAGES OF DISCOVERY AND THE COLONIAL CLAIMS OF SPAIN AND PORTUGAL IN THE FIFTEENTH AND SIXTEENTH CENTURIES *The map dramatizes Europe's global expansion in the fifteenth and sixteenth centuries.*

When Columbus landed in San Salvador, his three ships were met on the beach by naked and extremely friendly natives. Like all the natives Columbus met on his first voyage, they were Taino Indians, who spoke a variant of a language known as Arawak. From the start, the natives' generosity amazed Columbus. They freely gave his men all the corn and yams they desired and many sexual favors as well. "They never say no," Columbus marveled. At the same time Columbus observed how very easily they could be enslaved.

A Conquered World

Mistaking the islands where he landed for the East Indies, Columbus called the native peoples whom he encountered "Indians." That name persisted even after it had become clear that this was a new continent and not the East Indies. These native peoples had migrated across the Bering Straits from Asia onto the American landmass many thousands of years before the European voyages of discovery, creating communities all the way from Alaska to South America. The islands that Columbus mistakenly believed to be the East Indies came to be known as the West Indies.

Native Americans had established advanced civilizations going back to as early as the first millennium B.C.E. in two parts of what is today known as Latin America: Mesoamerica, which stretches from central Mexico into the Yucatan and Guatemala, and the Andean region of South America, primarily modern-day Peru and Bolivia. The earliest civilization in Mesoamerica, that of the Olmec, dates

to about 1200 B.C.E. By the early centuries of the first millennium C.E. much of the region was dominated by the powerful city of Teotihuacán, which at the time was one of the largest urban centers in the world. The first millennium C.E. saw the flowering of the remarkable civilization of the Mayas in the Yucatan region. The Mayans built large cities with immense pyramids and achieved considerable skills in mathematics and astronomy.

The first great interregional civilization in Andean South America, that of Chavín, emerged during the first millennium B.C.E. Regional cultures of the succeeding Early Intermediate Period (100–600 C.E.) included the Nazca on the south coast of Peru and the Moche on the north coast. The Huari–Tiahuanco culture again imposed interregional conformity during the Middle Horizon (600–1000). In the Late Intermediate Period, the Chimu Empire (800–1400) dominated the valleys of the Peruvian north coast. These early Andean societies built major ceremonial centers throughout the Andes, constructed elaborate irrigation systems, canals, and highways, and created exquisite pottery, textiles, and metalwork.

At the time of the arrival of the first Spanish explorers, the Aztec Empire dominated Mesoamerica and the Inca Empire dominated Andean South America. (See Map 10–3.) Both were very rich, and their conquest promised the Spanish the possibility of acquiring large quantities of gold.

THE AZTECS IN MEXICO The forebears of the Aztecs had arrived in the Valley of Mexico early in the twelfth century, where they lived as a sub-

Armored Spanish soldiers, under the command of Pedro de Alvarado (d. 1541) and bearing crossbows, engage unprotected and crudely armed Aztecs, who are nonetheless portrayed as larger than life by Spanish artist Diego Duran (16th century). Codex Duran: Pedro de Alvarado (c. 1485–1541), companion-at-arms of Hernando Cortes (1485–1547) besieged by Aztec warriors. Biblioteca Nacional, Madrid, Spain. The Bridgeman Art Library International Ltd.

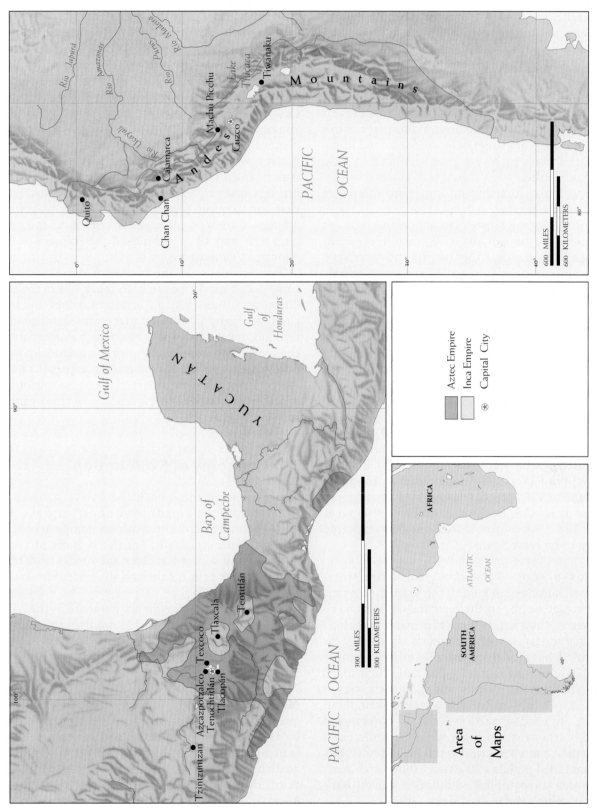

MAP 10–3 THE AZTEC AND INCA EMPIRES ON THE EVE OF THE SPANISH CONQUEST.

servient people. In 1428, under the leadership of Chief Itzcoatl, they rebelled against their rulers. That rebellion opened a period of Aztec conquest that reached its climax just after 1500. Their capital, Tenochtitlán (modern-day Mexico City), was located on an island in the center of a lake. By the time the Spanish conquerors arrived, the Aztecs governed many smaller tribes harshly, forcing labor and tribute from them. Believing that the gods must literally be fed with human bodies to guarantee continuing sunshine and fertility of the soil, the Aztecs also demanded and received thousands of captives each year to be sacrificed to their gods. Such policies left the Aztecs surrounded by terrorized tribes that felt no loyalty to them and longed for a liberator.

In 1519, Hernán Cortés landed on the coast of Mexico with a force of about 600 men. He opened communication with tribes nearby and then with Montezuma, the Aztec ruler. Montezuma initially believed Cortés to be a god. Aztec religion contained the legend of a priest named Quetzalcoatl who had been driven away four centuries earlier and had promised to return in the very year in which Cortés arrived. Montezuma initially attempted to appease Cortés with gifts of gold. The Indians had recently been ravaged by epidemic diseases of European origin, principally smallpox, and were in no position to oppose him. After several weeks of negotiations and the forging of alliances with subject tribes, Cortés's forces marched on Tenochtitlán, conquered it, and imprisoned Montezuma, who later died under unexplained circumstances. The Aztecs tried to drive the Spanish out, but by late 1521 they were defeated after great loss of life. Cortés proclaimed the former Aztec Empire to be New Spain.

THE INCAS IN PERU The second great Native American civilization conquered by the Spanish was that of the Incas, located in the highlands of Peru. Like the Aztecs, they had vanquished many neighboring states and tribes and by the early sixteenth century ruled harshly over several million subject people, whom they compelled to build their roads and cities, farm their lands, and fight their wars.

In 1531, largely inspired by Cortés's example in Mexico, Francisco Pizarro sailed from Panama and landed on the western coast of South America to undertake a campaign against the Inca Empire. His force included perhaps 200 men armed with guns and swords and equipped with horses, the military power of which the Incas did not fathom.

In late 1531, Pizarro lured the Inca chief Atahualpa into a conference, where he captured him and killed many of his followers. Atahualpa attempted to ransom himself by having a vast horde of gold transported from all over Peru to Pizarro. Discovering that he could not turn Atahualpa into a puppet ruler, Pizarro executed him in 1533. Division within the ranks of the Spanish conquerors prevented effective royal control of the sprawling Inca civilization until the late 1560s.

The conquests of Mexico and Peru stand among the most brutal episodes in modern Western history. One civilization armed with advanced weaponry subdued, in a remarkably brief time, two powerful peoples. Beyond the drama and bloodshed, the conquests made it very difficult for these Native American cultures to have a major impact on Western civilization. Some scholars believe, however, that the Iroquois tribes of North America set examples of freedom of speech, assembly, and religion that may have influenced the framers of the American Constitution.

The Spanish and the Native Americans made some accommodations to each other, but in the end European values, religion, economic goals, and language dominated. No group that retained indigenous religion, language, or values could become part of the new dominant culture or of the political power elite. In that sense, the Spanish conquests of the early sixteenth century marked the beginning of the process whereby South America was transformed into Latin America.

The Economy of Exploitation

From the beginning, both the native peoples of America and their lands were drawn into the Atlantic economy and the world of competitive European commercialism. For the Indians of Latin America and somewhat later, the blacks of Africa, that drive for gain meant various arrangements of forced labor.

There were three major components in the colonial economy of Latin America: mining, agriculture, and shipping. Each of them involved labor, servitude, or a relationship of dependence of the New World economy on that of Spain.

MINING The early *conquistadores*, or "conquerors," were primarily interested in gold, but by the middle of the sixteenth century, silver mining provided the chief source of metallic wealth. The great mining centers were Potosí in Peru and somewhat smaller sites in northern Mexico. (See "Forced Indian Labor at Potosí".) The Spanish crown was particularly interested in mining because it received one-fifth (the *quinto*) of all mining revenues. For this reason, the

Forced Indian Labor at Potosí

The Potosí range in Peru was the site of the great silver-mining industry in the Spanish Empire. The vast amount of wealth contained in the region became legendary almost as soon as mining began there in the 1540s. Indians, most of whom were forced laborers working under the mita *system of conscription, did virtually all of the work underground. The description that follows, written by a Spanish friar in the early seventeenth century, portrays both the large size of the enterprise and the harsh conditions that the Indians endured. At any one time, only one-third of the 13,300 conscripted Indians were employed. The labor force was changed every four months.*

❖ *How efficient does the description suggest the mines were? What would have been the likely effect of working so long underground surrounded by burning candles?*

According to His Majesty's warrant, the mine owners on this massive range have a right to the *mita* [conscripted labor] of 13,300 Indians in the working and exploitation of the mines, both those which have been discovered, those now discovered, and those which shall be discovered. It is the duty of the *Corregidor* [municipal governor] of Potosí to have them rounded up and to see that they come in from all the provinces between Cuzco over the whole of El Collao and as far as the frontiers of Tarija and Tomina....

The *mita* Indians go up every Monday morning to the locality of Guayna Potosí which is at the foot of the range; the *Corregidor* arrives with all the provincial captains or chiefs who have charge of the Indians assigned him for his miner or smelter; that keeps him busy till 1 P.M., by which time the Indians are already turned over to these mine and smelter owners.

After each has eaten his ration, they climb up the hill, each to his mine, and go in, staying there from that hour until Saturday evening without coming out of the mine; their wives bring them food, but they stay constantly underground, excavating and carrying out the ore from which they get the silver. They all have tallow candles, lighted day and night; that is the light they work with, for as they are underground, they have need of it all the time....

These Indians have different functions in the handling of the silver ore; some break it up with bar or pick, and dig down in, following the vein in the mine; others bring it up; others up above keep separating the good and the poor in piles; others are occupied in taking it down from the range to the mills on herds of llamas; every day they bring up more than 8,000 of these native beasts of burden for this task. These teamsters who carry the metal do not belong to the *mita*, but are *mingados*—hired.

From Antonia Vázquez de Espinosa, *Compendium and Description of the Indies [ca. 1620]*, trans. by Charles Upson Clark (Washington, DC: Smithsonian Institution Press, 1968), p. 62. Reprinted by permission of the Smithsonian Institution Press.

---

crown maintained a monopoly over the production and sale of mercury, required in the silver-mining process. Exploring for silver never lost predominance during the colonial era. Its production by forced labor for the benefit of Spaniards and the Spanish crown epitomized the wholly extractive economy that stood at the foundation of colonial life.

AGRICULTURE The major rural and agricultural institution of the Spanish colonies was the *hacienda*, a large landed estate owned by persons originally born in Spain (*peninsulares*) or persons of Spanish descent born in America (*creoles*). Laborers on the *hacienda* usually stood in some re-

lation of formal servitude to the owner and were rarely free to move from the services of one landowner to another.

The *hacienda* economy produced two major products: foodstuffs for mining areas and urban centers and leather goods used in mining machinery. Both farming and ranching were subordinate to the mining economy.

In the West Indies, the basic agricultural unit was the plantation. In Cuba, Hispaniola, Puerto Rico, and other islands, the labor of black slaves from Africa produced sugar to supply an almost insatiable demand for the product in Europe.

A final major area of economic activity in the Spanish colonies was urban service occupations, including government offices, the legal profession, and shipping. Practitioners of these occupations were either *peninsulares* or *creoles*, with the former dominating more often than not.

Labor Servitude All of this extractive and exploitive economic activity required labor, and the Spanish in the New World decided very early that the native population would supply that labor. A series of social devices was used to draw them into the new economic life imposed by the Spanish.

The first of these was the *encomienda*, a formal grant of the right to the labor of a specific number of Indians, usually a few hundred, but sometimes thousands, for a particular period of time. The institution stood in decline by the middle of the sixteenth century because the Spanish monarchs feared that the holders of *encomienda* might become a powerful independent nobility in the New World. They were also persuaded on humanitarian grounds against this particular kind of exploitation of the Indians.

The passing of the *encomienda* led to a new arrangement of labor servitude: the *repartimiento*. This device required adult male Indians to devote a certain number of days of labor annually to Spanish economic enterprises. In the mines of Peru, the *repartimiento* was known as the *mita*, the Inca term for their labor tax. *Repartimiento* service was often extremely harsh, and in some cases Indians did not survive their stint. The limitation on labor time led some Spanish managers to abuse their workers on the assumption that fresh workers would soon be appearing on the scene.

The eventual shortage of workers and the crown's pressure against extreme versions of forced labor led to the use of free labor. The freedom, however, was more in appearance than reality. Free Indian laborers were required to purchase goods from the landowner or mine owner, to whom they became forever indebted. This form of exploitation, known as *debt peonage*, continued in Latin America long after the nineteenth-century wars of liberation.

Black slavery was the final mode of forced or subservient labor in the New World. Both the Spanish and the Portuguese had earlier used African slaves in Europe. The sugar plantations of the West Indies now became the major center of black slavery.

The conquest, the forced labor of the economy of exploitation, and the introduction of European diseases had devastating demographic consequences for the Native American population. For centuries, Europeans had lived in a far more complex human and animal environment than Native Americans did. They had frequent contact with different ethnic and racial groups and with a variety of domestic animals. Such interaction helped them develop strong immune systems that enabled them to survive the ravages of measles, smallpox, and typhoid. Native Americans, by contrast, grew up in a simpler and more sterile environment and were completely defenseless against these diseases. Within a generation, the native population of New Spain (Mexico) was reduced to an estimated 8 percent of its numbers, from 25,000,000 to 2,000,000.

The Impact on Europe

Among contemporary European intellectuals, Columbus's discovery increased skepticism about the wisdom of the ancients. If traditional knowledge about the world had been so wrong geographically, how could one trust it on other matters? For many, Columbus's discovery demonstrated the folly of relying on any fixed body of presumed authoritative knowledge. Both in Europe and in the New World, there were those who condemned the explorers' treatment of American natives, as more was learned about their cruelty. (See "Montaigne on 'Cannibals' in Foreign Lands.") Three centuries later, however, on the third anniversary of Columbus's discovery (1792), the great thinkers of the age lionized Columbus for having opened up new possibilities for civilization and morality. By establishing new commercial contacts among different peoples of the world, Columbus was said to have made cooperation, civility, and peace among them indispensible. Enlightenment thinkers drew parallels between the discovery of America and the invention of the printing press—both portrayed as world-historical events opening new eras in communication and globalization, an early multicultural experiment.[4]

On the material side, the influx of spices and precious metals into Europe from the new Spanish Empire was a mixed blessing. It contributed to a steady rise in prices during the sixteenth century that created an inflation rate estimated at 2 percent a year. The new supply of bullion from the Americas joined with enlarged European production to increase greatly the amount of coinage in circulation, and this increase in turn fed inflation. Fortunately, the increase in prices was by and large spread over a long period and was not sudden. Prices doubled in Spain by midcentury, quadrupled by 1600. In Luther's Wittenberg, the cost of

[4] Cf. Anthony Pagden, "The Impact of the New World on the Old: The History of an Idea," *Renaissance and Modern Studies* 30 (1986): 1–11.

Montaigne on "Cannibals" in Foreign Lands

The French philosopher Michel de Montaigne (1533–1592) had seen a Brazilian native in Rouen in 1562, an alleged cannibal brought to France by the explorer Villegagnon. The experience gave rise to an essay on the subject of what constitutes a "savage." Montaigne concluded that no people on earth were more barbarous than Europeans, who take natives of other lands captive.

❖ *Is Montaigne romanticizing New World natives? Is he being too hard on Europeans? Had the Aztecs or Incas had the ability to discover and occupy Europe, would they have enslaved and exploited Europeans?*

Now, to return to my subject, I think there is nothing barbarous and savage in that nation [Brazil], from what I have been told....Each man calls barbarism whatever is not his own practice; for indeed it seems we have no other test of truth and reason than the example and pattern of the opinions and customs of the country we live in. There [we] always [find] the perfect religion, the perfect government, the perfect and accomplished manners in all things. Those [foreign] people are wild, just as we call wild the fruits that Nature has produced by herself and in her normal course; where really it is those that we have changed artificially and led astray from the common order that we should rather call wild. The former retain alive and vigorous their genuine virtues and properties, which we have debased in the latter by adapting them to gratify our corrupted taste. And yet for all that, the savor and delicacy of some uncultivated fruits of those countries is quite as excellent, even to our taste, as that of our own. It is not reasonable that [our human] art should win the place of honor over our great and powerful mother Nature. We have so overloaded the beauty and richness of her works by our inventions that we have quite smothered her. Yet wherever her purity shines forth, she wonderfully puts to shame our vain and frivolous attempts: "Ivy comes readier without our care;/In lonely caves the arbutus grows more fair;/No art with artless bird song can compare."[1] All our efforts cannot even succeed in reproducing the nest of the tiniest little bird, its contexture, its beauty and convenience; or even the web of the puny spider. All things, says Plato,[2] are produced by nature, by fortune, or by art; the greatest and most beautiful by one or the other of the first two, the least and most imperfect by the last.

These nations, then, seem to me "barbarous" in this sense, that they have been fashioned very little by the human mind, and are still very close to their original naturalness. The laws of nature still rule them, very little corrupted by ours; and they are in such a state of purity that I am sometimes vexed that they were unknown earlier, in the days when there were men able to judge them better than we.

[1] Propertius, 1.11.10.

[2] Laws, 10.

From *The Complete Essays of Montaigne*, trans. by Donald M. Frame (Stanford: Stanford University Press, 1958), pp. 153–154.

basic food and clothing increased almost 100 percent between 1519 and 1540. Generally, wages and rents remained well behind the rise in prices.

The new wealth enabled governments and private entrepreneurs to sponsor basic research and expansion in the printing, shipping, mining, textile, and weapons industries. There is also evidence of large-scale government planning in such ventures as the French silk industry and the Habsburg–Fugger development of mines in Austria and Hungary.

In the thirteenth and fourteenth centuries capitalist institutions and practices had already begun to develop in the rich Italian cities. (One may point to the activities of the Florentine banking houses of Bardi and Peruzzi.) Those who owned the means of production, either privately or corporately, were clearly distinguished from the workers who operated them. Wherever possible, entrepreneurs created monopolies in basic goods. High interest was charged on loans—actual, if not legal, usury. And the "capitalist" virtues of thrift, industry, and orderly planning were everywhere in evidence—all intended to permit the free and efficient accumulation of wealth.

The late fifteenth and the sixteenth centuries saw the maturation of this type of capitalism together with its attendant social problems. The Medicis of Florence grew very rich as bankers of the pope, as did the Fuggers of Augsburg, who bankrolled Habsburg rulers. The Fuggers lent Charles I of Spain more than 500,000 florins to buy his election as Holy Roman Emperor in 1519 and boasted that they had created the emperor. The new wealth and industrial expansion also raised the expectations of the poor and the ambitious and heightened the reactionary tendencies of the wealthy. This effect, in turn, aggravated the traditional social divisions between the clergy and the laity, the urban patriciate and the guilds, and the landed nobility and the agrarian peasantry.

These divisions indirectly prepared the way for the Reformation as well, by making many people critical of traditional institutions and open to new ideas—especially those that seemed to promise greater freedom and a chance at a better life.

In Perspective

As it recovered from national wars during the late Middle Ages, Europe saw the establishment of permanent centralized states and regional governments. The foundations of modern France, Spain, England, Germany, and Italy were laid at this time. As rulers imposed their will on regions outside their immediate domains, the "one" progressively took control of the "many," and previously divided lands came together as nations.

Thanks to the work of Byzantine and Islamic scholars, ancient Greek science and scholarship found their way into the West in these centuries. Europeans had been separated from their classical cultural heritage for almost eight centuries. No other world civilization had experienced such a disjunction from its cultural past. The discovery of classical civilization occasioned a rebirth of intellectual and artistic activity in both southern and northern Europe. One result was the splendor of the Italian Renaissance, whose scholarship, painting, and sculpture remain among western Europe's most impressive achievements.

Ancient learning was not the only discovery of the era. New political unity spurred both royal greed and national ambition. By the late fifteenth centu-

ry, Europeans were in a position to venture far away to the shores of Africa, the southern and eastern coasts of Asia, and the New World of the Americas. European discovery was not the only outcome of these voyages: The exploitation of the peoples and lands of the New World revealed a dark side of Western civilization. Some penalties were paid even then. The influx of New World gold and silver created new human and economic problems on the European mainland. In some circles, Europeans even began to question their civilization's traditional values.

REVIEW QUESTIONS

1. Discuss Jacob Burkhardt's interpretation of the Renaissance. What criticisms have been leveled against it? How would you define the term "Renaissance" in the context of fifteenth- and sixteenth-century Italy?
2. How would you define Renaissance humanism? In what ways was the Renaissance a break with the Middle Ages, and in what ways did it owe its existence to medieval civilization?
3. Who were some of the famous literary and artistic figures of the Italian Renaissance? What did they have in common that might be described as "the spirit of the Renaissance"?
4. Why did the French invade Italy in 1494? How did this event trigger Italy's political decline? How do the actions of Pope Julius II and the ideas of Niccolò Machiavelli signify a new era in Italian civilization?
5. A common assumption is that creative work proceeds best in periods of calm and peace. Given the combination of political instability and cultural productivity in Renaissance Italy, do you think this assumption is valid?
6. How did the Renaissance in the north differ from the Italian Renaissance? In what ways was Erasmus the embodiment of the northern Renaissance?
7. What factors led to the voyages of discovery? How did the Spanish establish their empire in the Americas? Why was the conquest so violent? What was the experience of native peoples during and after the conquest?

SUGGESTED READINGS

L. B. ALBERTI, *The Family in Renaissance Florence*, trans. by R. N. Watkins (1962). A contemporary humanist, who never married, explains how a family should behave.

R. H. BAINTON, *Erasmus of Christendom* (1960). Charming presentation.

H. Baron, *The Crisis of the Early Italian Renaissance*, vols. 1 and 2 (1966). A major work, setting forth the civic dimension of Italian humanism.

C. Boxer, *Four Centuries of Portuguese Expansion, 1415–1825* (1961). Comprehensive survey by the leading authority.

G. A. Brucker, *Renaissance Florence* (1969). Comprehensive survey of all facets of Florentine life.

G. A. Brucker, *Giovanni and Lusanna: Love and Marriage in Renaissance Florence* (1986). Love in the Renaissance shown to be more Bergman than Fellini.

J. Burckhardt, *The Civilization of the Renaissance in Italy* (1867). The old classic that still has as many defenders as detractors.

R. E. Conrad, *Children of God's Fire: A Documentary History of Black Slavery in Brazil* (1983). Not for the squeamish.

A. W. Crosby, *The Columbian Exchange: Biological and Cultural Consequences of 1492* (1973). A study of the epidemiological disaster that Columbus visited upon Native Americans.

E. L. Eisenstein, *The Printing Press as an Agent of Change: Communications and Cultural Transformations in Early Modern Europe*, 2 vols. (1979). Bold, stimulating account of the centrality of printing to all progress in the period.

W. K. Ferguson, *Europe in Transition, 1300–1520* (1962). A major survey that deals with the transition from medieval society to Renaissance society.

F. Gilbert, *Machiavelli and Guicciardini* (1984). The two great Renaissance historians lucidly compared.

L. Hanke, *Bartholomé de Las Casas: An Interpretation of His Life and Writings* (1951). Biography of the great Dominican critic of Spanish exploitation of Native Americans.

J. Hankins, *Plato in the Renaissance* (1992). A magisterial study of how Plato was read and interpreted by Renaissance scholars.

D. Herlihy, *The Family in Renaissance Italy* (1974). Excellent on family structure and general features.

D. Herlihy, *Women, Family, and Society in Medieval Europe: Historical Essays, 1978–1991*, ed. A. Molho (1998). A major medievalist's collected essays on medieval and Renaissance society.

D. Herlihy and C. Klapisch-Zuber, *Tuscans and Their Families* (1985). Important work based on unique demographic data that give the reader a new appreciation of quantitative history.

D. L. Jensen, *Renaissance Europe: Age of Recovery and Reconciliation* (1981). Up-to-date and comprehensive survey.

F. Katz, *The Ancient American Civilizations* (1972). An excellent introduction.

R. Kelso, *Doctrine of the Lady of the Renaissance* (1978). Noblewomen in the Renaissance.

C. Klapisch-Zuber, *Women, Family, and Ritual in Renaissance Italy* (1985). Provocative, wide-ranging essays documenting Renaissance Italy as very much a man's world.

P. O. Kristeller, *Renaissance Thought: The Classic, Scholastic, and Humanist Strains* (1961). A master shows the many sides of Renaissance thought.

I. Maclean, *The Renaissance Notion of Women* (1980). An account of the views of Renaissance intellectuals and their sources in antiquity.

L. Martines, *Power and Imagination: City States in Renaissance Italy* (1980). Stimulating account of cultural and political history.

S. E. Morrison, *Admiral of the Ocean Sea: A Life of Christopher Columbus* (1946). Still the authoritative biography.

E. Panofsky, *Meaning in the Visual Arts* (1955). Eloquent treatment of Renaissance art.

J. H. Parry, *The Age of Reconnaissance* (1964). A comprehensive account of exploration in the years 1450–1650.

P. Partner, *Renaissance Rome, 1500–1559: A Portrait of a Society* (1976). A description of the city from an insider's perspective.

J. B. A. Pocock, *The Machiavellian Moment in Florentine Political Thought and the Atlantic Republican Tradition* (1975). Traces the influence of Florentine political thought in early modern Europe.

I. A. Richter (ed.), *The Notebooks of Leonardo da Vinci* (1985). The master in his own words.

Q. Skinner, *The Foundations of Modern Political Thought; I: The Renaissance* (1978). Broad survey, including absolutely every known political theorist, major and minor.

Glossary

absolutism   Term applied to strong centralized continental monarchies that attempted to make royal power dominant over aristocracies and other regional authorities.

Acropolis (ACK-row-po-lis)   The religious and civic center of Athens. It is the site of the Parthenon.

Act of Supremacy   The declaration by Parliament in 1534 that Henry VIII, not the Pope, was the head of the Church in England.

agape (AG-a-pay)   Meaning "love feast." A common meal that was part of the central ritual of early Christian worship.

agora (AG-o-rah)   The Greek marketplace and civic center. It was the heart of the social life of the polis.

Agricultural Revolution   The innovations in farm production that began in the eighteenth century and led to a scientific and mechanized agriculture.

Albigensians (Al-bi-GEN-see-uns)   Thirteenth-century advocates of a dualist religion. They took their name from the city of Albi in southern France. Also called Cathars.

Anabaptists   Protestants who insisted that only adult baptism conformed to Scripture.

anarchism   The theory that government and social institutions are oppressive and unnecessary and that society should be based on voluntary cooperation among individuals.

Anschluss (AHN-shluz)   Meaning "union." The annexation of Austria by Germany in March 1938.

anti-Semitism   Prejudice, hostility, or legal discrimination against Jews.

apostolic primacy   The doctrine that the Popes are the direct successors to the Apostle Peter and as such heads of the Church.

Apostolic Succession   The Christian doctrine that the powers given by Jesus to his original disciples have been handed down from bishop to bishop through ordination.

appeasement   The Anglo–French policy of making concessions to Germany in the 1930s to avoid a crisis that would lead to war. It assumed that Germany had real grievances and that Hitler's aims were limited and ultimately acceptable.

Areopagus   The governing council of Athens, originally open only to the nobility. It was named after the hill on which it met.

Arete (AH-ray-tay)   Manliness, courage, and the excellence appropriate to a hero. It was considered the highest virtue of Homeric society.

Arianism (AIR-ee-an-ism)   The belief formulated by Arius of Alexandria (ca. 280–336 C.E.) that Jesus was a created being, neither fully man nor fully God, but something in between. It did away with the doctrine of the Trinity.

aristocratic resurgence   Term applied to the eighteenth-century aristocratic efforts to resist the expanding power of European monarchies.

Arminians (are-MIN-ee-ans)   A group within the Church of England who rejected Puritanism and the Calvinist doctrine of predestination in favor of free will and an elaborate liturgy.

Asia Minor   Modern Turkey. Also called Anatolia.

asiento (ah-SEE-ehn-tow)   The contract to furnish slaves to the Spanish colonies.

assignants (as-seen-YAHNTS)   Government bonds based on the value of confiscated Church lands issued during the early French Revolution.

Atomists   School of ancient Greek philosophy founded in the fifth century B.C.E. by Leucippus of Miletus and Democritus of Abdera. It held that the world consists of innumerable, tiny, solid, indivisible, and unchangeable particles called atoms.

Attica (AT-tick-a)   The region of Greece where Athens is located.

Augsburg (AWGS-berg) **Confession**   The definitive statement of Lutheran belief made in 1530.

Augustus (AW-gust-us)   The title given to Octavian in 27 B.C.E. and borne thereafter by all Roman emperors. It was a semireligious title that implied veneration, majesty, and holiness.

Ausgleich (AWS-glike)   Meaning "compromise." The agreement between the Habsburg Emperor and the Hungarians to give Hungary considerable administrative autonomy in 1867. It created the Dual Monarchy or Austria–Hungary.

autocracy (AW-to-kra-see)   Government in which the ruler has absolute power.

Axis   The alliance between Nazi Germany and Fascist Italy. Also called the Pact of Steel.

banalities   Exactions that the lord of a manor could make on his tenants.

baroque (bah-ROWK)   A style of art marked by heavy and dramatic ornamentation and curved rather than straight lines that flourished between 1550 and 1750. It was especially associated with the Catholic Counter-Reformation.

beguines (bi-GEENS)   Lay sisterhoods not bound by the rules of a religious order.

benefice   Church offices granted by the ruler of a state or the Pope to an individual. It also meant "fief" in the Middle Ages.

bishop   Originally a person elected by early Christian congregations to lead them in worship and supervise their funds. In time bishops became the religious and even political authorities for Christian communities within large geographical areas.

Black Death   The bubonic plague that killed millions of Europeans in the fourteenth century.

blitzkrieg (BLITZ-kreeg)   Meaning "lightning war." The German tactic early in World War II of employing fast-moving, massed armored columns supported by airpower to overwhelm the enemy.

Bolsheviks   Meaning the "majority." Term Lenin applied to his faction of the Russian Social Democratic Party. It became the Communist Party of the Soviet Union after the Russian Revolution.

boyars   The Russian nobility.

Bronze Age   The name given to the earliest civilized era, c. 4000 to 1000 B.C.E. The term reflects the importance of the metal bronze, a mixture of tin and copper, for the peoples of this age for use as weapons and tools.

Bund   A secular Jewish socialist organization of Polish Jews.

Caesaro-papism (SEE-zer-o-PAY-pi-zim)   The direct involvement of the ruler in religious doctrine and practice as if he were the head of the Church as well as the state.

cahiers de doleances (KAH-hee-ay de dough-LAY-ahnce)   Meaning "lists of grievances." Petitions for reforms submitted to the French Crown when the Estates General met in 1789.

caliphate (KAH-li-fate)   The true line of succession to Muhammad.

capital goods   Machines and tools used to produce other goods.

carbonari (car-buh-NAH-ree)   Meaning "charcoal burners." The most famous of the secret republican societies seeking to unify Italy in the 1820s.

categorical imperative   According to Emmanuel Kant (1724–1804), the internal sense of moral duty or awareness possessed by all human beings.

Catholic Emancipation   The grant of full political rights to Roman Catholics in Britain in 1829.

catholic   Meaning "universal." The body of belief held by most Christians enshrined within the Church.

censor   Official of the Roman republic charged with conducting the census and compiling the lists of citizens and members of the Senate. They could expel senators for financial or moral reasons. Two censors were elected every five years.

Chartism   The first large-scale European working-class political movement. It sought political reforms that would favor the interests of skilled British workers in the 1830s and 1840s.

chiaroscuro (kyar-eh-SKEW-row)   The use of shading to enhance naturalness in painting and drawing.

civic humanism   Education designed to promote humanist leadership of political and cultural life.

civilization   A form of human culture marked by urbanism, metallurgy, and writing.

classical economics   The theory that economies grow through the free enterprise of individuals competing in a largely self-regulating marketplace with government intervention held to a minimum.

clientage (KLI-ent-age)   The custom in ancient Rome whereby men became supporters of more powerful men in return for legal and physical protection and economic benefits.

Cold War   The ideological and geographical struggle between the U.S. and its allies and the U.S.S.R. and its allies that began after World War II and lasted until the dissolution of the U.S.S.R. in 1989.

Collectivization   The bedrock of Stalinist agriculture, which forced Russian peasants to give up their private farms and work as members of collectives, large agricultural units controlled by the state.

coloni (CO-loan-ee)   Farmers or sharecroppers on the estates of wealthy Romans.

Commonwealthmen   British political writers whose radical republican ideas influenced the American revolutionaries.

Concert of Europe   Term applied to the European great powers acting together (in "concert") to resolve international disputes between 1815 and the 1850s.

Conciliar Theory   The argument that General Councils were superior in authority to the Pope and represented the whole body of the faithful.

condottieri (con-da-TEE-AIR-ee)   Military brokers who furnished mercenary forces to the Italian states during the Renaissance.

Congress System   A series of international meetings among the European great powers to promote mutual cooperation between 1818 and 1822.

conquistadores (kahn-KWIS-teh-door-hez)   Meaning "conquerors." The Spanish conquerors of the New World.

conservatism   Support for the established order in Church and state. In the nineteenth century it implied support for legitimate monarchies, landed aristocracies, and established Churches. Conservatives favored only gradual, or "organic," change.

Consulate   French government dominated by Napoleon from 1799 to 1804.

consuls (CON-suls)   The two chief magistrates of the Roman state.

Consumer Revolution   The vast increase in both the desire and the possibility of consuming goods and services that began in the early eighteenth century and created the demand for sustaining the Industrial Revolution.

Containment   The U.S. policy during the Cold War of resisting Soviet expansion and influence in the expectation that the U.S.S.R. would eventually collapse.

Convention   French radical legislative body from 1792 to 1794.

Corn Laws   British tariffs on imported grain that protected the price of grain grown within the British Isles.

corporatism   The planned economy of Fascist Italy that combined private ownership of capital with government direction of Italy's economic life and arbitration of labor disputes. All major areas of production were organized into state-controlled bodies called corporations, which were represented in the Chamber of Corporations that replaced the Chamber of Deputies. The state, not consumers and owners, determined what the economy produced.

corvee (cor-VAY)   A French labor tax requiring peasants to work on roads, bridges, and canals.

Council of Nicaea   (NIGH-see-a) The council of Christian bishops at Nicaea in 325 C.E. that formulated the Nicene Creed, a statement of Christian belief that rejected Arianism in favor of the doctrine that Christ is both fully human and fully divine.

Counter-Reformation   The sixteenth-century reform movement in the Roman Catholic Church in reaction to the Protestant Reformation.

coup d'état (COO DAY-ta)   The sudden violent overthrow of a government by its own army.

creed   A brief statement of faith to which true Christians should adhere.

creoles (KRAY-ol-ez)   Persons of Spanish descent born in the Spanish colonies.

Crusades   Religious wars directed by the Church against infidels and heretics.

culture   The ways of living built up by a group and passed on from one generation to another.

cuneiform (Q-nee-i-form)   A writing system invented by the Sumerians that used a wedge-shaped stylus, or pointed tool, to write on wet clay tablets that were then baked or dried ("cuneus" means wedge in Latin). The writing was also cut into stone.

Curia (CURE-ee-a)   The papal government.

Cynic (SIN-ick) **School, The**   A fourth-century philosophical movement that ridiculed all religious observances and turned away from involvement in the affairs of the polis. Its most famous exemplar was Diogenes of Sinope (ca. 400-325 B.C.E.).

deacon   Meaning "those who serve." In early Christian congregations, deacons assisted the presbyters, or elders.

deism   A belief in a rational God who had created the universe, but then allowed it to function without his interference according to the mechanisms of nature and a belief in rewards and punishments after death for human action.

Delian (DEE-li-an)   An alliance of Greek states under the leadership of Athens that was formed in 478–477 B.C.E. to resist the Persians. In time the league was transformed into the Athenian Empire.

deme (DEEM)   A small town in Attica or a ward in Athens that became the basic unit of Athenian civic life under the democratic reforms of Clisthenes in 508 B.C.E.

demesne (di-MAIN)   The part of a manor that was cultivated directly for the lord of the manor.

divine right of kings   The theory that monarchs are appointed by and answerable only to God.

Domesday (DOOMS-day) **Book**   A detailed survey of the wealth of England undertaken by William the Conqueror between 1080 and 1086.

domestic system of textile production   Method of producing textiles in which agents furnished raw materials to households whose members spun them into thread and then wove cloth, which the agents then sold as finished products.

Donatism   The heresy that taught that the efficacy of the sacraments depended on the moral character of the clergy who administered them.

Duce (DO-chay)   Meaning "leader." Mussolini's title as head of the Fascist Party.

Duma (DOO-ma)   The Russian parliament, after the Revolution of 1905.

Electors   Nine German princes who had the right to elect the Holy Roman Emperor.

emigrés (em-ee-GRAYS)   French aristocrats who fled France during the Revolution.

empiricism (em-PEER-ih-cism)   The use of experiment and observation derived from sensory evidence to construct scientific theory or philosophy of knowledge.

enclosure   The consolidation or fencing in of common lands by British landlords to increase production and achieve greater commercial profits. It also involved the reclamation of waste land and the consolidation of strips into block fields.

encomienda (en-co-mee-EN-da)   The grant by the Spanish Crown to a colonist of the labor of a specific number of Indians for a set period of time.

ENIAC   The Electronic Numerical Integrator and Computer. The first genuine modern digital computer, developed in the 1940s.

Enlightenment   The eighteenth-century movement led by the philosophies that held that change and reform were both desirable through the application of reason and science.

Epicureans (EP-i-cure-ee-ans) School of philosophy founded by Epicurus of Athens (342–371 B.C.E.). It sought to liberate people from fear of death and the supernatural by teaching that the gods took no interest in human affairs and that true happiness consisted in pleasure, which was defined as the absence of pain. This could be achieved by attaining ataraxia, freedom from trouble, pain, and responsibility by withdrawing from business and public life.

equestrians (EE-quest-ree-ans) Literally "cavalrymen" or "knights." In the earliest years of the Roman Republic those who could afford to serve as mounted warriors. The equestrians evolved into a social rank of well-to-do businessmen and middle-ranking officials. Many of them supported the Gracchi.

Estates General The medieval French parliament. It consisted of three separate groups, or "estates:" clergy, nobility, and commoners. It last met in 1789 at the outbreak of the French Revolution.

Etruscans (EE-trus-cans) A people of central Italy who exerted the most powerful external influence on the early Romans. Etruscan kings ruled Rome until 509 B.C.E.

Eucharist (YOU-ka-rist) Meaning "thanksgiving." The celebration of the Lord's Supper. Considered the central ritual of worship by most Christians. Also called Holy Communion.

Euro The common currency created by the EEC in the late 1990s.

European Economic Community (EEC) The economic association formed by France, Germany, Italy, Belgium, the Netherlands, and Luxembourg in 1957. Also known as the Common Market.

European Union The new name given to the EEC in 1993. It included most of the states of Western Europe.

excommunication Denial by the Church of the right to receive the sacraments.

Existentialism The post-World War II Western philosophy that holds that human beings are totally responsible for their acts and that this responsibility causes them dread and anguish.

Führer (FYOOR-er) Meaning "leader." The title taken by Hitler when he became dictator of Germany.

Fabians British socialists in the late 19th and early 20th century who sought to achieve socialism through gradual, peaceful, and democratic means.

family economy The basic structure of production and consumption in preindustrial Europe.

fascism Political movements that tend to be antidemocratic, anti-Marxist, antiparliamentary, and often anti-Semitic. Fascists were invariably nationalists and exhalted the nation over the individual. They supported the interests of the middle class and rejected the ideas of the French Revolution and nineteenth-century liberalism. The first fascist regime was founded by Benito Mussolini (1883–1945) in Italy in the 1920s.

fealty An oath of loyalty by a vassal to a lord, promising to perform specified services.

feudal (FEW-dull) **society** The social, political, military, and economic system that prevailed in the Middle Ages and beyond in some parts of Europe.

fief Land granted to a vassal in exchange for services, usually military.

foederati (FAY-der-ah-tee) Barbarian tribes enlisted as special allies of the Roman Empire.

folk culture The distinctive songs, sayings, legends, and crafts of a people.

Fourteen Points President Woodrow Wilson's (1856–1924) idealistic war aims.

Fronde (FROHND) A series of rebellions against royal authority in France between 1649 and 1652.

gabelle (gah-BELL) The royal tax on salt in France.

Gaul (GAWL) Modern France.

German Confederation Association of German states established at the Congress of Vienna that replaced the Holy Roman Empire from 1815 to 1866.

ghetto Separate communities in which Jews were required by law to live.

Glasnost (GLAZ-nohst) Meaning "openness." The policy initiated by Mikhail Gorbachev (MEEK-hail GORE-buh-choff) in the 1980s of permitting open criticism of the policies of the Soviet Communist Party.

Glorious Revolution The largely peaceful replacement of James II by William and Mary as English monarchs in 1688. It marked the beginning of constitutional monarchy in Britain.

gold standard A monetary system in which the value of a unit of a nation's currency is related to a fixed amount of gold.

Golden Bull The agreement in 1356 to establish a seven-member electoral college of German princes to choose the Holy Roman Emperor.

Great Depression A prolonged worldwide economic downturn that began in 1929 with the collapse of the New York Stock Exchange.

Great Purges The imprisonment and execution of millions of Soviet citizens by Stalin between 1934 and 1939.

Great Reform Bill (1832) A limited reform of the British House of Commons and an expansion of the electorate to include a wider variety of the propertied classes. It laid the groundwork for further orderly reforms within the British constitutional system.

Great Schism The appearance of two and at times three rival popes between 1378 and 1415.

Green Movement A political environmentalist movement that began in West Germany in the 1970s and spread to a number of other Western nations.

grossdeutsch (gross-DOYCH) Meaning "great German." The argument that the German-speaking portions of the Habsburg Empire should be included in a united Germany.

guild   An association of merchants or craftsmen that offered protection to its members and set rules for their work and products.

hacienda (ha-SEE-hen-da)   A large landed estate in Spanish America.

Hegira (HEJ-ear-a)   The flight of Muhammad and his followers from Mecca to Medina in 622 C.E. It marks the beginning of the Islamic calendar.

heliocentric (HE-li-o-cen-trick) **theory**   The theory, now universally accepted, that the Earth and the other planets revolve around the Sun. First proposed by Aristarchos of Samos (310–230 B.C.E.). Its opposite, the geocentric theory, which was dominant until the sixteenth century C.E., held that the Sun and the planets revolved around the Earth.

helots (HELL-ots)   Hereditary Spartan serfs.

heretic (HAIR-i-tick)   A person whose beliefs were contrary to those of the Catholic Church.

Hieroglyphics (HI-er-o-gli-phicks)   The complicated writing script of ancient Egypt. It combined picture writing with pictographs and sound signs. Hieroglyph means "sacred carvings" in Greek.

Holocaust   The Nazi extermination of millions of European Jews between 1940 and 1945. Also called the "final solution to the Jewish problem."

Holy Roman Empire   The revival of the old Roman Empire, based mainly in Germany and northern Italy, that endured from 870 to 1806.

Home Rule   The advocacy of a large measure of administrative autonomy for Ireland within the British Empire between the 1880s and 1914.

Homo sapiens (HO-mo say-pee-ans)   The scientific name for human beings, from the Latin words meaning "Wise man." Homo sapiens emerged some 200,000 years ago.

honestiores (HON-est-ee-or-ez)   The Roman term formalized from the beginning of the third century C.E. to denote the privileged classes: senators, equestrians, the municipal aristocracy, and soldiers.

hoplite phalanx (FAY-lanks)   The basic unit of Greek warfare in which infantrymen fought in close order, shield to shield, usually eight ranks deep. The phalanx perfectly suited the farmer-soldier-citizen who was the backbone of the polis.

hubris (WHO-bris)   Arrogance brought on by excessive wealth or good fortune. The Greeks believed that it led to moral blindness and divine vengeance.

Huguenots (HYOU-gu-nots)   French Calvinists.

humanism   The study of the Latin and Greek classics and of the Church Fathers both for their own sake and to promote a rebirth of ancient norms and values.

humanitas (HEW-man-i-tas)   The Roman name for a liberal arts education.

humiliores (HEW-mi-lee-orez)   The Roman term formalized at the beginning of the third century C.E. for the lower classes.

Hussites (HUS-Its)   Followers of John Huss (d. 1415) who questioned Catholic teachings about the Eucharist.

iconoclasm (i-KON-o-kla-zoom)   A heresy in Eastern Christianity that sought to ban the veneration of sacred images, or icons.

id, ego, superego   The three entities in Sigmund Freud's model of the internal organization of the human mind. The id consists of the amoral, irrational instincts for self-gratification. The superego embodies the external morality imposed on the personality by society. The ego mediates between the two and allows the personality to cope with the internal and external demands of its existence.

Iliad (ILL-ee-ad) **and the Odyssey** (O-dis-see), **The**   Epic poems by Homer about the "Dark Age" heroes of Greece who fought at Troy. The poems were written down in the eighth century B.C.E. after centuries of being sung by bards.

imperator (IM-per-a-tor)   Under the Roman Republic it was the title given to a victorious general. Under Augustus and his successors it became the title of the ruler of Rome meaning "Emperor."

imperialism   The extension of a nation's authority over other nations or areas through conquest or political or economic hegemony.

imperium (IM-pear-ee-um)   In ancient Rome the right to issue commands and to enforce them by fines, arrests, and even corporal and capital punishment.

indulgences   Remission of the temporal penalty of punishment in purgatory that remained after sins had been forgiven.

Industrial Revolution   Mechanization of the European economy that began in Britain in the second half of the eighteenth century.

insulae (IN-sul-lay)   Meaning "islands." The multistoried apartment buildings of Rome in which most of the inhabitants of the city lived.

intendents (in-TEN-duhnts)   Royal officials under the French monarchy who supervised the provincial governments in the name of the king.

Intolerable Acts   Measures passed by the British Parliament in 1774 to punish the colony of Massachusetts and strengthen Britain's authority in the colonies. The laws provoked colonial opposition, which led immediately to the American Revolution.

Investiture Struggle   The medieval conflict between the Church and lay rulers over who would control bishops and abbots, symbolized by the ceremony of "investing" them with the symbols of their authority.

Ionia (I-o-knee-a)   The part of western Asia Minor heavily colonized by the Greeks.

Islam (IZ-lahm)   Meaning "submission." The religion founded by the prophet Muhammad.

Italia Irredenta (ee-TAHL-ee-a ir-REH-dent-a) Meaning "unredeemed Italy." Italian-speaking areas that had been left under Austrian rule at the time of the unification of Italy.

Jacobins (JACK-uh-bins) The radical republican party during the French Revolution that displaced the Girondins.

jacquerie (jah-KREE) Revolt of the French peasantry.

Jansenism A seventeenth-century movement within the Catholic Church that taught that human beings were so corrupted by original sin that they could do nothing good nor secure their own salvation without divine grace. (It was opposed to the Jesuits).

Judah (JEW-da) The southern Israelite kingdom established after the death of Solomon in the tenth century B.C.E.

Julian Calendar The reform of the calendar by Julius Caesar in 46 B.C.E. It remained in use throughout Europe until the sixteenth century and in Russia until the Russian Revolution in 1917.

July Monarchy The French regime set up after the overthrow of the Bourbons in July 1830.

junkers (YOONG-kerz) The noble landlords of Prussia.

jus gentium (YUZ GEN-tee-um) Meaning "law of peoples." The body of Roman law that dealt with foreigners.

jus naturale (YUZ NAH-tu-rah-lay) Meaning "natural law." The Stoic concept of a world ruled by divine reason.

Ka'ba (KAH-bah) A black meteorite in the city of Mecca that became Islam's holiest shrine.

Keynesian Economics The theory of John Maynard Keynes (CANES) (1883–1946) that governments could spend their economies out of a depression by running deficits to encourage employment and stimulate the production and consumption of goods.

kleindeutsch (kline-DOYCH) Meaning "small German." The argument that the German-speaking portions of the Habsburg Empire should be excluded from a united Germany.

Kristallnacht (KRIS-tahl-NAHKT) Meaning "crystal night" because of the broken glass that littered German streets after the looting and destruction of Jewish homes, businesses, and synagogues across Germany on the orders of the Nazi Party in November, 1938.

kulaks (koo-LAKS) Prosperous Russian peasant farmers.

Kulturkampf (cool-TOOR-cahmff) Meaning the "battle for culture." The conflict between the Roman Catholic Church and the government of the German Empire in the 1870s.

laissez-faire (lay-ZAY-faire) French phrase meaning "allow to do." In economics the doctrine of minimal government interference in the working of the economy.

latifundia (LAT-ee-fun-dee-a) Large plantations for growing cash crops owned by wealthy Romans.

Latium (LAT-ee-um) The region of Italy in which Rome is located. Its inhabitants were called Latins.

League of Nations The association of sovereign states set up after World War I to pursue common policies and avert international aggression.

Lebensraum (LAY-benz-rauhm) Meaning "living space." The Nazi plan to colonize and exploit the Slavic areas of Eastern Europe for the benefit of Germany.

levée en masse (le-VAY en MASS) The French Revolutionary conscription (1792) of all males into the army and the harnessing of the economy for war production.

liberal arts The medieval university program that consisted of the trivium (TRI-vee-um): grammar, rhetoric, and logic, and the quadrivium (qua-DRI-vee-um): arithmetic, geometry, astronomy, and music.

liberalism In the nineteenth century, support for representative government dominated by the propertied classes and minimal government interference in the economy.

Logos (LOW-goz) Divine reason, or fire, which according to the Stoics was the guiding principle in nature. Every human had a spark of this divinity, which returned to the eternal divine spirit after death.

Lollards (LALL-erds) Followers of John Wycliffe (d. 1384) who questioned the supremacy and privileges of the Pope and the Church hierarchy.

Lower Egypt The Nile delta.

Luftwaffe (LUFT-vaff-uh) The German airforce in World War II.

Magna Carta (MAG-nuh CAR-tuh) The "Great Charter" limiting royal power that the English nobility forced King John to sign in 1215.

Magna Graecia (MAG-nah GRAY-see-a) Meaning "Great Greece" in Latin, it was the name given by the Romans to southern Italy and Sicily because there were so many Greek colonies in the region.

Magyars (MAH-jars) The majority ethnic group in Hungary.

Mandates The assigning of the former German colonies and Turkish territories in the Middle East to Britain, France, Japan, Belgium, Australia, and South Africa as de facto colonies under the vague supervision of the League of Nations with the hope that the territories would someday advance to independence.

mannerism A style of art in the mid-to late-sixteenth century that permitted the artist to express his or her own "manner" or feelings in contrast to the symmetry and simplicity of the art of the High Renaissance.

manor Village farms owned by a lord.

Marshall Plan The U.S. program named after Secretary of State George C. Marshall of providing economic aid to Europe after World War II.

Marxism The theory of Karl Marx (1818–1883) and Friedrich Engels (FREE-drick Eng-ulz) (1820–1895) that history is the result of class conflict, which will end in the inevitable triumph of the industrial proletariat over the bourgeoisie and the abolition of private property and social class.

Mein Kampf (MINE KAHMFF) Meaning "my struggle." Hitler's statement of his political program published in 1924.

Mensheviks Meaning the "minority." Term Lenin applied to the majority moderate faction of the Russian Social Democratic Party opposed to him and the Bolsheviks.

mercantilism Term used to describe close government control of the economy that sought to maximize exports and accumulate as much precious metals as possible to enable the state to defend its economic and political interests.

Mesopotamia (MEZ-o-po-tay-me-a) Modern Iraq. The land between the Tigris and Euphrates Rivers where the first civilization appeared around 3000 B.C.E.

Messiah (MESS-eye-a) The redeemer whose coming Jews believed would establish the kingdom of God on earth. Christians considered Jesus to be the Messiah (Christ means Messiah in Greek).

Methodism An English religious movement begun by John Wesley (1703–1791) that stressed inward, heartfelt religion and the possibility of attaining Christian perfection in this life.

millets Administrative units of the Ottoman Empire that were not geographic but consisted of ethnic or religious minorities to whom particular laws and regulations applied.

Minoans (MIN-o-ans) The Bronze Age civilization that arose in Crete in the third and second millenia B.C.E.

missi dominici (MISS-ee dough-MIN-ee-chee) Meaning "the envoys of the ruler." Royal overseers of the king's law in the Carolingian Empire.

mobilization The placing of a country's military forces on a war footing.

modernism The movement in the arts and literature in the late nineteenth and early twentieth centuries to create new aesthetic forms and to elevate the aesthetic experience of a work of art above the attempt to portray reality as accurately as possible.

moldboard plow A heavy plow introduced in the Middle Ages that cut deep into the soil.

monophysitism (ma-NO-fiz-it-ism) A Christian heresy that taught that Jesus had only one nature.

monotheism The worship of one, universal God.

Mycenaean (MY-cen-a-an) The Bronze Age civilization of mainland Greece that was centered at Mycenae.

"mystery" religions The cults of Isis, Mithra, and Osiris, which promised salvation to those initiated into the secret or "mystery" of their rites. These cults competed with Christianity in the Roman Empire.

nationalism The belief that one is part of a nation, defined as a community with its own language, traditions, customs, and history that distinguish it from other nations and make it the primary focus of a person's loyalty and sense of identity.

natural selection The theory originating with Darwin that organisms evolve through a struggle for existence in which those that have a marginal advantage live long enough to propagate their kind.

naturalism The attempt to portray nature and human life without sentimentality.

Nazis The German Nationalist Socialist Party.

Neolithic (NEE-o-lith-ick) **Revolution, The** The shift beginning 10,000 years ago from hunter-gatherer societies to settled communities of farmers and artisans. Also called the Age of Agriculture, it witnessed the invention of farming, the domestication of plants and animals, and the development of technologies such as pottery and weaving. The earliest Neolithic societies appeared in the Near East about 8,000 B.C.E. "Neolithic" comes from the Greek words for "new stone."

Neoplatonism (KNEE-o-play-ton-ism) A religious philosophy that tried to combine mysticism with classical and rationalist speculation. Its chief formulator was Plotinus (205–270 C.E.).

New Economic Policy (NEP) A limited revival of capitalism, especially in light industry and agriculture, introduced by Lenin in 1921 to repair the damage inflicted on the Russian economy by the Civil War and War Communism.

New Imperialism The extension in the late nineteenth and early twentieth centuries of Western political and economic dominance to Asia, the Middle East, and Africa.

nomes regions or provinces of ancient Egypt governed by officials called nomarchs.

oikos (OI-cos) The Greek household, always headed by a male.

Old Believers Those members of the Russian Orthodox Church who refused to accept the reforms of the seventeenth century regarding Church texts and ritual.

Old Regime Term applied to the pattern of social, political, and economic relationships and institutions that existed in Europe before the French Revolution.

optimates (OP-tee-ma-tes) Meaning "the best men." Roman politicians who supported the traditional role of the Senate.

orthodox Meaning "holding the right opinions." Applied to the doctrines of the Catholic Church.

Ottoman Empire The imperial Turkish state centered in Constantinople that ruled large parts of the Balkans, North Africa, and the Middle East until 1918.

Paleolithic (PAY-lee-o-lith-ick) **Age, The** The earliest period when stone tools were used, from about 1,000,000 to 10,000 B.C.E. From the Greek meaning "old stone."

Panhellenic (PAN-hell-en-ick) ("all-Greek")   The sense of cultural identity that all Greeks felt in common with each other.

Panslavism   The movement to create a nation or federation that would embrace all the Slavic peoples of eastern Europe.

papal infallibility   The doctrine that the Pope is infallible when pronouncing officially in his capacity as head of the Church on matters of faith and morals, enumerated by the First Vatican Council in 1870.

Papal States   Territory in central Italy ruled by the Pope until 1870.

parlements (par-luh-MAHNS)   French regional courts dominated by hereditary nobility. The most important was the Parlement of Paris, which claimed the right to register royal decrees before they could become law.

patricians (PA-tri-she-ans)   The hereditary upper class of early Republican Rome.

Peloponnesian (PELL-o-po-knees-ee-an) **Wars**   The protracted struggle between Athens and Sparta to dominate Greece between 465 and Athens final defeat in 404 B.C.E.

Peloponnesus (PELL-o-po-knee-sus)   The southern peninsula of Greece where Sparta was located.

peninsulares (pen-in-SUE-la-rez)   Persons born in Spain who settled in the Spanish colonies.

Perestroika (pare-ess-TROY-ka)   Meaning "restructuring." The attempt in the 1980s to reform the Soviet government and economy.

petit bourgeoisie (peh-TEE BOOSH-schwa-zee)   The lower middle class.

Pharisees (FAIR-i-sees)   The group that was most strict in its adherence to Jewish law.

pharoah (FAY-row)   The god-kings of ancient Egypt. The term originally meant "great house" or palace.

philosophes (fee-lou-SOPHS)   The eighteenth-century writers and critics who forged the new attitudes favorable to change. They sought to apply reason and common sense to the institutions and societies of their day.

Phoenicians (FA-nee-shi-ans)   The ancient inhabitants of modern Lebanon. A trading people, they established colonies throughout the Mediterranean.

physiocrats   Eighteenth-century French thinkers who attacked the mercantilist regulation of the economy, advocated a limited economic role for government, and believed that all economic production depended on sound agriculture.

Plantation Economy, The   The economic system stretching between Chesapeake Bay and Brazil that produced crops, especially sugar, cotton, and tobacco, using slave labor on large estates.

plebeians (PLEB-bee-ans)   The hereditary lower class of early Republican Rome.

plenitude of power   The teaching that the Popes have power over all other bishops of the Church.

pogroms (PO-grohms)   Organized riots against Jews in the Russian Empire.

polis (PO-lis) (plural, poleis)   The basic Greek political unit. Usually, but incompletely, translated as "city state," the Greeks thought of the polis as a community of citizens theoretically descended from a common ancestor.

polygyny (po-LIJ-eh-nee)   The practice of having two or more wives or concubines at the same time.

polytheism (PAH-lee-thee-ism)   The worship of many gods

pontifex maximus (PON-ti-feks MAK-suh-muss)   Meaning "supreme priest." The chief priest of ancient Rome. The title was later assumed by the Popes.

Popular Front   A government of all left-wing parties that took power in France in 1936 to enact social and economic reforms.

populares (PO-pew-lar-es)   Roman politicians who sought to pursue a political career based on the support of the people rather than just the aristocracy.

Positivism   The philosophy of Auguste Comte that science is the final, or positive, stage of human intellectual development because it involves exact descriptions of phenomena, without recourse to unobservable operative principles, such as gods or spirits.

Pragmatic Sanction   The legal basis negotiated by the Emperor Charles VI (r. 1711–1740) for the Habsburg succession through his daughter Maria Theresa (r. 1740–1780).

predestination   The doctrine that God had foreordained all souls to salvation (the "elect") or damnation. It was especially associated with Calvinism.

Presbyterians   Scottish Calvinists and English Protestants who advocated a national church composed of semi-autonomous congregations governed by "presbyteries."

presbyter (PRESS-bi-ter)   Meaning "elder." A person who directed the affairs of early Christian congregations.

proconsulship (PRO-con-sul-ship)   In Republican Rome the extension of a consul's imperium beyond the end of his term of office to allow him to continue to command an army in the field.

Protestant Ethic   The theory propounded by Max Weber in 1904 that the religious confidence and self-disciplined activism that were supposedly associated with Protestantism produced an ethic that stimulated the spirit of emergent capitalism.

Ptolemaic (tow-LEM-a-ick) **System**   The pre-Copernican explanation of the universe, with the Earth at the center of the universe, originated in the ancient world.

Punic (PEW-nick) **Wars**   Three wars between Rome and Carthage for dominance of the western Mediterranean that were fought from 264 B.C.E. to 146 B.C.E.

Puritans   English Protestants who sought to "purify" the Church of England of any vestiges of Catholicism.

Qur'an (kuh-RAN)   Meaning "a reciting." The Islamic bible, which Muslims believe God revealed to the prophet Muhammad.

racism   The pseudo-scientific theory that biological features of race determine human character and worth.

raison d'etat (RAY-suhn day-TAH)   Meaning "reason of state." Concept that the interests of the state justify a course of action.

realism   The style of art and literature that seeks to depict the physical world and human life with scientific objectivity and detached observation.

Reformation   The sixteenth-century religious movement that sought to reform the Roman Catholic Church and led to the establishment of Protestantism.

regular clergy   Monks and nuns who belong to religious orders.

Reichstag (RIKES-stahg)   The German parliament, which existed in various forms, until 1945.

Reign of Terror   The period between the summer of 1793 and the end of July 1794 when the French Revolutionary state used extensive executions and violence to defend the Revolution and suppress its alleged internal enemies.

relativity   The scientific theory associated with Einstein that time and space exist not separately but as a combined continuum whose measurement depends as much on the observer as on the entities that are being measured.

Renaissance   The revival of ancient learning and the supplanting of traditional religious beliefs by new secular and scientific values that began in Italy in the fourteenth and fifteenth centuries.

reparations   The requirement incorporated into the Versailles Treaty that Germany should pay for the cost of World War I.

revisionism   The advocacy among nineteenth-century German socialists of achieving a humane socialist society through the evolution of democratic institutions, not revolution.

robot (ROW-boht)   The amount of labor landowners demanded from peasants in the Habsburg Monarchy before 1848.

Romanitas (row-MAN-ee-tas)   Meaning "Roman-ness." The spread of the Roman way of life and the sense of identifying with Rome across the Roman Empire.

Romanticism   A reaction in early nineteenth century literature, philosophy, and religion against what many considered the excessive rationality and scientific narrowness of the Enlightenment.

SA   The Nazi parliamentary forces, or storm troopers.

sans-culottes (SAHN coo-LOTS)   Meaning "without kneebreeches." The lower-middle classes and artisans of Paris during the French Revolution.

Schlieffen (SHLEE-fun) **Plan**   Germany's plan for achieving a quick victory in the West at the outbreak of World War I by invading France through Belgium and Luxembourg.

scholasticism   The method of study based on logic and dialectic that dominated the medieval schools. It assumed that truth already existed; students had only to organize, elucidate, and defend knowledge learned from authoritative texts, especially those of Aristotle and the Church Fathers.

scientific induction   Scientific method in which generalizations are derived from data gained from empirical observations.

Scientific Revolution   The sweeping change in the scientific view of the universe that occurred in the sixteenth and seventeenth centuries. The new scientific concepts and the method of their construction became the standard for assessing the validity of knowledge in the West.

scutage   Monetary payments by a vassal to a lord in place of the required military service.

Second Industrial Revolution   The emergence of new industries and the spread of industrialization from Britain to other countries, especially Germany and the United States, in the second half of the nineteenth century.

secular clergy   Parish clergy who did not belong to a religious order.

seigneur (sane-YOUR)   A noble French landlord.

Sejm (SHEM)   The legislative assembly of the Polish nobility.

serfs   Peasants tied to the land they tilled.

Shi-a (SHE-ah)   The minority of Muslims who trace their beliefs from the caliph Ali who was assassinated in 661 C.E.

Sinn Fein (SHIN FAHN)   Meaning "ourselves alone." An Irish political movement founded in 1905 that advocated complete political separation from Britain.

Social Darwinism   The application of Darwin's concept of "the survival of the fittest" to explain evolution in nature to human social relationships.

Sophists (SO-fists)   Professional teachers who emerged in Greece in the mid-fifth century B.C.E. who were paid to teach techniques of rhetoric, dialectic, and argumentation.

soviets   Workers and soldiers councils formed in Russia during the Revolution.

spinning jenny   A machine invented in England by James Hargreaves around 1765 to mass-produce thread.

SS   The chief security units of the Nazi state.

Stoics (STOW-icks)   A philosophical school founded by Zeno of Citium (335–263 B.C.E.) that taught that humans could only be happy with natural law. Human misery was caused by passion, which was a disease of the soul. The wise sought apatheia, freedom from passion.

studia humanitatis (STEW-dee-a hew-MAHN-ee tah-tis)   During the Renaissance a liberal arts program of study that embraced grammar, rhetoric, poetry, history, philosophy, and politics.

Sturm und Drang (SHTURM und DRAHNG)   Meaning "storm and stress." A movement in German romantic literature and philosophy that emphasized feeling and emotion.

suffragettes   British women who lobbied and agitated for the right to vote in the early 20th century.

summa (SUE-ma)   An authoritative summary in the Middle Ages of all that was allegedly known about a subject.

Sunna (SOON-ah)   Meaning "tradition." The dominant Islamic group.

symposium (SIM-po-see-um)   The carefully organized drinking party that was the center of Greek aristocratic social life. It featured games, songs, poetry, and even philosophical disputation.

syncretism (SIN-cret-ism)   The intermingling of different religions to form an amalgam that contained elements from each.

syndicalism   French labor movement that sought to improve workers' conditions through direct action, especially general strikes.

Table of Ranks   An official hierarchy established by Peter the Great in Imperial Russia that equated a person's social position and privileges with his rank in the state bureaucracy or army.

tabula rasa (tah-BOO-lah RAH-sah)   Meaning a "blank page." The philosophical belief associated with John Locke that human beings enter the world with totally unformed characters that are completely shaped by experience.

taille (TIE)   The direct tax on the French peasantry.

"Ten lost tribes"   The Israelites who were scattered and lost to history when the northern kingdom of Israel fell to the Assyrians in 722 B.C.E.

tertiaries (TER-she-air-ees)   Laypeople affiliated with the monastic life who took vows of poverty, chastity, and obedience but remained in the world.

tetrarchy (TET-rar-key)   Diocletian's (r. 306–337 C.E.) system for ruling the Roman Empire by four men with power divided territorially.

Thermidorean Reaction   The reaction against the radicalism of the French Revolution that began in July 1794. Associated with the end of terror and establishment of the Directory.

thesis, antithesis, and synthesis   G.W.F. Hegel's (HAY-gle) (1770–1831) concept of how ideas develop. The thesis is a dominant set of ideas. It is challenged by a set of conflicting ideas, the antithesis. From the clash of these ideas, a new pattern of thought, the synthesis, emerges and eventually becomes the new thesis.

Third Estate   The branch of the French Estates General representing all of the kingdom outside the nobility and the clergy.

Third Reich (RIKE)   Hitler's regime in Germany, which lasted from 1933 to 1945.

Thirty-Nine Articles (1563)   The official statement of the beliefs of the Church of England. They established a moderate form of Protestantism.

three-field system   A medieval innovation that increased the amount of land under cultivation by leaving only one-third fallow in a given year.

transportation   The British policy from the late eighteenth to the mid-nineteenth centuries of shipping persons convicted of the most serious offenses to Australia as an alternative to capital punishment.

transubstantiation   The doctrine that the entire substances of the bread and wine are changed in the Eucharist into the body and blood of Christ.

tribunes (TRIB-unes)   Roman officials who had to be plebeians and were elected by the plebeian assembly to protect plebeians from the arbitrary power of the magistrates.

ulema (oo-LEE-mah)   Meaning "persons with correct knowledge." The Islamic scholarly elite who served a social function similar to the Christian clergy.

Upper Egypt   The part of Egypt that runs from the delta to the Sudanese border.

utilitarianism   The theory associated with Jeremy Bentham (1748–1832) that the principle of utility, defined as the greatest good for the greatest number of people, should be applied to government, the economy, and the judicial system.

utopian socialism   Early nineteenth century theories that sought to replace the existing capitalist structure and values with visionary solutions or ideal communities.

vassal   A person granted an estate or cash payments in return for accepting the obligation to render services to a lord.

vernacular   The everyday language spoken by the people as opposed to Latin.

vingtieme (VEN-tee-em)   Meaning "one twentieth." A tax on income in France before the Revolution.

Vulgate   The Latin translation of the Bible by Jerome (348–420 C.E.) that became the standard bible used by the Catholic Church.

Waldensians (wahl-DEN-see-ens)   Medieval heretics who advocated Biblical simplicity in reaction to the worldliness of the Church.

War Communism   The economic policy adopted by the Bolsheviks during the Russian Civil War to seize the banks, heavy industry, railroads, and grain.

War Guilt Clause   Clause 231 of the Versailles Treaty, which assigned responsibility for World War I solely to Germany.

water frame   A water-powered device invented by Richard Arkwright to produce a more durable cotton fabric. It led to the shift in the production of cotton textiles from households to factories.

Weimar (Why-mar) **Republic**   The German democratic regime that existed between the end of World War I and Hitler's coming to power in 1933.

White Russians   Those Russians who opposed the Bolsheviks (the "Reds") in the Russian Civil War of 1918–1921.

zemstvos (ZEMPST-vohs)   Local governments set up in the Russian Empire in 1864.

Zionism   The movement to create a Jewish state in Palestine (the Biblical Zion).

Zollverein (TZOL-fuh-rine)   A free trade union established among the major German states in 1834.

Index

A

Aachen, 214, 216
Abelard, Peter, 276, 277
Abortion
  Cathars and, 239
  fascist Italy, 1035
  19th century, 824–825
  Roman Empire, 160, 162
  Soviet Union, 1033
  20th century, 1052
Abu Bakr, 207
Academy of Experiments, 464
Academy of Plato, 93, 102–103
Achaemenid dynasty, 63
Achilles, 42, 43
Acrocorinth, 46
Acropolis, 46, 76, 86, 88, *88*
Action Française, 970
Actium, battle of, 143
Acton, Lord, 802
Acts of Supremacy (1534, 1559), 341, 370, 404
Acts of Uniformity (1549, 1552, 1559), 372, 404
Adages (Erasmus), 340
Addison, Joseph, 595, 598
*Address to the Christian Nobility of the German
    Nation* (Luther), 356, 360
Adrian IV, pope, 250
Adrianople, battle of, 176, 196
Adrianople, treaty of (1829), 719
Ad Sacram Sedem, 438
Advancement of Learning, The (Bacon), 455
Aegean area, map of in the Bronze Age, *41*
Aegospotami, battle of, 82
Aeneid (Vergil), 152
Aeschylus, 78, 86
Afghanistan, Soviet invasion of, 1095
Africa
  decolonization, 1048, 1085–1089, *1088*
  early explorations of, 341–343
  imperialism and, 891–893, 895
  slavery in, 560, 741
Africa (Petrarch), 323
Africanus, Scipio, 123, 323
Agamemnon, 42, 43
Agamemnon (Aeschylus), 78
Agesilaus, 83–84
Agincourt, battle of (1415), 295–296
Agon, 43
Agora, 46, 56, *88*, 103
Agricola, Rudolf, 340
Agriculture
  in the Americas, 347–348, 583–585
  Athenian, 54
  Black Death and, 302–303
  Carolingian manor, 217–220, *219*
  collectivization, 984–986, 1038–1039
  18th century, 517–519, 528–531, *530*

enclosures replace open fields, 529–530
  Greek, 54, 58, 59
  Hellenistic, 102
  Middle Ages, 265, 266, 298
  Neolithic Age, 8
  in the 1920s, 967–968
  Roman Republic, 128, 130–132
Agrippa, 141, 143
Agrippina, 162
Aix-la-Chapelle, treaty of (1668), 440
Akhenaten, 24
Akkadians/Akkade, 11, 12, 13
Alais, peace of (1629), 431
Alaric, 197
Alba, duke of, 401, 405
Albanians, 1038
  collapse of Yugoslavia and civil war, 1106,
    1108–1109
Albert, Jeanne d', 391
Alberti, Leon Battista, 326
Albigensians (Cathars), 238–239, 382
Albrecht of Mainz, 358
Albret, Charlotte d', 333
Alcabala, 336
Alcaeus, *60*, 62
Alcibiades, 82
Alcmaeonids, 56
Alcuin of York, 217
Alemanni, 171–172, 175
Alençon, duke of, 403
Alexander I, king of Yugoslavia, 953
Alexander I, tsar of Russia, 674, 685, 717, *717*,
    724, 725
Alexander II, pope, 232
Alexander II, tsar of Russia, 803–805, 807
Alexander III, pope, 243, 250
Alexander III, tsar of Russia, 842, 844
Alexander V, pope, 312
Alexander VI, pope, 332, 333
Alexander the Great (Alexander III), 94, 99–100, *99*,
    101, 188, 930
  campaigns (map) of, *101*
  successors to, 100, 102
Alexandria, 104
Alexandria Eschate, 100
Alexis I, king of Russia, 503, 508, 509
Alexius I Comnenus, 205, 235
Alfred the Great, 241
Algarotti, Francesco, 467
Algeria, French in, 891
Alimenta, 158
Almagest (Ptolemy), 451
Alvarado, Pedro de, *344*
Amboise, conspiracy of, 391
Ambrose, bishop of Milan, 179
Americanization of Europe, 1057–1058
American Revolution, 572